S0-BYT-263

ISRAEL

ISRAEL

ITS LIFE AND CULTURE

I—II

BY

JOHS. PEDERSEN
PROFESSOR OF SEMITIC PHILOLOGY IN THE UNIVERSITY
OF COPENHAGEN

GEOFFREY CUMBERLEGE
OXFORD UNIVERSITY PRESS
LONDON

BRANNER OG KORCH
29, ST. KONGENSGADE
COPENHAGEN

FIRST PUBLISHED IN 1926
REPRINTED (PHOTOPRINT) 1946
REPRINTED (PHOTOPRINT) 1954

PRINTED IN DENMARK
BY
S. L. MØLLERS BOGTRYKKERI

THIS work was first published in the Danish language in 1920, and the present edition deviates only on a few points from the original. Here and there the text has been shortened a little, while in other places details have been further elaborated. Most of the alterations are due to the discovery of the Assyrian and Hittite Laws which were made known shortly after the first appearance of this book, the Hittite Law in particular giving valuable contributions towards our understanding of the formation of Israelitic culture. As an example illustrating Israel's position in the ancient cultures I have, in an additional note, given a short summary of the marriage laws in the different codes. On the other hand, I have left out a brief survey given in the Danish edition of the treatment of the psychology of Israel, and its relation to the general psychology of peoples as developed during the 19th century. The English translation has been undertaken, in close collaboration with myself, by Mrs. Aslaug Møller, M. A. of the University of Copenhagen, and I take this opportunity of thanking her for her great interest in the work, which has been made all the more difficult, as the character of the subject has sometimes necessitated the finding of expressions which, like their Danish equivalents, may strike the reader as peculiar and perhaps not in strict accordance with the common *ušus loquendi.* For further security it has been revised and the proofs read by Mr. H. Stewart Maclaren. The indices have been compiled by my wife. References to Bible texts apply to the Hebrew edition, and the translations are undertaken direct from the latter, the wording, however, having been kept as close to the Authorized Version as possible, while Hebrew names are generally written as in English. In the transcription of Hebrew and other Semitic words special signs have only been used wherever absolutely necessary; thus, *sh* is used for the Hebrew *shīn,* and the fricative pronunciation of the explosive mediæ after vowels is rendered by *h (th, ph,* etc.).

The cost of production of the English edition has been defrayed by the Danish Rask-Ørsted Fond, to which institution I wish to express my deep sense of obligation. In the preface to the Danish edition, which was dedicated to my colleague and friend Vilh. Grönbech, I said that I hoped to be able to continue with a work on the Israelitic cult and conception of the Holy. Hitherto I have unfortunately been prevented by other works from carrying out this plan, but I hope that it may prove practicable in a not too distant future.

Copenhagen, January, 1926.

Johs. P.

CONTENTS

and the cursed are in Sheol; also in the ocean. Restoration of health deliverance from Sheol, pp. 466—470.

Israelitic conception of universe expression of conflict between life and death, p. 470. Myths express the creation of land of man from desert-land and chaos; Yahweh's fight against chaos waters; fight against dragons; expresses victory of blessing over evil; genesis of world of life. Ocean must serve the blessing, pp. 471—474.

Relation of people to the land as that of family to property. Land of fathers, pp. 474—475. People a psychic whole; their life together with the fathers; fathers' history that of the people, pp. 475—476. Creation of land of man coinciding with that of people; exile of people revival of chaos and desert, pp. 476—477. Relation to other peoples and their world, pp. 477—479.

The earth a living thing; its soul must be respected, the year of sabbath, pp. 479—480. Division of animals. Tame animals known by the Israelites. Right of wild beasts, pp. 480—482. Clean and unclean animals; historically determined, pp. 482—483. Man not permitted to eat all parts of animals, in particular not the blood; would destroy totality of man and life of the animal species, pp. 483—484. Man master of animals. Right of wild beasts limited, pp. 484—485. Significance of species; its purity is to be maintained; mixtures impermissible, pp. 485—486. Plants, p. 486.

Celestial bodies guardians of light, belong to world of light, p. 487. Sun and moon govern time. Time is the development of events, action and fate. Times of same substance identical; time alive, pp. 487—488. Centres of time. Periods determined by their substance; totalities grouping round certain days *(mō'ēdh)*, pp. 488—490. History generations *(dōrōth)*, times with certain men as centres. Fused into eternity, i. e. primeval time *('ōlām)*, pp. 490—491.

The world is kept clean by normal conduct of life. Individual acquisition of Israelitic custom, pp. 491—492. Circumcision initiation into manhood, p. 492. Uncleanness breach of totality, closely allied to sin; must be kept out, pp. 492—493. Death makes unclean. Mourning rites expression of sorrow and fear of hurting the blessing; used at deaths and in misfortune. pp. 493—495. The violent death; the death in peace. Union with kinsmen, pp. 495—496.

CANAAN BEFORE THE IMMIGRATION OF THE ISRAELITES

CANAAN was settled for thousands of years before the history of Israel began. Scattered about the land there are from times immemorial relics of human habitation, mostly stone implements such as we know them from other parts of the world, i. e. roughly hewn flints, lances and arrow heads, knives and saws. The oldest dwellings were very primitive. The inhabitants settled in caves, which are to be found in great numbers in the mountains of Canaan. At Ḥarādjel in the region round Lebanon there is a cave 160 m. in length, with the remains of rhinoceros, wild horse, hart, bison, bear, cave-lion and primeval goat; in and near the cave there are fragments of earthenware as well as knives and flakes of flint. At Gezer in the southern part of the country caves were excavated, forming a whole system of corridors and provided with water reservoirs. Later on the people learned to build mud cabins against the walls of rocks, and soon the practice of making tiles of baked clay developed. The inhabitants left the hill country where they had originally settled, and came to live in the fertile valleys, where in the course of time cities sprang up.

From about 3000 B. C. Canaan begins to appear in the light of history. From the oldest times we only have glimpses here and there, but gradually the light becomes clearer; from the second millennium we know, at any rate, a good deal of the political conditions, while the excavations supply a fair amount of knowledge regarding the degree of civilization attained, all evidence pointing towards the fact that Canaan was inhabited by a heterogeneous population and became the meeting place of various cultures. This was the result of the very character of the country.

Unlike the great river valleys of Egypt and Mesopotamia

Canaan was not suited to shelter a closely packed population. In spite of the small area covered, the effect was rather scattering than uniting. The Jordan valley, which is often deep and narrow, but always irregular, divides Canaan into two parts, both of which chiefly consist of hill-country, intersected by valleys running from west to east. Of greatest importance are the coastal lowlands and the nearly eight mile broad plain of Jezreel, the towns of which came to play a leading part in the civilization of Canaan. North and south of this plain are the mountainous districts; towards the south the heights of Ephraim, the central part of the country, consisting of ranges which are sometimes bare and sometimes covered with copses and pastures, but everywhere intersected by numerous valleys, which for the greater part are very fertile. Towards the south these ranges lose themselves in the hill country of Judah, which rises to greater heights, sometimes 800—1000 m. above sea level. Also here there are fertile valleys, but the chief characteristics of the country are the great steppes covered with pastures which, however, towards the east merge into the desolate tracts round the Dead Sea.

The whole of the central and southern part of the country, the real home of the history of Israel, would necessarily isolate its population in small communities, though roads of communication are not lacking. But at the same time the roads of Canaan point towards the outer world.

Canaan is a narrow borderland dividing sea from desert, and consequently it naturally became the highway between northern and southern civilization. The main road passes through the plain of Jezreel, towards the south along the coastal plain as far as Egypt; towards the north it continues as far as Syria and from there goes on to Asia Minor, Mesopotamia and still remoter countries. Thus Canaan becomes the narrow strait through which the stream must pass between the northern and southern centres of culture. Towards the west the sea gives access to the islands and coasts of the Mediterranean. To the east and south lies the wide expanse of the desert, where live the people who are constantly moving from one place to another and are attracted to the country by the civilization developed in it.

It is not to be wondered at that many people meet here. The Old Testament preserves the tradition of the variegated population living in Canaan, when the Israelites came to settle there; but by means of the sources brought to light during the last hundred years — Egyptian, Babylonian, Assyrian and Hittite — this scanty information has come to loom against a wider horizon.

Even from the beginning of the third millennium a Semitic population is to be found in Canaan. They lived in the fortified towns, such as Megiddo, Jericho, Gezer, Lachish and Jerusalem, and their high degree of civilization appears, e. g., from the imposing tunnels in Gezer and Jerusalem. This population was closely related to the Amorites, who in the third millennium inhabitated the regions round Lebanon and from there spread towards the east of the Euphrates. This people must have played a great part as a connecting link between the East and the West. From that stock sprang the dynasty of the famous Hammurabi, which was of such importance in the cultural development of Babylonia. Through the Amorites the eastern culture spread along the routes of war and commerce, which to the north of the desert lead towards the west and down into Canaan. Here the Amorites were still the essential element of the population at the time that the Israelites came into the country. We find them in the centre of Canaan, round Shechem (Gen. 48,22; Judg. 1,34) and still more pronouncedly in Gibeon (2 Sam. 21,2); to the east of Jordan they drove out the Moabites from their northern border regions (Num. 21,21).

There is thus a practically unbroken communication through related peoples between Canaan and the countries of the Euphrates, and from the early part of the third millennium the eastern empires, by warlike expeditions, further secured the influence which they were free to exercise in the west.

This stream from the north was met from the south by another, especially strong influence, i. e. that of the *Egyptians*. That the Egyptians, who were much nearer neighbours than the Babylonians, had a strong cultural influence in Canaan appears from the archæological finds with the many articles of earthenware, statuettes, ornaments, scarabees, etc., not only in the southern towns like Gezer and Jerusalem, but also in the plain of Jezreel. As early as in the third millennium we know of warlike expeditions undertaken by the Egyptian kings as far as Palestine, and so the great eastern and western powers met in this place, politically as well as culturally. Canaan was the country through which their emissaries, their traders and their workmen passed, and it absorbed its ample share of cultural elements from both sides. This was the state of Canaan in the second and third millenniums. Whereas the Egyptian cultural influence more particularly manifests itself in an infinite number of small things, the Mesopotamian influence is visible in the brick walls of the cities, in seal cylinders, in weapons and, first and foremost, in the use of the Babylonian language and characters in the written documents. We come across gods who are well known in the cuneiform literature, such as Nergal, Nabu, Hadad, Shamash, Ninurta, and also Egyptians gods, such as Ptah, Osiris, etc., and more particularly Bes. The close intermixture of the two cultures is shown by the frequently mentioned example: the seal cylinder of Atanaḥili at Taanach from about 2000 B. C., provided with cuneiform characters and hieroglyphs, the king in Babylonian garments and offering prayers to Nergal, who is in Egyptian apparel.

From the middle of the second millennium the Egyptians became the political rulers of Canaan, but the Babylonian cultural influence persisted, and the Babylonian language and characters are used in international communication. The first centuries of the second millennium had, however, brought about great and radical changes, introducing new elements into Canaan.

In the north the *Hittites* pressed forward; their centre was in Asia Minor, and to the east of them, in northern Mesopotamia, the Mitanni settled, forcing back the Amorites.

Hittite peoples we meet with for the first time a little before 1900, when they raided Babylon and thus contributed to the fall of the first dynasty. From about 1500 we know them as building a state with a strong kingdom in Asia Minor. Their scriptures are in various dialects, showing their mixed character and the prevalence of Aryan elements. So Aryan tribes must to a certain extent have been the ruling race with them as with the Mitanni.

In the 14th century the Hittites are the dominating power in Syria. From the Amarna letters we see them maintaining themselves as a political power towards Egypt and extending their influence in Canaan. We find Hittite princes lika Labaya and Khiziri in the central and southern part of the country: in Jerusalem a prince is called after a Mitanni and Hittite divinity Khiba. A number of Aryan names are found. Excavations in Syria show that Hittite cultural influence was strong here for a long time after the fall of the great empire, and in Assyrian sources Syria often appears under the name of Khatti. Consequently we cannot wonder at Hittites being mentioned in the Old Testament. Uriah, the husband of Bathsheba, and Ahimelech, another of the circle of David, are Hittites (1 Sam. 26,6); Solomon had Hittite wives (1 Kings 11,1). Mention is made of Hittites in Hebron (Gen. 23), and Ezekiel says that the mother of Jerusalem was a Hittite (Ez. 16,3. 45).

From about 1700 B. C. an influence also makes itself felt from the west through Cypriote pottery, and this western influence spreads during the later centuries of the second millennium. From this period excavations have brought to light a good deal of Cretian and, generally, Ægæan earthenware. The great wave of migration which during this period moved the Ægæan peoples, also made itself felt in Palestine. The peoples came partly by sea and partly by land, and they bore down upon Canaan in their ox-carts, following the routes along the Syrian coast. They had to fight their way, but found a domicile in the broad coastal plain south of Carmel. Their descendants are the *Philistines,* who, during the older period of the history of Israel, for a time successfully attempted to extend their rule to the plain of Jezreel and the central highlands.

Also other Semitic elements were gradually introduced into the original Amorite population. The Old Testament distinguishes between Canaanites and Amorites, the former presumably having come into the country together with the closely related Phœnicians, who settled by the sea in the northern parts of the country. [1]

The frequent shiftings of the population were naturally accompanied by fights, but owing to the heterogeneous character of the land, they were also brought about in rather an imperceptible manner. There was no sudden transition between the steppes and the cultivated land, and to the east as well as to the west of Jordan there were regions where the nomads might continue their accustomed manner of living, until one day they went down to the plains and settled in the cultivated land. But even after they had acquired a fixed residence they would, for part of the year, go out with their herds and once more return to their old nomadic life. However, the nucleus of the population were residential peasants. They cultivated their fields with wheat and barley; their domestic animals were mainly sheep and goats, oxen, asses and swine. An important part of the property of landowners consisted in the vineyard and the olive grove. The old presses in which the grapes and the olives were crushed and pressed are still to be seen.

The centres of culture were the towns, round which were the fields and vineyards. As a rule the town was situated on a hill, by preference in the neighbourhood of some spring. It was surrounded by strong walls, which in the older times generally consisted of piled-up unhewn stone-blocks, but later on were built of hewn stone and baked clay, frequently provided with towers. A single gate would suffice (cf. Judg. 16,3), the principal object being that the town should not be too easily accessible. The streets were narrow, and the space in the house of the scantiest; the buildings were to give shelter for human beings and animals against sun and rain and to serve as store rooms. They were not intended as a setting for social intercourse, which took place in the open air, mostly in or round the gateway. Every town formed a special community, while the adjoining smaller towns, presumably open villages, stood in a relation of subordination to the former; in the Old Testament such villages are called the daughters of the larger town. A similar organization is also known from the Amarna letters. [1]

These letters, which for the greater part were written by Canaanite petty kings to their Egyptian overlords, are the source of our knowledge of conditions in Canaan about 1400 B. C. From the Old Testament we know that the towns of Canaan are sometimes governed by a local aristocracy, the Elders, sometimes by a king. In the case of a single town, Shechem, we learn how one type of constitution is substituted for another (Judg. 9).[1] Also in the Amarna letters mention is sometimes made of "lords of towns", in the case of towns which we know were ruled by kings, and a couple of letters have been written by the inhabitants of the town, which seems to show that there has been no king.[2] But usually the city was ruled by a monarch.

Unfortunately we are not told much of the inner life of the towns and the relation between king and people, but there are some few suggestions to the effect that this relation was the same as in Egypt and Babylonia. The community is identical with the king, who acts by himself on behalf of the people: and the people have no independent will as against his. A separate will they could only show through sedition, which also sometimes happened. The prince of Gubla relates that the population, as well as his own house and his women, asked him to conclude peace with the Amorites, but he refused to do so. The malcontents then rose against him, but were killed. It is characteristic that after that the people said: "How long art thou going to kill us? How wilt thou get people to live in the city[3]?" The town belongs to the king, and the subjects live in his town.

These petty kings living all over the country call each other brethren;[4] at times they make covenants, at other times they fight each other, partly by means of intrigues and calumny. They are the smaller luminaries, who derive their light from the great sun, the King of Egypt. Just as they own their subjects, so in the same manner Pharaoh owns them and the whole country. They may say that they protect the King's land for him;[5] they have their shoulders under his yoke, they are his governors and his slaves. They search for the most servile expressions, call themselves the stableboy of the King, a dog, his footstool, the dirt under his feet. They assure him that they prostrate themselves before him "seven times seven", some even "both on their breasts and their backs".[6] The King is the absolute despot. "Thou art King, by thy heart thou mayst act", writes the Babylonian King to the King of Egypt.[7] This plenitude of power possessed by the King is, however, not only of a material kind. He is not an ordinary human being, but a deity, and he is constantly addressed thus in the letters. "My Addu", one of the princes calls him.[1] He is the sun rising over the lands, and he is constantly addressed as "my lord, my gods, my sun".[2] We know from the Egyptians themselves that these are not empty words. The King possesses divine life and yields thereof to his subjects. He gives life to the country, and his vassals are imbued with his strength; they look to him and there is light. He is the strength of their souls which gives them power to maintain themselves.[3]

The great King sent out officials to act as intermediaries between him and the petty princes. An official of this kind, *rabiṣu,* seems to have had several princes under him, who had to render obedience to him and turned to him for advice. In cases of conflict he judged between them; difficult questions were put before him; he reported to Pharaoh on the various happenings and the enterprises of the princes, for which reason he often went from one place to another. In such cases the local princes must provide the necessary following for his protection. This *rabiṣu* is solemnly inaugurated, Pharaoh putting a ring on his finger.[4]

The relation between the King and the princes is ratified by gifts. The vassal kings must pay tribute to their overlord to add to his wealth and indicate their dependency. Pharaoh's *rabiṣu* comes to fetch it, or he sends a special envoy for it.[5] The petty princes must now and again fit out caravans and send them to the King with the produce of the country, besides slaves and slave girls,[6] at the same time communicating their requirements. In return they constantly demand gifts from the King as tokens of his approval, preferably gold and silver in abundance. They loudly demand their gifts. One complains that the neighbouring king has been more honoured than he, his envoy having received a horse from Pharaoh.[7] A prince whose envoy returns from Pharaoh without a gift, risks losing his throne.

The possession of Canaan added to the pomp and splendour of Pharaoh's majesty; from a practical point of view it meant that he controlled the thoroughfare to the northern countries. The caravans of the King are constantly passing through Canaan in a northerly or southerly direction, and the kings of the towns must support them. Their arrival is announced by messengers, and the petty kings have to supply them with meat and drink, probably also with men for their protection.[1] When the armies of Pharaoh came up in order to secure the frontiers against the northern and eastern states, orders were issued to the kings to prepare everything for the troops. Then wine, oil, grain and cattle must be kept ready, and the King of the town goes out in person with his warriors in order to receive the troops of his overlord.[2] Royal envoys are constantly passing through Canaan on their way to and from more remote countries, and whenever they come to a prince, they must be received and provided with everything necessary for their journey; they also must be given presents, just as they themselves bring a present from the King, if he is generously inclined. The Amorite prince Aziru was accused of not having received the envoy of the King with the necessary honours. He immediately wrote an eloquent apology to the great King, telling him that he had unfortunately been away and returned too late, but his brothers had given the envoy oxen and fowls, meat and strong drinks as well as horses and asses for the journey. And next time the envoy of the King will receive food, ships, oil and fine woods.[3]

Aziru, however, was not so innocent as he pretended to be. His principality lay near the frontiers of the Hittites, and in his exposed position he attempted to keep his balance between the two great powers by showing a fitting servility on both sides. At the same time he did all he could to extend his territory at the cost of various neighbouring princes, and presently he surrendered entirely to the Hittites. At the time of the Amarna letters conditions in Canaan became still more confused, owing to the invasion of the foreign tribes, the *Khabiru,* who threatened the petty kings in the north as well as in the south. The Khabiru, whose name has been identified with that of the Hebrews,[4] are probably one of the waves of migration, which now and again came from the desert, and there is every probability that in some way or other they are connected with the Israelitic immigrants. Concerning the centuries after 1400 B. C. we know very little: in spite of the wars with the Hittites, Egypt still kept her leadership in Canaan, though it is impossible to say how important it really was. In Canaan itself the inhabitants lived more or less as at the time of the Amarna letters. The petty kings resided in their cities, each of them the lord of his own small territory, without any community beyond that which arose out of covenants with the nearest neighbours, occupied in fighting other petty princes and invading tribes. Their subjects cultivated their fields and vineyards and tended their cattle; at the same time the caravans undoubtedly kept on passing through the country and exchanged the produce of Canaan with the commodities of foreign countries.

The Amarna letters show that the inner political conditions of Canaan were of a similar character to those of Babylonia in the third millennium, a number of city-kingdoms now and then making small coalitions. But the common ruler was a foreign monarch outside the country. The inhabitants of Canaan did not possess the strength of the Babylonians to shape a homogeneous national culture, nor was a Palestinian empire created before David. Therefore we cannot expect to find a strong social organization in Canaan like those of the surrounding empires, neither the strongly developed civil service of Egypt nor the feudalism prevailing in Egypt, Babylonia and Asia Minor. But, as appears from the excavations, the Old Testament and other sources, the Canaanites with whom the Israelites came to live were strongly influenced by all these peoples, and we can trace their influence in the social and legal life of Canaanite Israel.

In Babylonia we find, about 2000 B. C., a society moulded on the same principles as those flourishing among the Arabs, but these principles were in the Babylonian city-community and empire transformed to fixed and limited, partly doctrinarian forms. The members of the community are divided into certain strictly defined categories: king, patricians, plebeians and slaves. The solidarity of the kindred, the nucleus of the conception of man in the free society, is acknowledged to a certain degree, but in a limited and dogmatized form. The relation between men is not regulated by the free balance between the kindred groups, but it is regulated from above by rules determined by the principle of restoration which prevails in the free society, at the same time entirely transforming this principle.

The Hittites have gone much further. In their now published laws we trace only little of the old conception of man. Breach of life is not restored by life, but — if rightly understood — by the deliverance of a number of slaves. In these laws we almost seem to discern the modern conception of man as a sum of working-power. The slave is not placed outside the community; he is a sort of plebeian, valued as half a freeman. The rigorous rules for matrimonial and sexual life, so intimately connected with the conception of kin in the Semitic communities, are not to be traced in this culture, and in the Hittite laws we find a striking illustration of what is called "the doings of the land of Canaan" (Lev. 18,3). According to all this the relation of property to man has not the same intimate character as in the other societies here mentioned.

In the following an attempt will be made to show how these important cultures have affected Canaanite and thus Israelitic life, the Israelites partly assimilating their spirit and customs, partly reacting against them. We are not able to say whether the Assyrians — who had a colony in Asia Minor even before 2000 B. C. — have made their influence felt in Canaan during an older period. We have no direct evidence of their influence in this country, before they entered into the history of Israel as conquerors. But before and during the Israelitic period customs common to Assyria and the other northern states may have spread over southern Syria and Canaan. This seems suggested by the fragment of an Assyrian code which has now become known. How far the influence of Egypt has penetrated the inner life of Canaan we cannot say. But in the main the same certainly holds good of Palestine in the second millennium B. C., as later in history. Politically Palestine was the object of strife between Egypt and the northern kingdoms. From the point of view of culture it frequently received strong impulses from Egypt, but it has always belonged together with Syria and shared the culture with the northern regions, whatever the trend of the cultural current.

THE MAKING OF ISRAEL. HISTORY AND SOURCES.

This was the *milieu* into which the Israelitic shepherds penetrated, and where they settled. They had grazed their flocks of sheep and goats in the border lands round Canaan, but gradually they followed the road which so many other nomads had taken before them, and crossed the frontiers of the cultivated country. At first they lived in the mountains, where they might continue their wonted manner of living with their flocks. Like the Khabiru people they spread over the whole of the country and lived in small communities. Gradually, however, they were able to pass down into the valleys and conquer first one town, then another, or a group of them met a population with whom they could make covenants and with whom they lived on a friendly footing. We possess no knowledge of the details, but it was through a process of this kind that historic Israel came into existence.

The Old Testament seemingly furnishes a complete account of the making of Israel. It begins with Abraham proceeding from Haran in northern Mesopotamia or — according to another tradition — from Ur in southern Mesopotamia towards the west across Jordan. He first goes to Shechem, where he founds an altar; then towards the south to Bethel and further south to Hebron which, apart from a short excursion to Egypt, becomes his fixed abode. His grandson Jacob passes through Palestine, following the same route along which Abraham travelled south, settles among the Aramæans, marries and, with his wives and children, returns to Canaan. Famine compels them all to go to Egypt, where they settle as shepherds, multiply greatly and become extremely numerous. They leave Egypt, where they had to work as slaves, and, led by Moses, they pass by the mount of Sinai, where they make the covenant with Yahweh, and proceed from there further east round the Dead Sea, until, under the leadership of Joshua, they conquer the land which had belonged to their fathers.

One must admire the clearness with which this narrative has been put together. We see how one man, through the generations, gradually becomes a whole nation. But the very simplicity seems to bear testimony that we are dealing with an artificial story. History itself does not progress along straight lines, but by crooked and tortuous ways. The Israelitic usurpation of Canaan has been much more varied, as appears, among other things, from the old narratives of the Book of Judges. And no people is formed by natural descent from one common ancestor. In reality Israel was not complete when the immigration took place, its tribes having formed in the country itself. The Patriarchal legends and the story of the immigration show us the view taken by later Israel of its own making. As these legends have been handed down to us through the various written sources, they only came into existence when Israel had long been fully developed, and the spirit of later Israel speaks through them. But the material, of course, cannot be pure fiction; there must be old traditions behind them.

The first thing to be done is to cut the thread between the various groups of legends and to take them separately. We then get a narrative of Abraham, who lives at Hebron, but has immigrated from the east. We get a cycle of traditions centring round Jacob, who was connected partly with the founder of the Edomites, partly with the Aramæans, and finally a group of stories dealing with Israelitic tribes living in Egypt and round Sinai and later migrating into Canaan. As to Abraham, we are told so little that it is impossible to ascertain the actual part played by him in the history of old Israel. His name is connected with several places of worship, more especially Hebron. But the narratives centring round him have a marked didactic character.

Of much greater importance are the other two groups of traditions. The names of Jacob's sons are well known to us from historical times as the names of tribes. If, e. g., we read the blessing of Jacob (Gen. 49), it is clear that we are here dealing with tribes, not with individuals. But alongside with these there are a series of narratives, which undoubtedly deal with individuals. When a wedding is described, when it is told how Isaac and Ishmael play together, when we hear that Joseph's father presented him with a fine new coat, and when we listen to his strange adventures in Egypt, who then will be able to look upon this as tribal history? But when are the patriarchs tribes, and when are they individuals? Thus *we* ask in our eagerness to individualize our material, but this question is not in the spirit of the old legends, which do not acknowledge the sharp distinction between the history of the individual and that of the tribe. We here touch upon a fact which cannot be thoroughly grasped until we have made clear the Israelitic conception of man and community. From the Arabians and other peoples we know how tribes are formed; a prominent man gathers all his kindred around him, and others join them. They then form a perfectly solidary unity, and are called after him, while he acts on their behalf. When he dies, he is the father, not only of the sons of his loins, but of all who belong to the community of the group. He is not removed by death from his tribe, but continues to live in it and share its adventures; he is still the one round whom adventures centre. He is at the same time the tribe and its father, and to everyone who joins the tribe he thus becomes a father. There are Arabian legends to the effect that Kalb, being a North-Arabian tribe and having Maʿadd as their father, once formed a confederation with the southern tribes and thus got Ḳaḥṭān as their father.

In the same manner the formation of tribes must have taken place among the Israelites. Therefore the patriarchs are neither merely individuals nor the personifications of tribes; they are *fathers* who take part in the life of the tribe. The legends centre round them, intermixed with fairy tales and minor features, which the sons involuntarily stamp with their character, and all the great events happening to the tribe are ascribed to them. The difficulty which we experience in the transition from the individual to the tribal features, they do not feel. It can be said to Rebekah that "two nations are in thy womb" (Gen. 25,23), because every Israelite knew that she was going to give birth to two fathers of peoples. The story of the death of Jacob is typical. It runs: And Israel said unto Joseph, Behold, I die: but God shall be with you, and bring you again unto the land of your fathers. Moreover I have given to thee a *shechem* (i. e. a shoulder of mountain) above thy brethren, which I took out of the hand of the Amorite with my sword and my bow (Gen. 48,21-22). The first part of the account shows us a scene in Egypt: Jacob lies on his death-bed in his chamber and takes leave of his son Joseph, who has brought his two boys Ephraim and Manasseh. But the next word transfers us to quite a different sphere. The old man suddenly grows into a tribe, who has conquered an important part of the land of Canaan and leaves it to another tribe, Joseph, including two more tribes, Ephraim and Manasseh, who in the historical periods actually lived in those parts. It is clear that we are here dealing with tribal history.

The peculiarly vivid manner in which the fathers take part in the history makes it difficult for us to separate the material reflecting historical events and to refer it to definite periods. The narrators, it must be remembered, do not attach any great weight to the isolating of each individual period. That an intricate historical process is at the bottom of the legends, appears from several facts. Reuben, as the first born, must have been an important tribe, and at one time lived west of Jordan;[1] in historic times it is quite an insignificant tribe in the eastern Jordan country. Simeon and Levi in historic times are of no importance as independent tribes, and the remains of Simeon are closely connected with those of Judah; but from Gen. 34 it appears that they once played a part round Shechem. And why, for instance, have Zebulon and Reuben a common mother, though in historic times they have nothing to do with one another? Behind our traditions there is a history to which we cannot penetrate. Jacob, who was the father of them all, was probably at one time a tribe like the others living in the central hill country round Bethel and Shechem (Gen. 28; 48,22). As early as about 1500 B. C. Jacob is mentioned in an Egyptian inscription as a tribal or a local name in Palestine,[2] and Israel is mentioned in the same manner about 1230 B. C., being localized in Central Palestine. It is probable that Jacob was a Canaanite place name, from which the Israelites subsequently derived their appellation. That Jacob and Israel are identical probably means that the two tribes have coalesced, and as they give a common name to the whole nation, they must have been the nucleus round which the Israelitic people formed. In the above-mentioned inscription

Joseph was mentioned together with Jacob, but Joseph, in his turn, gradually dissappeared and was merged into new tribal formations (Ephraim and Manasseh). Their special connection with Jacob rests on the fact that they lived together, and Joseph took over the territory which Jacob at one time possessed, i. e. the region round Shechem; but as a father Jacob lived on, also within the Joseph tribe, and eventually became the father of them all.

Jacob's history is particularly bound up with that of two other peoples: the Edomites and the Aramæans. He has Aramæan wives and for a long time sojourns among his Aramæan kinsmen. Though the legends centring round him bear the impress of the later Israelitic conception of life, it cannot be taken for granted that they merely reflect conditions during the time of the kings, when the relation between Israel and Aram, as far as we know, had a somewhat different character. In this there may be reminiscences of a connection existing between the wanderings of the Israelites and those of the Aramæans.[1] Still closer are the ties connecting Jacob with Edom; they are twin brothers and live together for a long time. Nor do these legends seem to reflect the historical events of a later period, but to preserve a memory from the time of wandering. That there was at that time a connection between the two peoples appears from the fact that the God of Israel is associated with the hill country of Edom (Judg. 5,4; Deut. 33,2). This fact bears testimony that the old tribes had more to do with Edom than has been directly communicated by our authorities.[2]

That the immigration of Jacob led to the coming of other tribal elements is probable. What the relation was between that and the immigration legends of the Book of Joshua we cannot say. Unfortunately, even in its best sources, the Book of Joshua is so strongly influenced by later Israelitic views that it is difficult to distinguish between the old and the new. According to the Priestly Code the people under Joshua conquer the country from one end to the other, and then divide it among the tribes. According to the Yahwist the country is divided beforehand according to a common plan; after that the tribes to some extent act independently. But also in the latter version the tribes are fully established, and before and during the conquest the people form a unity under a common leader, while Judah, who does not play any part in the oldest history, comes to the front. But apart from this, some narratives are left of individual conquests (in particular Jericho and Ai) and the conclusion of a covenant (Gibeon), which may reflect old events, but undoubtedly is coloured by later ideas about olden times; to this must be added a list of cities which had not been conquered, but which remained Canaanitic (Judg. 1), the list dating from a time when Israel was the lord of the essential part of Canaan.

Coupled with these two groups of traditions relating to immigration are the narratives of the sojourn in Egypt and at Sinai. It is clear that these must reflect historical events. Yahweh is closely connected with Mount Sinai, and the events in Egypt have come to occupy a unique position in the conceptions of the Israelites, having attained a permanent place in their worship; and this can only be explained through the fact that Sinai and Egypt played a practical part in the life of the people. It is obvious that part of pre-historic Israel during their wanderings with Edom, and perhaps other peoples, as, e. g., the Midianites, have resorted to these regions and worshipped at Mount Sinai.[1] That Semitic nomads often penetrated into the Egyptian border lands we know on Egyptian authority, and they were sometimes employed in building the fortifications of the Pharaohs. It is told that the Israelites worked at Pithom and Raamses (Exod. 1,11). The former of these cities has of recent years been excavated; the excavator, Naville, was of opinion that it had been built by Raamses 2, and this has given rise to the theory that the Exodus took place in the reign of Merneptah, the son of the latter, about 1200 B. C.[2] This theory may be right, but that which makes the problem so intricate is that we do not know how great a part of pre-historic Israel remained in Egypt.

We must constantly bear in mind that it was pre-historic Israel which lived in Egypt; historic Israel and its tribes were created in Canaan. Therefore it is impossible to say what part of Israel they were, as they must have preceded all the subsequent tribal formations. But in all probability they formed the nucleus of the population, inasmuch as their traditions play a principal part for the whole of Israel during later years. It is probable that they were the fathers of the old tribes in the central part of the country, Israel, Jacob, Joseph, Benjamin, Ephraim, Manasseh.

The events centring round Sinai were of such importance that they became the basis of the life of the people. Here the Covenant was made with their God, out of which covenant grew the whole fabric of their existence. Moses, the great leader who had brought them out of Egypt, becomes the creator of the whole Israelitic type of life. Everything that is essential to the life of the people is derived from Moses, and all laws are given in his name. All this bears testimony to the vital importance of this period, but also to the fact that we cannot make a direct use of our sources in describing the Mosaic period. When everything authoritative is Mosaic, then every generation will naturally lend to the time of Moses its own manner of living and thinking. And this is what has happened. All the laws to be found in the Pentateuch date from a far later period. The Book of Covenant for instance, with its precepts about the three harvest festivals, presupposes that people live in fixed habitations, and that the ox is their most important domestic animal. Is it possible out of such a complex material to distinguish individual parts as Mosaic, because there is no direct évidence of their being of Canaanite origin? We must consider the codes throughout as the expression of Canaanite Israel's life. To separate certain clauses of these laws of historic Israel, and to prove that they were formulated by Moses is unthinkable. We must look upon Moses, as Israel looked upon him, i. e. as the original law-maker to whom all laws are ascribed. Apart from this we have no means of answering the question, what Moses was from an historical point of view.

What holds good of the laws also holds good of the narratives contained in the Pentateuch. Wherever we can look behind them, it is the later Israel we discern. A case in point is the story of the Golden Calf (Exod. 32). The priest Aaron makes a molten image of a calf, and together with the whole people holds a feast of worship to Yahweh. Then Moses, Yahweh's man, appears, destroys the calf and punishes the people very severely. The question of the worship of the bull-calf plays a great part in the life of Canaanite Israel: it is even their principal problem of cult. It could not possibly be of any interest to them before that time, seeing that they had formerly had nothing to do with bulls. Our narrative condemns the bull-worship, which was adopted in Canaan by so many Israelites and their priests: it says that Moses once and for all passed judgment on this practice; Israel is not permitted to worship the calf. Another example we find in Num. 16, where two stories have become mixed. In the one (from J. E.) two men, Dathan and Abiram, refused to obey the chief, Moses. Moses maintained that he had not been unjust to any one, and the Elders supported him. The matter is decided by divine judgment, and the rebels are swallowed up by the earth (16,12-15. 25-34 with some exceptions). In the narratives of the Priestly Code the two things are mixed. According to one part of the story it is a revolt against the priestly prerogatives. The chiefs or princes maintain that the whole of the people are holy and that Moses and Aaron have no special prerogatives. Once more the matter is decided by divine judgment, the rebels being told to perform one of the priestly functions, which were of importance in the later sanctuary of Jerusalem, viz. the offering of incense. The result is that the priests are proved to be right, the rebels being consumed by fire. Another part of the narrative raises a problem of a similar kind; here the Levites under Korah rise against Aaron and claim for themselves priestly dignity; Korah is well known as the name of a section of the Levites in the post-exilic temple.[1] The narrative reflects conflicts among the priests of Jerusalem, partly between the clergy and the laity, partly between the lower and higher clergy. In the same manner the narrative of Dathan and Abiram decides questions of principle as to the duty of rendering obedience to the leaders of the people.

Israel's old history presents many unsolved problems. The narratives of the sojourn in Egypt, the exodus and the wanderings in the desert have been elaborated from the point of view of fully finished Israel. We cannot prove in details what is the real, historical basis of the whole story. The chief actors are from a pre-historic Israel, preceding the tribal division and unknown to the later narrators. We altogether lack the means to decide the relation between Jacob's wanderings and the Sinai wanderings, and we cannot form a complete picture of the history of Israel's making. However, certain principal features are quite clear, and they give an impression of the manner in which Israel was made.

In consequence of the separatist character of Canaan the events connected with the immigration must everywhere be purely local. When the Khabiru peoples invaded the country, they appeared in various parts and threatened first one and then another city and its king; at the same time there is evidence that here and there they concluded covenants.[1] The same course was followed by the Israelites. They were not powerful tribes; their flocks consisted of goats and sheep, not, as those of the richer tribes, of camels. First they had to be content with the hill country. Here they lived in their tents, but in all probability they also used the numerous caves which for thousands of years had served as human dwellings[2]. We hear of the covenants they make, as, e. g., with Gibeon and with Shechem, which covenant, it is true, was broken. We hear of the conquests of individual towns, such as Jericho and Ai, and the Song of Deborah celebrates a great victory through which they gained access to the plain of Jezreel. New changes, new wanderings would take place. The Danites first settled at the plain of the Philistines, but later on they wandered in a body through the country to its northern border regions (Judg. 18). In the old narratives of the Book of Judges we find the Israelites in possession of a number of towns, more especially in the central part of the country. In that manner they gradually change their mode of life to that of the towns and begin to cultivate the fields, though at the same time they keep the flocks which they used to graze in the mountains. Sheep and goats still formed the greater part of their live stock. David kept his father's sheep (1 Sam. 17,15. 34); the wealth of Nabal is illustrated by his having three thousand sheep and one thousand goats (1 Sam. 25,2), while in the same manner the kid is the usual sacrificial animal (Judg. 6,19; 13,15 ff.; 1 Sam. 10,3); to these are added oxen, which pertain to the agricultural work and do duty as draught-animals for plough and cart, and which also in their turn become sacrificial animals (1 Sam. 1,24). On the other hand the Israelites refused to adopt the swine and the special cult connected with it.

The patriarchs are described as farmers. Abraham at Hebron sets a calf before his guests; Isaac sows and reaps (Gen. 26,12. 14); Jacob is blessed with the blessing of the peasant (Gen. 27,28); Joseph dreams that he binds sheaves in the field together with his brethren (Gen. 37,7). But at the same time they are described as Canaanite nomads wandering about with their flocks; Abraham and Lot wander about the southern part of the country (Gen. 13), the sons of Jacob in the north, and we learn how Joseph must go from one place to another and ask his way, before he finds them (Gen. 37,12 ff.). The conditions here described have undoubtedly lasted for a long time and been familiar to the narrator. Canaan was sufficiently diverse in character to accommodate people who were peasants and at the same time half nomads. Therefore the tent still existed together with the house. Jael who killed Sisera after the battle on the plain of Jezreel lived in a tent (Judg. 4,17; 5,24). There is a certain significance in the fact that the patriarchs are all the time described as tent-dwellers, even when residing in towns (Gen. 18,1, cf. 25,27); the tent was preserved in Israel as the true appellation of dwelling, and an extreme conservative party like that of the Rechabites demanded that the people should live in tents [1].

But even though the Israelites, to a certain extent, continued their wonted manner of living, immigration, nevertheless, meant a complete revolution in their lives. They gradually became accustomed to fixed dwellings and new habits. They had to learn peasants' work and to become familiar with new domestic animals. This could only happen, because they learned from the Canaanites. The patriarchal legends lay great stress upon the fact that the fathers lived protected by the right of hospitality among the natives, and so it must generally have been, while at the same time they make a way for themselves by means of the sword. Thus they came to live scattered among the old population, partly learning from them, and partly keeping their own characteristics. There was no other bond of unity between them than the ideal one — common characteristics and common history. On special occasions the feeling of unity might burst into flames, inspiring them to a common enterprise; but otherwise they lived apart, each group in its small community. In the course of time they adopted more and more of Canaanite civilization, through which process their mental outlook and ideals were gradually changed. This fusion and the conflict between Israelite and Canaanite form the main element of the cultural history of Israel.

An important epoch in this development is the Davidic Empire. It broke through the old order with the centre of gravity in the separate Israelitic communities, and introduced the West-Asiatic social idea of the king as the central figure. The monarchic idea was tantamount to a conversion to the Canaanite order, and this was further accomplished by the manner in which the empire was founded. The Israelitic communities are merged in an empire which, it is true, was Israelitic and had the God of Israel as its imperial God, but this empire also included the non-Israelitic inhabitants of the country. A non-Israelitic city, Jerusalem, was made the capital of the country, and David surrounded himself with many foreigners. He was the ruler of a country and an empire, and if we hear of no antagonism between Israelites and Canaanites in his empire, it can only mean that the Canaanites were merged into the Israelitic unity and thus disappeared, naturally infusing Canaanite life and culture into Israel. And so nearly every trace of the Canaanites vanishes, while at the same time Israel becomes more Canaanitic. To later generations this will come to signify that the Canaanites have been exterminated, and this may have given rise to the view which dominates the descriptions of the immigration.

Thus a revolution in the life centring round the cities was carried out, and the Israelitic communities became like those of Canaan; to a very large extent they adopted the legal customs of

Canaan and Western Asia, as appears from their law-codes. This meant a change in the conception of man and also in the mutual relation of men and their relation to the outer world. The old continuity of the family could not be maintained in its full extent, and so the old ideals were abandoned.

In many respects the all-Israel Monarchy meant a deep incision in the life of Israel. It should be the aim of the king to create a unity out of the many isolated communities, and to further a development like that completed in the third and second millenniums B. C. in Egypt, Babylonia and Asia Minor, when these countries were transformed to empires, with a uniform organization of officials and feudals, thus securing the civil and military administration under the leading monarch. But conditions in Canaan were not favourable to a development of this kind. The communities were too heterogeneous and their independence too deeply rooted. We do not know the details of the attempts at centralizing made by the king, but he never overcame the relative independence of the individual communities. What we see is that a smouldering conflict arises between the old family conception of right and wrong on one side and monarchy on the other, a conflict which may sometimes burst into flames. And the king's service — such a natural link in the whole social order of the neighbouring empires — was always felt to be an unjust encroachment on the rights of the citizens.

How utterly foreign to Israelitic habits the essence of the kingdom was felt to be, we see from the bitter description of the doings of the king, ascribed to one of the great representatives of the old order (1 Sam. 8). And the fact that monarchy has left no impression on the preserved laws, shows how little it has been assimilated to Israelitic popular life.

The most important change in the monarchic period took place in the larger cities, the centres of international trade and politics. Here new classes sprang up, appropriated the whole of the property, and thus obtained complete control of the cities. The remainder of the population, above all the small landed proprietors, degenerated and became a proletariat, living in poverty and misery. The relation between these dominant classes and the old leading families is not exactly known, but they seem to be associated with the king.

Thus the large cities created new social and ethical problems, and as a matter of course they became the dominant factor of evolution. In this respect Jerusalem acquired a leading position as the old monarchic centre. It not only possessed the oldest traditions of the monarchy, but also the chief temple of the empire. When the northern kingdom collapsed in 723 B. C.,[1] Jerusalem became the pivot round which everything turned. At its temple the priesthood developed the Israelitic cult through an increasingly elaborate technique, not inferior to that which is known from other great west-Asiatic temples.

However, Israel was not a homogeneous community. Besides the more or less Canaanized circles there were others who, with the greatest tenacity, clung to the old manner of living and the old ideals, i. e. people who had their abodes in the small towns and on the steppes. The latter also naturally adapted themselves to the conditions of Canaan and were changed by its culture, but they stand out in sharp contrast to the doings of the kingdom and the large cities. Their life and ideals are those of the peasants in the small towns and the shepherds on the steppes, as they were before the immigration. And from such or closely connected circles the prophets arise. Though in many ways imbued with the Canaanite conception of life, they still maintain the old ideals and denounce the social and cultic trend of the prevailing Canaanization. They maintain the right of the family and protest against the lack of respect shown to the old view of property. They were not alone, for in the laws there is a strong tendency towards maintaining the old. A vivid protest is heard all through the Old Testament against the attempt to create an aristocratic class, raised above obligations towards the people. We are all of us plebeians, it is said, for we have all been slaves in Egypt. No Israelite is allowed to despise the slave or the wretched, because as an Israelite he himself belongs to the same category.

In the very surroundings of the king conservative elements made themselves felt in the same direction, and we find a curious union between the ideals of the shepherds and the ideals of dominion prevailing in the Asiatic monarchy. At the fall of Jerusalem these conservative circles were the ones to determine the future. They collected the literature of the people and left their impress upon it, partly by elaborating it, and partly by curtailing the old writings and providing them with notes, which expressed their condemnation of those who had taken the lead in shaping the life of the people by carrying through the Canaanization.

Thus Israel's mental history does not move along one single line. Complexity prevailed in Canaanite Israel, just as it prevailed in Canaan before Israel. There were many stages of transition from those who without restriction adapted themselves to Canaanite customs and life to those who claimed to maintain the life of the wilderness. But upon the whole we are able to distinguish two main types: the old Israel of the small communities and the remodelled Israel of the great towns. Like the latter the former type has adapted itself to the life of Canaan; but the transformation is not so violent that the genuine conception of man and his position in the world has been radically converted. The other type was the result of a more intimate adaptation to the Canaanite spirit, but to this factor must be added the kingdom and the social changes of the great cities. The two types have existed alongside, fought each other and influenced each other. Sometimes open conflicts arose, as instanced by the different prophets. But this does not mean that the two types were sharply defined. Also strongly Canaanized circles kept Israelitic traditions and thought themselves good representatives of the latter, as, e. g., the kings. On the other hand, the ardent spokesmen of the old habits were imperceptibly imbued with Canaanite ideals; this holds good of the prophets and other representatives of the reaction against Canaanization. To this category belong the admonitions of the Deuteronomy, containing violent demands that all Canaanites should be exterminated. The authors of these claims did not know that the laws connected with their admonitions were nearly all purely Canaanite.

The object of the present work is to describe the conception of life in Israel as it was until the collapse of the nation. The fundamental psychological conception of the Israelites is the same throughout their history until their meeting with Hellenistic culture. In this respect Israel may therefore be described as a unity. But in other domains of psychic life its history makes itself felt, and here it is often possible to trace the two types mentioned above: the old Israelitic conception and its transformation under the influences of the different forces of Canaanite life — "Canaanite" here being a term used to designate the non-Israelitic population of Canaan as a whole, irrespective of such points of difference as it is impossible for us to trace.

The only sources at hand for an account of the mental history of Israel are the various books of the Old Testament which, each in its way, yield material towards the understanding of the psychology of Israel. Whenever it is a question of describing the values of life, one feels that the writings have been handed down to us by people belonging to the last stages of evolution and far removed from the life of oldest Israel. Nevertheless, the material at hand for the study of this life is not inconsiderable, though we might naturally wish for more.

Of primary importance are the *Books of Samuel* and, apart from the remarks and additions of the exilic compilers, the *Book of Judges,* giving vivid pictures of the life of oldest Israel; of a similar value are parts of the, unfortunately greatly curtailed, narratives of the *Books of Kings.* A picturesque description of the life of a small Israelitic community, untouched by the spirit of the large cities, we find in the *Book of Job.* It is impossible to decide when this work was composed, but on the other hand the time of composition is immaterial, as it has no connection whatsoever with the evolution determined by the influence of Jerusalem. The problem dealt with cannot have arisen in the oldest time, but, on the other hand, the description of life contained in it could not be fresher. The speeches of the *prophets* give evidence of ideals not to be found in the oldest Israel, but by their arguments they throw light on many particulars of the conflict between the old and the new order of things. Among the *Psalms* the royal hymns contribute a greatly needed material towards the understanding of the position of the king. Other psalms reveal different sides of life in Jerusalem and the cult connected with the temple.

As to the *Pentateuch* the admirable researches carried on during the latter generations have taught us to look on them as being composed of sources, each elucidating an epoch of the inner and outer history of Israel. There is no reason to deny that the analysis of the documents is on the whole correct, as far as concerns the distinction between the Priestly Code, the Deuteronomy and the Yahwist-Elohist. But as it will appear in the present work, the narratives cannot always be divided between Yahwist and Elohist as is generally done, just as it is unjustifiable to divide the old narratives of the Book of Judges. Far too frequently modern logic, in these respects, has blinded the critics and prevented them from discerning the inner logic of the narratives. As to the mutual relation of the various sources, far too much importance has been attached to the problem of the time of composition. The generally adopted opinion is that the Yahwist-Elohist dates from the earlier period, e. g. the ninth century, while the Deuteronomy dates from the seventh century, representing a later stage, and the Priestly Code from the Exile or the last stage of evolution. According to this view the history of Israel is moving along one line of development. But matters have been more composite.

The *Priestly Code* is mainly a compilation of laws, which no doubt was given its final form during or after the Exile. It is filled with theoretical constructions, but behind the constructions we discern old material. So the laws of cult represent the old traditions of the priesthood at the temple of Jerusalem, and the social laws in the "Law of Holiness" (Lev. 17-26), forming part of the Priestly Code, contain among pure constructions the old laws of kindred, which do not harmonize with later customs and manners, but which formed the kernel of the social life of the oldest Israel. The *Deuteronomy* contains a law-code, part of which bears the stamp of certain circles of the priesthood of Jerusalem, who claimed a monopoly on their temple, thinking in that manner to liberate Israel from Canaanite customs; for the main object of the book, in its present shape, is to protect the Israelitic community against Canaanite influence. The object of the historical section is to show that Israel has its special history from the desert and only courts disaster by associating with strangers. The social laws of the Deuteronomy are very incomplete; they represent the Canaanite laws, which are here fused with the specifically Israelitic conception. As to the *Yahwist* and the *Elohist,* the main law-code is to be found in the Book of Covenant containing a number of Canaanite laws which have prevailed in a wider or narrower circle of Israelitic city communities. It is of course impossible to say at what time these laws were adopted by the Israelites, but there is no reason to doubt that they held good in certain circles as long as Israel remained in Canaan.

Just as the Priestly Code abounds in constructions dating from the Exile, or a still later period, so the other codes are supplemented with admonitions, etc., referring us to the Exile or, at any rate, the last stage of the development of Israel. As for the laws themselves, there is no reason to deny that the great bulk of them were practised in Israel. They belong to different circles, thus giving evidence of the variety and lack of unity in Israel. It is impossible to fix certain dates for them. The laws of antiquity — setting aside mere constructions — are not created on a sudden by an author. They must be rooted in customs and in an historical social life. We can only say that the laws of the Deuteronomy and the Book of Covenant are almost thoroughly Canaanite, while those of the Priestly Code partly represent late constructions, partly laws of the oldest Israelitic conception, and partly laws of reaction against Canaanite customs.

As for the narratives of the Pentateuch, those of the Priestly Code and the Deuteronomy are evidently didactic constructions made from old material. Most important are the narratives of the Yahwist-Elohist, being richer and fuller than those of the other sources. But these cannot be taken as direct evidence of old Israelitic life. As we know them, they are composed with fine art and by skilled authors having a definite aim of composition. They contain elements reminding us of Judaism, as, e. g., the speculations on justice found in narratives centring round Abraham, or the speculations on the name of the God of Israel; the purely didactic character makes itself felt in many narratives, above all those of Abraham. There is a great difference between these narratives and those of the Book of Judges and of Samuel. They are told in a spirit imbued with the soul of Canaan and monarchy. But the narrators, whose object is a deliberate glorifying of the old order of things, still look towards the life of the shepherds and peasants as the true Israelitic life. Though also these parts of the Pentateuch must have been given their present form at a late period of Israelitic history, their value to us is very great, yielding glimpses of the old traditions which are much fresher than the narratives of the other sources. It is impossible for us to say whether they were completed before the Exile, but it is not probable. Great importance has been attached to the fact that the Yahwist-Elohist takes no account of the demand of the Deuteronomy, that the temple of Jerusalem should be the only one, from which fact it is concluded that the former must be from an earlier time. But the difference between the two parts of the Pentateuch cannot be explained as a mere difference of time. The Yahwist-Elohist belongs to circles which are quite different from those of the Deuteronomy. These circles considered life outside Jerusalem the true Israelitic life, and consequently they saw no reason to acknowledge the claims of the priesthood of the capital. Purely literary criticism is thus by no means sufficient to decide what is old and not old in Israel. All the sources contain elements pointing backwards to the old, and other elements which belong to the later development, these elements most frequently being greatly intermixed. It is the object of analytical research to find these various tendencies and thus to separate the old. In this manner we are able to form an imcomplete, but, nevertheless, vivid picture of the life in old Israel and the transformation it underwent within the historical period.

TRIBE AND CITY. SOCIAL ORDER.

The organization of the people of Israel we find most clearly expressed in the Priestly Code which, besides its body of laws, gives us a summary of the history of the people as it appeared to the learned Jews of the Babylonian Exile, when the empire had fallen to pieces. Ever since the sojourn in Egypt Israel has been divided into twelve tribes, sub-divided into families, which again consist of the houses of fathers. In this systematization the centre of gravity lies in the tribe. The people encamp with their tribe, each tribe by its own standard. When mention is to be made of the authorities of the tribe, these are Moses and Aaron and the princes of the tribes (Num. 1,44; 4,34.46), each tribe being represented by a prince *(nāśī')*, who is its leader during the period of migration; later on he presides over the distribution of land (Num. 2; 34,16 ff.), and he likewise, on behalf of his tribe, delivers the assessed tribute to the setting up of the tabernacle (Num. 7).

This system is rather artificial. The systematizing tendency of the priestly writer is well known; even the freebooters rallying round David in the highlands of Judah are divided into regular clans, each with its own head (1 Chron. 12). It was all the easier for the writer to systematize the tribes, as at his time they were of no practical importance. In the old sources the tribes are stamped by the irregularities of life.

The Jewish writer made an abstract division dependent upon conditions as they subsequently developed in Canaan, and as usual he projected them back to the time of the wanderings in the wilderness, in the same manner as he describes a sanctuary from the temple in Jerusalem and places it in the desert. Like other Bedouins pre-Canaanite Israel in all probability ranged itself in tribal divisions, which were very closely banded and kept together during the immigration. Such groups fought their wars and made compacts in the various parts of the country. They settled together in the hill-country and in towns lying close together. We are thus told that the Danites lived together in the cities of Zorah and Eshtaol (Judg. 18,11). When they allied themselves to the Canaanites, as is described in Gen. 34, they enlarged their community, and out of these groups grew the tribes of Israel.

We must not imagine these old tribes as being too large. The bond which held them together was that they all felt like one family. The Danites were called a family (Judg. 18,11), and Ephraim, later on such a powerful tribe, felt its honour as the first tribe threatened by Abiezer, who could muster only three hundred warriors (Judg. 7,16; 8,1-3). It is a question if it is at all correct in the oldest times to speak of tribes in the later Israelitic sense of the word. Those who belonged together settled all over the country in small communities, without any regular intercourse between the groups. Because each tribe lived an isolated life among the Canaanites, their peculiarities were developed.

We learn that the Danites, for some reason or other, migrated from the south-western to the north-eastern part of the country, without creating great disturbances in the whole of the people (Judg. 17—18), and there was no question whatsoever of a permanent leader of each tribe. When danger called, a leader came to the fore, rallied his community around him, and as many others as he could attract, or the prominent men of a certain circle turned to a chief and asked him to be their leader, as the Gileadites did with Jephthah.

Through wanderings and covenants old tribes disappeared and new tribes sprang up. Thus Jacob and Joseph disappeared, and Ephraim and Manasseh were formed. The Abiezerites are only mentioned in connection with Gideon; they were merged in Manasseh. The same probably held good of Jair, who formed a community, the tent-villages of Jair (Num. 32,41).[1] We possess no information whatsoever to the effect that Jacob's wives, and even his daughter Dinah, at one time should have been tribes; this being inferred from a mechanical view of the Patriarchs as artificial personifications of the tribes.[2]

According as the Israelites gained a firmer foothold, the tribes grew more definite, while at the same time their geographical position became more established. The centre was the highlands in the middle of Canaan, where Ephraim and Benjamin were settled. The latter name means the southern; it bears, at the same time, testimony to the importance of the geographical point of view and to the fact that the still more southerly tribe, i. e. Judah, is not included in Israel. Nor is this tribe mentioned in the Song of Deborah, but only acquires importance to Israel through David; the greater part of it was undoubtedly, like Jerusalem, non-Israelitic, and only by David was it assimilated with the Israelites, though there is ample evidence that the assimilation was never quite complete. [1]

There is other evidence to the fact that the names of the tribes mainly denote territories. In the Song of Deborah Gad is designated as Gilead (Judg. 5,17), the name of the region inhabited by this tribe; it describes how the warriors march out *from* Ephraim, from Machir, from Zebulon. Gideon sent messengers "throughout all Manasseh", "in Asher, in Zebulon, and in Naphtali" (Judg. 6,35). Asher is otherwise known to us from an Egyptian inscription as the name of a district. [2] When using the term "tribe" among the Israelites, we must not identify it with the Arabian tribe. Among the Arabians the tribe is the principal factor of social organization, because it comprises those who wander together, and who share common experiences. In the nomadic existence companionship is very close, and no foreign elements can be introduced among the members of the tribe. The foundation of the Israelitic tribal system is of a similar kind, and therefore the old tribes are large families. But when the tribes were extended over a larger area, it would necessarily make their common life together less intensive and so weaken the importance of the tribe.

That the tribal life in the older period was of importance is seen from the fact that the tribes appear as exclusive unities. The Song of Deborah addresses them separately with praise or blame, and it is evident that the question of participation or non-participation in the wars is decided by each tribe separately. Each tribe has its own history and its own physiognomy, which we still clearly discern, even as late as in the days of the monarchy; it appears from the blessing of Jacob (Gen. 49) and the blessing of Moses (Deut. 33) in which each tribe is characterized [3]: Judah is the lion gaining strength through rapine, a born ruler rich in milk and wine, in cattle and fields; Issachar lacks energy and has submitted to the Canaanites; Asher lives on the fat of the land; Benjamin is a tribe of warriors, always on the look-out; Gad must constantly fight the Bedouins. Thus each tribe has its own life and its own pecularities, and when it is said: Dan judges his people, as one of the tribes of Israel (Gen. 49,16) it means that the tribe keeps order within its special sphere. Therefore it is also called *shēbheṭ* or *maṭṭe,* two terms meaning the ruler's rod.

The tribe is to a certain extent an obscure point in the history of Israel. It must have been of real importance, but the extent of this importance we do not know. It flourished at the time of the Judges, which was surely attributable to the fact that the tribes, at that time, were still fairly small and rather isolated in their relation to each other. The Israelitic life in caves, in tents and in villages would not dissolve the force of tribal coherence. Even when the invaders conquered walled towns, this would at first agree very well with the tribal conception, seeing that a tribe settled in a couple of towns lying very close to one another, as was done by the tribe of Dan. When Israel gradually increased by the absorption of other racial elements, and the country upon the whole became Israelitic, the peculiar stamp of the individual tribes would in part be obliterated, and the community within them in any case grow less intensive. Monarchy strengthened the national unity, and the tribal feeling was swallowed up by national consciousness. When the empire had perished entirely, the tribe acquired importance through the interest taken by posterity in the past; the part it played here is a reflection of the period when Israel owned the whole of the country and the tribes were its territorial parts.

In the olden times, when the tribes were a factor in the life of the people, they would act partly together and partly against each other, but these conflicts were local and of a limited character. An event like the one chronicled in the last chapters of the Book of Judges cannot have taken place, as it is related, in the early period. It is an account of an Ephraimite who was violated by the city of Gibeah in Benjamin, and all the tribes gather against Benjamin and punish it for its crime (Judg. 19-21). The whole of the account is an expression of the ideas formed by the Jews of a later generation of life and manners in old-time Israel[1].

Whatever the significance of the tribe at a certain period in the history of Israel, it has nowhere left tangible traces. In no respect do the laws take account of the tribe, neither as regards property nor bloodfeuds nor the general relation to one's neighbour.

Whether tribal organization prevailed among the Canaanites we do not know, but it is not probable. With the Canaanites the chief thing was the city and its environs, and in the course of time this also came to hold good among the Israelites. The towns tended towards becoming independent communities, little worlds apart, such as they were at the time of the Canaanites. And this development would naturally be favoured by the fact that the influence of the tribe diminished, while it spread over a larger territory.

Even in the oldest times the *town* had its independent importance. Gideon was settled in Ophrah, which belonged to the Abiezrites, and his activity was chiefly limited to this circle. On his military expedition he turns to the cities of Succoth and Penuel, and these two cities act, each on its own responsibility, as separate communities (Judg. 8). There was a connection between Ophrah and Shechem, which was likewise ruled by the kin of Gideon. According to Gen. 34 Shechem was at one time ruled by the Hamor kin, and we see this city make a covenant with the sons of Jacob. When Abimelech obtained power over Shechem, he was the ruler of two cities, Ophra and Shechem, and he tried to add a third, i. e. Thebez. Thus an extended city monarchy was formed which, however, did not last very long. Time after time we see the city act as a unity. The cities of Ziph and Keilah take sides in the war between Saul and David (1 Sam. 23). The city of Jabesh was attacked by the Ammonites (1 Sam. 11), and it had no tribe to feel the attack as directed against itself and to rise instinctively against the assailants. It received help from other Israelites, but we see that as a city it formed an independent community.

As a rule it was undoubtedly a single family which dominated the city, such as the Abiezrites in Ophrah and the Hamor sons in Shechem, and in a smaller town, such as Bethlehem, the whole town considered itself one family (1 Sam. 20,6). It had a common sanctuary and common religious festivals (1 Sam. 9; 20,6). It might be a city which had a particularly important place of worship, and the ruling family of which was a family of priests such as Nob (1 Sam. 22,19). The unity of the city community was so strong that the responsibility was common to all. Saul put to death the whole of the city of Nob because one of its leaders had helped David (1 Sam. 22,19), and we see Gibeon standing forth to demand revenge against Saul (2 Sam. 21). The responsibility for blood guilt resting upon the whole of the town has been recognized by the Deuteronomy: If a man is found slain in a field, the citizens of the nearest town must come forth and with certain rites declare the city to be not guilty of the murder (Deut. 21,1-9).[1]

Among the laws it is first and foremost the Deuteronomy which shows us the importance of the city, even though it must have played a no less important part in the laws of the Book of Covenant. We may call it a municipal law in the proper sense of the word, for it is the town it reckons with as the responsible factor, thus increasing the authority of the elders of the city. We have already seen that the city is threatened with blood guilt, because of a murder committed in its vicinity. The Deuteronomy introduces cities of refuge for certain kinds of man-slayers. If a murderer has taken refuge in a city of this kind without sufficient justification, the elders of this city, when having investigated the matter, must fetch him back and deliver him into the hands of the kinsmen of the slain (Deut. 19,12); elsewhere it is ordained that he shall not be taken into the city, before he has "stood at the entering of the gate of the town" and declared his cause in the ears of the elders (Josh. 20,4). If parents have a particularly vicious son, then he can be brought before the elders and thereafter stoned by all the men of the city (Deut. 21,19-20). If a man accuses his newly wedded wife of unchastity, then it is the elders of the town who pass judgment. If he is right, then the men of the city stone her before the house of her father. If her father proves her to be innocent, then it is the elders who chastise and amerce the man (Deut. 22,13-21). "The elders at the gate" (25,7-9) are the authority to whom people turn.[2]

Thus the city becomes the dominating community in Israel. Its interior life is governed by the elders. There are suggestions to the effect that these representatives of the citizens played a part in the cities during the time of the Amarna letters, and in Israel they were of great importance in all the towns. We are not to look upon this institution as an artificial one. The elders do not form a council, chosen and governing according to automatic rules. An elder, *zāḳēn,* is, properly speaking, only a man with a *zāḳān,* i. e. full beard. The elders are the grown-up men of the powerful families who *de facto* have the power to rule. It is a matter of course that they must belong to the "men of valour", *gibbōrē ḥayil,* the proprietors and warriors who are able to bear the burden of the community. Just as the men of Kuraysh sat together in Mecca at the Kaʿba and decided what should be done, so the Israelitic townsmen meet "at the gate" and speak of the affairs of the town. All day long the elders move about the gate, where they are always sure of finding company, and can commune about all sorts of matters, great and trivial. Everything of any importance takes place in their presence. If a field is bought, the buyer and seller go there and ratify the purchase before the elders. There are always witnesses, and the elders are co-responsible for the legality of the transaction (Ruth 4).

The citizen who could not reckon himself among the "men of valour" as a matter of course stayed away from the assembly of the elders. It rested with those who already belonged to the circle, whether they were willing to receive him among them. The elders are identical with the city; they comprise the whole body of citizens helping to support its life. We hear, by mere chance, that there were seventy-seven elders in Succoth (Judg. 8,14). One single family might acquire such power that it excluded the others, or at any rate dominated their will (Judg. 9,2).

The manner of consultation adopted by the assembly of the "men of valour" of a small town is described, vividly and in a few words, in the Book of Job (29,7-11): In the open space at the gateway the men are assembled. One matter occupies the thoughts of all; one chief after another sets forth his advice. Then comes the great chief who has hitherto been missing; he says what he thinks of the matter, and immediately all bend before him. The elders may more or less follow one single man; they may even, as in the case of Shechem and Abimelech, acknowledge one man as their chief. But on the whole the responsibility rests with all the "men of valour", life itself determining who is to have the greatest influence.

There are different names for these powerful men. They are called *nādhībh, nāghīdh, nāśī*, and very often *śar*, "chief". In olden times the *śārīm* did not form a special class; they were only men of prominent importance (cf. Job 29,9). The "men of Succoth", "the elders of Succoth" and the "chiefs of Succoth" are thus used promiscuously of the responsible men of this town (Judg. 8,5.6.8.14.15.16).

In the course of time every Israelite became a member of a city community, either a large town or a village, and so "elders" would always necessarily be the elders of a town. When mention is so often made of the "elders of Israel" (1 Sam. 4,3; 8,4; 2 Sam. 3,17; 5,3, etc.), it does not imply another institution besides the one mentioned above, but only the responsible Israelites from the various cities and villages. Upon the whole the term "elders" always signifies those who are possessed of authority. In a great house like that of David it is possible to speak of the "elders of his house" (2 Sam. 12,17, cf Gen. 50,7); a trusted slave is an "elder" (Gen. 24,2), nay, every community must have its elders, i. e. those possessed of authority.[1] Therefore, to the Israelite it is a matter of course that also pre-Canaanite Israel was ruled by elders. As an abstraction of a late period in the history of Israel the writers of the Pentateuch make them a connecting link between Moses and the people.

As a matter of fact the character of the organization of pre-Canaanite Israel can not have been very different from that of the small towns in Canaan as, e. g., those which are known from the Book of Job. Thus the old Israelitic organization might develop imperceptibly out of nomadic conditions. Unfortunately we have no objective description of the life and social order in the large cities from the days of the kings, corresponding with the description of a small town given in the Book of Job. We have the indictments of the prophets and the plaints of the Psalms and the laws of the Deuteronomy. From this law-code it appears that the town retained its old character as the essential Israelitic community, forming a unity with self-government and common responsibility. As in olden times the elders and *śārīm* are the governing and responsible men (1 Kings 21,8; 2 Kings 10,1; 23,1); the king did not change the inner organization of the towns.

Just as Abimelech, when king of Shechem, had a *śar* to represent himself in this town, so there was now a *śar* at the head of the larger cities (1 Kings 22,26; 2 Kings 23,8), while King Solomon installed royal officials, *niṣṣābhīm,* all over the country (1 Kings 4,7 f.). But these officials did not do away with or replace the inner organization of the town. They merely represent the interests of the king, i. e. to get taxes and corvée-workers out of the towns, but as to ways and means they were, as it seems, left to themselves. The kings failed to shape a new order, so as to make the kingdom and the old town-centres organic links of a common whole. In his self-conceit the king might try to encroach upon the rights of a citizen. If so he would have to reckon with the elders; but because of his power he might sometimes make the elders betray those of their own community, as is shown by the stories of Ahab and Jehu (1 Kings 21; 2 Kings 10). Monarchy remained an alien institution in the social body of Israel, and many circles would not acknowledge it.

Nevertheless, the influence exercised by monarchy on the social conditions of the towns was great. Even if the kings did not reorganize the cities, they created new organizations. They maintained an army, they established roads, aqueducts, built fortresses, palaces and temples. Money and men for all this they took from the cities, but for the administration they needed officials. The *Śārīm* were, as we have already seen, the men of the old powerful families, the natural leaders and bearers of the town. Now we meet with a new kind of *śārīm,* a class of officials associated with the king. They are the officers of the army, of different rank according as they command the carriages, or the guard, detachments of 50, 100 or 1000 man, or the whole army. To the same class belong the civil service, and these *śārīm* with the *sōphēr* or chancellor at their head are known to us from the Books of Kings and the reports of Jeremiah (36-38). The *śārīm* are the staff of the king and are mentioned together with him as the basis of power. They form a new aristocracy, a limited class as opposed to the people, *hā'ām.* In the small towns this new aristocracy may not have made itself felt. But in the large cities, and above all in Jerusalem, the new class dissolved the power of the old families. It may be that in many cases the royal *śārīm* class had developed out of the old "men of valour". But the king could raise men who pleased him, and the old order of property was not respected. It is very likely that the Israelitic king tried to do the same thing as had been done in Egypt by the Pharaohs of the 17th and 18th dynasty, i. e. to create a feudalistic state and to supplant the old proprietors with his officials, thus maintaining these as his feudals — an order of things for which the Genesis makes the Hebrew Joseph responsible. This is word by word what is told in the anti-royalistic description of the king assigned to Samuel: And he will take your good fields and vineyards and oliveyards and give them to his slaves (1 Sam. 8,14).

At any rate the new nobility was different from the old one. The *śārīm* of the new time were dependent upon the king, not upon themselves. They did not have the feeling of responsibility, as the ties connecting them with the poor fellow-citizens were broken; and so they crushed them instead of upholding them. What this meant in the psychic life of Israel we shall see later on [1].

The military order was the only royal organization effected. A similar organization of the whole administration of the country was never accomplished. It is only in the idealized description of the time of the wanderings in the deserts that the systematizisers of the Pentateuch create a picture of a wholly organized Israel, abstracted from the military order of the monarchy: at the head the leader, beneath him the elders and the people, there being certain officials for Thousands, Hundreds, etc.

Besides the ruling families we find the poor Israelites, but also other classes. The description of the latter we will preface with a question: what became of the earlier population, those whom we briefly call the Canaanites? The relation between

Israelites and Canaanites was not uniform. At the very beginning a number of towns were conquered with the sword and their population exterminated, but it is not likely that this extermination has been very extensive. The great fusion followed, above all during the monarchic period. Certain Canaanite towns for a long time retained their independence, but in the course of years they were overcome by the Israelites. It is stated on several occasions that their inhabitants were not exterminated; the Israelites made them *lāmás.* We are told that all Amorites and Canaanites were gradually made *lāmás* (Josh. 16,10; 17,13; Judg. 1,28.30.33.35; 1 Kings 9,21), this term characterizing them as corvée-workers. We are also told that Solomon did not use the Israelites as bondmen, but only the former population. This information (1 Kings 9,22) does not seem very trustworthy, seeing that Jeroboam was the ruler over "all the burden of the house of Joseph" (1 Kings 11,28), and that all the people complained of their yoke. The kings did not spare the Israelites, neither for the army nor for their corvée-work (1 Sam. 8,11-17). But the Canaanites were the corvée-workers par excellence; this designates them as citizens of a lower rank. There is no doubt that these reduced Canaanites may be recognized in the class of the *gērīm,* the "sojourners".

The term *gēr* is used of anyone living associated to a community which is not his own. He may be an Israelite (Judg. 17,7-9; 19,16) or a stranger. He may be a traveller, only sojourning there for some days as a guest (Job 31,32). But the word has its special sphere as a designation of a great class of fellow citizens who are not born Israelites, but attach themselves to the Israelitic community. That their importance was considerable may be inferred from the fact that the laws very often mention them together with the native Israelite *(ʾezrāḥ).*

It is true that a fairly large number of foreigners lived in Canaan. David's guard consisted of hired foreigners, and we learn that in Samaria certain bazaars were inhabited by Aramæan merchants (1 Kings 20,34). But the *gērīm* alluded to in the laws cannot be identical with these foreigners. They form a limited social class, closely allied with the Israelites, and making an important part of their most intimate institutions. They can only be the conquered, not wholly but nearly assimilated early population. Just as the early population of Peloponnese lived as *perioikoi*, with personal freedom and right of property, but excluded from the privileged society of the patrician citizens, thus also the *gērīm* of Israel occupied an intermediate position between the free Israelitic burghers and the slaves.

As a rule they were poor. In a town conquered by the Israelites the latter appropriated the landed property, and the Canaanite *gērīm* were reduced to penury. They are mentioned among the poor and miserable who are to be allowed to gather the after-math on fields and in vineyards (Lev. 19,10; 23,22; Deut. 24,19). Like the widows and the fatherless they are to enjoy the tithe of the Levite (Deut. 14,29). Generally they supported themselves as paid workmen (Exod. 20,10; Lev. 22,10; 25,6.40; Deut. 24,14, etc.), and thus a new class of plebeians arose in Israel, as was in former times the case in Babylonia; but Israel did not make special laws for them. On the contrary, it is emphasized that *gēr* and freeman are to be judged according to the same principles (Deut. 1,16). The Israelite is not allowed to oppress him, but is pledged to love him and treat him as an Israelite, not forgetting that Israel is itself a plebeian nation which has been *gēr* in Egypt (Exod. 22,20; 23,9; Lev. 19,33 f.; Deut. 10,19; 24,17 f.; Ez. 22,29, etc.). These constantly repeated admonitions, which even recur in writings full of hatred against the foreign, especially the Canaanite spirit, can only mean that these *gērīm* have gradually become so closely allied with the Israelites that the original difference has vanished.

The laws of cult fully confirm that it is so. It is true that the "Law of Holiness", which forbids the buying of Israelitic slaves, recommends the buying of slaves from the *gērīm* (Lev. 25,45 f.), and the Deuteronomy says that the Israelites ought to leave it to a foreigner and a *gēr* to eat animals not slaughtered (Deut. 14,21). But another text ordains the same purification for an Israelite and a *gēr* guilty of this sin (Lev. 17,15). The same fidelity towards Yahweh is demanded from the *gēr* as from an Israelite (Lev. 20,2; Ez. 14,7); and on the occasion of many important acts of cult it is expressly stated that they are to be performed by Israelites and *gērīm* alike (Lev. 16,29; 17,8-16; 22,18; Num. 15,29; 19,10). The eating of the passover is conditioned by the *gēr* being circumcised; but if he is so, he takes part in this feast like an Israelite (Exod. 12,44 f. 48 f., cf. Num. 9,14). It is evident that the assimilation has become so intimate that the difference between native Israelites and *gērīm* is only a social one, i. e. as between patricians and plebeians.

But even this difference could be diminished. It is mentioned as a sinister possibility in the Deuteronomy (28,43) that *gērīm* shall rise at the cost of the genuine Israelites. It is taken into account by the "Law of Holiness", when it is demanded (Lev. 25,47 f.) that a man shall be redeemed by his family, if he has been forced to sell himself to a rich *gēr*. To such heights a *gēr* was able to rise. It is a matter of course that despotic monarchy was very favourable to the rise of the plebeian class. How the relation of the *gērīm* was regarding landed property in earlier times we do not know in detail. Though as a rule they must have been deprived of fields, it does not necessarily follow that they always were so. At any rate in the course of time they acquired landed property in the same manner as Israelites. Otherwise Ezekiel would not have claimed as their right that they should be entitled to a share together with the Israelites in the distribution of land projected by him for the restored people (Ez. 47,21-23). Here there is no other difference between Israelites and *gērīm* than the genealogy. We may imagine that even this difference at last has been superseded.

The difference between Israelites and *gērīm* was obliterated all the more easily, as a class possessing nothing or very little also arose among the native Israelites. Like the Babylonian and Hittite laws the Old Testament reckons with the hired workman *(śākhīr)* as a link in the social order, and this class is not only recruited from the *gērīm,* but also from the Israelites (Deut. 24,14). The hired workmen are personally free, but they are not much better off than the slaves. They work hard without enjoying the benefit of their efforts (Job 7,1-2; 14,6). They are mentioned among the miserable who ought not to be oppressed; every day their wages are to be rightly paid (Lev. 19,13). In many cases they may have been attached to a particular employer, perhaps for periods extending over a year as in Babylonia (Lev. 22,10; 25,50; Is. 16,14; 21,16 cf. Ham. § 273). This class naturally increased in the days of the kings, when so many Israelites had to leave their inheritance and were reduced to the class of the poor.

On the lowest rang of the social ladder stand *the slaves*, the unfree servants, generally of foreign birth and acquired in war or by purchase. But it is a typical symptom of the conditions developed in Israel that the laws reckon with an Israelite selling his own daughter (Exod. 21,7) or going into slavery, perhaps with his family. This debasement is always caused by debts; for the creditor can indemnify himself with the person of the debtor (2 Kings 4,1, in case of theft Exod. 22,2).

The laws bear witness to the energetic endeavours towards limiting the serfdom of Israelites. According to the Book of Covenant and the Deuteronomy, an Israelitic slave is to be released after six years of servitude, if he does not prefer to stay (Exod. 21,2 f.; Deut. 15,12-18). If he takes a wife with him into servitude, she shall be released together with him. But if his master gives him a wife, she belongs to the master, together with the children she may have born. The Deuteronomy requires of the master that he shall provide the released with gifts, so as to enable him to maintain himself. The "Law of Holiness", on the other hand, does not acknowledge the serfdom of an Israelite. If he is involved in debt to such an extent that he cannot maintain himself, then he shall have the position of a *gēr* who gradually clears his debt by hired labour; for slaves are only to be bought among foreigners and *gērīm*. And if an Israelite is forced to sell himself as a slave to a *gēr*, his family must redeem him (Lev. 25,39 ff.).

The slave was entirely in the hands of his master. It is true that it shall "be revenged" if the master smites the slave so that he dies under his hand, and if he mutilates the latter, he (or she) is to be released; but with these exceptions he is entitled to chastise his slave at discretion, and even if the slave dies one or two days after the chastisement, the master is quit (Exod. 21,20-21; 26-27). The slave has no independent family, but belongs to the house of his master. Of course the slave may be released at any time. The exact character of the relationship of the released slave to his former master we do not know. In any case we may take it for granted that he passed to the class of hired labourers and *gērīm,* and he may in this quality be supposed to have attached himself permanently to his former master.[1]

The strong flux and reflux to be discerned in the social order of Israel also distinguishes the sharp division between slaves and freemen. Monarchy acts in the same manner. The despot looks upon all as his slaves; in the Old Testament this is acknowledged, in so far as even the highest men of the empire are called the slaves of the king. "Slave" is not a special term for a caste standing outside the community. It denotes a subordinate, and as a class designation it means those of lowest order; but there is no absolute distinction between them and other classes. This development may to a certain extent have been furthered by Canaanite habits; for we discern simular tendencies among the peoples who have particularly influenced life and conditions in Canaan, i. e. the eastern Semites and the Hittites; especially the latter, in their laws, treat the slaves as a sort of plebeian, their value being half that of free men.

All the classes making up the life of the town are characterized by the men. It is the man who acts outwardly and represents the family. Behind him stands the woman, whose sphere is in the house and within the circle of the family, and who does not appear independently in public. An exception is made by the *hetæras* (designated in the translations as "harlots"). They do not follow the laws of women fulfilling their appointed task, but, leaving the normal sphere of women, they converse freely with men. The hetæra goes about the city without restriction, trying to attract the attention of men, as it is said in a scoffing ditty: Take an harp, go about the city, thou hetæra that hast been forgotten; make sweet melody, sing many songs, that thou mayest be remembered (Is. 23,16). We get the impression that there has been a fairly considerable number of hetæras, and they are often visited by strangers (1 Kings 22,38; Josh. 2; Judg. 16,1). The part played by the hetæras in the other old communities is a similar one. The Babylonians and Assyrians had definite rules for them in the laws; thus in Assyria they are not allowed to go about veiled, this being the privilege of the married women; it is not likely that this has been the case in Israel, seeing that Tamar veils herself when playing the part of an hetæra (Gen. 38,15). In the preserved laws of Israel we are only told that a priest is not allowed to marry an hetæra (Lev. 21,7.14). From this it is to be inferred that ordinary men sometimes married women of this class.

The hetæras have not the honour of normal women. They may frequently have been foreigners, or at any rate have sprung from the lower classes; but they were not always without a family (Josh. 2,12.18; 6,17.25). If they bore children, they might enjoy their motherhood, as shown by the narrative about the judgment of Solomon (1 Kings 3); but we may be sure that these children only swelled the ranks of the lowest order. Exceptionally a child of this kind could succeed and become a powerful chief, partly admitted to his father's house, though not without opposition on the part of the other children. Such was the fate of Jephthah (Judg. 11,1) as, on Arabian soil in the Umayyad family, that of the renowned Ziyād, acknowledged as a brother by Moʿāwiya, but commonly named Ziyād, *son of his father*. Generally such children must have belonged to the class of the fatherless in the truest sense of the word. The term "fatherless", designating one of the categories of the miserable, cannot refer to the fatherless sons of landed proprietors, these taking over the inheritance of the deceased and therefore not being miserable. It only has a meaning when applied to those who have lost a poor father, and have no family to rely upon, or to those who have never had a father, i. e. the sons of hetæras.

Thus the population of the towns became, on one hand, more homogeneous, the strange elements being absorbed in the common Israelitic, but Canaanized, community; and, on the other, all the more mixed from a social point of view. It was a necessary result of the whole development that the old tribal feeling was weakened, whereas the importance of the city grew stronger.

The city is the community to which the man belongs, and which he longs to return to; and in his city he shall be buried (2 Sam. 19,38). When designating a man one mentions him by his name, his family and his city, possibly his tribe. Mention is made of the Tishbite Elijah (1 Kings 17,1), the Jezreelite Naboth (1 Kings 21,1), Micah from Moreshet, Jeremiah from Anathoth, etc. When the tribe is mentioned, it is probably meant to indicate the district in which the city lies. The feeling of nationality and city both absorb their share of the tribal feeling and help to dissolve the latter.

However, the city is not the unit which is nearest to the heart of the man. Its importance lies chiefly in the fact that it shelters his family. It is true that the town has left its impress on a number of laws, but it never becomes the basic factor of life. When the men of a town try to get hold of a man-slayer, it is not because they themselves want to settle the matter with him, but in order to deliver him into the hands of the revenger, i. e. the family of the slain. And we have seen that, what in the olden times formed the basis of the unity of city as well as of tribe, was the family community. When asking what was the foundation of their feeling of unity, we receive the answer from patriarchal history: it depended upon the fact that they were one family and descended from a common ancestor.

THE FAMILY, THE FATHER'S HOUSE AND THE PEOPLE.

The *mishpāḥā* (clan or family) is, in the later genealogical scheme, a connecting link between the tribe and the household or father's house (Num. 2,34). In a story like that of the casting of lots after the theft of Achan, this genealogical scheme appears very clearly; the lot is first to be cast among the tribes, then among the houses of the thus marked-out family *(bāttīm),* and finally among the men of the house (Josh. 7,14). In so far the use of the word *mishpāḥā* seems clear enough, in that it must rather be regarded as an expanded household and is more limited than the tribe.

However, the undefined character of the tribe, in the olden time, when the idea was a living one, shows that this division is not so simple as it may seem. The line of distinction between the terms of tribe and family might be fluid. The Danites, who generally form a tribe, are sometimes designated as a family (Judg. 13,2; 18,11). The seeming incongruity is not sufficiently explained by saying that they originally formed a family and subsequently a tribe. [1] The Danites say to the priest whom they force to accompany them towards the north: "Is it better for thee to be a priest unto the house of one man *(bayith)*, or that thou be a priest unto a tribe and a family *(mishpāḥā)* in Israel?" (Judg. 18,19). When at the same time they apply both of these names to themselves, it can only mean that they are not at all strictly defined. It can also be said of a young Bethlehemite that he is of the family of Judah (Judg. 17,7).

On the other hand, there is no sharp distinction between the father's house and family. The Israelites are told to kill the paschal lamb according to their families (Exod. 12,21), but it is also said that it must be done "according to the house of their fathers". When Abraham bids his slave go "unto my father's house and to my family" (Gen. 24,38-41), it is clear that these two denominations mean very nearly the same thing. Sometimes we come across the word "family", where, according to the system, we should expect "father's house". The Deuteronomist says in an admonitory speech: "Man, woman, family or tribe" (29,17), thus passing from the individual directly to the family. An example of this we also find in the history of Saul. When Samuel says that "all the desire of Israel is on him and his father's house", Saul answers that his is the least of all the families of the tribe of Benjamin [2] (1 Sam. 9,21), and in the parallel story, where the election of the king takes place by the casting of lots, it is first cast between the tribes, then between families and, within the family taken, Saul is singled out. There is no father's house between Saul and his *mishpāḥā*.

As a matter of fact, one cannot define tribe, family and father's house as materially limited quantities, so that many father's houses make a family *(mishpāḥā)*, and many families a tribe. Tribe, when still a living term, was not essentially different from the family *mishpāḥā)*, the family not being an external, clearly limited quantity, but the appellation of those who are of common blood or, as the Hebrews say, of common flesh, and the family extends as far as the feeling of unity makes itself felt. Therefore, the line of distinction must necessarily be fluid. A father's house is in itself a family, *mishpāḥā*, and a tribe may be so.

In the family the chief thing is kinship. When the *mishpāḥā* is used as the connecting link between the father's house and the tribe, then it is due to the fact that it presupposes the father's house. But in later times there have surely been cases where families divided themselves among different tribes. [1] The difference between *mishpāḥā* and the father's house is presumably that the *mishpāḥā* has a wider scope, but not that it arises through a multiplication of father's houses. The father's house is a community centring about one man, the father of the house. If we take him as our starting point, then his house comprises all who call him father; his family is all who claim community of kin with him; and this also includes the house; Shimei was "of the family of the house of Saul" (2 Sam. 16,5) and David says to Saul: "What is my father's family in Israel?" (1 Sam. 18,18); he might just as well have said "house" as "family". Self-evident though it may sound, yet we must draw attention to the fact that there is a vital difference as to whether we emphasize the external, quantitative idea and only consider the family as a closely defined group, or whether we look upon the family as being defined by internal characteristics so as to be present wherever the latter make themselves felt.

For the Israelite it is a matter of course that common flesh makes common character. Therefore family, *mishpāḥā*, is the designation of those who are of the same kind, have the same essential features, and it is the essential factor of the community. Israel is a confederation of families (Jer. 2,4; 31,1); its two kingdoms are two families (Jer. 33,24), nay, the whole people is one *mishpāḥā*, one family as against all the other families of the earth. "You only have I known of all the families of the earth", says Amos (3,2).

All that forms a whole, a homogeneous community with its own characteristics, is a *mishpāḥā*. Therefore, not only Israel but the whole world consists of families. Abraham receives the promise that through him "shall all families of the earth be blessed" (Gen. 12,3), and the same is said to Jacob (Gen. 28,14). It is the natural appellation for all human beings, because it comprises them all, each according to their characteristics. All non-Israelitic people consist of families, the Canaanites as well as all distant nations (Gen. 10,5.18). The prophet asks Yahweh to "pour out his fury" upon the foreign people, "the families that call not on thy name" (Jer. 10,25); all the families of the earth shall come to worship him (Zech. 14,17 f.). The characteristic feature of these examples, which might be supplemented with many more,[1] is that the idea of the *mishpāḥā* is the basis of all definitions, and that it immediately presents itself whenever the Israelite wants to define a community.

Mishpāḥā is chiefly used of a community of human beings, but there are also other communities with their distinctive marks and characteristics. When the Israelite speaks of animals and other living beings outside the human world, he divides them into species *(mīnīm)*, but once in a while the priestly writer also speaks of their families. Not only men and women, but also animals left the Ark arranged in families (Gen. 8,19), and in Jeremiah Yahweh says: "And I will appoint over them four families: the sword to slay and the dogs to tear, and the fowls of the heaven and the beasts of the earth to devour and destroy" (Jer. 15,3).

None of the social definitions is so living as that of the *mishpāḥā*. The tribe becomes a territory, and the "house" is first and foremost the household, but the family is always those who are determined through kinship; there is no external definition of any kind in this idea, the chief feature being whether one has the common stamp in oneself. So flexible is the term *mishpāḥā* that it can be used wherever there is a whole bearing the impress of a common character. The Israelites, whom Micah thunders against, form one family (Mic. 2,3), because they are all guilty of the same transgressions. Also Jeremiah speaks to this "evil family" (8,3). And the family not only expands in scope so as to comprise all of those who share in the common characteristics; it comprises all of the same stamp throughout the ages. Amos says expressly that he speaks to the family who were "brought up" from the land of Egypt (3,1).

When the word *mishpāḥā* can be used in this extremely living manner, then it is naturally because the very idea of kinship is not defined by external, mechanical limits. *Mishpāḥā* are those who are of common flesh and blood, but it signifies more than what is immediately communicated through it; it is the expression of a common character, of a psychic community. Therefore we cannot wonder that the Israelites once in a while, instead of *mishpāḥā,* use the word *ḥayyā,* signifying those related as a community of life. For the family is the source from which life springs, and those who are one in kin have community of life.[1]

This community is also expressed by the word *'eleph,* which means those intimate with each other, the community of those who belong together. In an older period this denomination, which so often occurs among other Semitic peoples, has certainly been used very frequently, but it has been supplanted by *mishpāḥā.* An old exclamation reads: Return Yahweh! The myriads of Israel's communities of kin! (Num. 10,36). The community of kin is the basis of the social order; we see the word used in the same sense as *mishpāḥā.* Gideon says: My *'eleph* (community of kin) is poor in Manasseh, and I am the least in my father's house (Judg. 6,15). The people consists of tribes and communities of kin (1 Sam. 10,19). As the city may form a *mishpāḥā,* it may also form an *'eleph* (Mic. 5,1, cf. 1 Sam. 23,23).

Even though the principal feature in the definition of families is not the external limitation, the communities of kinsmen naturally have a certain average extent, and *'eleph,* the old denomination of community, gradually comes to signify a definite number, a thousand. While it gives way to *mishpāḥā* as the name of a community of kin, it merges into the military organization, as denoting a section fighting under the same captain, the army being divided into tens, hundreds and thousands. This arrangement, which is already mentioned in the books of Samuel (1 Sam. 8,12; 17,18; 22,7; 2 Sam. 18,1), is probably a result of the organization of the monarchy. The authors of the Priestly Code adopt it in their classification of the Israel of the time of the wilderness (Num. 10,4; Josh. 22,21.30).[1]

The nucleus of *mishpāḥā* is *bēth 'ābh,* the father's house. The word *bayith* is a common Semitic word, denoting the dwelling, house or tent, but at the same time all of those who live in and round the building — i. e. the household.[2] Whereas the tribe and the city have been of varying importance to the lives of the Israelites, the household everywhere preserved its importance as the centre of life, because it represents kinship in its most intimate sense. The laws and manner of thinking of the Israelites are throughout stamped by it.

The patriarchal legend begins with the following words: "Now Yahweh said unto Abram: Get thee out of thy country and from thy family and thy father's house." (Gen. 12,1). The Yahwist from the very start gives an example of the obedience of the ancestor. It was a hard and unusual order which Abram thus received; and when, at a later period, he looks about him for a wife for his son, he reminds his trusted slave of the strange fate he experienced, i. e. to be forced to leave his father's house (Gen. 24,7); likewise, when speaking to Abimelech, he makes that his excuse for having concealed his true relation to Sarah: When Elohim caused me to wander from my father's house, I said to her: This is the kindness which thou shalt show unto me: At every place whither we shall come, say of me: He is my brother! (Gen. 20,13). When he is not in his father's house, he is without protection and safety. When Jacob leaves the house of his father, it is therefore in the certain hope that he will be able to return to it. If the patriarchs bear witness to the importance of the tribe, then it is still more characteristic that their history is a family history. Only thus can the Israelitic narrators imbue it with the reality of life.

Everywhere in the Old Testament we come across the father's house; wherever a man goes, he takes his "house" with him. When David went to the Philistines with his men, they lived there, "each with his own house" (1 Sam. 27,3), and the same is said in connection with their moving to Hebron (2 Sam. 2,3). When the old world perished in the deluge, and the new world came into existence, then Noah was saved, he and his house going into the Ark (Gen. 7,1.13). On this occasion we are informed who belong to a house: Husband, wife, sons and their wives and, of course, also daughters.

The man is always mentioned first, being the founder of the house; after him the wife who helps him to maintain the family, and then the children. When a man arrives at years of discretion, he leaves his father and mother and lives in community with his wife, founding a new house. In so far the father's house seems to be an externally well-defined institution, being those who live together. But the community goes far deeper. The decisive factor is not to live together, but to take part in the community of the house. The house forms a "breeding group", *mōledheth* (Gen. 12,1). That which keeps the father's house together, is the strong bond of kinship; it is that strength which unites the *mishpāḥā*, only that it is here to be found in its strongest form, seeing that the circle closes narrowly round the headspring.

These common characteristics, imparted by the house to its various members, are not lost, even when the son breaks away and founds his own house. The married son is still a member of his father's house. The sons of Noah belong to Noah's house, even though they are all married and have their own houses. When it is told that Joseph nourished his father and his brethren and all his father's house with bread (Gen. 47,12, cf. 50,8), then it does not mean that the brethren are outside the father's house. The father and the brethren are mentioned as the most important, and to these must then be added all the *others* who belonged to Jacob's house.

If the house is once formed, it continues its growth and lives on through propagation, as long as there are any descendants whatsoever. "Is there yet any that is left of the house of Saul, that I may show him kindness for Jonathan's sake?" asks David, and he gets the answer that Meribbaal, the son of Jonathan, is still alive (2 Sam. 9,1-3). Meribbaal is a grown-up man, but he is still reckoned as of the house of Saul, seeing that Saul was strong enough to leave his impress on the house so far. The house of the strong remains forever. His strength is living forever in the descendants, who continue to multiply, and they call it his house, because they still feel his flesh in themselves.

In history the strong cohesion of the family extends upwards and downwards. The family is not merely a *bēth 'ābh,* the father's house, but also a *bēth 'ābhōth,* the house of fathers. A great and strong man like David introduces an entirely new blessing into his family and thus founds a new house. But even though not all are able to impart as much as the greatest, yet everyone of the long series of fathers contribute towards its special stamp. Each of them gives what he has to give, and together they create the peculiar essence of the house. When a man is going to die, he sets his house in order (Is. 38,1). His will is determined by the earlier fathers, and now he hands it over to posterity. Thus the continuity of the father's house is maintained.

It is the continuity which makes the father's house and family. Unless special emphasis is laid on the idea of household, institution, the two words are rather used indiscriminately, which has already been shown through certain examples. Even the priestly writer who aims at a certain systematization, uses them promiscuously. There is, however, the shade of difference that the "house" has a more intimate character, because it indicates a closer kinship with the man in question, whereas the family *(mishpāḥā)* is apt to be used in a wider sense. "Family" in instinctively felt as a more comprehensive term than household, though there is no absolute difference, which for that matter is the natural consequence of the house having no upward or downvard limit, as far as time is concerned. If the house of Issachar exists as long as Issachar has any descendants, then the tribe of Issachar may just as well be called the house of Issachar as in 1 Kings 15,27, and so we also hear of the house of Ephraim (Judg. 10,9) and the house of Levi (Exod. 2,1; Ps. 135,20). But seeing that the *mishpāḥā* normally has a wider scope than the house, the road is open to the later custom of letting the house designate those most narrowly related, and the family the larger community, whose common ancestor must be traced further back.

Just as every whole is a family, it is also a house, that which makes a whole, the psychic community, being identical with kinship. Every community is a community of kinsmen with a common ancestor, the bearer of the unity. Not only the tribes, but the whole of the people form a house, the house of Israel. Wherever those of one mind form a community round a common leader, they are a house; the leader who stamps it with his personality is its father, and those who join him are his sons. We often hear of such communities of prophets, whose members are the sons of prophets.[1] The Rechabites, whose unity consisted in their following the nomadic ideal, formed a house, the father of which was the founder, Jonadab son of Rechab (Jer. 35,18). The artisans form a house, where we would speak of a guild (Neh. 3,8). Wherever we would speak of categories and classes bearing the stamp of unity, the Israelite sees a house. He may speak of "the house of the evildoers" (Is. 31,2), just as the wise is "the son of the wise" (Is. 19,11), the poor "the son of the needy" (Ps. 72,4), the stranger "the son" of a stranger (Ps. 18,45). All living beings consist of this kind of unities, and the various characteristics and possibilities of every individual makes him a part of many wholes. A man may at the same time be the son of his own father and of Jonadab ben Rechab, while he is also the son of the shepherds, of the just, etc., all his characteristics making him a part of wholes, and it depends upon circumstances which of these at the moment is the most prominent. But the whole most deeply rooted and of the strongest influence is generally that which belongs to him by birth, i. e. the kinship of the father's house.

Those who form a whole make an *'am,* which word is usually rendered by "people". One of the peculiarities of this word is that it can be used both in the singular and in the plural, very nearly with the same sense. When it is said in several places that a man is to be cut off from his *people* (Lev. 17,4; 20,3.6), and in other places that a man or a woman is to be cut off from his or her *peoples* (Gen. 17,14; Exod. 30,33.38; 31,14; Lev. 7,20 f. 25.27 et al.) it naturally means the same thing. When death approaches, Jacob says: "I am to be gathered to my *people*" (Gen. 49,29), while it is generally called to be gathered unto ones *peoples* (Gen. 25,8.17; 35,29; 49,33; Num. 20,24; 27,13; 31,2; Deut. 32,50 et al.).

This fluctuating *usus loquendi* expresses the Israelitic conception of the relation between the whole and the unit. The whole is entirely in the individual and *vice versa.* [1]

The word first and foremost stands for the kinsmen, those who are bound together by close ties. In them the life of the individual has its source and its base. The absolute annihilation consists in being driven out of one's community, in being cut off from one's *'am.* It only happens with the person who has violated the fundamental laws of life, and thus himself has severed the string that binds him to life. The one who lives normally lives among his kinsmen and through death passes into the large community of kinsmen who have gone before him.

It is again the family confronting us in the word *'am.* A distinction is made between the nearer and more distant part of one's *'ammīm,* kinsmen. A priest is not to be defiled by the bodies of his kinsmen, except by those nearest in kin: father and mother, son and daughter, brother and sister. That is to say, *'am* centres in the father's house and designates its members. The "people" which Jacob brought with him from the land of the Aramæans, and which he divided into the two bands (Gen. 32,8), are all of those who formed his house (Gen. 35,2.6). But like *mishpāḥā* it extends beyond the narrow limits of the family, as far as kinship makes itself felt. The kinship becomes thinner and thinner the further one gets away from the centre; but it is not always easy to say exactly where is ceases.

It is the community which forms wholes, and the whole consisting of human beings is always an *'am.* It may be the father's house, it may be the city, it may be the empire or the people. [2] The Israelite does not attach much importance to a sharp line of distinction. The woman who has committed adultery and is convicted of it, becomes a curse in her people, says the law (Num. 5,27). Her "people" is the community to which she belongs, and from which she springs; the word has no other meaning. When in the laws mention is constantly made of "your people", and when, for instance, it is said that one must not bear a grudge against any of the sons of one's people (Lev. 19,18), it does not appear directly from the text how far this division extends. We may only say that it denotes the community to which each individual belongs.

No human being can exist except as a member of an *'am*. That which is possessed of life naturally tends towards becoming a people. When Joseph is afraid that Jacob is not going to give Manasseh the right blessing, he is comforted by the promise that Manasseh also shall become a people (Gen. 48,19). To be a "non-people" is the same as to perish (Deut. 32,21). The natural manner in which to become a people is by the multiplication of the family. But if two communities join and live together, then they immediately become one people (Gen. 34,16.22). It is the unity in the many which makes the people. Having community is the same as being one people (Gen. 11,6). Disruption means the destruction of the people (Ezek. 36,19).

The Israelitic community bears the impress of the man. It is characteristic that *'am,* the word which means kinsmen in all kinds of communities, in the related Arabian language stands for the family of the father and its members. When the Hebrew says *'am,* he is also first and foremost thinking of men. Women of course also belong (e. g. Judg. 16,30), but as a rule no count is taken of them. "The people of Niniveh are women", says Nahum (3,13), and such an unnatural community must perish. Therefore *'am* is used to designate the warriors, the community of men in the proper sense of the word,[1] and at the same time it also denotes the community of worship of the men of the city.

Homogeneity always creates an *'am*. It may be the miserable (2 Sam. 22,28; Ps. 18,28); it may be the faithful (Is. 51,7); it may be the ordinary people who form a whole as against the priests (Is. 24,2; Jer. 19,1; 28,1.5; Hos. 4,9), as against the prophets (Jer. 29,1), as against the elders (Ruth 4,9), as against those in power (Jer. 26,16; 43,4) or the king. The ants form an *'am* (Prov. 30,25), and so also the locusts (Joel 2,2).

'am thus means the same as the father's house and the family, because it arises out of kinship. The three definitions centre in the same idea: The father, the rise of the family. The father's house is most closely attached to him, the "family" extends further, and the "people of kinsmen" furthest of all; it is the most flexible of

the three conceptions, seeing that it denotes the entirety extending the furthest: the nation, the people. It denotes all of those who take part in the whole of the common history. This totality acquired firmness and strength during the period of the fusion and the fights with the foreign people in and outside Canaan, and during the time of the monarchy it was further established. It became the whole of greatest importance besides the family. It left its stamp on the culture and laws of the Israelites, and, for instance, with the prophets it forms the basis of religion and ethos. When *'am* is constantly used to designate the whole of the Israelitic community, then it has not broken away from its fundamental meaning of community of kinsmen. [1] The unity of Israel depends on kinship, the community of soul arising out of a common character and a common history, and it is expressed by dating the people back to a common ancestor.

Every community forms a unity, but the unity is not mechanical; it does not consist in obliterating the individual, but in imbuing him with the common character and spirit of the community. Those who belong to the community call each other by terms such as *'āḥ,* brother, *'āmīth,* kinsman or *rē'a,* fellow, neighbour. The three expressions all occur in one of the admonitions of the law: Thou shalt not go up and down as a talebearer among thy kinsmen, neither shalt thou stand against the blood of thy neighbour (fellow): I am Yahweh! Thou shalt not hate thy brother in thine heart, thou shalt in any wise rebuke thy kinsman and not suffer sin for his sake. Thou shalt not avenge nor bear any grudge against the children of thy people, but thou shalt love thy fellow (neighbour) as thyself: I am Yahweh! (Lev. 19,16-18). It is clear that the three terms are used promiscuously and have the same meaning, i. e. a member of the community of kinsmen, and of this there are many examples. [2]

The most comprehensive of the three words is *'āḥ,* being well known from all Semitic languages as the name of the brother. It means in the first place: The one with whom one has common parents. In polygamous Israel there are many brothers who only have a common father; also these are brothers, but the brotherhood is not the same. When it is said: Jacob did not send

Benjamin, Joseph's brother, with his brethren (Gen. 42,4) then the word is first used of full brotherhood, afterwards of what we call half-brotherhood. If emphasis is to be placed on the full brotherhood, it is said "his brother, his mother's son" (Gen. 43,29). In the same manner Tamar, the daughter of David, in 2 Sam. 13,5.7.8 is called the sister of Amnon, whereas in verses 1 and 4 she is called the sister of his brother Absalom. In our languages we meet the same fluctuating *usus loquendi*, but with the Israelites it extends over a wider field. When looking at more remote degrees of kinship, the same phenomenon presents itself. Lot is the son of Abraham's brother, and he is sometimes expressly called his brother's son (Gen. 12,5). Nevertheless, they are called brothers (Gen. 13,8; 14,14.16). When Abimelech has broken with his nearest of kin on his father's side, and goes to his mother's brothers in Shechem, we hear that he is their brother (Judg. 9,3). Jacob is Laban's sister's son, and yet he is called his brother (Gen. 29,12.15), just as Bethuel is called the brother of Abraham, his father's brother (Gen. 24,48); but it does not prevent Jacob from distinguishing sharply between his brothers and Laban's brothers (Gen. 31,37.54 cf. 32).

It would be incorrect to conclude that the word, as with us, means own brother, while in all other contexts it is used less strictly. Like kinship, brotherhood extends as far as the feeling of consanguinity exists. Kinship is strongest near its origin in the father's house, and so also brotherhood. Brothers may be more or less intimately united; in relation to the half-brother two full brothers are termed brothers, and all the three of them call themselves brothers in relation to the cousin, etc. In other words, the idea of "brother" corresponds exactly with the idea of family. Wherever there is a *mishpāḥā,* there are also brothers, for they are the bearers of kinship. Whether we say that Abraham's servant looks for a wife to Isaac in his master's family or among his master's brothers amounts to the same thing (Gen. 24,4.27. 38).[1] When Samson wanted to marry a Philistine woman, his father said to him: Is there never a woman among the daughters of thy brothers or among all my kinspeople, that thou goest to take a wife of the uncircumcised Philistines? (Judg. 14,3). The kinsmen of the father are the brothers of the son. In this manner mention is often made of brothers, without our being able to say how close the relationship is. When Job's good fortune returned, his "brothers and sisters" came to celebrate the occasion with him (Job 42,11), meaning: his kinsfolk. Brotherhood always follows kinship in its various shades of meaning. The city-community is a *mishpāḥā,* and consequently the fellow-citizen becomes a brother. When speaking of Elimelech to the elders of the city, Boaz calls him "our brother Elimelech" (Ruth 4,3), and Abimelech is the brother of the Shechemites, because he is of the kin of the rulers of this city (Judg. 9,18), just as Ittai from Gath is the brother of the other men from this city (2 Sam. 15,20). Members of the same tribe are brothers, because they form a *mishpāḥā.* David says that the Judæans are his brothers, his bone and flesh (2 Sam. 19,13), just as the Danites are brothers (Judg. 18,8). But also the whole of Israel forms one family, one house; therefore all Israelites are brothers (Exod. 2,11; Lev. 10,6; 2 Sam. 19,42; Jer. 34,14 et al.). This generally is the extreme limit. It is presupposed as a matter of course in the Deuteronomy. In the year of release this law demands that one shall forgive one's brother his debt: Of a foreigner thou mayest exact it again, but that which is thine with thy brother, thine hand shall release (Deut. 15,3). Here the contrast is clearly defined: the kinsman, the brother on the one hand, the foreigner on the other.

Wherever there is social unity, we have brotherhood. Through the pact of amity David became the brother of Jonathan (2 Sam. 1,26). And the pact may extend beyond the limits of the community of the people, as happened when Solomon and Hiram became brothers (1 Kings 9,13), and as happens whenever a foreigner is received into a community as a residential guest.

As *'āḥ* belongs to "the house" and to *mishpāḥā,* in the same manner *'āmīth* belongs to *'am* from which it is derived; it has the same flexibility as this idea, and there is no place where we can fix its exact limit.[1]

rē'a, fellow (neighbour), is like the brother the person with whom one has community, but this word does not quite designate the kinsman in the strictest sense. It is used about neighbours, fellow-citizens, compatriots (Exod. 2,13; 11,2; 20,16), the one whose wife, ox and ass one daily has before one, and with whom one lives in community. The special sphere of the word is a community, the kernel of which is not blood relationship but friendship. It is true that brotherhood is also used in this comprehensive sense, but if one wants to be sure not to be misunderstood, one says *rē'a* (Deut. 13,7; 2 Sam. 13,3; Prov. 17,17 et al.). The word therefore is often used together with *'ōhēbh,* a friend (Ps. 38,12; 88,19; 122,8; Pr. 17,17); it may be used for the beloved (Jer. 3,1; Hos. 3,1; Cant. 5,16), and it denotes "fellow" in all the more transient and superficial relations, where the Israelites see wholes and communities forming, because there is a fellowship.[1]

The question which was once put to Jesus: Who is my neighbour? was thus not so easy to answer in ancient Israel. The neighbour, the fellow, is the one with whom one lives in community, but there are many kinds of communities. However, there are some of these which are more intimate than others, such as the city community and the national community, but both are based on the community which is more intimate and living than all others, and from which all life springs: the strong community of the kindred.

THE FORMATION OF THE FAMILY.

The unity of the family is so strong, because it rests on a solid foundation, i. e. common descent, which makes common blood, flesh and bone. The presupposition of the making of the family is marriage, and upon its character depends the character of the family. In marriage man and wife meet, each from their own family. Which of the two has then the power to mould the new community arising out of their union? There are peoples, where the woman is the dominating factor in the making of the family. She remains with her own kindred and there receives the man, and the children exclusively count kin through their mother.

Among other peoples the opposite is the case. But the relationship is often very complicated, and the relation of the children to the kin of the father and mother respectively is decided according to special rules. But marriage also offers other problems. What is the basis of such a union of two families? In some nations the families must be far removed, in others quite close. There are peoples who have very definite laws as to who are to marry each other.

If we ask whether in Israel the man or the woman is the determining factor in the making of the family, this question is easily answered. It is the man who dominates, the family being called a father's house. But, on the other hand, the Israelites never went so far as the Muhammadan poet who says that the mothers of mankind are only "vessels" which receive the children without leaving any impress on them.

The importance of marriage in the lives of the Israelites has found its expression in the two accounts of the creation of man. When the world came into existence, and the order of the world was created, all was crowned by the creation of man and woman. On their union was laid the blessing to which later generations owe their existence. In both accounts man and woman are indissolubly bound together, but the closeness of the connection is differently expressed. The Priestly Code expresses it in the manner that man and woman together make *'ādhām* (man). The passage reads: God created man *(hā-'ādhām)* in his own image, in the image of God created he him, male and female created he them (1,27).

Singular and plural are used indifferently about the same being. Man is a whole consisting of two parts, the man and the woman. Nothing is said of the relation between them, except that they are indispensible to each other, and not till they are united do they together form a whole human being.

The Yahwist, on the other hand, relates how Yahweh first created man, i. e. the man. The man is in himself man, but he lacks something that he may be so wholly. It is not good that man should be alone. He must have someone to help him, and this help-meet he finds in woman. She is taken out of him, and thus she must be there, in order that he may be man wholly. She is part of him; that which makes her fit to make him whole is that she is of the same flesh as himself. When the parents have brought up the son so far that he is becoming a man, then he leaves the house of his father and founds a new house, thus uniting himself with the woman and becoming a man, man wholly.

Thus the shade of difference between the two accounts is that, according to the former, the man and the woman together make man, while according to the latter the man is man proper, though the woman is necessary in order that he may be man wholly. This shade of difference cannot be explained through a difference in time between the two narratives. The relation between man and woman was considered in rather the same manner throughout the whole of the history of Israel; and, like other Israelitic authors, the priestly writer in his genealogies exclusively reckons with men. No more can it be explained by the fact that the priestly account should be of foreign origin, whereas the Yahwist represents the Israelitic point of view. There are certain things which seem to point in the direction that both accounts are due to foreign influence; but they both describe something which the Israelite can recognize. The difference originates in the different points of view of the two narratives. The priestly writer wants to describe the creation of the various genera. Man — woman make a separate genus as contrasted with plants, birds, fishes, etc. The genus man is of dual sex, just as male and female specimens are required to represent the genera of the animals. The Yahwist wants to describe the order of the world in which man lives, the centre of gravity and distribution of power, and then the man must necessarily occupy a prominent position. The man is the ruler; it is he who provides the bread and makes the soil yield up its wealth. The woman is dependent upon him, but not like the animals; she is closely connected with him and part of him. Her task is to bear him children. She is his indispensible help-meet in the maintenance of the family.

The man's position in the family is expressed by his being its *ba'al,* the meaning of which word is the possessor and the master. But these two meanings spring from another still deeper. *Ba'al* always presupposes a psychic community, a whole, and *ba'al* designates the ruling will within this. The word does not mean one-sided sovereignty; wherever that is meant, *'ādhōn* is used. The conqueror who sets his foot on the neck of the enemy will never be called the *ba'al* of the vanquished. In order that a man may become a *ba'al* there must be an intimate relation, and he exercises his power within its limits. Therefore the word is hardly ever used in an isolated sense; the relation in which the person in question is *ba'al* is always mentioned, unless it appears directly from the context.

When the father of the household is called its *ba'al,* then it implies that he is the strong will within the narrow circle. He is the *ba'al* of his wife and she is *ba'al*-taken by him. He is the *ba'al* of his domestic animals, of his field and the whole of his property. It is probably due to chance that he is nowhere called the *ba'al* of his slave, even though the word *'ādhōn,* master, is also here appropriate.[1]

The word *ba'al* therefore not only characterizes the man as the master of the house, but also tells us something of the character of his rule. He is not an isolated despot, but the centre from which strength and will emanate through the whole of the sphere which belongs to him and to which he belongs.

When a man is called father, it really implies the same thing, kinship and authority also being expressed by the name of father. To the Israelite the name of father always spells authority. Naaman is called father by his servants (2 Kings 5,13). The priest is called the father of the cultic community, of which he is the head (Judg. 18,19), and Elijah is called father by his disciple (2 Kings 2,12).

Round the man the house groups itself, forming a psychic community, which is stamped by him. Wives, children, slaves, property are entirely merged in this unity. Nearest to the father are to a certain extent the children. They are his flesh and bear his name. The slaves are either born in the household or foreigners; in the former case they belong more intimately to the circle than if they are bought or captives. But they never leave their impress upon the house, the man being strong enough to counteract any foreign influence. The foreign characteristics of the slave only leave insignificant traces, and he falls quite into line with the house in its entirety. The position of the house-born slave in many ways closely resembles that of the children: he is "the son of the house" (Gen. 14,14; 15,2 f.; 17,12.27; Jer. 2,14); and if he has belonged to the house for a long time, he may as the "elder of the house" come to stand in very close relationship to the father of the house. He performs important tasks on behalf of the house father (Gen. 24), and even the possibility that he may inherit is hinted (Gen. 15,4). The slave is subject to circumcision (Gen. 17) and is admitted to the family worship. How closely he is received into the household appears from the fact that the slave of a priest may eat of the holy thing which is forbidden to the strange guest or the paid labourer, nay, even to the daughter who is married to a stranger (Lev. 22,10-12).

Where does the man find the woman who is most fit to help him to found a house? In this respect the Israelites do not possess the same fixed and rigorous rules as so many other peoples. But the leading principle is that the woman must not be so far removed from the family of the man as to introduce quite new and strange elements, which the husband cannot assimilate. She would disrupt the house and remove the children from the family characteristics of the father. This finds its classical expression in the story of Abraham, who seeks a bride for his son Isaac and therefore sends his slave to far-off countries and his own deserted kindred, because in Canaan he lives among strangers. Abraham says expressly to the slave that he shall seek out his *mōledheth* (Gen. 24,4), his *mishpāḥā* and his *bēth 'ābh* (Gen. 24,38.40). The principal object is to find someone who is of the same flesh and blood; thus the flesh and blood of Abraham will continue purest in the progeny of Isaac. We meet the same thing in the story of Jacob, and we are here at a point where the Israelites cling most stubbornly to their old traditions. That which was quite natural to the Abraham of the Yahwist was also to be carried through in the post-exilitic time, and the Book of Tobit is, to a certain extent, built upon this motive.

However, there are limits to the closeness of the degree of relationship permitted. By the regulations of Lev. 18 it is ordained what female relations the man is not permitted to marry. The prohibited degrees are first of all in an upward and downward line: sister, mother and child's daughter. But together with the mother are mentioned the other wives of the father and their daughters, and somewhat farther on we meet father's and mother's sisters, as well as the wife of the father's brother and, moreover, son's wife. And it is not permitted to marry a wife and her daughter or a daughter's daughter, neither a woman and her sister.

The reason of these prohibitions is not to be looked for in the experience that marriages between near relatives make unhealthy progeny, which for that matter is rather doubtful, and at any rate it could not prevent a man from marrying the wife of his father's brother. The reason lies deeper; it must be looked for in the intimate character of relationship as well as of marriage. The one like the other is in itself a deeply rooted, all-pervading psychic community, and yet so different that they cannot be united in one person.

This holds good of mother, sister and daughter, but also of the sisters of the father and mother; they belong to the father and mother and are therefore his own flesh (Lev. 20,19). The wives of the father are the "nakedness" of the father, that is to say the feeling of shame is abolished between them; they form a psychic unity with the father, and thus have entered into a relationship with his sons, which cannot be reconciled with a new relationship, through which they are united with one of these sons, in the intimate but different relationship of a wife. The same principle prevents marriage with the wife of brother and father's brother. Through her marriage such a woman bears the impress of her husband and his nearest male kin; and she cannot stand in two relationships, intimate but of a different kind, to the same man. But the law in the latter case is less strict than in the case of mother and sister, because the relationship here is less strong. If a man marries his brother's or father's brother's wife, the marriage will prove a failure and childless (Lev. 20,20-21), whereas he who married his mother or sister would be put to death.

The wife of the mother's brother is not among those excluded, because the relationship through the mother is less strong than through the father. Daughter of brother and daughter of father's brother, mother's brother, father's and mother's sister are outside the forbidden degrees. The cousin is of the same kin, though so far removed that marriage is possible, and therefore she is the natural bride of the man. When it is not permitted at the same time to marry mother and daughter or sisters, then the reason must be that through their mutual relationship with the man they would come to be related in such a way as to burst the relation already existing between them through their mutual kindred.

The object of the marriage laws in Lev. 18 and 20 is to preserve the kin and family; for this can only be done when the source of its propagation is kept pure and not polluted by encroaching upon other fundamental relations. The law does not only forbid connections with women standing in another intimate relationship to the man or belonging to another man; it also abhors any sexual intercourse in which the other part is not a woman. The keen interest shown by this law in these doings and its violent reaction against them — still more violent than in Babylonia — is explained by the text itself telling us that these were Canaanite habits: "For all these abominations have the men of the land done, which were before you, and the land is defiled" (Lev. 18,27). Behind the Canaanite customs stand, as we now know, the Hittites. The laws of this people testify that they acknowledged the right to sexual intercourse with the nearest relatives, such as mother, daughter or son, when no coercion was used; it even seems that pederasty has been legally regulated. And as for bestiality, it is to be punished with death, to be sure, but the king may render pardon.[1] It is against these habits that the Israelitic law reacts thus strongly.

But this reaction has not been equally strong on all points nor in all Israelitic circles, and we have evidence of marriage between half-brothers and half-sisters. This custom is of usual occurrence in Egypt, probably originating in the royal house, which is anxious not to be mixed with other families; but it is also said to be found among the Phœnicians, where it may have been imported by the Hittites.[2] The Israelitic patriarch Abraham pretended that his wife Sarah was his sister, and in one of the accounts thereof it is said that she was in reality the daughter of his father, but not of his mother (Gen. 20,12), while the story of Amnon who ravished his half-sister Tamar, presupposes that he might make her his wife, if his father's consent were obtained (2 Sam. 13,13). In reality it was not so far from the daughter of the father's brother to the father's daughter, but that kind of marriage may more easily have taken place in greater households, where the various wives had separate establishments.

On the other hand, the demand that marriages should take place only among those of the same kin is not absolute, and there is even ample evidence that the Israelites had connubium with other peoples. Through that fusion the Israelitic empire was created. But in certain circles there was a tendency to maintain the Israelitic peculiarities as against the surrounding peoples. In the end these tendencies prevailed, but only when the whole of the people had been mixed with the Canaanites and strongly imbued with the Canaanite spirit. This reaction must, as a matter of course, result in the strong reprobation of marriages with non-Israelites, for the connubium was the nucleus of the fusion, because it united Israelitic and foreign families. "And they took their daughters to be their wives and gave their daughters to their sons and served their Gods" (Judg. 3,6). So the later Israelite judges of the earlier history. The reactionaries expressed their view concerning marriage with non-Israelites in admonitions attached to the law-codes, in which such connections were strictly forbidden (Exod. 34,15 f.; Deut. 7,3 et al.).

The contracting of marriage naturally cannot be a matter which only concerns the individual; it must be a matter concerning the family. The initial step is taken by the parents of the man; in any case it is they who form the resolution and carry it out. We hear nothing of Abraham asking Isaac's opinion and, at any rate as the story now stands, Samson gets his wife through the intercession of his father (Judg. 14,2), seeing that it is his house and his name which is going to be maintained.

When the young woman passes from her own family into that of her husband, it is thus two family spheres meeting. The

Israelitic wedding-ceremonies, of which we unfortunately hear so little, tend towards gradually fusing the two circles. Her family give some of the best they possess, their flesh and blood, and to put things on an equal footing it is invariably demanded that the family of the bridegroom should give something to that of the bride. If they do not give a jewel as valuable as a daughter, they must give something of what belongs to them. They give a bridal sum, *mōhar,* of their property, not merely as a material compensation, but as a mental balancing of what is given by the family of the bride; for in the eyes of the Israelite also property is a living thing, and is part of his soul. Thus the family of the bride are not wholly givers, that of the bridegroom not wholly takers, and the bond between two families is strengthened.

When the marriage is consummated, the house of the man has planted another shoot, which — if all goes well — will grow and, in its turn, send forth new shoots. The man founds a house, identical with that of his father, and yet something new, and the root of this transplanting is marriage. Marriage yields the strength, making the newly planted life grow, that it may expand through the generations by means of its progeny. The young woman takes her place in the new family, as a helpmeet towards maintaining its life. But she does not lose the connection with her own family. It is only at a royal wedding that it can be said to a bride: Forget also thine own people and thy father's house! (Ps. 45,11). The woman thus holds a dual position. The law of priests tells us that the priest may only defile himself for the bodies of those nearest to him, and it mentions father, mother, son, daughter, brother and virgin sister, whereas he must not come near the body of a married sister (Lev. 21,1-4; Ez. 44,25). This is in exact accord with the fact that the whole of his family may eat of the holy thing, but not his daughter, if she is married to a man who is not himself a priest (Lev. 22,12). So the married woman no more belongs entirely to her own family, nor does she wholly belong to that of her husband. The wife is not mentioned among those for whom the priest may defile himself. And if the man dies, or she is repudiated, then she generally returns to the house of her father, where she lives as a widow. She now once more belongs there, and if her father is a priest, she is again permitted to eat of the holy thing (Lev. 22,13). It is also told of Tamar that, after the death of the husband, she returned to the house of her father (Gen. 38,11), though she did not live there in the same manner as in the days when she was a virgin. She had not given her husband children, and her efforts were still directed towards fulfilling this wifely duty. When she is falsely accused of unchastity, it is also considered a crime against the family of her husband (Gen. 38,24), to which she is thus to a certain extent still bound. It is mentioned as a rare sign of fidelity towards the deceased husband that Ruth clave to her husband's mother and his family instead of remaining with her own.

The position of the wife in the family is characterized by her being *ba'al*-taken by her husband. In this is expressed both the intimacy and the subordination. That the relation between man and woman, also among the Israelites, is an intimate one, is shown by many examples, but that it was at the same time a relation of subordination, cannot be disputed. The man is the centre of the family, the woman his helpmeet; her desire is towards the husband, "but he rules over her". It is expressed by her being called by his name (Is. 4,1; Tob. 2,8). The will of the husband is the will of the house; the woman must often act by underhand means and use cunning in order to have her way. A typical example of this kind of woman's cunning is when Rebekah makes the blind father give Jacob his blessing. No less typical is the example of the clever Abigail, who, behind the back of her husband, tries to atone for his foolishness in relation to the strong captain of the freebooters (1 Sam. 25).

From her family the wife generally received a present to serve as a tie between her and her father's house [1]. It gives her a support and a certain independence in her relation to her husband. She may have her own property, as, by the way, a slave may, and we sometimes hear that she has her own tent (Gen. 24,67; 31,33; Judg. 4,17), but it is the duty of her husband to support her. She has the benefit from his property (Gen. 31,16), and upon the whole she must share good and evil with him. He may give her a bondmaiden, who is entirely subject to her will, as when

Abraham gave Hagar to Sarah. But it is Abraham who permits Sarah to humiliate Hagar, and it is he who must turn her out at the demand of Sarah (Gen. 16). If the husband loses his property and must become a slave for debt, it is a matter of course that she goes with him (Exod. 21,2 f.). The position of the woman was greatly dependent on the strength of the family which she had to support her. To a certain extent she continued to belong to it, and if she were wronged, then she must apply there for redress. Monarchy and the development of the great towns did not have a favourable effect upon the old-fashioned type of marriage. The pact became looser, and the harems, introduced on a large scale by the kings, tended to kill intimacy.

The position of the wife in the household is that of the husband's helpmeet, and first and foremost her duty it to give him children; thus she is assisting him in creating a "house" and in upholding him within his family. She is first and foremost a sexual being [1], and as such she entirely belongs to her husband. Thus, according to the legislation, she cannot, by vowing a sacred vow without the will of the husband, evade her duties towards him (Num. 30), and the capital offence is for her unfaithfulness towards her husband. It is *his* family which she must multiply. In that respect the Old Testament knows no pity. Those who commit adultery, men as well as women, are punished by death (Lev. 19,20; Deut. 22,22 ff.). All marriage laws show that, in this respect, right and wrong are determined from the standpoint of the husband. He is fully entitled to sexual intercourse with other women than his wife, as long as he does not violate the rights of some other man, but for a woman a corresponding act is a deadly sin.

Everything is grouped round the man; it is his life which is to be continued in the family. Therefore polygamy is a natural type of marriage among the Israelites. It is not the outcome of masculine licentiousness, but a mere consequence of the fact that two or three wives do more than one to satisfy the husband's demand for progeny. Polygamy is one of the ethical demands of old Israel, because the maintenance of the family is the greatest of all. Under the old simple conditions there was nothing in polygamy to violate the idea of marriage. That a man may feel affection for more than one woman, is a natural consequence of the whole of the Israelitic conception of woman's psychic characteristics, but as a rule it ends by his preferring one to the others, and the slighted wife will be in a very bad position. When Laban gave his two daughters to Jacob, he made it a condition that he was not permitted to have other wives beside them (Gen. 31,50).

This pronounced one-sidedness which places the centre of gravity in the man only, appears with particular clearness in the divorce-laws, for it seems as if the husband, without further ado, can dissolve the marriage — whereas we hear nothing of women possessing the same freedom — in the same manner as he may put away his children (Is. 50,1; Jer. 3,8; Hos. 2,4). The reason for divorcing a wife was generally her childlessness, the normal state of affairs being that the husband is closely united with the woman who has born him sons (Gen. 29,34).

It is peculiar that in the old accounts there are several examples of childless wives being most loved by their husbands, as, for instance, Rachel and Hannah. But they are the very exceptions, which derive their particular interest from the fact that the art of the narrator appears in his showing the tragedy of these women, who enjoy privileges to which they feel they are not entitled. Rachel says that she is dying with grief, because she has no children (Gen. 30,1). Through the whole of the Old Testament the cry for children is heard from all women, as everywhere, to this day, in Oriental countries; and first and foremost for male children (1 Sam. 1,11), these being the direct perpetuators and bearers of the husband's family, whereas girls must help in the growth of some other family.

Motherhood is the patent of nobility of a woman; through it she acquires her place in life and a share in the family. Even the slave woman feels so exalted when she has become a mother, that she can look down upon her childless mistress. Whatever the opinions of the Israelite regarding women, for the mother he knows only respect; here the bonds of blood as well as authority are operating. A man is nearer to his mother than to his wife.

Samson's wife does not hesitate to deceive her husband, but no mother would ever deceive her son. And when Samson's wife complains that he has not told her of the riddle he put unto the Philistines, he answers her in the following manner: Behold I have not told it to my father nor my mother, and shall I tell it thee? (Judg. 14,16). It is therefore in exact accord with the old Israelitic manner of thinking, when the mother of the king in later Israel holds the position of honour as *g^ebhīrā,* even though this institution probably has its prototype in foreign (Egyptian) customs.

As a mother the woman has her share in the authority of the husband over the children. When a bride was to be chosen for the son, it was not unusual for the mother to have her say in the matter (Gen. 24,55; Judg. 14,2). And even though the authority of the father is constantly maintained in his relation to the children, father and mother are always mentioned together. It is said: Honour thy father and thy mother, that thy lot may be happy and thy days long upon the land which Yahweh thy God giveth thee (Exod. 20,12; Deut. 5,16 cf Lev. 19,3). Here respect towards both parents is laid down as the basis upon which life rests. It supports the strength of the family, because the relation between parents and children is the innermost kernel of the community of kindred. If anyone presumes to smite or curse his parents, then he is as a diseased member, and is to be removed and put to death (Exod. 21,15.17; Lev. 20,9). Here is a fundamental point of Israelitic morals, and time has not brought any changes in this respect. In the great register of sins, drawn up by Ezekiel, the slighting of the parents takes the first place (Ez. 22,7).

It is so important that a son is born to a man that other considerations must give way to it. The Deuteronomy ordains that a newly-married man is not to go to war or to carry out other tasks drawing him away from the house (24,5). Other peoples have similar regulations, the object of which is to permit the man to devote himself to the protection of his wife, until she has given birth to her child. [1]

Israelitic law and practice put no limits to the endeavours of the man towards getting progeny. If the number of children born in his marriage with free women is insufficient to him, then he may have as many children with slave-women as he chooses. The position of the slave-woman differs from that of the wife, in that she lacks the protection of her kindred, and consequently is unable to maintain her rights towards the husband. She is frequently, but by no means always, a foreigner (Gen. 31,15), and in that case she is either a captive of war (Judg. 5,29; Deut. 21, 11-14) or she is purchased, e. g. from Phœnician traders (Ez. 27,13; Am. 1,9). If she is an Israelite, then her father must have been so deeply in debt that he has been obliged to sell her (Exod. 21,7; Is. 50,1; Neh. 5,5). The law tries to regulate her rights, so that she is not undefended from the caprices of her lord and master, and the vital point is then that she has been raised to the family through the very fact that her master has conversed with her conjugally (Exod. 21,8-11 of a Hebrew slave-woman, Deut. 21,10-14 of a foreigner). Her children may share in the inheritance (Gen. 21,10; cf. Judg. 11,2), but are not always recognized by the children of the real wives.

The wife would not always look upon the slave-woman as a rival; on the contrary, she sometimes looked upon her as a helpmeet towards fulfilling the task she herself is unable to fulfil. When Sarah did not bear Abraham any children, she said to him: Behold now, Yahweh has restrained me from bearing. I pray thee, go unto my slave; it may be that I may obtain children by her (Gen. 16,2). How this is to be understood appears from the story of Rachel. When she is grieving that, unlike Leah, she cannot bear Jacob any children, she says to him: Behold my slave Bilhah, go in unto her; and she shall bear upon my knees, that I may also have children by her (Gen. 30,3). When Bilhah gives birth to a son, Rachel says: God has given me my rights, and has also heard my voice and has given me a son; therefore called she his name Dan (Gen. 30,6). And when Bilhah gives birth to a second son, then Rachel says: With great wrestlings have I wrestled with my sister, and I have prevailed (30,8). Even Leah, who has several sons, gives her slave to Jacob, when she has ceased bearing. The words of Rachel show that she looks upon herself as a mother. The delivery of the slave-girl is made her own, in that it takes place upon her knee. Thus she appropriates the honour of motherhood, and it consists in her having helped her husband to progeny.

When the women call for children, it is true that they aim at something for themselves — the joy and honour of motherhood. But their claim can never rival that of the husband, because they render themselves entirely subservient to it. Their joy is in giving birth to *his* children. When the woman from Tekoah presented herself before David and told him the story of her two sons who had fought with each other, in which fight one of them had lost his life, then she did not only complain that the family — by demanding the delivery of the slayer that they might kill him — deprived her of her only son and bread-winner; she said: And so they shall quench my coal which is left, and shall not leave to *my husband* name nor remainder upon the earth (2 Sam. 14,7). Her misery consists in the fact that her husband will thus leave no progeny.

It follows from the whole character of the formation of the family that a man is nearest to the family of his father. The father's brother is a closer relation than the mother's brother. This appears from the prohibition against marrying the wife of the father's brother, but not that of the mother's brother. One of the words used to indicate relationship, *'am,* is as mentioned above in Arabic the denomination of father's brother, and the usual Hebrew word for father's brother, *dōdh,* has come to mean a friend who is particularly close to one; on the other hand, there is not even a special word for mother's brother in the Hebrew language. It is told as something quite natural that Abraham and his brother's son Lot are wandering together; each with his own tents and his own flocks, it is true, but still together.

This is the fundamental rule, though it does not exclude the case of a man feeling kinship with his mother's family, and in certain cases it may manifest itself very strongly, this being the result of the mother constantly keeping up the connection with her own family. Where polygamy prevails it is quite natural that those who, besides having the same father also have the same mother, are bound together by particularly close ties. This feeling forms one of the principal features in the narratives of Joseph and Benjamin and of Absalom and Tamar, but we have also many other examples (Judg. 8,19). If the sons are numerous and come to stand up against each other, it happens, as in the case of Abimelech (Judg. 9,1), that the one or the other turns to the mother's family for help against his half-brothers.

In a single instance we hear of the husband living among the kindred of the wife and being dependent upon them. This is the case with Jacob, who lives with Laban. When he has fled, and Laban has overtaken him, the latter says: These daughters are my daughters, these children are my children, and these cattle are my cattle, and all that thou seest is mine (Gen. 31,43). But the dependency of Jacob is due to the circumstance that he has taken service with Laban. That by marrying the daughters he really founded an independent house, appears both from his complaint against Laban that he may not act independently in his own house, but must serve Laban, and from the statements of the daughters that they are independent of their father's house. They have no more share in it, but, on the other hand, they share in the house and property of Jacob (Gen. 31,14 ff.).[1] Thus even this account confirms the patriarchal order.

The family of the mother may be so much more important than the kindred of the father that it makes itself most strongly felt. We know men who are not named by the name of the father, but by that of the mother, as, e. g., Joab and Abishai, the sons of Zeruiah (1 Sam. 26,6; 2 Sam. 2,13 and others); they are thus named, because Zeruiah is the sister of David. The sons of the daughter of Saul are reckoned as of the family of Saul, for which they had to pay dearly (2 Sam. 21,8). There are also examples of a man taking the name of the family of his wife, whereas the contrary should be the case (Ezr. 2,61; Neh. 7,63), and from the latest years of the history of Israel we hear of a man who continues his house through daughters. It is told (1 Chr. 2,34 ff.) of a man by the name of Sheshan that he had only daughters and no sons. But he had an Egyptian slave, and to him he gave his daughter. The slave has no family, but belongs to the house of his master, and through this marriage Sheshan obtains sons in his family. These examples only show that the relation between the kindred of the husband and wife can be so unevenly balanced that the equilibrium is shifted, and the centre of gravity, contrary to all custom, comes to lie in the mother. For the patriarchate is not the result of a theory to be carried through doctrinally. It rests upon the certainty that the soul of the man is the stronger; and if in certain cases this is not so, then it may happen that the patriarchate cannot be absolute, for every man has in him the kindred of the mother as well as of the father.

We know examples of a man having wives who are not received into his house, but who live in another town and remain among their own family. Samson had a Philistine wife at Timnath; she lived with her father, and he came to visit her there (Judg. 14; 15,1). Gideon, who himself lived in Ophrah, had a wife living in Shechem (Judg. 8,31).

It is natural that the children of such marriages must come to stand in a somewhat closer relationship to the mother than those born in normal marriages, but it would be an error to take cases of this kind as a proof that the matriarchate should have existed in a people whose whole manner of thinking was so patriarchal as that of the Israelites. In reality the dominant feature of the matriarchate is lacking, viz. that the children are not reckoned as of the family of the father. The story of Abimelech, who was born of Gideon's wife at Shechem, begins as follows: And Abimelech, the son of Jerubbaal went to Shechem unto his mother's brothers and communed with them and with all the family of the house of his mother's father (Judg. 9,1). Here Abimelech is characterized as the son of Gideon, in the same manner as it is said that she bore *him* this son, whom *he* named (8,31) and who must have lived outside his mother's family or, in all probability, with the father. If further proof is required, his own mother's family is called a "father's house".[1] We now know that it was a habit with the Assyrians to let the wife live in her father's house, and it also may have been a common practice in the other northern nations. But an Assyrian marriage of this kind is no less patriarchal than the marriage in which the wife is living in the house of her husband. The law even expressly says that such a wife is responsible for her husband's obligations, guilt and sin, and in everything that does not concern the property of her father she is fully dependent on him.

The Israelitic conception of marriage and its importance in the life of the people as the organ of the formation of families, finds one of its most typical expressions in the so-called law of Levirate marriages, which is preserved in the Deuteronomy. As this part of the law is of such vital importance, it is here given verbatim: If brethren dwell together, [1] and one of them die and have no son, [2] the wife of the dead shall not marry without unto a stranger; [3] her husband's brother shall go in unto her, and take her to him to wife, and enter into a Levirate marriage with her. And it shall be that the first-born which she beareth shall maintain the name of his brother which is dead, [4] that his name be not put out of Israel. And if the man like not to take his brother's wife, then let his brother's wife go up to the gate unto the elders and say: My husband's brother refuseth to maintain a name for his brother in Israel; in that he will not enter into a Levirate marriage with me. Then the elders of the city shall call him and speak unto him, and if he stand to it, and say, I like not to take her; then shall his brother's wife come unto him, in the presence of the elders, and loose his sandal from off his foot and spit in his face, and shall answer and say: So shall it be done unto that man that will not build up his brother's house. And his name shall be called in Israel: The house of him that has his sandal loosed (Deut. 25,5.7-10).

This law has caused difficulties to later Judaism, because it is in conflict with the laws concerning the prohibited degrees of kindred. The law is then interpreted in the manner that if a man die without issue, the brother in the natural course of events inherits his wife and property; but he may get rid of her by means of the ceremony already described, and in certain cases he is obliged to do so. [5] The meaning of the old law is, however, a different one. The ceremony which takes place at the gate is an ignomy to the man in question. He is now a marked man, and he and his house forever must suffer under it. No one can force the man to do what is requested of him; but if he refuses, he cannot any more be looked upon as a normal citizen among his people. The only restriction on the validity of the law is that the brothers must live together, and from the context this means in the same town. Naturally these precautions cannot be taken in such cases where the husband has left his kindred.

Great uncertainty has prevailed regarding the interpretation of this passage of the law; now stress has been laid upon consideration for the widow, now upon the maintenance of the family property, now upon other circumstances.[1] If we do not go beyond the text, the meaning is clear enough. The object of the law is to get progeny for a man without sons, that his name may be preserved and his house not be blotted out. If a man, after having contracted a marriage, dies without sons, then he dies entirely. It is this blotting out of life which is to be avoided. His nearest of kin, the brother, must perform this office of love in order to protect him from extermination. The wife, whose object in life it is to bear him a son in whom his life is resurrected, must be enabled to do her duty towards him. It is this which is expressed by the fact that the first-born of the new marriage — which is thus not a new one, in so far as the brother does not act on his own behalf, but only on that of his dead brother — shall "stand upon" the name of the dead. The name once more comes to life in him. The widow acts on the same motives as Sarah or Rachel, when bidding their husbands "go in unto" their handmaidens. It is the honour of the wife to supply the man with progeny, in which his life may be maintained. If the brother of her husband refuses his help towards this object, it is due to his lack of love for the deceased brother, and it is also a violation of her rights, in that he prevents her from fulfilling her most exalted duty.

When the brother is mentioned as the one to take this obligation upon himself, it is because he is the nearest of kin to the deceased and best suited to act in his name, just as he is the man from whom it is most fair to exact the fulfilment of this duty. There are few laws in Israel which in such a characteristic manner show us the position of the man and the woman and their demands on life: the man as the one who raises up the family and lives in it, the woman as his helpmeet.

An illustration of this law we find in Genesis, Chap. 38, which deals with the house of Judah. Judah had three sons: Er, Onan and Shelah. To Er he gave as wife Tamar, but shortly afterwards Er died, because he displeased Yahweh. Judah now ordered Onan to fulfill his duty towards his brother and to get progeny for him through Tamar, but, being wicked, he was unwilling to do this service of love unto his deceased brother, and so Yahweh also let him die. Tamar is now sent back to her family in order to wait until the second brother of her husband, Shelah, be grown. She waits in vain. She learns that Shelah is grown, and yet she is left at her father's house. Tamar, however, is an energetic woman, who knows how to maintain her honour. By disguising herself as a hetæra she attracts Judah, the father of her deceased husband, and she conceives by him, as had so long been her ardent wish.

The manner in which her behaviour is judged appears very clearly from the story itself and is expressed in the appreciation of Judah; first he believed her to have been guilty of inchastity, but later on he learns how the matter really stands; she is right, and he is wrong; she has thought more of her husband than he of his son. Israelitic women have looked up to her as an example, a woman who knew how to show endurance and cunning and set aside all other considerations in order to attain the great victory, namely to give the husband progeny.

It appears from this story that the natural thing would have been for the brother to have procured progeny, as demanded by the deuteronomic law — first the elder brother, then the others. But it is not necessary; it can, in cases of emergency, be done by the father. The Yahwist expresses no surprise that Tamar goes to her father-in-law, even though it is an irregular proceeding. The irregularity is that the father of the deceased becomes the one to get him progeny, though a brother is still alive.

But if neither the father nor the brother lives, then the duty falls upon the nearest agnate outside the narrow circle of the house, and an example of this is supplied in the Book of Ruth.

Elimelech is dead in foreign parts, leaving a widow Naomi; later on both of his sons die, each leaving a widow, Orpah and Ruth. When Naomi wants to return to her own kindred, the two daughters-in-law go with her for part of the way, until Orpah takes the earnest advice of her mother-in-law and turns back, whereas Ruth goes with her. Naomi says that she advises the daughter-in-law to return, as she is too old to give birth to more sons, and even if she should give birth to sons, she would not demand that the young women should wait until they grew up; they had better stay and get new husbands. But Ruth declares that she will never desert her mother-in-law.

It is not the individual affection of Ruth for Naomi which the narrator wants to praise in her. This affection exists, and is beautifully expressed, but the feeling of Ruth is of a much deeper and more far-reaching kind; she acts in loyalty towards her husband and his family. The Israelitic wife thinks and acts like Ruth — and yet she is no Israelite! This is what the narrator wants to point out to his countrymen. Naomi herself knows how to appreciate this loyalty: if she had sons who could get them progeny, it would all be very simple. But she does not see her way to procure them progeny, so why monopolize their youth? They still have possibilities in other houses; as regards the house of her husband and sons, all hope is extinguished; she justly calls herself "the bitter" (1,20). That which lies behind Naomi's feelings is that the house of her husband is blotted out by the death of her childless sons. Her soul is bound up with the house of her husband. Every Israelitic woman will understand this: The hand of Yahweh has stricken Naomi, and that cannot be helped.

Ruth like Tamar is an example of womanly heroism. She might have taken the advice of Naomi and would perhaps have had a rich future before her in other families, and her desire for children might then have been amply fulfilled. But for Ruth it was not sufficient to get children; she wanted to fulfil her obligation of honour towards her deceased husband; it is first and foremost to him that she owes progeny, and, against all likelihood, her perseverance at last attains its goal. There are neither brothers, nor even a father; but there is one kinsman sufficiently close to be a "maintainer". Boaz buys the property of Elimelech and his sons, and "moreover I purchase the Moabitess, the wife of Mahlon, to maintain the name of the dead upon his inheritance, that the name of the dead be not cut off from his brethren and from the gate of his place" (4,10).

Boaz marries Ruth, and she gives birth to a son called Obed. It is characteristic that the women now praise Naomi for this child, and Naomi becomes nurse unto it. The new-born son maintains the name of the deceased and thus also makes reparation to her as the mother of a house. Boaz is not the brother of Ruth's deceased husband, but still a near kinsman, and in the solemn declaration which he makes, on taking over Ruth, he pronounces that he will perform the office of love towards the deceased which, according to the Levirate law, is incumbent upon the brother, i. e. to maintain the name of the dead. [1] Here we have the essence of this law: the endeavour to get for this man a house, a posterity in which his life is continued, even if it is not done in the normal way. In that manner he is safeguarded against that which is the great terror of the Israelite: to perish from the family and to be blotted out.

THE PROPERTY OF THE FAMILY.

The connection existing between the man and his property will only be quite clear to us when we have fully realized the psychological totality of the man, but in this context we shall content ourselves with considering the close connection between property and family.

This close relation or solidarity appears most clearly wherever conflicts arise. When, through the Monarchy, the Israelites had developed a powerful institution, which did not harmonize very well with their old traditions, there was ample occasion for conflicts. If the King were the absolute centre of power, why then should he respect the distribution arising out of the old family-division? All Israelites were his subjects, his slaves.

The story of Ahab shows us a conflict of this kind. He wishes to possess a vineyard in Jezreel which belongs to Naboth, and offers him full compensation in money or a still better vineyard elsewhere, but Naboth answers in great fright: Yahweh forbid me that I should give the inheritance of my father unto thee! The Phœnician Queen Jezebel, however, finds a way. She cunningly succeeds in getting Naboth sentenced for blasphemy, and the king takes over his property (1 Kings 21). That such behaviour on the part of a monarch is not unique appears from the history of David. By one word David deprives Meribbaal of his lawful inheritance and gives it to his faithless calumniator (2 Sam. 16,4), and while Meribbaal maintains that the accusation is false, he must still divide his property with his accuser (2 Sam. 19,30). And how often do we hear the prophets complain of the great men who, rallying round the monarchs, do violence to the inheritance of people. "Woe unto them that join house unto house, that lay field to field till there be no place, that they may be placed alone in the midst of the world!" says Isaiah (5,8). And from the same time we have the curses of Micah: "Woe to them that devise iniquity, and work evil upon their beds! When the morning is light they practise it, as soon as it is in the power of their hand! And they covet fields and take them by violence; and houses and take them away; so they oppress a man and his house, even a man and his heritage!" (2,1.2). The mighty are no better than common thieves that remove the bound (Hos. 5,10).

That which makes the strongest impression in the account of Naboth, is the terror ringing through his answer to the proposal of the king; he uses the strongest words which can be used by an Israelite. It is not that the king wants to deprive him of a material value. There is no question about that; the king is willing to pay the full value of the piece of ground, nay, more than that, and he leaves it to Naboth himself to fix the sum of compensation. But Naboth cannot part with the property which he has inherited from his fathers, without committing sacrilege against himself and his kindred, so closely do kindred and property belong together. Therefore, the crime of Ahab is a double one.

When Isaiah and the other prophets blame the princes, the main point is not that they appropriate the property of other people without paying for it, though this also happened. Their offence is that they avail themselves of the unfavourable position of a man, in order to purchase his property, thus violating the family privilege of solidarity with the property. The prophet maintains the old moral principle, in that he claims that the property shall remain with the family.

In the olden times this moral principle was maintained by the family itself, and in all the laws of the Old Testament it is taken for absolutely granted that no one sells his landed property without being forced to do so. But if he gets into such difficulties that he can hold it no longer, then his kindred take care that it is not sold to the highest bidder. Property is not a material sale-commodity. It follows its own laws, which are identical with those of the formation of the family. If it is on account of poverty that a man must sell his property, then the son is also poor and cannot take it over, but the property must then follow the line of kindred. It must be bought by the nearest relative, and as will appear from the above, this naturally means the nearest agnate. In the so-called Law of Holiness there is a regulation to this effect, among other regulations with which it does not seem to harmonize.

It is said: If thy brother be waxen poor and sells some of his possession, then his nearest redeemer shall come to him and redeem that which his brother sold. And if a man have no redeemer (and consequently must sell to a stranger) and recovers and can afford the redemption, then let him count the years it has been sold and restore the overplus to the man to whom he sold it, that he may return into his possession. But if he cannot afford to redeem it, then that which is sold shall remain in the hand of him that hath bought it until the year of *yōbhēl;* and in the year of *yōbhēl* it shall go and return into his possession (Lev. 25, 25-28).

We are here confronted with two different regulations, the one regarding the year of *yōbhēl,* the other regarding the redemption, and for the time being it is the latter which interests us. Redemption or restitution, *ge'ullā,* means the getting back of something which has been lost, the restitution of a breach. The breach to be avoided here is that the property, by being thrown on to the highest bidder, should pass out of the hands of the family. That section of the law of redemption which says that the redeemer is to buy the field from the needy, contains no unnatural or doctrinary demand. It is the natural expression of the family feeling, and no outer force secures its fulfilment: only the will of men to maintain their family and its demands. We understand who the redeemer should be, in that another section of the same law shows us that it is first the brother, then the brother of the father and finally the son of the latter. Property follows exactly the same line as kindred. But the law contains no sentimental regulations that the kinsmen should assist the needy by keeping the property *for his person.* If he has not the strength to keep it for himself, he must lose it. The centre of gravity passes from him to a relative; he loses in importance what the relative gains, but the family, as family, loses nothing. The property is not left to chance, but remains in the kindred with which it is familiar.

This law accords so well with the manner of thinking of old Israel, that it cannot be a doctrine invented by the later compiler. By mere chance we also possess historical evidence of its having been applied. In the story of Jeremiah we read: Jeremiah said: The word of Yahweh came unto me saying: Behold, Hanameel, the son of Shallum, thy father's brother, shall come unto thee saying: Buy thee my field that is in Anathoth; for it is thy right to purchase it according to the right of redemption. Then Hanameel, my father's brother's son came unto me in the court of the prison according to the word of Yahweh, saying unto me: Buy my field in Anathoth, which is in the country of Benjamin; for the right of inheritance is thine, and the redemption is thine. Buy it! Then I understood that it was the word of Yahweh, and I bought the field of Hanameel, my father's brother's son, that was in Anathoth, and weighed him the silver, even seventeen shekels of silver. And I wrote it down in a document and sealed it, and took witnesses, and weighed the silver in the balances, etc.

(Jer. 32,6-11). Later on it is told that Jeremiah went away into the land of Benjamin to take possession of the field in the midst of his own kindred (37,12). [1] The cousin must have become poor, so the prophet takes upon himself the duty of redemption, and thus the field passes into his possession. There is no question of any help to the cousin.

We possess no evidence of the family having had community of property in the sense that all the members of the family had equal rights of property to a certain piece of ground. A community of this kind would also have been very peculiar when considering the character of the family. It is true that the family forms a solid community, and in so far its property may be called common property (Gen. 34,23). But its members do not form a homogeneous mass. It centres in the fathers of the houses, each of whom has his own responsibility. Further, all laws presuppose that every man has his own property as divided from that of his neighbour, and the very basis of the laws, maintaining that the property must remain in the family, is that it is a kinsman who possesses it and is responsible for it. It is Naboth who possesses the property in Jezreel of which Ahab wanted to acquire a part. Those who belong to his house have a share in the property, to the same extent as they have a share in him. It is true that the wife, as we have seen, may have her own private property, which she brought from her kindred; but the fundamental point of view is that she shares in the possession of the husband. Leah and Rachel say to Jacob, when he has acquired great wealth with Laban: For all the riches which God has taken from our father, that is ours and our children's (Gen. 31,16). The property is bound up in the man, that is to say the house. [2]

The great social revolutions, during the time of the Monarchy, brought about several breaks in the regular transference of property, without redemption, from generation to generation. We see how the laws are at work to counteract this. The motive power in the old law — the family's strength to maintain itself — was vitiated in many cases, and attempts were made to remedy these breaks by purely mechanical means, which those in power were of course not particularly eager to carry into practice. We must not forget that those preparing the later laws were not always those who *possessed* the power, but those who thought that they *ought* to possess it, because they looked upon it as their right to represent the traditions of old Israel. The lawgivers are groping in the dark in order to maintain the old traditions; but, as a matter of fact, they were all vain endeavours to stem the tide. That they must be vain we understand, when we see the kind of remedies invented by the laws against the evils in question.

The Deuteronomy says: At the end of every seven years thou shalt make a release. And this is the manner of the release: Every creditor that lendeth ought unto his neighbour shall release it; he shall not exact it of his neighbour or of his brother; because there has been announced release unto Yahweh. Of a foreigner thou mayst call for payment again, but that which is thine with thy brother thine hand shall release (Deut. 15,1-3).

A sharp distinction is made between the Israelite and the stranger. There is no direct mention of landed property, but this indeed is implied, the object of the law being to prevent Israelites from becoming deeply involved in debt and thus being ruined. The man is to be kept in the same relation to property in which he was born; the lawgiver has taken the analogy from the laws, which permit the normal life to rest after a period of seven years. The result of the law would then be, either that the weaker would not get help, or that energy must relax, and that the strength which was to maintain the property of the family would be paralyzed. [1]

Ezekiel has an ordinance which, it is true, only applies to the prince, but the tendency of which is the same; and his prescription shows that it is still fresh in his memory, whence come the attacks on the right of property of the families. He says: If the prince give of his property unto any of his sons [2], it shall belong to his sons; it shall be their possession as landed property. But if he give a gift of his inheritance to one of his slaves (i. e. subjects), then it shall be his to the year of liberty; after it shall return [3] to the prince; only his sons shall keep their landed property. [4] Moreover, the prince shall not take of the people's inheritance by oppression, so as to thrust them out of their possession; but he may give his sons property out of his own possession; that my people be not scattered every man from his possession (Ez. 46,16-18).

In another place (45,8) Ezekiel says straight out that his object is to guard the old rights of the family against the wrongs of the prince. The latter must not interfere with the property of others, and in his own he must respect the principle of kindred. He is entitled to give of his property to his sons, who are his heirs. But if he gives outside his own kindred, the gift is only a loan until the year of release; then it must return. The law regarding the year of release is, as applied by Ezekiel, a novel thing: the restitution of property to the former owners. Still, it rests on an old idea. In the Book of the Covenant the seventh year is a year of release for Hebrew slaves (Exod. 21,2 cf. Deut. 15,12; Jer. 34,14-17), and this idea is taken up by Ezekiel and extended to include the restitution of all property; it should be a matter of course that the year of release not only applies to the property of the prince, but to that of the whole people. Ezekiel has gone one step further than the Deuteronomy, which expressly only mentioned the remission of debts. We do not know how often this "release" *(d^e^rōr)*, which in this case has become considerably more than release, should take place. It is possible that Ezekiel has taken the period from the old slave-law and thought of every seventh year; but it is also possible that he thought of a longer term, as we find it in the Priestly Code.

In the latter it is stated that every fiftieth year is to be sacred; it is celebrated by the blowing of rams' horns *(yōbhēl)*, for which reason it is called the *yōbhēl*-year. In that year "release" is to be called all over the country, and everyone shall return to his property and his kindred. This is to be understood as meaning that every Hebrew slave is to be released and every purchase of landed property annulled (Lev. 25 cf. 27,17 ff.; Num. 36,4). This law thus annuls the sale of real property in the strictest sense of the word. The buying of that kind of possession in reality only becomes a leasehold for a certain number of years. The payment shall be arranged accordingly, so as to become a royalty for the number of years left until the next year of *yōbhēl* (Lev. 25,14-17).

It is characteristic that this law is expressly said not to apply to houses within walls (apart from the Levite cities); here we only have the reservation that the bargain may be relinquished, in case the seller can find the money within twelve months. On the other hand, the law applies fully to houses in small open towns, which are reckoned with the arable land (Lev. 25,31). The conservative tendency of the lawgiver appears very clearly from this ordinance. It is the soil, the fields, which are to be saved for the original owners. In the large fortified cities there are other laws. They are something new and strange in Israelitic life and do not depend upon the old Israelitic ideas of kindred and property. But in the country, where the old state still prevails, it must be protected against the modern forces which are likely to undermine it.

We have already seen that this law is combined with another, i. e. that of redemption by a kinsman, which latter law in a characteristic manner expresses the old-Israelitic conception of the internal cohesion of the family and its connection with the soil. The reason why it was taken up in this context was simply that it existed and so could not be neglected, for it was made entirely unnecessary by the law of the *yōbhēl* year. If the property, in any case, must return to the original owner, why then should a relative in the meantime go and buy it? The two laws are fundamentally different. The law of the release provides for the property, so that, if it comes to one who is inefficient and cannot hold it, it is directed into other channels of the stream of kindred. The law is a living law, imbued with real life. In case there is a ne'er-do-well in the family, he is not to be permitted to involve his kindred in his ruin. The nearest of kin is required to step in and maintain the claim of the family, so that it shall not be weakened by strangers taking its property. The object of the law of the *yōbhēl* year is, by might and main, to preserve the property for the person into whose hands it has come, whether he is worthy or not. It is the expediency of despair, of the same kind as the demands of the Deuteronomy for the remission of debts, but still more radical in its conservative tendency. The law of redemption only aims at maintaining the unity of the family; if the family is not strong enough to maintain the property, then it must go down. The Priestly Code doctrinally wants to check the development of life, in order that the inefficient may have the same property, as if they had been efficient; the family must be maintained at its former level.

Life, however, proved stronger than doctrines. As far as is known the *yōbhēl* ordinances have never been observed. According to Nehemiah (10,32) the demand put forth in the Deuteronomy as to the remission of debts was one of the ordinances which the Jews, at the reformation of Ezra, bound themselves to keep, which seems to indicate that at the time when this was written down, a certain weight was attached to it.[1] In later years the Jews managed to circumvent this unpractical law by means of a proviso made beforehand, *prosbol,* invented by Hillel.

Thus, though these laws were of small or perhaps no practical importance, they are extremely interesting to us, in that they bear testimony to the old-Israelitic conception of kindred and property, being an expression of the reaction against the forces counteracting it, which forces, as we have already seen, were closely connected, partly with the city-culture, and partly with the monarchy.[2]

Even for the man who is able to maintain his right of property there will, sooner or later, come a time when he must relinquish it. On the death of the father the property normally passes to the son or sons. The heir in the strictest sense of the word is the first-born; he maintains the name of the father over the landed property. In the Deuteronomy there are given certain rules, according to which the first-born is to have two-thirds of the inheritance, even though the mother is less beloved by the husband (Deut. 21,15 ff.).

From the point of view of inheritance the children of slave-women are not on the same level as the progeny of the free-born wives. If there are no other children than those of the slave-women, then they must take over the inheritance, since, after all, they are nearer than strangers. Sarah turns out Hagar and Ishmael saying: The son of this bondswoman shall not be heir with my son (Gen. 21,10). This presupposes that the right of inheritance of the sons of slave-women was a thing to be reckoned with, at any rate to a certain extent. But later on it is stated that Abraham gave to Isaac all he possessed, whereas the daughters of the concubines only got certain gifts (Gen. 24,36; 25,5). Here, as in so many other cases, there may have been a certain vagueness, and much may have depended upon the will of the father. Of Jephthah we hear that he was turned out by his brothers, who were the sons of free women. For it is said that he himself was the son of a hetæra, and the other sons would not permit him to inherit with them (Judg. 11,2). If there is no progeny whatsoever, things may occur so unhappily that a slave falls heir to the property[1] (Gen. 15,3).

Considering the Israelitic ideas of the family, it is quite natural that the son should take over the inheritance. It is the son who continues the life of the father, and therefore it is rather exceptional, when it is told of Job that he gives his daughters inheritance among their brethren (Job 42,15), because the daughters normally pass to another man and help to reproduce *his* life. In the Old Testament it is, therefore, constantly presupposed that the man has sons; if he has not, it is looked upon as an unlucky and abnormal case, but also the abnormal may occur, and then an expedient must be found to reduce the damage as much as possible. This the various lawgivers also attempt to do, and here again we see them using various remedies.

In the Priestly Code it is ordained that, in certain circumstances, daughters may inherit. In this context it is said: If a man die and have no son, then ye shall cause his inheritance to pass unto his daughters. And if he have no daughter, then ye shall give his inheritance unto his brethren. And if he have no brethren, then ye shall give his inheritance unto his father's brethren. And if his father have no brethren, then ye shall give his inheritance unto his kinsman that is next to him in his flesh, and he shall inherit him (Num. 27,8-11). Setting aside the new elements of this law — i. e. the right of inheritance of daughters — that which we are told is that the inheritance passed to the brother of the man, then to the father's brother, etc. or the same line which the property would follow, in case the man could not maintain it while he was still alive. This is the old law of inheritance. If there is no son, the property follows the normal way of the formation of the family through the kindred of the husband; it passes unto a lateral branch, but still remains in the family. When the woman from Tekoah complains to David that she has wicked kinsmen on her husband's side who want to exterminate his name, then it rather reflects on their character, when it is known that they themselves may take over the inheritance in case the man be childless (2 Sam. 14,7).

Beside this law stands the Levirate Law. The object of the latter is, as we have seen, to get progeny for the man who is dead without sons, to "maintain his name in Israel". The intention is to continue his life, but it also includes the taking over of his property. We do not know to what extent the Levirate Law has been the rule in old Israel. It always expresses an office of love on the part of the brother. If he is actually the natural heir, it is clear that it is a great sacrifice on his part; for then he might let the deceased be blotted out and take over the inheritance for himself and his progeny. This view, in all probability, underlies the demand of the Deuteronomy to brand with a serious ignomy the man who refuses to fulfil the law. The presupposition is that it is really a great sacrifice he is making.

A peculiar application of the principle of the Levirate Law is to be found in the Book of Ruth. In so far as it is only a question of getting progeny for the man, the story is clear enough, but when we come to the problem of property, we are confronted with several difficulties. When Boaz has resolved to fulfil his duty towards the deceased, he goes right up to the gate of the town, saying to the nearest redeemer: Naomi that is come again out of the country of Moab selleth a parcel of land which was our brother Elimelech's.[1] And I thought to advertise thee, saying: Buy it before those sitting here and before the elders of my people. If thou wilt redeem it, redeem it, but if thou[2] wilt not redeem it, then tell me that I may know; for there is none to redeem it beside thee, and I am after thee. And he said: I will redeem it. Then said Boaz: But buying the field of Naomi, thou buyest[3] also

Ruth, the Moabitess, the wife of the dead, to raise up the name of the dead upon his inheritance. And the kinsman said: I cannot redeem it for myself, lest I mar mine own property; redeem thou my redemption, for I cannot redeem it (Ruth 4,3-6). After that it is told that the first redeemer, in confirmation of his words, plucked off his sandal, and Boaz called those gathered round the gate to witness that he bought all that belonged to Elimelech and his two sons of the hand of Naomi, adding that he bought Ruth in order to raise up his name that was dead.

The first redeemer is by the writer treated with delicate raillery. He is at first willing to take over the field, but when he hears that he must take Ruth into the bargain, and that the name of him that was dead is to be "raised up upon" the inheritance, he suddenly discovers that the property after all does not suit him. Not so with Boaz, who is willing to undertake the obligations. But the whole position of the redeemer and Naomi in this matter causes us serious difficulties. How can the childless Naomi become possessed of the field of her dead husband? In no Israelitic law is there any suggestion of a widow being able to inherit her dead husband's property, and such a proceeding would be against the general Israelitic conception of the essence of the family. Of course the widow retains what has been given her by her own family. If she has a son, then she remains with him, and he honours her, as an Israelite ought to honour his mother. If he is not full-grown, then she takes him with her and sees to his education (1 Kings 17,9 ff.). If she has no sons and does not succeed in getting her husband sons under the shelter of the Levirate Law, then she must return to her kindred. If she has no relations who are able or willing to take care of her, then she has nothing to rely upon except the charity which the Old Testament constantly admonishes the Israelites to show to everyone lacking the natural support of kindred: the miserable *gērīm,* fatherless and widows. And how should there be room for her? The inheritance follows its natural line within the family of the husband, to those who are nearest to him.

Nor do we, at the beginning of the story, get the impression that Naomi possesses a field. If so it would not be necessary for Ruth to glean ears of corn in the fields of other people, and that she should be made happy by being given a pittance to take home to her mother-in-law. But there are other points which are not clear. What has happened to the field in the meantime? As the Israelites, in the same manner as the Arabians and Babylonians, had rules for the care of property during the absence of the owner (Exod. 22,6 ff.), it would be natural that the property should have been taken over by another. But we hear nothing of such a proceeding; besides, it is not very probable that the owner of landed property should go and settle permanently in a foreign country. To this it must be added that the whole of the position of the redeemer is very peculiar. The redeemer is the next agnate, and thus, according to the most natural conception, the heir. How then can he be made to buy the property of his near kinsman from a widow who does not belong to the family?

And why is Boaz to *buy* the field? It is not to belong to him, but shall remain in the possession of him that is dead through the son, whom Boaz is to procure him. Also the expression that he buys Ruth is very peculiar. Though it is not expressly stated, the natural conception of the Levirate Law is that the brother-in-law, without further ceremony, takes over the wife of the deceased. The two things — the taking over of the widow and the maintenance of the property for the brother — in the old law come to the same thing. But in our account a distinction is made, Boaz buying both field and widow. It is possible that the law in Lev. 25,25 relating to the redemption of a field which is on the point of passing out of the family, has also acted here. But with the intermixture of this point of view the proper meaning of the Levirate Law becomes eclipsed.

In spite of the antique colouring of the Book of Ruth, it must not be forgotten that it is of a very late date. It begins in a romantic manner: "Now it came to pass in the days when the judges ruled that there was a famine in the land", and it describes the old customs as something belonging to former days. And though it preserves so vividly the old Israelitic family feeling, it seems as if it is far removed from the old law of property. On this point we must not be guided by the narrative.

That the Levirate Law has not preserved its strength as the regular solution of the problem of the inheritance of those without sons, appears from the fact that the Priestly Code looks for a very different expedient, which, for that matter, cannot be said to exclude the Levirate Law, but which takes no account of it whatsoever. It is the above-mentioned law dealing with the inheritance of daughters. In Num. 27,1-11 it is stated in a similar form as the one used by the Muhammadans in their collections of traditions: On a special occasion a person came, laying before the lawgiver a special case, and his judgment was made of general application. The daughters of Selpachad (this is the correct reading of the name) came to Moses saying that their father was dead in the desert, without leaving any son. His name was threatened by extermination, and therefore they asked him to give them a position among the brethren of their father. Moses agreed to their request, and thus the order of inheritance became fixed, i. e. first the son is to inherit, then the daughter; only then comes the brother, and after him the brother of the father.

An attempt has been made in this law to trace the influence of the matriarchate, but these traces are still weaker than those found elsewhere, or, rather, none at all. For the object of the law is not to safeguard the family of the woman, but exclusively, as it is said in plain terms, to secure the name of the *man,* even if he has no sons, and particularly in order to secure the lasting connection between the kindred and property of the man. When it is to take place through the daughters, it can only mean that their children carry on the name of the grandfather, which is at variance both with the spirit of old Israel and that of the matriarchate.

Thus it is by no means a remainder of something old, but must be considered a new and very radical measure in Israelitic life since, according to the old law, the daughter should pass unto another family and assist in continuing the name of its men. The new law is well conversant with the old, i. e. to let the inheritance pass unto the collateral lines. But when attention is called to the daughters, then the tendency is the same as in the Levirate Law: to keep the inheritance for the main line and not to let the name of the deceased disappear. But the Levirate Law is far more in harmony with old habits, having as its basis the old conception of the relation of man and woman in the formation of the family.

These laws are pervaded by a similar tendency, the presupposition of which is that the name of the man is not sufficiently maintained through brother, uncles and cousins. He must himself have progeny in order to be protected against death. We have seen that the family of the woman may be so superior that she becomes the dominating factor, but that is the exception, and can only take place when the two families are disproportionate. The law of inheriting daughters will make the woman the person to continue the name. But the position which is here given to the woman, is so greatly at variance with the old conception of the family and the relation of woman to man, that it never came to be of any practical importance.[1]

As a matter of fact, the law does not solve the problem. The presupposition is evidently that the daughters are unmarried, but when they marry the inheritance passes to a new man, and his name is mentioned over it. When it does not go back to the family of the deceased — and this is what the law wishes to avoid — it can only remain in the family of the new man, *his* sons being the heirs. In a supplement to the law (Num. 36) an attempt is made to remedy this by demanding that such women are only permitted to marry men of the "tribe of the family of their father", an unreal expression which rather shows that we are here dealing with abstract legal speculations. The supplement in reality takes it for granted that it is the new husband who becomes the owner; the old manner of thinking is in his very blood — but then nothing has been attained by the whole of the law.

Thus also this law bears upon the old fundamental Israelitic conception that it is the man in whom everything centres, and the law is further testimony to the importance attached by the

Israelites to the fact that the man should never be separated from the property which he had inherited from his house and its fathers.

These, then, are the outlines of the social conditions under which the Israelites lived. In order to understand what is implied by them we must make a thorough investigation of the Israelitic conception of life.

I

THE SOUL,

ITS POWERS AND CAPACITY

THE SOUL

ISRAELITIC psychology seems near and familiar to us, because such a great number of its forms of manifestation are part of our own mental capacity. We use biblical definitions, such as spirit and heart, when expressing states of mind, but it is not to be taken for granted that the words mean the same to us as to them. The words express a life determined by the totality-conception, but the Israelitic view of life is determined by other factors than ours. If we want to understand the mind of the Israelite, we must first of all examine what the psychic terms mean in their own context.

The Israelitic conception of man is made clear to us through the myth of creation; even though the latter is adopted from other nations, it still preserves the stamp of the Israelitic manner of thinking. Like the Egyptian God Chnum, Yahweh, as a potter, moulded man of clay or earth, and into the moulded image he breathed his breath, in which manner man became a living soul. It is not the object of the narrator to analyse the elements of man, but to represent his essential character. The basis of its essence was the fragile corporeal substance, but by the breath of God it was transformed and became a *nephesh,* a soul. It is not said that man was supplied with a *nephesh,* and so the relation between body and soul is quite different from what it is to us. Such as he is, man, in his total essence, is a soul.

In the Old Testament we are constantly confronted with the fact that man, as such, is a soul. Abraham started for Canaan with his property and all the souls he had gotten (Gen. 12,5), and when Abraham had taken booty on his warlike expedition against the great kings, the King of Sodom exhorted him to yield the souls and himself keep the goods (Gen. 14,21). Seventy souls of the house of Jacob came into Egypt (Gen. 46,27; Exod. 1,5). Whenever a census is taken, the question always is: How many souls are there? In these and in numerous other places we may substitute persons for souls.

But if we read the priestly account of the creation, we learn that it is not only man who is a soul, but also the animals. The animal world in its various genera consists of mere souls. It is a swarm of living souls who fill the earth. [1]

That which the Israelite understands by soul is, first and foremost, a totality with a peculiar stamp. It is the different features of character which compose the essence of the souls and make the world a motley swarm of souls. A righteous man regardeth the soul of his cattle, says the proverb (Pr. 12,10). The Israelites are told: Ye know the soul of a *gēr;* ye were *gērīm* in the land of Egypt (Exod. 23,9). He who lives among strange masters is a soul stamped by the special conditions under which he lives; the word expresses his whole manner and being, his pursuit of security, his fear of arbitrariness and the pain he feels under oppression.

Sensation forms the basis of the making of mental images, but all senses act together in one and constitute an immediate perception. The most important are, of course, the sensations of vision and hearing. It is characteristic that the word which means to see, *rā'ā,* not only means the impression received through the eye, but it also applies to the hearing, to the touch and, upon the whole, to the reception of any mental impression: one "sees" heat, misery, hunger, life and death. [2] It shows how little interest the Israelite takes in distinguishing the various kinds of sensation.

The sense of touch gives strong, but less definite impressions of the soul. Isaac tried to identify Jacob by touching him, but still he was mistaken. The Hebrew says that he *feels* the darkness (Exod. 10,21), for in the darkness the sense of touch must take the place of the sense of vision. Taste is more narrowly circumscribed, but also this sense may be identified with an ordinary mental sensation; the pious man tastes that Yahweh is good (Ps. 34,9), the housewife tastes that her merchandise is good (Pr. 31,18). Taste designates shrewdness, presumably because it is a particularly critical sense. A sense which is greatly weakened with us, i. e. the sense of smelling, plays a great part among primitive peoples, and so also among the Israelites. Isaac smelt the clothes of his son, and the sense of smelling inspires one of his sayings: See, the smell of my son is as the smell of a field which Yahweh has blessed (Gen. 27,27). Men have known each other's smell, and the smell entered into the consciousness of friends of each other. We know this, because when people become abhorrent to each other, then it is said that they have become stinking to each other. [1]

All sensations act together in the making of the mental image. To the soul of a man pertain his appearance, his voice, the more or less hairy quality of his skin, his smell. To this must be added his manner of acting, all that he has done, all that belongs to him, which elements together constitute his soul. Among all the impressions received of him continuity obtains, the one immediately calling forth all the others, and of course, first and foremost, those which stamp the essence of his being with its special characteristics.

Therefore, the soul is at the same time something visible and invisible. Instinctively one senses only individual parts of the man one meets. One perceives a figure with a certain expression, certain movements, a certain manner of speech, etc. This momentary impression only becomes the idea of a soul when the whole of its background is imagined, so that it finds its place in a whole. Thus we get the idea of the man in question, and this is what primitive peoples call soul. It is always present in the man, lies behind all that he does, manifests itself therein. If that is known, then all the individual impressions of the man in question will immediately call forth the totality. If, e. g., one hears his voice, then, if one *knows* it, one knows he is the son of so and so, and has such and such habits, etc. The sound of the voice produces the totality. It is this totality which primitive peoples are always looking for. If they meet a man whom they do not know, they ask who he is, in order to know to what totality they must refer the impression which they receive of him. If he answers: I am Saul, the son of Kish, then they have the totality image. They know Kish, the rich peasant; they are aware of his importance in Benjamin; they are familiar with the history of his kindred, and thus the essential character of Saul is defined; they know his soul. The ideas of the soul are thus the outcome of a pronounced sense of reality. Primitive peoples will not be content with the single, isolated impression, but demand to have it in its proper context.

The word generally rendered by soul is in Hebrew called *nephesh,* which word in various forms is found in all Semitic languages, and which presumably is the old Semitic designation of the soul. The Israelites had other words denoting the soul; the ones most frequently in use being *rūaḥ,* spirit, and *lēbh,* heart. The three expressions are not identical, but the likeness is greater than the difference. The two latter also designate the soul as the distinctive essence.

Caleb was to enter Canaan, because his spirit was different from that of the other men who were sent to spy out the land (Num. 14,24). It means that he was of quite a different essence. There are people in whom there is a spirit of whoredom (Hos. 5,4), a spirit of deep sleep (Is. 29,10), a spirit of uncleanness (Zech. 13,2); others in whom there is a spirit of grace (Zech. 12,10); it defines their stamp and character. "The spirit of the terrible ones is as a cold rain" (Is. 25,4). [1]

The heart also designates the whole of the essence and the character. Concerning Samson we know that he was quite different from other people; he bursts seven ropes as a thread, and if he is locked in a city, he runs away with its gates. What is the secret of this enormous strength? The cunning woman succeeded in coaxing it out of him: He told her all his heart and said unto her: There has not come a razor upon mine head, for I have been a Nazarite of God from my mother's womb; if I be shaven, then my strength will go from me; and I shall become weak and be like any other man. And Delilah saw that he had told her all his heart . . . (Judg. 16,17-18). The words of Samson imply more than that he told her things which "lay near to his heart". Samson's heart is the whole of his peculiar stamp and essence, his strength and the conditions thereof — in short, his being a Nazarite. When Saul had been anointed king, God gave him another heart (1 Sam. 10,9). It means that the whole of his essence changed; he was no more a common soul, but a royal soul.

The soul is thus an entirety with a definite stamp, and this stamp is transmuted into a definite will. The Israelite has no independent term for will as we understand the word. He does not recognize the will as an independent feature or force of the soul. The soul is a totality; its sensations penetrate it entirely and determine its direction; the will is the whole of the tendency of the soul. We perceive that when considering the Hebrew expressions of volitional processes.

Abraham says: If it be with your soul to bury my dead from me . . . (Gen. 23,8). Yahweh wants a priest who "shall do according to that which is in my heart and in my soul" (1 Sam. 2,35). We may even find passages such as: If it be your soul, [1] then let none go forth nor escape out of the city (2 Kings 9,15). In these places we can only render *nephesh* by volition, but this does not express what is implied by the Hebrew term: that the will is not something apart, but the tendency of the totality of the soul.

The soul can never exist without volition, because its special character directs it along a certain course. Where special emphasis is put on the tendency of the soul, the word heart is often used. When Jonathan wanted to go over to the garrison of the Philistines, and consulted his armour-bearer, the latter gave him the following reply: Do all that is in thine heart: go thither; behold I am with thee according to thy heart (1 Sam. 14,7). [2] When Pharaoh had been influenced by the plagues of Egypt, his heart was directed towards letting the Israelites leave the country, but when they had gone, "the heart of Pharaoh and his servants was turned against the people" (Exod. 14,5). It means that their will was turned in another direction. The direction of the heart determines the act. The discontented spies spoke discouragingly of Canaan and kept the hearts of the children of Israel from entering it (Num. 32,9). Jeroboam fears that the hearts of his subjects shall return to the royal house of David, if they go up to Jerusalem in order to do sacrifice (1 Kings 12,27). If their hearts have turned from Yahweh, then the prophet begs of him to "turn their heart back again" (1 Kings 18,37). The strong soul may turn the direction of the weak soul. If God "touches" a heart, then it is he who determines its will (1 Sam. 10,26).

Behind such expressions we are apt to trace a mood. It is true that feelings are involved, but they are not characterized with the passivity which we instinctively attribute to the emotions of the heart. With the Israelites the heart is the soul, being the organ which at the same time feels and acts. Therefore the skill of him who wants to do great acts consists in bending the hearts towards himself. It was this which David realized, and which Absalom for a time succeeded in doing. When Abimelech wanted to rule the Shechemites, he succeeded in bending their hearts towards himself (Judg. 9,3). This does not imply a merely sentimental affection for him on their part, but it means that they bent their will after his, and really acted as his adherents.

The relation between *nephesh,* soul, and *lēbh,* heart, is not that the heart is the designation of certain special functions. The heart is the totality of the soul as a character and operating power, particular stress being laid upon its capacity; *nephesh* is the soul in the sum of its totality, such as it appears; the heart is the soul in its inner value. One may just as well say "that which is in your soul" as "that which is in your heart". But whereas it can be said that Jacob came to Egypt with seventy souls, it cannot be said that he came there with seventy hearts.

The heart is the soul as an operating force, and the same holds good of the spirit, *rūaḥ.* But whereas the heart is at the same time the centre of the soul and the substance gathering round it and determining its strength, the spirit is more particularly the motive power of the soul. It does not mean the centre of the soul, but the strength emanating from it and, in its turn, reacting upon it. Man in his totality is a *nephesh,* but he has a *rūaḥ* and a heart. The heart and the spirit act upon the centre and urge it in a certain direction, towards action. "Every one whose heart stirred him up, and every one whom his spirit made willing came and brought Yahweh's offering" (Exod. 35,21).

The prompting to action is expressed by saying that the spirit is roused. Yahweh raised up the spirit of the kings of the Medes in order to destroy Babel (Jer. 51,11). He raised up the spirit of Cyros, so that he made a proclamation throughout all his kingdom, giving permission to the Jews to return and rebuild the temple (Ezr. 1,1; 2 Chr. 36,22), just as he raised the spirit of Joshua, Zerubbabel and the people to build the temple (Hag. 1,14). It is the motive power of the soul — the energy, as we would say — which is raised and leads the soul to certain acts. If a spirit of jealousy has been raised in a man, then it drives him forth to action, and does not cease until the innocence of the wife has been proved, or reparation has been made to the husband (Num. 5,14.30). When the prophet tells Israel that a new heart will be given them, and a new spirit will be put into them (Ez. 11,19; 18,31; 36,26), then it means that the soul of the people will be of quite a new kind and of a new essence, which will urge it to entirely different acts. But when all is said and done, all the terms by which the soul is expressed convey the same thing, because the soul is a connected whole. It is the spirit of the man which seeks God, as well as his soul and heart (Is. 26,9).

It is not an isolated part of the man that acts, but the soul in its totality. When Isaac asks Esau to go hunting and get him some venison "that my soul may bless thee before I die" (Gen. 27,4 cf. 19.25.31), it does not mean that he wants to utter good wishes for his son, but that he will execute a real act: with all the strength of his soul he will make the blessing for his firstborn. In the same manner it is the soul that swears (Lev. 5,4). It is the soul that sins, not only in thoughts and passing feelings, but in real acts (Lev. 4,2.27; Num. 15,27; Ez. 18,4.20). It is the soul that offers its sacrificial gift to Yahweh (Lev. 2,1). The soul hears the words spoken, but also touches carrion or other unclean things, and thus becomes unclean (Lev. 5,2 f.; 22,6). The soul may perform a trespass on the holy things of Yahweh (Lev. 5,15) and commit actions which are forbidden by the commandments of Yahweh (Lev. 5,17.21). A soul which is not righteous may drink blood (Lev. 7,27; 17,12) or eat carrion (Lev. 17,15). In all of these cases *nephesh* is generally used as the most comprehensive denomination of the totality of the soul; but also the heart may be mentioned as the acting power. The heart of the perpetrator of violence will work iniquity, because it violates those who are sorely tried (Is. 32,6).

The soul can not, as long as it is a soul, desist from being a connected whole, characterized by volition and action. Therefore the Israelitic manner of *thinking* is of a different kind from ours. What we call objective, that is to say inactive, theoretical thinking without further implications, does not exist in the case of the Israelite. He naturally knows mind-images, which are only flashes, or so peripheric as to leave no deeper impress upon the soul. And yet there is a decisive difference between what is outside and what is inside the soul. That which is received into the soul must influence the character of the whole, just as, in its turn, it takes its character from the given stamp of totality. He who writes truth and faithfulness on the table of his heart (Prov. 3,7) lets these forces enter into his soul and determine its direction.

The mental process which takes place while something makes its way into, or rises in the soul, the Hebrew, like ourselves, designates as that which "rises up". By that he is not thinking of neutral mental images rising before the soul as in a kaleidoscope. When something rises "upon the heart", then it immediately influences the will. It came into the hearts of the Judæans to bring silver to the house of Yahweh (2 Kings 12,5) implying that their will drove them to do it. "And they built the high places of Tophet, which is in the valley of the son of Hinnom, to burn their sons and daughters in the fire; which I commanded them not, neither came it into my heart", it is said in Jeremiah (7,31 cf. 19,5; 32,35). The last sentence means that it has not been the will of Yahweh.

The expression is used parallel with *zākhar*, to remember, call to mind, commemorate. When the soul remembers something, it does not mean that it has an objective memory image of some thing or event, but that this image is called forth in the soul and assists in determining its direction, its action. When man remembers God, he lets his being and his actions be determined by him. The Psalmist says: Seek Yahweh and his strength, seek his face evermore! Remember his marvellous works that he has done; his wonders, and the judgments of his mouth (Ps. 105,4 f.). To remember the works of Yahweh and to seek him, i. e. to let one's acts be determined by his will, is in reality the same. The Israelite constantly asks his God to remember him, but just as often he begs him not to remember his sins; the sins are to pass out of Yahweh's soul and not to influence his actions.

When Shimei asks David not to remember the curses which he uttered in his hour of humiliation (2 Sam. 19,20), then we also quite instinctively understand the meaning thereof. But the peculiarity about the Israelite is that he cannot at all imagine memory, unless at the same time an effect on the totality and its direction of will is taken for granted. Therefore *zākhar* may also mean to begin an action, to proceed to do something, as when Elihu says: Proceed *(zᵉkhōr)* to magnify his work, which men sing of (Job 36,24). New and large experiences make one forget the lesser; they are displaced from the soul and exercise no influence. When the new heavens and the new earth are created, then the Israelites no more shall remember the former, and it shall not rise in their hearts (Is. 65,17, cf. Jer. 3,16). It means that the new order of things shall fill their soul, so that the old no more stirs any emotion in it.

That something is remembered, and that it rises up upon the heart, thus means the same thing. For such stirrings in the soul *nephesh* is never used, though it ought to be possible to do so, but once we also find *rūᵃḥ*. Ezekiel says: And that which riseth upon your spirit shall not be at all (20,32), and in another place: I know the risings of your spirits (Ez. 11,5) i. e. that which rises upon your spirit and determines its impulse to act. [1] As a rule, however, the word used is the *heart.*

A man lays a matter "upon his heart" when he takes it up, and lets it act upon his soul. "The righteous perisheth, and no man layeth it to heart", it is said (Is. 57,1), in the same manner as Jeremiah complains that the whole country has perished because no man laid it to his heart (12,11). [2] In both cases it is said that nothing is done by anyone, because neither the righteous nor the country plays any part in their souls. When a man lays something to his heart it is an understood thing that it must create action (Mal. 2,2).

We now and again find the expression to "speak upon someone's heart". Shechem spoke upon Dinah's heart (Gen. 34,3). An Ephraimite had a concubine who left him; he then followed her in order to "speak upon her heart" and make her return with him (Judg. 19,3). Joseph spoke upon the hearts of his troubled brethren (Gen. 50,21, cf. 2 Sam. 19,8). In all of these cases the question is, through the word, to act upon the soul, to fill it out of one's own soul and thus to act upon its direction.

To lay something to heart is the same as to "set one's heart to" something. Amnon tells his sister Tamar not to set her heart to this matter (2 Sam. 13,20). When Moses turned the waters of the Nile into blood, the magicians of Egypt did the same thing with their enchantments, and Pharaoh no more "set his heart to this" (Exod. 7,23).[1] In both cases it is a question of receiving something into the soul and letting it act upon it. The expression implies more than mere superficial attention. David's men, who remained faithful to him during the sedition of Absalom, asked him not to go forth during the fight, because his life was too valuable, whereas their own lives did not mean so much: "For if we flee, they will not set their heart to us" (2 Sam. 18,3), or in other words, it will not influence them and their actions. To "fix one's heart to" something is, therefore, very nearly the same as an incipient action. Ezra fixed his heart *(hēkhīn)* to study the torah of Yahweh (Ezr. 7,10), in the same manner as Hezekiah fixed his heart to seek Yahweh, the god of his fathers (2 Chron. 30,19, cf. 1 Sam. 7,3). One steals the hearts of men, when one steals their will. This was what Absalom did, when with cunning and light promises he made people follow him (2 Sam. 15,6). Jacob stole the heart of Laban by fleeing from him in secret and thus, by devious ways, escaping from his influence (Gen. 31,20).

For the Israelite *thinking* was not the solving of abstract problems. He does not add link to link, nor does he set up major and minor premises from which conclusions are drawn. To him thinking is to grasp a totality. He directs his soul towards the principal matter, that which determines the totality, and receives it into his soul, the soul thus being immediately stirred and led in a certain direction. In the Hebrew dictionary we look in vain for a word which quite corresponds to our "to think". There are words which mean "to remember", "make present" and thus to act upon the soul. There are words expressing that the soul seeks and investigates; but by that is not meant an investigation which analyses and arranges according to abstract views. To investigate is a practical activity; it consists in directing the soul towards something which it can receive into itself, and by which it can be determined. One investigates wisdom, i e. makes it one's own. [1]

The chief elements of thinking are: to seek (investigate), to appropriate and thus to determine the will. The knowledge is the appropriation, the reception into the soul. It is not an abstract recognition or a perception of details, but an appropriation of the totality and, first and foremost, of its main features. Therefore, the knowledge of a thing, a man or whatever else, is identical with intimacy, friendship, fellow-feeling. To know wisdom is the same as to possess wisdom, and also the same as to have the wisdom for sister (Prov. 7,4). It stamps throughout the Israelitic use of the words meaning to know and learn, *yādha'* and *'lp.*

In accordance with this the *ideas* of the Israelite are neither abstractions nor details pieced together, but totalities. He takes hold of the essential, that which more particularly characterizes the idea, and lets the details subordinate themselves to that, and so his thought is ruled by the general idea. If, for instance, he calls up the image of a Moabite, then it is not an individual person with a number of individual qualities, which also include the fact of his coming from Moab. The features which make the specially Moabitic character, create a *type* which is the sum and substance of Moabitic features. This type is called *mō'ābh*, and the individual Moabite, *mō'ābhī*, is a manifestation of it. We are so trained to take our starting point in the individual that we instinctively apply the term of personification to this manner of dealing with the general, suggesting that it is something artificial, a manner of speaking. But this is not so; on the contrary, it is the starting point of thought. All that contains the common characteristics forms a unity, the type, and the homogeneousness impresses it with a common will. Therefore it acts as a unity and is treated as a unity. Moab and Edom speak and act when their king negotiates with Israel, because what is Moabitic and Edomitic manifests itself entirely in their words and deeds.

The Hebrew language is full of what we term collectives, because the Hebrew always perceives the general. But our use of "collective" is a manifestation of our own individualism, in that by this term we rather imply a collection of individuals. Perhaps we ought to say: general or totality denomination or denominations of species, seeing that the determining factor is not whether there are many examples or only one, but, on the contrary, that it is the species which reveals itself in the individual or individuals in question. For instance, *'ēṣ* means the idea of a tree, that which has the characteristics of a tree, and it equally denominates the single specimen and a whole collection; in the same manner *'ādhām* is man and mankind in one, *'īsh* man and men, *rekhebh* carriage and carriages, etc. The individual is only a form of the predominant type. In certain denominations of kind, the individual may be designated by a derivative ending *ī (mō'ābh — mō'ābhī),* which implies that the individual is that which is derived. But in many cases the same form is equally used of one and many, and this shows that the relation of the individual to the species is not, as it were, an isolated section, but a specimen, in which the kind presents itself. This is the relation between the individual and the family. The individual Moabite is not a section of a number of Moabitic individuals, but a revelation of "Moabithood", just as the individual cow is a fully qualified representation of "cowhood". It is therefore immaterial whether one says *a* lion or *the* lion; it is the species of lion, as manifesting itself in one or perhaps several specimens. The herds of the Israelite are attacked by *the* lion and *the* bear (1 Sam. 17,34; Am. 5,19). Noah sent forth *the* raven and *the* dove (Gen. 8,7.8).

With the Hebrews that which we call abstract stands in another relation to the concrete than it does with us, seeing that there is no distinction between the two things. *tōbh* is at the same time "goodness", the fact of being good, and "a good person", or, in other words, goodness in all its manifestations. Therefore, there is no sharp distinction between the various classes of words; this is one of the fundamental characteristics of the Semitic languages. To the root *mlk* the signification of "kinghood" attaches itself, and according to the modification of the word it may mean the king, the kingdom and the fact of acting as a king.

In the same manner the Israelites unite, where we would separate, and, on the other hand, they often separate what to us is united. An independent idea always arises where there is an independent characteristic. When we speak of going, going in, going out, going up or going down, then it is for us the same action, only performed in a different manner and leading to different results, because we have an abstract idea, i. e. to "go", which may be supplemented now in one, now in another direction. To the Israelite these are perfectly different actions, seeing that he considers the totality-character of the action with its special stamp; for each of them he has a special appellation.

When we say that a man goes *from* one town to another, then the prepositions are meant to designate a starting point and a point of arrival, and for us the two towns play no other part in the sentence. To the Hebrew conception it is as if the man passes from making a *part* of the totality of one town to making a part of the totality of another town. The word *min,* which we translate by "from", characterizes something as a component of a totality. Therefore we must sometimes translate *min* by "in" or "at" or even "towards"; when, for instance, it is used to designate a journey towards the east, it implies that the traveller is in the east, forming a part of the totality of these regions; if it had been expressed by the preposition *l*ᵉ, it would mean that he was not in the east, but was going there.

That which interests the Israelite is not the strict limitation of the idea, but the determination of its peculiarity. This manifests itself in his language, and makes it practically impossible to translate a Hebrew account into any modern language. For us each word in its context has its definitely limited sense; but even though a special shade of meaning predominates, the Hebrew constantly feels the idea of totality acting through it. When the word *b*ᵉ*rīth* is to be translated, now by right, now by duty, and now by law, etc., then in every one of these various connections it imparts to us a new sense. For the Israelite there is always the same idea underlying it; it only presents itself in various forms. Herder, whose book on the spirit of Hebrew poetry contains so much deep observation, also has his attention directed towards this. He mentions as a case in point the root-word: he has passed away. "A number of terms for loss, disappearance, death, futile advice, empty trouble and work progress in soft transitions; and when transporting oneself to the time of the wandering, to the leave-taking, to all the situations of pastoral life, then, even in the most remote meaning of the word, there rings an echo of the old primeval sound, the image of the first sensation".[1] We have had the same experience with all the Hebrew ideas which have presented themselves, and we shall repeatedly meet it again.

It is not for the Israelite to analyse in the sense of limiting and dissolving into elements, whereas he is at his best when characterizing. When he is to describe something, he mentions the outstanding characteristic features. The bull he calls "the strong", the sun "the warm", the moon "the white", the grasshopper "the eater", the goat "the long-haired". In such characterizations, or where an expression is to be found for the passions which fill the soul, he is a master. On the other hand, he rarely satisfies us when we demand a distinct limitation of details, as, for instance, in the description of a building. No one has ever yet been able to say for certain how Noah's Ark looked, or to draw a distinct picture of Solomon's temple from the description in the Book of Kings (1 Kings 6). The narrator mentions a number of details, undoubtedly those which presented themselves to him as the most important, at the time when he was to call forth the totality image. But for us it is not possible to form a whole out of these details, which seem to us casual and badly arranged.

Hebrew, like other Semitic languages, has preserved its primitive character and gives an immediate expression of the processes of thought. The words that make the language, call forth images, but the Israelite sees more in them than something that is different from the actual matter. The matter lives in the word. The Hebrew language is principally composed of two kinds of words, nouns and verbs, the nouns designating the souls, the things, the ideas, that which is and acts, the verbs designating the action, the activity, the movement issuing from the souls and acting upon them.

To a certain extent one word is sufficient to form a sentence. If I say *'īsh,* then it calls forth the image of a man, i. e. there is a man; if I say *kāthabh* the image of writing is called forth, i. e. some one writes. Speech consists in that an image, which is thus called forth by the word, is extended and modified by being combined with others. The combination may consist of nouns only; in that case it is a nominal phrase, or it can be determined by the verb, thus becoming a verbal phrase. The simplest extended verbal phrase reads *ḳᵉṭaltīkhā* "I kill you". The mode of expression shows us that the phrase is not the result of the piecing together of various elements, but that it forms a whole, which is governed by the fundamental idea of killing *ḳṭl;* to this fundamental idea is subordinated the denomination of him from whom the action issues, — *tī,* i. e. I — and to this idea of killing issuing from me, is added whom it is directed against: *khā, you.* We have no reason to suppose that the thinking process is different in a sentence such as: The man kills an ox, in Hebrew: kill-man-ox. The action of killing is the chief thing; into that image is fitted the man from whom it emanates, and into this new whole is fitted the ox, against whom it is directed.

A continued totality-formation of this kind is also found in the nominal combinations. If I say *'īsh ṭōbh* "man good", then I combine man and goodness in one image, which we would either express by "a man is good", or "a good man". If I say "oxen brass" (2 Kings 16,17), then I call forth an image combining oxen and brass: brass oxen. This combination may be so intimate that two nouns also formally coalesce into one conception, through that which is called the *status constructus.* It is formed by putting first the word in which the chief interest centres, but it is designated as a link of the immediately following, this being specially emphasized, and so the form of the former word is modified. "House — mán" means that the two pictures form a unity, but the house belongs to the totality of the man. Thus three boys can be designated either as "triad boys" or "boys triad" or "triad — bóys". The nominal phrase is formed by modifying the image presented, thus enriching it by assimilating new nominal images. Gen. 41,3 reads literally: septiad-cows others ascending after-them from-Nile poor-appearance and-thin-flesh. The unity-image "septiad-cows" is more closely defined by its being another than the one which formerly appeared. It is seen ascending, etc. Every new link modifies and enriches the totality-image already given.

The nominal phrases proper are static; they picture situations. The Israelite does not know the logical progress which leads us from one idea to another. That which stirs his mind-images is the action, the event. Therefore Hebrew descriptions are dominated by the verbal phrases. The vividness of the description is created by the verbs, which constantly succeed each other and form the stages of the progressive narrative.

First and foremost the verb expresses the *occurrence* of the action; then from whom it issues and against whom it is directed. However, it may sometimes be of importance to call attention to one of the two latter factors, and this is done by placing it in the foreground. The time of the action, which for us is the principal thing, is of no importance to the Hebrew. When an action is born, then it takes effect, but it has been prepared by other actions, and new actions group around it, and it is this cohesion of actions which interests him. As in the case of all Semitic verbs, no attention is paid to time; but there are two verbal forms by which the actions designated are characterized; either it is a complete independent action, or a nascent, preparatory or supplementary one. The former is expressed through the simplest form of the verb, usually called the perfect, the latter by the form which is usually called the imperfect. [1]

Let us analyse 1 Sam. 13,14: And now thy kingdom does not exist (impf.), sought has Yahweh (perf.) a man after his own heart, and Yahweh has commanded him (impf.) to be captain over his people, because thou hast not kept (perf.) that which Yahweh commanded thee. — The main point in the chain of sentences is the second: Yahweh has sought a man after his own heart. It is preceded by the preparatory situation, the background of the action of Yahweh: The kingdom of Saul on the point of being dissolved; after that follows the concomitant action, which broadens and complements the principal action. Last of all the argument sets forth something accomplished, which contributes to the constitution of the principal action.

The question whether an action is an independent, self-contained whole or something complementing another, naturally cannot be answered according to definite rules; this the author must decide according to his own feeling. The natural thing would be that the account was entirely ruled by the perfects, and so it is in Aramæan and Arabic; but the Israelites (like the Moabites) in this matter followed their own course, using far more imperfects than perfects. By means of these, the so-called consecutive imperfects, they link the actions more strongly together than their Semitic kinsmen. If we look at the account of the creation in the first chapter of the Bible, then it begins with a perfect: God has created the heaven and the earth. In the following this is complemented by the description of the details of the creation, which are communicated in consecutive imperfects. The term of "consecutive" is not quite appropriate, seeing that what is expressed is not so much succession as context, i. e. the fact that the action associates itself with the preceding.

Just as the word-images form new wholes by being united in one sentence, so also the sentences form totalities by being connected with each other, in that they concentrate round the specially emphasized main points. Israelitic *logic* is dominated throughout by this totality-formation. We arrive at a conclusion by setting up two premises, a major and a minor, each of which is a complete unity; as their logical consequence we set up a new phrase which makes a third unity. We *draw* a conclusion from what is given and thus carry the thought further. The Israelite does not argue by means of conclusions and logical progress. His argumentation consists in showing that one statement associates itself with another, as belonging to its totality.

This appears most clearly when we consider the Israelitic use of particles designating such contexts. A word corresponding to the Latin "ergo" we look for in vain, but there are several particles which we must render by "for", "therefore", etc. One of them is *lākhēn.* It consists of two elements: the preposition *la,* which means connection, continuity, and *kēn* which, properly speaking, means "standing place", [1] but is used as a demonstrative particle, "that", "such circumstances", the whole word meaning "connected with these circumstances". It means that what is now going to be told is connected with the preceding as an indissoluble unity. The continuity may have the character of what we would call a logical sequence, as in 1 Sam. 27,6: And Achish gave him (David) Ziklag that day; *therefore* Ziklag pertaineth unto the kings of Judah until this day. — Or what we would call a moral consequence, as when the prophets constantly say after having described the sins of the people: Therefore Yahweh says, now I will take my revenge on you (Is. 1,24; 10,24; 16,7; 27,9; Jer. 2,9; Mic. 3,12 et al.).

Readers of the Old Testament cannot help noticing the apparent looseness with which such a "therefore" is often used. This is because it does not really mean therefore; it does not indicate consequence, but connection. It is not necessarily connected with the immediately preceding; it belongs to the totality which has gone before it. Thus, e. g., Jer. 16,21. Here a threat is uttered against the Israelites, introduced by a *lākhēn.* This cannot refer to the immediately preceding sentence, where the prophet speaks of the strange peoples and their gods; but this mention of the strangers subordinates itself to the preceding remarks on the apostacy of the Israelites, and to the totality thus formed the punishment of the Israelites pertains. [2]

As a rule the best rendering of the word would be: under these circumstances. Isaiah once describes the behaviour of drunkards and finishes by saying that Yahweh is going to pass judgment on them. Then he turns to the inhabitants of Jerusalem, lecturing them severely and beginning his speech with the following words: *lākhēn* hear the word of Yahweh! (Is. 28,14). It is evident that it is not a conclusion, but that he merely suggests a connection between the drunkards and the other sinners and their destinies. When Ezekiel threatens an awful judgment and then continues: *lākhēn* fathers shall eat their children and the children shall eat their fathers (Ez. 5,10), then the connecting word clearly indicates that in the following he will further elaborate the description given in the preceding. It indicates what is going to happen under present conditions.

A small word in the preceding sentence sometimes indicates that it is to be supplemented with a sentence introduced by "therefore". Words of this kind are *ya'an, ya'an 'asher* and *kī,* which for want of a better translation may be rendered by "because": *Because* ye despise this word and thrust in oppression and perverseness and stay thereon, *therefore* this iniquity shall be to you as a breach ready to fall (Is. 30,12-13). As a matter of fact the two words "because" — "therefore" only indicate that the two sentences point towards each other and are mutually dependent upon each other to form a whole. The causal connection which, to a certain extent, we are entitled to trace in these sentences cannot be maintained in the case of a statement like the following: "*Because*" I will cut off from thee the righteous and the wicked, "*therefore*" shall my sword go forth out of his sheath against all flesh from the South to the North (Ez. 21,9). Here we would, e. g., have to say "inasmuch" in the first sentence and "under these circumstances" in the second.[1]

So far from initiating a logical step forward this word, in accordance with its nature, sometimes rather introduces a contrast. After Cain has complained of his fate, to have to roam about without protection, Yahweh says: *lākhēn* whosoever slayeth Cain, vengeance shall be taken on him sevenfold (Gen. 4,15). In the Greek translation it is here and in a few other places (Gen. 30,15; Judg. 11,8; 1 Kings 22,19) rendered by "not thus", which in itself is not incorrect. But we must not think that the word here appears in a new sense; it means "belonging to the given situation", and it is best rendered by "under these circumstances".[2]

Very closely related with the word described above is *'al-kēn,* which means "on those circumstances". In many cases the two words may be used indiscriminately, but there still seems to be a shade of difference between them. Both indicate that the following sentence forms a unity with the preceding. But *'al-kēn,* as a rule, introduces sentences which in themselves are a complete whole, united with the preceding in a new and greater whole. This relative independence is rarely to be found in the sentences with *lākhēn;* the latter, by their very character, most frequently lead beyond themselves, since they describe undeveloped or supplementary actions and situations. For instance: And Esau said to Jacob: Feed me, I pray thee, with this same red pottage, for I am faint; *therefore* was his name called Edom (Gen. 25,30). In this and similar cases [1] *'al-kēn* is used, and consequently this expression is generally connected with the perfect, whereas *lākhēn* as a rule introduces sentences with imperfect or imperative, possibly nominal phrases.

Upon the whole the Hebrews had no special particles indicating a logical context. Besides those already mentioned there are particles indicating that the following phrase has a supplementary, subordinate character, i. e. *kī* and *'ᵃsher.* They are demonstrative words of interjection, the latter presumably strictly speaking meaning "place". [2] The most comprehensive is *kī.* It may mean that something is now coming to which we must pay attention as, e. g.: the cry of Sodom, *lo,* it is great (Gen. 18,20). Therefore it is frequently used in oaths: I sware . . . *lo,* Solomon thy son shall reign after me (1 Kings 1,30). In the same manner as *lākhēn* it connects a phrase with the preceding, thus indicating that it belongs to its totality. Job wishes that he were dead and adds: under those circumstances *(kī)* I now lay resting (Job 3,13; cf. 7,21). It here introduces a sentence communicating the consequence of an imagined fact; the same is the case in 1 Sam. 13,13: Thou hast not kept the commandment of Yahweh thy God, which he commanded thee; in this case *(kī)* would Yahweh have established thy kingdom, etc.

kī often connects a phrase with the preceding by way of contrast: Ye shall surely not die, *no,* God doth know that your eyes shall be opened, etc. (Gen. 3,5). This use, which is very frequent, is analogous with the use of *lākhēn* and indicates that the two statements are joined together into a whole.

As we have already seen, *kī* may emphasize a principal statement, but more frequently it is used like *'ᵃsher* in order to introduce secondary phrases. The best manner of describing them would perhaps be as "connecting particles", and the general name of the sentences would then be: collateral-circumstantial phrases. It is extremely characteristic of the whole Israelitic manner of thinking that no distinction is made between the various kinds of these connected sentences. All that we have to distinguish as argument, consequence, cause, effect, simultaneousness, further explanation ("seing that") and relative sentences, is to him one thing only, i. e. a supplementary insertion into the given whole. The two connecting particles must, according to the context, be rendered by: as, whereas, seeing that, though, for, that, since, or a relative pronoun.

Let us analyse Gen. 45,5-6: And now ye shall not grieve nor let it burn in your eyes *that* ye sold me hither; *for* God sent me before you to preserve life; *for* this (is) two years (in which is) the famine in the interior of the land, and yet (there are) five years *while* no earning or harvest. The words "that" and "for" are a rendering of *kī*, "while" of *ʾasher*. The former of these words introduces a sentence, supplementing the preceding one by more closely defining its action. This whole is further supplemented by a detail relating to the fact that they are not to grieve at having sold Joseph. The whole formed by these three sentences is further supplemented by the inclusion of the idea that they must not grieve at having sold Joseph to preserve life. This supplementary feature we call an argument; the Hebrew only says that it communicates a fact, which is subordinated to the principal idea. The individual parts may be combined into minor wholes, before they are absorbed in the great totality. The last "while" forms a whole with a *part* of the preceding ("years"), which is thus modified before it is absorbed into the given whole. In that case we would use a relative sentence ("in *which* there shall neither be earning nor harvest"). In such expressions is generally used *ʾasher:* the man, *lo* I saw him, i. e. the man I saw. But also *kī* can be used in the same manner (Gen. 3,19; 4,25; Deut. 14,29; Is. 54,6; 57,20; Ps. 90,4; Prov. 30,23).[1]

Thus Hebrew thinking, as expressed in the language, does not distinguish between the various manners of connecting sentences, whether the thing to be expressed is a temporal or causal connection or only the adding of supplementary qualities. The thinking process of the Hebrew consists in forming wholes round certain centres. Thus he builds up his sentences and connects them, arranging them as primary and secondary parts of a whole.

One final example to illustrate the Israelitic manner of thinking. 2 Kings 22,19 sounds "verbatim": "Given" *(ya'an)* thinness-heart-yours and-you-bent before-face-Yahweh by-hearing-thine "namely" *('asher)* spoke-I against-place-this and-against-inhabitants-its for-to-be to-ruin and-to-curse and-thou-torest clothes-thine and-thou-wepst before-face-mine and-also hear-I saying-Yahweh. — The first word indicates that the whole sentence presupposes a new sentence with which to form a whole. The image of the king's uneasiness is presented in an imperfective verbal phrase. We now see the king standing uneasy and humbled before Yahweh. The picture is supplemented by the fact that the king hears. A collateral-circumstantial phrase introduced by *'asher* develops a detail of the resulting picture; we are told what the king hears. The king thus described tears his clothes and weeps. Then the picture is finished — for the time being. But the introductory word implied that this picture was to be introduced into a whole together with another. This other picture contains a person who acts: Yahweh, the listener. The picture now consists of two principal elements: the humble listening king, weeping, with torn clothes, and the listening Yahweh. The action consisting in the king's hearing, entails the action of Yahweh's hearing. And so the picture is complete, but in the following it is supplemented by a new picture connected with the former: under those circumstances *(lākhēn)* Yahweh will let him die in peace.

Where many pictures are accumulated in nominal phrases, it may be difficult to follow the narrative, because they constantly form new wholes, without the details being sharply defined. The Hebrew has his strength in the description of simple situations, where the pictures are called forth by a few characterizing words and are quickly replaced by others, action following upon action. This kind of description we find in the old accounts of the Genesis and the historical writings of the Old Testament. One of the most beautiful examples is the account of Jacob's meeting with Rachel, Gen. 29,1-14.

"Then Jacob went on his journey and came into the land of the people of the East. And he looked and beheld a well in the field, and lo, there were three flocks of sheep and goats lying by it; for out of that well they watered the flocks; and a great stone was upon the well's mouth. And thither all the flocks were wont to gather; and they rolled the stone from the well's mouth, and watered the sheep and goats, and put the stone again upon the well's mouth in his place. — And Jacob said unto them: My brethren, whence be ye? And they said: Of Haran are we. And he said unto them: Know ye Laban, the son of Nahor? And they said: We know him. And he said unto them: Is he in peace? And they said: He is in peace; and behold, Rachel his daughter cometh with the sheep and goats. And he said: Lo, it is yet high day, neither is it time that the cattle should be gathered together; water ye the sheep and goats, and go and feed them. And they said: We cannot, until all the flocks be gathered together, and till they (the shepherds) roll the stone from the well's mouth; then we water the sheep and the goats. — And while he yet spoke with them, Rachel came with her father's sheep and goats; for she kept them. And it came to pass, when Jacob saw Rachel, the daughter of Laban his mother's brother, and the sheep and goats of Laban his mother's brother, that Jacob went near, and rolled the stone from the well's mouth, and watered the flock of Laban his mother's brother. And Jacob kissed Rachel, and lifted up his voice and wept. And Jacob told Rachel that he was her father's brother, and that he was Rebekah's son; and she ran and told her father. And it came to pass, when Laban heard the tidings of Jacob his sister's son, that he ran to meet him, and embraced him, and kissed him, and brought him to his house. And he told Laban all these things. And Laban said to him: Surely thou art my bone and my flesh. And he abode with him the space of a month."

That which makes a description like this so clear and yet so comprehensive, is the author's genius in selecting the essential features. He does not lose himself in details obscuring the totality, but leaves the principal features to stand alone and develop freely with all their associations. Secondly, and this is closely connected with what has already been said, as soon as a picture has been described, with its essential characteristics, it is replaced by another. The events carry us quickly from one significant situation to another.

We are rapidly carried with Jacob from Canaan to Haran; the description is not burdened by any irrelevant collateral circumstances. Then a picture is painted, in a few words, of the flocks gathering round the well, and we are told what we must necessarily know of this well.

The next scene describes the conversation of Jacob with the shepherds. In these few words a number of pregnant pictures are held up before us. First the situation: Jacob, the wanderer, who stands talking with the strange shepherds. Though chary of speech, they tell us sufficient to indicate their *milieu;* they come from Haran, belong to Laban, the kinsman of Jacob, and he has peace, i. e. he lives in the complete harmony that makes happiness, and now his daughter appears with the sheep and goats. Thus the situation is fitted into the whole centring round Jacob. Our feeling of the situation is intensified, because it falls so closely into line with the pictures which already have attracted our interest. We are now informed of the impression which all this makes upon Jacob; it is indicated in a few words and in an indirect manner; he tries to get rid of the shepherds in order to be able to meet Rachel alone (v. 7), in which, however, he does not succeed, and at the same time we are told something new: the stone covering the well is so heavy that only all of the shepherds together are able to move it.

Thus this scene ends; the new one (v. 9-12) is created by the arrival of Rachel. For the time being only three things are told: Rachel arrives; Jacob moves the stone from the well and waters the herd; he weeps and kisses Rachel. But behind the scanty words there is a wealth of matter: the overpowering feeling of kindred. When Jacob sees the daughter of his near kinsman, all his strength swells in him, and he alone moves the stone which it takes all the herdsmen together to roll from the mouth of the well.

He can no longer master his emotion, but bursts into tears. Then event rapidly succeeds event; Rachel runs home, Laban arrives, takes Jacob to his dwelling, confirms the relationship, and now we are at the goal: the reception of Jacob into his kinsman's house.

The very language shows how Israelitic thought is dominated by two things: *striving after totality* and *movement.* Properly speaking it only expresses that the whole soul takes part in the thinking and creates out of its own essence. The thought is charged with the feeling of the soul and the striving of its will after action. This characterizes the Hebrew manner of argumentation. We try to persuade by means of abstract reasoning, the Hebrew by directly influencing the will. In expressing a thought he makes the souls of his listeners receive his mind-image, and thus the matter itself; but at the same time he produces an effect by the feeling and will which he puts into the words. His argumentation therefore consists in assurance and repetition. The "*parallelismus membrorum*" has become his natural manner of expression; he expresses his thought twice in a different manner, the result of which is a totality with a double accent: "Therefore the wicked shall not stand in the judgment, nor sinners in the congregations of the righteous" (Ps. 1,5). When the Preacher wants the reader to see that "to everything there is a season" then he proves it by constantly repeating first one thing, then another (Eccles. 3). Upon the whole the book of the Preacher is characteristic of Israelitic argumentation. He repeats and repeats, and it seems to us that he practically ends where he began.

But also in an older book we find an example elucidating the Hebrew manner of argumentation; the prophet Amos says (3, 2-6.8): You only have I known of all the families of the earth; this being so (*'al-kēn)* I will punish you for all your iniquities. Do two walk together except they be agreed? Does a lion roar in the forest, without getting prey? Does a young lion growl out of his den, except when he has made booty? Does a bird fall in a snare upon the earth, where no gin is for him? Does a snare spring up from the earth, without catching anything at all? Shall a trumpet be blown in a city, and the people not be afraid? Shall there be evil in a city, and Yahweh has not done it? When the lion roareth, who will not fear? When the Lord Yahweh has spoken, who would not prophesy?

Modern readers are disposed to understand this in the following manner: all occurrences in nature are as a rule due *to their proper cause;* hence, when the prophet speaks, as Amos did in the utterance of v. 2, it may be inferred that it is because he has heard Yahweh's voice commanding him to do so.[1] But it is not the task of Amos to give proof of the causal proposition, nor would his examples be very appropriate for that purpose. Some of these examples would rather seem to prove that things have an effect, and the first example neither yields cause nor effect. Amos says that Yahweh only knows Israel; every Israelite would acknowledge that. But with this fact he connects the prediction of their punishment, and this connection he corroborates — like the Preacher — by a series of examples showing close connections between occurrences. These connections being necessarily admitted, the people will be impressed with the connection — i. e. between the love and punishment of Yahweh — set forth by him. The final clause, emphasizing the close connection between the activity of Yahweh and that of the prophet will intensify the impression of the words of Amos.

When modern logicians have characterized the correct manner of thinking as an interplay of simple, i. e. essentially empty but sharply defined space images, then we see at once the contrast between this and the Israelitic ideal of thinking. The Israelite does not occupy himself with empty nor with sharply defined space images. His logic is not the logic of abstraction, but of immediate perception.

It is characteristic that the problems treated in the Old Testament are problems pertaining, not to thought, but to life, and that what they seek are not logical results. Psalm 73, e. g., deals with the problem that the wicked are faring well in this world. But the object is not to solve the problem logically; the Psalmist attempts to rid himself of it, and this he obtains through a *conviction* that the happiness of the wicked is only of a transitory kind. This is also the case with the Book of Job. It is a story charged with passion and reasoning, but passion is the deepest. There is no logical progress in the argument; from his friends Job demands friendship and moral support, from God a practical maintenance of justice in which he may find rest. Nor does the conclusion, the answer of God, contain any logical solution, but only a practical one, which puts an end to the complaints of Job.

All the Hebrew words most commonly used to designate the process of thinking reveal the movement of the soul in the direction of activity. The one most frequently employed is *ḥāshabh,* which partly means the valuation, partly the plan. It is used in such phrases: Wherefore hidest thou thy face and *holdest me* thine enemy? (Job 13,24) and also when Job complains that his maids *count him* a stranger (19,15). But the chief meaning of the word is the planning. The sinner *plans* wicked deeds in his bed (Ps. 36,5 cf. 140,3); there are those who "think" to make Israel forget the name of his God (Jer. 23,27). These are only a few of many instances of the fact that this, the most important word for thinking, contains the plan, the direction of the mind towards action. And the corresponding noun, *maḥshebheth,* always indicates the plan, i. e. the action such as it appears in the mind. The proverb says: Many are the "thoughts" in a man's heart (Prov. 19,21), and the continuation: "nevertheless the counsel of Yahweh, that stands", shows that the thoughts are plans, thoughts of action. The contents of the thoughts are different, according to the nature and will of the soul. It may be peace (Jer. 29,11), and it may be wickedness (Is. 55,7; 59,7; Jer. 4,14 et al.), but it may also be the completion of a building. The builder of the tabernacle was filled with wisdom "to devise thoughts, to work in gold and in silver and in brass", etc. (Exod. 31,4; cf. 35,32.33.35; 2 Chr. 2,13). "Thoughts" here as elsewhere mean plans, i. e. the accomplished work as a mental image, involving its execution.

The word *dimmā,* which means to imagine, to form mental images, also implies that these images must be transplanted into action. Isaiah says: Howbeit he meaneth *(yᵉdhamme)* not so, neither does his heart think *(ḥshb)* so, but it is in his heart to destroy and cut off nations not a few (Is. 10,7). The thought is here the act, such as it lies in the soul of the man and is to be carried out by the latter. Just as it is said: to remember to act, when speaking of an action commencing in the will, in the same manner it is said: to imagine to act (Num. 33,56; Judg. 20,5). When it is said to Esther: Think not with thyself that thou shalt escape in the king's house, more than all the Jews (Esth. 4,13), then the reason of the admonition is that it would not be a *real* thought, of the kind which involves carrying into effect.

Close to this word lies *zāmam:* Yahweh has *thought* and done that which he spoke against the inhabitants of Babylon, says Jeremiah (51,12). The good wife "thinks of fields and buys them" (Prov. 31,16). "Yahweh hath done that which he has thought, he hath fulfilled his word" (Lam. 2,17). The word always expresses the elaboration of something leading directly to action.

There are certain Hebrew words, the generally adopted translation of which is "to meditate", conveying to us the idea of something stationary or something which moves backwards and forwards without attaining any result. This manner of thinking is very familiar to the Hebrew, but only as a disease indicating confused thoughts; the normal thought leads directly towards the result. Nor does such a word as *hāghā* mean the stationary, quiescent, but the active thought. It means to make oneself familiar with something and thus to be determined to act. The Israelites are to meditate on *(hāghā)* the law day and night, (Ps. 1,2) but it means that they are to receive it as a determining element in their souls and act by it (Josh. 1,8). When they remember the days of yore and meditate on *(hāghā)* all the work of Yahweh (Ps. 77,13; 143,5), then it means that the striving of their souls becomes influenced by it. The wicked ones "imagine" violence and deceit (Ps. 38,13; Prov. 24,2). The kings of the earth who set themselves against Israel and his great god, *imagine* vain things (Ps. 2,1).[1]

The word *śīaḥ*, which also circles round the process of thought, indicates the absorption of the soul, its orientation towards something to which it is led or towards which it directs itself. We can render it by: remember, take to heart, consider.[2] It is often used of the lamentation arising out of remembrance, but like the other words for thinking it is never used of disinterested reflection.

Thus thinking is not theoretical, but of a pronouncedly practical character. He who understands how to think well is wise. *Wisdom* is a property of the soul or, rather, a faculty, an ability to produce, a skill in shaping the very thought which yields the right result. An Israelite, Bezaleel, was filled with the divine spirit, particularly with wisdom and understanding to devise thoughts and to work in gold, and in silver, and in brass (Exod. 31,4; 35,31 f.). It is generally the heart which is mentioned when speaking of the wisdom of a man. It is said that God gave unto the man just mentioned wisdom of heart (Exod. 35,35; cf. 28,3; 36,1.2.8). A wise and obedient heart is Solomon's prayer to Yahweh, which prayer is granted (1 Kings 3,9.12).

Wisdom is essential in the making of a soul. If a man lacks wisdom, then he has no heart. Jeremiah says of his countrymen that they have eyes without being able to see, and ears without being able to hear; they are a foolish people without a heart (Jer. 5,21), whereas Job, when he wants to maintain his understanding as against that of his friends, says that also he has a heart (Job 12,3). This is the consequence of the heart designating the soul as an inner power. It does not imply that wisdom should be the property of a special part of the soul. Wisdom is the faculty of the whole of the soul, just as the will is the direction of the whole of the soul.

And it may just as well be said that thinking is practised by *nephesh* or *rūaḥ*. It is said: My soul calleth to mind and thinketh in me (Lam. 3,20), or: My soul knoweth right well (Ps. 139,14).[1] The wise are filled with a spirit of wisdom (Exod. 28,3). The plan of the temple was in David's spirit, i. e. was created by it (1 Chron. 28,12). Understanding is created by the spirit in man (Is. 29,24; Job 32,8).

All mental activity points in the direction of action. But what is the place that *action* occupies in the psychological process? According to European psychology action first originates in the region of ideas; then it is penetrated by feeling, which in its turn makes it to be determined by volition; this again leads to resolution, which is followed by action. Thus the activity of the soul is completed; the result of the action lies entirely outside its sphere, being added as a new element. The one who acts trusts to his good intentions and feels no responsibility regarding the result, as long as the intentions were good.

For the Israelite — as for primitive peoples generally — the mental processes are not successive, but united in one, because the soul is always a unit, acting in one. But no more are the action and its result to be distinguished from each other or from the mental activities; they are implied in the actual mental process. This is to be attributed to the fact that the soul is wholly present in all its works. The actions are not sent away from the soul, they are the outer manifestations of the whole of the soul, the traces of its movements; its "ways" the Hebrew calls them.

The action and its accomplishment are a matter of course, once the thought is there. The essence of the thought is, as we have seen, directed towards the action. There are mental images which appear and disappear immediately, without leaving any deeper trace; these are of no importance in the psychological process. But as soon as the thought is fixed, the action is at once a matter of course. This kind of fixed thought the Israelite calls *'ēṣā,* counsel. Thoughts are fixed by counsel, says the proverb (Pr. 20,18). Counsel implies wisdom and understanding, i. e. the power to act (Jer. 18,18; Ez. 7,26; Prov. 8,14; Job 12,13). The counsel is an expression of the character of the soul. The good man counsels peace (Prov. 12,20); it means not only that he causes others to keep peace, but that his actions bear the impress of peace. When Zechariah says that the counsel of peace shall be between the ruler and the high priest (6,13), then it means that they must act in full mutual accord. When the Israelites had assembled on account of the crime of Gibeah, it was said to them: Give word and counsel! It means more than a proposal, something that is to be discussed. It is their will, their resolution, the action which rises in their souls. Their counsel was: And all the people arose as one man, saying: None of us will return, before we have punished Gibeah (Judg. 20,7-8).

When the deed is done and carried into effect, it does not mean that the counsel has now fulfilled its task and led up to the action as something new. On the contrary, the carrying into effect is the manifestation of the very counsel. This the Israelite expresses by saying that the counsel *stands, tāḳūm* (Is. 14,24; 46,10; Prov. 15,22; 19,21), stands firm, *ta'amōdh* (Ps. 33,11), — in other words the counsel by no means ceases because it is carried out. In a still more characteristic manner he says that the counsel is *filled* (Ps. 20,5) or *made whole* (Is. 44,26); it means that the carrying into effect is the normal expansion of the counsel. Therefore counsel and action are identical. The prophet says: Woe unto them that seek deep to hide their counsel from Yahweh, and their works are in the dark (Is. 29,15). Those who at the time of Isaiah awaited the great work of Yahweh said: Let his work make speed and hasten that we may see it, and let the counsel of the Holy One of Israel draw nigh and come that we may know it (Is. 5,19).

If the counsel is not carried into effect, then this implies a judgment on him in whom it originates. It means that he has not made a good counsel. Everything depends on whether he is able to put strength into it. He who has the great strength of soul, gives mighty counsel (Is. 28,29), irresistible thoughts which are immediately carried out. The ruler must have the power to make counsel full of strength. The great king of whom Isaiah speaks has the "spirit of counsel and strength", i. e. strength of soul to make good, strong counsels which remain and are fulfilled. Conversely, the leader of the armies of the Assyrian king says scornfully to Hezekiah: Thou speakest lip-words as counsel and strength for war (2 Kings 18,20; Is. 36,5), i. e. he can do nothing because his counsel lacks strength; it is vain words.

The "redeless" man is he who lacks wisdom (Deut. 32,28; Jer. 49,8). He has not the power to create actions, imbued with the strength of life. When enemies are standing face to face with each other they are waging a mental war. The all-important thing is to carry through the fight, and to strike at the central part of the adversary, where action is created. The strong has the power to "confuse" the counsel of the enemy (Is. 19,3) or to destroy it (2 Sam. 15,34); thus it is dissolved and cannot take effect, and the soul which created it is paralyzed. Yahweh is so strong that he breaks all counsels directed against him (Is. 8,10; 14,24; Ps. 33,10).

The counsel is the most typical expression of the character of the soul; it is the sum of its essence, because it contains the fully accomplished action.

In the Proverbs the saying recurs several times that the counsel of one person does endure, but that many counsellors win the day (11,14; 15,22; 24,6). Of course people may advise each other, discuss matters between them and arrive at a common result, but the general mentality of the Israelites being what it was, a consultation with them must be of an entirely different type from what it is with us. For us a council is a number of individuals who put forth proposals and argue with each other, whereas, among the Israelites, there must be a psychic community between men sitting together. An assembly of this kind is called *sōdh.* The unity is not complete, each man having his own counsel, but the object of their gathering is to arrive at one counsel. One after the other sets forth his counsel, and thus they act upon each other's will. A "palaver" of this kind has not taken place in quiet, the excitable Hebrews having often declaimed and shouted all at the same time. But the decision is arrived at when the strongest, he whose counsel is the most vigorous, makes it penetrate into the souls of the others, and thus bends their will to his. In this manner they become one heart. The counsel is made all the stronger, because so many put their strength into it. But the strong man, he who framed what may be called the counsel of the people's soul, he is the counsellor, *yō'ēṣ.* Counsellor he may be called, but the counsel is not only something which he gives to the others; it is his will, determining the unity, to which he himself and the others belong. Such a man was Job. We hear how it was when he came to the council; all the others were silent, and no one offered further counsel when he had spoken (Job 29).

Very close to the word "counsel" or "frame counsel" lies another, the peculiar significance of which we are hardly able to render, i. e. *hō'īl.* It means at the same time the action, as it has been shaped and resolved in the mind, and the action, as it is being translated into a result. When the Israelites had suffered their defeat at Ai, Joshua complained bitterly before Yahweh saying:

Alas, oh Lord Yahweh, wherefore hast thou at all brought this people over Jordan, to deliver us into the hand of the Amorites, to destroy us? Would to God we now *hō'alnā* and sat on the other side Jordan (Josh. 7,7), thus implying their resolve as well as the carrying through of their staying on the other side of the river. Samuel said: Yahweh will not exterminate his people for his great name's sake; for Yahweh *hō'īl* to make this his people (1 Sam. 12,22). Hosea says: Israel *hō'īl* went after impurity (?Hos. 5,11). Moses *hō'īl* and declared the law before the Israelites (Deut. 1,5). This everywhere indicates the action, as it is borne in the soul of him who acts. Therefore the word sometimes leads up to an imperative, by which another is exhorted to create an action. David says: *hō'ēl* bless the house of thy servant (2 Sam. 7,29; cf. Judg. 19,6; 2 Kings 5,23; 6,3).

If we ask at what stage of the mental process the action takes place, the answer is undoubtedly that the action lies in the very idea as soon as it has assumed a permanent character. God says: The end of all flesh is come before me (Gen. 6,13). That which has come before the face of God is what he sees. He sees the end of the world before him, and thus it is a fact. Other expressions of the same kind can be used. The Danites ask the Levite whether their journey is going to be successful, and he answers: Go in peace, your way wherein you go is before *(nōkhaḥ)* Yahweh! (Judg. 18,6). Yahweh has seen their way, the fulfilment of the object lies in his soul, and thus it is a matter of course. Pharaoh says to Moses: Evil is before *(neghedh)* you (Exod. 10,10), i. e. you are men who see and therefore do evil deeds. When the penitent says: I acknowledge my transgressions, and my sin is ever before me (*neghdī*, Ps. 51,5), then it means that he is familiar with his sinning, that he always feels it in himself. When Job says of his misfortune: These things hast thou hid in thine heart, I know that this is with thee (10,13; cf. 23,13), then it means that it is with *('im)* God, or that he sees it, and this in its turn is identical with his doing it.

This is the close context between the action and the idea, the consequence of which is that words meaning "hear", "observe" may often be more suitably rendered by "obey". When a man hears the word of God, it is to be taken for granted that he acts accordingly.

The consequence is that the man is responsible for his acts and their results, not only for his intentions. A distinction is impossible, because there is no such thing as "good intentions". The intention or will is identical with the totality of the soul which creates action. In reality the Israelite has drawn this conclusion, or rather, it is for him a matter of course. When Abimelech took the wife of Isaac, he did not know what he did, but yet he had to bear the responsibility for his act to its full extent. When Jonathan broke the commandment of his father—that no one was to taste any food throughout the day — then he must die, and he recognizes it himself, though he knew nothing of the prohibition (1 Sam. 14). Manslaughter and bodily hurt is judged according to the actual deed and its extent, not according to the more or less evil intention. It may happen, it is true, that a power outside oneself may guide one's hand (Exod. 21,13), and in that case there is a chance that a man may flee to a sanctuary, but even so he does not escape responsibility and the duty to make amends.

We see that consciousness plays a subordinate part in the psychological basic conception. The question is what actually is in the soul, and it may be there without our knowing it. When we speak of the *perceptions* of the soul, we must clearly realize that. For the primitive peoples perceptions are not only images appearing before the consciousness, but they contain the very matter. This holds good whether we look at things from the point of view of the perceiver or the perceived. The soul is wholly in everything belonging to it or emanating from it; therefore it must also be wholly in the impress which it leaves on another's soul. That which fills a man's soul, with that he is in real contact; it becomes the operating power of his soul, and he acts upon it. There is what has been called "a physical and mystical" connection between them.[1] It is this act of intimate appropriation which is called to *know*. This holds good of human beings, as well as of animals. If animals when conceiving see something streaked they have "streakedness" in them, and will throw streaked young (Gen.

30). The primitive peoples decline foreign ideas which they do not know, because they cannot tell whether they are able to grasp them; they do not know what such ideas contain, and where they are going to lead the will.

It is this reality of the idea which is likewise implied by the Israelitic conception of action. If the act lives in the man, as an idea, then it is fully present in him, and he bears the responsibility for it.

From this it will be understood that it is not due to chance when the Israelite has no special term for what we call causal connection, no more than he has a word which we may render by cause. He does not consider an action as something isolated, directly determined by the immediately preceding; he does not judge "post hoc, ergo propter hoc". All that happens is to him a link in a comprehensive continuity, i. e. the character and capacity of the entire soul, because the action expresses the soul, such as it is. A wicked act may wreak ruin upon its perpetrator; not because the one wicked deed must directly wreak ruin, for this is not always the case, but because a soul that perpetrates wicked deeds must also wreak ruin.

The conception of the act is analogous with the conception of the idea, there being a main factor around which all the other elements centre. We have seen how this characterizes the narrative of the Israelite. The verb stands as a king, surrounded by all the subordinate phrases. And the context between the principal action, as expressed by the verb and all the circumstances connected with the former, is to him just as firmly established as is the causal connection in our mind.

Thus the context between that which happens cannot simply be recognized externally. The events are not connected by mutual concatenation, but through the continuity of the soul in which they originate.

An idea arising in the soul always has a tendency to maintain itself through action. The question is then, whether it is something transient, which is quickly driven away and leaves only insignificant traces, or whether it is firmly established, possessing strength for normal development. But every idea contains this possibility, since it is the natural law.

According to its power to maintain itself, the reality of an idea is determined. If it possesses firmness and strength, then it is real; if it does not, it is unreal. Whence the ideas come into the soul cannot always be controlled. They may come from other souls about one, as when one meets a man, or they may rise from the very depths of the soul. It is in all cases the soul which takes charge of them and bears the responsibility for them, because if they are at all possessed of strength to maintain themselves they must act upon the entirety and thus also upon the will. This we see where there is a question of *dreams*. They are a reality, just as well as other ideas.

We often hear of dreams in the Old Testament. God speaks in a dream to Abimelech, and at once he acts accordingly (Gen. 20). Yahweh appears before Jacob in a dream at Bethel, and Jacob is surprised that Yahweh is also in this place (Gen. 28,16), so real is his dream. Through dreams God influences the soul and leads it in the direction he desires. When Jacob had been for a long time in the service of Laban, God appeared before him in a dream, said that he was the God of Bethel, and that Jacob was to return to his native country (Gen. 31). Thus the resolution becomes firmly established in the soul of Jacob and is succeeded by action. By a dream Laban is restrained from doing him harm on the road (31,24).

That dreams are realities follows from the whole Israelitic conception of the idea. When in his dream Jacob sees a ladder, then it is as real as any other. When it is told that Solomon dreamt a dream at the outset of his kingship, and the narrator adds: And he awoke, and behold, it was a dream (1 Kings 3,15), then it does not mean: It was only a dream. On the contrary. Just because the dream so utterly rises from the depths of unconsciousness it is particularly significant. For Solomon the whole blessing of his reign is given with this good dream, and he confirms it by making great sacrifices. The dream is so real that a needy Babylonian, who in a hymn implores his God to alleviate his misery, asks to get a happy dream.[1]

These dreams are easily understood, because the whole of their content lies clearly in them. If they are true and fixed, then the contents must also some day project themselves in outer events. But there are other dreams which are not so simple, because they contain peculiar images, the context of which is not immediately apparent. The man who is visited by such dreams does not know them, nor the direction in which they may lead his soul. Then his mind becomes filled with unrest and anxiety. Thus it was with Pharaoh (Gen. 41,8) and his chief butler and chief baker (Gen. 40,7), and thus it was with Nebuchadnezzar (Dan. 2,1 ff.).

The unrest is doubly strong, because it comes from his own soul: the dream is fixed in it; the soul has taken a direction which he himself neither knows nor controls, because the dream is the manifestation of a context which is strange to him. Therefore it must be interpreted by one who is able to penetrate deeper and to see through the context. This must not be understood in the sense that the dream is a kind of allegory, a series of pictures in which a power outside oneself indicates what it intends to do; or in other words, a purely mechanical means of communication from gods to man. This is at variance with the old conception of the action and of the work of the divinity. It is true that the dream is a communication from God to man, but it does not clash with the psychological process. The dream is a communication from God, because it is a direct outcome of reality itself.

In order to understand this, we ought to consider how the event is conceived. It is created in the souls which experience it. As shown above, an act may lie in the soul of a man, as a counsel, quite real, but still dormant, in so far as it has not found an outward expression; in the same manner any event may lie latent in the souls experiencing it, before it appears in an outward form. In these souls it may produce effects before having directly manifested itself outwardly, because it fills and forms the souls and makes them something which they themselves do not know. Such effects are the dreams, which must always be considered as the outcome of the latent event and parallel with its very outbreak.

When Pharaoh in his dream sees seven lean-fleshed kine eat up seven fat-fleshed ones, and then seven thin ears of corn devour seven rank and full ears, then there is a connection between these events and the seven good and the seven bad years which followed in Egypt. But this connection is quite different from any kind of connection with which we reckon. It is the outcome of the fact that these years, which Pharaoh shall live to see, already live as a reality in his soul, without his knowing it. He carries these years in his soul, and therefore his soul must create dreams of abundance and hunger. The same event may naturally produce many dreams; the expert who sees deeply enough may then see that it is this same event underlying them. Therefore Joseph said to Pharaoh that his two dreams are one (Gen. 41,25).

In the dream the event is caught. He who has a dream has, through his dream, received the matter itself, because it is the matter that through the dream acts in the soul. And *vice versa:* Through the dream the man makes the matter his own: it is in his will, and he is responsible for it.

How dangerous dreams may be, Joseph himself was to experience. It is told: And Joseph dreamed a dream, and he told it his brethren; and they hated him yet the more. And he said unto them: Hear, I pray you, this dream which I have dreamed. For behold, we were binding sheaves in the field, and lo, my sheaf arose and also stood upright; and behold, your sheaves stood round about, and made obeisance to my sheaf. And his brethren said to him: Shalt thou indeed reign over us? Or shalt thou indeed have dominion over us? And they hated him yet the more for his dreams and for his words. And he dreamed yet another dream, and told it his brethren and said: Behold, I have dreamed a dream more; and behold, the sun and the moon and eleven stars made obeisance to me. And he told it to his father and to his brethren, and his father rebuked him and said unto him: What is this dream that thou hast dreamed? Shall I and thy mother and thy brethren indeed come to bow down ourselves to thee to the earth? And his brethren envied him; but his father observed the saying (Gen. 37,5-11).

So strong was the hatred of his brothers against Joseph that they decided to avail themselves of the opportunity to kill him. When he came to them at Dothan, where they stayed with their herds, they said: Behold, this dreamer cometh! Come now therefore, and let us slay him and cast him into one of the pits and we will say some evil beast hath devoured him, and we shall see what will become of his dreams (Gen. 37,19-20). It ended by their selling him as a slave in order to get rid of him.

Whence comes this violent hatred among the brothers? First of all it is owing to the fact that the dream is something real. But it is not sufficient to say that they hated him because they feared that his dreams should be fulfilled. The presupposition of the whole story is that the man is responsible for his dreams. Even his father, whose favourite he is, rebukes him for his dreams. When Joseph has the power to dream as he did, then this implies a claim. He has had king's dreams, but this can only happen to a king's soul. The fact of being the ruler, before whom the others throw themselves, has passed into his soul and makes it the soul of a ruler, with the demand of the ruler for the subjection of the others. That which happens at a later period, when Joseph stands as the vizier of Egypt, and the brothers lie in the dust before the powerful ruler, is no new situation. It means that the dream of Joseph persisted, was real. His soul was really the soul of a ruler; it *must* have that kind of dream. Thence the hatred of his brothers. Through his dreams Joseph has become a potential ruler, and some day this potentiality will be fulfilled, unless it be extirpated. Therefore they want to kill him or, at least, to get him out of the way; thus they prevent the persistence of his dream or, what comes to the same thing, they prevent his soul from carrying through its claim, to unfold itself according to its nature. It has become crushed in the very beginning of its growth.

When Gideon was at war with the Midianites, he one night in secret went with his servant to the furthest outposts of the enemy, and here he listened to a warrior who told a dream to his comrade. The account of his dream reads: He said: Behold, I dreamed a dream and lo, a cake of barley bread tumbled into the host of Midian, and came unto a tent and smote it that it fell, and overturned it that the tent lay along. And his fellow answered and said: This is nothing else save the sword of the Israelite Gideon, the son of Joash; for into his hand God hath delivered Midian, and all the host (Judg. 7,13-14). When Gideon heard that, he thanked his God, returned to his people and said: Arise, for Yahweh hath delivered into your hand the host of Midian.

With the dream the matter is settled. The Midianites lack the strength of victory; their soul is inferior, a soul of defeat, and therefore it must create dreams of defeat, whereas victory is created in the soul of Gideon. The outcome of the succeeding battle is simply the consequence of all this. The dream of defeat and the defeat itself are only two different manifestations of the same idea: that the Midianites were weak souls which could create nothing but defeat.

In order to dream well, one must have a strong soul. It is possible to form ideas that lie so far out in the periphery that what they stir is quite unimportant. The direction of a will may be counteracted by another and thus be stopped or diverted. Of course dreams can also be so unimportant that they contain no reality, and such dreams are called *shāw'*, false, empty. They are only air, an illusion without any strength. Ordinary people may often have such dream images, which disappear without leaving any deeper impress (Ps. 73,20; Job 20,8). It is that kind of dream which the false prophets dream and tell the people (Jer. 23,32; Zech. 10,2).

The strong warriors, so full of vitality, dream dreams of victory which are reality. How the others fare is told by Isaiah when he speaks of the enemies, gathering for an unsuccessful war against Jerusalem: Just as the hungry eat in dreams and then wake up with empty souls, as the thirsty drink in dreams and then wake up faint, with worn-out souls, so shall the multitude of all the nations be that fight against Mount Zion (Is. 29,7-8). Isaiah does not say that this holds good of the dreams of all who are hungry and thirsty; but it often does so, because he who is languishing lacks the strength that may give life to his dream and fill it with reality. And this impotence is to be the lot of the enemies of Jerusalem. The victory they have created in their souls turns out to be an illusion.

Israel had a whole class of men and women with a peculiar capacity for dreaming. It was the power of the *prophets* to dream strong dreams which were real. They were true, because they were filled with strength of soul from God, or as the Israelite also expresses it: their dreams had been sent by Yahweh. The main thing is then to find the prophets who have true dreams. We know that a hard fight has taken place between the various prophets. We hear the echo of it in Jeremiah: I have heard what the prophets say, that prophesy lies in my name, saying I have dreamed, I have dreamed. How long? Is this (really) in the heart of the prophets that prophesy falsehoods, yea, they are prophets of the deceit of their own heart; which think to cause my people to forget my name by their dreams which they tell every man to his neighbour, as their fathers have forgotten my name for Baal. The prophet that (really) hath a dream, let him tell his dream, and he that hath my word let him speak my word faithfully. What community is there between the chaff and the wheat? saith Yahweh (Jer. 23,25-28). And he continues: I am against them that prophesy false dreams, saith Yahweh, and do tell them and confuse my people by their lies and by their lightness, without my having sent them nor commanded them; therefore they shall not profit this people at all, saith Yahweh (v. 32, cf. 29,8).

The question whether the dream is a reality cannot be decided by external means. It rests in the quality of the soul of the dreamer, but even he who is able to dream true dreams may have untrue dreams, phantasms that disappear. Jeremiah accuses the prophets of holding forth such valueless, fortuitous inventions as dreams. If they have a real dream, then they must also produce it. But that which they say cannot have its root in reality; he asks whether there is really anything in their souls. The answer is implied in his own words; they are lying souls that deceive and produce deceptive untruths. Jeremiah rejects the dreams of the prophets, because their contents conflict with the laws of reality, such as he knows it. Thus they cannot be real dreams, and must have been created by lying souls.

For the Israelites dreams retain their character far into historical times. One of the late prophets, Joel, looks forward to a time when all Israelites shall have the power to see visions and dreams (Joel 3,1). From the time of Herod Josephos tells a story which is entirely in the old spirit: The chief priest Matthias once on fasting day, i. e. on the day of atonement, had to withdraw and let another be appointed in his place. For on the preceding night Matthias had dreamt that he lay with his wife, and this made him unfit to perform his priestly office.[1] Thus the dream is considered equal to the action itself.

This conception of the dream is not due to chance, but is closely connected with the fundamental conception which sharply distinguishes between what is and what is not in the soul; that which maintains itself in the soul is truth. Nor is it an isolated phenomenon. Alongside of the dream stands the vision; there is only the difference between them that the vision is received when awake.

That which characterizes the *vision* as well as the dream is that the seer sees irrespective of distance. This sensitive faculty is different from the so-called normal sensation. We all know how we may be conscious of the presence of a person, though we are neither able to see nor to hear him. This immediate perception is developed among primitive peoples to an extent unknown to us, and it is also found among the Israelitic seers. They look right across distances of space and time. If some asses have run away, then the visionary may look through space and see them return, (1 Sam. 9,20). The same phenomenon is well known among the Arabs and most other peoples.

Of the greatest importance is the prophet's seeing through time. Events are created by the souls meeting other souls, being an expression of the actual character of these. The faculty of the prophet is a fellow feeling with the souls, which permits him to see what they are going to be, what experiences they are bound to have. He sees this as something which already is. When Jeremiah was called to King Zedekiah, he said that Yahweh had permitted him to see all the women of the royal household being brought forth to the king of Babylon's princes (Jer. 38,22). Elisha saw Hazael as king of Aram, before any one had been able to consider this possibility (2 Kings 8,13). Thus the prophets hear what is coming. When Elijah had conquered the prophets of Baal, the reason of the lasting drought had been removed. Now he hears the sound of abundance of rain: Ahab can eat and drink in peace, the rain is there (1 Kings 18,41) — and yet no one else can see any cloud in the sky. Jeremiah hears the trumpets of the enemy; the whole land is laid waste and ruined (Jer. 4,20), and yet others have seen nothing of any enemy.

The peculiar thing is that the prophet makes himself contemporary with events which, to other people, have no direct connection with the present. He sees the souls in a state which is to come. But he only does so, because what is coming is connected with what *is*. He is able to look into the souls and see what they contain. It is real at the moment he has seen it and it has taken the shape of a firm idea in his soul. And because it lives in his soul he assists in maintaining it and is responsible for it, just as the dreamer is responsible for his dreams.

The soul is responsible for the ideas it contains, and it must act in accordance with them, because they harmonize so closely with its essence and general character. Therefore it is of the greatest importance what ideas fill the soul. When the king is going to the war, his soul must be filled with victory before the fight. If the victory can be created in him by firmness and strength, then it is a fact, for the remainder is only a manifestation of his actual being; if he does not win, then it is because he did not after all go to the war as a soul of victory. By thus creating the victory before the fight the prophets play a great part, and of all this we find an account in the Book of Kings (1 Kings 22).

It is told that when Ahab made ready to go against the Aramæans then, on the suggestion of his friend king Jehoshaphat, he first enquired at the word of Yahweh. He gathered about him four hundred prophets and put the following question before them: Shall I go against Ramoth in Gilead to battle, or shall I forbear? And they said all with one voice: Go up, for Yahweh shall deliver it into the hand of the king. And the king of Judah asks whether there are more prophets, and Ahab answers that there is one more, Micaiah the son of Imlah, "but I hate him; for he does not prophesy good concerning me, but evil". While a messenger is sent to fetch Micaiah, the prophets repeat their prophecies: "Go up against Ramoth in Gilead and prosper, for Yahweh shall deliver it into the king's hand." One of the prophets, Zedekiah the son of Chenaanah, made him horns of iron and he said: Thus saith Yahweh: With these shalt thou push the Aramæans, until thou have consumed them.

Of the appearance of Micaiah the Book of Kings tells the following: And the messenger that was gone to call Micaiah spoke unto him, saying: Behold now, the words of the prophets declare good unto the king with one mouth; let thy word, I pray thee, be like the word of one of them, and speak that which is good. And Micaiah said: By the life of Yahweh, what Yahweh saith unto me, that will I speak. So he came to the king. And the king said unto him: Micaiah, shall we go against Ramoth in Gilead to battle, or shall we forbear? And he answered him: Go and prosper! for Yahweh has delivered it into the hand of the king. And the king said unto him: How many times shall I adjure thee that thou shall tell me nothing but that which is true in the name of Yahweh? And he said: I see all Israel scattered upon the hills as sheep that have not a shepherd. And Yahweh said: These have no master; let them return every man to his house in peace. — And the king of Israel said unto Jehoshaphat: Did I not tell thee that he would prophesy no good concerning me, but evil? And he (Micaiah) said: Hear then *(lākhēn)* the word of Yahweh! I saw Yahweh sitting on his throne, and all the host of heaven standing by him on his right hand and on his left. And Yahweh said: Who shall beguile Ahab that he may go up and fall at Ramoth in Gilead? And one said on this manner, and others said on that manner. And there came forth a spirit and stood before Yahweh and said: I will beguile him! And Yahweh said unto him: Wherewith? And he said: I will go forth, and I will be a lying spirit in the mouth of all his prophets . And Yahweh said: Thou shalt beguile him, and prevail also; go forth and do so! — Now therefore, behold, Yahweh hath put a lying spirit into the mouth of all these thy prophets, and Yahweh hath spoken evil concerning thee. But Zedekiah, the son of Chenaanah, went near and smote Micaiah on the cheek, and said: How came it to pass that the spirit of Yahweh went from me to speak unto thee? And Micaiah said: Behold, thou shall see in that day when thou shalt go into an inner chamber to hide thyself. And the king of Israel said: Take Micaiah, and carry him back unto Amon the governor of the city, and Joash the king's son, and say: Thus saith the king: Put this fellow in the prison, and feed him with bread of affliction and with water of affliction, until I come in peace. And Micaiah said: If thou return at all in peace, Yahweh hath not spoken in me (1 Kings 22,13-28).

In this pithy narrative we see how events are created. The king is confronted by war, which is action in the preeminent sense of the word. The important thing is to create victory, and to do this he must seek assistance; he must have prophets who are able to see him as a victor and to put the victory into his soul. The prophets do not give abstract information of something which is to happen in the future. The victory depends upon whether the king has the strength within himself; they are to see whether he has this strength. But if they are able to see it, then the victory is seated as a reality, also in their souls, and they act towards creating it in that of the king. The four hundred prophets act together with the king in order to make him a soul of victory, and each of them is responsible for the victory.

The narrative of Micaiah is saturated with the idea that a responsibility rests with the prophet. The king hates him, because he is not wont to see anything good; the messenger *implores* Micaiah to join the others and to see something good. Of course this is not a wanton request to fall in with the views of the king; the vision of the prophet is the outcome of the power and will of his soul, and the messenger, by his request, tries to influence the latter. But Micaiah is not master of his will in the sense that according to his caprices he may see the one or the other; he can only give the king victory in case he really sees it in him, and this he expresses by saying: Only that which Yahweh saith unto me will I speak.

Ahab realizes at once that Micaiah is prophesying falsely, when he prophesies victory, and he demands that Micaiah shall tell him what is actually in his heart. When the prophet then does as he is told, he is punished by being thrown into prison. And yet the action of the king is throughout consistent. A sentimental good will does not exist; Micaiah sees evil things for the king; thus he wills evil things for him. He creates defeat instead of victory in the soul of the king, and therefore he must be struck down.

That which happens here is of the same kind as that which happens with other primitive peoples before a war, a hunt or other acts of similar importance. By the observance of special rites they create victory in themselves and defeat in the enemy, before they sally forth. Thus Elisha created the victory of Israel over Aram by letting King Joash send forth an arrow of victory against it while the hand of Elisha rested on his, and in our narrative the prophet Zedekiah does something of a similar kind by butting with horns of iron. If the victory rites fail, the day is lost. The sayings of the prophets make part of this kind of victory rites; if they cannot create visions of victory, there is no victory.

In our narrative the king is in a difficult position. The four hundred prophets say victory, and Micaiah visions defeat. Ahab adopts the will of the many, but then he must strike down Micaiah and try to frustrate his vision and so also its effect in his soul. The king has no external means with which to decide the matter. The decisive factor is where the strength lies, he must feel quite instinctively whether he has the victory in his soul; it is there that it has to be created. The party which is able to create the certainty in him must possess the truth.

If the prophet is filled with a divine spirit, then he has the strength to see reality, and reality there is, in that it is seen and perceived in the soul. In that case it must manifest itself in an outward form, at the eventual accomplishment of victory. It may happen that the prophet speaks foolish and idle words; but it may also happen that Yahweh fills him with false ideas; then the souls are confused, and misfortune is there. If the prophet does not possess the power of vision, then his vision is a lie *(sheḳer* 1 Kings 22,22 f.) or emptiness *(shāw'* Ez. 12,24; 13,6 ff.). The vision is not as the good counsel that persists; it immediately perishes *('ābhadh)*. The fulfilment is the test of the truth of the prophet (Deut. 18,22). If it does not take place, then the vision never was real, and the prophet is a powerless juggler untouched by the spirit of Yahweh.

When the prophets set forth their visions, they express themselves in the form which is called perfect, i. e. that which indicates the complete and independent action. It is not a special use of this form, a "prophetical perfect", which is applied in a figurative manner. That which the prophet sees takes place simultaneously with his vision; the outward fulfilment is not an entirely novel thing; it is simply a further elaboration of a context implied in the vision. All this is the outcome of his fundamental psychological conception, according to which the image of the soul, the motion of the will and the carrying out of the action form a complete whole. Starting from these presuppositions we understand that the Hebrew does not require special verbal forms in order to express time.

The soul is constructed with a view to action, but the presupposition of its being able to act is that the construction is firm. The best characterization of the soul is as an organism, which at any time centres and ranges itself round a point of gravity. This point of gravity is the centre of force in which action is created, and this centre must be firm and strong; otherwise the soul must not be stiff but pliable, so that it subordinates itself to its centre.

Of the man who acts it is said that he fixes his heart to his action *(hēkhīn)*. Ezra fixed his heart to study the torah (Ezr. 7,10). Samuel encourages the people to fix their hearts to do the will of Yahweh (1 Sam. 7,3; cf. 2 Chr. 30,19).[1] The heart is fixed and *strengthened* for the action.

It is generally the heart which denotes this organized strength of soul. The stout-hearted are the strong men who create the great deeds (Ps. 76,6). He who has lost the power to live and to act has no heart. Jeremiah speaks of the dreadful day, when misfortunes pour in upon Judah; priests and prophets stand horror-stricken, and the hearts of kings and princes shall perish (Jer. 4,9). A very vivid picture Hosea gives us of him without heart, when he compares Ephraim with a heartless dove fluttering here and there (Hos. 7,11). The same prophet says that whoredom and wine and new wine take away the heart (Hos. 4,11), thus implying that not only they deprive people of the power of reflection, but that the vitality, the energy and power to create perish. The Proverbs constantly warn against letting light women take away one's heart. "Who so committeth adultery with a woman loses his heart: he that doeth it, destroyeth his own soul; he is smitten with dishonour, and his ignomy shall not be wiped away" (Pr. 6, 32-33). She steals his whole strength and vitality.

Peoples outside our sphere of culture do not consider the soul primarily as a thinking organism, the activity of which lies at the surface under the control of the consciousness. For them the soul is a depth of forces, and this also holds good of the fundamental Israelitic conception. To be filled with soul means to be imbued with strength. "Spirit" is frequently the denomination of this strength, where stress is not to be laid on the centre of the soul. "But truly I am full of power by the spirit of Yahweh, and of judgment, and of might, to declare unto Jacob his transgression and to Israel his sin", says the prophet (Mic. 3,8). When Joshua is said to *have spirit* (Num. 27,18) or to be full of the spirit of wisdom (Deut. 34,9), then it means that his soul is filled with powers which make him a chief. The "spirit of counsel and might" is what the ruler must possess (Is. 11,2). When the Old Testament sometimes sets up flesh and spirit as contrasts, then it is not because it distinguishes between soul and body as two entirely different forms of existence, but it is weakness as against strength. "Their horses are flesh and not spirit" (Is. 31,3) means that they are weak and lack the strength distinguishing the soul.

It is this strength which the Israelite desires; he can never get enough and demands it from his God. "Give thy strength unto thy slave", says the Psalmist (Ps. 86,16). God is mighty in strength of heart (Job 9,4; 36,5), a spirit of inexhaustible powers.

The power is drawn from the contents of the soul; it imbues the centre of action with strength and stamps the act. The fulness of the soul is therefore the same as its might or strength: Thou shalt love Yahweh thy god with all thine heart, and with all thy soul and with all thy might (Deut. 6,5). The word which here is rendered by "might" *(meʼōdh)* means the quantity, the fulness. One must put the whole of the soul into one's action. In order to be able to act the soul must have contents; it demands to be filled. This demand for contents is the desire.

The *desire* comprises everything that may add to the capacity of the soul, both the ideal values and the satisfaction of the claims of the body. The soul desires to eat meat (Deut. 12,15.20 f.), to get its share of the sacrificial gifts (1 Sam. 2,16); the thirsty soul desires to drink, the rutting ass desires to have its rut satisfied (Jer. 2,24). When the Levite comes from his country sanctuary to the temple of Jerusalem, then he comes with all the desire of his soul (*'awwat naphshō,* Deut. 18,6), that is to get everything that a Levite, i. e. a priest, demands in his capacity of a priest: the right to do sacrifice, to share in the incomes of the temple, in short, the position, the honour which his soul, i. e. that of a priest, may demand. David has a king's soul, his desire is to rule over Israel (2 Sam. 3,21, cf. 1 Kings 11,37). The desire of the Israelite is the remembrance of Yahweh and his name (Is. 26,8). The nature of this desire depends upon the peculiar qualities of the soul and prevailing circumstances. The soul always desires that which it must contain in itself in order to be filled.

There is a connection between the desire and operation of the soul, but also a difference. In the desire the soul attracts substance; it is of a less active character than the action; the desire is not the outcome of strength, but a demand for strength. Therefore the spirit is not mentioned as the agent of desires. The heart has desires (Ps. 21,3; 37,4), but they are particularly characteristic of *nephesh.* The proverb warns against being a *ba'al nephesh* (Pr. 23,2), i. e. to be full of desires. Such greedy people are called "strong of soul" (Is. 56,11), have a "wide soul" (Pr. 28,25). They demand to be filled with more than they have the capacity of holding; they make their soul as wide as Sheol (Hab. 2,5). For Sheol has a wide soul (Is. 5,14) and is able to receive all living things.

When the soul gets all it desires, then it is *filled* or *sated.* The soul is daily to be filled or sated with meat and drink (Jer. 50,19; Ps. 78,18). If the man goes hungry, the soul is empty (Is. 29,8) and pines away (Ps. 106,15). The soul delights in fatness; then it is *made good* (Is. 55,2; Jer. 31,14.25; Pr. 11,25; 13,4). When the heart is fed with meat and drink, it is supported (Gen. 18,5; Judg. 19,5.8; Ps. 104,15), and the soul is strengthened. Meat and drink determine the growth of the soul to such an extent that desire of other things is called hunger and thirst; the soul thirsts after God (Ps. 42,3; 63,2).

When the soul is filled, it is happy, it is made full with joys (Ps. 16,11); it is also said that the heart becomes *good*. When the great festival celebrating the inauguration of the temple was over, and the souls of the Israelites were filled with new strength, they went home "joyful and good of heart" (1 Kings 8,66). When a man is comfortably lodged (Judg. 19,6.9), or when the heart is supported by meat and wine, then it becomes good, happy (Judg. 16,25; 18,20; 19,22; 2 Sam. 13,28; 1 Kings 21,7; Ps. 104,15; Ruth 3,7; Esth. 1,10).

It is the nature of the soul to be full and happy. To make it happy and strong is therefore to "restore the soul", to make it once more into a soul. He who mourns wants to have his soul restored (Lam. 1,16). When, through the marriage of Ruth, Naomi finally found progeny for her husband and son, it was a restoration of her soul (Ruth 4,15); hitherto it had been checked and not been able to unfold itself according to the nature of a soul. The pious man has his soul restored by the law (Ps. 19,8). Joy expresses itself in the exultations of the soul, the rejoicings of the heart (1 Sam. 2,1; Ps. 13,6; 28,7; 84,3). The mighty man who fills the soul of the weak, "causes the widow's heart to exult" (Job 29,13) just as the Israelite exults in Yahweh, when his soul is filled with happiness (Ps. 34,3; 35,9; 146,1).

When the soul is filled, it grows, expands. Through false desire after honour or whatever it is, it is filled so strongly that it cannot hold what is in it and expands beyond its capacity. It then swells like a boil (*'uppelā*, Hab. 2,4). The heart becomes fat (Is. 6,10), high (Ps. 131,1; Pr. 16,5) or wide (Pr. 21,4); it lifts itself above those with whom its fulness in reality places it (Deut. 17,20; Ezek. 31,10), it "boils up" and thus makes itself greater than it naturally is (*zādhōn*, Deut. 17,12; 18,22; 1 Sam. 17,28; Ob. 3 et al.), nay, it may even be foolish enough to make itself as the heart of God (Ezek. 28,2.6).

This demand to be filled beyond its capacity is strongly rebuked in the Old Testament; but it is only the caricature of that which is the happiness of the soul: to be filled, to thrive, to expand. God gave to Solomon "largeness of the heart" even as the sand that is on the sea shore (1 Kings 5,9), a great soul, rich in contents and strength. Jeremiah says that in the days of bliss the people shall come and have their share of Yahweh's wealth of grain and wine and oil and cattle. "Their soul shall be as a watered garden" (Jer. 31,12). Like fruitful soil it must expand and thrive.

If the soul is not nourished but is stricken by misfortune, then it becomes *bitter* (Judg. 18,25; 1 Sam. 1,10; 22,2; 30,6; Job 3,20 et al.), and this at the same time designates the soul as miserable and sorrowing, as lacking natural courage and energy. While he who is glad exults out of the goodness of his heart, the unhappy cries for sorrow of heart (Is. 65,14). The unhappy soul is always restless (2 Kings 6,11), trembles (Is. 15,4), quakes and quivers (1 Sam. 4,13; 28,5; Jer. 4,19).

As the happy soul is wide, so the anguished soul is narrow. Job speaks in the anguish of his spirit (7,11), and so do many psalmists; others are able to confess: Thou hast made expansion for me when I was in narrowness (Ps. 4,2; cf. 143,11). This anguish is identical with lack of strength: Thou faint in the day of adversity, thy strength is small (Pr. 24,10).

The anguished soul is *empty;* and as such the soul of the hungry is designated (Is. 32,6). The miserable has poured out his *nephesh,* i. e. emptied it of its fulness and strength. The soul of Job is poured out in him (Job 30,16); the exile, who is perishing for longing of the holy place, pours out his soul in himself (Ps. 42,5); Hannah lies dissolved in tears before Yahweh and beseeches him to put an end to her misery of childlessness; she behaves like a drunken woman, but says to Eli, who rebukes her, that she has poured out her soul before Yahweh (1 Sam. 1,15). These expressions must not, in accordance with our *usus loquendi,* be interpreted as signifying: to make known one's feelings. It means to stand forth in all one's sorrow, helplessness and lack of strength. He who is stricken by misfortune therefore begs God not to empty his soul (Ps. 141,8), i. e. to deprive it of the amount of strength and vitality, possessed by it. The healthy soul is firm, well-organized. The diseased, miserable soul is confused (Ps. 6,4), faints (Ps. 107,5) [1] or languishes (Jer. 15,9).

The heart is the entirety of the soul as a power; therefore the miserable may say that his heart has left him (Ps. 40,13), that it is turned within him (Lam. 1,20), but he may also say that the heart, like *nephesh,* is emptied. The miserable are to pour out their hearts like water before God (Lam. 2,19; Ps. 62,9), i. e. to humble themselves, to surrender the whole of their own strength. "A trembling heart and failing of eyes and fainting of soul", thus Deut. 28,65 describes the state of perfect dissolution which the Israelites run the risk of incurring. In a situation like that "the heart falls" (1 Sam. 17,32).

Or we are told that the heart *melts* (Lev. 26,16; Ps. 107,26). When the Israelites approached Canaan under the leadership of Joshua, the hearts of the Amorites melted, neither was there any spirit in them (Josh. 5,1 cf. 2,11); the inhabitants of the town of Ai fared likewise; their hearts melted and became as water (Josh. 7,5). The spies melted the hearts of their brethren by speaking of the mighty peoples living in Canaan (Deut. 1,28; Josh. 14,8). Hushai says that in defeat he whose heart is as the heart of a lion shall utterly melt (2 Sam. 17,10). All of these expressions imply that the courage fails, but also something more: it is the strength, the creative power which disappears. The soul, the firm whole, falls to pieces and is utterly dissolved; although its essence is action and production, it is unable to undertake anything. "The mighty men's heart in Moab at that day shall be as the heart of a woman in her pangs" (Jer. 48, 41; cf. 49,22); it is not only the lack of courage, but the weakness, the pain and the helplessness which is described here.

This abnormal state is described by the hands becoming faint (Is. 13,7; Ezek. 21,12). The heart is cold and faint *(pūgh* Gen. 45,26; Ps. 38,9); warmth is required to make it strong. The heart vacillates to and fro like the wave *(mūgh,* Ezek. 21,20); it collapses *('āṭaph,* Ps. 61,3), withers *(yābhēsh,* Ps. 102,5); it becomes lean or soft *(rakk,* Deut. 20,3.8; 2 Kings 22,19; Is. 7,4; Jer. 51,46); it is bent or shrinks *(nikhna',* Lev. 26,41; 2 Kings

22,19): it becomes broken or crushed *(shbr,* Ps. 69,21). It is this kind of broken, faint souls in which the Yahweh of later Israel took particular delight (Is. 61,1; Ps. 34,19; 51,19; 147,3). Jeremiah, who knew mental suffering from experience, gives a vivid description of the state of the broken soul: Mine heart is broken within me; all my bones are soft; I am like a drunken man and like a man whom wine hath overcome (Jer. 23,9). This state of hopeless dissolution he might also have described by saying that his heart had passed away (Gen. 42,28). The soul was no longer entirely soul.

This might more particularly be expressed by saying that the spirit was destroyed. The spirit is strength itself and therefore vanishes with it. In the powerless there is no spirit any more (Josh. 5,1); his spirit is weakened like the light that is on the point of being extinguished (Is. 61,3); it is broken or crushed (Is. 65,14; Ps. 34,19; 51,19);[1] it collapses (Ps. 142,4; 143,4) and slackens like a loosely hanging bow (Ps. 32,2; Pr. 19,15); it becomes of no account (Is. 57,15; Pr. 16,19; 29,23). He whose heart is paralyzed, his spirit fails (Is. 19,3). Either it disappears altogether, or it rushes about at random, a spirit of giddiness, which staggers in all that it undertakes, as the drunken man staggereth in his vomit (Is. 19,14). When a man is rendered entirely paralyzed, as by deadly hunger or thirst (Judg. 15,19; 1 Sam. 30,12), by fainting (1 Kings 10,5) or by death, the spirit is gone; then only the weaker of the component parts of the soul are left.

It is in accordance with all this that the Israelite says: the soul as soul is *living* or, which comes to the same thing, is *life*. The Israelite may say: "God holdeth our soul in life" (Ps. 66,9), but with this he does not mean to say that life and soul are two different things which have been united. Spirit is the spirit of life (Gen. 6,17; 7,15.22), because it is identical with the vital force. If "spirit and life" enter into dead bones, then they again become human (Ezek. 37,5.6.10).

We hear so often in the Psalms that the merciless enemy demands the soul of his adversary (35,4; 38,13; 40,15; 63,10; 70,3; 86,14 et al.). The pursued always cries shame on him who seeks his soul or pursues it and lays snares before it. We hear the miserable lamenting that the dangers reach unto his very soul (Jer. 4,10; Jon. 2,6; Ps. 69,2). They who are in danger of their lives "flee to their souls" (2 Kings 7,7), and if they risk their lives, then they "put their soul in their hands" (Judg. 12,3; 1 Sam. 19,5; 28,21; Ps. 119,109; Job 13,14); they "go with their souls" (2 Sam. 23,17); the valiant "throws away his soul", as Gideon did in order to save his compatriots (Judg. 9,17); he "despises his soul as regards dying" (Judg. 5,18).

This does not mean that *nephesh* means life or soul interchangeably; still less does it mean, as has been maintained, that *nephesh* does not mean soul at all, but only life.[1] For this would not carry us one step further; if it is said of *nephesh* that it eats, speaks, acts, then we could only render it by life, with the reservation that life here means something else than is generally represented by the term. But the fact is that soul as well as life with the Israelites means something else than it usually does with us. The soul is not only the upholder of certain states; it is the full soul-substance with special qualities and powers. And life is not an abstract colourless something, which forms the basis of the souls, not mere existence without any qualities. Life is always stamped in certain capacities and powers, which means that life only manifests itself as soul. The world is filled with a whirl of souls; we might also say: a whirl of lives, of lives of the human genus, of lives of animal genera, of lives of plants.

Life is an organism of values, a real substance. He who takes a mill to pledge, takes the soul to pledge, says the law (Deut. 24,6), because the mill forms the basis of daily nourishment and so of life; but it means more than the purely physical, all functions and values of life being connected with food. Life and soul is something which can be taken (1 Sam. 24,12; 1 Kings 19,4; Ezek. 33,6; Ps. 31,14; Pr. 1,19). It does not only mean that the person in question is deprived of the ordinary functions of life; it means that his soul is appropriated with its substance, its strength and its values. Therefore one must either give a soul for a soul, as required according to the law of blood-feud, or possibly ransom one's soul. That a soul is exterminated from its kin means more than that physical life is drained off a man. It implies that a soul organism with the whole of its contents, all that belongs to it and characterizes it, is uprooted and removed.

As there are many forms of life, so are there also many degrees. The great soul, which is full of forces, has much life, the weak one only little. The more one possesses of values of life, of strength, the more life one possesses. Physical strength is not all, but it plays a great part. When one eats and drinks, one gets life. The proverb mentions goat's milk for food and life (Pr. 27,27). When Samson was fainting with thirst and then found a fountain and drank of the latter, "his spirit came again, and he revived" (Judg. 15,19). It does not simply mean that he escaped dying, but that he gained vitality. Life and death are not two sharply distinguished spheres, because they do not mean existence or non-existence. Life is something which one possesses in a higher or lower degree. If afflicted by misfortune, illness or something else which checks the soul, then one has only little life, but all the more death. He who is ill or otherwise in distress may say that he is dead, and when he recovers, he is pulled out of death.[1]

When the Israelites were ill after the circumcision, they sat, each in his place in the camp, until they "became alive" (Josh. 5,8). When they were assailed by poisonous snakes, which killed them with their bites, Moses turned to Yahweh, and asked him to save them. And Yahweh said unto Moses: Make thee a saraph and set it upon a pale, that every one who is bitten, when he looketh upon that, shall live. And Moses made a serpent of brass, and put it upon a pale, and it came to pass that if a serpent had bitten any man, when he beheld the serpent of brass, he lived (Num. 21, 8-9). This does not mean that he escaped death, in the sense that he retained his existence, though weakened by the poison; it means that life and strength and health returned to him, i. e. he was healed. He is made alive "from" or "out of" a disease (2 Kings 1,2; 8,9; Is. 38,9).[2] Illness is death, healing life.

This application of the words "life", "live" and "make living" is not a special, isolated use of the word, so that *hayyīm* partly meant life, partly recovery. It always means life, but the Israelitic conception of life is such that in certain cases it must cover the idea of recovery. But it comprises all the forms of the free expansion of the soul. When in his old age Jacob had been persuaded that his son Joseph lived as a mighty ruler in Egypt, "his spirit revived" (Gen. 45,27). In its sorrow it had shrunk, had lost its fulness and strength or, briefly, life; but now it gained new life, became alive. The unhappy says: Thou which hast shewed me (or us) great and sore troubles, give thou me (or us) life again; bring me (us) up again from the oceans of the earth! (Ps. 71,20). Another says: Wilt thou be angry with us forever? Wilt thou keep thine anger to generation after generation? Wilt thou not receive us again: that thy people may rejoice in thee? (Ps. 85,6-7). It is quite characteristic of Yahweh that he "revives the spirits of the humble and the hearts of the contrite ones" (Is. 57,15). Life is the opposite of misery, identical with joy. God "maketh not the wicked live" (Job 36,6), i. e. he does not make him happy, does not grant him expansion and prosperity.

Just as this can be expressed by *receiving* spirit, so it may also be called to be "ensouled", i. e. to *receive nephesh.* Slaves and other workers must rest on the sabbath in order to be "ensouled" (Exod. 23,12), as Yahweh did (Exod. 31,17). David stopped somewhere, exhausted from his flight, and was "ensouled" (2 Sam. 16,14). All of these cases imply a fresh acquisition of strength, in which manner the person in question gains more life and thus more soul.

That life is not a mere empty idea of existence, but identical with the happiness and expansion of the soul appears constantly from the Old Testament. "What man is he that desireth life and loveth many days, that he may see good?" asks the Psalmist (Ps. 34,13). The "fountain of life" is with God (Ps. 36,10); therefore man does not only live on bread, but on his words, whereby the soul of the Israelite is filled with joy. Life is all that fills the soul, makes it "wide" and full of matter. When the king asks God for life, his wish is not exhausted by being granted a long life, but it means that the king desires to become a rich and great soul, exuberantly full of strength, so that there is enough for him and his people. When the Israelites say: Live the King! (1 Sam. 10,24; 2 Sam. 16,16; 1 Kings 1,25.31.34.39; 2 Kings 11,12), then it is this kind of strength they are thinking of. The soul of the king must not sicken and shrink in weakness and misery. "The king live for ever!" they also say (1 Kings 1,31; Dan. 2,4; 3,9; 5,10; 6,7. 22). For life shows its strength in not perishing. The life of the king must be preserved through the generations in his sons.

Thus life has many forms, but also a very different substance, from the miserable who cries out from death to the king and the still stronger powers who have more life than other souls. All that operates in this world is life. The man who breeds lambs and horses "makes them live" (2 Sam. 12,3; 1 Kings 18,5). He who grows corn "makes corn live" (Hos. 14,8), because he takes care that it may thrive and grow according to its own nature. One makes an undertaking live by finishing it, elaborating it according to its special kind (Hab. 3,2). When one rebuilds a town, one makes it live (1 Chron. 11,8). As long as the stones of the town lie in ruins, they are dead, but when the town is rebuilt, they are made to live (Neh. 3,34). For life means to have a definite stamp, to work in a definite form, and the stones act according to their peculiarity, when they are being built into a wall.

Flesh is alive, as long as it is in its natural state (Lev. 13,14 ff.; 1 Sam. 2,15), and this also holds good of water. When running water is called living,[1] then it is not exactly the motion which justifies this appellation, but the fact that it is the nature of the water to be running. Time is living when it manifests itself through its contents, rain, sowing, harvest or whatever else it may be. "When this season becomes alive" (Gen. 18,14; 2 Kings 4,16.17) therefore must mean: When the season recurs in which we now find ourselves.

From all this it appears that the Israelite does not distinguish between a living and a lifeless nature. All is living which has its peculiarity and so also its faculties. A stone is not merely a lump of material substance. It is, like all living things, an organism with peculiar forces of a certain mysterious capacity, only known to him who is familiar with it. Thus, like all other beings of the earth, the stone has the quality of a soul, and so also can be made familiar with other psychical forces and filled with soul-substance. The earth is a living thing. It has its nature, with which man must make himself familiar when he wants to use it; he must respect its soul as it is, and not do violence to it while appropriating it.

Life and soul are both denominations of the many forms of existence with which the world is teeming, each possessed of its peculiar quality, of will and strength; the difference between the two ideas is the veriest nuance. The soul is life in its distinctive form; life is the strength and peculiarity formed in the soul. No wonder that the two ideas are not always kept apart in language. Just as *nephesh* is often used to denote life without defining the form it takes in the soul, so roots of words denoting life *(hyy)* are often used, where one would rather expect *nephesh.*

It is said: Yahweh my God, thou hast brought up my life from the grave (Jon. 2,7); we know numerous examples of *nephesh* being used in this context. Further: The enemy pursues my soul and overtakes it and treads down my life upon the earth (Ps. 7,6). And: my soul is sated with troubles, they have thrust my life down into Sheol (Ps. 88,4), "soul" and "life" here being synonymous. David says to Saul: Who am I, and who my life or my father's family in Israel? (1 Sam. 18,18). As it stands, "life" here means "soul", and the same holds good, even if we make a small alteration in the text and read: what is the life of my father's family?

nephesh hayyā "living soul" is a frequently occurring appellation of the whole welter of the earth. But also *ḥayyā* "the living" is used independently, as denoting the souls, chiefly of animals, though it is also used of the souls of human beings in the same manner as *nephesh.* It is said: Enemies "throw my living unto the earth" (Ps. 143,3). "His living abhorreth meat and his soul his favourite dish" (Job 33,20). "His soul draweth near unto the grave, his living to the destroyers" (Job 33,22). "He has delivered my soul from going into the pit, and my living shall see the light" (Job 33,28, cf. 36,14; 38,39). Such sayings are to us a confirmation of the indissoluble unity of the two ideas: soul and life.

The life of the soul is wide of range. The conscious thought and feeling, moving on the surface of the soul, is not by the Israelite identified with the whole soul. The will is not identical with more or less profound wishes; it is seated deeply in the actual centre of the soul and is identical with its very essence and character. Under the soul of the man, which he himself knows, there may lie another, stronger and more comprehensive; which one day suddenly bursts out and transforms an average man into a giant. Perhaps a man with a penetrating vision, a prophet, is required to call this to life; he inaugurates it, and the new soul bursts out in the man, as a flame bursts from the spark.

Thus it was with Saul. As an ordinary young man he went out one day with his father's servant to look for some asses; when he came to the seer, he was received with strange words: Samuel would tell him all that was in his heart (1 Sam. 9,19). The latent forces at the bottom of his soul were what Samuel was to call forth and to make active.[1] This happened on the following day. Samuel anointed him and kissed him and consecrated him a king. It is not an outward ceremony of a formal kind. The kingdom cannot be given to Saul, unless he has the power in himself to take it. He possesses this power, though he has not known it; the consecration makes it living and calls it forth; gradually Saul also feels it himself; it is confirmed in him through some events with which it was bound up by Samuel.

When Saul left Samuel, God changed his heart and gave him another (1 Sam. 10,9). The kingly soul which had lain dormant deep down in him, welled forth and made itself felt. The violent force of the new soul had to find a vent; when he met with a crowd of prophets, it burst into ecstasy and, drunken with enthusiasm, Saul went about among the prophets.

The narrative of the consecration of Saul shows us the close connection between the person of the old chieftain and that of the prophet. Common to both of them are the enormous forces which burst into actions, different to those of normal men. The force does not always pulsate with the same violence. It comes upon them suddenly, when the soul of power stirs within them; this we know best from the *prophets*.[2]

We learn from the books of Samuel that he who was at a later period called a prophet *(nābhī')* before that time was called a seer (1 Sam. 9,9). To see visions both asleep and awake was at all times the activity of the prophet. In so far any man might have visions as well as dreams; but the seer is specially disposed for that kind of thing and sees more deeply. He sees the context of events, and he looks right through space and time. These powers the prophet always possesses. One might go, at any time, to a man like Samuel, and against payment make him see for one, just as the Arabians might turn to their *kāhin*'s. But the forces had to be renewed, and at times they exploded violently. This happens in the ecstatic state.

We hear nothing of ecstasies in connection with Samuel or with the old Arabian *kāhin*'s, but this is undoubtedly due to the fact that we generally hear very little of them . Still the ecstatic state may have played a more or less important part in the various circles. We know that it is a well-known phenomenon among other peoples of the same kind of culture as the Israelites. The Canaanites were familiar with it; in Syria it played, during later years, a very great part, and it was particularly practised in Asia Minor within the Hittite area of culture. It is *a priori* rather probable that the stream of ecstatic phenomena spreading over the near East had received various affluents from the spring in Asia Minor.

The prophetic ecstatic state might be called forth by certain means. At the time of Saul we hear of prophets playing psalteries, tabrets, pipes and harps (1 Sam. 10,5). When King Jehoram asked Elisha for a prophetic word, the prophet caused a minstrel to be brought, and through his playing he was thrown into ecstasies (2 Kings 3,15). The Canaanite prophets performed dances, and called upon their God with short outcries, all the time cutting themselves, after their manner, with knives and lancets till the blood gushed out upon them (1 Kings 18,26-29). The latter was of rather common occurrence, for it is mentioned as the distinguishing mark of a prophet that his body is covered with wounds (Zech. 13,6), this being at the same time a result of the ecstatic state and the means to revive it. The phenomenon is known from the Attis priests of Asia Minor. Intoxicating drinks such as wine possibly played a part (Is. 28,7). The prophet sometimes goes into the solitude (1 Kings 19,8; 2 Kings 1,9); here he may sit silent or hold discourses with God. In later literature we often hear of such long prayers as the precursors of a prophetic vision (Dan. 9,21), and also fasting is sometimes mentioned as a means to prepare for an ecstatic state (Dan. 10,3).

Prophetism is generally something which must be learnt. With other peoples men possessed of such gifts often had to spend many years in fatiguing and painful attempts before they fully developed these powers. Among the Israelites we do not hear so much of this, but we know that the young rallied round an older leader, and that they experienced the ecstatic state together. This was of very common occurrence. When Ahab consulted the prophets, they all stood in ecstasy before him and spoke as with one voice (1 Kings 22,10.12). How a mental state of this kind might spread, we learn from the history of Saul. When he met the ecstatic prophets, he was himself seized by ecstasy (1 Sam. 10,10-11), naturally because he was susceptible. But that it has been considered an ordinary psychological fact appears from another story. It is told that Saul sent messengers to a crowd of prophets, one after the other; but none of them returned, because they were all seized with the ecstasy of the prophets. And Saul fared no better, when at last he came there himself. He at once began to behave ecstatically, stripping off his clothes and throwing himself on the ground, where he lay naked all that day and all that night (1 Sam. 19,19-24).

What happens in the ecstatic state is that the soul bursts its frame. The consciousness of self disappears altogether, and the violent movement in the forces of the soul find expression in strange gestures. The ecstatic utters broken, stammering exclamations (Is. 28,10.13?), his spittle falls down upon his beard, and he acts as a madman (1 Sam. 21,14). He is beset by tremblings and shakings as Daniel (10,10); he may become dumb as Daniel (10,15) or Ezekiel (3,26; 24,27; 29,21; 33,22). Perhaps he falls to the ground stunned, as Saul or Ezekiel, who lay as in bands (Ezek. 1,28; 3,25 et al.; Dan. 10,9). After his first vision Ezekiel sat for seven days staring before him (Ezek. 3,15).

Conversely, the ecstatic state may find expression in violent gestures. Elijah ran before the carriage of Ahab in the direction of Jezreel, though without knowing it (1 Kings 18,46). In violent agitation Ezekiel, after his vision, went to Tell Abịb, before he sat down like one dumbfounded (3,15); sometimes he clapped his hands and stamped his feet (6,11; 21,19). The prophet rushes about on mountains and in valleys (2 Kings 2,16). "The madmen" the prophets were called, because their behaviour appeared perfectly absurd.

If it were only arbitrariness which characterized the prophet, his experiences would be without interest, but this is by no means the view which he himself or the Israelites take of the matter. Those for whom the activity of the soul is limited to thoughts and actions in a definite plan, under the control of consciousness, will generally only look upon the ecstatic state from a negative point of view, as a suspension of the healthy life of the soul. But for the peoples to whom the soul is a large fund of forces, far larger than what lies on the surface, the ecstatic state is only an expression of the man possessing other powers than those which make themselves felt in everyday life. If the ecstatic behaves differently from other people, it is because he is filled with unusual powers which, of course, must express themselves in an unusual way.

This unusual, supernormal power is divine. The prophet says that the hand of God comes upon him (2 Kings 3,15; Ezek. 1,3; 3,14.22; 8,1; 37,1); it seizes him (Is. 8,11). But it does not mean that it is an external force guiding him. God forces him by entering into his soul and filling it; the *rūaḥ* acting in him is God's. It is called that God's spirit comes upon him (1 Sam. 10, 6.10), falls upon [1] him (Ezek. 11,5), enters into him (Ezek. 2,2; 3,24), is given in him. The most vivid expression is perhaps that God dons him like a garment (Judg. 6,34; 1 Chron. 12,19; 2 Chron. 24,20).

This is the case both with the heroes and the prophets, when ecstasy wells up in them. They receive a new soul, a divine soul acting in them. Therefore the prophets do not deliver their sayings as their own, but "Yahweh says" the words they utter; it is God who speaks through them. It is characteristic of the false prophets that they speak out of their own hearts.

Starting from these presuppositions the Israelite understands that the prophet must do strange things. The divine soul is so violent in him that it paralyzes him and throws him hither and thither. Several of the prophets have spoken thrillingly of the violent emotion which the soul of God stirs in them. Jeremiah cries: My bowels, my bowels! I am pained at the walls of my heart; my heart thrilleth in me; I cannot hold my peace (Jer. 4,19). Isaiah complains: My loins are filled with pain; pangs have taken hold upon me, as the pangs of a woman that travaileth; I broke down so that I could not see. My heart panted, fearfulness affrighted me; dawn, my yearning, has he turned into fear unto me (Is. 21,3-4). The fear of the prophet does not originate in some external thing; he feels that he is not the master of his own soul; it is commanded by another mighty soul. It is not he himself who takes his vocation; it is a burden, which is thrust upon him. "O Yahweh, thou hast beguiled me, and I was beguiled; thou hast overwhelmed me and prevailed." In these words of Jeremiah (20,7) we see the prophet's own conception of the state of his soul.

In this state, when self-consciousness is suspended and the bounds of the soul disrupted, the prophet receives his strong sensory impressions. A new world opens before him. Strange figures come and touch him. While Isaiah stood in a state of ecstasy and saw the temple filled with the glory of God, a seraph came and touched his mouth with a glowing stone (Is. 6,6). He saw Yahweh himself and his seraphs; he heard them crying one unto another, and everything was filled with a dense smoke (6,1-4). Elisha saw Elijah disappear in a chariot of fire with horses of fire (2 Kings 2,11). Another time he saw a mountain, filled with chariots and horses of fire (2 Kings 6,17). This kind of fire-phenomena often make part of the visions of the prophets (Ezek. 1; Dan. 10). The prophet sees armies approaching, sees ruin and destruction round him, all of which to him are revelations of a deeper context, out of which the events are developed.

It is not always immediately apparent what is the context revealed by the visions. That which held good of dreams also holds good here. Jeremiah sees a seething pot, and the face thereof is towards the north (Jer. 1,13); it is misfortune boiling from the north. He sees two baskets with figs, good and bad (Jer. 24); they are the two elements of which the people are composed. Amos sees a basket with summer figs, which signifies that the end of Israel is come; the connection is here a similarity of words like the one we find with Jeremiah, who sees a branch of an almond tree as evidence that he is to be a watchman.[1] It is often an external vision which calls forth the inner vision in the prophet. Elijah hears the voice of Yahweh in a faint rustle of the wind (1 Kings 19,13). But it is not necessarily so.

The Israelite always sees the strange gestures of the ecstatic in the light of what lies behind them. The state is not judged from the gestures, but the gestures from the state, from the unity of which they are the outward expression, and this agrees entirely with the whole of the fundamental Israelitic psychological conception. Together with the wild gestures we see the other results of the supernatural power: the strong vision of the prophet and the mighty deeds of the hero. It is the same divine power which makes Saul lie down on the ground crying aloud, and which makes him sally forth at the head of his men to carry home the victory from the enemy.

The state of ecstasy bears witness to the variety of the contents of the soul, in that it calls forth new elements which do not ordinarily make themselves known; it shows us the elasticity of the soul, its power to transcend and burst its limits. This power is also displayed in the vision. The prophet sends parts of his soul out through space and time.

In his vision Daniel is removed to the palace of Shushan and the river of Ulai (Dan. 8,2). It does not mean that the soul leaves the body. The soul still cleaves to the body, but part of it has been sent to far-off regions. When Gehazi, the servant of Elisha, followed the Aramæan chieftain Naaman, in order to appropriate the gift which Elisha had refused, he was on his return greeted with the words that the heart of Elisha had gone with him, when he met Naaman in the road (2 Kings 5,26). Elisha has the power to send forth his heart, i. e. his soul, and to let it take part in what happens afar. This is what we know from many other peoples.

Thus the prophets send out parts of their souls in order to watch for developing events. In Isaiah we read: Go set the watcher, let him declare what he seeth. And if he see a riding company, couples of horsemen, a riding company on asses, a riding company on camels, then let him attend diligently with much heed! — He cries: I see![1] Oh Lord, I stand continually upon the watch-tower in the daytime, and I am set in my ward whole nights. And behold, here cometh a riding company of men, with couples of horsemen. And he resumed and said: Babylon is fallen, is fallen, and all the graven images of her gods he hath broken unto the ground (Is. 21,6-9).

This text is in all probability correctly explained by the prophet sending out part of his soul as a watchman; it stands in the watch-tower, where it suddenly sees the vision which it then brings.[2] In reality this agrees well with Israelitic psychology. The experiences of Ezekiel were of a similar kind. While he sat, surrounded by the elders in his house at the river Chebar, God's hand seized him by the forelock, a spirit lifted him up between heaven and earth and led him to the temple of Jerusalem, where he saw the glory of God; and he was taken from one place to another in the temple and saw various groups of Israelitic men and women who practised non-Jewish cults. He heard God exclaim and saw the carrying out of the punishment of the infidels, and Yahweh's glory departed from the temple. "And a spirit lifted me up in the vision and led me to the exiles in Chaldæa, by the spirit of God. And the vision which I saw departed from me. And I spoke to the exiles the word of Yahweh, as he had shown it me" (Ezek. 8-11).

The scene is here very vividly described. The prophet sits in Mesopotamia, surrounded by his countrymen. He is then led towards Jerusalem, where he sees what happens; and his soul again returns to the soul seated in Mesopotamia. He had that kind of experience on several occasions. Once he was led down into a valley and saw a number of dead bones being restored to life, and another time he was led to a mountain outside Jerusalem from which he saw the town, and he was led about in the resurrected temple. On these voyages of the soul Ezekiel is accompanied by a man, sometimes by God himself, who explains to him all that he sees. Amos has the same experience; the visions he sees are constantly accompanied by speech with Yahweh. In his vision Zechariah sees an angel explaining the vision to him, and he hears

Yahweh and the angel hold converse on it. It is characteristic that this angel is called "the angel who spoke *in* me" (Zech. 2,2).

That which happens when the prophet thus sends out his soul in order to gather experiences, is the same which anyone can experience in dreams, for also the dreamer sends out his soul to the places he sees.

When the soul is thus rushing out on its own account, it may be exposed to the malice of evil-minded human beings. It is a common idea among the peoples that men and women, by means of certain manipulations, are able to lure and get wandering parts of souls into their power, thus obtaining a control over the whole of the soul and possibly killing it. Examples of this occur in various parts of the world, and it seems as if we also have an example of this with the Israelites. Ezekiel 13,17-21 [1] reads as follows:

Likewise, thou son of man, set thy face against the daughters of thy people, which prophesy out of their own heart; and prophesy thou against them. And say: Thus saith the Lord Yahweh: Woe to the women that sow bands on all wrists and veils(?) upon the head of every stature to hunt souls. Ye hunt the souls from my people, and make souls alive for yourselves. And ye pollute me before my people for handfuls of barley and for pieces of bread, in that ye slay souls that should not die and save souls alive that should not live, by your lying to my people that hear your lies. Wherefore thus saith the Lord Yahweh: Behold, I am against your bands, wherewith ye hunt souls...[2] and will tear them from your arms, and will let the souls go, the souls that ye hunt, souls to... Your veil also will I tear and deliver my people out of your hand, and they shall be no more in your hand to be hunted; and ye shall know that I am Yahweh.

What it is these women do, is not quite clear, but it seems as though by their wiles they pursue and kill souls for payment. Another question is then what it means that they make souls alive for themselves. It probably means that they use their tricks to hurt some and to favour others.

The soul is thus not sharply defined regarding space. It has its centre, and from this it extends so far as it works and makes itself felt. When a man sends word across the land, then his soul is in it and works directly in the souls.

Therefore, a human being cannot be isolated, as this is contrary to its disposition. It must act, i. e. act on others and itself be acted upon by others; in that manner the souls are brought into real contact with each other. This openness towards other souls, or this pliability is part of the fundamental character of the soul, and for that the soul is created; when being born it exists only as a link in an organism, the family. And life consists in constantly renewed combinations with souls.

Between those who are thus connected there is a mutual interchange of strength of soul. Friends receive from each other, father from son, disciple from master. The strength in the one may be handed over to the other. Elisha asked to be given two-thirds of Elijah's spirit, and this was granted him (2 Kings 2,9.15). In the same manner some of the spirit of Moses was taken and handed over to the seventy elders, and it had at once such a strong effect that they were seized by ecstasy (Num. 11,17.25). Also before Moses died, he transferred by the imposition of hands some of the contents of his soul to Joshua (Num. 27,20).

When souls are united, they get a common will and thus form a psychic unity. The mutual point of gravity lies in the whole. Totalities of this kind are constantly created. When the Israelite confronts an assembly of human beings, who to him at that moment are impressed with one character, then he considers them a unit. The word *nephesh* rarely occurs in the plural, because souls which are together are generally taken as a unit. Abraham says to those from whom he buys his burying place: If it be "with your soul" that I should bury my dead... (Gen. 23,8), because the owners of this piece of ground in his eyes are as one person. The discontented Israelites say: Our soul is dried away (Num. 11, 6) and: Our soul loathes this light bread (Num. 21,5), because they are in the same condition and, at that moment, of one character. When confronting Yahweh the Israelites therefore always say "our soul": "Our soul waiteth for Yahweh" (Ps.

33,20), "Our soul is bowed down to the dust" (Ps. 44,26), just as they are to lay his law in "their heart and in their soul" (Deut. 11,18).

When in his formation of ideas the Israelite, as we have seen, starts from the general, the whole, it thus closely corresponds with the nature of the soul. It is partly an entirety in itself and partly forms an entirety with others. What entireties it is merged in, depends upon the constant interchange of life. There are those who are determined by a purely momentary situation. "Might your soul be in my soul's stead", says Job to his friends (Job 16,4); in their relation to him they form a unity, but then it is only a passing state.

Every time the soul merges into a new entirety, new centres of action are formed in it; but they are created by temporary situations, only lie on the surface and quickly disappear. There are other entireties to which the soul belongs, and which live in it with quite a different depth and firmness, because they make the very nucleus of the soul. Thus there may be a difference between the momentary and the stable points of gravity in the soul. But none of the momentary centres of action can ever annul or counteract those which lie deeper.

The deepest-lying contents of the soul are, it is true, always there, but they do not always make themselves equally felt. In the great moments, when the man is to act in the highest sense of the word, his soul is shaken, his feeling penetrates into the remotest corner of his soul and makes the whole of its contents present. Then all momentary centres of will disappear; the man is completely himself; all the powers of the soul are concentrated and act completely together. The proper pride swells; the man lays the whole of his mental capacity and strength into the action he creates. In such moments it is felt what it is that fills the soul of the man and, in the deepest sense of the word, creates its contents.

The soul is thus unlimited in more than one dimension, i. e. both in breadth and in depth, in space and in time. Starting from its centre it acts in the family, in the friends, in its works, and if we seek to the bottom of it, then, before we are aware of it, we pass from the soul of the individual into the family, from which it has sprung.

The close connection between the soul and all that originates in it, is the presupposition of the strong power of the *word*. This *power* does not consist in the word being something purely material, acting by its very existence in the same manner as a projectile. On the contrary, the power of the word consists entirely in its mental essence.

The word is the form of vesture of the contents of the soul, its bodily expression. Behind the word stands the whole of the soul which created it. If he who utters a word is a strong soul, then the word expresses more reality than a weak soul can put into it; for reality is only another expression for the ability to maintain oneself, to realize. He who utters a word to another lays that which he has created in his own soul into that of the other, and here then must it act with the whole of the reality it contains. He who speaks good words to another, creates something good in his soul, and he who speaks evil words, creates unhappiness in his soul.

When an Israelite pronounces blessings on another, then these are not empty though kindly wishes for the future. With the words: Thou art blessed! and: Thou art cursed! he has created a blessing or a curse in his soul, and laid it into that of the other. If the blessing be strong, then it will show its real power by growing and expanding. But it is not only when this happens and the fruits are gathered that it comes into existence. It is there at the same moment that it has been planted in the soul. If the blessing does not grow and expand, then it may be because the soul that received it did not possess the power to absorb it, but it may also be because the word was only a "lip-word" (2 Kings 18,20; Prov. 14,23), a body without soul, an empty case, in that there was not behind it a soul which might lend to it life and strength. It is therefore in full agreement with the general view when the Israelites, by the verbal form denoting the causative, do not distinguish between *making* a man into something and *saying* that he is so.

Thus no distinction is made between the word and the matter

described, and consequently the Hebrew denominations of a word may just as well apply to the matter. This holds good both of *dbr* and *'mr*. The most ordinary term for "word", *dābhār,* also implies an action, that which happens, the event with all that it implies (Gen. 15,1; 22,20); it is said: make a *dābhār* (Gen. 20,10; 22,16; 44,7). Abraham's servant who returned with Rebekah told Isaac "all the *d*ᵉ*bhārīm* he had made" (Gen. 24,66); it means all he had said, done, heard and experienced. The word means an affair, a matter and all the circumstances attached to it. It is used in a perfectly concrete manner about that which is. When Yahweh killed the cattle of the Egyptians, not *dābhār* of that of the Israelites was killed (Exod. 9,4). In the same manner *'ōmer* is used (Job 22,28): if you decide *'ōmer,* it shall be established unto thee.[1]

For the Israelites there is upon the whole no difference whatsoever between the idea, the name and the matter itself, and this is also implied by what has been said of the idea. It is not an abstraction, but the very reality underlying the momentary manifestations; and it is wholly in all that belongs to it, both in the detail, in the name and the idea.

The soul may manifest itself in other ways than in words. It may manifest itself in the expression of the face. An evil glance has the same effect as a verbal curse, and is equally feared, just as the soul is warmed and strengthened by friendly glances. And that which fills the soul may express itself in what we might call *secondary actions,* of the kind frequently attempted by the prophets.

One of the prophets whom Ahab consulted went about butting with a horn of iron, thus implying the victory of the king over the Aramæans. Isaiah went about naked and barefoot for three years, which signified that the Assyrians should thus be dragged away naked and barefoot (Is. 20,2-3). Jeremiah put on bands and yokes, which meant that Judah and the other smaller West-Asiatic states should subject themselves to the king of Babylon (Jer. 27). When he was in Egypt, he took great stones and hid them near Pharaoh's house, and upon these stones Nebuchadnezzar should set his throne and thus plunder the land of Egypt (Jer. 43). With a whole artillery Ezekiel once laid siege against a tile, upon which he had portrayed the city of Jerusalem (Ezek. 4). In the same manner the marriage of Hosea with a faithless woman was to express the relation of Yahweh to his people. And he named his children by names such as Want-Grace and Not-my-People, which should be of importance for the destiny of the people, in the same manner as when Isaiah named his children by names such as Quick-Spoil and Lightning-Plunder. The weight attached to this kind of incident appears from the circumstantial manner in which the whole thing was done. First Isaiah, in the presence of witnesses, wrote the name of the child on a tablet; then his wife conceived, and when the child was born, it was called by this significant name.

These actions may be called symbolic, but they are more than images. Their significance is analogous with that of the dream-images and depends upon the context of the events. When, e. g., Isaiah walks about barefoot, it means that the Assyrians are to be carried away barefoot. This must be understood in the way that the event, i. e. the carrying off of the Assyrians, is present and lies latent in the souls out of which it is to be created. Thus it also lies in the soul of Isaiah, and the fact that he himself walks about barefoot is a parallel manifestation of this barefoot carrying-off. But by energetically maintaining such a secondary manifestation of the carrying-off, he maintains the latter, because there is an indissoluble connection between the individual case and the whole. The same construction must be put upon all the other actions.

Such actions or things which point beyond themselves to an underlying context, the Israelite calls *token, 'ōth* or *mōphēth;* the latter of these words is, however, only used of events. The rainbow, the circumcision, the sabbath are tokens carrying the covenant in them. A cord in a window (Josh. 2,12) may be a token. A stone may be a token of a compact between human beings (Gen. 31) or with God (Josh. 24,27). An unusual event is a sign indicating an underlying mighty power of the soul (Exod. 4,8.9.17 ff.; 7,3; Deut. 4,34 et al.). The signs or tokens are realities; they are not naked things nor facts which are nothing but symbols or indications of some underlying element. The contents of the soul are manifested in them and fill them. If one spoils the token, then its mental implication is broken.

He who can penetrate to the bottom and see through the contexts can also see the tokens bearing upon them. The birth of the child Immanuel is a token (Is. 7,11.14), a secondary outcome of the misery of Israel, lying ready to break forth. The token does not need to be anything very particular. As a token of the greatness of his soul Saul is to meet various persons on his way (1 Sam. 10,1-7). It becomes a token, because it refers to a context, which is seen and established by the sharp prophetic vision of Samuel, who has descried it at a distance. When Gideon prays that the dew may fall in a different manner on a woollen blanket than on the ground around it, then he also therein finds a token, a secondary effect of the underlying divine power, which likewise puts the victory into his soul (Judg. 6,17).

All this implies a conception of the body different from the one we hold, and it agrees with all that we have already observed. To the mind in question nothing is in itself lifeless, but everything has the character of a soul and must therefore be susceptible to the contents of a soul. A stone may be full of strength as well as a staff. Elisha laid his strength into his staff and gave it to Gehazi, who was to go to Shunem with it and by this means heal a young man (2 Kings 4,29). A similar strength lay in the staff of Moses.

All that the man possesses and that belongs to his sphere is penetrated by his soul; this holds good of that which is nearest to his body, his clothes; it holds good of his tools, his house, his animals, the whole of his property.

In the mantle of Elijah there was such a strength that with it he could divide the waters of Jordan, and when Elijah had disappeared, Elisha was able to do the same (2 Kings 2,8.14). A little box or case could be filled with soul, from the strength of which the owner draws.[1]

This corporeal conception is confirmed when we observe in details the Israelitic idea of soul and body.

The Israelites are quite able to distinguish between soul and body, as when Isaiah says: He shall consume both soul and flesh

(10,18). But no distinction is made between them as two fundamental forms of existence. The flesh is the weaker, as the grass which withers and disappears; the soul is the stronger. The soul is more than the body, but the body is a perfectly valid manifestation of the soul.

When in the story of the creation it is told that God breathed the spirit of life into the man of clay he had moulded, it must not be construed in the manner that the clay is the body, the spirit of God the soul, which is seated and acts within the body. The man of clay was a dead thing, but by the breath of God he was entirely changed and became a living soul. Soul and body are so intimately united that a distinction cannot be made between them. They are more than "united": the body is the soul in its outward form.

If the soul is life, then it is closely united with the physical breath. We would express it thus that the breath is the condition of life. But the Israelite does not in this manner distinguish between life and its conditions or manifestations. Here his fundamental law always holds good, viz. the whole acts through all the details. All that pertains to the life of the soul, *is* the soul, and this more particularly must hold good of its most important functions.

Therefore the *breath* is the soul. It may just as well be said that God created "breath" as that he created "spirits" or "souls" (Is. 57,16). When the Israelites conquered Canaan, "they smote by ban all the souls that were therein with the edge of the sword, neither was any breath left" (Josh. 11,11 cf. 14; 10,40; Deut. 20,16). In the same manner the family of Jeroboam was destroyed; "no breath" was left to Jeroboam (1 Kings 15,29), and the last verse of the Book of Psalms reads: Let every breath praise Yahweh (Ps. 150,6).

The Hebrews consistently maintain that the breath is the soul entirely. It is the breath that thinks: "The breath of man is the candle of Yahweh searching all the inward parts of the belly" (Prov. 20,27). Job asks Bildad: How hast thou counselled him that hath no wisdom? and how hast thou plentifully declared sound wisdom? To whom hast thou uttered words? and whose breath came forth from thee? (26,4). The breath is here the wise, acting soul which makes good counsel. Quite naturally it is therefore said that it is the breath of God which gives life (Job 33,4), just as it gives wisdom (Job 32,8).

In the same manner it must be understood, when the *heart* has become one of the principal denominations of the soul, life being particularly bound up in its functions. From the heart life issues. We would admit that, if it were a question of physical life only. But to the ancients the whole of the life of the soul is a unity. When the Israelite speaks of the heart, it is not so that he first thinks of the bit of flesh within his body, and then "metaphorically" of the activities of the soul which he is likely to connect with it. The heart, it is true, is a bit of flesh, but it is always filled with life, the central element of man and beast, indissolubly connected with the entirety of the soul. Ezekiel says that Yahweh will take out the stony hearts of the Israelites and give them a heart of flesh, that they may keep his ordinances (Ezek. 11,19; 36,26). Here we see how the normal life of the soul is connected with the heart in its very function as a heart of flesh. The Israelite cannot think of the heart without at the same time considering the entirety: all life connected with its activity. Like any other part of the body the heart is not entirely material. Therefore the Israelite can say that the heart of flesh thinks and acts.

Also the *blood* is the soul. Life is very closely connected with this red fluid which runs through the body; if it runs out, life itself runs out. The connection may be expressed by the soul being *in* the blood: "The soul of the flesh is in the blood" (Lev. 17,11), and also from another point of view the blood belongs to the soul, is in it (Gen. 9,5; Jer. 2,34). But as a rule it is said that the soul *is* the blood, or the blood is the soul: "But flesh with the life thereof which is the blood thereof, shall ye not eat" (Gen. 9,4); "the soul of all flesh is the blood thereof" (Lev. 17,14). "The blood is the soul", says the law deliberately (Deut. 12,23).

As the blood so also the *bones,* the solid frame of the body. If the bones are strong and firm, then the soul is strong; it manifests itself just as well in them as in the heart or any other vital organ. Therefore the bones are the soul. They are vexed and tremble (Ps 6,3; Job 4,14); they rejoice (Ps. 51,10); they praise Yahweh (Ps.

35,10). When the man is weak, rottenness enters into his bones (Hab. 3,16); the bones are consumed and paralyzed (Ps. 31,11; 32,3); they are dissolved, as it is said of the marrow that it wears away (Ps. 32,4), and of the heart that it is broken (Jer. 23,9).

The bodily sensations are felt right through the soul. To drink and eat is good for the soul; it fills and "sustains" it. He who goes without food afflicts the soul (Lev. 16,29.31; 23,27.32; Num. 29,7; Is. 58,3.5.10). And, on the other hand, that which particularly pertains to the soul is felt in the body. When the heart has been considered so significant as to be used synonymously with the soul, it is probably not only because the Israelite knows the importance of the heart to life, but because he instinctively felt the movements of the soul in the beats of his heart.

The feelings are like a gnawing anxiety in the *bowels*. "My bowels, my bowels, I am pained at the walls of my heart!" cries Jeremiah (4,19).[1] The bowels *(mēʿīm, raḥᵃmīm, ḳerebh, beṭen)* roar like waves in violent motion, whether for terror (Is. 16,11) or pity (Jer. 31,20) or anger (Is. 16,11), or when the woman in love feels the presence of the beloved (Cant. 5,4). They "ferment" (Lam. 1,20; 2,11) or "boil" (Job 30,27) with the person in despair. The words of the tale-barer go down into the innermost parts of the belly (Pr. 18,8; 26,22). All mental activity is exercised by them. The bowels think (Is. 19,3), form plans and make counsels (Ps. 5,10), are full of wisdom (1 Kings 3,28).

The bowels remember the law (Ps. 40,9), and the belly preserves the wisdom (Prov. 22,18), for the belly is identical with the soul. The Psalmist says: Our soul is bowed down to the dust, our belly cleaveth unto the earth (Ps. 44,26) or: Mine eye is consumed with grief, yea, my soul and my belly (Ps. 31,10). When the belly is weak, the soul is weak, and when the soul is weak, the belly is weak.

The person in despair feels as if pricked in his *reins* (Ps. 73, 21); he feels as if there is an invisible arrow in them (Lam. 3,13) and that they are cleaved asunder (Job 16,13). In great pain the reins are consumed (Job 19,27),[2] and therefore the reins are the soul. They rejoice (Pr. 23,16), instruct the man (Ps. 16,7). Heart and reins are often mentioned together as appellations of the soul, its essence and its function. He who knows souls is he who examines and tests reins and heart (Jer. 11,20; 17,10; 20,12; Ps. 7,10; 26,2; Pr. 17,3; 21,2). It is the whole of the soul, not a special part or aspect of it, which is denominated by reins. When Jeremiah says of his enemies that God is "near in their mouth, and far from their reins" (Jer. 12,2), then it means that their soul has nothing to do with God. And the Psalmist, who, wondering, thinks how God created him, says: For thou hast possessed my reins; thou hast covered me in my mother's womb (Ps. 139,13).

Also the *liver* may be mentioned as a denomination of the soul, though not so frequently as with the Assyrians or Arabians. In the Lamentations we read: My liver is poured out upon the earth (2,11), which reminds us of other manners of expressing dissolution of soul. [1]

It is not only in the inner parts of the body that the soul expresses itself. It is manifested in the whole carriage of the body. The strong soul treads firmly upon the ground, has solid and well-knit limbs. The weak and timid soul has "a melting heart and the knees smite together" (Nah. 2,11). He has "feeble hands" as Ishbaal when Abner was killed (2 Sam. 4,1); thus men are going to fare when the hostile armies pour into the country (Jer. 6,24, cf. Is. 13,7). Ezekiel, who is particularly rich in violent terms for the dissolution of the soul, says: When they say unto thee: Wherefore sighest thou? thou shalt answer: For the tidings; because it cometh, and every heart shall melt, and all hands shall be feeble, and every spirit shall faint, and all knees shall be weak as water (Ezek. 21,12, cf. 7,17). When all becomes well again, the feeble hands will be strengthened and the trembling knees gain power (Is. 35,3, cf. Ezek. 22,14).

In the *head* the soul is prominent. It bears honour, as it bears disgrace or, upon the whole, responsibility. A crime comes over the head of a man when he bears the responsibility of it (Ezek. 9,10; 11,21; 16,43 et al.). To be the keeper of a man's head (1 Sam. 28,2) is the same as to guard his life. "A man's head" is the same as a man.

The soul shows more particularly in the face and its expression. When the soul is healthy and strong, the *eyes* are shining and bright. The man who is faint and has lost his strength complains that the light of his eyes is gone from him (Ps. 38,11). The eye is dulled and consumed; it fails (Deut. 28,65; Ps. 6,8; Lam. 4,17). The eyes of the hungry when eating are enlightened (1 Sam. 14,27. 29); the same effect has the commandment of the Lord on the pious (Ps. 19,9). Ezra begs God that he may make them alive and enlighten their eyes.

Through the eyes one can read the soul and know whether it contains something good or something bad (Jer. 21,10; 24,6; 44, 11; Am. 9,4). The envious has an evil eye (Pr. 23,6; 28,22), the benevolent a good eye (Pr. 22,9); the proud has "high eyes" (Ps. 18,28; Pr. 6,17, cf. Is. 10,12). Therefore the eye is also an expression of the soul. The eye desires that which it sees and which pleases it (1 Kings 20,6; Ezek. 24,16.21.25; Lam. 2,4). The eye may mock at his father and despise to obey his mother (Pr. 30,17). The eye is full of anxiety for the loss of any property (Gen. 45, 20). It is the eye that spares the enemy and forgives (Deut. 7,16; 13,9; 19,13.21; Is. 13,18; Ezek. 5,11; 7,4.9 et al.).

The angry snorts; the "breath of the nostrils" is therefore an expression of anger (Job. 4,9); in fact nose and anger become identical terms.

The soul and its moods are reflected in the *face*. It becomes jaundiced in fright (Jer. 30,6) and red in terror (Is. 13,8; Joel 2,6; Nah. 2,11), but also in anger it becomes as flames, and flame *(ḥārōn)* becomes the term denoting anger, whereas redness *(ḳin'ā)* is used to designate indignation. He who sees a man's face sees his soul. If the face be stiff or hard, then the soul is unbending (Ezek. 2,4), perhaps even brazen (Deut. 28,50). If the face is ill-favoured, then all is not well with the soul; it is sad, angry (Gen. 40,7; Pr. 25,23). But if the face is pleasant, then the soul is good and spacious. "A merry heart maketh a cheerful countenance; but by sorrow of the heart the spirit is broken" (Pr. 15,13).

The Power may be particularly concentrated in individual parts of the body. The strength of Samson was bound up with his hair. Through the bodily touch strength is transferred. Elisha restored to life the son of the Shunammite by stretching himself upon the child (2 Kings 4, 32-35).

All of these examples show how the Israelite sees the soul manifesting itself in the body. It bears witness to his psychological observation and his sense of reality. He concludes not from the movements of the body to an underlying soul, which uses and moves the body, but in the activity of the soul he sees the soul itself. When, e. g., a man looks at something, then the eye at that moment is the particularly active part of the soul, but this activity includes the whole of the soul, just as it reacts upon the whole of the contents of the soul. Therefore the soul *is* at that moment eye.

When considering all this we are face to face with the consequence that flesh is soul, or rather that the soul may be flesh, and this in reality is the exact exposition of the Israelitic manner of thinking. Like the souls of animals and all other created beings, the soul of man is a soul of flesh. Are there then souls which are not flesh? Yes, the divine souls. This does not mean that God is without a body, a reasoning so subtle as that being far from the Israelite. Every soul must have a body, a form in which it lives. But the divine beings are not made of the same fragile substance as man. They have more soul, and the more soul the less flesh, for flesh is only a weak form of soul. Flesh and soul are not contrasts as two absolutely different forms of existence; but they are contrasts, in so far as the one stands highest, the other lowest in the graduated forms of life. At the top stand soul and strength, at the bottom flesh and weakness.

Starting from these presuppositions we understand what is said in the Old Testament of flesh and spirit. No contrast is ever hinted at as existing within the individual between the weak flesh and the strong soul. When mention is made of a contrast between flesh and soul or spirit, then it is man or creation at large, which, wholly flesh, is contrasted with the superhuman souls, in particular with God. Thus it is said: Now the Egyptians are men, and not God; and their horses flesh and not spirit (Is. 31,3). Or in a psalm: In God have I put my trust, I will not fear what flesh can do unto me (Ps. 56,5).

Man is flesh and therefore cannot set himself up against God; it is foolish to trust in man instead of in God. "Cursed be the man that trusteth in man, and maketh flesh his arm, and whose heart departeth from Yahweh" (Jer. 17,5). God has not eyes of flesh or seeth not as man seeth (Job 10,4). If he had eyes of flesh he would have a soul of flesh and make weak counsel as the soul of man. The fact that the souls of men are flesh is why the soul of God cannot commune directly with them. But, on the other hand, it is the idea that man "is but flesh, a breath that passeth away and cometh not again" which rouses the pity of God and makes him forgive his sins (Ps. 78,39). Here we meet thoughts which particularly refer us to later Israel; but that which is of special interest to us, viz. the fundamental psychological view, is the same as in the early days.

Just as the Israelite mentions the heart or the bones or other parts of the body, he also mentions the flesh when he is thinking of the human entirety, or in other words the soul. "My soul longeth, yea, even fainteth for the courts of Yahweh; my heart and my flesh crieth out for the living God," says one of the psalmists (Ps. 84,3) and another: "My soul thirsteth for thee, my flesh longeth for thee in a dry and thirsty land" (Ps. 63,2). Job says of him who lies on his sick-bed: Only *his* flesh hath pain within him, and *his* soul mourneth within him (Job 14,22).

In exactly the same manner we must understand the well-known verse of the psalm: Therefore my heart is glad, and my glory rejoiceth; indeed my flesh shall rest in safety. For thou wilt not leave my soul in Sheol, neither wilt thou suffer thy devoted to see the grave (Ps. 16,9-10). Here there is no contrast between the soul which rejoices and is saved from the grave, and the body that lives in safety. Heart, honour, soul, flesh are different manifestations of the same, the whole of man, the happy man who trusts in God that he may have life and joy, not misfortune, disease, death, all that is combined in the denomination: the grave or the realm of the dead.

Therefore we sometimes find Israelitic authors mentioning the flesh, where we would consider it more natural to mention the soul, as when, for instance, the Preacher warns against letting "thy mouth cause thy flesh to sin" (5,5), or when the Proverbs say that an indulgent heart is "life to the beings of flesh"[1] (Prov. 14,30) or that his exhortations are life to those who find them, health to all their flesh (4,22). It does not mean that they cure diseases of the body, but that they give life to the whole person. And when in the law it is said that "the flesh which hath boils on its skin" (Lev. 13,18) is to go and be shown to the priest, then it does not only mean a body, but a person in his entirety, a soul. All such sayings are no more peculiar than those which mention the heart as thinking and acting.

"All flesh" means all souls which are displayed in bodies of flesh, i. e. weak, perishable souls. The term includes both human beings, animals and, though it is not expressly stated anywhere, surely also plants and whatever else that is weak and perishable.

The Israelitic view as regards the relation between body and soul, which in its fundamental features is the same as with other peoples, remote from European culture, it is difficult for us to recreate or re-experience, because we are always operating with sharply defined dimensions. The relation between soul and body we prefer to imagine as two circles which either do not touch at all or overlap slightly. And when we hear that in the eyes of the Israelites the body belongs to the soul, we would perhaps be apt to make this clear to ourselves by letting the soul be represented by a limited diagram, e. g. a circle, while the body forms a section of it. But this would be at variance with the Israelitic view. The soul is not a closely defined whole. It is a force, acting through all its parts. The whole of the soul is in the reins, in the heart, in the flesh, just as, on the other hand, the flesh stamps the whole of the character of the soul.

Consequently we must not consider as materialistic the Israelitic view of the relation between soul and body. We must bear in mind how the proposition that the soul of man is flesh, is indissolubly connected with the converse, i. e. that flesh is soul. Flesh is volition, action, goodness — all that to us is most obviously contrasted with the material. If we imagine a man in a moment of action, e. g. a king who kills his enemy, then it is his right hand that performs the act. In this right hand lies at that moment the entire soul of the king: its glory and might, its hatred and cruelty and all that otherwise goes to make a warlike royal soul.

When the soul can be said to be entirely in the body, it consequently does not mean a spacial limitation. As we have seen, the intimate relation between body and soul does not exclude the manifestation of the soul outside the body, at the same time that it manifests itself within it.

When we have thoroughly realized the relation between body and soul, then we also understand what it means to have one flesh, or to have common bones and flesh or blood. If members of one family have common flesh, then they also have community of soul. Their life bears a common impress. It appears from their flesh, the features reveal their common character; and it makes itself felt through their actions, which are stamped by a definite will and definite powers.

The father's house makes one soul. It has its centre in the man, but acts in all the members of the family through the common character and will. As far as the common impress extends, so far the psychic community pervades. But the impress may change with changing conditions. Each of the fathers' houses makes a special soul in contrast with the others; but still they bear a common impress formed through the common history, and this common soul, the people's soul, is nearly as deeply seated as the soul of the family. In moments of great distress it may become dominating. The Israelite has cultic feasts which strengthen the family soul, and others which strengthen the people's soul in him.

When *death* occurs, then it is the soul that is deprived of life. Death cannot strike the body or any other part of the soul without striking the entirety of the soul. Therefore it is also said to "kill a soul" or "smite a soul" (Num. 31,19; 35,15.30; Josh. 20,3.9); it may also be called to "smite one as regards the soul", i. e. to smite one so that the soul is killed (Gen. 37,21; Deut. 19,6.11; Jer. 40, 14.15; with *rāṣaḥ* Deut. 22,26). There can be no doubt that it is the soul which dies, and all theories attempting to deny this fact are false. It is deliberately said both that the soul dies (Judg. 16,30; Num. 23,10 et al.), that it is destroyed or consumed (Ez. 22,25.27), and that it is extinguished (Job 11,20).

Sometimes it may be said that the soul departs when it dies (Gen. 35,18), just as it is said that the soul returns when it is revived (1 Kings 17,21-22). But such expressions do not imply that death consists in the departure of the soul from the body, so that the soul is untouched, but only goes elsewhere. How would it be possible to reconcile an idea of this kind with the quotations given above? Both soul and body lose their lives at the same time, because they are a unity.

To lose one's life means the same as to lose one's strength, one's potentiality. Therefore death is most appropriately described as an emptying out. "He has emptied out his soul unto death", it is said of the suffering martyr (Is. 53,12). As it is possible to be more or less alive, so one is also able to be more or less dead. When Nabal heard of the danger to which he had been exposed, on account of his unwise behaviour towards David, "his heart dies within him" (1 Sam. 25,37). The paralysis affecting his heart was incipient death, which was accomplished when shortly afterwards he passed away entirely. We have seen how the diseased and miserable man says that he is already in death.

The dead is a soul bereft of strength. Therefore the dead are called "the weak" *(r^{e}phā'īm)*.[1] "Now thou art become weak" is the greeting with which the fallen king of the Babylonians is received in the realm of the dead (Is. 14,10). The weakness of the dead appears in that they peep and mutter (Is. 8,19; 29,4). The dead is still a soul, but a soul that has lost its substance and strength: it is as a misty vapour or a shadow.

Even after death the soul still maintains its intimate relation with the body. The dead body is still the soul. It is a law among the Nazarites that they are not allowed to defile themselves for the dead as long as they are in their consecrated state; it is expressed by their not being permitted to come near the "soul of one dead" (Num. 6,6). In the same manner the priest is forbidden to defile himself for the souls of his relations, except those nearest to him (Lev. 21,1.11, cf. 19,28; Num. 5,2; 9,6.7.10).

As long as the body is a body, the soul is closely connected with it. That which is done to the body is done to the soul. When the worms gnaw the dead body, the soul feels it (Job 14,22; Is.

66,24). Therefore the mutilation of dead bodies has a particularly horrible effect. The Philistines practised this on Saul, cutting off his head and hanging up his body (1 Sam. 31,9.10). When the murderers of Ishbaal came to David, their hands and feet were cut off after they had been killed, and their bodies were hung up (2 Sam. 4,12). A man takes the head of his enemy with him (1 Sam. 17,54), thus maintaining mastery over his soul.

When the body is flung on fields or roads, there is a danger that birds or other animals may defile it and thus also the soul. This was the case with Jezebel (2 Kings 9,10), and Jeremiah threatens that the same fate will overtake the whole of the people (Jer. 16,4). A most pathetic example of a mother's love is given in the history of Saul. When his sons, who had been delivered for blood-feud, lay cast abroad on the fields, their mother Rizpah covered them and defended them, and this she did from autumn unto spring against the birds of the air and the beasts of the field, until David took the matter in hand (2 Sam. 21,10-14). The complete destruction of the dead body which takes place when it is burnt, the Israelite only knows in such cases where a soul is to be utterly destroyed (Gen. 38,24; Lev. 20,14; 21,9; Josh. 7,25; 2 Kings 23,16-18; Am. 2,1).

When the body is laid down into the grave together with the fathers, the soul is at rest there; here it is at home, and here it is safe. If it is not laid in the grave, it is anxious and rushes about restlessly. The soul is not quite tied to the dead, as it is not even tied to the living. At the same time that it is in the grave, it may appear on earth and interfere with the fate of the survivors.

Such a soul *(ʾōbh)* may be called forth by means of secret arts. We have one well-known example of this, viz. the raising up of the soul of Samuel by the witch of Endor (1 Sam. 28). Upon the whole there is sufficient testimony to the use of this manner of communicating with the souls of the dead, even though other currents, tending in an opposite direction, made themselves felt among the Israelites.

THE BLESSING

The soul is a whole saturated with power. It is the same power which acts in the centre and far out in the periphery, as far as the soul extends. It makes the soul grow and prosper, in order that it may maintain itself and do its work in the world. This vital power, without which no living being can exist, is called by the Israelites *b^erākhā,* blessing. The Israelite does not distinguish between the power, as it acts in the soul, and as it manifests itself outwardly. For him the capacity and the result is the same: where the capacity exists, the result of its action is a matter of course. The blessing, therefore, means at the same time something internal and something external. Blessing is the inner strength of the soul and the happiness it creates.

The blessing may be stronger or weaker and, according to the different peculiarities of the souls, it may be of an entirely different kind. When the welter of souls is so diverse, then it is because a different blessing has been laid into the different kinds of souls. When God had created all the animals in the sea and the winged beings under heaven, he blessed them and thus gave them strength to maintain their kind, as he had made them (Gen. 1,22). And he blessed man, male and female, giving them the power to multiply and to have dominion over all creation (Gen. 1,28; 5,2).

Every Israelitic tribe has its peculiar characteristic. Judah is the ruler, rich in victory and fertility; Asher lives on the fat of the land; Issachar has settled among strange tribes and become a servant unto tribute, etc. It all originates in the fact that a different blessing has been put into each of them. To Levi has been given the blessing of forming the priestly caste, ministering to the holy oracle and serving in the sanctuary; and he received this blessing, because he was more eager than others to crush those who worshipped Yahweh after the Canaanite fashion, against the traditions of Israel (Exod. 32,29). The sabbath is blessed above all other days; therefore ordinary work cannot be performed on it (Exod. 20,11, cf. Gen. 2,3). All that has the vitality, also has the blessing, for the blessing is the life-power. We learn by chance how it was said, when juice was found in the grape: Destroy it not, for a blessing is in it (Is. 65,8). It is the blessing of the grape to contain juice, just as it is the blessing of the kneading-trough to be full of dough.

There are people who succeed in everything they undertake, others who fail in everything. There is in so far nothing strange in this. But for the old Israelites this was not a matter of chance. It depended upon the blessing of the man, but this again implies that it depended upon some gift or capability of the man himself; with that his outward fate becomes a matter of course. It is the conception of the soul which manifests itself in this.

To a man's psychic totality belongs the whole of his sphere, everything that surrounds him. If the soul is strong, then it must leave its impress on all his undertakings. The blessing is felt in the *counsel* of the man, thus already implying his action. He has the strength with which to fill it, and he makes good counsel, which persists. The counsel of the blessed is attended willingly.

To make strong counsel must be in the power of the chief and the king. He must have sufficient blessing, both for himself and his people. The counsellor is the same as the ruler. "Is there no king in thee, is thy counsellor perished?" asks Micah (4,9). It is he who lays the plans and creates the actions on behalf of the people (Is. 1,26; 3,3; Job 3,14). The looked-for ideal king is to be called "Wonderful-Counsellor" (Is. 9,5). It does not mean that he has good counsels to suggest to others, but that he may conceive the good counsels for the whole of his community. A soul of "counsel and might" shall act within him (Is. 11,2).

In order to be able to conceive good counsel, the king employs the help of others. His is the responsibility and honour, but others contribute towards creating the good counsel in his soul. The king is surrounded by men who are blessed with a special blessing, i. e. to assist with counsel. We know it from the history of David. When, during the rising of Absalom, he fled from the capital, barefoot and weeping, Hushai came to him in order to accompany him, but David asks him to go back and make believe to join Absalom in order to break the counsel of Ahithophel (2 Sam. 15,34). David did not know what Ahithophel counselled, but he knew that he was blessed with the blessing of conceiving counsel; he was the man to be broken. As soon as David heard that Ahithophel was among the followers of Absalom, he exclaimed: Turn the counsel of Ahithophel into foolishness, Yahweh (2 Sam. 15,31). For it is said that the counsel of Ahithophel was as if a man had enquired at the oracle of God (16,23).

The blessing of David was stronger than that of Ahithophel and Absalom. Yahweh confused the soul of Absalom so that he preferred the counsel of Hushai to that of Ahithophel, and this sealed his fate. Yahweh was not with his soul; therefore he must act as a fool and conceive counsel which could not be carried into effect. Misfortune did not strike him from without, but in the centre of his soul; it was he himself who created it. And he must inevitably involve Ahithophel in his fall. When the latter saw his counsel falling dead, he at once saddled his ass and rode home, where he put his house in order and hanged himself. It was not necessary for him to wait until Absalom had lost his fight against David. At the same moment that his counsel was broken, he himself was broken and had no more to do with life.

In this fight David proved the real king. A king must be blessed with the greatest blessing, because the whole of the people must derive its blessing from him. If his blessing is eclipsed by that of another, then it is as if he had lost it.

David was richer in blessing than any other Israelite. If his life was not always without sorrows, yet it was happy, and one long series of blessings. He is described to Saul as "a mighty valiant man, and a man of war, and wise of speech, and a comely person, and Yahweh is with him" (1 Sam. 16,18); mention is also made of his handsome body and beautiful eyes (1 Sam. 16,12). His appearance was that of a blessed man.

As is described in one of the narratives, the blessing of David made itself felt at once during the fight with Goliath. In this part of the story he is still a youth, of insignificant stature, but fair to look upon. He trusts that Yahweh is with him, and Saul strengthens his confidence with these words: Yahweh shall be with thee! And so it also came to pass. By his cunning and quick movements he slings a stone against the great Philistine who, caught unawares, falls upon his face on the ground, and then David slays him with his own sword. That Yahweh was with David appeared from his cunning and quickness of resource, from his courage and sureness of touch.

The blessing all the time took greater and greater effect in David. It appeared from his ability of making friends. He understood to bend the wills of others to his own, not by compulsion, but in such a manner that he poured his own will into their souls. Saul entrusted him with great tasks, and he accomplished them all. He became a great leader of armies which returned victorious, and one day the women sang: Saul has slain his thousands, and David his ten thousands.

Then begins the overwhelming drama which unfolds itself in the conflict between Saul and David. What makes this drama so powerful is that it reflects a psychic conflict. A fight for happiness one may call it, but happiness which has its seat in the soul and implies its growth or death. A peculiar colouring is lent to this conflict, in that it does not take place between enemies who openly attack each other, but between a chief and the man nearest to him.

Saul himself had begun in the same manner as David: a glorious and stately youth of noble origin, a head higher than any of the people (1 Sam. 9,2). On the morning when Samuel anointed him, a new soul had been born in him, and he knew who he was. Soon after that he had the chance of proving it. When the Israelitic city of Jabesh was threatened by shame and defeat and all others stood about weak-handed, Yahweh's spirit rose in him; he poured strength into their wills, collected an army and gained the victory for his people. He now stood as the one who was to be the king, because the blessing was his.

But it was the fate of his soul that Yahweh should leave it and give his blessing to David. When David had won his victories, the crisis was brought about. It was all right as long as David's warlike deeds were performed in the name of Saul and given to him. But the very moment when the two were compared, and the deeds of David were extolled above those of Saul, Saul became less than his own man, and it was clear that the blessing was taken from him. In order to maintain himself, Saul had to get David out of the way. While David sat playing the harp to Saul, the latter flung his javelin at him, but David escaped it twice. "And Saul was afraid of David, because Yahweh was with him, and was departed from Saul" (1 Sam. 18,12); so strong was the blessing of David that Saul could not even hit him at a distance of a few yards.

Then David was sent away as a leader of armies, and his blessing grew and grew. He won new victories and new friends; he succeeded in all that he undertook, and Saul became still more afraid of him.

Then Saul tries a new expedient. He promises his daughter to David, if he can get him trophies of a hundred Philistines; this excessive demand must surely be the death of him. But David brings back the foreskins of two hundred Philistines and is united with Saul's daughter. "And Saul saw and knew that Yahweh was with David, and that Michal, Saul's daughter, loved him. And Saul was yet the more afraid of David; and Saul became David's enemy continually" (1 Sam. 18,28-29). The blessing of Saul had passed to David. He had taken his renown as the greatest warrior; where anyone else would have failed, David carried home the victory. And now at last he had taken away from Saul the soul of his own daughter, just as he had already taken away his son's. What was left in the soul of Saul which David had not sucked out?

Jonathan, the son of Saul and David's friend, tries to solve the conflict. He can do it in one way only: by making Saul look at the blessing of David as something which belongs to him. "He hath not sinned against thee, and his works have been to theeward very good. For he did put his life in his hand, and slew the Philistine, and Yahweh wrought a great salvation for all Israel; thou sawest it, and didst rejoice; wherefore then wilt thou sin against innocent blood, to slay David without a cause?" (1 Sam. 19,4-5). Then Saul changed his mind, and David came back to him once more.

But it was a false harmony. Soon David performs great deeds, and again Saul hurls his javelin at him. David only escapes by means of a stratagem. But Saul cannot let him be. He must pursue him who has deprived him of his blessing, and smite him down in order to maintain himself. He feels deserted by all. His own son has supported his slave David as his "eavesdropper" (1 Sam. 22,8), a graphic description of the trusted man, who keeps close to him in order to deprive him of his blessing.[1] He rushes about in the desert, in mountains and valleys in order to find David, and these events reach their climax in the meeting between Saul and David.

David is still the blessed. While Saul is vainly roaming about in search of his enemy, David without any difficulty gets Saul into his power so that he may take his life if he wants. There are two different versions of the story. In the one Saul, without knowing it, sits down in a cave, in the dim background of which David stays with his men; in the other David goes at night into the camp of Saul and finds him and all his men asleep. In both versions of the story David only secures evidence that he has held the life of Saul in his hands, in the former by cutting off the skirt of Saul's robe, in the other by taking his javelin. In that manner he won a much greater victory than if he had killed him. He humbled Saul by his generosity, and Saul realizes at once that this is the final decision of the conflict between them: in the fight for the blessing he stands the loser.

According to the one version Saul burst into tears saying: Thou art more righteous than I: for thou hast rewarded me good, whereas I have rewarded thee evil... Yahweh reward thee good, for that thou hast done unto me this day. And now, behold, I know well that thou shalt surely be king, and that the kingdom of Israel shall be established in thine hand. Swear now therefore unto me by Yahweh, that thou wilt not cut off my seed after me, and that thou wilt not destroy my name out of my father's house (1 Sam. 24, 18-22). In the other version the answer of Saul in its vivid curtness sounds: Blessed art thou, my son David; thou shalt act and thou canst (26,25). These words are still more significant than the others. Saul acknowledges that David has the blessing.

He has now received his life as a gift from his own servant. He cannot lower himself more — only complete extermination could still threaten him.

Saul's behaviour is typical of a man who has lost the blessing. Aimlessly he rushes about from one place to another, attempts first one thing and then another in order to strike down David, to regain the blessing and thus maintain himself. When his fight with David is lost, his soul is exhausted. The enemies gather against him, he knows no counsel, and during the night he steals away to the witch of Endor as a last expedient to conjure Samuel back from the dead. With great art the scene of this night of tragedy is described. Samuel is brought up from the depth and confirms the sentence which has been passed on Saul. And Saul falls down in a faint, while the woman stands besides him, terror-stricken. She manages to restore him to life, in so far that he is able to stagger out into the night, out to the fate which must overtake him, who has no blessing. Soon after that the hopeless fight against the Philistines took place, and in Mount Gilboa Saul died by his own hand. Even after death he did not escape plundering and ill-treatment, until the men from Jabesh took the matter in hand because of the benefaction he had conferred upon them in his youth.

The tragic pathos of the figure of Saul is not the outward conflict, but the fact that he who had the blessing should lose it. The narrator has pictured his soul in its growth and strength, and we see how it is gradually emptied out and shrinks, more and more vacillating and divided within itself, making plans which are foredoomed to fail, and yet driven afresh to action, because he has to fight in order to maintain his blessing and so to keep his own soul. In this tragedy death does not come as the solution of a hard knot into which life has been twisted by misery. It is a link in the tragedy: the extreme stage in the dissolution and ill-treatment of the soul. As the background of the picture of the mutilated bodies of Saul and Jonathan we must see the humbled chief who implores his own vassal not altogether to destroy his name out of his father's house. He just succeeded in maintaining his name for posterity; but he came very near losing even that.

There is a curious difference between the characters of Saul and David. Saul is the single-minded chief, whose actions are necessary in order to maintain himself; David has the blessing and makes it felt, but he does not uphold it openly before Saul and is all the time hesitating to take up the fight. He conquers Saul without lifting his hand against him, and when Saul is dead, he, the mortal enemy of Saul, may stand forth as heir, being the son-in-law of the king. He acts as the blood-avenger of Saul, laments his death in song and thanks the Jabeshites for their kindness to him. Without appearing, at any point, as an open assailant, he humbles the family of Saul into the dust and takes upon himself all its royal blessing. The kingdom of Ishbaal becomes his, in that Abner hands it over to him, when he and Ishbaal no longer live in harmony. Ishbaal is naturally still a danger to David's possession of the kingdom, but soon afterwards he is murdered, David reaps the fruit — and is at the same time able to stand forth as his blood-avenger. Meribbaal, the son of Jonathan, who might still maintain the claims of the house of Saul, he treats very kindly by letting him eat continually at his own table. Thus his inferior position is established, and he is unable to move; but David is the benefactor, not the enemy of the house of Saul. And what is still left of the house of Saul, David must necessarily hand over to the Gibeonites, in order to fulfil their lawful demand for blood-vengeance.

How much cunning and how much sincerity is there in David's relation to Saul? Surely none can unravel the threads of this tangle. There is no reason to doubt that his friendship for Jonathan was unfeigned, and that his hesitation to lay hands on the chief whose bread he ate was sincere. But somewhere or other the sincerity ceases. He clings to this house, at the same time destroying it utterly. He is clever enough to preserve his relation with the house of his old chief, and yet to deprive it of all the honour and blessing belonging to it, while he himself takes its place.

The curious thing is that David, apparently in every case, does the very thing he ought to do, according to his position towards Saul, and in that very manner he conquers his house entirely. It was his blessing to be able to succeed in this duplicity. It was also displayed in the dangerous double-dealing which he carried on with the Philistines. He was in the pay of king Achish, and represented himself to him as an enemy of the Israelites; when he went out reconnoitring, he even made Achish believe that it was the Israelites he attacked. Now the decisive battle between Saul and the Philistines was drawing near. When the army of the Philistines advanced, their chiefs *forced* David to keep back. Thus he kept on a good footing with Achish, and at the same time did not prejudice his relation to Saul.

Even during the greatest affliction of his life, when his son raised the standard of revolt against him, even then the blessing did not fail him. Yahweh confused the soul of the rebellious son, and David regained his power. The blessing acted through the whole of his reign. He gathered men round him, by whose assistance he could subdue all the neighbouring kingdoms and gain a power for his people which it otherwise never possessed, neither before nor after. A royal blessing had been given him; his throne stood firm and, before he died, he had the happiness of seeing one of his sons as his successor.

In the *patriarchal legends* we read how the blessing came to Israel. It began with Abraham. Yahweh told him that he was to be blessed, that he should be blessed with a great name, and that in his seed all the nations of the earth should be blessed. Wealth grew up around him, and he became a great chief. From Abraham the blessing passed to Isaac.

That the blessing is handed down from father to son is a consequence of its being a power of the soul. It must go with the family, because there is a psychic community in the latter. When Isaac is blessed with the blessing after Abraham, then it is a confirmation of the oath with which Yahweh gave Abraham his blessing (Gen. 26,3). It is the soul of Abraham that lives on in Isaac. It is Abraham who, through the whole of his manner of living, deserved the blessing of Isaac (Gen. 26,5.24).

Both of Abraham and Isaac it is told that they had experiences which brought them into conflict with Abimelech. When the latter had violated the rights of Abraham, fertility at once stopped in his house, and only when amends had been made to Abraham did the wife and maidservants of Abimelech again begin to bear children.

So great was the blessing of Abraham that no one could molest him unpunished. Abimelech realized at once whom he had before him. He overwhelmed Abraham with presents and told him to move about freely in the country. A blessing of this kind he was bound to conciliate. So also the history of Isaac. It ends by Abimelech coming and proposing a covenant, establishing their mutual friendly relation. And he does not conceal his reason: Thou art the blessed of Yahweh (Gen. 26,29). When a man has the blessing in him, one ought not to oppose him but, on the contrary, to seek his friendship.

From Isaac the blessing is carried on to Jacob. In him it manifests itself as a capability of managing everything, and in this his story reminds us of that of David. Jacob was always the weaker, and yet all the time he won happiness. His blessing appears particularly in his cunning. By cunning he conquered his older and stronger brother, and by cunning he conquered the artful Laban, who himself had once circumvented him.

The story of the stay of Jacob with Laban shows how the blessing followed him constantly, how Laban exploited it, and how at last Jacob himself succeeded in getting the full profit (Gen. 30). Laban readily admits that Yahweh has blessed him by Jacob. Before Jacob came, he was not a rich man, but now prosperity welled up around him, and by arts of soothsaying he found out that the blessing came from Jacob. Yahweh blessed him, wherever Jacob set his foot, but Jacob was not inclined to let somebody else reap all the profit that his blessing produced, and now he threatens to go away. But for Laban it was of the greatest importance to keep such a valuable shepherd, under whom his herds throve and multiplied exceedingly. Therefore he was quite willing to agree to the proposal of Jacob which, for that matter, sounded very generous.

Most goats have the quality of being dark, some few are speckled; most sheep are white, some few are black. Laban was now to select all the ring-streaked and spotted goats and all the black sheep, and Jacob should keep all the black goats and white sheep. Such pied kids and black lambs that were thrown were then to belong to Jacob. Laban was eager enough to accept the proposal. He removed carefully all the animals in question and took care that a couple of days' journey was set between them, so that a mixture of his and Jacob's flocks was out of the question. But this time it was Laban who walked into the trap. When the animals gathered at the watering troughs, they were in the habit of pairing-off, and Jacob now took care that the goats, at the moment of conception, had some streaked and spotted rods before them, and that the sheep set their faces against the black goats. Thus he achieved the result that the goats threw speckled kids and the sheep black lambs. But this was not all. They were only the strongest animals which he treated in that way. The feeble ones were left to take care of themselves, and thus they threw young of their own colour. But in that way Laban received the feeble, worthless young, whereas Jacob kept all the strong ones. And Jacob became overwhelmingly rich in sheep and goats, in slaves and slave-girls, in camels and asses (Gen. 30,43). [1]

When Jacob has the power of making the herds and whatever else he has to do with thrive, this and the cunning he displays towards Laban are both of them expressions of the same blessing, the power to succeed. Through this blessing God deprives Laban of his wealth and gives it to Jacob (Gen. 31,9).

Jacob handed over his blessing to his sons. We see it following Joseph in all he does, even during his period of degradation. When he arrived in Egypt and was placed in the house of his Egyptian master, Yahweh was with him, and he prospered in all that he undertook (Gen. 39,2 f.). The Egyptian made him overseer of his house, and for the sake of Joseph Yahweh blessed all that belonged to the Egyptian, just as at one time Laban was blessed for the sake of Jacob. "The blessing of Yahweh was upon all that he had in the house and in the field". And when, by the wicked wiles of a woman, Joseph had fallen from grace and been put to prison, Yahweh was still with him. He gained friends, became the overseer of the prison and the prisoners, and in all things he was successful (Gen. 39,21-23). His blessing later on raised him to the highest post in Egypt and made him the saviour of the whole of his family.

The Israelites tell these stories of the blessing of the patriarchs with special affection, because they are the stories of their fathers, and so also of themselves. They derive their souls from their fathers, and how good to have fathers who are rich in blessing! From that they draw the blessing which gives themselves happiness in this life. It passes like a family heirloom through the souls, from generation to generation. The soul of Isaac, it is true, is the soul of Abraham, but in a new shape. Yahweh states expressly to Isaac that in him he confirms the blessing of his father; the first-born has claims on the blessing of the father; it is his birthright. The father speaks it into him before his death, and with him rests the main responsibility that it is maintained in and, in its turn, maintains the family. It is only by deceit that Jacob succeeds in getting the best blessing.

It is not only the family which receives its share of a man rich in blessing. Life consists in the constant meeting of souls, which must share their contents with each other. The blessed gives to the others, because the strength instinctively pours from him and up around him. The important thing is to ally oneself closely with the blessed and to get one's share of his gifts. Both Jacob and Joseph, in strange countries, were possessed of the power to spread blessing among their surroundings. Wherever the man who has the blessing in him goes, happiness must spring up, and others must get blessing, because he has the mysterious power of the strong soul to inspire them with his strength. David created happiness for the whole of his people, as is the task of a good king. When the king is as he should be, then the rain falls in season, fertility spreads in the country, and the righteous flourish (Ps. 72).

It is the hope of Israel some day to become such a strong fountain of blessing among future peoples when the great catastrophe takes place (Is. 19,24). It is the same hope and demand which manifests itself in the patriarchal legends. Abraham, Isaac and Jacob each gets promise that all peoples are to obtain blessing by him (Gen. 12,3; 18,18; 22,18; 26,4; 28,14). Israel must be among the peoples as the chief among his men; the best men seek him in order to have their share of his blessing. The blessing of Israel must be the greatest, nay, the only one, and those who want blessing must come there for it, just as all peoples must seek blessing in the God of Israel (Is. 65,16; Jer. 4,2; Ps. 72,17). The strength must be looked for where it is to be found.

The blessing is a mental gift, and as such it has its root in something which partly loses itself in mystery. Behind the blessing of the individual stand the fathers; from them he has derived it, and its strength depends on their power. When all is said and done, it rests in powers which lie behind all human capability. When a man is blessed, it may also be expressed in the way that God is with him. This conception we meet time after time in the narratives. We have seen how it was expressed to Isaac (Gen. 26, 2.28). Samuel, one of the great men of Israel, had already, as a small boy, been destined to blessing. It appeared while he was growing up that Yahweh was with him (1 Sam. 3,19). Thus Yahweh was with Saul (1 Sam. 10,7) until the moment of the great crisis, when David took the blessing, and Yahweh left Saul in order to follow David. The whole of the life of David is the story of how a man fares when Yahweh is with him. The narrator does not forget to mention it at the various stages of David's successful career (1 Sam. 16,18; 18,12.14; 20,13). Now and again he interrupts his narrative in order to recapitulate as follows: And David went on and grew great, and Yahweh, the Lord of hosts, was with him (2 Sam. 5,10). Nathan says to him: Go and do all that is in thine heart, for Yahweh is with thee (2 Sam. 7,3 cf. 9; 14,17). There are not many kings about whom this is expressly said; Hezekiah is one of the few of whom it is said that Yahweh was with him; all that he undertook to do, in that he succeeded (2 Kings 18,7).

This expression that Yahweh or God is with one is only another term for the blessing. There are sufficient statements to show that the two appellations are used interchangeably. In this there is nothing strange. The blessing is concentrated in Yahweh, therefore one can only have blessing in harmony with him.

We must not consider the expression as a suggestion of the arbitrariness of the blessing, as though the superhuman powers of chance caprices granted the happiness of life now to one, now to another, whosoever the man might be. The blessing, it is true.

originates in God, but as a power of the soul. The seat of the blessing is in the soul of the man, and it is also there that God works. Happiness cannot be given to the man as something lying outside him, because the whole of his sphere is part of the entirety of his soul.

It would perhaps seem natural to interpret the Israelitic view of the divine activity according to the formula of Leibniz; on one side the resolve and action of man, on the other side the outward result, and in the middle the strength of God bridging the two halves of the event. But the Israelite acknowledges no empty space between action and result; the latter lies in the former. And the action of God does not fall outside man, but in the very centre of the soul; that which it gives to man is not only something external, but the energy, the power of creating it. When God gives Jacob wealth, it means that Jacob has the power to create wealth.

Therefore the divine power within the man is his own strength, which fills him with pride and confidence. When Yahweh's *mal'ākh* came to Gideon, he greeted him with the following words: Yahweh is with thee, thou mighty man of valour! And Gideon said unto him: Oh my Lord, if Yahweh be with us, how then could all this befall us? And where be all his miracles which our fathers told us of, saying: Did not Yahweh bring us up from Egypt? But now Yahweh has forsaken us, and delivered us into the hands of the Midianites. And Yahweh looked upon him and said: Go in thy might that thou hast, and thou shalt save Israel from the hands of the Midianites. I send thee! (Judg. 6,12-14).

The greeting: "Yahweh is with thee!" is a homage and acknowledgment of the strength of Gideon; and when Gideon rejects it by referring to the weakness of his people against the enemy, Yahweh confirms his saying: Go in thy might that thou hast! There is no question of any distinction between the strength of Gideon and that of Yahweh. Gideon gains the honour of Yahweh being with him, because the strength with which Yahweh acts in him is his own.

The term commonly used to denote that a man succeeds or prospers, is *ṣālaḥ* or *hiṣlīᵃḥ*. It means the power, the ability to live. In one place Ezekiel compares Jerusalem with a vine and asks whether it is more than any tree, but he answers himself: Behold it is cast into the fire for fuel; the fire devoureth both the ends of it, and the midst of it is burned. Is it meet for any work? (Ezek. 15,4). The word used in this case is *ṣālah*. In the following the sentence is repeated in this form: Can it be made into any thing? — Also elsewhere Ezekiel uses this term about the vine. He speaks of a vine-tree planted in good soil, by great waters, that it might bring forth branches, and that it might bear fruit, that it might be a goodly vine. But it shall not prosper *(yiṣlaḥ)*. It is to be plucked up by the roots thereof, loose the fruit, wither when touched by the east wind (Ezek. 17,8-10). The same negative expression is used of a girdle which is destroyed and worthless (Jer. 13,7.10). In a positive connection it is used of weapons which are forged for the war and are fit to defeat the enemy (Is. 54,17).

This word thus means the same as blessing. It designates the efficiency as an inner power to work in accordance with its nature, and at the same time success, prosperity and the carrying out of that for which one is disposed.

The two things are a unity, so that one can never judge from the word whether the ability or the result is being particularly considered. When a man begins his undertaking by asking the oracle whether it is going to succeed *(yiṣlaḥ*, Judg. 18,5), then it is just as well a question of the power as a question of the result. When the king is going into the war, and the prophets are to put victory into his soul, then they cry to him: Go up and prosper *(haṣlaḥ)*, Yahweh delivers the enemy into the hands of the king (1 Kings 22,12.15; cf. Ps. 45,5).

A king who did not prosper was Jehoiachin. He was a king for some few months only, and during an extremely unhappy period. Jeremiah states without mercy that he is a man created for calamity. The words are: Write ye this man childless, a man that shall not prosper *(yiṣlaḥ)* in his days; for no man of his seed shall succeed *(yiṣlaḥ),* sitting upon the throne of David and ruling once more in Judah (Jer. 22,30). He is compared with a worthless vessel which is cast out, just as the girdle of Jeremiah which was destroyed. There is no "reason" given for it. It is due to a lack in his soul; he lacks the blessing of efficiency.

The intimate connection between ability and accomplishment also stamps other words. The word *yākhōl* more particularly means ability; we render it by "can". The Hebrew, it is true, is able to emphasize the ability, but not as something isolated. He who "can", also carries into effect. In reality there is only a faint shade of meaning between this and the above-mentioned word. Jeremiah says to his people: Thou hast spoken and done evil things, and thou couldst (Jer. 3,5); it means that the people has carried out its wicked intention, just as the lying spirit which spoke in Ahab's prophets "could" (1 Kings 22,22). Saul said to David: Blessed art thou, my son David, thou shalt really act, and thou always *canst* (1 Sam. 26,25). As contrasted with Saul, David "could", i. e. fortune favoured him, because he was blessed.

He who "can" is the same as he who carries through his counsel. The wicked "intended evil, but they could not" (Ps. 21, 12). Their counsel was empty fancy which they could not fill with the strength of the blessing and make a real counsel. The persecutors of Jeremiah stumble and *can not,* but are greatly put to shame, for they have the strength of Yahweh against them (Jer. 20,11). And with particular strength it is said about Moab: When Moab appears wearying himself at the high place and comes to the sanctuary to pray, he *can not* (Is. 16,12). The people of Moab come to the holy place in order to be inspired with strength, but all power is dead within them; no strength pours into them, however great are the efforts they make.

The victor "can" over against the opponent. When Naphtali was born, Rachel said: God's wrestlings have I wrestled with my sister, and I "could" (Gen. 30,8). When Jacob fought his divine fight, before entering Canaan, it is said that the strange God only gave up the fight when he saw that he "could" not against him; but Jacob might say that he had fought against God and "could",

i. e. prevailed (Gen. 32, 26.29). To that extent the power itself contains the very victory, and now and again we come across sayings of a similar kind (Judg. 16,5; 1 Sam. 17,9; Hos. 12,5; Ps. 13,5).

The blessing is the power of the soul which creates all progress; it contains the strength to produce, as well as the mysterious power which really causes it to be produced, and it contains the full power to find and use the necessary means. Therefore it is related to *wisdom,* for the latter consists in the very possession of the "insight" out of which one creates the power to make counsels that persist. What wisdom is, appears from a place in the Book of Job, where Job speaks of God: With him is wisdom and strength, he has counsel and insight. Behold, he breaketh down, and it cannot be built again; he shutteth up a man, and there can be no opening. Behold, he withholdeth the waters, and they dry up; also he sendeth them out, and they overturn the earth, etc. (Job 12,13-15). Thus the wisdom of God consists in his irresistible fulfilment of what he has in his mind. Wisdom is the same as blessing: the power to work and to succeed.

It is more or less implied in all the words which signify understanding. Characteristic is such a word as *hiśkīl,* which at the same time signifies to have understanding, insight, energy and the production of good results. Sometimes stress may be laid so strongly on the inner activity that the thought of outward action is eclipsed (e. g. Deut. 32,29). But as a rule the idea of the totality prevails so strongly that it means to be wise and happy, and we are not able to say where the emphasis is laid. When Solomon receives the promise that he shall "have understanding" in all he does (1 Kings 2,3), then this implies much more than can be rendered by our translation, because we are far removed from the conception of life out of which the word is created. The "understanding" is the special blessing of the chief. It was given to David as his birthright. When the Philistines marched out to battle, David proved that he had more of this quality than the other men of Saul, and he gained great honour (1 Sam. 18,30); this appeared in all he did (1 Sam. 18,5.14). Jeremiah entertained the hope that some day there would be good "shepherds", who might guard the people "with knowledge and understanding" (Jer. 3,15; cf. Josh. 1,7.8). He had to acknowledge with sorrow that the present shepherds did not possess the understanding; therefore this herd did not prosper and was scattered (Jer. 10,21).

Understanding is thus the same as blessing, a power to live and accomplish the purpose one has set oneself in life. Therefore man desires knowledge and was easily caught when the serpent persuaded him to eat of the tree in the garden of Eden. For "it was pleasant to the eyes and the tree was desirable to gain wisdom" (Gen. 3,6). It does not mean that the fruit gave theoretical knowledge, but that it gave blessing, power to live, and the strength to get happiness and to prosper in the world. [1]

The blessing thus comprises the power to live in its deepest and most comprehensive sense. Nothing which belongs to action and to making life real can fall outside the blessing, which is always a power in the soul.

The man who has the blessing within himself is *bārūkh,* full of blessing. We render this word by "blessed", but ought not to put a passive meaning into it, as if it designated one on whom a blessing had been pronounced. It does not designate a man with whom something has been done, but a man possessing a power, a capable, vigorous man, full of *b^{e}rākhā.* [2]

From him who is thus filled with blessing, power must radiate in all directions. We have seen how all things grew round Jacob, David and the other great types of blessing. But first and foremost it must make itself felt in those nearest to them.

The father, the main pillar of the house, carries the whole of the family. On his blessing rests its prosperity; all the members of the house: wives, children, slaves, animals, property must draw from it, and thus be upheld through it. But he is only a single link in the long chain of fathers who have carried the blessing of the families. From the fathers he has received it, and to the sons he passes it on by saying it into them before his death. It is the blessing within himself which he passes on. When Jacob blessed the sons of Joseph, he said: Yahweh before whom my fathers Abraham and Isaac did walk, the God which fed me all my life long unto this day, the *mal'ākh* which redeemed me from all evil, bless the lads (Gen. 48,15 f.). And he says expressly that the blessing which he now gives to the boys is closely connected with the one which he himself received (Gen. 48, 3-4).

How serious is the act of blessing appears from the story of Isaac, when he blessed Esau and Jacob. The blessing cannot be taken back, because it is not idle breath. If once uttered, then the soul of him who uttered the blessing has really created it, and it must act by the power which has been put into it. That which at one time has been real cannot be undone, but it can of course be counteracted. The blessing can only take effect when he who pronounces it can put real strength into it, and when the person blessed is susceptible. Balaam was a man who had special gifts for blessing: "For I wot that he whom thou blessest it blessed, and he whom thou cursest it cursed" (Num. 22,6). But he cannot arbitrarily create blessing or curses in whomsoever he wishes, which was demonstrated when he was to curse Israel. Yahweh inspired him to bless it, because it was blessed (Num. 22, 12, cf. 23,20). It had the blessing of Yahweh in itself, and Balaam could only work in harmony with reality, not in spite of it.

The act of blessing another, *bērēkh,* means to communicate to him strength of soul, but one can communicate to him only of the strength one has in oneself. He who blesses another gives him something of his own soul. In reality there is no greater difference between the transference of blessing which takes place directly, when the weak keeps close to the strong, and the one which takes place by the word of blessing. Only the latter is more concentrated. The strength of the word of blessing depends upon the power that the word possesses to hold the real contents of a soul. By means of the word something is laid into the soul of the other, but behind the word stands the soul which created it. He who himself is not possessed of the blessing can create nothing in others.

The blessing connects the souls, and so it must be, because it consists in a communication of the contents of the soul. The souls must come into close contact, in order that the current between them may become alive. Before Isaac could collect himself to give Jacob his blessing, he ate of the food which the son brought him, and drank of his wine. He kissed him and sniffed the smell of his clothes and his body. Now that they were close to each other, the soul of the father could communicate itself to that of the son. The bodily nearness is generally, if not always, a presupposition, and it is made more intimate by the touch, most often by the laying of hands on the head of the person in question. When Moses was to consecrate Joshua, he laid his hand on him and communicated to him some of his honour (Num. 27, 18-20). It is really equivalent to his blessing.

Like all soul-substance the blessing can be put into a thing, penetrate what we call things just as well as it can penetrate a human body. Elisha once sent his servant with his staff to Shunem, in order to render help to the son of the woman who had shown him kindness. It was a costly treasure which the servant brought; it was full of the blessing of Elisha, and he had to guard it well. Elisha commanded him not to bless any one on the way, and not to let himself be blessed by anybody (2 Kings 4,29). The blessing the servant had upon him he was to preserve intact, and not to cede any of it or confuse it by having other souls mixed up in it with greetings.

We know that the kneading-trough and all the tools have their blessing. A stone may possess a greater blessing than the greatest chief, and the same holds good of a chest such as the Ark of the Covenant. All property is penetrated by the blessing of its owner; therefore any gift is a psychic gift, never anything dead, material. He who gives a gift, gives something of himself, to the increase of the strength of the other man. Therefore a gift is just as well a blessing as the good word, or whatever else by which a man puts part of his soul into that of another. The gift is not rarely called a blessing. Caleb received Hebron as a blessing from Joshua, and himself gave his daughter a piece of land as a blessing (Josh. 14,13; 15,19 and Judg. 1,15). Jacob gave to Esau as a blessing a great deal of his herd (Gen. 33,11), and Abigail, the wife of Nabal, brought the following blessing to David: two hundred loaves, two sacks of wine, and five sheep ready dressed, and five measures of parched corn, and an hundred cakes of raisins, and two hundred cakes of figs (1 Sam. 25,18.27, cf. 1 Sam. 30,26; 2 Kings 5,15).

Thus people give each other blessings in one way or the other, and whichever form the blessing takes, it implies an exchange of the contents of the soul. Human intercourse is impossible without blessing. Intercourse is community, and it is against the nature of the soul to have community without communicating and receiving. When people meet, they bless each other. We call it a greeting and know how to value the kindness which may lie in it. For peoples like Israel the greeting is a formality which entails a deep reality, as all other forms with primitive peoples. He who has travelled in the desert knows what it means to meet a man who does not salute, but pulls the kerchief down over his face and passes on.

The *greeting* is the establishment or confirmation of psychic communion. Therefore it is tantamount to a blessing, and it is necessary for the beginning of intercourse. When, against Samuel's wishes, Saul had done sacrifice in Gilgal and then went out to meet the prophet "that he might bless him" (1 Sam. 13,10), he received no blessing in return, but was met with the harsh question: What hast thou done? From that moment the relation between Saul and Samuel was broken. When David wanted to get into closer contact with Nabal, in order to profit by his riches, and on that occasion sent his men to him, it was reported to Abigail with the following words: Behold David sent messengers out of the wilderness to bless our master (1 Sam. 25,14). In our ears it would rather sound like irony, but it was meant in all sincerity. David gives blessing in order that a connection may be brought about between him and Nabal, and gifts given or received. When Jehu rode off on his murderous expedition to Samaria, he met with Jonadab ben Rechab. Then he stopped, blessed him and asked whether his heart was with him. And when Jonadab answered in the affirmative, they shook hands, and now they were fellows in the fight (2 Kings 10,15-16).

When friends separate, they bless each other in order to confirm the fellowship, and each gives to the other so much of his soul that the community can be maintained, even when they are far away from each other. Rebekah leaves her home with the blessing of her family (Gen. 24,60). Laban rebukes Jacob that, with his secret departure, he had deprived him of the privilege of kissing his sons and daughters and blessing them (Gen. 31, 28; 32,1). The close bodily contact imparted in the kiss or, according to the degree of intimacy, in other forms of blessing, always pertains to the leave-taking (Gen. 47,10; 2 Sam. 13,25; 19,40). We also find this natural, but with the ancients it was essential, because the blessing was a reality, and friends must necessarily feel each other's souls in themselves.

Great assemblies, cultic or non-cultic, must necessarily conclude with a blessing, so that every one may take away with him the strength of the community. It is expressly said, both of the gathering which Joshua held after the distribution of the land (Josh. 22,7), and of the festival which David gave, when the Ark was carried up on Zion (2 Sam. 6,18). And as soon as the festival was over, David went home in order to bless his own house and resume his position as the head of the family. Also on such occasions the blessing is mutual. After the great festival at the inauguration of the temple, the people blessed the king and then went each his different way (1 Kings 8,66).

Upon the whole blessings must be mutual. When souls open to one another, the current between them must be interchangeable. Also the lesser people may, according to their humble means, bless the great. Thus they confirm the blessing which the great naturally possess, and thus they contribute to its increase. Job, who in his days of prosperity gave so much, was richly blessed by the poor. The loins of the miserable blessed him when they were warmed in the fleece of his sheep (Job 31,20). He who receives a present, blesses the giver (2 Sam. 14,22). Naomi blessed the man who permitted Ruth to glean ears of corn on his field (Ruth 2,19.20; cf. Deut. 24,13).

The king is blessed by his subjects. When David lay on his death-bed, the king's servants came to him to bless him saying: God make the name of Solomon better than thy name (1 Kings 1,47). He who manifests his blessing in a valiant deed is blessed by others, because he has the blessing. In the blessing lies homage. Jael is blessed in the Song of Deborah, because she killed Sisera (Judg. 5,24), and David praises the clever Abigail who saved him from blood-guilt by redressing the offence of her husband (1 Sam. 25,33). Melchizedek blesses Abraham because he has conquered the great kings (Gen. 14,19).

Yahweh is exalted above all blessing, it is said in one of the latest writings of the Old Testament (Neh. 9, 5). This does not imply that people shall refrain from blessing him, but, on the contrary, that he cannot be blessed enough. His claim to blessing is so great, because all blessing is concentrated in him. Whenever he has given another proof of the great strength of his soul, the praising and corroboration of his wealth must be carried forward.

The blessing manifests itself in a great variety of ways. The blessing of the fish is determined by its motion in the water, that of the bird by its life in the air. Men and women have a different blessing, each according to their kind; but there are certain fundamental features which constantly recur when the Israelites speak of the blessing.

Firstly, it is the power to multiply. On this point the Israelitic spirit has remained the same throughout the times, and it is not impossible that, properly speaking, the Hebrew denomination of the blessing expresses this power. [1] It is quite as important as existence, and the history of the Creation deliberately emphasizes the fact that it is a blessing which has been given to everything alive. The herbs carry seed, the trees fruits with kernels; this is more important than any other of their peculiarities. And when man and woman were created, the first blessing of God to them was: Be fruitful and multiply.

In the narratives of the fathers the chief subject is constantly the same: the blessing to be fruitful and multiply. Noah receives this blessing when he leaves the ark (Gen. 9). Abraham receives the promise on his departure from home: And I will make of thee a great nation, and I will bless thee and make thy name great, and thou shalt be a blessing (Gen. 12,2), which blessing is confirmed several times: And I will make thy seed as the dust of the earth, so that if a man can number the dust of the earth, then shall thy seed also be numbered (Gen. 13,16). The leading motive of the narrative of Abraham is the anxiety about the fulfilment of this prophecy. It might very easily have miscarried, and for a long time Abraham remained childless. He had a son by one of his slave-girls, but in the proper sense of the word this could not be called a son; still Yahweh constantly confirms his promise, and Abraham believes him. Only when Sarah has become so old that according to human standards it is not thought possible that she could give birth to a child, a son is born to Abraham. And all the time they are harping on the same string, how easily it might have miscarried, for a greater misfortune cannot be imagined.

Over and over again the patriarchal legends recur to the blessing of being as the stars of the firmament and the sand of the beach. Isaac inherits the blessing from his father, and to him it sounds: I will bless thee and multiply thy seed for my servant Abraham's sake (Gen. 26,24). When Jacob has his revelation at Bethel, it sounds: Thy seed shall be as the dust of the earth, and thou shalt spread about to the west and to the east, to the north and to the south (Gen. 28,14, cf. 3). Another of the narrators says: I am El Shaddai, be fruitful and multiply! A nation and a community of nations shall be of thee (Gen. 35,11 P), and when Jacob, before his death, sees the sons of Joseph before him, he gratefully recalls this blessing (Gen. 48,4).

The Israelites instinctively consider blessing to mean numerous progeny. When Jacob is on the point of blessing the sons of Joseph, and Joseph attracts his attention to Manasseh being the elder, Jacob says: I know it, my son, I know it; he also shall become a people, and he also shall be great, but only his younger brother shall be greater than he, and his seed shall become a multitude of nations (Gen. 48,19). To be blessed and to have a large progeny amounts to the same thing.

The patriarchal legends express the ideal of the Israelites and their deepest hope. To be numerous, to spread all over the earth is their supreme desire. They wish that people shall say with Balaam: Who can count the heap of dust in Jacob, and number the quantity of dust of Israel? (Num. 23,10).

Does this mean that the Israelites wish to be many, because the many can better maintain themselves than the few, e. g. against enemies? This factor has undoubtedly been of great importance, but it is not the only one, nor even the most important. When a man has progeny, it means that his soul persists, nay, which is more, it grows. It spreads in his sons and the sons of his sons, and the more numerous they are, the greater the soul becomes. The progeny is not something which comes after the man, divided from him. It is, as is constantly said, the man himself who multiplies. It is the joy which the Israelite takes in life, expressing itself in this demand for multiplying. Death is the great enemy. Always to live and to defy Death is happiness. This happiness fills the heart of the Israelite when he feels his soul expand and stretch across the whole world.

The blessing is tantamount to the continued existence of the family, because the Israelite lives in the family. It is expressed by the term that a man gets a house. An example of what it means appears in the story of David. We have already seen how the blessing worked in his soul, in everything he did. But when the great blessing in a solemn hour was pronounced unto him, the principal thing was first and foremost his persistence in the house. The words are the following: And when thy days be fulfilled and thou shalt sleep with thy fathers, I will set up thy seed after thee, which shall proceed out of thy bowels, and I will establish its kingdom. It shall build a house for my name, and I will establish the throne of its kingdom for ever.[1] I will be its father and it shall be my son. If it commit iniquity, I will chasten it with the rod of men and with the stripes of the children of men; but my mercy shall not depart away from it, as I took it from Saul, whom I put away before thee. And thine house and thy kingdom shall be established for ever before thee; thy throne shall be established for ever (2 Sam. 7,11-16). David confirms the blessing with these words: Therefore now let it please thee to bless the house of thy servant, that it may continue for ever before thee; for thou, O Lord Yahweh, hast spoken it, and with thy blessing let the house of thy servant be blessed for ever (2 Sam. 7,29).

It is obvious that the speech of Nathan to David is composed at a later period, though entirely in the spirit of old Israel. The great blessing of David is that his soul, as the royal soul it is, shall live through the ages, in that he shall always have successors sitting on his throne. Through it he must grow and become still greater. The firmness of the house of David becomes typical of the Israelites. When Jeroboam founds a royal house, it is said that if he will maintain it, it shall be "a sure house, as I built for David, and I will give Israel unto thee" (1 Kings 11,38). The blessing of the man takes effect in that his son gets a house, and the son gets a house the moment he occupies the place of a father and takes over the authority and the responsibility which the father has hitherto held (1 Kings 2,24).

A surely established house is the blessing which the man desires above everything else; it was that which was denied to Eli, because his sons degenerated. At one time the blessing had been given unto him that his house should always walk in front of Yahweh as priests. But the blessing departed from them and was given unto another. "And I will raise me up a faithful priest, that shall do according to that which is in mine heart and in my mind, and I will build him a sure house, and he shall walk before mine anointed for ever" (1 Sam. 2,35). One little remnant is left to Eli: "One man I shall not cut off from mine altar in order to dull thine eyes, and to grieve thine heart, but all the rest of thine house shall die in the flower of their age" (1 Sam. 2,33). If all the successors of Eli are to be entirely exterminated, then it is his soul which is thus paralyzed, because it is the same strength which acts in the soul of the man and that of his progeny. That the soul should be filled with sufficient strength to grow and thrive interminately through his progeny, that is the blessing which the man desires above everything else.

To "beget children unto Death" is the same as to "labour in vain" (Is. 65,23). He who has no progeny labours in vain; all the energy he uses in this life he pours into the void.

For women the blessing more particularly consists in giving

birth to children; it is really the only blessing she knows, for her soul is made to be the helpmeet of the man in the propagating of his soul. When a woman remains childless, then she must do all she can in order to acquire the blessing. Rachel ate a fruit which was supposed to quicken the power of reproduction (Gen. 30,14 ff.). Hannah went up to the temple in Shiloh and implored God to bless her with children, which blessing was given to her in abundance. After she had given her firstborn to the temple, Eli once more blessed her and her husband, and she gave birth to three sons and two daughters (1 Sam. 2,20 f.).

It follows as a matter of course that the blessing of the woman is derived from that of the man. It was the blessing of Abraham which opened the womb of Sarah, just as Abimelech's wives were stricken with barrenness because of the transgression of Abimelech. The wife can never receive a blessing equal or superior to that of her husband; even when she has the very greatest blessing, it always acts in the service of the man.

When the young woman is sent from home in order to go to the house of her bridegroom, her family puts blessing into her, before she goes away, and the aim of the blessing is always that she may bear her husband children. When Rebekah left her home, the blessing of her family was: Our sister, be thou the mother of thousands of ten thousands and let thy seed possess the gate of those which hate them (Gen. 24,60). Leah and Rachel are the types of women rich in blessing, who bore their husbands strong sons, and their names are sometimes mentioned in the nuptial blessing. When Boaz had married Ruth, people said to him: Yahweh make the woman that is come into thine house like Rachel and like Leah, which two did build the house of Israel, and do thou worthily in Ephratah, and create a name in Bethlehem. And let thine house be like the house of Pharez, whom Tamar bore unto Judah, of the seed which Yahweh shall give thee of this young woman (Ruth 4,11-12). When Tobit brought home Sarah from Ecbatana, his mother-in-law said to him: The Lord of heaven guide thee back and grant me to see thy children by my daughter Sarah, in order that I may rejoice before the Lord! And her father speaks in a somewhat similar manner (Tob. 10,11-12).

It is a common blessing which is given to the young people; but first and foremost the blessing applies to the man, and the father and mother of the woman rejoice, because they are able to give him the helpmeet who is necessary in order to make the blessing work.

Progeny goes before everything else, but more was required. When God blessed Abraham he "is become great; and he hath given him flocks and herds and silver and gold, and man-servants and maid-servants and camels and asses" (Gen. 24,35). It is the power to create wealth and prosperity in the herds, which is described in this place. Add to this the prosperity which the peasant must have. "Isaac sowed in that land and received in the same year an hundredfold, and Yahweh blessed him. And the man waxed great, and went forward and grew until he became very great; and he had possession of flock and possession of herds, and great store of servants" (Gen. 26,12-14). The first part of the blessing of Jacob reads: See, the smell of my son is as the smell of a field which Yahweh hath blessed. Therefore God give thee of the dew of heaven, and the fatness of the earth and plenty of corn and wine (Gen. 27,27-28). The Israelitic blessing is that of peasants and shepherds.

It is the same strength which manifests itself in the power to found a large family and in the power to make everything flourish round one. In both cases the blessing consists in the power of fertility; fertility in the family, in the field and in the herd.

That blessing is fertility we see time after time. In the sabbath year all is to lie fallow, but it is written: I will command my blessing upon you in the sixth year (Lev. 25,21). The blessing is the fertility which gives them abundance, so that they also have sufficient for the year, when they do not breed. When Job thinks of his lost happiness, then he speaks of how he waded in cream, and rivers of oil flowed around him (Job 29,6). With bitter irony he describes the happiness of the wicked and thus indirectly tells us what he understands by blessing: Their seed is established in their sight with them, and their offspring before their eyes. Their houses are safe from fear, neither is the rod of God upon them. Their bull gendereth and faileth not; their cow calveth, and casteth not their calf. They send forth their youths like a flock, and their little ones dance. They take the timbrel and harp, and rejoice at the sound of the organ. They spend their days in happiness, and in peace they go down to Sheol (Job 21,8-13). It is the fertility in family and herd which here plays the principal part. The bull never leaps in vain, the cow calves at the right moment. In this unfailing fertility we have the kernel of the blessing. Cattle, sons and daughters were also what Job received in abundance, when the blessing was given him afresh (42,12).

In the laws we find the same striving for blessing as otherwise, and here again fertility is a principal factor (Exod. 23,25-26; Deut. 7,12-14; 11,14-15; 12,15; 16,17). Blessing is the kernel of life, the very life itself. At the end of the Deuteronomy a great blessing gives an epitome of all that an Israelite, at the time of consolidated Israel, understands by the power and happiness of life. It reads (Deut. 28,1-13):

And it shall come to pass if thou shalt hearken diligently unto the voice of Yahweh, thy God, to observe and to do all his commandments which I command thee this day, that Yahweh thy God will set thee on high above all nations of the earth, and all these blessings shall come on thee, and overtake thee, if thou shalt hearken unto the voice of Yahweh thy God. Blessed shalt thou be in the city, and blessed shalt thou be in the field. Blessed shall be the fruit of thy body, and the fruit of thy ground, and the fruit of thy cattle, the increase of thy kine and the young of thy sheep. Blessed shalt thou be when thou comest in, and blessed shalt thou be when thou goest out. Yahweh shall cause thine enemies that rise up against thee to be smitten before thy face, they shall come out against thee one way, and flee before thee seven ways. Yahweh shall command the blessing upon thee in thy storehouses and in all that thou settest thine hand unto; and he shall bless thee in the land which Yahweh they God giveth thee. Yahweh shall establish thee an holy people unto himself, as he has sworn unto thee, if thou shalt keep the commandments of Yahweh thy God and walk in his ways. And all people of the earth shall see that thou art called by the name of Yahweh, and they shall be afraid of thee. — Yahweh shall make thee plenteous in goods, in the fruit of thy body, and in the fruit of thy ground, in the land which Yahweh sware unto the fathers to give thee. Yahweh shall open unto thee his good treasure, the heaven to give the rain unto thy land in his season, and to bless all the work of thine hand; and thou shalt lend unto many nations, and thou shalt not borrow. And Yahweh shall make thee the head and not the tail, and thou shalt be above only, and thou shalt not be beneath; if that thou hearken unto the commandments of Yahweh, thy God, which I command thee this day, to observe and to do them.

We see that the blessing comprises everything in life. Wherever the blessed goes, happiness shall flourish, and whatever he undertakes shall succeed. And the principal features are the growth of the family and fertility in abundance around him. This is what he calls "life" and "good" (Deut. 30,15). In this respect the Israelites have not altered. Even the later prophets speak of the blessing in the same manner (Joel 2,14; Zech. 8,12 f.; Mal. 3, 10-11).

Blessing is the positive strength of life, and for the Israelite it chiefly manifests itself in fertility. But to this must be added a feature which has already been glanced at. In the Deuteronomy it was said: "Yahweh shall cause thine enemies that rise up against thee to be smitten before thy face; they shall come out against thee one way, and flee before thee seven ways". The power to confuse the enemy, to conquer him and to defeat him, is an essential part of the blessing. It is contained in the blessing of Jacob that the peoples shall subject themselves to him (Gen. 27, 29), and success in war is mentioned in the blessing of Balaam, as being characteristic of Israel (Num. 24,17-18). This blessing is not given equally to all Israelites; there are two tribes in particular which are stamped by it, and these are Judah and Joseph.

The blessing of Judah is as follows: Judah, thou art he whom thy brethren shall praise; thine hand is in the neck of thine enemies; thy father's children bow down before thee. Judah is a lion's whelp; from the prey, my son, thou art gone up; he stooped down, he couched as a lion, and as a lioness; who shall rouse him up? The sceptre shall not depart from Judah, nor the ruler's staff from between his knees as long as people come to Shiloh (?); and to him the obedience of the people is due. He binds his ass unto his vine, and his ass's colt unto the branch of the vine; he washes his garments in wine, and his clothes in the blood of grapes. His eyes are red with wine, and his teeth white with milk (Gen. 49, 8-12).

If we compare this blessing with that of Joseph we see that the main features are the same: Joseph is a fruitful branch of vine, a fruitful branch by the well, whose shoots run over the wall (?). The archers have sorely grieved him, and shot at him, and assailed him; but his bow abode in strength, his powerful arms moved quickly, with the help of the mighty bull of Jacob. By the God of thy father, who shall help thee! by Shaddai, who shall bless thee with blessings of heaven above, blessings of the deep that lieth under, blessings of the breasts and of the womb. The blessings of thy father are stronger than ... blessings, the glory of everlasting hills; they shall be on the head of Joseph, and on the crown of the head of him that was the consecrated ruler among his brethren (Gen. 49,22-26).

In these two blessings lies the highest which the Israelite can attain. The blessings of breasts and mothers' wombs is fertility in the family and among the cattle. The blessings of the heaven and primeval deep is the life-giving waters which create the fertility in the field. It is that which makes vines so strong that one may tie asses to them. Cattle and fields prosper, so that the country is flowing with wine and milk. And to this must be added the conquering of all enemies. Like the lion Judah falls on them, and chases them off or slays them.

Throughout the history of Israel these three things are the main points of what is understood by blessing. But we must not forget that the blessing is the entire power of life, the strength underlying all progress and self-expansion.

HONOUR AND SHAME

A great blessing belongs to a great soul as its ability and strength. Conversely, the blessing reacts upon the soul. If it grows, then it fills the soul with new substance, extends it, increases its value and thus its self-consciousness. This substance of the soul, giving it a peculiar stamp, is the honour of the man. Honour is not that which the man himself or others, with more or less justice, think of him. Honour is that which actually fills the soul and keeps it upright. The question of its nature is in so far the central question in the understanding of the soul, involving the very nerve of life: what is it that makes the soul of the Israelite great, wherein consist the values of life?

No single answer can be given to this question. The widely different currents running through the history of Israel must in this place, if in any, leave their impress. Where should they make themselves felt, if not in the very contents and values of the soul?

Among the writings which reveal most of the Israelitic conception of life-values is the Book of Job. The values stand out so clearly here because they are lost, but still live as a craving in the writer. In eloquent words Job describes the quality of honour which he himself had lost, and which is now remembered with such great bitterness. His exact words are:

Oh! that I were as in months past, as in the days when Eloah preserved me; when his lamp shined upon my head, and when by his light I walked through darkness; as I was in the days of my autumn, when the confidence of Eloah was upon my tent; when Shaddai was yet with me, when my boys were about me, when my steps were washed in cream, and the rock poured me out rivers of oil; when I went out to the gate above the city, when I prepared my seat in the market-place. The young men saw me, and hid themselves; and the aged arose and stood up. The nobles refrained talking and laid their hand on their mouth. The chiefs held their peace,[1] and their tongue cleaved to the roof of their mouth. Unto me men gave ear and waited, and kept silence at my counsel. After my words they spoke not again, and my speech dropped upon them. And they waited for me as for the rain; and they opened their mouth wide as for the late rain. I smiled to them when they were not confident; and the light of my countenance kept them from falling. I chose out their way, and sat as chief, and dwelt as a king in the army ... When the ear heard me, then it blessed me; and when the eye saw me, it gave witness to me. Because I delivered the poor that cried, and the fatherless, who had none to help him. The blessing of him that was ready to perish came on me; and I caused the widow's heart to sing for joy. I put on righteousness, and it clothed me; my justice was as a robe and a turban. I was eyes to the blind, and feet was I to the lame. I was a father to the poor, and the cause which I knew not I searched out. And I broke the jaws of the wicked, and plucked the spoil out of his teeth. Then I said: I shall die with my nest, and I shall multiply my days as the sand. My root is spread out by the waters, and the dew lieth all night upon my branch. My glory is fresh in me, and my bow is renewed in my hand (Job 29; verses 21-25 are put before verse 11).

This description takes us into the midst of a small harmonious Israelitic community, the centre of which is Job. He is a man rich in blessing, successful in all that he undertakes. And his blessing is typically Israelitic. He lives surrounded by sons, and fertility wells up around him, both in the herd and the field; milk and oil flow in currents. It is this rich blessing which creates the honour of Job. His honour, which is renewed daily, consists in being able to give.

If we want to see Job in his highest manifestation of honour, we must follow him to the market place, to see him in the circle of the upholders of the little community. They are in the midst of their consultation, but as soon as Job arrives, the old men bow before him, and the greatest chiefs keep silent when he speaks. Why do they do that? Job has no external authority which forces them to bow before him. They keep silent because Job's counsel is really the best. He has strength of soul to put into his counsel so that he is always able to create that which persists and leads to the goal. Therefore they all listen to him; they are like the dry field which greedily sucks the rain. Job is the great *counsellor*.

He has the strength to uphold both himself and the others; all take refuge with him, in order to be supported by his strength. As a counsellor Job shows his ability most strongly in the market place, when he puts his will into the strongest and thus bends them to his will. But wherever he goes, he must be the counsellor because he has the strength, which must also penetrate the surroundings. He remembers how a smile from him would strengthen the weak, and Eliphaz confirms it by his words: Behold, thou hast instructed many, and thou hast strengthened the weak hands. Thy words have upholden him that was falling, and thou hast strengthened the feeble knees (4,3-4).

The same honour which Job wins by giving counsel to the strong and strength of soul to the weak, he acquires through giving gifts to the poor. For it is the same blessing which acts in his power to make counsel, and in the wealth which he creates around himself. From him the poor can get all they need. He made the heart of the widow exult; he clothed those who were poor and miserable; their loins blessed him when they were being warmed by the wool of his sheep. No poor man could perish entirely in that community; he always could turn to Job for assistance. To help the lesser is, in the eyes of Job, something far greater than a duty; it is a privilege.

In the Book of Job the conception of honour is based upon a safely established harmony. The community forms a closely connected circle, a society of friends where all belong. Each communicates to the other of the blessing he possesses, but he who communicates most has the authority and honour, because he upholds them all. Thus honour maintains harmony in the community, because it is determined by the relation between giving and taking. Honour is not a mechanically established factor which the man possesses, howsoever he may be; on the contrary, it is identical with the very being of the man. At the moment when the blessing departs from him, so that he can no longer give, he has also lost his honour. Job himself has described it to us in bitter words. The harmony has crumbled to pieces; his friends are not to be found; those nearest to him do not know him, his wife and children hate him. His slave does not answer him; boys who formerly concealed themselves from his strength, show him contempt (19,13-19); rabble which he would have disdained to have set with the dogs of his flock, deride him (30,1). So close is the connection between giving and taking in this community.

The Book of Job gives us valuable evidence of a harmony which, in spite of everything, it has been possible to preserve in an Israelitic community; it shows us that there was an Israelitic town-life, different from that in the great cities which the prophets reveal to us.

In the oldest Israel the rule of the chiefs rested entirely on this realistic foundation. Jephthah and Gideon were judges, i. e. chiefs, because they were the greatest. They counselled the people and gained the victory. When their tribesmen conferred upon them the honour of the chief and subjected themselves to them, then it was only an expression of actual conditions: they were the greatest, and the others received strength from them. Saul's dominion was based on the same foundation of reality. He was a chief because he had the soul of a chief, in their relation to which the others ought to be receivers. He manifested it when he saved his people from the Ammonites; but this deed was only an expression of the greatness which he already possessed and which would necessarily entitle him to be the greatest, who was to uphold the others. And the kingdom which was conferred upon him was the people's manner of confirming that it had been the receiver, and that he was the great one, who gave to them all.

As Job says, the honour of the chief must be renewed. He must always be the one who gives to all; otherwise he ceases being a chief. It was that which brought about the tragedy in the life of Saul. It does not imply that he is the only one who performs great deeds. The great chief is surrounded by a company of heroes, who would not be worth much, if they did not maintain their honour by valiant deeds. But the honour is to be given to the chief. Thereby his men acknowledge that he is still greater, and that in their strength they are dependent upon him. When Joab revenged himself upon Abner, against whom he bore a grudge, it was a violation of his relations with David, the friend of Abner. Joab cannot maintain a claim of honour against his chief. He showed that he understood it when he laid siege to the capital of the Ammonites, and when the chief preparations had been made, he sent a messenger to David saying: Now therefore gather the rest of the people together, and encamp against the city and take it, lest I take the city and my name be called over it (2 Sam. 12, 28). This honour is due to David, because Joab cannot maintain a special honour beside that of David. His deeds are performed to the glory of his king.

The same relation which Joab occupied towards David, the latter at one time had occupied towards Saul. When the conflict had broken loose, Jonathan tried to settle it by making Saul consider the valiant deeds of David as done in his honour. But all attempts were in vain. The fact was that the deeds of David had been held up as independent deeds, equal and superior to those of Saul. At the very moment when the women sang: Saul hath slain his thousands, David his ten thousands! Saul was no longer the greatest, the one on whom everybody was dependent. David had become greater than he. He knew what it meant, and it is said: And Saul was very wroth, and the saying displeased him; and he said: They have ascribed to David ten thousands, and to me they have ascribed but thousands, and now he will surely get the kingdom (1 Sam. 18,8). Saul would either have to fall as Job, or to defeat David. It was a fight for the blessing; but the central point of the fight was the fact that the blessing created greatness of soul, honour, and so also demands.

Honour is not an individual possession; as a result of the very construction of the soul it must, like the blessing, spread from the individual. First and foremost it is a family property. The son possesses the honour of his father and is bound to manifest it. When Gideon had died, it followed as a matter of course that his sons must become chiefs. But it also extends beyond the family. The chief and his men create honour for each other; the whole of the community which is dependent upon the chief, has its share in his honour and maintains the demands of honour.

Thus the Ephraimites claimed to be the strongest family or tribe, whose honour the others had to acknowledge. This appeared when Gideon had fought the Midianites and conquered the two mighty chiefs. The Ephraimites had not been present, but when the battle was decided, they were called to keep guard upon some wading-places, and there they killed two other chiefs, Oreb and Zeeb. The Ephraimites burst out upon Gideon and rebuked him that he had gone to war without them. Why this anger? The answer is implied in the words of Gideon. He says: What have I done now in comparison of you? Is not the gleaning of the grapes of Ephraim better than the vintage of Abiezer? God hath delivered into your hands the princes of Midian, Oreb and Zeeb, and what am I able to do in comparison of you? (Judg. 8,2-3). The continuation runs: Then their anger was abated toward him when he had said that.

The words of the Ephraimites imply a rebuke of Gideon and his family, because they have taken the whole glory. They themselves have hitherto possessed the greatest honour, and now the Abiezerites come and, by their deed, deprive them of that glory! Gideon is a wise man and turns aside in time. His answer is not warranted by the immediately preceding events; for it is, after all, he who has gained the battle and carried the greater burden. His words are warranted by the relation between his family and the Ephraimites. Honour rests upon the proportion between giving and taking. To maintain one's honour means to be able to prove oneself the giver and counsellor, and that one can only do when one possesses more than the others. The Ephraimites have hitherto been the family to whom the others had to take recourse. Gideon knows that if he is to maintain the honour of being the greatest, which he has gained through his victory, then it must be through a fight between his family and the Ephraimites, in which the Abiezerites will have to show that they really possess the greatness which is claimed by their victory. The consequences of this step Gideon dare not take, and so he yields his victory to the Ephraimites by yielding them the greater honour. This decides the matter. A Bedouin-tribe might have acted like Ephraim, but not all Bedouin chiefs would have answered like Gideon.

There was also another Israelite who would not do it, and that was Jephthah. When he had won his great victory over the Ammonites the Ephraimites became anxious about their honour and threatened Jephthah to burn his house — he was to be humbled and reduced.

But Jephthah proved what sort of man he was. He gathered his men and inflicted a crushing defeat upon the Ephraimites; he took possession of the passages of Jordan, and when the fugitives betrayed their Ephraimitic parentage by saying *sibbōleth* instead of *shibbōleth,* they were slain (Judg. 12,1-6).[1] As to the further development of these events we know nothing, the Book of Judges only containing detached narratives, which show us the life of that period in isolated instances. But both narratives give us glimpses of a conception of life of which we have otherwise little evidence in Israel.

The narratives dealing with the Ephraimites show us the sensitiveness of honour in the oldest Israel. It was always necessary to be on one's guard in order to maintain it. As we have already seen, Gideon was a man of honour, and yet, when on his expedition against the Midianites he came, with his starving men, to the city of Succoth and asked for a little bread, he received the answer: Are the hands of Zebah and Zalmunna now in thine hand, that we should give bread unto thy men that are weary? And he took the elders of the city and thorns of the wilderness and briers, and with them he taught[2] the men of Succoth (Judg. 8,15-16). Nor did Penuel, which acted in a similar manner, fare any better.

The doubt which these citizens entertain about Gideon's power to win is a doubt of his strength, and consequently an insult. Gideon wants full reparation, and therefore he does not strike at once. He first shows his greatness by really proving victorious, and as a victor he maintains himself against the doubters by chastising them.

The chief must maintain his honour throughout; he cannot in any single point let himself be surpassed by a lesser man. The old Israelites now and again strive with each other in order thus to maintain their honour. But it is not empty play; it is a real fight to maintain oneself, because the honour is the reality which keeps the man upright. We find one example of this in the Books of Samuel (2 Sam. 2). Once when Joab and Abner met, each with his company of men, they agreed to hold a sort of tournament. They wrestled, but the wrestling quickly came to an end, in that the men smote each other down. The ensuing fight seems to consist in a race, in which the object of the pursuer was to overtake the pursued and take his armour away from him. During this fight a strange episode occurred. Abner is pursued by Asahel, the brother of Joab, much younger, but light of feet. Abner cries to him: Turn thee aside to the right or the left, and lay thee hold on one of the young men and take his armour (v. 21). Asahel refuses to hear, and after a little while Abner says: Turn thee aside from following me! Otherwise I shall smite thee to the ground, and how then should I hold up my face to Joab, thy brother? But Asahel still refuses to hear, and it ends by Abner thrusting his spear backwards and into the body of Asahel.

Abner is the full-grown chief, the head of the whole of his company of heroes. If he is vanquished, then all his men will be put to shame, and he will no more be the great chief. When the younger man is on the point of vanquishing him, there are only two possibilities before him: either to strike him down or himself to lose his position. Still, there is a third: to persuade him to turn aside. Of course Asahel knows what is at stake. He might vanquish one of the younger men and win honour thereby, but his claims are great; he will not be content with less than what, as a matter of fact, he is able to gain. Abner then has no other expedient than to maintain himself by striking the other down.

To fall at the hand of a lesser man is insupportable for a chief. When Gideon had caught the two chiefs of the Midianites, he first wanted his boy to strike them down, but they were too mighty for him. Then they said: Rise thou and smite us down; for as the man is, so is his strength! (Judg. 8,21). They presumably mean: A great man is required in order to strike us down. To fall before a chief and not before a boy is what befits them. When Abimelech had received a mortal hurt from a piece of a mill-stone flung against him by a woman, he had to ask his armour-bearer to give him the death-thrust, that it should not be said of him that a woman slew him (Judg. 9,54).

The old conception of honour is imbued with ideality. Honour is not a thing which one possesses and enjoys. It does not consist in being free of labour and trouble, but, on the contrary, in making the greatest effort, in being the one who carries the greatest burden: in giving most, in acting most. To be a chief does not imply to be able to force something upon the community, to keep it down. It is not necessary for the chief always to go about and keep his people under control. His position depends on the acknowledgment of something underlying his actions, an actual greatness. Therefore, the outward victory is not everything to him; the all-important thing is that the victory should manifest the fact that he is the greatest.

When Nahash, the king of Ammonites, attacked Jabesh, it was neither in order to plunder the town nor to strike it down at all costs. He wanted to humble it, to force it to render up its honour to him; but it should be through a real fight, otherwise the whole deed would be without value. The city was free to turn for help to its kinsmen before the decisive step was to be taken (Judg. 11).

By means of deceit Abimelech had made himself the ruler of Shechem, but his rule did not last, because it was built on a crime. Still, Abimelech was able to maintain himself for some time. We hear of the rising against him (Judg. 9). Gaal, the son of Ebed, is the leader. He asks the men of Shechem whether Abimelech really possesses sufficient greatness to make him their chief; his fathers were not chiefs, but had served their fathers. Abimelech is warned by his confidential man, Zebul, and approaches with his warriors. Next morning Gaal stands with Zebul at the gate and sees Abimelech coming. Zebul then says to Gaal that now is the time to show what his big words are worth, and to march against Abimelech to fight him. Gaal then gathers his people and goes against Abimelech, but is put to flight. This settles the matter — for the time being. Abimelech withdraws again, and Zebul chases Gaal out of the town (Judg. 9,40-41).

It has been said that this version is impossible. After all that has taken place, how can Gaal and the head man of Abimelech stand as "boon companions" within the gate? But this is quite in the old spirit. Gaal wants to be chief, and this matter can be decided in one way only, i. e. by his measuring his strength against Abimelech and striking him down. Zebul and Gaal both realize that and, Gaal being defeated, Abimelech must consider the matter as settled. Gaal is done for; now Zebul can chase him out of the city without any kind of opposition. It is quite a different matter that the rising also has other roots, and that the fight between Shechem and Abimelech therefore breaks out afresh (ib. 42 ff.).[1]

The conception of honour with which we become acquainted in the Book of Judges does not appear to be essentially different from that of several other peoples, but most closely related it is to that of their Arabian kinsmen. An Arab of the old type knows nothing higher than to fight and thus to gain honour as the first among his fellows. During the battle he seeks the most dangerous post, and directs his efforts against the most valiant adversary. He does not attempt to go in hiding, but shouts his name aloud, so that everybody may know whom they have before them. He wants to be the one whose help is sought by others, to whom guests turn for shelter, and who distributes his gifts to all comers. Honour consists in independence. If one cannot give, then one can, at any rate, forbear receiving. "Rather would I swallow the dust of the earth, than that a mighty man should look down upon me in his mightiness", says Shanfara. We know Arabians like the newly appointed Shanfara, or like Imra'alkais, who go into the desert to live among jackals and suffer all the bitterness of want in order to maintain their honour: not to owe anything to anybody, not to submit to anybody.

This Arabian ideal of a chief we recognize in the Book of Judges. When Gideon and the two Midianite princes were confronting each other, they were three specimens of the same type. Jephthah acts exactly as a Bedouin chief would do. But also the extreme type of honour, that of Shanfara and Imra'alkais, is suggested in Israel by a figure like that of Samson. Also he is denied by his family and is bound to live in caves; but he passes from one valiant deed unto another, in order to maintain his pride: not to put up with insults. He was a man who rent a lion, as he would have rent a kid, so why should others not bend down before him? Whenever the Philistines insulted him, they were made to pay for it; when by wiles they had solved his riddle, and he had to pay thirty state-garments, then he slew thirty of their kinsmen and took their spoil. When they had taken his wife, he burnt their fields, and when he had been delivered into their hands, he struck them right and left with a jaw-bone.[1]

Samson performs none of these valiant deeds in order to achieve something. One cannot help feeling impressed by the recklessness with which he moves freely among the Philistines, while at the same time beating and chastising them. His mighty actions are all the outcome of his greatness. He does not gather wealth, but a great soul like his must do great deeds and maintain itself when assailed. It is just as impossible to subdue Samson as it was to subdue Shanfara. When, through cunning and a woman's wiles, the Philistines had got him into their power, they tried to subdue him by putting out his eyes and setting him to the humiliating task of grinding. But they were unable to lessen his soul. When they were together at a great feast, the captured giant was led in by a slave, that they might exult at the sight of his humiliation. Samson asked the slave to lead him to the middle pillars. He took hold of them and broke them, so that the whole of the house collapsed and buried everyone who was in it, the Philistines and himself. "So the dead which he slew at his death were more than they which he slew in his life" (Judg. 16, 30). The grandeur of Samson's death surpasses that of all other Israelitic heroes, and he maintained his indomitable pride until the last. Before he took hold of the pillars, he cried to Yahweh for strength to avenge his *one* eye. More all the Philistines together could not outweigh!

If we compare these heroes of the oldest Israel with Job, we find essential points of similarity. Honour in both cases depends upon harmony: he who is filled with honour is the giver and the counsellor, the upholder of the others. His honour is throughout dependent upon the fact that he is the stronger. Jephthah gains honour while protecting his tribe, Job while he leads the will of the others and upholds the life of the poor. And yet they are two different types. The heroes of the Book of Judges represent the Bedouin spirit in the newly immigrated Israelites, to whom life is a constant fight. That which makes honour is first and foremost valiant deeds. Job, on the other hand, is the great chief of the fellahs; he represents the life of the small town. For him honour is to counsel and at the same time to gain wealth which he may distribute to others. The life of the fighting and plundering nomads is to him a strange world. The difference appears most strongly when he is stricken by misfortune. When it is announced that nomads have taken his property, his honour is not roused to make a fight for it. All his striving ceases; he sits down with nerveless hands saying: Yahweh gave, Yahweh has taken away, blessed be the name of Yahweh! His honour is taken away, and so all is over. How far he is from Samson! whose striving never dies, or from Shanfara, who has lost all in the family and proceeds to new destines, perfectly convinced that "for the noble there is on this earth refuge against ignomy."

The Bedouin, as we know him in his ideal form, can never lose honour as long as his will is towards it, because the kernel of honour is courage and valiant deeds; even through misery and want he is able to maintain his honour. But a man like Job loses honour when losing prosperity, just because wealth and prosperity form an essential part of his honour. In the days of his prosperity Job stands out so beautiful and strong, because we see him within his own circle, where he is the constantly active person, imparting his gifts on all sides. When he has fallen, he can only complain and ask for the restoration of that which has been lost. With this type it is not courage creating honour, but wealth and prosperity.

Of these two types it is the latter which is typically Israelitic. Jephthah, Samson and Saul stand forth in the Israelitic literature as solitary relics of the past. But even the type of Job was not preserved in its purity. The presupposition of this type is *harmony*. The great man acquires wealth in order to give to others, and he is great, because he upholds. We know that this harmony was dissolved. The great profited by their strength to gather and collect, but they acquired wealth only in order to enjoy, not in order to give. They did not support the community, but impoverished it and calmly left the weaker to starve. They lived in luxury, in houses of hewn stone, and trampled the poor underfoot (Is. 1,23; 3,12-14; 5,8 ff.; Am. 5,11-12; 8,4-5; Mic. 2,1-5, etc.).

It is the new city culture which bore this bitter fruit. It was the indomitable maintenance of self which had supplanted the old conception of honour in this demand for *possession,* instead of giving and upholding.

The great wants honour without giving, merely because he possesses. He is no longer a counsellor. The old chief gained honour by uplifting the wills, at the same time making them subservient to his own. He became great by making others great. The man of the new type first and foremost thinks of maintaining himself. He wants to *rule* rather than to counsel; he becomes great by humiliating others, not by raising them. He wants to *have* the honour and to enjoy it by letting others give without giving anything himself. Therefore, he does not fight, like the Israelites of the older type, in order to grow through the combat and to maintain his actual greatness. He prefers to avoid fighting, and if he must, then the chief thing for him is not to measure himself against the enemy and to become the greatest, but to achieve a result: to obtain dominion, to crush the enemy.

Such claims are put forward by the despot, who is first and foremost thinking of his own greatness, desiring to take rather than to give. With this claim corresponds the humbleness of the lesser. He must give all, subject himself entirely to the strong. With the love of dominion of the great corresponds the *fear* of the lesser. He has no independent honour to maintain, but must trust to the mercy of the stronger. He must often gain his end by wiles, always turn aside; for him fighting is out of the question; he cannot openly maintain his cause, but achieves prosperity and progress by throwing himself before one who is greater. But this prosperity is sufficient to him; however gained, it is his self-maintenance, and all prosperity and self-maintenance is to him identical with honour. The honour is in the result, in the thing acquired.

This timidity, in a greater or lesser degree, characterizes average Israel and in particular leaves a strong impress on the Patriarchal legends. Jacob always turns aside, but gains happiness by devious ways and by humbling himself. Seven times he throws himself down before Esau (Gen. 33,3). Upon the whole one throws oneself in the dust before one's superior, or before one from whom one expects to achieve something. One honours a man by humbling oneself in the dust before him and calling oneself his slave. We know these habits from the Tell-el-Amarna tablets, from which it appears that they are in the old Canaanite spirit. Up or down, so it was in Canaan, and so it came to be in Israel. It is then rather obvious that it is not only the development of the large city which has bent the old Israelitic conception of honour, but that the Canaanite spirit, which in all respects penetrated into the soul of the Israelite, also here has the main share in the transformation. And this influence was particularly favoured by the introduction of a monarchy in the Canaanite spirit. It is expressed symbolically in the relation between Saul and David. Saul represents throughout the old type, while in the character of David — as already suggested — we recognize a good deal of the later type.

The image of the man possessed of honour as it stands out in the old sources, we may picture more in detail. The soul manifests itself in the *body*. One can judge from the appearance of a man that he is a chief. Saul was "from his shoulder and upward higher than any of the people". When Gideon had caught the two Midianite chiefs, Zebah and Zalmunna, and asked what manner of men they were whom they had killed at Tabor, he received the answer: Each one resembled the son of a king (Judg. 8,18). It makes part of the praising of a king to call him the fairest of the children of men (Ps. 45,3). The strength of the limbs, the harmoniously built stature bear witness to the nobility of the soul. Meribbaal, the son of Jonathan, was lame (2 Sam. 9). But then he was also a poor invalid who could not maintain himself, neither in relation to David nor to the chief of his own warriors, Abner. Of course it was out of the question that men with bodily defects should be able to do service as priests (Lev. 21,16-24), and so also eunuchs are excluded from the cultic community (Deut. 23,2).

But honour is also to be read in the face and the countenance. The proud man looks freely about him. If he loses his honour, then his face is covered with shame; he lowers his face and veils it from the eyes of others.[1]

Honour must appear in the *garments* worn, because the soul of the man penetrates everything that belongs to his entirety. The miserable sits with his shame in the ash-heap, without clothes. But the apparel of the king is splendour and glory, smelling of sweet odours (Ps. 45,9). There may be garments, so penetrated by a definite psychical substance, that they are indissolubly connected with its forms of manifestation. This holds good where special importance is attached to the functions. Thus with the priests. There cannot be any doubt that certain parts of the clerical costume were heirlooms, in particular the ephod, the scapular. The honour and glory of the priest is bound up with his garment (Sir. 50,11). Therefore it can only be worn by him who is qualified for it; but if he is, then the garment also invests him with full honour of his vocation, "consecrates him to be a priest", gives him "honour and glory" (Exod. 28,2 f.). The anxiety lest the holy garments should be defiled, appears from the careful ritual for the Day of Atonement, preserved in Mishna.

The king also has his appurtenances pertaining to the kingly honour, viz. diadem and sceptre. They have passed from generation to generation, still more or less penetrated by the kingly soul and thus transmitting its honour.[2] When Pharaoh takes the ring off his finger and puts it on the hand of Joseph, then this implies a real conferring of honour (Gen. 41,42). When a man assumes his holiday attire and puts on his jewellery, then he is not the same as in his everyday clothes. If he is struck by misfortune, then he cannot wear jewellery (Exod. 33,4 ff.). He cannot even wear his normal garments, but rends them and dons a piece of coarse cloth, which is not worn by men possessed of honour, and also the widow has her own special dress (Gen. 38,14.19). Thus the clothes follow and partake of the total character of the soul. He who defiles himself, e. g. by "a wòman in her issue" or by unclean food, thus also shall get unclean clothes (Lev. 15,27; 17,15). And he who enters the sphere of the sanctuary, must not only consecrate and cleanse his body, but also his clothes (Gen. 35,2; Exod. 19,10.14).

Property is called that which is "taken", "appropriated" or "gathered" (*'ᵃḥuzzā, ḳinyān* or *miḳne, rᵉkhūsh).* There is a particularly intimate association between the man and his property, which is penetrated by and absorbed into his soul. This association is expressed by his being its *ba'al.* It is not mere chance when the Hebrew language, in its terms, does not distinguish between the partitive and the possessive: to make part of and to belong to someone. Property is partly real estate, partly cattle[1] and slaves, partly gold and silver and whatever a man may possess. It follows from the whole general conception that property must make a very considerable part of the honour of a man, nay, is often equal to the whole honour.

Property makes the man *great.* Isaac became very great, having possession of sheep and goats, cattle and slaves (Gen. 26,13 f.). The soul becomes great or *heavy* through wealth. "Abram was very heavy through property" (Gen. 13,2). The word which we generally translate by "honour", *kābhōdh,* strictly means "heaviness", the fact of being heavy; it indicates the heavy substance of the soul and is most particularly used about wealth. Laban's sons say of Jacob, who has become rich in cattle by tending their father's herds: Of that which was our father's has he made himself all this "heaviness" (Gen. 31,1). Whether *kābhōdh* is here rendered by wealth or honour is immaterial, seeing that it means both. The eyes of the Israelite shine when in possession of gold; the more gold, the more honour. The prophet announcing the conquest of Niniveh says to his countrymen: Take ye the spoil of silver, take the spoil of gold; for there is none end of its store and glory out of all the precious furniture! (Nah. 2,10). And the Psalmist who is sorely troubled by the wealth of the wicked says: Be not thou afraid when one is made rich, when the glory of his house is increased (Ps. 49,17); for the rich will have to render up wealth and honour. Wealth, treasures and honour are indissolubly connected terms in the eyes of the Israelites (Pr. 22,4; Eccles. 6,2; Esth. 1,4; 5,11).

Appreciation of wealth is a human feature, but for non-modern peoples wealth means more than material gain, and so also for the Israelites. It fills and uplifts the soul and makes it grow in value; blessing acts in it and honour swells. This intimate relation between soul and property is the decisive factor in the law of inheritance. We have seen how the property is connected with the family to whose soul it has been made familiar.

The relation between man and property is a mutual one. Property is imbued with the essence of the owner, and on him it reflects honour or shame. The man is wholly responsible for his property. This general principle of "primitive" peoples must have held good in old Israel. But in the city-cultures of western Asia the old conception of property has been modified. There is a tendency to slacken its intimate connection with man, to take it as something to be utilized. So the responsibility of the man for his property is weakened and reduced to the duty of giving a fixed compensation in case of damage. If, for instance, an ox gores a man and hurts him, the owner, according to the law of Hammurabi, is generally not responsible; he is only responsible if he knows that the ox is apt to gore, and has failed to make it harmless. And even in this case he is only obliged to pay a fine if the ox kills a free man, and a smaller one if it kills a slave (§§ 250-252). A similar rule prevails among the Hittites, of whose conception it is still more characteristic.

In Israel this law is formulated in the following manner: If an ox gore a man or a woman that they die, then the ox shall be surely stoned, and his flesh shall not be eaten, but the owner of the ox shall be quit. But if the ox were wont to push with his horn in time past, and it has been testified to his owner, and he has not kept him in, but that he has killed a man or a woman, the ox shall be stoned, and his owner also shall be put to death. If there be laid on him a sum of money, then he shall give for the ransom of his life whatsoever is laid upon him. Whether he have gored a son or have gored a daughter, according to this rule shall it be done unto him. If the ox shall push a man slave or a female slave, he shall give unto their master thirty shekels of silver, and the ox shall be stoned (Exod. 21,28-32).

In this law we find the idea of the Babylonian and Hittite in a modified form. Only if the ox is known to be in the habit of goring and it kills a man, the owner bears full responsibility and is treated as a manslayer. Thus the law represents a compromise between the Canaanite and the Israelitic spirit. From the laws of retaliation many other examples of this will appear.

When wealth is honour, then it is because it is strength. It is not only *kābhōdh,* heaviness, but also *ḥayil,* strength (Gen. 34,29; Is. 10,14; Job 20,15 *et al.*). The word comprises both blessing and honour. It designates the capability of the soul, its strength and efficiency, valour. It comprises mighty deeds and wealth, all that in which strength manifests itself. A "mighty man of valour", *gibbōr ḥayil,* is the proper appellation for a man of honour of the old type. It is used both of Gideon, of Jephthah, of the father of Saul, of young David (Judg. 6,12; 11,1; 1 Sam. 9,1; 16,18), indicating men who possess the blessing and manifest it in courage and mighty deeds and in the power to succeed. It designates the nobility, those possessed of great property and having great obligations.

The blessing always creates honour, simply because of its creating prosperity. "The shoot of Yahweh shall be beauty and honour, and the fruit of the country shall be exaltation and glory, for them that are escaped of Israel" (Is. 4,2). Still, not only wealth, but long life is honour (Pr. 3,16), and first and foremost the possession of sons. The prophet says: Their honour flieth like a bird, away from the birth, and from the womb, and from the conception (Hos. 9,11; cf. Esth. 5,11). Blessing, honour, life and joy are expressions which are very closely connected (Ps. 21,6; Pr. 21,21; 22,4).

Honour being identical with the substance and weight of the soul, it must be individual in its kind. The chief has his honour, the lesser man his. The older man has more honour than the younger; one must be *zāḳān,* a full-grown man, in order to possess full honour. We have seen how impossible it is for Abner to let himself be conquered by the younger. Job best describes the greatness of his honour by saying that the old men bent before him, and the depth of his humiliation is characterized by his being mocked by people who are younger than he (Job 29,8; 30,1). The demand that honour shall be shown to the old is in full accordance with the Israelitic view of life, which sees the blessing act in him who has a long life. Honour is shown to a man as a father, because he grows through the family. The fact of being many makes the soul great and full of honour.

Woman also has her honour. In the Proverbs woman is often praised as the wife; the passionate songs of the Canticles praise her as the beloved, but, upon the whole, woman is not praised as woman among the Israelites. For her life is full of sufferings and labour. The scantiness of sources from the oldest Israel unfortunately yields us very little information about woman — but still some. It is a woman, Deborah, who stands forth urging the tribes to fight, and it is the women who, with their songs, render honour to the returning warriors and reprove the less victorious chief. We know these urging, glorifying and mocking women from the Bedouins. It is the man who performs the deeds; the woman is to share his honour with him, and it is she who keeps alive his energy. A different, although analogous, type of woman we meet in Abigail, who with her cleverness must remedy the harm which the impetuousness of her husband is on the point of calling down upon the house.

The honour of a woman is to bear a man's name through marriage. If she does not obtain this, she is dishonoured (Is. 4,1). And her honour as a wife she only maintains by multiplying and continuing the name of her husband through posterity. As a mother the woman is honoured; childlessness is a shame which she can hardly survive. Only when Rachel gives birth to a son, is she able to say: God has taken away my shame (Gen. 30,23). Hannah is so bowed down by her childlessness that she nearly dies with shame. [1] The woman who gives birth to a son no longer needs to be afraid; she has fulfilled her task, her soul has acquired merit (1 Sam. 4,20). Jerusalem is sometimes called a childless widow, when its state of deepest degradation is to be characterized. A childless widow is entirely destitute of honour and has no great hope of acquiring any. And still less honour has perhaps the woman who has been repudiated by her husband, because she could not fulfil her task of supplying him with children. Even the hetæra, standing outside the circle of honourable women, rejoices in her child and will not give it to another (1 Kings 3, 16 f.).

To bear a man's name and to increase it is the honour of the woman. The dishonoured virgin is bowed down with shame, because she has been taken by the man without his giving her a name. And the faithless wife degrades herself and sins against her own soul, because she has given it to her husband and takes her name from him, while at the same time giving herself to another, whose name she does not bear (cf. Hos. 2,7). When the law forbids a priest to marry a whore or a profane woman, or a woman put away from her husband (Lev. 21,7), then it is the woman without honour who is here mentioned in her three typical forms.

That a woman may enjoy a fair amount of freedom appears from a number of examples. She goes about tending her sheep, and in the evenings she meets the shepherds at the well. Likewise, Rebekah is not given into marriage, before she herself has consented. But because of her mentality woman must accommodate herself to the soul of her husband and become part of him, and there are examples showing how intimate the relation could be.

But when considering the average type of Israelite, we are struck by the lack of chivalry characterizing his relation towards woman, and this entirely agrees with the conception of honour and the relation of the stronger towards the weaker which gradually came to prevail. Abraham, this ideal Israelite, calmly gives up his wife and her honour in order to save his own precious life, and this narrative must even have been a great favourite, seeing that it is told three times, once about Isaac (Gen. 12.21.26). When he goes down into a foreign country, he says to his wife: Say, I pray thee, thou art my sister, that it may be well with me for thy sake; and that I shall not lose my life because of thee (Gen. 12,13). A more glaring proof that the old conception of honour has been lost, it is hard to find. Abraham prefers to tell a lie and to sacrifice his wife rather than to run the risk of getting into a disagreeable position. And it must be presumed that Sarah found it quite natural, seeing that she agrees. This is then the good wife according to the Israelitic ideal.

There are other narratives of a similar kind, one in the Book of Judges (chap. 19): An Ephraimite and his concubine go to lodge in the house of a man in Gibeah. The men of Gibeah break into the house in order to do violence to the strangers. The owner of the house offers them his daughter who is a virgin, that they may do with her as they want. However, they seize the strange woman and abuse her until she dies.—We not only hear nothing of the man defending his concubine, but in the eyes of the narrator the host evidently seems particularly generous, in that he offers to sacrifice his daughter. This narrative, it is true, dates from a late period, but it is also found in an older story about Lot, who in a similar position makes the men of his town an offer of the same generous kind (Gen. 19). The foundation of both narratives is that the right of hospitality towards a man is more sacred than the life and honour of a woman.

It is probable that this view of woman was less pronounced in old Israel, where strength was tantamount to the privilege of protecting the weaker. That changing social conditions exercised a great influence on the position of the wife is easily discerned. The harems which the mighty subsequently introduced into Israel, deprived marriage of its intimate character, and here, as in other respects, new and foreign elements in Israel can be traced to monarchy. The degradation of woman did not imply loss of influence; but her manner and so also her influence came to be of a different kind. There is a world of difference between the old types of women, such as Abigail or Hannah or Tamar, and the refined "kine of Bashan" in Samaria who, according to the description of Amos, recline on their elegant ivory couches, insatiably demanding wine and pleasure, or the fine ladies who, in the days of Isaiah, tripped about the streets of Jerusalem displaying all the arts of the demi-monde.

He whose soul is filled with strength is heavy of substance, *nikhbādh,* i. e., properly speaking, he who gets himself heaviness. When we translate it by "honoured", we must not consider it as something passive, something which is exclusively given to the man from without. It is an expression of self-glory, of something which the man possesses within himself. Honour fills the soul and "lifts" it (2 Kings 14,10), by honour the soul exalts "its horn" (Ps. 112,9). Power fills with "glory and honour" (Ps. 8,6). When it is said of Samuel: The man is filled with honour *(nikhbādh),* all that he saith cometh surely to pass (1 Sam. 9,6), then it means, not only that he is honoured by other people, but that he has the "heaviness", the strength within himself to be able to act as a proper seer. In the same manner it is said of Shechem that he is the "heaviest", most *nikhbādh* of his house (Gen. 34, 19), just as David was full of honour, one who had great weight and authority in the house of Saul (1 Sam. 22,14).

But in order to be a whole, honour must be acknowledged by others. A type like the Arabian Shanfara, who is deserted by all, but maintains his honour by not being dependent upon anybody, is an extreme case; he has the honour within himself, though independence after all is only something negative. The normal honour is that which makes others dependent. He who receives, increases the honour of the giver by acknowledging that he receives; the weak honours the great by submitting to his will. Children honour their parents by obedience, and in the same manner the Israelite honours his god by acknowledging that he receives everything from him. The chief gains great honour when strong men join his following and thus show that they are dependent on him, subject to his will. When Saul had quarrelled with Samuel, he asked the latter to honour him before the elders of his people by turning back with him (1 Sam. 15,30).

Thus also the weaker may give something to the stronger. He always gives him something of himself, in submitting his will to him; thus he increases and strengthens the will of the strong, while at the same time he himself derives volition from him. It happens in that the receiver blesses the giver. Thus it must be according to the law of souls; when the stream of blessing emanates from the strong in the shape of good gifts, it must return with blessing from the weak, who strengthen and increase his greatness. Thus the greater and lesser uphold each other with their blessings. In the harmonious community the blessing of the receivers is created directly from what they receive. Therefore there is a direct ratio between the honour which the man receives and that which he gives. He takes the honour which he himself has as the substance of his soul. But the despot demands that the lesser are to give him all; their whole will they are to bend to his, and they are to render him all the honour, whether he gives or not.

The great has greatness within himself, but the lesser yields him actual greatness by honouring him. It is not only because the word of the lesser has its real power, but first and foremost because the receiver, through his word, subjects his will to that of the great, and thus really makes him great. God has the honour within himself, but through his hymns of praise man *renders* him honour, strengthens and increases it (Ps. 29,1; 96,7). He extols his deeds, announces the greatness of his power and his dominion all over the earth (Ps. 66,2-4). Thus he increases his greatness and honour, makes him "heavy" (Is. 24,15; Ps. 22,24). Yahweh is enthroned on the hymns of praise of Israel.

The praise, the blessing with which the lesser honours the greater, is called *t^ehillā*. But it does not only mean the words of praise or the action of praising. It means the honour and power which fill the soul and make it rich and great. "Moab's *t^ehillā*", which has disappeared from its capital (Jer. 48,2), is the power and strength of the country, the same thing which another prophet calls its *kābhōdh* (Is. 16,14). Babel was the *t^ehillā* of the whole earth, because its honour and strength extended so far (Jer. 51, 41), in the same manner as the *t^ehillā* of God fills the whole earth (Hab. 3,3). When human beings, in their joy at what they have received, render God *t^ehillā,* they yield him the honour he has and thus strengthen it.

One always honours a man by letting him assert his will; one honours him whom one countenances in a court of justice (Exod. 23,3), and Eli must bear the blame for having honoured his sons more than Yahweh (1 Sam. 2,29). But in particular one honours the man by making him greater than oneself. One rises in the presence of him who has greater honour (Job 29,8), and, as already mentioned, one honours one's superior by throwing oneself before him.

The man is honoured by *gifts*. The presupposition of the value of the gift and its extremely great importance among the different peoples, is that it is never merely material, but that it is filled with spiritual values. Therefore, the character and effect of the gift cannot be established by mechanical rules; it depends upon what lies in it, the gift being a form of blessing. The great receives honour by giving, and the lesser must give, as an expression that he owes something to the great. The guest one specially wants to honour is given more than the others. Therefore Benjamin's mess was five times as much as that of his brothers when they were entertained as the guests of Joseph in Egypt (Gen. 43,34).

He who gives has a direct claim on honour, because he gives. When the *mal'ākh* of Yahweh had promised Manoah a son, Manoah asked: What is thy name, that when thy sayings come true we may do thee honour? (Judg. 13,17). We see how simple is the conception of honour. It is rendered at the moment when the gift is at hand, neither before nor after, because honour at that moment is due to the giver. He who gives knows what he does; honour is something which is due to him, and he demands it as his right. Without any kind of false modesty one may beforehand negotiate about the honour. When Balak demanded the assistance of Balaam in order to curse the Israelitic troops, he promised him to honour him much and to do whatever he asked (Num. 22,17; 24,11). When Balaam did not fulfil the demands put to him, Balak could not but think that it was due to his doubting whether he would really be honoured for his help (22,37). It is true that it also should come to pass that Balaam was not honoured, but this was due to the intervention of a stronger power, which prevented him from serving Balak (24,11).

The eagerness with which the soul demands the maintenance of its honour is *ḳin'ā*, which word seems to be related to "red" and probably refers to the red colour appearing in the face when a person's honour is violated. It is characteristic that it is most frequently used about Yahweh, who demanded that Israel should show him all honour.

As we have already seen, honour is called *kābhōdh,* heaviness, because it is the same as the substance of the soul, its weight and value. But one may just as well speak of the *greatness* or the strength of the soul. When it is said in an appeal to God: Thine, O Yahweh, is the greatness, and the power, and the glory, and the victory, and the majesty (1 Chron. 29,11), then all of these words are synonyms: the fulness and volume of the soul, or in other words: honour. One speaks of a man's *gā'ōn,* possibly *gē'ūth* his "highness". The great soul is not only "heavy", it is also "high". When it is said that the "highness" of the Babylonian King has fallen down into Sheol (Is. 14,11), it does not mean something outside him, but the king himself in his greatness and plenitude of power. Yahweh's *gā'ōn* is his might and power (Mic. 5,3), Jordan's *gā'ōn* is the luxuriant vegetation of the valley, in which it manifests its blessing and its essence (Jer. 12,5; 49,19; 50,44; Zech. 11,3). Mention is often made, in a disapproving tone, of the "highness" of various people, because there are limits to the swelling of the honour of man and his consequent demands. [1]

A related term for honour is *tiph'ereth,* glory. The warrior acquires "glory" when he slays his enemy (Judg. 4,9). The glory of young men is their strength (Pr. 20,29). The meaning is the same: the substance and might of the soul, its honour. Yahweh led out his people from Egypt in order to create for himself a name of glory; his glorious arm supported Moses and divided the waters (Is. 63,12.14). Israel shall be to him "in praise, and in name, and in glory" (Deut. 26,19); when he sent it into exile "he delivered his strength into captivity, and his glory into the enemy's hand" (Ps. 78,61). [2] When the king stands forth in his full power, he shows his *hōdh* and *hādhār* (Ps. 21,6; 45,4), in the same manner as Yahweh, when acting in all his strength (Ps. 111,3), "dons" honour and majesty (Ps. 104,1; Job 40,10). The two words always designate the soul in its highest manifestation of power. The author of the Proverbs rises to such heights in his praise of the good wife that he calls strength and *hādhār* her clothing (31,25); *hōdh* may mean the violent snorting of the horses (Job 39,20). When Yahweh causes his voice to be heard and lets his arm come down in uncontrolled anger, with flames and tempest and hailstone, then one feels what is the *hōdh* and *hādhār* of his voice (Is. 30,30; Ps. 29,4). Both of these words indicate the outward manifestation of strength, but first and foremost the inner strength and merit. When we read in Daniel: My *hōdh* was turned in me into misery, [1] and I retained no strength (Dan. 10,8), then this implies the strength of the soul which fills it and upholds it.[2] And the same meaning *hōdh* has Num. 27,20, where it is said that Moses is to put some of his *hōdh* into Joshua that Israel may be obedient to him. It is the inner strength and worth which fills Moses and gives him authority. But this invisible strength, which is equal to honour, manifests itself outwardly. It radiates from the might of the strong, penetrates the surroundings and fills the space around him (Ps. 96,6). We have already seen that *tehillā* is not very different from this meaning.

All this shows that there is only very little difference between honour and that which the Israelite calls "heart". Honour is the substance of the soul as a value, the heart its substance as an acting power; but the value consists in this very power, and we have seen how close is the connection between these terms. When Samuel says to Saul: I will tell thee all that is in thine heart! (1 Sam. 9,19), then he might just as well have said: I will make known unto thee thine "heaviness", thy "greatness", thine "highness", or any other of the terms for honour. And when it is said to the king: Yahweh give to thee according to thine heart! (Ps. 20,5), then it means: all the demands which thy soul in its greatness may set forth, i. e. in accordance with the heaviness of thy soul, thine honour.

The difference is a mere nuance, conveyed by a different accent, but both of them indicate the soul as it is in its entirety. The honour of Yahweh is Yahweh himself, as he appears in all his greatness and might. When Joseph instructs his brothers to make known to their father "all mine honour in Egypt" (Gen. 45,13), then it means the character and being of Joseph with all the worth and authority which he has in this country. When the Psalmist asks: How long shall mine honour be turned into shame? (Ps. 4,3), then it is not a question of anything beside his soul, but of the soul itself in its strength and honour. It is said: Enemies persecute my *soul* and take it, tread down my *life* upon the earth and lay mine *honour* in the dust (Ps. 7,6), and between these three expressions there is in reality no difference. Consequently we cannot be surprised that the *usus loquendi* goes one step further and now and again turns "honour" into the region which generally pertains to the "heart", i. e. activity, such being always the case with the various conceptions among the Israelites. We hear that the glory rejoices (Ps. 16,9) and sings praise to God (Ps. 30,13); it summons its strength to give praise to him (Ps. 57,9; 108,2). "In their assembly mine honour shall not join", says Jacob of the tribes which his soul is reluctant to acknowledge (Gen. 49,6). "Honour" and "glory" in particular are terms frequently used of the soul of Yahweh, as it manifests itself and acts among mankind. [1]

As strength and wealth fill the strong soul with honour, so misfortune atrophies the soul with *shame.* The unfortunate may say that he is "sated" with shame. It is the same as if he would speak of being "sated" with hunger. It is the emptying out of the soul, the breaking of its uprightness, and therefore it paralyzes its power to act. He who has been shamed, sits down with nerveless hands, deprived of all initiative.

What is it then that causes the Israelite shame? Of course the opposite of that which fills him with honour. The old Israelites for whom life consisted in courage and valiant deeds, were on their guard if anyone offended them by doubting whether they had sufficient strength to perform these deeds. Not to possess sufficient courage to maintain one's honour is the shame. The Old Testament knows the picture of the shameful warriors who steal into the town after having fled from the battle (2 Sam. 19,4).

Just as the victory at all times creates honour in Israel, in the same manner defeat is shame. Jeremiah says: A voice of wailing is heard out of Zion: how are we spoiled! we are greatly confounded, because we have forsaken the land, because they have overthrown our dwellings (Jer. 9,18). Egypt is shamed, in that she is conquered and put into the hands of the people of the north (Jer. 46,24). Bel is put to shame when he succumbs (Jer. 50,2, cf. 48,1). In so far this may be acknowledged by every Israelite. But with the shifting of the conception of honour a significant difference makes itself felt, in that the shame is more and more transferred to the result. When honour consists in thriving, then defeat, the failure to carry out one's undertaking, becomes a shame, Samson may fall with honour, because he has preserved his inner greatness, the indomitability of his soul; but in the eyes of later Israel the fall is identical with shame, just as wealth and prosperity are identical with honour. "Israel shall be shamed from its counsel" (Hos. 10,6), when it cannot be carried through, and the prophets are shamed when they cannot see visions (Mic. 3,7), or when they see false visions (Zech. 13,4).

It is "shame" not to have blessing. The peasants and wine dressers are covered with shame when locusts come and devour their crops (Joel 1,11). When the rain fails, when the shepherds lack water in the pits, and the arable land lies dry, then they are shamed and confounded (Jer. 14,3-4). Poverty is shame, the direct consequence of wealth being honour (1 Sam. 18,23). "Wherefore came I forth out of the womb to see labour and sorrow that my days should be consumed with shame?" asks Jeremiah (20,18). Trouble, misery and misfortune, like hunger, are in themselves a shame (Ezek. 36,30).

The source of shame, but also its proper essence, is weakness. Ezekiel describes the realm of the dead, considering with particular joy the princes of the north and the Phœnicians who lie there covered with shame: There be the princes of the north, all of them, and all the Zidonians, which are gone down with those slain in their terrible misery, shamed from their might; and they lie uncircumcised with them that be slain by the sword, and bear their shame with them that go down to the pit (Ezek. 32,30). Their strength has failed them, now they lie in weakness together with those who perished in the most horrible manner. In this enormous defeat, in this hopeless weakness, lies their shame. In the same manner the King of Babylon fared (Is. 14,19).

Shame consists in lacking "heaviness", in having a lowly, empty soul. A soul like that cannot prosper, and conversely misfortune reacts upon the soul and empties it. The Old Testament has vivid descriptions of the dissolution entailed by defeat and humiliation. The shame "breaks the heart" (Ps. 69,21). Those defeated are struck with terror, shake and tremble, become like the grass, "their hand is made short" (Jer. 37,27). The defeat deprives the soul of its worth and shakes its self-confidence. The same word is used to signify the feeling of him who is struck by misfortune, of the thief who is caught in the offence (Jer. 2,26), of him whose nakedness is uncovered, and of him who has committed treachery (Jer. 6,15; 8,12).

Shame spreads through the whole of the region of the soul. The shamed "clothes himself in his shame" (Ps. 35,26; 132,18; Job 8,22). Like honour it can be read in the face (2 Sam. 19,6; Jer. 7,19; 51,51; Ps. 44,16 *et al.).* It is only the brazen person, like the harlot, who bears her shame with head erect (Jer. 3,3). Therefore he who is full of shame covers his head or beard (2 Sam. 15,30; 19,5; Is. 25,7; Jer. 14,3-4; Mic. 3,7). When Tamar had been ravished, she rent her garment, strewed herself with ashes, laid her hand on her head and went on crying (2 Sam. 13,19). One smites one's thighs, stamps with one's feet and clasps one's hands (Ezek. 21,17.19 ff.; 22,13; 25,6), which movements are quite as direct an expression of sorrow and shame as tears.

As shame, like honour, finds expression in the body, so one may cause shame by disturbing the latter. One shamed one's enemy by thrusting out his eyes, as Nahash wanted to do (1 Sam. 11,2) or by cutting off his thumbs and great toes (Judg. 1,6 f.). The cutting off of the hair is a shame which the repulsed must bear (Jer. 7,29). With this iniquity Isaiah threatens the ladies of Jerusalem (Is. 3,17), and the same prophet threatens his people, saying that the hairs of their heads, as well as of their beards and abdomens, shall be shaven off (7,20). Also the laying bare of the body is a shame, in particular when the secret parts of it are thus discovered. As distinguished from many other peoples the Israelites are very sensitive on this point (*vide* Gen. 2,25; 8,22 ff.), and this, of course, particularly holds good of the women (Is. 47,3; Jer. 13,26; Ezek. 16,37; Nah. 3,5). The messengers whom David sent to the king of Ammon were insulted, both by having their beards shaven off and "their garments cut in the middle, even to their buttocks" (2 Sam. 10,4-5). They were so ashamed that they could not show their faces at home before their beards had grown to their former length. If one pulls off the sandal of a man, one puts him to shame, just as when one spits in his face (Num. 12,14). It was the privilege of the widow thus to affront her brother-in-law when he refused to help her to get progeny for her dead husband (Deut. 25,9 cf. Test. Sebulon. 3).

Thus shame is caused through actions, but it can also be done by words. The power of the word is strong, whether it contains honour or shame. The old heroes were sensitive to words, such as appears from the behaviour of Gideon, when the men of Succoth expressed their doubt as to his ability of conquering adversaries. Goliath shamed the ranks of Israel with his insulting words, which no one could disprove, until David appeared (1 Sam. 17,10.26.36). The harsh words which Saul uttered to Jonathan of his friend David, whom he called a "son of death", filled him with such violent shame that he kept away from the table of the king, though it was the second day of the feast of the new moon (1 Sam. 20,34). Any lack of due acknowledgment is shame. When David sat crying on the day when Absalom was vanquished, he shamed his warriors (2 Sam. 19,6). They returned with victory and were therefore entitled to be honoured by the acknowledgment of the king.

Shame follows the conception of honour as its shadow. Where honour is the absolute maintenance of self, there shame must consist in being unable to maintain oneself. And where honour consists in having progress and prosperity, even if one must receive it from someone stronger, then shame will consist in not getting the assistance confidently expected. "Therefore shall the strength of Pharaoh be your shame, and the trust in the protection of

Egypt your confusion", says the prophet (Is. 30,3, cf. 20,5). "Thou shalt also be shamed by Egypt, as thou wast shamed by Assyria", says Jeremiah (2,36). Those who have feeble gods, are shamed by them, as Moab is shamed by Chemosh and the house of Israel by their self-chosen gods (Jer. 48,13; Is. 1,29). Through prophets and psalms constantly rings the confidence that Yahweh will not let his faithful suffer shame.

Honour always contains two elements: greatness in oneself and greatness in one's relation to others, whether there is an equilibrium between the two poles or not. Through defeat or disappointment one becomes of less account than others. "Thou makest us a reproach to our neighbours", the Psalmist complains (Ps. 44,14). From the prophets we often hear that the destruction of Israel is to be its shame among other peoples: Your mother shall be sore confounded, she that bare you shall be ashamed, behold, she shall be the hindermost of the nations, a wilderness, a dry land, and a desert (Jer. 50,12). Defeat humbles so that one becomes less than others, and the others enforce the humiliation by making "a wide mouth" and gnashing their teeth (Is. 57,4); also by clapping their hands, hissing and wagging their heads (Lam. 2,15; 3,46). The vanquished enemy is utterly humbled; he must throw himself on the ground and let the conqueror put his foot on the back of his neck.

It is characteristic that in the Old Testament we hear more of shame than of honour where fighting and enmity are concerned. For the average type of Israelite fighting is something unnatural, unreasonable. As mentioned above, he fights the combat in order to get rid of it; therefore the object of the fight is the complete confusion of the enemy. It is in this spirit that Jeremiah says: Let them be confounded that persecute me, but let not me be confounded; let them be dismayed, but let not me be dismayed; bring upon them the day of evil, and destroy them with double destruction (Jer. 17,18). He does not ask to be given honour by maintaining himself against the enemy, nor does he ask that he himself may be made great, but that his adversary may be humbled.

The Psalms are imbued with this spirit: "Let them be ashamed and confounded together that seek after my soul to destroy it; let them be driven backward and put to shame that wish me evil" (Ps. 40,15; cf. 35,4; 70,3; 71,13). So frequently do such exclamations occur that they almost become a kind of stock phrase. He who complains is surrounded by enemies persecuting him; to strike them down, to humble and put them to shame is his desire.

All this belongs to an Israel which has a different conception of honour from the old one. Honour consists in prospering and getting rid of him who counteracts prosperity. He who has the power will keep the others down, so that they are not to approach him and threaten his power. The weak man knows that he must humble himself utterly, but his desire is to get on top and see the powerful under his feet. The Israelite knows to the full both the joy of the conqueror when he is able to gloat over the conquered and put his foot on his neck, and the stinging pain stirred by the mockery of the conqueror in the heart of the conquered. He "enjoys the sight" of the crushed adversary, exults exceedingly at his fall. And how often was he not himself to yield to others this kind of enjoyment, whether he found his enemy among his own or among strangers!

The weak wants to rule because he cannot uphold, and to strike down others in order that he may maintain himself. We meet it constantly in later Israel. The Israelite is the suppressed who must humble himself, but he must have help in order to become the superior who is able to suppress others. When Moab mocks the humbled Israelites, then the prophet expresses his joy, because he has a god who can strike down Moab, that Israel may plunder him and trample on him (Zeph. 2,8-10). In this exultation at the fall of the enemy lies a good deal of the gloating of the weak over the fall of the mighty.

These features of the Israelitic conception of life do not give evidence of the culture of Israel in its flourishing period; they are closely connected with the currents which gradually bore down upon this people and carried off the old harmonious culture. [1]

NAME.

THE soul in its entirety, with all its blessing and honour, finds expression in the name, *shēm*. The word *shēm* is found in all Semitic languages and belongs to the absolutely certain ur-semitic components.

Firstly, the name is the appellation characterizing each individual soul. In so far it may be said that the name is part of the soul, seeing that it is possessed by it like the body, and everything wherein it manifests itself. But, fully as much as any other part of the soul, it characterizes the whole of the soul, such as it is. To know the name of a man is the same as to know his essence. The pious "know the name" of their God (Ps. 9,11; 91,14), i. e. they know how he is. The more he makes himself felt, the better his name is made known; his people are to know it fully when some day he shall appear in all his fullness of might and lead them to victory (Is. 52,6), just as all the peoples of the earth will also come to know it (1 Kings 8,42). He whose name one knows fully, one loves. Yahweh knew the name of Moses, in that he had chosen him, and Moses had found grace in his sight (Exod. 33,12.17). Shulamite praises the loveable presence of her chosen by saying that his name is as ointment poured forth (Cant. 1,3).

This identity between the soul and the name is necessary from the general psychological view. It is to be understood quite literally that the name is the soul. It was to the *name* of Yahweh that Solomon built his temple (1 Kings 3,2; 5,17.19; 8,17.20.29). When Yahweh took up his abode in the temple "he put his name there" (Deut. 12,5.21; 14,24; 1 Kings 8, 29; 9,3; 11,36; 2 Kings 21,7; 23,27) or "let his name dwell there" (Deut. 12,11; 14,23; 16,2.6.11; 26,2). When people go up in crowds to Jerusalem, they go up to the name of Yahweh (Jer. 3,17). Israel trusts in the name of Yahweh, longs for it (Ps. 33,21; Is. 26,8); to that extent it is identical with himself.

Therefore the name acts. The name of Yahweh supports the king (Ps. 20,2), it deals wonderfully with Israel (Joel 2,26). It might just as well have been *nephesh* or *kābhōdh* or any other denomination of the soul. The name of the child unborn is covered with darkness (Eccles. 6,4), for no one knows its soul. The name is so identical with the soul in the whole of its weight and extent that it can be said that the name of the wicked shall rot (Prov. 10,7), a characteristic and picturesque expression of the dissolution and ruin of the soul, which description is not in need of improvement through textual corrections.

Just as "honour" may sometimes be used to designate the soul of Yahweh as it manifests itself before mankind, in the same manner it may sometimes be said that the name of Yahweh comes from afar in its flaming might (Is. 30,27). It designates him as he appears in the figure of a warrior in the whole of his might, with foaming lips and his breath as an overflowing stream. When Israel receives the promise that an angel is to come and lead it, the name of Yahweh being in him (Exod. 23,21), then it means that Yahweh has laid some of his soul into his, so that he may act with the strength of Yahweh and with his authority.

There is a deep meaning in the expression: to act in or with (the preposition can be translated both ways) one's name. Of course it means, in the first place, that one mentions him in whose name one acts; but in reality it means the same as if the person in question had done it himself. The act is done as he would have done it, with his authority and on his responsibility. David sent his servants to Nabal, whom they addressed "in the name of David" (1 Sam. 25,9). Therefore the affrontery of Nabal was as insulting as if it had been pronounced to David himself. When Jezebel, in the name of Ahab, sent letters to the elders of Jezreel (1 Kings 21,8), it meant that the letters spoke with the authority of the king. Commands which are issued in the name of the king are upheld by his authority and, it is said in the narrative from the Persian court, cannot be reversed (Esth. 3,12; 8,8.10).

To speak in the name of God is something which cannot be done by everyone. It means speaking on behalf of God but, according to the view of an older period, it is more than speaking according to his will and commandment. It implies speaking with the spirit of God, and it presupposes that the person in question has something of God's soul in him. It is that which happens with the prophets. They speak in the name of Yahweh (Deut. 18,19; Jer. 26,20; 44,16), for they are inspired with divine soul, and thus become possessed of the power to utter strong words. To utter lies in the name of Yahweh is, therefore, a violation both of their own soul and of that of Yahweh (Jer. 14,15; 23,25; 27,15; 29, 9.21.23; Zech. 13,3). To speak in the name of Yahweh is to speak strong words. He who swears, swears by his name, thus filling himself with divine soul.

Of course it is not only *speaking* that can be done in the name of Yahweh. In his name the Israelites fight and trample their enemies (Ps. 44,6). It does not only mean that they fight with Yahweh's approval, but that it is his strength which inspires them in the fight, as is said of the ideal king: And he shall stand and guard in the strength of Yahweh in the majesty of the name of Yahweh his God (Mic. 5,3). All peoples act and live in the name of their god, and so also Israel (Mic. 4,5).

The name grows with action, because the soul with its honour is in it. According as David won victories over the Philistines, his name became very "precious" (1 Sam. 18,30). Nathan prophesied that he would be a great ruler; God would exterminate his enemies and create for him a great name, as the names of the great ones on the earth (2 Sam. 7,9). Such a name his son likewise gained on account of his wisdom. The name of Solomon spread abroad among the peoples (1 Kings 5,11), just as it is said of Uzziah that because of his exceeding power his name reached as far as Egypt and to peoples in far-off countries (2 Chron. 26,8.15).

The name is *renown;* it is more than report. When it is said of a man who accuses his newly wedded wife of not being a virgin when he married her, that he "brings up an evil name upon her" (Deut. 22,14.19), then it surely means that he gives her a bad reputation among people. And when the enemies of Nehemiah tried to frighten him that there might be an evil name which they could reproach him with (Neh. 6,13), then it evidently means that they would be able to speak evil of him. But it also implies more. The outward reputation cannot be separated from the inner value. Either it is false and must be struck down, or it persists and then reacts upon the centre of the soul. When the name of Solomon reaches the people in far-off countries, then it does not mean that he is being spoken of there, but that the might of his soul extends so far and acts there. It is he himself reaching to these remote regions and making himself felt there. The soul is not limited to what is directly seen. It reaches across the world, as far as it acts.

The name is the very peculiarity and power of the soul. It is greatness of soul rather than report. The inhabitants of the plain of Shinar said: Let us build us a city and a tower whose top may reach unto heaven, and let us make us a name, lest we be scattered abroad upon the face of the whole earth (Gen. 11,4). If they can build themselves a tower which reaches towards heaven, then they have acquired honour, a greatness without bounds, and there is no limit to the works which they can perform. If they have come so far, then they will not be scattered and dissolved; the honour inspires them with power and gives them strength to keep together. This was their thought, but Yahweh saw it before it had gone too far. He rushed down, confused their language and scattered them, and thus the power resting in their unity was dissolved. The city with the tower, which could only be built by a strong people, and which when fulfilled would renew and increase their strength, came to naught, and mankind had to be content with a lesser name.

There is solid logic in the narrative, which rests upon the interaction between great achievement and great name. The narrator cannot mean that the tower should keep the peoples together, because it was visible everywhere; this is not implied, and for that matter could make no difference whatsoever when it was a question of spreading and keeping together. And one only spoils the beautiful construction of the story by splitting it up into two parts, each of which would only be a poor fragment of the whole.[1] The narrative gives us an insight into the manner of thinking of old Israel. Name is honour, that is to say, power. The deeds spring from the inner strength of the soul. The men of name, *'anshē hash-shēm,* were the old giants, born of the women who had been visited by the sons of gods. They were men of power, whose honour swelled with great deeds. A man of name one must be in order to be able to fill the place of a chief among the people (Num. 16,2). The Israelites say with pride that they themselves and the peoples allied to them are *b^{e}nē shēm,* sons of name. The name, the renown, is their ancestor.

To have a name means the same as to have greatness. Israel received a name and greatness from his god (2 Sam. 7,23). When Yahweh says to Abraham: I will bless thee and make thy name great (Gen. 12,2), then it means that through his prospering, through wealth and posterity, he is to grow and increase in substance that he may become great and fill the earth. Thus name is the same as honour. It can be said ironically of the shameless woman that she becomes a name among women (Ezek. 23,10). To have one's name among the three heroes of David (2 Sam. 23,18.22), not only means to be mentioned among them, but to be filled with their greatness.

The relation between name and renown is the same as between honour and praise. The name is the character and greatness of the soul, but others may act upon it by raising or lowering it. To proclaim the name of Yahweh is tantamount to ascribing greatness to him (Deut. 32,3); by saying: "Yahweh is the God over Israel!" one helps in making his name great (2 Sam. 7,26). Yahweh's name is sung, extolled, proclaimed, blessed; it is praised and exalted; it is remembered with rejoicing, honoured and made holy. This is done because Yahweh himself gains a name through his mighty deeds, which make his soul infinitely great. Therefore his name is glorious in all the earth, and great in might among the peoples (Jer. 10,6; Mal. 1,6.11; Ps. 8,2.10). The praising of Yahweh corresponds with his name (Ps. 48,11). He is given the name which he has gained for himself. To act for the sake of one's name means to act as one must, in order to maintain the greatness of soul which one possesses.

The intimate relation between soul and property is expressed by its being called after the name of the owner (Ps. 49,12). This means both that it belongs to the soul and that it takes part in its honour. [1] When Joab lay besieging Rabbah, the capital of the Ammonites, he sent the following message to David: "I have fought against Rabbah and have taken the city of waters. Now therefore gather the rest of the people together and encamp against the city and take it, lest I take the city, and my name be called over it" (2 Sam. 12,28). The name is gained by means of actual deeds. When David takes the city, it makes part of his honour. The woman bears the name of the man because she belongs to his entirety; she is part of the sphere which together makes his honour.

Every part of the contents of the soul can, as we know, be actually present in an object; so also the name. The name of Yahweh lay in the temple, in the Ark, in all sacred things. A pillar upon which the valiant deeds of the man are written contains his name. It is mentioned on it, but to the Israelite it implies more than that. His deeds, the contents of his soul, are in this pillar and accomplishes that which his soul can accomplish. When the Babylonian and Assyrian kings were so eager to put up inscriptions proclaiming their deeds, then it was not only the inclination to tell which urged them to do it. They would make sure that their renown, their name in all its real greatness, should live and act for ever. They raised pillars on their property, and these *name pillars* were erected by the victorious kings in the territories which they had conquered and subjected to their will. [2]

Of this kind of pillars we presumably also hear in the Old Testament. Of David it is told (2 Sam. 8,13): "And David made a name when he returned from smiting Aram in the valley of salt, eighteen thousand men" — Aram evidently being a scribal error for Edom. The sentence as it stands hardly means that David got for himself a warrior's renown; he did that in defeating the enemy, not afterwards. It rather means that, like the Babylonian kings, he made for himself a name pillar. It is then told that he put *n^eṣībhīm* in the whole of Edom, and the Edomites became his slaves. The word means "something which has been put up", and it may mean a governor (1 Kings 4,19); but it may also mean a pillar (Gen. 19,26), and in that case it is a pillar of victory which puts the name of David over the conquered territory. The word seems to have a similar meaning in a few other places. When Saul is about to depart from Ramah, Samuel says to him that when he arrives at God's Gibeah, where the *n^eṣībhīm* of the Philistines are, then at the entrance of the city he is going to meet with a company of prophets (1 Sam. 10,5). The natural thing is, in this place, to think of something which can be used as a local designation, or, in other words, rather "pillar" than "governor". In that case they were pillars which the Philistines put up with their names, in which manner the place was subjected to them. It was a pillar of this kind which Jonathan subsequently overturned (1 Sam. 13,3), thus inaugurating the war of liberation against the Philistines. As in Edom, David put up *n^eṣībhīm* in Damascus (2 Sam. 8,6).

Such pillars were sometimes shaped like a hand, [1] this being the expression of strength. When Saul had conquered the Amalekites, he set up for himself "a hand" in Carmel, south of Hebron (1 Sam. 15,12). In this hand lay the valiant deed of Saul, and so also his name and honour. Of Absalom there is the following narrative: Now Absalom in his lifetime had taken and reared up for himself a pillar which is in the king's dale, for he said, I have no son to keep my name in remembrance, and he called the pillar after his name, and it is called to this day Absalom's hand (2 Sam. 18,18). This narrative shows the reality implied in such a pillar, which thus, like that of Saul, had the shape of a hand. It contains the name of the man, and so protects his soul against extermination, when it cannot be preserved in a natural manner by being maintained in the son. The pillar is equal to the name, and the name is equal to the soul. A custom like the one here described was not uncommon in Israel, as the words of Yahweh relating to the eunuchs would otherwise have been different: Even unto them will I give in my house and within my walls a hand and a name better than that of sons and daughters;

I will give them an everlasting name that shall not be cut off (Is. 56,5). The tombstones are to preserve the name of him who is dead, that the soul shall not become extinct; but in the Old Testament we only hear of them once, viz. on the grave of Rachel (Gen. 35,20).

The man fills his name with the whole of his being and impresses it. There is no doubt that it was a common wish to call one's children by good names to which good forces were attached. We know that among the Jews of a later period it was common to choose the name of one of the ancestors, especially that of the father's father. Though this custom cannot be traced in the older period,[1] it undoubtedly has its root in it. Many names, in their very significance, contain something good. Names like: "Yahweh helps", "Yahweh gives", "Yahweh makes fast", establish the divine protection. We know from the prophets names which are meant to express directly the being of the bearer: Graceless, Not-my-people, Jezreel (Hos. 1) or With-us-God (Is. 7,14, cf. 9,5). When it is said that the name of Yahweh is Jealous-God (Exod. 34,14), then it implies that such is his essence.

The most important feature about the name is, however, not its linguistic significance, but the association with which it is charged. When one of the children of Isaiah is to be called Quickspoil Lightning-plunder (8,3), then it means that it is to be bound up with the defeat of the people. From the many explanatory names of the Old Testament we see that the name is given by association with some experience or other. It is impossible that a Hebrew should not know the linguistic value of "Benjamin". But it does not exclude the possibility that for him the name may be essentially connected with ideas of quite a different kind. The substance of a name must, to a very large extent, depend upon the contents imparted to it by those who have formerly borne it.

If one is to enter into relation with somebody, one must know his name, and if one knows it, then one may use it and thus exercise influence upon him, not because one knows the linguistic significance of the name, but because his soul is wholly in it. Therefore the strange God, with whom Jacob wrestled at Jabbok, refused to reveal his name (Gen. 32, 30), and the same holds good of the *mal'ākh* of Yahweh when he came to Manoah prophesying the birth of Samson (Judg. 13,18). Manoah is only told that the name was wonderful; a god naturally has a wonderful name.

If a man changes his character entirely, and the contents of his soul are altered, he often must have a new name. Also elsewhere it is a well-known custom that people are given a new name when entering upon a new phase, and that they frequently have several names. In the Old Testament Abram gets a new name at the time that the blessing is given to him (Gen. 17), and Jacob was given a new name when, after a long struggle, he had won a blessing from the god of the new country (Gen. 32). Joseph received a new name as a ruler (Gen. 41,45), just as Daniel and his friends received new names at the court of the great king. When Nebuchadnezzar made Eliakim his vassal, he changed his name to Jehoiakim (2 Kings 23,34), just as he, later on, changed the name of Mattaniah to Zedekiah (2 Kings 24,17). Eliakim was given a name which, from the point of view of language, was not very different from the former, but the great king wished to show that the king of Israel henceforth was something quite different, and what he was he received from him. When, some day, Israel attains its full happiness, it will be called by a new name, which Yahweh himself shall give it (Is. 62,2; 65,15). All the ignominy and misery accumulated in the name of Israel will be done away with and a new life begin, while the enemies who are now exulting must deliver up their names for curses (Is. 65,15).

If one wants to proclaim a man's identity, one does not only mention his own name. In older writings one generally mentions his father, also the name of his native place. To these is generally added that of a more remote ancestor, whose name has been so great that it stamps the family throughout the generations. Shimei is called the son of Gera, of the family of the house of Saul (2 Sam. 16,5); in Gera and Saul we have the two names which are the chief components of his essence. Gideon is the son of Joash of the family of Abiezer (Judg. 6,11), etc. But if we are to know a man of special importance, then we ought to know the whole succession of his fathers. Samuel and Saul are represented by a long succession (1 Sam. 1,1; 9,1). David himself was the great founder of a house, greater than that of any of his ancestors, but, for all that, the Chronicles show his genealogy, which carries us back to primeval ages.

The long lists of names are, of course, not enumerated because, e. g., David is to be distinguished from others of the same name, but in order to show what kind of man he is. The man bears the name of his fathers, and the meaning of that now appears quite clearly. The name is the soul; the heritage consisting in the name is not an empty appellation, a sound, but the substance of a soul. In the heritage of the name the psychic community is expressed. The house bears the name of the father of the house, and this implies that his soul imbues the whole of the family with everything that belongs to it. After his death the name is taken over by the son; it means that he does not die. His soul, with all its substance, great achievements, wealth, blessing, honour, everything which fills the name, lives on in the son.

We are unable to understand this manner of thinking, unless we look upon it from the psychological standpoint of the Israelite. We must realize what is implied by the soul not being limited to the ego, the conscious, finished personality. The soul is in everything that fills it, in the renown, in the property, in everything wherein it works. Therefore the soul may live, even though the ego disappears. The supreme desire of the Israelite is life, i. e. strength as it acts in the blessing and is shaped in the honour. He desires that life is never to run out, but is to be constantly renewed. Therefore, he desires sons more than anything else on this earth. It is his desire to live which demands them; for the son bears his name, in him his life and soul live continually.

The progeny, the "seed", is identical with the name. "For as the new heavens and the new earth, which I will make, shall remain before me, saith Yahweh, so shall your seed and your name remain" (Is. 66,22). The old view has not changed in this respect. It is really a promise to Abraham himself and the other patriarchs that the earth is to be blessed by their seed, because it is identical with their own soul.

The Israelites hailed their king with the cry that he should live for ever, and in the cult he desired to gain eternal life (1 Kings 1,31; Ps. 21,5; 45,7; 61,8). This greeting, which was also offered to other oriental kings, [1] is to be understood quite literally. The king is to have the blessing that his soul may never die. Throughout the ages his name is to remain eternally; before the sun (i. e., as long as it shines) his name is to send forth shoots (Ps. 72,17). When David was dying, and Solomon had taken his place on the throne, people came to David in order to bless him, and they did so in the following words: "Your god make the name of Solomon better than thy name, and make his throne better than thy throne!" And David blessed Yahweh "which hath given one to sit on my throne this day, mine eyes even seeing it" (1 Kings 1,47-48). It can never be an insult to a man that the son makes the name greater, because it is his own honour which is increased by it.

The extermination of the name is the strongest expression of annihilation. The Israelites in their anguish beseech their god that their enemies may not succeed in exterminating their names from the earth; even if he deserts them, and they are struck by misfortune, he cannot surely let it go so far (Josh. 7,9; 2 Kings 14,27). Just as eager is later Israel to exterminate the names of their enemies, first and foremost those of the Canaanites (Deut. 7,24; 9,14; 12,3), but all who do not submit themselves to the glory of the god of Israel shall fare likewise, all the wicked ones (Deut. 29,19; Zeph. 1,4; Job 18,17). "I will cut off from Babylon the name and remnant, and progeny and posterity, saith Yahweh. I will also make it a possession for the bittern, and pools of water" (Is. 14,22 f.).

The extermination of the name is so dreadful, because it implies complete annihilation. In the name lies the whole substance of the man's soul; if it is killed, then there is only absolute emptiness. When Saul had been in the power of David, and David had proved his superiority to him, he burst into tears, and in his impotence he could only utter this prayer: Swear now therefore unto me by Yahweh that thou wilt not cut off my seed after me, and that thou wilt not destroy my name out of my father's house! (1 Sam. 24,22). Saul's father's house is the family of his father

Kish. If his seed be exterminated, then there will only be an empty gap, where he had hitherto filled his position in the family and made the house of his father tower conspicuously.

Nothing has such an effect in Israel as the danger that the name may be exterminated. Therefore it was the main point in the feigned complaint laid before David by the woman of Tekoah, who accused the relatives of her husband of wanting to cut off her husband's name and remainder upon earth (2 Sam. 14,7). To "exterminate" as one wipes out something *(māḥā)* or to "cut off" from the family (Num. 27,4; Ruth 4,10), those are the characteristic terms of this absolute death. In order to prevent it, the brother of the deceased must come to the fore and offer disinterested help, as demanded by the Levirate law. By providing progeny for his brother he maintains his name *(hēḳīm,* Deut. 25,6; Ruth 4,5.10); he guards his soul against obliteration.

To the extermination pertains oblivion. The enemies of Jeremiah say: Let us destroy the tree with the meat [1] thereof, that his name may be no more remembered (Jer. 11,19). Thus the enemies say of Israel (Ps. 83,5), and Israel of his enemy (Exod. 17,14; Deut. 25,19). As name and renown belong together, so do also life and *memory.* He who lives acts upon other souls; as long as he acts, he is not dead. We know the close connection which, in the eyes of the Israelite, exists between the soul and all the sensations and ideas involved. The word memory or remembrance, *zēkher,* is used in exactly the same manner as *shēm,* in order to designate the name, and so also the soul. "The memory of the just is for blessing, but the name of the wicked shall rot", says the proverb (Prov. 10,7). The memory of Yahweh is the same as his name (Exod. 3,15; Hos. 12,6; 14,8; Ps. 97,12; 102,13). When the unhappy man cries out that the memory of Yahweh is not in Sheol (Ps. 6,6), then it surely means that he is not mentioned there; nobody thinks of him; but it means still more: he is not there, he does not act in Sheol.

One makes a name alive by mentioning it. The name immediately calls forth the soul it designates; therefore there is such a deep significance in the very mention of a name. Yahweh wants to be mentioned and remembered; it is chiefly done in the holy places (Exod. 20,24), and ought not to be done in the wrong place and season. Where misfortune abides, one must not mention his name (Am. 6,10); his soul is violated by being made present at misfortune. One must not mention his name in connection with that which lacks the reality of life (Exod. 20,7; Deut. 5,11). But, above all, one must not forget it (Jer. 23,27). It is a different matter with the other gods. Their names must not be mentioned or remembered (Exod. 23,13; Deut. 18,20; Josh. 23,7; Hos. 2,19), for in that manner one contributes towards keeping them alive and their soul upright.

The man wants to be remembered; thus his name is made to live. The substance of his soul must be so strong that it does not perish, but works through the generations. If he has no sons, then he may seek compensation in setting up a memorial, into which his name has been laid so as to be preserved. It may have its value, perhaps even if he has sons. But it can never be full compensation for the life which the name continues in the new souls through the descendants. It sounds very strange when Yahweh says to the most rejected people, the eunuchs, that to them will be given a memorial and a name better than that of sons and daughters (Is. 56,5).

That which the son receives from the father are flesh and blood — a body; also certain abilities and habits, demands for influence, power, in short, blessing and honour, the whole substance of the soul, and that is what is called the name. The body is only a single part of the whole of this inheritance. That which was in the souls of the fathers is his; therefore it is of such vital importance who the fathers are. But psychic community being the principal thing, then the fact of being the son of a man does not only mean being the son of his body. It is true that under normal conditions the contents of the soul are inherited through the natural channels of propagation. But it also happens in life that people inherit the contents of their souls from others than their natural fathers. When Elisha cried out: Father, father! to Elijah (2 Kings 2,12), then it surely implied more than a mere expression of reverence. And, in any case, we must keep this in mind, if we want to understand the genealogies of the Old Testament. When Ethiopia, Egypt and the African Phut and Canaan are mentioned as brothers (Gen. 10,6), then the idea of the author is not to tell us of community of races or "natural" descent, but it means that the four peoples have psychic relationship or, as we would put it, relationship of culture and history. And this is also the case when Elam, Ashur, Arphaxad, Lud and Aram are mentioned as the sons of Shem, though they belonged to different races.

If a man has no sons himself, he may adopt a stranger and make him his son, saying his name into him. Of this kind of adoption, which plays a great part in the different laws of Mesopotamia, [1] we hear nothing in the Old Testament, presumably by chance. But we have analogous examples. When Rachel remained childless, she gave her slave Bilhah to her husband and made the child her own by letting the girl bear upon her knees (Gen. 30,3). To be adopted by the mother cannot be of the same importance as to be adopted by the father. The child was, whatever else, the offspring of the husband; but in becoming the child of the legitimate wife it got a higher position and a greater share in the name of the father, and, at any rate, Rachel became possessed of the honour of motherhood. We also hear of the grandfather adopting grandsons; Jacob adopted Manasseh and Ephraim as his sons with the following words: And my name shall be named in them, and the names of my fathers Abraham and Isaac, and they shall grow into a multitude in the midst of the earth (Gen. 48,16). Joseph even let the children of his grandson Machir be born on his knees (Gen. 50,23). This, however, is not adoption in the strictest sense of the word, grandsons having the name of their grandfather and the name of his fathers in them. That which happens is partly a confirmation of this, partly an elevation. The children are raised one generation, so as to be on an equal footing with their father and his brothers, who take their name directly from the grandfather. Thus they attain more greatness and greater right to the inheritance (Gen. 48,6).

It is not every son who has an equal share of the name and soul of the father. The first-born has received the first strength of the father, and it raises him above his brothers. "Reuben, thou art my first-born, my might and the beginning of my strength", says Jacob (Gen. 49,3). The eldest son always acts with a certain authority and feels a greater responsibility than the others, as was shown by Reuben when the brothers wanted to kill Joseph (Gen. 37,22). The right of the first-born, which Esau sold to Jacob, implies the abilities and claims which are to be maintained by him who has most of the father in him. It is in consequence of this that he receives a greater inheritance than the others. The Deuteronomy sees fit to point out that this rule must be followed, whether or not the mother of the first-born is the favourite wife of the man. The important factor is not the mother, but the fact that he is the first-fruit of the strength of the man. On the same occasion we are told that the inheritance of the first-born was two-thirds (Deut. 21,17). Over against the first-born stand all the other sons. It is not likely that the inheritance gradually lessened with each son. Therefore it is doubtful whether the promise of David to Bath-sheba that her son Solomon should be made a king would come under the censure of the Deuteronomy. It is true that Adonijah was older, but he was not the first-born.

Thus the name is the soul in its full capacity and, at the same time, that which connects the generations. Life is not something individual, to be shaped according to the needs of each individual. Man is only what he is as a link in the family. He derives his life from the family, shares it with the family and leaves it to be continued in posterity, though not as an impersonal force. It is a definitely shaped life which man takes over, distinctive, great or small; his task is to renew it and to hand it over to those who come after him, as rich as he received it or, if possible, still richer.

If we know the soul of the Israelite, then we also know his view of life: this firm and strong power, which always is a community and yet appears in individuals, which swells in the great and flags in the small, which is constantly taken over and must still be maintained, and which, before all, craves to be able to carry on its activity, infinitely and without ever running out.

II

COMMON LIFE AND ITS LAWS

PEACE AND COVENANT.

WHEN we look at the soul, we always see a community rising behind it. What it is, it is by virtue of others. It has sprung up from a family which has filled it with its contents, and from which it can never grow away. The family forms the narrowest community in which it lives. But wherever it works, it must live in community, because it is its nature to communicate itself to others, to share blessing with them.

Loneliness, the lack of community, the Old Testament only knows as something unnatural, an expression that life is failing. It is the suffering who speak of being alone, men like Jeremiah and Job. "I sat alone because of thy hand, for thou hast filled me with bitterness", says Jeremiah (15,17). The horror of loneliness is described in powerful imagery: "I am like the *ḳā'āth* bird of the wilderness. I am like an owl among the ruins. I watch, and I am as a sparrow alone on the housetop" (Ps. 102, 7—8). When Hosea is to give a true description of the misery of his people, he calls it "a wild ass alone by himself" (Hos. 8,9). These similes from the animal world express the abnormal: As bird and wild ass belong in their flock, and outside this are abandoned, so it is with human beings.

Community is found wherever the blessing is, community being a common participation of blessing. A community like the one described by Job is characterized by the harmony arising, in that the whole of the community is penetrated by the blessing. This harmony the Israelite calls *shālōm*, the word which is usually rendered by peace. Its fundamental meaning is totality; it means the untrammelled, free growth of the soul. But this, in its turn, means the same as harmonious community; the soul can only expand in conjunction with other souls. There is "totality" in a community when there is harmony, and the blessing flows freely among its members, everyone giving and taking whatever he is able to.

Soul is will. A community of souls must therefore mean that one will more or less prevails among the souls. "Let there be no strife, I pray thee, between me and thee, and between my herdmen and thy herdmen, for we be brethren", says Abraham to Lot (Gen. 13,8). Nothing is more unnatural than strife between brothers. It may happen when a demoniac spirit possesses them and confuses their souls, as may at times occur in an army which has a mighty God against it (Judg. 7,22; 1 Sam. 14,20). Or it takes place in a dissolved community, where all human order has been made to give way to chaos. When everything collapses in Israel, every individual will fight his brother and his neighbour (Is. 19,2); no one will be able to trust his neighbour, but a man's enemies will be the men of his own house (Mic. 7,5-6); every one alone will they have to totter out through the breaches of the palaces lying in ruins (Am. 4,3).

According to the evidence of prophets and psalms this dissolution is in full progress in the Israelitic towns. Strife and murder rage in Jerusalem, says Isaiah (1,21). Jeremiah cannot trust anyone. "For even thy brethren and the house of thy father, even they have dealt treacherously with thee; yea, they cry after thee with full throat; believe them not, though they speak fair words unto thee!" (Jer. 12,6). "All my men of peace watched for my fall" (Jer. 20,10). The Psalms give us a glimpse of the sinister life in a community where "they speak vanity every one with his neighbour" (12,3), watch for each other like wild beasts of prey, desire to trample on each other and eat of the flesh of each other, where the man is betrayed by those who are nearest to him. "I am a fear to mine acquaintance; they that see me in the street flee from me. I am forgotten as a dead man out of mind; I am like a broken vessel. For I hear the slander of many; fear is on every side, while they take counsel together against me, devise to take away my life" (Ps. 31,12-14). We hear complaints from one who is attacked by his own "man of peace" in whom he trusted and who ate his bread (Ps. 41,10).

It is the life in the great towns, and in particular Jerusalem, of which these and many similar exclamations show us such desolate glimpses, displaying a state of dissolution. Here we are told what peace is not; and yet there are suggestions of what it ought to be. The "man of peace" is he with whom one shares one's bread, whom one relies upon, and from whom one would least of all expect enmity. When an embittered psalmist proclaims that the table of his enemies shall "become a snare before them and their men of peace" (Ps. 69,23) [1] then it shows how close is the community between those who have peace.

We must, as it were, feel our ground towards the implication of the word, whose substance is so obvious to every Israelite. When it is said of a man or a family that there is peace, what then does it imply? The word itself says that it denotes harmony, agreement and psychic community; but it does not say directly how deep and intimate the community is. As a matter of fact, this community may be extremely different. People may meet in peace for a while, without its meaning anything but mutual inviolability, and the souls may be so firmly united that they are entirely penetrated by one will, that they are one. This intimate community is to be found in the family. Peace prevails among brothers.

David, the great ideal of the Israelites, who otherwise was so successful in all he undertook, had little peace within his family. First he lost the son whom Bath-sheba had born to him. He made every sacrifice in order to induce Yahweh to permit him to live. He refused to take part in the meal of his men, and the nights he spent in a mourning garment, lying on the ground (2 Sam. 12, 16-17). Of his surviving sons there were several who caused him sorrow. Amnon violated his half-sister Tamar; Adonijah openly revolted against him and was elected king by a circle of adherents. A grosser breach of peace could not be imagined, but what did David do? He was very angry, but could do nothing. Peace was broken, but could not be made whole because it had been broken by those who were to uphold it. If David had removed the guilty, he would have made whole the breach with a new breach. He could do nothing, because he loved them too dearly (2 Sam. 13,21, the Greek translation; 1 Kings 1,6).

The son who made David suffer most, was, however, Absalom. First he killed Amnon, who had violated his sister Tamar. To a certain extent he was justified in doing so: the deed of Amnon must be avenged. But still he killed his half-brother, his father's son. The attitude of David is determined by conflicting feelings, and therefore his whole behaviour is wavering. David weeps and wails, and Absalom flees, but is later on recalled. Then he raises the standard of revolt against his father. If a stranger had done that, David would have gathered his men, quickly and energetically, and struck him down. But in this situation he acts throughout with a curious mixture of energy and stupefaction. He flees at once up Mount Olivet, barefoot, weeping, with his head covered. As usual he is able to find the expedient leading to a favourable result, but behind all his commandments lies the fear of victory. This unscrupulous man, who could use the most brutal means when he wanted to strike down his enemies, was, as it were, paralyzed when he was to fight his own son.

When the army was mustered, his chief interest was that the son should not be killed, and his first question was about his safety, when news of the issue of the battle came to him. When he heard that Absalom was killed, he sacrificed the whole of his dignity as king and leader of the army in order to retire and lament the loss of his son. There is no glimpse of joy that a dangerous sedition has been subdued; only despair at the loss of his son. His warriors sneaked into the town, ashamed of their victory, as if they were an army in defeat, while David went to his chamber and wished that he had died instead of his son. All his energy and vitality was broken, until Joab made him summon his strength to preserve the outward appearance of his royal dignity (2 Sam. 16-19).

There is no difficulty in understanding the behaviour of David, nor his weakness with regard to his sons. And yet his whole attitude appears in a different light when viewed from the standpoint of the Israelitic conception of the family.

We already know wherein it consists: the family is a common life, an organism which grows and spreads in the shoots which it is constantly sending forth. The symbol of the plant or the tree naturally suggests itself, and the ancients themselves already made use of it. When *we* speak of genealogical trees, the symbol, properly speaking, can only be applied with certain limitations. We are thinking of the individual as owing his existence to the preceding generation; but he emancipates himself more and more, until as a grown-up man he has his point of gravity entirely in himself. In the eyes of the Israelites, however, the symbol is fully applicable; indeed, it is rather more than a symbol, for tree and human species are two entirely analogous forms of life. Just as the branch not only owes its existence to the trunk and the root, but constantly sucks its nourishment from it, in the same manner the individual holds his life only in connection with his family. It is that which is expressed by the sons bearing the name of the father.

That the son places himself outside the family and raises the standard of revolt against his father, is so utterly unnatural that no law can take account of it. It is more absurd than a kingdom divided against itself; it is a unity, a soul that is at war with itself. If the son sets himself against the father, then he is as a diseased member of a body, and the father who, by the acts of the son, is forced to remove him, is as a man who cuts his own flesh.

This is not only a symbol. The strong community between the members of the family has its physical presuppositions, resting upon the fact that their bodies are made of the same substance. They have the same flesh, bones and blood. "What profit is it, if we slay our brother and conceal his blood", says Judah to his brothers when they are on the point of committing violence against Joseph. "Come, and let us sell him to the Ishmaelites, and let not our hand be upon him; for he is our brother, *our flesh*" (Gen. 37,27). In the marriage laws "the flesh" [1] is even the usual appellation of those related. But one can also say "flesh and bone". Laban says to Jacob: "Thou art my bone and my flesh" (Gen. 29,14), and the same term Abimelech uses in relation to the Shechemites (Judg. 9,2). In both of these cases it is a question of relationship through the mother. Even with her family which, however, plays a less important part, the man shares flesh and bone. As far as the relationship extends, flesh and bone are common. Therefore David can say to the Judæans that they are his bone and flesh (2 Sam. 19,13), just as he says it to his relative Amasa (v. 14). Indeed, when all is said and done, the community of all Israel depends upon their having common flesh and bone (2 Sam. 5,1).

These terms imply that there is a likeness between those related. The flesh and the parts of the body grow out of some other body, and bear its impress upon them, having grown directly from out of the loins of the father, and thus literally being his flesh. Thus anyone can see that the people of Esau are distinguished by their hairy bodies, whereas the people of Jacob are smooth.

It is the chance development of this *usus loquendi* which has made the Israelite speak more of flesh and bone than of blood. With the Arabians the opposite is the case. In actual fact blood is as essential a part of the community as flesh and bone, indeed, perhaps the most important, for in the blood life is seated. This means that when blood is shed, life expires with it. But it also means more. It means that when human beings belong together and have common blood, then they also have common life. The corporeal community of the family is only one expression or manifestation of the common life pervading it. And it means that it has a common soul, for body and soul are, as we know, only two terms for the same thing.

By the unity of the family it is implied that its will and strength acts in the man. We are given exact information of a man, who his father is, and what family he belongs to; without that piece of information his being would not be defined. When Gideon received his summons, he answered at once that his family was the least in Manasseh, just as he himself was the least in his family (Judg. 6,15). The family forms the background of a man's actions, the blessing depending upon its strength and character. But the very example of Gideon shows that a man may rise above the level of his family, and of this we also have other examples. However, this does not mean that he rises above the family; he invariably pulls it up with him.

Therefore, the conflict between men becomes a conflict between families. If a man rises in the world and gains honour and blessing, the family immediately follows him; and if he is made to fall, it shares his fall, unless it has the strength to uphold him and thus to maintain itself. The latter can take place through blood-vengeance, which in its old form is one of the most pronounced outcomes of the solidarity of the family.

The Israel of the Old Testament never abandoned this fundamental view of the relation between the individual and his family. When Goliath flouted and threatened the Israelites, Saul promised that, whoever killed the giant, his father's house should be made a privileged house in Israel (1 Sam. 17,25). This form of promise is perfectly natural to the Israelite. A man cannot be a nobleman when his family is not free; his family's lack of honour would prey on his own and deprive him of nobility and glory.

This appears most clearly in those who attain to the highest dignity, i. e. the kings. When Saul is made a king, it is not only he, but his family that is elevated. "In whom is all the pride of Israel? Is it not in thee, and in all thy father's house?" says Samuel to him (1 Sam. 9,20), and when he falls as a king, it is *his house* which loses its royal dignity (2 Sam. 3,10). As long as the house of Saul was in power, the rule of David was not safely established. Every member of Saul's family had in himself an inborn claim to share the glory of rulership. Yahweh had chosen David, not only before Saul, but before Saul and his house (2 Sam. 6,21). The object of David would therefore necessarily be to neutralize all who were of the house of Saul. He showed all his cunning, in that he succeeded in doing it without breaking his covenant with Jonathan, as this covenant laid obligations upon him which might counteract his aim.

And David himself, from the very first, always made his own family rise with him. When he went into the desert and commenced his life as a captain of freebooters, his brothers and the whole of his father's house rallied round him (1 Sam. 22,1). They are solidary with him, and quite naturally follow his destiny. When David has gained the power, the chief thing for him is to keep it for his house. The prophet Nathan tells him that his house shall be established for ever (2 Sam. 7,16), just as it is his house that was stricken when he committed his crime with Bath-sheba (2 Sam. 12,10). Monarchy belongs to his house, and when Jeroboam has taken the north country from Rehabeam, it is still "David's house" which he fears (1 Kings 12,26).

Monarchy belongs to a family, because the blessing cannot be the possession of an isolated individual. It must necessarily spread to all with whom his soul is organically united. This refers to all forms of blessing, also the one which the priest possesses. Therefore priesthood is also identified with one family. In Shiloh it was Eli who, in the older period, officiated in the temple. As a matter of course the sons succeed and partake of the privileges of priesthood. It had been given to Eli's father's house, with the promise that it should possess it forever. But the sons of Eli degenerated; they were not the true souls of priests, and had to perish. Their father is irresistibly involved in their ruin; the arm of Eli and his father's house is cut off, so that none of his family reaches old age, and priesthood is given to another (1 Sam. 2,27 ff.). So families of priests replace each other.

It is the family feeling which is the most fundamental part of the soul of the man, nor is it touched in vain. When Jacob saw the daughter and herds of his kinsman at the well's head near Haran, family feeling stirred his strength so violently that he alone could lift the stone, which otherwise required the united strength of all the shepherds. And Laban confirmed the family feeling by saying: Surely, thou art my bone and my flesh (Gen. 29,14).

Kinship is given with birth, but we know that it is not merely a community of body, seeing that not only those who are related in the flesh make part of the unity. When once the wife has been received into the family of her husband, she enters into its psychic unity, and this not only holds good of her, but of all that attaches itself to the sphere of the family. This is most vividly illustrated by the old narratives.

Achan of the tribe of Judah, who takes part in the fights of the Israelites under Joshua, has purloined a good deal of silver, a wedge of gold and a costly Babylonian garment from the spoil, which was consecrated to Yahweh for destruction. The garment he has hidden, but the consequences are obvious, the Israelites suffering a severe and unexpected defeat when they go against the town of Ai. Joshua complains before Yahweh, and the reason of their defeat is made known to him: Yahweh is enraged, because part of his spoil has been stolen. The oracle is asked, and soon Achan is taken and unreservedly confesses his guilt. "And Joshua took Achan, the son of Zerah, and the silver, and the garment, and the wedge of gold, and his sons, and his tent, and all that he had, and they brought them unto the valley of Achor, all Israel standing by. And Joshua said: Yahweh shall trouble thee this day, for thou hast troubled us. And all Israel stoned him with stones, and burned them with fire, after they had stoned them with stones" (Josh. 7).

There is another narrative of quite a similar kind in the Pentateuch (Num. 16). Two men, Dathan and Abiram, have revolted against the rule of Moses, which to them seems intolerably despotic. But Yahweh takes the part of Moses. The two men and their families are isolated, all Israel standing aloof from their tents, where the rebels are now left alone with their wives and children. At the prayer of Moses the earth opens and swallows up Dathan and Abiram; alive they go down into Sheol *with all that appertains to them.*

From these events we learn that the man forms a complete unity with the whole of his family, his "house" and his property. Psychic community means, above all, a common will and so a common responsibility. The man is the centre of this common will. He does not act for himself alone, but for the whole of his house. Whatever he has done, the house, the family has likewise done, for together they form an organism so closely knit that no single part thereof can be separated as something independent. The two examples are by no means the chance outcome of blind passion in the souls of Moses and Joshua; on the contrary, they only express what is natural to the Israelite, and we constantly find proofs thereof.

When Pharaoh had deprived Abraham of his wife without knowing what he did, because Abraham himself had deceived him, Yahweh plagued him and *his house* with great plagues (Gen. 12,17). And the same thing happens in the parallel narrative, where the guilty person is Abimelech not Pharaoh. He is threatened with death, together with all that pertains to him (Gen. 20,17), and later on we hear that judgment has already fallen upon his wives and slave-women, in that they are unable to bear children (v. 18). When the Danites steal a graven image from a man by name of Micah, and he overtakes them, they threaten to kill him — but not him only: Thou might "gather" thy soul and the souls of thy house (Judg. 18,25). It is always taken for granted that, when a man perishes, he also involves his house in his ruin. Jacob reproves Simeon and Levi for the act of violence they committed against Shechem, and then says: The Canaanites shall gather themselves together against me and slay me, and I shall be destroyed, I and my house (Gen.. 34,30). On the other hand, when the flood came and destroyed the whole world, only Noah was saved, because he was just and walked with God; but it is a matter of course that he is not saved alone; the whole of his family follows him (Gen. 6,18; 7,1). In the same manner Lot with his family is saved out of the destruction of Sodom, because of his relationship with Abraham who interceded on his behalf (Gen. 19).

The words of Jacob to his unruly sons show that it is not only the man, the head of the house, who involves the others in ruin. They are all solidary, and every member holds the destiny of the family in his hands. When Samson has set the Philistines a riddle which they cannot solve, they frighten his wife to entice him to declare the riddle, threatening her all the time to burn her and her father's house (Judg. 14,15); Rahab at Jericho saved herself and her father's house by her treason (Josh. 2). And the woman of Tekoah, whom Joab sent to David, says, when David promises to take her cause in hand: The iniquity be on me, and on my father's house, and the king and his throne be guiltless (2 Sam. 14,9).

The community of the family is a common participation of the good, but also of the evil forces of life. As the blessing acts throughout, so also the curse. Whether it be said in so many words or not is in itself immaterial; the misfortune must strike the "house" when it strikes the man. When Joab has killed Abner, David says: Let it rest on the head of Joab and on all his father's house; and let there not fail from the house of Joab one that has an issue, or that is a leper, or that plies a distaff, or that falls on the sword, or that lacks bread! (2 Sam. 3,29). This is so deeply rooted in the Israelites, that even a man like Jeremiah, in whom certain features of individualism are to be traced, says that if a prophet, priest or ordinary man speak of the "burden" of Yahweh, then Yahweh will visit that man and his house (Jer. 23,34).

It is this common responsibility which makes the catastrophes in Israel so great. The man cannot fall as an individual, but it is as with the trees in the wood, of which Cæsar tells us: all the trunks were cut at the roots, and when one fell, the fall spread incessantly from one end of the wood to the other. Or we ought, rather, to make use of another picture: When the tree falls, one cannot save single branches from the fall.

It is not only Zimri who, on his own accord, kills the ruling king, Elah, together with the whole of his father's, Baasha's house (1 Kings 16,11 f.). The most glaring example before us is the fate overtaking the dynasty of Ahab. Through his prophet Yahweh himself informs Jehu what he is to do: "And thou shalt smite the house of Ahab thy master, that I may avenge the blood of my servants the prophets, and the blood of all the servants of Yahweh on Jezebel. For the whole house of Ahab shall perish, and I will cut off from Ahab him that pisseth against the wall (i. e. men), and him that is shut up and left in Israel; and I will make the house of Ahab like the house of Jeroboam, the son of Nebat, and like the house of Baasha, the son of Ahijah" (2 Kings 9,7-9). This commandment Jehu carried out with conscientious thoroughness, and not one of Ahab's family was left alive.

In a similar manner the first royal family of the north country perished in its sins, because Jeroboam had practised Canaanite cults. These were "the sins of the house of Jeroboam" (1 Kings 13,34; 14,10.14; 15,29; 16,3; 21,22; 2 Kings 13,6).

It rings through the prophetic sayings against the various kings. When Isaiah threatens Ahaz, he mentions expressly himself and his people and his father's house as the objects of the punishment of Yahweh (Is. 7,17), just as Amos announces that the sword of Yahweh will be directed against the house of Jeroboam the Second (Am. 7,9); and when Jeremiah advises King Zedekiah to surrender himself into the hands of the Babylonian king, he does not forget to emphasize that Zedekiah thus may save his own life and that of his house (Jer. 38,17).

How far does this community and responsibility extend? The question cannot be answered with a formula. The community extends as far as the relationship. The kernel is the family: husband and wife, sons and daughters, slaves and everything that belongs to the household. It is always "the house" that shares the same fate. But the house, as we know, has no formally fixed bounds; it extends as far as the relationship makes itself felt. It may just as well be said that the family *(mishpāhā)* follows the man, as that the house does it. It is told of Bethel that when the Israelites took it by treason, all the citizens were cut down, with the exception of the traitor and his family (Judg. 1,25). And Yahweh says that if any man begin to sacrifice children to Melech, then he will exterminate that man and the whole of his family (Lev. 20,5).

Generally speaking we may say that this community does not extend widely, and here there is a significant difference between Israel and the Arabians, where community extends through a whole tribe. An investigation of blood-vengeance will show us that it is mostly *families* who go against each other, and they *may* even be rather closely related.

The union of the family or the house is so firm, the harmony so deep, that neither of the two words, union or harmony, is quite sufficient. Peace in the house is a common will and a common responsibility, not dependent on the various individuals. The peace of the family is not something which is first created by the goodwill of men: it is given with life, and its dissolution means the ruin of life. The house stands and falls as a whole. Whether a man says "I" or "my house" is really immaterial. When David says: Although *my house* be not so with El, yet he hath made with *me* an everlasting covenant (2 Sam. 23,5), the two terms cover each other entirely.

No other peace relation has such an intimate character as that of the family. But it is not the only one.

The Israelite belongs to various wholes; the most important are, as we have already seen, the town and the nation. There are examples of the town community being so firm as to be classed with the solidarity of the family. When Ahimelech, priest of the sanctuary of Nob, had helped David to escape, Saul not only caused him and all the priests to be slain, but "Nob, the city of the priests, smote he with the edge of his sword, both men and women, children and sucklings, and oxen, and asses, and sheep, and goats, with the edge of the sword" (1 Sam. 22,19). The town forms a community under the elders; peace consists in the blessing acting throughout the community. How deeply it goes depends upon several things. Nob was hardly greater than that it formed one large family. Sometimes the unity may be stronger than at other times. We know from the Arabian towns how the families or, rather, the tribes of the town might be fighting among themselves, but as soon as they were attacked from without they might form a solid unity. This was probably also the case in Israel.

Apart from the family the totality which has the strongest hold upon the Israelites is that of the people. The unity of the people rests upon a common being and a common history, or in other words, upon a psychic community. In point of fact the unity of the people may be just as strong as the unity of the family. The prophets speak to the people as one being with a common responsibility. It may be called a stricken man, covered with wounds (Is. 1,5-6) or a woman who commits adultery (Ezek. 16; Hos. 2; 4).

Those of the same people thus stand in a similar state of peace towards each other as those of the same kin, and just as the house is centred in the father, so the soul of the people is centred in the king. When David has committed a crime, a pestilence is sent upon the whole people, but from this very narrative it appears that there might be some doubt of the full co-responsibility of the people. David said to Yahweh: Lo, I have sinned, and I have done wickedly; but these sheep, what have they done? Let thine hand, I pray thee, be against me, and against my father's house! (2 Sam. 24,17; 1 Chron. 21,17). David denies the common responsibility [1] of the people, but it is characteristic that it does not occur to him to touch the unity of the family. The responsibility rests with him and his house.

Thus it may, in more than one sense, be doubtful how widely the responsibility extends, but there can be no doubt that peace must normally extend to the whole of the people, and in this there is always a certain community of will, a strong fellow feeling, even if it cannot compare with the family feeling in intensity.

Community goes deeper than to the one generation; it extends backwards as well as forwards through history. We see this wherever we consider the family. From fathers to sons the same soul grows through time; it is the same in preceding and succeeding generations, just as at any time it is common to the whole family. When at the gathering of the people Joshua says: I and my house, we will serve Yahweh (Josh. 24,15), then he takes upon himself an obligation, which also concerns his family through the generations. The blessing which was given to Abraham keeps on acting in his successors, first in Isaac, then in Jacob and all his sons, and so in the whole of Israel. This community of blessing is the consequence of Abraham having commended his sons and *his household after him* to do justice (Gen. 18,19).

Whatever the fathers do of good or evil acts in the successors far down through the generations. It is that which is expressed in the law by the well-known words that Yahweh visits the iniquity of the fathers upon the children unto the third and fourth generation of them that hate him, and shows mercy towards thousands [2] of them that love him and keep his commandments (Exod. 20,5-6). What is done to the descendant is also done to the father. This determined David's treatment of the house of Jonathan (1 Sam. 20,16; 24,22), and we are several times confronted with the thought when there is a question of manslaughter and violence.

When Ahab had perpetrated his deed of violence against Naboth, Elijah said to him that the dogs were to lick his blood in the place where they had licked the blood of Naboth (1 Kings 21,19). Sin must entail misery. A certain remission is granted to Ahab; it will not happen in his days (v. 29). But the poison is in the family, and some day it must come out. It happened with his son Joram when Jehu killed him. Jehu expressly calls to mind these words, which were spoken to Ahab: Surely I have seen yesterday the blood of Naboth, and the blood of his sons, saith Yahweh, and I will requite thee in this plot, saith Yahweh (2 Kings 9,26). Retribution came over Ahab, in that his son was killed. Conversely, when Abimelech, the son of Gideon and a slave girl, has usurped the power and slain his brothers who were born in wedlock, we hear that Jotham asks the men of Shechem, whether they have dealt truly and sincerely by Gideon and his house in making Abimelech a king (Judg. 9,16.19). What they do against the sons of Gideon, they do against Gideon himself.

All this shows us the family as the fundamental factor of life to which everything comes home. That which is in the family is shared by all its members, but not in such a manner that each has a share of the whole. The family is embodied in every man, with all its blessing, all its substance, and so also its responsibility. One may say that he is the family, because it manifests itself completely in him.

This is in close agreement with the law of thought. The thought is directed against the conception of the whole, and sees it entirely in its individual parts. The soul is wholly in the body, and, as in the case of the family, its single parts are wholly in each member. The view has been advanced[1] that it is the social order or the relation between the family and the individual which forms the starting point of this fundamental law in the thinking of all primitive peoples. However, there is no indication of the one or the other being "first". But what can be established with certainty is the complete harmony between thinking and the general conception of life.

This law of community is the basis of the Israelitic conception *history*. The pride with which the Arabs or the Scandinavians, the heroes of Firdawsi enumerate the valiant deeds of their ncestors, also filled the Israelites when they spoke of the peaceful, ighty and generous Abraham, or the rightly blessed Jacob who, y means of his cunning, conquered the strong; for they entertain o doubt that the mental possessions of the fathers are theirs. nd if the Israelite has not so many valiant deeds to pride him- elf in, then he has the promises given by his strong god to the athers. "Remember Abraham, Isaac and Israel, thy servants, to whom thou swarest by thine own self and saidst unto them, I will multiply your seed as the stars of heaven", says Moses to ahweh in a critical situation (Exod. 32,13, cf. Deut. 9,5); with the fathers he made a covenant and gave them Canaan, thus also giving it to their successors (Gen. 12,7; 13,15; 17,8, etc.).

The relation to the fathers cannot be decided merely by the sons deriving the substance of their souls from them. It is true that the fathers form a long succession through the generations, but the differences in point of time are not decisive. Israel is Jacob who has spread out in the many. The fathers are constantly present and take part in the life of the family. Therefore the relation between fathers and descendants is mutual. Just as the blessing of the fathers is inherited by the sons, in the same manner the greatness of the sons reacts upon the fathers. In face of this view of history it is of no importance to distinguish sharply between what has been done by each generation. The Israelites to whom Amos spoke had come up from Egypt (3,2); this can be said, because every Israelite shared in this experience. The fathers live according to the same laws as their successors, and they share the experiences of posterity. Jacob as a man and Jacob as a people are so intimately connected that no one can keep the two apart. But, starting from these presuppositions, we understand that the patriarchal legends must contain the history of the people in a condensed form, but also that they cannot be interpreted according to hard and fast rules.

The fathers make part of the peace, or, rather, in them it is centred, and in them it has its origin. One is born into a peace-relation, which is determined by one's fathers. Peace-relations are, however, not limited to those of the same kin, but may be entered into with others through friendship.

The old Israelites knew how to value *friendship.* We often hear complaints from those who have lost it, and one of the many unfortunates who expresses his feelings in the Old Testament also describes his longing for friendship: "Two are better than one, because they have a good reward for their labour. For if they fall, the one will lift up his fellow, but woe to him that is alone, when he falleth; for he has not another to help him up. Again, if two lie together, then they have heat, but how can one be warm alone? And if one prevail against him, two shall withstand him; and a threefold chord is not quickly broken" (Eccles. 4,9-12). The greatest eulogy of friendship is, however, to be found in the story of David and Jonathan.

It is told: "The soul of Jonathan was knit with the soul of David, and Jonathan loved him as his own soul. And Saul took him that day, and would let him go no more home to his father's house. Then Jonathan and David made a covenant, because he loved him as his own soul. And Jonathan stripped himself of the robe that was upon him, and gave it to David, and his garments, even to his sword, and to his bow, and to his girdle. And David went out whithersoever Saul sent him, and ever prospered; and Saul set him over the men of war, and he was accepted in the sight of all the people, and also in the sight of Saul's servants" (1 Sam. 18,1-5).

Friendship is a community of souls. Two souls enter into a union and form one whole. It means that they are ruled by a common will, this being the substance of the covenant. It is confirmed by mutual assurances and by Jonathan arraying David in his clothes and arms. Clothes and armour pertain to the honour of the man, make part of his soul. When Jonathan gives to David clothes and arms, penetrated by his soul, then it is at the same time an outcome and a confirmation of the community existing between them.

One cannot be the friend of a man at the same time that one

is the friend of his enemy, inasmuch as this would make division in the will and entirety of the soul. The friendship of Jonathan with David, which is so intimate that it rules his soul entirely, cannot clash with his family-relation to Saul without involving the deepest conflicts.

At first all is harmony. Saul received David into his house and honoured him more than his other men. He was received into the peace of the family. But when the blessing of David became too much for Saul and threatened him with ruin, the harmony was broken. The position of Saul is clear; he hates David and must do all he can in order to maintain himself as his superior, and if it had been anybody else, the position of Jonathan would have been the same as that of his father. It was no less his honour and blessing which was threatened. If David grew to be the greatest, then the soul of Jonathan would be crippled, and the chiefdom, which his very birth entitled him to maintain, would be lost.

But a new soul had been born in Jonathan. He had mingled his soul with that of David; the centre from which his acts spring does not lie in the family, in Saul, but close to David; for in the unity of the fellowship of souls it is the strong soul which determines the direction of the common soul. Or, rather, he has two centres. As long as harmony prevailed between Saul and David, the point of gravity had not been shifted; as soon as this harmony is broken, it is separated into two points of gravity.

The task of Jonathan must necessarily be that of the conciliator. For his own sake he must try to unite Saul and David. And there is only one possible way to do it, viz. by persuading Saul that the great honour which David has gained is not the honour of a chief, but honour gained for Saul. We have already seen that this is the course he takes. He supports his point of view by showing that David formerly performed valiant deeds, which were quite as great and which Saul gladly accepted.

This was the first effort of Jonathan to preserve the harmony of his own soul. He succeeds, but only by setting aside reality. It is not here a case of "good will" and pious wishes. The question is: who *is* the greater. And reality itself gives a distinct answer. David wins a new victory, and Saul again sees clearly that the blessing of the chief is David's.

Jonathan is one of the tragic figures of the Old Testament. He had the spirit and also the blessing of a chief; he showed it when, in his youth, he made his way across the deep ravine between Gibeah and Michmash and, only attended by his armour-bearer, created such a confusion in the camp of the Philistines that utter dissolution prevailed, and they suffered a terrible defeat. His fate was the meeting with David. When the blessing of David has grown so strong as to be irreconcilable with that of Saul, it is impossible for Jonathan to follow the claim of kindred and to fight David. The soul of the latter acts in him; if David takes away chiefdom, he takes nothing from Jonathan, for Jonathan has identified his happiness with that of David.

When Saul has tried to kill David, the two friends meet. David wants to know whether Saul's hatred of him is of a transient nature, or whether he really wants to strike him down. Jonathan must excuse his absence and secretly bring the news to David. David's position is entirely dependent upon the covenant with Jonathan; on the strength of that he asks Jonathan to show him love and to help him. Jonathan could and — according to the claim of kindred — should bring David to Saul and surrender him into the hands of his father. But this is what David wants to avoid. He relies on the covenant; if it is broken, the whole foundation of his position is taken away. If this is the case, he prefers that Jonathan himself should slay him (1 Sam. 20,8). But Jonathan again gives him assurances of his friendship. He wants to try the mood of Saul and, if it be inimical, to help David to escape.

The crisis in their relation occurs on the following day. At the common meal on the day of the new moon Saul misses David. When he asks for the absent one, Jonathan answers that he has permitted David to go home to his family to partake of a sacrificial meal. "Then Saul's anger was kindled against Jonathan, and he said to him: Thou son of a perverse rebellious woman, do not I know that thou hast chosen the son of Jesse to thine own confusion, and to disgrace thyself, and thy mother's shame. For as long as the son of Jesse liveth upon the ground, thou shalt not be established, nor thy kingdom. Therefore now send and fetch him unto me, for he shall surely die. And Jonathan answered Saul his father and said unto him: Wherefore shall he be slain? what hath he done? And Saul cast a javelin at him to smite him, whereby Jonathan knew that it was determined of his father to slay David. So Jonathan arose from the table, in fierce anger, and did eat no meat the second day of the new moon, because his father had done him shame" (1 Sam. 20,30-34).

One may say that it is the outcome of a diseased mind, when Saul hurls the javelin at his own son, and thus the Israelite would also judge. But it must only be understood in the manner that a healthy soul does not attempt to kill its own son seeing that he never has occasion to do so. The disease is not a spontaneous outbreak in the soul of Saul. It lies deeper; it is the very foundation that is dissolved, because the absolute validity of the relationship has been shaken. All the words and acts of Saul are fully consistent.

Jonathan has already failed in the claim of kindred by letting David escape after what had happened. Saul is firm on the right of the family. There is no other blessing and honour than the one a man has with his family, and no obligation can clash with that of the claim of kindred, because this is the deepest of all. He says justly that Jonathan has sacrificed his honour; he has not maintained the absolute claim of his father's house against David; kindred claimed that he should support the fight of his father, in order to strike him down who had a greater blessing than he and therefore wanted to take his blessing. This applies to the claim of Jonathan himself to the honour of chiefdom, which it is equally his right and his duty to maintain. But Jonathan frankly refuses the direct request of his father to bring David before him, and thus the story reaches its crisis. Jonathan has placed himself outside the family, he is a degenerate son; when Saul flung the javelin at him, he did the natural thing, that which was implied in the claim of kindred — that which David later on was to have done to Absalom and the other sons who rebelled against him.

In reality there is no possibility of a solution of the conflict in the soul of Jonathan. The strife does not come from without, but depends upon his being placed in two soul-relations which are at war with one another. Without a breach of something which, according to its nature, must not be broken, it cannot be done. But the real conflict arises because his covenant with David has become so strong that it is as intimate as the covenant which in any case claims to be the deepest, the covenant of kin.

When David is roaming about in the desert, pursued by Saul, Jonathan comes to him in order to support him and imbue him with new strength by renewing the covenant and strengthening their community. His words are strange; he says that David is to become a king and himself only next unto him (1 Sam. 23,17). He who had the task to maintain in himself the claims of a whole family gladly gives way, in order that David may become the highest. So great is the power exercised by David over his soul, that it determines his own will and its demands. All that which filled and guided the soul of an Israelite, the history of the family and the claim of the name, submits to this power.

We do not hear more of Jonathan. It is his faithful friendship for David which is constantly remembered; he has become the type of a friend, and with justice; he sacrificed everything to his friendship. But the tragic thing about him is that, from his own presuppositions, he sacrificed too much. According to the old Israelitic moral conception he became a lesser man, because he sacrificed that which no one had the right to give up: the claims of kin.

It would have been interesting to know more of his relation to Saul after the events on the day of the new moon. From the ensuing occurrences it appears that he has not renounced the family; he has only placed it on a lower level. But what was the attitude of Saul towards Jonathan after that unhappy day? We may imagine that his soul was so weakened by what occurred to him that his actions were characterized by uncertainty. He was incapable of putting his son out of the family. When the Philistines came back, and Saul, broken and despairing, had to go out and wage the last hopeless fight in order to preserve and maintain its blessing, then Jonathan at any rate stood at his side, together with his brothers, and followed the claim of kindred. He followed his father to his death and shared with him the ignominy of defeat. His fate was eventually determined by the family with which, by reason of his birth, he was to share everything, but which his own history had prevented him from maintaining to the full.

David confirmed the covenant with Jonathan in his lamentation over the slain: "I am distressed for thee, my brother Jonathan; very pleasant hast thou been unto me; thy love was to me wonderful, passing the love of woman" (2 Sam. 1,26). But when in the same lamentation he says: Saul and Jonathan were lovely and pleasant, in their lives and in their death they were not divided! then there is decidedly a note of discord, considering the part which David played in the lives of the two men.

After the death of Jonathan the covenant with him on several occasions influenced the actions of David. He asked once: Is there any that is left of the house of Saul that I may show him kindness for Jonathan's sake? And when it turned out that there was a son of Jonathan, Meribbaal, he gave to him the land of Saul, but received him into his house (2 Sam. 9,1-13). Even though there is always a certain duplicity of motive in David's relation to the house of Saul, his behaviour bears testimony to the strength of the covenant. His covenant with Jonathan claims kindness to the sons of Jonathan. And when he delivered the descendants of Saul to the vengeance of the Gibeonites, he spared the life of Meribbaal on account of the Yahweh-oath which he and Jonathan swore to one another.

The friendship between Jonathan and David shows us the covenant of unrelated persons in its strongest form. Here the community of soul is whole, as strong as that of kin, nay, kinship must give way to friendship. "My brother" David calls Jonathan, as if they were of the same kin.

One is *near, ḳārōbh,* to him with whom one is related. It is not only the external nearness which is implied in the word, but the fellowship, the spiritual community (Exod. 32,27; Lev. 21,2; 25,25; 2 Sam. 19,43; Job 19,14; Ps. 15,3; Ruth 2,20; 3,12 *et al.).* Therefore it is generally impossible to decide whether it is the natural relationship or the covenant of friends which forms the basis, a proof that in kinship it is the spiritual element to which chief weight is attached. The word has nearly the same significance as *mōdhaʿ*, "him whom one knows" (Prov. 7,4 Ḳᵉrē, Ruth 2,1), for in this word the intimacy is expressed, and a similar idea is suggested by *ʾallūph*. Also the word *rēʿa* interchangeably means friend and kinsman. The friends are "knit together", therefore the friend is called *ḥābhēr,* which also means the kinsman (Judg. 20,11).

We see that the *usus loquendi* only distinguishes vaguely between the relation of kin and friendship. Both are called *shālōm* or *bᵉrīth,* peace or covenant. These two words are of different origin and scope, but they do not designate different kinds of relationship. *shālōm* means the state prevailing in those united: the growth and full harmony of the soul, *bᵉrīth* the community with all the privileges and duties implied in it.[1] Therefore both words may be used together, a "covenant of peace" (Ezek. 34,25; 37,26) being only a stronger expression for covenant. The two words are often used interchangeably (e. g., Gen. 26,28 f. 31; 1 Kings 5,26; Ps. 55,21), and if it does not appear from the context, we cannot see whether mention is made of kinship or friendship. It is true that *bᵉrīth* is chiefly used of community entered upon by unrelated persons, but this is because there is most reason to speak of this kind of peace-relations; and the word being used to designate all duties and privileges, it must necessarily, nay, first and foremost, include relationship. There are also other designations of the covenant.[2] To enter into a covenant is to "establish" or "set" or "give" a covenant or to "make peace".

Kinship is the nucleus of the psychic community. Every other kind of community must conform to it, if the soul is to be kept healthy and free from deep-rooted conflicts. He who is full of blessing has the ability to attach souls to himself; as the Preacher says in his own way: "he who stands alone can do nothing". No human being can do anything except through a connection with other souls. The proverb says that when the ways of a man please Yahweh, he maketh even his enemies to be at peace with him (Prov. 16,7). The power to make friends was perhaps the greatest quality of David, and that which most of all conditioned his happiness. It was also this ability which created the happiness of Joseph. Even when he was thrown into prison in Egypt, Yahweh was with him "and showed him mercy, and gave him favour in the sight of the keeper of the prison" (Gen. 39,21).

The covenant must always contain a certain community of will, for the soul is determined by will. Those who are united have a common aim. The one becomes "whole with" the other *(shālēm,* Gen. 34,21; 1 Kings 8,61; 11,4; 15,3.14). The more intimate the union, the more they communicate to each other of their being, and then it becomes the stronger who imparts his character to the fellowship. For the stronger it is a question of making covenants in order to carry through one's aims; for the weaker to make a covenant with the strong in order to enjoy his strength.

Abimelech, who has turned away Isaac because he became too powerful, later on comes to him with a couple of his men. And when Isaac asks what he comes for now, after having turned him away, he says straightway: "We have seen that Yahweh is with thee, let us make a covenant! Thou wilt do us no hurt, as we have not touched thee, and as we have done unto thee nothing but good, and have sent thee away in peace; for thou art the blessed of Yahweh." They made the covenant, and Isaac let him depart in peace (Gen. 26,26-33). The mighty one who may become disagreeably strong, him the king sends away from his territory. But if it proves that he is *very* powerful, so powerful that he far surpasses the king, then it is good to enter into a covenant with him; for the covenant consists in doing good to one another.

It is in the nature of things that the covenant excludes essential points of controversy between those united. In a story parallel with the one just communicated, it is told how Abimelech made a covenant with Abraham (Gen. 21,22-32). During the negotiations Abraham mentions that the shepherds of Abimelech have violently taken away some of the wells of Abraham, and he presents Abimelech with some lambs as a proof that the wells are his. In accepting the lambs Abimelech acknowledges the right of Abraham, and the covenant thus entered upon excludes future strife on that point.

The peace entered upon between human beings consists in *mutual confidence; shālōm* is the full manifestation of the soul, and if souls are united, then their *shālōm* consists in their acting together for the common prosperity. The Deuteronomy forbids Israel to receive Ammonites or Moabites into their community. "Thou shalt not seek their peace nor their prosperity", it is said (Deut. 23,7, cf. Ezr. 9,12). The covenant consists in this common endeavour. In a community where there is peace, manslaughter is out of the question. To introduce blood into a community of peace belongs to the great crimes. It was that which Joab did when he killed Abner and Amasa, who both of them were his rivals, but lived in peace with David and therefore, naturally, also with the house of David and his surroundings.

To do something in peace means doing it in harmony with those with whom one has to deal. The king of the Ammonites said to Jephthah: Israel took away my land when they came up out of Egypt, from Arnon even unto Jabbok and unto Jordan; now therefore restore those lands again in peace! (Judg. 11,13) "in peace" meaning that the souls of Jephthah and the king of the Ammonites are to be united and their wills made identical in this matter.

The union of souls may be more or less intimate. Therefore there is a great difference between covenants. When the king of the Ammonites demands an action on the part of Jephthah in peace, then the peace is limited to one special matter. But in every kind of peace and covenant there is a tendency to spread, according to the nature of the soul. If part of another soul enters into the soul, then it will be entirely penetrated by it. Hence the caution which the Israelites, like other peoples, show towards those with whom they associate. If they have entered into contact with them, then they must leave traces in the soul, and then the all-important question is whether they have something to put into it which cannot harmonize with that which it contains beforehand.

The oldest Israel was not afraid to make covenants with the

older populations of Canaan; in point of fact it was through covenants of this kind that Israel came into existence. The fight with the Philistines they could only carry on because at the same time they had peace with the Amorites (1 Sam. 7,14). Even at a very late period this natural relation persisted, until the assimilation was to all intents and purposes an established fact. How a covenant of this kind could be entered upon and what it implied, we learn from a narrative, as the one dealing with Jacob's relation to Shechem (Gen. 34).

It is told how Dinah, the daughter of Leah, was ravished by Shechem, the son of Hamor. But he came to love her and asked his father to get him the damsel to wife. Father and son now go to Jacob, who likewise has his sons around him. Hamor asks these strangers to give their daughter to his son, adding: "And make ye marriages with us, and give your daughters unto us, and take our daughters unto you. And ye shall dwell with us, and the land shall be before you; dwell and trade ye therein, and get you possessions therein." And Shechem exclaims impatiently: "Ask me never so much dowry and gift, and I will give according as ye shall say unto me; but give me the damsel to wife."

The sons of Jacob had not forgotten the outrage done to their sister, but they did not openly demand reparation; they followed a different course. They declared: "We cannot give our sister to one that is uncircumcised, for that were a reproach unto us. But in this will we consent unto you: if ye will be as we be, that every male of you be circumcised, then will we give our daughters unto you, and we will take your daughters to us, and we will dwell with you, and we will become one people." To this Shechem and Hamor agree, and Shechem makes haste to fulfil his obligation, in order to become possessed of the greatly desired woman.

Hamor and Shechem then go to their fellow-townsmen within the gate and say to them: "These men are at peace with us, and will dwell in the land and trade therein, for the land, behold, it is open to them; we take their daughters to us for wives, and we give them our daughters. Only herein will the men consent unto us for to dwell with us, to be one people, if every male among us be circumcised, as they are circumcised. Their cattle and their substance and every beast of theirs is ours, if only we consent unto them, so that they will dwell with us."

The men of the city agree and let themselves be circumcised, but while they lie in fever from their wounds, Simeon and Levi arrive, kill the sick men and carry away Dinah. And now all the sons of Jacob join them, falling upon the slain, plundering and spoiling the whole of the city and carrying away all women and children besides all cattle and goods. The cautious Jacob blames the two who had taken the initiative in this matter, viz. Simeon and Levi. Now they have made Jacob "to stink" among the inhabitants of the country, "and I being few in number they shall gather themselves together against me, and slay me; and I shall be destroyed, I and my house."

This narrative in vividness and strength is on a level with the best stories of the Genesis. Each scene stands out clearly and fully, giving us a series of pictures of life in Canaan. On one side stand Shechem and his father Hamor; they are a family of chiefs, and behind them stands a whole city. On the other side stands Jacob with all his sons and all the people rallying round him. Also they form a compact whole centring in Jacob, a family with a common responsibility and fate. The responsibility lies most heavily on Jacob; it is he who makes the decisions, and he knows his responsibility. "I am only few in number", says he; a small nomadic community they form, but the unity is strong. Jacob can say that he *is* the community.

The persons acting loom large enough, for Shechem and Hamor are a whole town and Jacob a whole family. But he who hears the narrative knows that they have still greater dimensions as regards depth, Shechem being the ancestor of the well-known city of the same name, situated in Mount Ephraim, and Jacob being the ancestor of all Israel. Thus we look behind the two principal actors into two worlds of peoples; it is the Israelitic community of peoples standing over against that of the Canaanites. Behind the history of the family rises the history of the peoples.

The act which starts the course of events is a deed of violence. Shechem ravishes one of the daughters of Jacob, but after the brutal deed his love is awakened, and his soul attaches itself intimately to that of Dinah.[1] This community of souls can only persist in case she becomes his wife. But now difficulties spring up. The Canaanite and Israelitic families are strangers to one another. If, through his daughter, Jacob is going to give part of his soul to the soul of the Canaanite family, then it cannot take place as an isolated event. By that the families become psychically connected, and this one event entails, as its necessary consequence, an entire community of life between the two parties. They are going to live together, to marry, to trade together, to get common property, in short: to become one community. Both parties look at the matter in exactly the same way. It is well worth noticing the art of the narrator in the description of the negotiations. The father, Hamor, states the matter in its wider aspects, with its consequences for the two communities. The son, Shechem, only thinks of one thing, that is to get Dinah for his wife, and he offers to sacrifice anything for this end, though of course, like his father, he knows the significance and scope of the event.

There might be great obstacles to such a psychic mixture between an Israelitic and a Canaanite or, as it is called, a Hivite community. The sons of Jacob mention only one thing, viz. the circumcision. It was of such vital importance to them that it could not be lacking in peoples with whom they were to live in close fellowship. Hamor and Shechem agree to it, and Shechem lets himself be circumcised as soon as possible in order to get his wife. But they have made a promise on behalf of the whole of their city; therefore their townsmen must follow them, and how this happens the narrative describes in a special scene.

They go unto the gate where the townsmen gather, saying: "These men are at peace with us." It means that the covenant *is* made. But in order that the covenant may be carried through, it is necessary that all the men of the city must be circumcised. In reality the men of the city were obliged to do what was required of them. The family who were their chiefs had made the covenant, and so they had also done it themselves. They could only protest by breaking the peace prevailing in their own community and by removing their own chiefs, but this would entail the breach of a double peace: first the peace within their own circle, including their chiefs, and then the peace with Jacob which they had already concluded through their chiefs. But the Shechemites were loyal people — besides, the new pact was advantageous — and they let themselves be circumcised.

Now the sons of Jacob had got their way with them. In time of peace Simeon and Levi enter the city and kill the men lying suffering from wound-fever, and the other men of the house of Jacob complete what they have begun. They plunder and spoil the assassinated men. Jacob sees at once what may be the consequences of the deed. Behind this city stand the other Canaanites, and it is now to be feared that they will rise and take their revenge on the cruel breakers of a covenant.[1]

That which makes this act of violence so serious is that the sons of Jacob have "laid blood in peace". And yet it is perhaps not in this respect that the breach is greatest. The Israelites would surely say that they had not made a real peace, but only a feigned one, for with a man who has violated one's sister one cannot make a covenant. The revolting thing is rather that they have dealt wantonly with what is most sacred of all: with peace itself. Instead of maintaining their violated honour openly, they cunningly seek shelter behind a feigned covenant, in order to strike against their adversaries. In this is the violation of peace, for it can never be used to shelter manslaughter without being violated in its innermost essence.

The narrative of Shechem and Dinah gives us a vivid picture of the life of the people in old Israel, and in particular it gives us an idea of the significance of the covenant, even when it was violated. The people with whom one made peace and covenant entered into a psychic community with the other party of the covenant. The two parties formed common customs and views, a common life; he who was superior communicated of his essence to the other party. Through the peace with the inhabitants of Canaan Israel changed. It adopted new customs of all kinds and learned to look at life in a new manner. Once the covenant is made, no limit can be fixed for the exchange of the substance of souls. When at a later period, under the influence of the opposition of the prophets, attempts were made to counteract the effects of the Canaanite religion, it necessarily must lead to a complete prohibition against any kind of covenant with the Canaanites (Exod. 23,31; 34,12; Judg. 2,2). But at that time the transformation of Israel towards Canaanite customs and ideals was to all intents and purposes carried into effect.

If a covenant is entered upon with a non-kinsman, the responsibility becomes mutual, just as between kinsmen. In both cases it is a psychic community, which means that the wills become identical. Perhaps it appears most strongly within the family itself, for the wife who always shares the responsibility of her husband and suffers ignominy and death together with him, does not share this responsibility on the strength of kinship, but because she has entered into the psychic unity of his house by being received into the covenant with him. As it is said, she has become his fellow, the wife of his covenant (Mal. 2,14; Prov. 2,17). And the same holds good of the men he gathers round him, his slaves.

But also outside the "house" the common responsibility of those united by a covenant holds good. When Jehu was engaged in exterminating the house of Ahab, he met the brothers of the king of Judah, Ahaziah. When, quite innocently, they told him that they were on their way to the Ephraimitic princes with whom they were at peace, Jehu caused them to be apprehended and slain, forty-two men in all (2 Kings 10,12-14). They had done Jehu no harm, and did not concern him, in so far as they belonged to another kingdom, but they had entered upon a covenant with his enemy, and thus they were his enemies. The least help rendered may be sufficient to create a full share in the responsibility. Friend wholly, or enemy wholly, this is the moral law of the ancients.

Conversely, common enemies join people together in peace-relations. The two Aramæan princes Toi and Hadadezer were at war with one another. When David fought with Hadadezer and defeated him, Toi sent his son to David in order to strengthen the peace between them (2 Sam. 8,9-10).

When princes thus make a covenant, the people, as a matter of course, are included in it. And the covenant between the peoples is always tantamount to a certain community, as great as circumstances permit. First and foremost the parties have common friends and enemies, for no one can have psychic community with two conflicting parties. In the covenant of peoples this plays an important part. They join together in order to fight against a common enemy.

New combinations always create confusion in older covenants and bring about conflicts. Thus Judah had a covenant with the realm of Damascus; later on the king of the latter, Benhadad, made a covenant with Baasha, the king of Ephraim. So when Baasha attacked Asa, king of Judah, he sent presents to Benhadad in order to strengthen the covenant between them, at the same time urging Benhadad to break his league with Baasha. The king of Damascus acknowledged the claim of the older covenant and broke his peace with the kingdom of Israel (1 Kings 15,18-19).

The peace between the peoples implies commercial intercourse and the exchange of cultural characteristics. David and Solomon had a covenant with Hiram of Tyre; Tyre supplied wood, etc., while Israel supplied Tyre with food. Later on, when Ahab had made a league with Tyre, it entailed the introduction of Phœnician cults into Israel. The two peoples, united by a covenant, must strengthen each other. Amos blames Tyre, because they forgot the brotherly covenant and sold Israelites as slaves to Edom (Am. 1,9).

But it is not necessary that the covenant should place the parties on an equal footing. It gives psychical community, but within the community the strongest will is the ruling one. When Israel makes a covenant with Ashur or Babel, then it means that Israel subordinates itself to the will of these mighty kingdoms. Therefore a prophet like Hosea complains of such covenants (Hos. 12,2). They must always entail the stronger power leaving its impress on the weaker. When Nebuchadnezzar came to Jerusalem and carried off the king and all the princes, he made a covenant with Zedekiah and put him on the throne, at the same time that he seriously weakened the kingdom. The covenant consists in Zedekiah and Nebuchadnezzar having one will, viz. that of Nebuchadnezzar. If Zedekiah opposes it, he has broken the covenant and violated the sacred thing (Ezek. 17).

It often happens that such a covenant is forced upon the vanquished. When Ahab had defeated Benhadad he imposed certain conditions on him, and then made a covenant with him (1 Kings 20,34), this covenant being an expression of the subordination of Benhadad to the will of Ahab. Thus it is said of the Aramæan kings who subordinated themselves to David, that they "made peace with Israel and served them" (2 Sam. 10,19; 1 Chron. 19, 19). The community is there, but the common will is not determined by an equal exchange; it is the one party that determines it.

A covenant of this kind Nahash was willing to enter upon with the city of Jabesh. The town was to suffer ignominy, in that all the inhabitants should lose their right eyes; thus they were made entirely subservient to him, but the compact meant mutual inviolability, community under the will of Nahash. If the covenant is there, it must also make itself felt. Less than mutual inviolability it cannot signify. The Gibeonites, under false pretences, made Joshua enter into peace and covenant *(shālōm* and *bᵉrīth)* with them, so that they were allowed to live, and the elders of the congregation sware unto them. When it became known how matters stood, all the protests of the people were of no avail. Joshua and the other chiefs had bound the people, and the Gibeonites might safely say to Joshua: We are in thine hand, and as it seemeth good and right unto thee to do unto us, do! (Josh. 9,25). The covenant was also maintained, but they had to subordinate themselves and to serve as slaves at the temple.

In reality the covenant rarely contains full equality. Within the community of the family, it is the man to whom the others subordinate themselves, and within other communities where peace reigns, it is the chief to whom they submit. And when two parties unite in the covenant, the one will generally be a greater giver than the other. The covenant is always a psychic community, but within it everybody must give and take as much as he can.

Therefore wisdom is required in order to make covenants; the man must be on his guard that he shall not become only giver. If it were a question of material gifts only, then the matter would be quite simple, but other values are implied; the covenant signifies a greater or a smaller right to demand.

A covenant of far-reaching consequences was the one which Abner made with David, after he had tired of Ishbaal, his former master (2 Sam. 3). Abner set to work very cautiously. First he sent some men to Hebron, where David sat as the chief of his Judæan tribesmen, and he bade them ask David whether he was willing to enter into a covenant with him. At the same time he worked among the elders within the former territory of Saul and paved the way for a covenant with David. David knew how to make covenants; he had shown that from the very beginning, and not least when he lived in the household of Saul. He made it a condition of the covenant with Abner, that Michal, the daughter of Saul, and his former wife, who had been given to another, should be restored to him. Thus he once more renews the bond connecting him with the house of Saul. He makes a covenant with Abner, as the son-in-law of Saul; his honour is re-established, and he associates himself strongly with the claims of the family of Saul; now he is able to take the kingdom; he does not receive it as a gift on the part of Abner. David makes the covenant, and everything seems to be in good order.

But this covenant also entails consequences for Abner. He had given so much that he also must be able to demand something in return; he must necessarily supersede Joab. Joab sees it at once, and as he has, furthermore, a claim for revenge on Abner as the slayer of his brother, he kills him.

David is now in a difficult position. His covenant with Israel is the covenant with Abner, who during complete peace has been killed by his own man; what is then to become of the new covenant? David kept the covenant. He mourned for Abner, bewailed him as a brother, lamented him in song and, briefly, treated him as if he were his own kin, thus confirming the covenant.

But what about Joab? David rid himself of him by pronouncing a curse upon him and laying the deed "on the head of Joab, and on all his father's house". But he does not take the consequences, for if so, he would have to get rid of him entirely. On the contrary, he even forces Joab to take part in the mourning rites. One might suppose that the attitude of David towards Joab implied a certain recognition of the fact that it was an act of vengeance with some element of justice. But this is not the case. Joab had no vengeance to wreak against the peace of David, and we see that David on his death-bed is tormented by the thought that he did not kill Joab, in spite of the blood-guilt which he bore so close to the house of David. In his relation to Joab David shows the same lack of ethical consistency, the same duplicity which we constantly observe in him. He cannot do without Joab, his strongest man; he maintains half of his relation towards him, and makes use of his strength, while at the same time he keeps the covenant with Abner, which excludes peace with Joab, and so he takes all that can be got out of both covenants.

Where peace and covenant prevail, gifts must be given. It follows from the whole character of the covenant; where there is a psychical community, gifts must pass from the one to the other, this being at the same time an outcome and a strengthening of the covenant.

The great importance which in Israel is attached to the *gift* has already been mentioned on several occasions. One honours the man by giving him gifts; one blesses him with one's gift, but, in any case, one strengthens the peace and the covenant through it. We know the basis of the value and power of the gift. It is not something material, but part of the psychic entirety of the man. Gifts are therefore always spiritual gifts. Like good words and good deeds they carry something from the soul of the one into the heart of the other; they not only bring tidings of good will, they bring good will itself, because they belong to the entirety of the soul. The gift is not an expression of sentiment; it is a necessary result of a real relation between men, and itself creates or strengthens a relation of this kind. Therefore the gift is not voluntary in the sense that it can be given or not given at discretion. Where the relation requires it, the gift is a duty, and at the same time it also creates obligations; he who receives has the duty to give and *vice versa:* he who has given has the claim to receive.

Thus, for instance, in the case of marriages. The relatives of the woman give their daughter; the balance must be maintained, and in their turn they receive gifts, *mōhar*. Thus both parties have given something which at the same time is material and spiritual. As to the size of the gift, negotiations are carried on beforehand, it being her relations who put forth their claims. If the bridegroom is a generous man, who dearly loves the desired woman, then it may be that he says, like Shechem when he woed Dinah: Ask me never so much dowry and gift, but give me the damsel to wife! (Gen. 34,12). Laban makes Jacob serve him seven years for each of his wives; a chief may demand valiant deeds from a man for his daughter (Judg. 1,12; 1 Sam. 17,25); David had to procure Saul a hundred foreskins of Philistines as the price of his daughter Michal (1 Sam. 18,25; 2 Sam. 3,14). But the usual thing in Israel was that fifty shekels of silver should be given as a gift for a wife. [1]

"The man of gifts gets all the friends", says the proverb (Prov. 19,6). It is the power of the gift towards making covenants which David used when he lived as a captain of freebooters in the desert of Judah. When he had obtained spoil, he sent some of it to the elders of Judah with the following words: Here ye have a blessing from the spoil of the enemies of Yahweh! (1 Sam. 30,26). He imparts to them blessing by the gift, and therefore has the right to be blessed by them in return; it is in this that the covenant consists. In relation to the shepherds of Nabal he behaved in a different manner. He gave them protection, lived peaceably with them; therefore he was also entitled to a gift from Nabal (1 Sam. 25,7-16). A gift is useful towards creating a covenant; but it may naturally also revive a covenant when on the point of expiring. Asa of Judah sent silver and gold to Benhadad in order to re-establish the covenant of their fathers, and so also of themselves, which covenant, however, they had let waste away. The effect made itself felt in due time. Benhadad broke with Baasha, the enemy of Asa, and compelled him to withdraw (1 Kings 15,18-19).

The gift always implies compulsion, because it entails a will that must act. One must be cautious in receiving a gift when one does not know what it implies. It may mean obligations which no one can grasp, and it may signify that which is worse: a demand for humiliation and subjection. The strange thing about the gift is that it may at the same time elevate and weigh down. No one can judge from its outward extent what is implied by it; this depends on what lies behind it, and is connected with the power of the gift to create honour. The great gives to the lesser; thus he helps him and makes him dependent. The lesser gives to the great in order to obtain something, or as an expression that he is dependent upon the great. But also the lesser is honoured by the gift of the great, in that it is an honour to receive from a really great man, to receive of his blessing and glory.

To live is to live in covenants: the great art of life consists in being able to make good covenants, and it is practised with the greatest nicety by him who understands how to deal wisely with the gift. The Israelite for whom property was such a large portion of the substance of life, was a master of this art; and in this respect he is the same, whether we look for him in the older or younger writings of the Old Testament.

Abraham, who proved so small when he was to risk his life for the sake of his wife, appears in his full greatness when people offer him gifts. When he wanted a burial-cave for his wife, the owner at once offered to give it to him as a gift. But Abraham knew what it meant: only against full payment would he receive it. And when the owner then demanded the exorbitant price of four hundred shekels, Abraham paid it without protest. He was the one who had given most.

The same qualities he showed when he had conquered the mighty kings who had plundered Sodom and Gomorrah. When Abraham returned with the spoil and the liberated prisoners, the king of Sodom came and asked to have his men back, but offered Abraham to keep the spoil himself (Gen. 14,21). Abraham might, with good justice, have done so; it was he who had taken it, and he demanded that his allies should have their share. But for himself he did not want to keep anything. By his offer the king of Sodom made it *his* gift, and Abraham did not want that another, with any show of right, should be able to say that he had made him rich (14,23).

Thus Elisha refused to accept a gift from the Aramæan chief whom he had healed (2 Kings 5,16), and in the same manner another prophet acted towards Jeroboam (1 Kings 13,7). Neither wanted to lose the honour of being the one who gave most. But it is a different proceeding when King Benhadad sent one of his men to Elisha with a gift consisting of every good thing of Damascus, forty camels' burden, with the order that they should say to the prophet: Thy son Benhadad sent me to thee! (2 Kings 8,8 f.). This implies that the gift proceeds from a lesser person who wants to honour the strong in order to acquire some of his strength.

Jacob was a man who understood the art of life, and naturally he also understood the use of gifts. This he proved in his relation to Esau. The peace between the two brothers was broken; Jacob had, by deceit, appropriated the blessing of his elder brother and had fled from his vengeance. Now he returned with his numerous family and the great wealth which he had acquired at Haran. He sent men to his brother in order to re-establish peace, but they returned unsuccessful. Esau approaches with four hundred men. Jacob is horror-stricken. If he is now to lose his wealth and his progeny, then he has lived in vain; he implores his god to help him.

The thought of measuring his strength against that of his brother and winning, through fight, the blessing he won by cunning, never occurs to him, but he uses all his wisdom, which was by no means inconsiderable. From his herds he selects a large gift for Esau. It is divided into small groups, which are sent out in advance to meet his brother. Every group is led by men who are to tell Esau of their errand: it is something which Jacob, the slave of Esau, sends to Esau. And there is to be a fair distance between the groups, so that every one is to come as a fresh surprise; in that manner Esau also gets time to reflect before he reaches Jacob, and if he harms one, the others are able to get away.

Esau must necessarily get the impression that by this gift Jacob subordinates himself to him. Jacob gives as the slave of

Esau and in order to acquire his protection. The gift takes effect. Esau meets Jacob without lifting his sword against him, and Jacob prostrates himself on the ground seven times, as the vassals of the Amarna letters before the great king. The words of Esau to Jacob aim at establishing the meaning of the gift. He asks what Jacob intends to do with the droves he met on the way, and is assured that they are the gifts of Jacob in order to obtain the grace of his lord Esau. Esau further establishes this meaning by saying that he does not need the gift, and Jacob affirms once more that the gift is given by the inferior, standing before Esau as before the face of God. Then Esau takes the gift, and thus his hands are tied; the peace between the two has been sealed.

But this peace was of a peculiar kind. Jacob has humbled himself before Esau, has subjected himself to him as his vassal, and now he must go with him to Seir as a dependent; he has given away his independency for the remainder of his life. The whole thing is a matter of course, so much so that it is not necessary to mention it expressly. Esau only says: Now let us take our journey, and let us go, and I will go before thee (Gen. 33,12).

But Jacob is master of the situation. He has gained the covenant which saves his life; now the great thing is to get rid of the covenant which is going to make him a lesser man, and he sees his way to do so. "He said to him: My lord knoweth that the children are tender, and the flocks and herds are suckling with me; and if men should overdrive them one day, all the flock will die. Let my lord, I pray thee, pass over before his servant; and I will lead on softly, according as the cattle that goeth before me and the children be able to endure, until I come unto my lord unto Seir. And Esau said: Let me now leave with thee some of the folk that are with me. And he said: What needeth it? Let me find grace in the sight of my lord. So Esau returned that day on his way unto Seir. And Jacob journeyed to Succoth..." (Gen. 33,13-17).

The amusing thing about this story is that Esau quite realizes what is at stake, and yet is deceived. By receiving the gift he has concluded the covenant, though like the lord with his vassal, and he acts accordingly. Jacob calls himself the slave of Esau; Esau calls Jacob his brother, and Esau demands that Jacob shall go with him. As Jacob now devises that it will delay a great lord like Esau too much if he is to take the caravan of Jacob with him, Esau wants to make sure of his share in Jacob by letting some of his men escort the expedition. But then Jacob makes an appeal to the chivalry of Esau. Why that suspicion? He ought to show him the confidence to permit him to follow in a few days. This appeal does not fail to influence the Bedouin. Trusting to the words of Jacob he goes towards his home in the south — whereupon Jacob hurriedly steals off towards the west.

One must admire the objectivity with which the figures of these two brothers are delineated, so as to stand out clearly in contrast to each other. But that which imparts life and substance to the sparse narrative is the sure touch with which it handles the mysterious virtue of the gift, its power to create a covenant and to give substance and character to the covenant.[1]

Whenever the great ones are approached, gifts must be laid before them. Thus one prepares the way, creates the possibility of the covenant, and shows that one wishes to get some of their blessing. One does not appear empty-handed before one's own king (1 Sam. 10,27), nor before other rulers. When the sons of Jacob, for the second time, had to go to Egypt in order to ask Joseph for grain, their father caused them to bring a gift out of the produce of the country: mastic, honey, tragacanth, resin, pistachio-nuts and almonds (Gen. 43,11).

The vassal must always send gifts to his lord. At one time the Israelites had to send gifts to the Moabites (Judg. 3,15.17 f.), and later on the stream flowed equally, now towards the east to Assyria, now towards the south to Egypt, exactly as in the days of the Amarna letters. As his slave and son Ahaz sends the treasures of temple and palace to Tiglath Pileser (2 Kings 16,8), and it was a costly present, implying the subjection of Judah under Ashur. The same was done in the kingdom of the north by Jehu, Menahem and Hosea. In David's days the opposite was the case; then all the neighbouring peoples sent presents to him (2 Sam. 8), and so it still was in the days of Solomon: vessels of silver and vessels of gold and garments and armour and spices, horses and mules poured into the palace of Solomon (1 Kings 10,25, cf. 5,1). The ideal of Israel is that the whole world should send presents in abundance to the king at Jerusalem, thus confirming that he is the one with whom they must look for a covenant when they want blessing (Ps. 72,10).

But it is a mutual relation. By his gift the vassal, as the inferior, confirms the covenant by a present; the master, on his part, must confirm the covenant, as the superior, by a gift. We know it from the Amarna letters. Not only the Egyptian king himself, but also his envoys, must be given presents.[1] He must also give presents to the others, to his equally situated "brethren" and to the small vassals. They never can get enough; the better the gifts from the great, the more honour. The gift is carefully balanced, and if it is too small, the vassals protest loudly. We have a single example of a Judæan king receiving a gift from the overlord. It was Merodach Baladan, who sent gifts to Hezekiah at the time when he was ill (2 Kings 20,12; Is. 39,1). A king must honour his well-deserving men by a gift (2 Sam. 11,8).

The gift makes peace and gives obligations; it "pacifies anger" (Prov. 21,14). Its power to make peace is expressed in one of the appellations for it, *shalmōnīm,* the connection of which with *shālōm* is obvious.[2] But it must not have the effect to disrupt deeper lying obligations. The prophets are constantly complaining that the princes violate justice for bribes (e. g., Is. 1,23; Mic. 3,11). What is reproved is the light acceptance of gifts from anyone who offers them; for the gift must, when accepted, necessarily lead to favouring the giver.

The value of the gift is by no means unimportant, but it is not decisive, because everything depends upon its spiritual value. That which is close to one, which is imbued with one's soul, is worth more than many treasures. Jonathan loved David as his own soul. When he made the covenant with him, he stripped himself of the mantle he wore and gave it to David, and the same he did with the remainder of his apparel, nay, even his sword, his bow and his girdle (1 Sam. 18,3-4). Clothes and weapons form part of the essence of the man, and have an intimate share in his soul. What Jonathan does is only the consequence of what has taken place: that his soul and that of David were united and mingled, and this union is further strengthened by its being carried through and receiving its tangible expression.

Any kind of bodily touch must strengthen the covenant, because the body forms part of the entirety of the soul. The very being together strengthens it; normally peace prevails between those who live together. Friends must seek the company of each other. The brothers of Ahaziah, king of Judah, who journeyed up to the royal house of the kingdom of the north, with whom they had a covenant, went up to "the peace of the sons of the king" (2 Kings 10,13). The covenant is confirmed by the shake of the hand, which one gives one's friends, and still more by the intimate touch through the kiss.[1]

All this is the expression of the mutual blessing, for it is the secret of the gift that it is a palpable form of blessing. Those who have peace with one another impart a mutual blessing, and if one gives blessing, then one creates peace and covenant. Those who meet and separate bless each other with good words, and through them they give each other peace. "Peace to you!" is the usual greeting (Gen. 43,23; Judg. 19,20). In that way something is given, which means well-being for the other; but peace contains still more. It is given by him who greets, and thus it contains a community between the two, a mutual touch which at least must mean inviolability.

"Is there peace?" (2 Kings 5,21). "Is thy coming peace?" (1 Sam. 16,4; 1 Kings 2,13). "Whether they be come out for peace — or whether they be come out for war?" (1 Kings 20,18). This is the constant question when one meets people whose will one does not know. It is also the decisive question, because peace is the condition of all common life or, if one chooses, identical therewith. If the answer is Peace! then all is well. How one answers when not wanting to have or to give peace we learn from the answer of Jehu when he approaches the capital, and the king sends his messengers to ask whether there is peace. Jehu says: What hast thou to do with peace? (2 Kings 9,18-19).

That men and women give each other a real gift when they give each other peace, it is hardly necessary to say. He who lays the blessing into the other, at the same time strengthens the growth of his soul and the community between them both. When Toi, the king of the Aramæans, sent his son to David to bless him and give him peace (2 Sam. 8,10), he thereby increased the peace of David, his well-being and the covenant between them. The man "demands peace" for the one with whom he wishes to maintain or maintains a relation of friendship. It means that he puts the energy of his soul into it. [1] This is the substance of the covenant: to benefit one another.

If the blessing is lacking, peace disappears. When Israel was visited by calamities because of the unexpiated deed of blood of Saul against the Gibeonites, David asked the latter: Wherewith shall I make the atonement that ye may bless the inheritance of Yahweh? (2 Sam. 21,3). The peace is broken because their blessing is lacking. When it is revived, peace and psychic community are healed. Blessing and peace are so closely knit together that they may be entirely identified. When the king of Assyria was laying siege to Jerusalem, he said: Make a blessing with me and come out to me, and then eat ye every man of his own vine and every one of his fig tree, and drink ye every one the waters of his cistern (2 Kings 18,31; Is. 36,16). To make a blessing with him is the same as to make a covenant with him, because the covenant consists in mutual blessing.

When a solemn covenant is concluded, it generally takes place with the observance of certain rites. The character of these is not artificial; one inaugurates the covenant with one of the actions in which this pact manifests itself and is constantly being confirmed.

When Zedekiah made his covenant with Nebuchadnezzar, it was confirmed by *handshakes* (Ezek. 17,18). When the priests at the time of Ezra made a league to rid themselves of their foreign wives, they shook each other's hands in confirmation (Ezr. 10,19), and so one gives one's hand to the king for confirmation that one enters into a covenant in which he predominates (2 Kings

10,15). It can be inaugurated by a kiss, as when Samuel kissed Saul after having anointed him (1 Sam. 10,1).

If it is a question of a more important covenant, it is frequently inaugurated by a *common meal*. The meal is the daily nourishment of the community among those related. Food gives life and strengthens the soul; the common strengthening makes common life. To eat with enemies would be inconceivable. He who is to maintain a special strength within himself, must not weaken it by eating with others (1 Kings 13). The common meal presupposes psychic community and strengthens it still further. "Yea, my man of peace in whom I trusted, which did eat of my bread, hath lifted up his heel against me," says a lamenter (Ps. 41,10). A stronger breach cannot be imagined. The common meal and the peace cannot be separated.

When the covenant is inaugurated by a meal, it is presupposed to have begun. The souls are united, but now the union is confirmed and approaches kinship in strength. When Jacob and Laban, the two kinsmen, had been divided, but once more came together and made a covenant, Jacob offered a large common sacrificial meal. The kinship was confirmed once more, and the divine powers of the family were acting in the strengthening of the community.

It is not immaterial who gives the meal. In the covenant strengthened by the meal every one has his place, and he who at table occupies the place of the father of the house has the place of honour. When David received Meribbaal at his table, he received him into the covenant of the house, but at the same time Meribbaal acknowledged David as his house-father. When Jacob and Laban made their covenant, it was Jacob who gave the meal. When Abimelech and the captain of his army sought Isaac and asked him to make a covenant with them, he prepared a meal for them (Gen. 26,30). The following morning the covenant, thus confirmed, was further strengthened by mutual oaths, and after that Isaac let his guests depart. The relation within this covenant is determined at once by the fact that it is Abimelech who asks for it. Isaac is the superior, and he gives the meal as the house-father. When Abner entered into a covenant with David, he arrived at Hebron with twenty men, and David prepared a meal for them (2 Sam. 3,20). He who has community of table with another "enjoys his salt" (Ezr. 4,14). A particularly intimate covenant is therefore called a "covenant of salt" (Num. 18,19; 2 Chron. 13,5).[1]

There is naturally a difference between the community of the family and other covenants, in that the latter are less stable. They are neither so intimate nor so lasting, and people who are united by a general covenant may in certain cases conclude individual covenants. This happens when their mutual relation enters upon a new phase. The people make a covenant with their king. Thus Israel concluded a league with David when they made him a king (2 Sam. 3,21; 5,3), and the same we learn of other kings (2 Kings 11,17). The consciousness of the covenant is naturally not always present. But when those who belong together are united in a new, common resolution, then the Israelite expresses it by making a covenant about it. The wills are united and meet in a special point. Thus king Zedekiah made a covenant with his people "to declare the liberation of slaves," so that everybody let his Hebrew slave and slave-girl go free, in accordance with the demands of the law (Jer. 34,8 ff.). One may call it an agreement, but that which takes place is that the wills, that is to say the souls, are united in one will, viz. that which the king enforces. When later on they repent of it and neglect to liberate the slaves, it is the covenant they have broken.

When the new code of laws had been found under King Josiah, he gathered the people and caused the words of the new book to be read to them. "And the king stood on the pillar and made the covenant before Yahweh to walk after Yahweh and to keep his commandments and his testimonies and his statutes with a whole heart and a whole soul, to perform the words of the covenant that are written in this book. And all the people stood to the covenant" (2 Kings 23,3). We find a similar scene described in the book of Joshua (chap. 24). Joshua gathers the people at Shechem, where they declare their willingness to worship Yahweh as their god. "So Joshua made a covenant with the people that day, and set them a statute and an ordinance in Shechem" (24,

25). Joshua and the people already have a covenant with each other; he has long been the chief of the people. But now the covenant is made afresh, in that it gets a new common will, viz. the one determined by the speech of Joshua.

This kind of separate covenant is constantly entered upon in daily life, whenever men unite about something. When men trade with each other, they are united; for by exchanging property they exchange souls. With the enemy one cannot trade, as this would create a conflict in one's soul, for the property of the enemy would act against the entirety of the soul. Trading is attended by gestures expressing union. In the olden times the one took off his sandal and gave it to the other (Ruth 4,7); later on a glove or a piece of cloth was given. [1] He who goes bail for another, becomes the debtor of the creditor and confirms the new relation with a handshake. In all of these cases it is a question of a covenant made. It generally happens between people who beforehand have a covenant with each other. But within the earlier covenant a new one is formed, centring in the specified object and creating a special common will.

The separate covenants may be of comparatively small importance, but they may also be particularly intimate. The Israelites have a term for such a particularly intimate union of souls shared by close friends; they call it *sōdh*. "Together we made the union sweet in Elohim's temple," says the psalmist of a friend, by whom he later on felt deserted (Ps. 55,15); and Job complains that those he loves turn against him, "the men of his *sōdh*" detest him (Job 19,19), i. e. the friends of his heart with whom he had an intimate covenant. [2] The word more particularly denotes the intimate circle rallying round him in order to create a common counsel (Ps. 83,4; Prov. 15,22). To have *sōdh* with God is another expression for the intimate covenant (Ps. 25,14; Prov. 3,32; Job 29,4).

The community formed through the covenant creates a new will, which changes the individual wills and goes beyond them. The point of gravity may lie nearer to the one than to the other, but never altogether with the one party. Therefore it often manifests itself in some external thing which lies outside the two parties and of which neither is predominantly the master, in the same manner as when two are joint holders of a pawn which is given into the keeping of a third. Thus Jacob and Laban deposited their covenant in a pillar or heap of stones, which thus became the witness between them. From that vengeance must come, if one of the parties should pass it by to do the other harm as a breaker of covenant (Gen. 31,44-48; 51-52). That which happens here must be interpreted as an outcome of the power of the Israelites to concentrate a psychical element into a body. Altars, pillars of stone, circumcision and the sabbath, all the outward manifestations of the Israelitic cult are witnesses to or "tokens" of the union of souls, the covenant between Israel and its god.

Peace and covenant are thus two expressions of the common life of the souls. All life is common life, and so peace and covenant are really denominations of life itself. One is born of a covenant and into a covenant, and wherever one moves in life, one makes a covenant or acts on the basis of the already existing covenant. If everything that comes under the term of covenant were dissolved, existence would fall to pieces, because no soul can live an isolated life. It not only means that it cannot get along without the assistance of others; it is in direct conflict with its essence to be something apart. It can only exist as a link of a whole, and it cannot work and act without working in connection with other souls and through them. Therefore the annihilation of the covenant would not only be the ruin of society, but the dissolution of each individual soul.

The covenant is not a thing to be dealt with as one pleases. It goes deeper than everything else, because it is the presupposition of all life. Therefore it is holy and has its roots in the divine powers. It receives its consecration in holy places, in the temple or under a holy tree (Judg. 9,6; 1 Sam. 23,18; 2 Sam. 5,3; 2 Kings 11,4; 23,3; Jer. 34,18). It is consecrated by sacrifices, whether these be of an ordinary kind (Exod. 24,5 ff.: Ps. 50,5), or whether they be specially adapted to the essence of the covenant (Gen. 15; Jer. 34). And when it is inaugurated by a meal, then that also is of a sacred nature. The gods of the two parties are in the union. The covenant sets such great forces into motion that it works throughout, to the very foundation of the united communities. All this can only be hinted at in this place in order to show how deeply founded the covenant is.

The covenant is the creator of all rights and duties. Therefore it is identical with right and duty; even of the least privilege or the least duty the Israelite can say that it *is* the covenant, for the covenant is present in it.[1] The basis of all Israelitic ethos is the common feeling, love, and according to the nature of the compact it must, in its innermost essence, be a family feeling. One of the Hebrew denominations of love, *raḥᵃmīm,* perhaps points directly to the relationship through its context with *reḥem,* mother's womb.[2] As the mother's womb is the source of the formation of families, so it is also the fountain of family feeling.

The old law of love finds its direct expression in a single place when it is said: Thou shalt love thy neighbour as thyself (Lev. 19,18). In this claim the Israelite expresses his idea of the mutual relation of mankind. The life which the individual holds is not private property, but something common, which he shares with others, first and foremost the family, and then the others with whom he has a covenant. Love is not a more or less superficial sentiment. It is identical with peace itself, with the unity of wills. When "the counsel of peace" prevails between two persons (Zech. 6,13), then there is love, because the wills are identical. To "speak peace" with one another and to "speak love" are two manners of expressing the maintenance of the common covenant;[3] it is practised by those who "know" each other, because knowing indicates a thorough, mutual feeling.

It is not strange that the Israelite should use the strongest expression for connection and context when he is to speak of love. Shechem's soul "clave" to Dinah, was "bound to her" (Gen. 34, 3.8), just as a man "cleaves to" his wife (Gen. 2,24). The soul of Jacob was "bound up in" the soul of Benjamin (Gen. 44,30), as Jonathan's was "bound up in" David (1 Sam. 18,1), because he loved him as his own soul. The heart is "with" the beloved person (Judg. 5,9).

In love the soul acts in accordance with its nature, because it is created to live in connection with other souls, with the family and those whom it receives into the peace of the family. The commandment to love is thus not a dogmatic invention, but a direct expression of the character of the soul and the organism of family and people. It means that the individual acts for the whole, and the whole for the individual, and this is not an abstract or an unnatural claim, but only the substance of normal life. He who keeps the law of love, shows that his soul is sound.

PEACE AND SALVATION.

PEACE and blessing are so closely united that they cannot be separated. Where there is blessing, there must be peace, because the latter is always the entirety of the soul, its free development.

shālōm under all circumstances designates that which is free and intact. The corresponding adjective is used of just weights (Deut. 25,15; Prov. 11,1), of whole stones (Deut. 27,6), of full and abundant reward (Ruth 2,12, cf. also Am. 1,6.9). And in exactly the same manner the verb is used of a work fulfilled (1 Kings 7,51; 2 Chron. 5,1) and a finished wall (Neh. 6,15). One makes a house "whole" when one finishes the building of it (1 Kings 9,25), and makes a dwelling whole when it is once more reared from its ruins (Job 8,6). One makes one's promise whole when it is fulfilled; a counsel becomes whole when it is carried through (Is. 44,26). *shālōm* designates at the same time the entirety, the fact of being whole, and he who is whole (e. g., 2 Sam. 17,3; Mic. 5,4; Job 5,24).

In its root the word has nothing to do with the passive and negative, which we are apt to put into our translation "peace", but also this fundamental conception has, in the course of time, been transformed by the new currents which came to prevail in Israel.

In the olden time peace is not in itself the opposite of war. There are friends and there are enemies; peace consists in complete harmony between friends and victory in the war against enemies, for in that consists the full development of the soul. One has "peace" in the fight when one conquers the enemy. When Gideon was on his way to the fight with the Midianites, and had his hostile encounter with Succoth and Penuel, he said to the men of Succoth: Therefore when Yahweh hath delivered Zebah and Zalmunna into mine hand, then I will tear your flesh with the thorns of wilderness and with briers. And in Penuel he said: When I come again in peace, I will break this tower (Judg. 8, 7-9). Both expressions mean the same thing: to have peace is, in the mind of Gideon, to conquer the two chiefs. David returned in peace, when Absalom was defeated (2 Sam. 19,25.31). When Ahab wanted to go to war with the Aramæans, Micaiah said to him: If thou return at all in peace, Yahweh has not spoken by me! (1 Kings 22,28).

We must not consider this as if peace were the release from fighting which follows upon victory. This "peace" would also belong to the vanquished; and Gideon had not finished the fight because he had gained the battle. Peace is victory itself, because the man develops through it. The great warrior is he who always has "peace" in his battles. Deutero-Isaiah extols Cyrus on his victorious course by proclaiming how he conquers peoples and tramples upon kings. "He pursued them and passed in *peace* even by the way that he had not gone with his feet" (Is. 41,3). Such a ruler is Yahweh: "He maketh peace in his high places" (Job 25,2). To return home in peace from the war means to return with victory (Josh. 10,21; Jer. 43,12). Nay, the Israelite may say that his war has "peace" (2 Sam. 11,7), if it succeeds and is victorious.

The man always has *shālōm* if he succeeds in his enterprise. When the Danites told the priest Micaiah to ask the oracle whether their way should be prosperous or not, the priest answered: Go in peace! [1] before Yahweh is your way, wherein ye go (Judg. 18,6). This means that their journey is going to succeed. When a man goes on a journey, whether away from home or homewards, the journey is to take place in peace. [2] This expression implies that everything is as it should be. The relation to those he leaves behind is harmonious; the journey is successful, and on his return he finds everything well and comfortable. When it is said that the Israelites are to return in peace after having carried on judicial proceedings for the under-judges appointed by Moses

(Exod. 18,23), then it means that the dispute is settled; the harmony is complete, and they return with their work well done.

We see how comprehensive and positive is the meaning of *shālōm;* it expresses every form of happiness and free expansion, but the kernel in it is the community with others, the foundation of life. Peace, strength and life belong together, because peace must be where the blessing is, the positive force of life. "Yahweh will give strength unto his people; Yahweh will bless his people with peace," it is said in the hymn (Ps. 29,11). "Life and peace" Yahweh has given to Levi, his caste of priests, according to the words of the prophet (Mal. 2,5); its peace is identical with its power to create blessing for the people. Therefore peace comprises all that the Israelite understands by "good". "Thou hast removed my soul out of *shālōm;* I forgot what is good", wails Jerusalem (Lam. 3,17, cf. Jer. 8,15; 14,19). When Yahweh intervenes, the world will be amazed at "all the goodness and all the *shālōm* that I procure unto Israel" (Jer. 33,9). Good is that which acts upon the soul in accordance with its nature and makes it expand, and so peace is the same as joy. "How beautiful upon the mountains are the feet of him that bringeth good tidings, proclaimeth *shālōm,* announceth good, publisheth salvation" (Is. 52,7); Israel receives the promise: In joy shall ye go out, in peace shall ye be led (Is. 55,12).

The relation of peace to evil is as light to darkness (Is. 45,7; Jer. 29,11). Evil is in its strongest form a breach, *shebher,* an infringement upon the whole, which is peace. Breaches are most frequently mentioned by the prophets, in particular by Jeremiah. His own soul is scarred with breaches (10,19), because his people is broken: For the virgin daughter of my people is broken with a great breach, with a very grievous blow (14,17, cf. 8,21; 30,12). For the land is devastated, far and wide; misery hangs over the people, the turmoil rages, an immense breach (4,6.20; 6,1; 30,15; 50,22). The word includes the annihilation of all peace. He who has no peace in his soul has a broken spirit; such a miserable person must be the care of Yahweh (Ps. 51,19; 147,3, cf. 69,21). [1]

He who has *shālōm* has everything, because it implies all the harmony and happiness which any one can take. Therefore peace is the first and last in life. If one wants to know something of a man, then one asks: Has he peace? He who has sent his sons with the herds sends a messenger to them in order to get tidings of their peace and that of the herds (Gen. 37,14). "Hast thou, thy husband and thy son peace?" Elisha tells his servant to ask the woman of Shunem. In the answer to this question all is implied. When Jacob asks the shepherds whether Laban has *shālōm,* then it means: Does he live in the close harmony of the family, in a friendly relation to his fellows, has he health and prosperity, is he successful in his undertakings, do the cattle thrive, etc.? If the Israelite can answer this brief question in the affirmative, then he has no more to wish for in life.

The preaching of the prophets is chiefly about peace, first and foremost about the peace not possessed by their people, because they themselves have forfeited it. Jeremiah and Ezekiel constantly speak of the prophets who preach *shālōm,* though there is no *shālōm* (Jer. 6,14; 8,11; 28,9; Ezek. 13,10.16), and Micah accuses them of proclaiming *shālōm,* as long as they are given something to eat (Mic. 3,5). From this it appears how great a part it has played in their sayings, and no wonder, for peace is the same as the very growth of life.

To have *shālōm* means to be unhurt and unchecked. When Jacob went travelling, he came "whole" *(shālēm)* unto Shechem (Gen. 33,18), no harm having come to him. If someone is in peril of his life, then he has "peace" in that he lives. Gideon was visited by Yahweh's *mal'ākh,* and he could not but fear that he should die, but then the words sounded in his ears: Peace be unto thee; fear not; thou shalt not die (Judg. 6,23). When David received a messenger from the battle with Absalom, his first question was: Has the young man Absalom peace? (2 Sam. 18, 29) meaning: Is he alive and unhurt? It was this peace which Absalom, according to Ahithophel, desired for the people, but not for his father, whose life he wanted to take (2 Sam. 17,3). [1]

The growth and well-being of the body is necessarily implied. "There is no *m^ethōm* in my flesh, no *shālōm* in my bones," cries the miserable one (Ps. 38,4). Both expressions mean wholeness, and that is normal development, growth and health. When the sick man is healed, he rejoices at having found peace. When Hezekiah had recovered from his illness, he praised Yahweh in song, saying: My bitterness was healed to peace. (Is. 38,17).[1]

Health entails a long life, and without that peace is not worth much. "A number of days without end" is claimed for the king (Ps. 21,5), and the whole of the Old Testament is pervaded by the idea that a long life is essential to happiness. According to the ten commandments this is the reward for honouring one's father and mother, and in the Proverbs it is said that if one shows obedience to them, length of days and long life and *shālōm* shall be added to one (Prov. 3,2).

The Israelites have embodied their conception of the ideal life in two kinds of descriptions, partly where they speak of the fathers in primeval times, when the people were created, partly in the expectations of the future, which the prophets picture. In both kinds of descriptions the immense length of life plays a prominent part. The fathers reached years which far exceeded ordinary measures, and the further back we get, the greater is the age. In Zechariah it is said of the future: There shall yet old men and old women dwell in the streets of Jerusalem, and every man with his staff in his hand for very age (Zech. 8,4); and still more powerfully the book of Isaiah describes the happiness of Jerusalem: There shall be no more thence an infant of days, nor an old man that hath not filled his days, for the child shall die an hundred years old, but he who misseth an hundred years[2] shall be reckoned accursed . . . for as the days of a tree are the days of my people . . . (Is. 65,20.22). Thus also Job after his rehabilitation lived a hundred and forty years (Job 42,16).

To die in the midst of one's days is always a misfortune, and long life a valuable possession. It is this spirit which, carried a little further, has created the proverb: For a living dog is better than a dead lion (Eccles. 9,4). No vigorous people entertain a desire for an early death. But the decisive thing is the weight which the Israelite attaches to long life, because life to him is corporeal life. Honour and valiant deeds cannot obtain a value counteracting it, because honour is bound up with the growth of the body.

Round such a human life in health and prosperous growth twines all other peace created by the blessing: fertility within the family, so that the name never dies out, and fertility in the field, where all vegetation flourishes. In the vine-tree there is "peace", in that it yields its fruit, while at the same time the earth yields its crops and the sky its dew (Zech. 8,12). On the pastures peace flourishes in all vegetation growing out of the earth (Jer. 25,37). When the man has peace in the proper sense of the word, then all his fields have peace, which means that they bring forth wheat in abundance (Ps. 147,14).

Thus peace spreads everywhere with him who is blessed. He himself is peace, his house is peace, everything that belongs to him is peace. When he examines his homestead, he only sees *shālōm;* nothing is wanting, and nothing fails (1 Sam. 25,6; Job 5,24). But the fountain of peace is the seat of the blessing, i. e. the soul. If one has no peace there, then all other peace must likewise perish. When David drew near his death, he felt how the peace of his soul was threatened by guilt, and he did all in order to remove it from himself, that he and "his seed and his house and his throne" might win peace everlasting from Yahweh (1 Kings 2,33). Peace is the blessing which it was essential to preserve whole and intact, so that it might expand without being infringed upon by evil.

In the preceding description of a life in peace we have already seen features pointing away from the old active and energetic conception of *shālōm*. Emphasis is laid, less on energy and victory than on quiet development. In this we see the forms of the new Israel, and the best illustration of the conception of peace of this type is a description in the Book of Job. It reads: He shall deliver thee in six troubles, yea, in seven shall no evil touch thee. In famine he shall redeem thee from death, and in war from the power of the sword. Thou shalt be hid from the scourge of the tongue, neither shalt thou be afraid of destruction when it cometh.

At destruction and famine thou shalt laugh; neither shalt thou be afraid of the beasts of the earth. For thou shalt be in covenant with the stones of the field, and the beasts of the field shall be at peace with thee. And thou shalt know that thy tent is peace, and thou shalt visit thy homestead and miss nothing. Thou shalt know also that thy seed shall be great, and thine offspring as the herbage of the earth. Thou shalt come to thy grave in thy vigour, as a shock of corn is carried up in its season (Job 5,19-26).

To this description, which has several parallels (e. g., Ezek. 34,25-30), there is a positive as well as a negative side. Peace is growth and expansion, fertility in husbandry and family, health and strength throughout life. But this also implies that everything evil must be kept away. Neither fight with the sword nor curses can hurt, and the hostile powers keep quiet. Emphasis is wholly laid on the untouched growth. In the negative sense, the fact of being untouched, lies the difference between this ideal and that of the old fighting Israel. This Israel wants to flourish without fighting. We have already seen how this difference stamps the conception of honour.

In the oldest Israel peace is maintained by being united with others to the furthest possible extent. In the family and the nearest circle peace follows as a matter of course. With strangers one seeks peace by uniting oneself with them in the covenant, and wherever this is not possible, one maintains peace by fighting and becoming victorious. The possibilities of life are unnumbered because there is no limit to the covenants. Israel, having come to rest, wants prosperity in security, and therefore the home world and the outside world are divided by a gulf. Enemies cannot be tolerated within the horizon, and therefore they must either be exterminated or struck down in such a manner that they are conquered once for all.

The change must have been effected rapidly and almost imperceptibly, men like Gideon, Jephthah, Saul and others being rather exceptions in the historical life of the Israelites. The timid ideal from the Book of Job must indicate the average conception of the small Israelitic towns. This negative ideal of being freed of every enemy necessarily means a lack of the old courage and energy. When the old order of communities was dissolved through the social revolutions, the lack of energy was still furthered, because the peace was broken and its instigating power lost. When the king took over the West-Asiatic claims to world empire, the timid Israelite adopted this claim; but he wished that it should be granted him as a gift, without efforts on his part. The reaction against the intermixture with the Canaanites unites with the new claims. Israel is not a people like other nations, but something apart, outside and above the nations. It can no more converse freely with them, making covenants, giving and receiving. A narrowing of Israel results, and new ideals are born, centring in the absolute rulership of Israel. The Israelitic peace now consists in Israel being the only nation acknowledged in Canaan and all other nations being its inferiors.

We may imagine that such ideals were limited to certain circles, but, nevertheless, they exercised great influence. We see them fully elaborated in the Deuteronomy, which claims the complete extermination of all the non-Israelitic peoples of Palestine: Thou shalt make no covenant with them, nor show mercy unto them (Deut. 7,2). In a special code of war the relation to other peoples is established in the following manner: When thou comest nigh unto a city to fight against it, then proclaim peace unto it. And it shall be, if it make thee answer of peace, and open unto thee, then all the people that is found therein shall be tributaries unto thee, and they shall serve thee. And if it will make no peace with thee, but will make war against thee, then thou shalt besiege it. And when Yahweh, thy God, hath delivered it into thine hands, thou shalt smite every male thereof with the edge of the sword. But the women, and the little ones, and the cattle, and all that is in the city, even all the spoil thereof, shalt thou take unto thyself, and thou shalt eat the spoil of thine enemies, which Yahweh thy God hath given thee. Thus shalt thou do unto all the cities which are very far off from thee, which do not belong to the cities of the peoples living here. But of the cities of these people, which Yahweh thy God doth give thee for an inheritance, thou shalt save alive nothing that breatheth; but thou shalt utterly destroy them... (Deut. 20, 10-17).

Nothing can be clearer than this law: All the Canaanites are to be exterminated; all other peoples, with whom Israel comes to war, are made slaves or cut down. In accordance with this David receives the promise that all his enemies are to be exterminated (2 Sam. 7,9). From this point of view the history of the immigration has been told. Not only the Priestly Code and the remarks related with those of the Deuteronomy, but the very narratives of the Book of Joshua take it for granted that all Canaanites ought to be exterminated. A characteristic narrative is that of the Gibeonites. They dress up as people coming from afar, and implore peace from Israel. Joshua and the chiefs let themselves be deceived and conclude the covenant with them, but after that make them slaves (Josh. 9). The whole of this narrative is an illustration of the claims of later Israel, as laid down in the Deuteronomy. Israel is to exterminate the Canaanites, but can make covenants with people from far-off countries. And so mighty was immigrated Israel that people came from afar to make covenants with it! One must not ask what people it might be which would think of wandering far away to Canaan in order to obtain a covenant with the crowds of nomadic Bedouins crossing Jordan. Our narrative deals with an ideal Israel, which exterminates all the neighbouring peoples and governs all others. [1]

We know it from the prophets' descriptions of the great peace which Israel some day is to obtain. It is most clearly expressed in one of the pictures of the future drawn in the latter part of the Book of Isaiah: And the sons of strangers shall build up thy walls, and their kings shall minister unto thee, for in my wrath I smote thee, but in my favour I have mercy on thee. Therefore thy gates shall be open continually; they shall not be shut day nor night, that men may bring unto thee the wealth of the Gentiles, whilst their kings are brought. For the nation and kingdom that will not serve thee, shall perish; yea, those nations shall be utterly wasted. The glory of Lebanon shall come unto thee, the cypress, the pine tree and the elm together, to beautify the place of my sanctuary; and I will make the place of my feet glorious. The sons also of them that afflicted thee shall come bending unto thee; and all they that despised thee shall bow themselves down at the soles of thy feet. They shall call thee city of Yahweh, the Zion of the Holy One of Israel. Whereas thou hast been forsaken and hated, so that no man went through thee, I will make thee an eternal excellency, a joy of many generations. Thou shalt suck the milk of the Gentiles, and shalt suck the breast of kings,[1] and thou shalt know that I am Yahweh, thy Saviour and thy Redeemer, the mighty One of Jacob. For brass I will bring gold, and for iron I will bring silver, and for wood brass, and for stones iron; I will make peace thy overseer and righteousness thine exactors. Violence shall no more be heard in thy land, wasting nor destruction within thy borders; but thou shalt call thy walls Salvation and thy gates Glory (Is. 60,10-18).

The peace here described consists in the fact that all strange peoples subject themselves entirely to Israel and yield all their treasures to it. They fawn before it (cf. Ps. 18,45). All peace is given to it; "like a flowing stream" their honour and wealth is led to it (Is. 66,12). This implies a claim to rule, nurtured by the ideals of the world-conqueror and extended beyond all bounds. In so far the claims go much further than those of the Book of Job. But behind it lies a community with the ideals of Job, viz. in the claim of security. In this we have a characteristic feature of the Israelitic conception of peace.

Security has always been an essential element of peace, but in the olden times it means mutual security among those who live in peace. Security consists in being able to trust one another, to abandon oneself to mutual confidence. The oldest fighting Israel only demands this feeling of security from those with whom it is in peace. Enemies are enemies, and one must take the dangers of life and fight against them. Later on the Israelite shudderingly looks towards the desert land with the uncertain Bedouin existence which he himself led at one time. The land of peace Jeremiah calls the safe land, as contrasted with the jungle of Jordan (Jer. 12,5). The Bedouin tribe Cain, which must roam about in uncertainty, is a cursed one. Esau, who led the uncertain life far from the fatness of the earth, all the time fighting for a foothold with the sword, derived the strength to do so from the blessing of his ancestor, but the Israelite comes very near to calling it a curse. And the same holds good of the Arabian, Ishmael, whose hand is against every man, and every man's hand against him (Gen. 16,12). Fight is the same as horror, something contrary to nature. "We have heard a voice of trembling, horror and no peace", says Jeremiah (30,5, cf. Ezek. 7,25). It recurs over and over again in the Book of Job. "Their houses are at peace and safe from fear" (21,9). "The wicked man travaileth with pain all his days, and the number of years that are laid up for the oppressor. Terrors sound in his ears; in peace the spoiler may assail him" (15,20-21).

One demands security from enemies, and if one must fight, one fights only to get rid of them. We are constantly confronted with this view. "Ye shall do my statutes and keep my commandments and do them, that ye may dwell in the land in security" (Lev. 25, 18-19). Security and satiety with fertility is the ideal. In the Deuteronomy it is put before everything else. "Ye shall go over Jordan, and dwell in the land which Yahweh your God giveth you to inherit, and he shall give you rest from all your enemies round about, so that ye dwell in security" (Deut. 12,10). When Israel looks back upon its history, then it praises its god who "delivered you out of the hand of your enemies on every side, and ye dwelled in security" (1 Sam. 12,11). To the compiler of the Book of Judges there is something abnormal in the old narratives of unrest and fights, these being the results of the transgressions of the people. The normal state is security: "The country had peace for forty years;" and we can see how this ideal spreads. In the blessing of Jacob Benjamin is praised as the greedy wolf which daily obtains prey (Gen. 49,27); in the blessing of Moses [1] the same tribe is the special favourite of Yahweh, because it lives in security, sheltered behind its mountains (Deut. 33,12, cf. v. 27-28).

The prophets' descriptions of happiness bear throughout the impress of this ideal. "And the work of righteousness shall be peace, and the effect of righteousness quietness and security forever. And my people shall dwell in habitations of peace, and in dwellings of security, in rest of happiness" (Is. 32,17-18). And one of the later prophets proclaims that when peace comes, no terror shall come near Israel, all assailers are to fall, "no weapon that is formed against thee shall prosper, and every tongue that shall rise against thee in judgment, thou shalt paralyze" (Is. 54,17).

The Israelite cannot accomplish this himself, but receives it from his strong God. In his care he is safe against enemies. "I will lay me down in peace and sleep, for thou, Yahweh, makest me dwell (even) alone in security." Thus says the man full of confidence, who knows that he has a strong helper (Ps. 4,9). He walks in safety as the herd following the shepherd, secure beside the strong. There is something idyllic about the picture, until suddenly we are told: Thou preparest a table before me in the presence of mine enemies (Ps. 23,5). The enemy is gnashing his teeth in impotent rage, but he is not able to do anything; then the Israelite enjoys his safety to the full.

Peace as safety does not only consist in friends trusting each other, but in the certainty that the enemy is impotent so that he cannot move. Therefore peace is identical with domination. This, by a curious transition, develops into the demand for the *abolition of war*. What this means appears from a description of the ideal king, reading: Rejoice greatly, O daughter of Zion; shout, O daughter of Jerusalem; behold, thy king cometh unto thee; he is just and victorious, lowly and riding upon an ass, and upon a colt, the foal of an ass. I will cut off the chariot from Ephraim, and the horse from Jerusalem, and the battle bow shall be cut off, and he shall speak peace unto the nations, and his dominion shall be from sea even to the sea, and from the river even to the ends of the earth [1] (Zech. 9, 9-10).

The Israelites need no weapons, because their king is the ruler of the whole world. The prophet says further: It shall yet come to pass that there shall come people, and the inhabitants of many cities. And the inhabitants of one city shall go to another, saying: Let us go speedily to conciliate Yahweh, and seek the Yahweh of hosts; I will go also. Yea, many people and strong nations shall seek the Yahweh of hosts in Jerusalem and conciliate him. Thus saith the Yahweh of hosts: In those days it shall come to pass that ten men shall take hold out of all the languages of the nations, even shall take hold of the skirt of a Judaic man, saying: We will go with you, for we have heard that God is with you (Zech. 8,20-23).

That which happens in this ideal age is that the mighty God of Israel inverts everything. At the present time the Israelites are oppressed, ruled by others, but one day they will get full power and *shālōm.* All thought of fighting against them drops quite naturally, other peoples only think of pacifying the mighty God of Israel, and with humble prayers they tug at the mantles of the Israelites, in order to be permitted to go with them and have a share in their peace.

We find the same ideal in Isaiah's descriptions of peace: The people that walk in darkness see a great light; they that dwell in the land of gloom, upon them shines the light. Thou multipliest the exultation [1] and increasest the joy; they joy before thee according to the joy in harvest, and as men rejoice, when they divide the spoil. For thou hast broken the yoke of his burden, and the staff of his shoulder, the rod of his oppressor as in the days of Midian. For every boot of war trampling in noise, every garment soiled with blood is burned as a spoil of the flames. For unto us a child is born, unto us a son is given, and the government shall be upon his shoulder, and his name shall be called Wonderful-Counsellor, The Mighty God, The Acquirer of Spoil, The Prince of Peace, for the increase of his government, for peace everlasting over the throne of David, and over his kingdom, to strengthen and to establish it in justice and righteousness from henceforth even for ever. The zeal of the Yahweh of hosts will perform this (Is. 9,1-6).

Between the various descriptions there are slight shades of difference, but in general we are confronted with the two ideas: War is abolished, and the world-rule passes to Israel. The world peace means that *Israel* has peace, because it is so mighty that all peoples voluntarily submit to it — and if they do not, they themselves will be the losers. Therefore there is in reality no difference between the above-mentioned description of the ideal king and the one in which, after having re-established full harmony within Israel, he shall strike at its enemies and plunder them, whereas other peoples in great crowds are coming to seek his protection (Is. 11,10-14).

From Israel peace spreads and encompasses the whole earth. All war between the peoples ceases, and about this we read in the Book of Isaiah: And it shall come to pass in the end of the days that the mountain of Yahweh's house shall be established in the top of the mountains, and shall be exalted above the hills. And all nations shall flow unto it, and many people shall go and say: Come ye and let us go up to the mountain of Yahweh, to the house of the God of Jacob that he may teach us his ways. And we will walk in his paths, for out of Zion goes instruction, and the word of Yahweh from Jerusalem. And he shall judge among the nations and do justice to everyone, and they shall beat their swords into ploughshares, and their spears into pruninghooks; nation shall not lift up sword against nation, neither shall they learn war any more (Is. 2,2-4). With Micah we find the same prophecy with the following continuation: But they shall sit every man under his vine and under his fig tree, and none shall make them afraid; for the mouth of the Yahweh of hosts hath spoken it. Let all the people walk every one in the name of his god, but we will walk in the name of Yahweh our God for ever and ever (Mic. 4,4-5).

The abolition of war concerns the whole world, but its starting point is Jerusalem, because power and wealth are concentrated in this place. The peoples must acknowledge the God of Israel as the mightiest; therefore they must look to him for instruction, and he decides everything for them. But when they have one ruler, who decides all points of issue, then nothing is left to fight for, and everyone can sit down peaceably under his vine. This prophecy distinguishes itself from the others by mentioning the mutual relation of the strange peoples. But also here peace is determined by the complete rule of Israel and its God. [1]

War is always evil, because it prevents the undisturbed enjoyment of fruition and prosperity. Zechariah says: For before these days there was no hire for man, nor any hire for beast, neither was there any peace for him that went out or came in, because of the affliction; for I set [2] all men everyone against his neighbour. But now I will not be unto the residue of this people as in the former days, saith the Yahweh of the hosts (Zech. 8, 10-11). The prophet here speaks of a time when Israel had no peace within itself, and so no fertility. But now there is to be inner harmony, no enemies, but fertility beyond all bounds.

War is, however, only one of the troubles which may prevent the Israelite from enjoying undisturbed prosperity. In the description from the Book of Job already quoted, Eliphaz says: Thou shalt not be afraid of the *beasts* of the earth, for thou shalt be in covenant with the stones of the field, and the beasts of the field shall be at peace with thee (Job 5,22-23). What is implied by this saying is not immediately apparent. If the covenant with the beasts means an intimacy, a reception of them into the world of man, then it is merely the natural form of life as we know it among the people who live with and in nature: the wild beasts make part of the whole and have their rights, but man must make himself familiar with them and receive them into his world.

Unfortunately we know very little of the views of the oldest Israel concerning animals which are not domestic animals, but in any case we know that later Israel did not acknowledge other animals than those which were useful to them. And the probability is that the covenant mentioned by Eliphaz is not different from the one mentioned by Hosea; its contents are purely negative, inasmuch as it consists in the animals keeping away (Hos. 2,20). The covenant with the beasts of the field is based upon an idea appearing in two variations: either the beasts of the fields are to be exterminated or they are to be entirely transformed.

In a description of happiness given by Ezekiel, we read: And I will make with them a covenant of peace, and will cause the evil beasts to cease out of the land; and they shall dwell safely in the wilderness and sleep in the woods ... And they shall no more be a prey to the nations, neither shall the beasts of the land devour them; but they shall dwell safely, and none shall make them afraid (Ezek. 34,25.28). Here the beasts of prey are to be exterminated.

There is a difference between this and the famous description of happiness in Isaiah: The wolf shall dwell with the lamb, and the leopard shall lie down with the kid, and the calf and the young lion and the fatling together, and a little child shall lead them. And the bear shall graze with the cow, their young ones shall lie down together; and the lion shall eat straw like the ox. And the suckling child shall play on the hole of the asp, and the weaned child shall stretch his hand towards the cockatrice's eye. [1] Nobody shall hurt nor destroy in all my holy mountain (Is. 11, 6-9). We hear the echo of these words from a later prophet: The wolf and the lamb shall graze together, and the lion shall eat straw like the bullock, and dust shall be the serpent's meat. Nobody shall hurt nor destroy in all my holy mountain, saith Yahweh (Is. 65,25).

The key to the understanding of these sayings is in those last words. It is not a poetic glorification of nature, but a real claim on the part of Israel. Beasts of prey must either, as with Ezekiel, be exterminated so that man can sleep safely anywhere, or they must be utterly revolutionized and become like tame animals. Lion and bear are to eat hay and grass, but not the cows and lambs of the Israelites, much less the Israelites themselves.

It is perfectly obvious what is the kernel of these descriptions. The security of Israel, its prosperity and undisturbed joy at its growth and fertility is the centre of life. Round this centre everything else must be arranged. Beasts of prey must disappear or be transformed, and strange people must fare likewise: either they must be exterminated or they must subordinate themselves to Israel and increase its happiness.

The fear of fighting causes *rest* to become the ideal. In every people rest must of course be an indispensable link in the economy of life. But there is a decisive difference between the two conceptions as to whether rest is considered a necessary means towards a higher aim, i. e. to gain strength for the effort, or whether it must in itself be considered the supreme state. And it cannot be denied that the mental development of Israel carried it far in the latter direction.

This appears in the words of the Yahwist when he tells of primeval man, to whom work in the soil is assigned as a curse: Cursed is the ground for thy sake; in sorrow shalt thou eat of it all the days of thy life (Gen. 3,17). He would prefer to see everything shooting up without any effort on his part. It is well worth noticing what associations are connected with the various expressions for work. Except in the case of actual production *(maʿ*^{a}*śe)* or produce *(m*^{e}*lāʾkhā),* there is a connotation of trouble, unhappiness, misery *(ʿml, ygʿ, ʿny)* or slavery *(ʿbd)*. The work, the strenuous effort is not the pleasure, but the misery of life. Rest is the same as happiness (Ruth 1,9).

For the people rest meant unchallenged possession of the country, without the trouble of maintaining it. The Deuteronomy dates the happiness of the people from the time when rest began to prevail in the country. "For ye have not as yet come to the rest and the possession, which Yahweh your God giveth you," says Moses (Deut. 12,9, cf. 1 Kings 8,56) — the rest which the old generation from the time of the wanderings in the desert could not obtain, because of the stubbornness of their hearts (Ps. 95,11). The picture of happiness, of peace, we have in the herd peacefully gathering under the care of the shepherd beside the "waters of rest" (Ps. 23,2). This picture reminds us involuntarily of its opposite, a description given by one of the prophets: But the wicked are like the troubled sea, when it cannot rest, whose waters cast up mire and dirt; there is no *shālōm,* saith my God, to the wicked (Is. 57,20).

The ideal life of the Israelite becomes that of the weak under the complete protection of the strong. In calm and security he lives with his happiness; when he works, his God puts so much therein, that he obtains much greater results than his efforts would normally produce. He buys grain and milk and wine "without money" (Is. 55,1). His crops are so abundant that his "threshing shall reach unto the vintage, and the vintage shall reach unto the sowing time;" if he lies down to rest, he is not to be frightened; evil beasts disappear, and if the enemy comes, then five shall be able to chase a hundred, and a hundred ten thousands (Lev. 26). Life passes smoothly, in complete security, because it is given to him by his God.

When a man has experienced some of all this happiness throughout a long life, then he becomes "full of days" (Gen. 15,15; 25,8; 35,29; Job 42,17); and when he dies "in a ripe old age"

(Gen. 15,15; 25,8; Judg. 8,32; 1 Chron. 29,28), after having fulfilled the "number of his days" (Exod. 23,26), then the harmony is complete. But his death must be what also we call a natural death. It is to come on gently, without violence, for it is a misfortune to die by the sword (Jer. 34,5); quick, violent death strikes down the man who commits outrage (1 Kings 2,6, and, conversely, 2 Kings 22,20; 2 Chron. 34,28) or those who, like Eli, have called down the curse upon themselves. The growth of man must be like the growth of the plant. If it dies after having completed its growth, death holds no terror; it is as the ripe fruit dropping off the tree or — as said by Eliphaz (Job 5,26) — as a shock of corn carried up in its season. He who dies a death of this kind dies in *peace.* He passes in security and harmony from this life into the great community of the fathers and rejoins the kinsmen who have gone before him. With them he rests in peace on his new bed (Gen. 15,15; Is. 57,2), while his name still lives on in his sons.

There is no better illustration of this ideal of life than the already suggested image of the plant or the tree, which also constantly occurs to the mind of the Israelite. The man who fails is like the barren tree of the desert, on the salt stony steppe, but the true Israelite is "as a tree planted by the waters, that spreadeth its roots into the river, and shall not see when heat cometh, but its leaf shall be green, and it shall not wither in the year of drought, neither shall it cease from yielding fruit" (Jer. 17,8). "The righteous flourisheth like the palm-tree, he groweth like a cedar in Lebanon. Those that be planted in the house of Yahweh flourish in the courts of our God. They bring forth fruit in old age; they are green and full of sap" (Ps. 92,13-15). [1]

There is in this ideal a joy in the life on earth which always characterizes the Israelite; but in the old type of society it is always coloured by the strong feeling of community in family life and the great claims of honour on him whom life has given much, and this lifts the joy of life far above the transient enjoyment of the moment and stamps it with the nobility of ideality. But all this joy at the unfolding of life implies a weakness, which appears very clearly in the descriptions of happiness given by the prophets.

Where fighting and strenuous effort is the supreme happiness of life, man himself holds happiness in his hand. He who demands to grow in complete security without fighting makes claims which the powers of life can rarely satisfy. Where this ideal is put forth in its full extent, it can only be realized through a complete revolution of life. An ideal of this kind easily leads to pessimism, or it must simply persist as a claim on the future.

When we compare the oldest conception of *shālōm* with the one which came to prevail later on, we see clearly that a great change has taken place in a negative direction: peace having become the opposite of fighting and strenuous effort. The development takes place imperceptibly, but its extremes are sharply distinguished.

There is in the ideal of later Israel not only a curious lack of realism, of acknowledgment of life as it is, but also a distinct limitation. In the welter of countless souls it is only man who has the right to live according to his nature; animals which do not subordinate themselves to man are to be exterminated. And within the human world it is the Israelites who have all the claims on life. Peace does not spread all over the world according to the old conception of the nature of peace, i. e. that bars fall away and the covenant makes brothers, who all give and take. Peace is established according to the ideal of the world-ruler, placing a lordly people in the centre and subordinating all the rest.

This difference in the conception of peace corresponds closely with the alteration in the conception of honour, when its immediate character changed, and the old upholder of the community was transformed into the despotic ruler. The ruler who, regardless of consequences, maintains himself against his people is of the same type as the people of rulers who only maintain themselves against other peoples. And in both cases it is, as far as Israel is concerned, a question of the claims of the weak. That it is Canaanization and the ideals of monarchy which have been at work here, of that there can be no doubt.

---

shālōm is the most comprehensive denomination of happiness, as it designates the healthy development in all forms, both of the harmony within the covenant and of all progress in life. But it is not the only one. Another related idea should also be considered, because it emphasizes other elements, viz. that which is expressed by *tᵉshūʿā, yᵉshūʿā* or *yēshaʿ*.[1] When the Jews of the Hellenistic period were to translate this word into Greek, they used a word which played a very great part at that time, i. e. *soteria,* one of the words which later on came to designate a fundamental idea in the New Testament. The word *salvation* has throughout become charged with the contents of the *soteria* of the New Testament, and when it is used to render the above-mentioned Hebrew words it is apt to cause ideas from the domain of the New Testament to be transferred into these Old-Israelitic terms. Salvation instinctively suggests the idea of something beyond, a deliverance from the misery of this world into another world. When we use the word with relation to the Old Testament, we must know that the meaning is a different one, life and happiness here always being bound up with this earth.

The Hebrew word is derived from the root *yshʿ,* which means "to be wide, spacious". What is implied by this we already know. The soul is wide when it develops without checking forces; salvation, like *shālōm,* is the development of the soul.

In the olden times it means victory in battle. Great salvation Samson obtained on the day when he killed a thousand Philistines with the jaw-bone of an ass (Judg. 15,18). When Jonathan made his bold attack on the Philistines and created the mighty victory, but was threatened by death because of his transgressions, the people said: Shall Jonathan die, who hath wrought this great salvation in Israel? God forbid! As Yahweh liveth there shall not one hair of his head fall to the ground, for he hath wrought with God this day (1 Sam. 14,45).

Salvation is not something negative. It consists in having the strength and acting with it, so that it makes itself felt. David gained salvation when he rendered all the neighbouring peoples subservient to him; he subdued the Philistines, Moabites, Ammonites, Edomites and Aramæans, "and Yahweh saved David whithersoever he went" (2 Sam. 8,14).

The chief must be a saviour; he must have the strength to obtain victory for his people. Such saviours were the judges who conquered the enemies attacking the Israelites (Judg. 2,18; 3,9.15; 6,14; 8,22). When Saul had become a king, there were people who asked in derision: How shall this man save us? (1 Sam. 10,27). If the chief does not have the blessing to uphold the others with his strength, he is no chief.

Salvation, however, as a rule contains a certain negative element: to liberate from danger or misfortune. The word is often used with terms expressing: to deliver, to rescue *(pillēṭ, hiṣṣīl, ḥālaṣ)*, because he who needs salvation generally has been threatened or oppressed. One is saved out of the hand of the enemy, because the enemy has been superior in power or threatened to be so (Judg. 6,14; 12,2; 1 Sam. 4,3; 7,8; 9,16 *et al.)*. But this is not the main point. The positive: to acquire victory, is the all-important thing. Samson was not oppressed when he gained salvation, neither was David.

To save another means to communicate to him of one's strength, and thus to give him the power to maintain himself. With pride Job asks one of his friends: How hast thou helped him that is without power? How savest thou the arm that hath no strength? (26,2). And he continues: How hast thou counselled him that hath no wisdom, and plentifully declared sound knowledge? This was what Job himself had done manifold times, when his word upheld him that was falling, and strengthened the weak knees (4,4). To save consists in letting one's blessing act in another and thus to give him *shālōm*. And it can be done by counsel, by encouragement, by a direct transference of strength, or by intervening for the benefit of one's neighbour.

When the king is saluted with the cry: Save, O king! (2 Sam. 14,4; 2 Kings 6,26),[1] then it means that he is to give of his strength. It is said in the special cases where one desires his help, but as a general exclamation it means an acknowledgment of the fact that he is to create happiness. He derives this strength from Yahweh, whom one consequently addresses with the cry: Yahweh, save the king! (Ps. 20,10), i. e. give him strength.

The difference between peace and salvation is that peace is rather the lasting state of harmony and happiness, salvation the momentary acquisition thereof. We have seen that Israel, as the years went by, laid greater and greater stress upon peace as something which man cannot take on his own accord, and this, in the very nature of things, must to a still higher degree characterize salvation. Only Yahweh is so strong that his own arm obtains salvation for himself (Ps. 98,1; Job 40,14). The Israelites get all their salvation from him; he does not suffer Israel to say: Mine own hand hath saved me (Judg. 7,2).

This difference also implies that salvation more particularly denotes victory over one's enemies; but in reality it comprises all acquisition of happiness. Eliphaz describes the benefits conferred by Yahweh on the good in the following manner: He giveth rain upon the earth and sendeth water upon the fields, to set up on high those that be low; that those which mourn may be exalted in salvation (Job 5,10-11).[1] On the other hand he says about the wicked: His children are far from salvation, and they are crushed in the gate, without anyone saving them (5,4). Like victory in the court of justice, rain and fertility are included in salvation.

The opposite of salvation is trouble, *ṣārā,* the state of narrowness. The sick man obtains salvation when he is cured. "Save my soul!" cries the miserable man from his sick-bed when his bones are wasted away (Ps. 6; 38). A sinner who acknowledges that he himself has caused Yahweh to break his bones, i. e. to strike him with illness, asks for permission once more to rejoice at his lord's salvation (Ps. 51,14). The girl who is subjected to violence (Deut. 22,27), the man who is persecuted by enemies (Ps. 7,2; 40,14-15; 59,3 *et al.*), he who never succeeds in anything he undertakes, who is oppressed and plundered (Deut. 28,29.31), who suffers misery and hunger (Ps. 34,7) — all desire salvation, the attainment of the happy state when they are delivered from evil.

Salvation, which in its root simply means victory and prosperity, is in its subsequent development entirely penetrated by the ideal of peace which gradually developed in Israel: unchecked prosperity, happiness in security under the protection of the strong God, the abolition of all dangers. This salvation is vividly described in one of the Psalms:

"Happy[1] he that dwelleth in the secret place of the most high, that abideth under the shadow of Shaddai, that saith to Yahweh: My refuge, my fortress, my God, in whom I trust! Surely he delivereth thee from the snare of the fowler, and from the noisome pestilence. He covereth thee with his feathers, and under his wings thou findest shelter. His truth is thy shield and buckler.[2] Thou shalt not be afraid for the terror by night, nor for the arrow that flieth by day, nor for the pestilence that flieth in darkness, nor for the plague that rageth at noonday. A thousand fall at thy side, and ten thousand at thy right hand; but it will not come nigh thee. Only with thine eye thou beholdest and seest the reward of the wicked. Surely, thou hast Yahweh as thy[3] refuge; the Highest hast thou made thy habitation. There shall no evil befall thee, neither shall any plague come nigh thy dwelling. For he giveth his angels charge over thee, to keep thee in all thy ways. They bear thee up in their hands, lest thou dash thy foot against a stone. Thou treadest upon the lion and adder; the young lions and the dragons thou tramplest under feet." — "Because he hath set his love upon me, therefore will I have him. I strengthen him because he knoweth my name. He calleth upon me, and I will answer him; I deliver him in trouble and honour him. With long life I satisfy him, I let him experience my salvation" (Ps. 91).

Salvation is the word embodying the whole contents of the hymn. It consists in the weak human soul having strength conferred upon it by its God when utterly submitting itself to him. It is developed, "gets space", in that everything evil which might check it is kept away from it. The plague rages around him, striking down all others, but not him. All who might check him are bound with solid chains; the wild beasts are so changed that he who is saved can trample on them as he likes, for they cannot hurt him. This salvation is identical with the peace which the prophets promised their people.

This demand, that everything evil and everything which checks is to be removed, is carried somewhat further in the thought of the *confusion of death.* In one of the great descriptions of salvation in the Book of Isaiah, it is said that the people are to gather on Zion for an abundant meal, and the veil that covered their faces shall vanish. Then death shall be annihilated and the tears of Israel wiped off their faces, but the enemy Moab shall be broken and trodden down into the dunghill (Is. 25,6-12).

The position of the peoples is not quite clear in this place, but the most obvious interpretation is that they are to acknowledge the greatness of Israel and its God,[1] and by submitting to them get a share of their happiness, whereas those stubbornly inimical, like Moab, are to be struck down entirely. All kings who will not bend before them are already rendered harmless (24,21-23). It is clear that Israel is the centre. It is the Israelites whose tears are to be wiped off, and they shall be able to continue undisturbed their life on earth, because death can hurt them no more.

In this ideal of salvation the Israelites have gone far from the old conception of peace. In the old communities, where the cohesion of kindred is still a living factor, an artificial annihilation of death is not required in order to preserve life. Generations supersede each other, but they do not die, because it is the same life which constantly springs up in posterity. Behind the new ideals lies the dissolution of the old order of things produced by the composite and artificial life of the cities.

But salvation is never like the Hellenistic *soteria,* a deliverance from corporeal life. This would be contrary to the fundamental psychological conception, nowhere abandoned in the Old Testament. One is saved *for* the world, not *from* the world. A special immortality of the soul is consequently out of the question.

It is said in Psalm 16,9-11, after the singer has praised Yahweh for all the happiness he has granted him: "Therefore my heart is glad, and my glory rejoiceth; nay, my flesh resteth in security. For thou wilt not leave my soul to Sheol; thou wilt not abandon thy devoted to see the grave. Thou lettest me know the path of life, the fullness of joy in thy presence, pleasures everlasting at thy right hand." The happiness of the soul is identical with that of the body, and it consists in security, prosperity and happiness. Life on earth is to be lived in untouched security, without being threatened by all the evil that rises into the world of man from the grave.[1]

It is the same thought which in another of the Psalms is expressed in the following manner: Surely, God redeemeth my soul from Sheol, for that he taketh care of me (Ps. 49,16). Or: My flesh and my heart faileth, but God is the strength of my heart and my portion for ever (Ps. 73,26). The pious goes through the world without being threatened by its numerous dangers. What does it matter that he himself is weak, when he has a God who forever will give him strength and guard him? But as distinguished from Isaiah 25,6 these psalms do not mention the abolition of natural death in the fullness of time, when satiation is complete.

When the thought of the abolition of death grew upon Israel, it meant, as already mentioned, the continuation of earthly life, without infringement or interruption. The thought was carried further and supplemented by the idea that also some of those departed should have their share in the great salvation; this then would necessarily take the shape that their bodies should be resurrected. It appears in connection with the abolition of death in the above-mentioned saying, which reads: Thy dead men shall live, my dead bodies[2] shall arise. Awake and sing, ye that dwell in dust; for the dew of light is thy dew, and the earth casteth out the dead souls (Is. 26,19). It is the departed Israelites who return to an earthly life.

With these thoughts, which we find once more in the Book of Daniel (12,1), we have, however, wandered far from old Israel and well into Judaism. But in this place it is of interest to demonstrate their connection with ideas, the roots of which strike far down into the older Israel, even though also other factors have been at work than the ones here indicated.

RIGHTEOUSNESS AND TRUTH.

As frequently mentioned, peace has its presupposition in the character of the soul. In order to be able to develop in full harmony the soul must be healthy; this healthiness the Israelite calls righteousness. Righteousness does not imply neutral, unconditioned justice on all hands; the ethics of the Israelite acknowledge neither neutral nor unconditioned acts. Justice is the mental quality on the strength of which peace is maintained; therefore it is at the same time the kernel of peace and blessing.

Righteousness is the presupposition of the right action. In order to realize wherein it consists, we must go back to the fundamental psychological conception. The action is created by the whole of the soul; the more the whole of the soul is implied, the more it acts in accordance with its nature, i. e. healthily and rightly. The integrity of the soul is therefore an expression of its righteousness. This integrity can be expressed in different ways. David desires for his son a whole *(shālēm)* heart to keep the commandments of Yahweh (1 Chron. 29,19). Here and in a single other place (2 Chron. 25,2) a word is used of the same root as the one denoting the full development of the soul. But where it is a question of the integrity as an inner presupposition, or, in other words, the health of the soul, the root *tmm* is used.

"Innocence" is a fairly accurate translation of this word, when by that it is understood that no secondary wills have their seat in the soul so as to counteract the main will in which its contents centre. "In the innocency of my heart and purity of my hands have I done this," says Abimelech (Gen. 20,5); in "innocency of heart" David lived before Yahweh (1 Kings 9,4). The psalmists constantly maintain that this is what they themselves do (Ps. 7,9; 26,1.11; 101,2).

With this "innocence" or integrity the righteous wanders. [1] He acts in integrity, and his acts are integrity, i. e. entirety; this is expressed by his way being whole (Prov. 13,6; Job 4,6). When he acts in this manner, then he is himself whole, *tāmīm* or *tām*; [2] thus he is characterized as healthy and normal. When Jacob is described as a man who is *tām* and lives in tents (Gen. 25,27), then it means that he is an orderly man, who lives the life of normal people, as distinguished from Esau, who roams about the steppe and makes himself the enemy of everybody.

A *pure* heart *(nāḳī, ṭāhōr, zakh)* is the same as a whole heart, for it implies a soul the integrity of which is not broken by foreign wills or contaminating elements. The opposite is a divided heart (Ps. 12,3).

Other expressions designate the righteous soul as firm or straight, thus also qualifying it as normal. In order to be able to act in its entirety, the soul must have a firm construction. It must have a safe centre, round which its contents arrange themselves, while at the same time it possesses the pliability, which is the presupposition of its being able to live and act in connection with others.

"Firm" is called *kēn* and *nākhōn*. It implies righteousness, both in the man who is as he ought to be and in his acts or "ways". To make the heart firm *(hēkhīn)* is the presupposition of the act, viz. the good, normal act, and therefore it is an expression of the health and righteousness of the soul. [3] In the Psalms disgust is expressed for those who do not make their hearts firm (Ps. 78,8); it was that which the friends of Job encouraged him to do (Job 11,13).

When the soul is whole and firm, it is likewise straight, *yāshār* or *nākhōaḥ*, expressions which we also find in our own and various other languages, denoting that it does not use indirect means, but acts in entire agreement with the laws of its nature. And, like the other appellations, this is used of the soul itself, as well as of its actions. [4]

From all this it appears how realistic is the Israelitic view of life. To act rightly is not to act according to rules which are forced upon the man from without. The good man acts rightly, because he acts entirely in accordance with the nature of his soul. But the soul exists only as a link in a covenant; it maintains its nature by maintaining the covenant.

All of these factors we find concentrated in the words righteousness, justice (*ṣedheḳ, ṣᵉdhāḳā*) and truth (*ʾᵉmeth, ʾᵉmūnā*). They always denote the healthy and normal, that which is in entire accord with its being, i. e. that which is "whole". "Noah was a just man and whole in his generations" (Gen. 6,9; 7,1); he was the perfect Israelite, described as "wandering in integrity and working righteousness and speaking truth with his heart" (Ps. 15,2, cf. 1 Kings 3,6). A just and true god (Zech. 8,8) is a god who throughout agrees with the being of a god, in the same manner as just balances are scales which weigh justly and have whole and intact weights (Lev. 19,36; Deut. 25,15; Ezek. 45,10; Job 31,6), and just sacrifices are sacrifices such as they should be (Deut. 33,19; Ps. 4,6; 51,21), whereas just and true ways are right ways leading to the goal (Gen. 24,48; Ps. 23,3).

Israelitic psychology does not distinguish between ability and will. The healthy soul is that which is able to act according to its nature; therefore firmness and strength are implied in justice and truth. We often see *strength* figuring prominently where it is a question of justice, in particular when it is Yahweh who acts. He thus says: Righteousness is gone out of my mouth, a word that returneth not (Is. 45,23), or: I strengthen thee, yea, I help thee; yea, I uphold thee with the right hand of my righteousness (Is. 41,10). Thus Yahweh may say, because with him there is "righteousnesses" and strength (Is. 45,24). The Israelite never tires of laying stress upon the righteousness of his god, and this always implies that he has infinite strength. Some verses of a psalm may be mentioned as one example among many: I set forth the powerful works of Yahweh; I make mention of thy righteousness, even of thine only. O God, thou hast taught me from my youth, and hitherto have I declared thy wondrous works. Even when I am old and greyheaded, O God, forsake me not, that I may proclaim thy strength, unto every generation that is to come[1] thy power. Thy righteousness, O God, is very high, thou hast done great things; O God, who is like unto thee? (Ps. 71,16-19).

It is the ability to maintain oneself which is implied by righteousness, to have a soul constructed in such a manner that it could maintain itself through all actions. In that consists the strength of the soul, but also its *truth.* Truth is that which can be maintained by the soul, that which has the strength to exist and act in the entirety of the soul. A statement which one makes is true if it can be maintained in all its consequences, a promise is true if it persists and is manifested in action. The judgment always falls back upon the soul. It is the soul which produces truth, and it depends on its quality whether that which it produces is true, i. e. something which exists because it is the expression of the working of a healthy and strong soul.

A true soul can only speak the truth, and the soul is true when throughout constructed as a normal soul — normal, not in the sense of average, but in the same manner as a building without faults of construction may be called normal.

It is a soul of this kind which the Hebrew calls *ne'ᵉmān,* true: reliable and strong at the same time, because it has the ability to hold and maintain its essence, and this denomination naturally also applies to the actions and the words which are created by the soul.

The prophets are true when they speak that which is really in their souls, and when the soul is strong. The former is of course essential. "How many times shall I adjure thee that thou tell me nothing but that which is true in the name of Yahweh!" says King Ahab to Micaiah, who at first deludes him with happy prophecies (1 Kings 22,16). When Elijah has raised from the dead the son of the widow of Zarephath, she says to him: Now by this I know that thou art a man of God, and that the word of Yahweh in thy mouth is truth (1 Kings 17,24). His raising of the dead boy points towards a psychic strength which must produce truth. A prophet must be true *(ne'ᵉmān)* in order to be a prophet, to have the necessary strength of soul, that his words shall not fail to take effect. Such a man was Samuel (1 Sam. 3,19). A "true house", like the one which Yahweh gives his friends, is a family which maintains itself throughout the generations and never dies out (1 Sam. 2,35; 25,28; 2 Sam. 7,16; 1 Kings 11,38).

A "true and faithful witness" (Jer. 42,5) is a man who steadfastly clings to that which is in his soul. When it is said that Yahweh swore unto David "truth from which he will not turn" (Ps. 132,11, cf. 2 Sam. 7,28), then this denotes words which he maintains, for, as it is said: "Yahweh God of hosts, who is like unto thee? Yahweh is strong, and thy truth is round about thee" (Ps. 89,9). It is said of Moses, when he stood with uplifted arms during the battle against Amalek, that his hands were "truth" until the going down of the sun (Exod. 17,12). It means that they had the firmness and strength to be kept in the uplifted position. Rahab demanded from the Israelitic spies a "true sign" that they would spare her (Josh. 2,12); by that is meant a real sign, viz. one which has the power and strength to express and maintain the contents of a soul, in this case their promise. And to mention another illustrative example: it is said in the Book of Jeremiah that Yahweh planted Israel as "a true seed", but now it is changed into a strange vine (Jer. 2,21), [1] "true" here meaning the same as healthy, normal, vigorous, good, in opposition to the unhealthy, abnormal, strange.

The Israelite expresses his adherence to an order, a suggestion, a promise, etc. by saying *'āmēn,* "true". [2] Thus he makes it truth for himself. His god is the god of *'āmēn* (Is. 65,16), because he has the strength to carry out his words.

Thus justice as well as truth means the strength to maintain oneself. But this only gives us one phase of these ideas. The self-maintenance which they express is not the unbridled, lawless one; it always has the covenant as a presupposition. The soul only exists in organic connection with other souls, and it can only act through being united with others; thus it becomes a link in a totality which creates a centre of will. To be just and true means to subject the whole of the contents of one's soul to this centre of will, to identify one's will with that of the totality.

Only towards those outside the covenant is justice the same as harsh self-maintenance. When Israel and their god strike down their enemies, it is always an act of justice, because there is no covenant with them (Judg. 5,11; 1 Sam. 12,7; Mic. 6,5). The question is then: with what men is it possible to make a covenant? We have seen that the Israelites gradually drew the line more and more narrowly.

The righteous is always "whole" with those with whom he has entered upon a covenant. His heart is whole *(shālēm)* with Yahweh because he lives in his covenant; it is also expressed by his being fast to him or for him.[1]

"Among the righteous *(yᵉshārīm*, 'straight') there is favour", says the proverb (14,9), thus expressing a matter of course, because the righteous are those who live in normal relations of covenantship with each other. Therefore righteous is the same as good (2 Kings 10,3; Ps. 25,8). With full security the Gibeonites might leave it to Joshua to deal with them as was "good and righteous" in his eyes, because his will through the covenant had been determined by a totality of which they formed a part (Josh. 9,25). "Is there righteous *(yāshār)* with thine heart, as my heart is with thy heart?" Thus asked Jehu of Jehonadab ben Rechab, when he was on the point of exterminating the whole of the royal family (2 Kings 10,15).[2] He might just as well have asked: Is there peace between thy heart and mine? Righteousness or justice is the kernel of peace; it is impossible to imagine the one without the other. "He walked with me in peace and righteousness", says Yahweh of Levi (Mal. 2,6).[3]

Love and justice are mutually necessary. Solidarity with those in the covenant only he can have whose soul is healthy, so that it submits harmoniously to the common will. But if one has love, then one must also act according to the law of the covenant. When "mercy and truth are met together, righteousness and peace have kissed each other", as is the expectation expressed by the psalmist (Ps. 85,11), then Israel has reached its highest. "The love of Yahweh is from everlasting to everlasting upon them that fear him, and his righteousness unto children's children" (Ps. 103, 17). Righteousness manifests itself in love, because it consists in maintaining the covenant. Therefore the pious says confidently: As for me I shall behold thy face in righteousness, I shall be satisfied, when I awake, with thy likeness (Ps. 17,15).

When the Shechemites had helped Abimelech to kill the seventy sons of Gideon, they were rebuked by the only survivor, Jotham. He asked them among other things to consider whether they had "acted in truth and integrity" ("entirety", *tāmīm*) by making Abimelech their king, and "benefited Jerubbaal and his house" (Judg. 9, 16.19). What they do towards the sons of Gideon, they naturally do towards Gideon. If they benefit him they act *truly*, because in that way they act in accordance with the covenant between them and him. Truth and love always go together, because truth is tantamount to justice and, like the latter, consists in maintaining the existing covenant. One is entitled to truth and love from one's family and one's people, because one stands in a relation of peace with them. [1]

Justice and truth thus both denote the maintenance of the covenant, and at the same time capability and will. But it is not to be understood in the way that they denote, now the maintenance of self, now the maintenance of the covenant; they always denote both at the same time, because the individual soul is not something apart. He who maintains the covenant maintains himself, because he forms a spiritual totality with those with whom he has a covenant. But the covenant may be more or less intimate. The most intimate covenant is that of the family. The upholding and maintenance of the family is the strongest claim of justice on the man; the community is here so intensive that the unity between the maintenance of self and the maintenance of the covenant is a matter of course. But the covenant extends far, the whole of the people being included in it. Also here the essential thing for the man is to make the claim of totality his own. Thus justice at the same time contains a privilege and a claim. The healthy soul is the one which has the ability to maintain the privileges as well as the requirements.

Where then is the standard of the balance between the privileges and the claims? It follows as a matter of course from the nature of the covenant. The covenant does not make mankind one homogeneous mass. The common, as well as the individual soul, is a firmly constructed organism, where everyone holds his place. He holds his place according to the honour his soul acquires; and honour is identical with his ability to give and take. Justice consists in maintaining one's own honour and that of others in giving and taking in accordance with the position occupied within the covenant. Justice and truth are expressions of the realism of old Israelitic culture; it gives every man his due and exactly as much as he can receive.

But all the time the covenant is presupposed. This Nehemiah enjoined on his countrymen when he started clearing up in Jerusalem. To the strangers who enjoyed great privileges in that town he said: Ye have no portion, nor right, nor memorial in Jerusalem (Neh. 2,20). They do not belong within the covenant, and therefore have no claim to a position in it.

Within the family it is only just that the father of the house, in all cases, should maintain his authority, nay, that the lesser members of the family should sacrifice themselves for him. The woman must sacrifice herself for her husband because his life is always more valuable than hers. When a man gains new honour, so that he rises above another, then he is entitled to maintain it and suppress the other family. When David had conquered the house of Saul, and after that received Meribbaal, the son of Jonathan, into his house, it was a just demand on the part of David that Meribbaal should follow him in adversity (2 Sam. 19,26). Meribbaal himself acknowledges the dictate of justice: "For all my father's house were but dead men before my lord the king; yet didst thou set thy servant among them that did eat at thine own table. What right therefore have I yet to cry any more unto the king?" And Meribbaal declares himself satisfied when David takes half of his property from him and gives it to the slave who slandered him. He has no right whatsoever, because his family has been brought low. When Jehu was anointed king and had killed Ahab, the men of Jezreel struck down all his sons, who were in their charge. Jehu says to the murderers: Ye be righteous! Behold, I conspired against my master and slew him. But who slew all these? (2 Kings 10,9). Jehu is right, provided the presupposition holds good. If it is just that he has become a king and has killed Ahab, then it is also just that the sons of Ahab should be killed.

Justice is most frequently a claim on the stronger, the claim implying that he receives the weaker into his will and self-maintenance. He must help him so that he shall not perish. "Did not thy father eat and drink and do right and justice, and then it was well with him. He rightened the poor and needy; then it was well", says Jeremiah (22,15-16). Job showed his righteousness by giving to the poor because his honour is sufficiently great to do it.

Therefore righteousness is a *kingly virtue*. More than any other the king is he who maintains the covenant. In justice and truth he strikes down his enemies (Ps. 45,5) and gains security for his people (Jer. 23,5). In justice he makes happiness flourish (Ps. 72,2 f.), in justice he helps the weak within the people and upholds them (Is. 11,4); in order to be a true king he must show justice towards the *whole of his people* (2 Sam. 8,15), i. e. to maintain his people outwardly and to uphold everyone within the covenant in the place where he stands. If he fails to do this, he is neither a just nor a true ruler. Jeremiah says of the rulers of his day that they "are not the rulers of the country by truth" (9,2), for they do nothing but evil, and there is no mutual security in the country.

On the other hand, justice claims that he shall maintain himself as the guiding will among the people, and that the latter shall follow him. But this maintenance of self is not different from the other. He maintains himself and his honour by the very fact of being the giver whom the people follows willingly. Job was followed willingly and reaped honour within his community as long as the blessing was with him. It was a just claim on his part. But at the very moment that the blessing left him, he had no longer any claim on justice. Even the lowest could despise him, this being just on their part.

On righteousness the Israelite founds his trust in life, for also his god makes part of the covenant. When Yahweh storms and thunders in all his terror, then it is always *his* god who maintains his honour. With him he has community, and Yahweh will always help his people, because he is a just god who maintains the covenant in which he stands. For righteousness' sake he must procure salvation and practise mercy. He who prays confidently appeals to justice: "Hear me, O God of my righteousness!" (Ps. 4,2). "Hear, Yahweh, the right, attend unto my cry, give ear unto my prayer" (Ps. 17,1). This is the fundamental chord struck in the Psalms. The weak Israelite is only to submit his soul entirely to the strong soul of his god; in that his justice consists.

Righteousness is thus the mutual acknowledgment of souls; but it is still more, viz. their mutual maintenance of each others' honour. The acknowledgment can never exclusively be a feeling or a mood, but it must manifest itself in action. To consider a man full of honour and to make him full of honour are the same thing, according to the psychological conception of the Israelites.

He who detracts from the honour of his neighbour disturbs the covenant, because he disturbs its construction, its inner harmony. He abolishes the natural equilibrium between himself and his neighbour, and thus he loses his righteousness, which is the very maintenance of the will of the covenant. Justice demands that equilibrium shall be re-established between the wronged and him who commits the breach, for thereby the covenant is healed. To re-establish this relation is to *justify* a man. To justify a man means to obtain for him the place due to him within the covenant.

The wronged is righteous in relation to him who has done him wrong, because his will, in opposition to that of the other, agrees with the demands of the covenant. "Thou art more righteous than I", Saul says to David, "for thou hast rewarded me good, whereas I have rewarded thee evil" (1 Sam. 24,18). David is righteous in his relation to Saul, because his goodness is a maintenance of the demands of the covenant. He has, as is told in another similar narrative, shown righteousness and truth by not killing Saul, when he had a favourable opportunity to do so without running any risk (1 Sam. 26,23).

When Elihu blames Job, because he has made his soul righteous in his relation to God (Job 32,2), then it means that Job maintains having fulfilled the claim of the covenant, whereas God has not done so. Jeremiah and Ezekiel may even say that the faithless kingdom of the north has had its soul justified by the degenerate Judah (Jer. 3,11; Ezek. 16,51.52), seeing that, in comparison with Judah, it stands quite close to the will of the covenant.

But when the injured is thus said to be righteous, this, however, only implies a psychic presupposition which is bound up with a claim. The wrong-doer has infringed upon his soul. It is healthy and normal, but through the wrong it has been checked in its normal development, which should be a simple effect of its health. In so far both the wrong-doer and the wronged have lost their righteousness, neither possessing it intact. But the wrong-doer has lost it from within, the wronged has suffered derogation of it from without, but is otherwise healthy. Therefore the wronged can be re-established by getting back what he has lost, and thus he may again take the place for which the strength of his soul qualifies him. Thus he once more becomes thoroughly righteous. [1]

To justify is thus to restore to a normal condition. The temple is justified when it is being restored, cleansed of impurity and once more turned into a sanctuary (Dan. 8,14). The mightier justifies the mean and the poor (Ps. 82,3), in that he secures for them a tolerable existence, and this is his prerogative as a member of the covenant. It is simple justice that everyone obtains the very position for which he has the inner qualifications. It is the righteous who is to be justified (Deut. 25,1; 1 Kings 8,32); he who justifies the unrighteous acts against the covenant and is abhorred by Yahweh (Is. 5,23; Prov. 17,15). It is only a reckless person like Absalom who can stand forth and say that any one who feels wronged shall come to him, then he will justify him (2 Sam. 15,4). This indirectly implies that the person in question will be proved right, whether justly or not.

This being so, we might expect that *hiṣdīḳ*, i. e. "justify", would be used in the sense of giving *everyone* his due within the covenant, but in fact it is only used to denote re-establishment, satisfaction of violated claims or the fulfilment of an incompletely satisfied claim. It means to make whole, viz. to restore to the man the position within the covenant to which he is entitled. Where no such violation exists, but where it is a question of imparting to the soul of a man the sureness and firmness corresponding with his position in the covenant, then one says: to make true. "Truth" is more strongly centred in the inner soul than "justice", both of them denoting the firm construction of the soul and its will and power to maintain the covenant, and both denoting their outward realization. But whereas "justice" equally covers all of these shades of meaning, "truth" mainly centres in the first-mentioned.

To make a man true, *he'emīn,* means the same as to rely on him. It implies confidence in his having the will and power to maintain the claims of the covenant, as they must shape themselves for him in the position which he holds within the covenant. Faith, *'emūnā,* is the mutual acknowledgment conditioning the covenant. Without mutual confidence the covenant cannot exist. The weaker members of the covenant help to uphold the stronger by their confidence. They *make* him "true", i. e. firm, sure and strong.

The proverb warns against believing in the calumniator. "When he speaketh fair, believe him not, for there are seven abominations in his heart" (Prov. 26,25). Such were the kinsmen of Jeremiah: "Believe them not, though they speak fair words unto thee" (Jer. 12,6; cf. Mic. 7,5). Their souls were very far from being whole and firm; to consider a soul firm and thus to contribute to its firmness, that is to "make true", to believe in it.

Warmth and pliability are essential that the soul may believe, faith being a manifestation of a covenant-relation, a mixture of souls. It is told of Jacob that when the sons returned with the message that Joseph was alive, his heart was cold and dull — both qualities are implied in *pūgh* — in that he did not believe them (Gen. 45,26). The life that is necessary in order that souls may come together was lacking in his sorely troubled heart. Only when he saw the wagons which Joseph had sent to carry him, "his spirit revived" (v. 27), and he believed them.

It is clear that greater strength is generally required in him who "justifies" another, than in him who "makes true", i. e. believes in another. The former is to reinstate a man into the position he comes from, as it were to put him back where he belongs. But he from whom nothing is required except faith, shall not alter anything; he is only to acknowledge and confirm the man who is already sure of his position.

This expresses itself in the *usus loquendi,* justification denoting a more powerful and direct action upon another. One says "to justify a man", whereas not "to make a man true", but to create truth in or for a man. [1] To believe in a man, and to believe in his words and acts is, of course, the same thing; he who has the confidence makes the word of the man true, just as he makes the man true, and in the same manner he who believes that Yahweh has revealed himself to Moses makes this fact true (Exod. 4,5).

Justification is rather the claim of the weak in relation to the strong, faith and confidence the claim of the strong in relation to the weak. Yahweh justifies, but demands faith, and the greater he becomes, the greater faith he demands, for to believe is the same as to honour. Indeed, the covenant with Yahweh gradually develops into a demand that the Israelite is to render him all honour; this is *just.* Abraham showed Yahweh confidence, and therefore Yahweh considered him righteous [2] (Gen. 15,6).

That which the Israelite understands by justification he also calls to judge, *shāphaṭ, dīn, hōkhīaḥ.* [3] The quality of the judge must be righteousness: the will, but also the power to maintain the covenant. The chief or king judges his people by helping them to conquer their enemies. This is well known from the Book of Judges. Here no mention is made of any activity which we would call judicial. The chief maintains the claims of the covenant by getting for his people a place among the others, and thereby he "judges" it.

But with that his activity is not exhausted. He is to uphold the covenant both outwardly and inwardly, and the inward equilibrium he maintains by supporting those who are about to fall, and by checking those who want to take too much. He judges a man by thus asserting his influence and putting him in his right place. The unrighteous is judged in that his house perishes (1 Sam. 3,13); the strong judges the fatherless, the widow, the poor and the oppressed by protecting them and giving them tolerable conditions of life, as claimed by the covenant (Is. 1,17.23; 11,4; Jer. 5,28; Ps. 10,18; 82,3; Prov. 29,14). He who judges must determine what the will of the covenant requires, and also carry it out. When Lot, who lived in Sodom by right of hospitality, wanted to protect his guests against the attacks of the Sodomites, the latter considered it presumption on the part of Lot to set his will against theirs. "This one fellow came in to sojourn, and he will needs be a judge", they exclaimed angrily (Gen. 19,9).

The righteous demands that Yahweh should judge him. "He pleaded my cause and delivered me out of thine hand", says David to Saul (1 Sam. 24,16), and he also judged David from their hands who rose against him during the revolt of Absalom (2 Sam. 18.19.31). To "judge" in this place — as to justify — means to help to gain the victory. The psalmists demand that Yahweh should "judge" them, in accordance with their righteousness and his justice (Ps. 7,9; 26,1; 35,24; 43,1). They demand it with the same confidence with which the poor demand "judgment" from the king, because their covenant with Yahweh makes it a duty of honour for him to uphold all who do not break the conditions of the covenant. And when it is expected that Yahweh is to come and judge the earth (e. g. Ps. 82,8; 96,13; 98,9), then it means that he is to ensure the final victory of the covenant by striking down all its enemies, i. e. all the enemies of Israel. "Thou hast maintained my right and my judgment; thou satest in the throne judging right. Thou hast rebuked the nations, thou hast destroyed the unjust, thou hast put out their name for ever and ever" (Ps. 9,5-6).

The word, which for lack of a better translation must be rendered by "judge", must consequently not be taken in a one-sided legal sense. One constantly "judges" in the daily life, because one must constantly act so as to uphold the covenant, i. e. the whole of the common life of the community. Everything in which this kind of "judging" manifests itself is called *mishpāṭ*. [1]

This word is used to denote the decisive actions, by which a broken relation is established, the judicial proceeding as well as the word or act by which right is being recreated. [2] But it is not the fundamental sense from which the others have developed. As directly derived from the root of the word is the significance of all the daily actions maintaining the covenant, viz. the true relation between human beings; the word denotes what a man may claim and what he is to do towards others or, in other words, the right and duty of everyone. The king's *mishpāṭ* (1 Sam. 8,9, cf. 10,25) is what the king, according to his position within the covenant, must demand and grant. The strange peoples which the Assyrians sent to Samaria, did not know the *mishpāṭ* of the god of their new country, the manner in which he was to be treated, what he gave and claimed (2 Kings 17,26).

Therefore everyone has his special *mishpāṭ* according to his position within the covenant. The priests have the *mishpāṭ* to get a certain share of the sacrificial meat (Deut. 18,3; 1 Sam. 2,13). The firstborn has his *mishpāṭ* (Deut. 21,17), the widow and the fatherless theirs. He who breaks the covenant in such a manner as to make the breach irreparable, has death as his *mishpāṭ* (Deut. 19,6; 21,22); death is what the quality of his soul must necessarily lead up to.

The word — we usually render it by "right" — thus denotes the mutual relation of men, their whole manner of being, the nature of their souls, their habits, appearance, behaviour. The *mishpāṭ* of the Phœnicians was to live in peace and security (Judg. 18,7), the *mishpāṭ* of Elijah to walk about in a woollen mantle with a girdle (2 Kings 1,7). The *mishpāṭ* of Samson was not to taste unclean food and intoxicating drinks, but also that his mother (previous to his birth) was forbidden to do so (Judg. 13, 12). The *mishpāṭ* of David when he lived among the Philistines, was that on his plundering expeditions among the peoples on his southern frontier he would slay everyone he met, that no one was to bring tidings of him (1 Sam. 27,11).

mishpāṭ is the manner of proceeding, the way in which something is done. The cupbearer has his manner of handing his cup to the king; the goring bull has a certain way in which it is to be treated; the king has a special manner in which, at important decisions, he places himself on a pillar in the sanctuary; the Israelitic warriors had a certain manner of compassing Jericho, under the leadership of Joshua, and all this is called their *mishpāṭ*. [1]

The word thus denotes the standard of one's behaviour, that which one is wont to do — custom; David ordained that those who kept watch over the camp train should have the same share of the spoil as those who went to the battle, "and he made it a statute and a *mishpāṭ* for Israel unto this day" (1 Sam. 30,25). In other words, *mishpāṭ* means the law for the actions of mankind, the same as *ḥōḳ* (the established), *tōrā* (instruction), *miṣwā* (tradition), and so it is used everywhere in the legal codes. And not only the law of mankind; it denotes all law, all lawfulness. When the Preacher says that everything has "time and *mishpāṭ*", and that a wise man's heart discerneth both time and *mishpāṭ* (8,5.6), then it means that everything has its special lawfulness, its circumscribed manner.

The laws and codes of mankind, no more than other laws, are something which has been enforced from without, something which infringes upon the soul. The law is in its very essence the free development of the soul, the maintenance of its peculiar essence. We see it so clearly from the very manner in which the Israelite uses the word *mishpāṭ*. The law consists in that every human being maintains his soul after its special kind. This implies that he maintains the covenant and confirms the position of his brothers in it, for the covenant is part of the essence of his own soul, or rather, he is himself a link in the covenant. He who thus develops his own kind does what is the usual thing, what is done by good people, and thus he maintains the harmony of the covenant; his action is normal.

mishpāṭ thus has its root in the very essence of the soul. It is "straight" as is the normal soul. To bend *mishpāṭ* is the same as to disturb the relation, to dissolve the harmony which conditions the maintenance of the covenant. It is a breach of the covenant which must not take place (Exod. 23,6; Deut. 16,19; 24,17; 27,19; 1 Sam. 8,3).

mishpāṭ, right, justice, virtually means the same as *ṣedheḳ*. Both expressions inform us of the state of the soul and the resulting relation to other souls. But in the case of *mishpāṭ* chief stress is laid upon the latter, and there is about it only a slight suggestion of the outward expansion which the healthy soul must enjoy, and which plays such a great part in the case of *ṣedhekḳ*. The health of the soul, the harmonious growth within the covenant, the direct union with the other souls, is always implied in both of them.

Right and love belong together, as well as justice and love. They are the two virtues which the prophets demand from their people. "Practise right and love", says Micah (6,8). "Keep love and right", says Hosea (12,7). "I will sing of love and right", thus begins one of the Psalms. And if the soul has right and love within itself, then it is healthy, strong, and may say with the prophet: Truly, I am full of power by the spirit of Yahweh, and of "right" and of might (Mic. 3,8). It is a matter of course that when a soul is healthy, normal, just as it should be, then it also has the power to maintain itself.

Thus justice and truth are not something abstract or something standing firm outside mankind. Truth is not something established, a distant goal, which one gradually approaches. It is a power within the very soul, which must constantly be created and upheld through the life lived in common with mankind. It is justice which creates the possibility of life; it is the strength that flows through the souls and enables them to uphold the community in the harmony which is the condition of its structure and thus of its very existence. Justice is at the same time a power and a claim: the power and the claim to maintain one's own honour and that of one's neighbour, i. e. to maintain life as it appears in the covenant.

Old Israel does not distinguish between right and duty; both are united in the covenant and the law, which is an expression of the standard according to which the soul must act when it follows its own nature. The covenant is different with every man, according to the position it gives him. The house of David has the covenant of royalty, the house of Levi the covenant of priesthood (Lev. 24,8; Num. 18,19; 25,12; Mal. 2,8; Neh. 13,29; 2 Chron.

13,5). It means that they are kingly and priestly souls, to whom pertains the maintenance of all the resulting rights and duties. But there are rights and duties which apply to all Israelites, because they are all in the same covenant. This is expressed in the *law*.

Every law is a *mishpāṭ,* because it is a manifestation of right, the right. As we have seen, it is also called "the established" *(ḥōḳ),* "ordainment" or "tradition" *(miṣwā),* "instruction" *(tōrā)*; further it is called *'ēdhūth,* which presumably means custom. All of these expressions designate the law as a custom, a habit, that which normal people do. Thus it is said that Sheol opens her mouth wider than is *ḥōḳ* (Is. 5,14). It became *ḥōḳ* in Israel that the young women bewailed the daughter of Jephthah (Judg. 11,39); the moon, the stars and the sea each has its *ḥōḳ* (Jer. 31,35-36); *miṣwā* means the instruction as to their conduct given by the older to the young, the instruction of the teacher (Prov. 2,1; 7,1-2), or of the father (Prov. 6,20.23), or of another superior instructor (Jer. 35,14); *tōrā* is also instruction, both of parents and of teachers, but in particular of the priests, i. e. that which they obtained through the oracle.

Whether the law be written down or not, does not decide its character. The old Arabians had no written laws, and yet their life was as firmly regulated as that of the Babylonians, whose statutes were carved in stone. "This is not done" is said of that which is against the law (Gen. 29,26; 34,7; 2 Sam. 13,12). It is this spontaneity which makes the law so strong; it rests on a solid basis, because it is a direct expression of the construction of the soul.

The Israelites have cast part of their laws into sentences which are written down in the codes; other laws for their actions we must read between the lines in their other writings. All the laws are referred to Moses, an expression of the fact that they make the foundation of the life of the people and therefore must originate in its founder. At the great climaxes in the history of the people the latter solemnly undertook to respect the laws (Josh. 23 f.; 2 Kings 23; Neh. 8-11).

The most fundamental law is that of *kinship.* It is expressed in the commandment that people should honour father and mother (Exod. 20,12; Lev. 19,3; Deut. 5,16); this law is the basic condition of all life and happiness, and he who breaks it is to be exterminated (Exod. 21,15; Lev. 20,9; Deut. 21,18-21). But in reality the law of kinship underlies all the other laws, because the peace of the family is the foundation of everything. He who infringes upon the right of a man, strikes his family, and if the person stricken cannot himself repair the breach, then the kinsman must come to his assistance and restore the family; this is the most elementary claim of justice. The relation between men, the maintenance of which the laws claim, is in so far a relation between families.

The law is that every man respects his neighbour, such as he is, in his totality. First of all his life must be respected; this is included in "the ten words" (Exod. 20,13; Deut. 5,17, cf. Lev. 19,16), presuming of course that he has not forfeited his life. The law of unlawful manslaughter is bound up with the law guarding against violence and bodily hurt (Exod. 21,12 ff.; Deut. 17,8-13; 19,21; 21,1-9).

He who takes the life of a man takes his soul; for it is the soul in its normal development which must be respected, this also including his house. No one is permitted to violate his marriage covenant (Exod. 20,14; Lev. 20,10; Deut. 5,18; 22,22.23-29), or to steal one of his children (Deut. 24,7). The law reads: Thou shalt not covet thy neighbour's house, thou shalt not covet thy neighbour's wife, nor his manservant, nor his maidservant, nor his ox, nor his ass, nor anything that is thy neighbour's (Exod. 20,17; Deut. 5,21, cf. Lev. 19,20). The totality of the man is himself and his house, everything that belongs to him, including his property; it is to be respected as well as his life (Exod. 20,15; Lev. 19,11; Deut. 5,19; 23,25-26). In the three pithy words: *lō' tirsāḥ, lō' tin'āph, lō' tighnōbh* "thou committest not murder, thou committest not adultery, thou committest not theft" the law expresses the respect shown by normal individuals towards each others' integrity: life, house, property. This principle must be maintained in the daily life together, in trading (Lev. 19,35 f.;

25,14.17), and when conflicts arise (Exod. 23,1-3.6-8; 20,16 *et al.).*

The law of the Israelites strongly enforces *mercy* towards the weak. They also are included in the covenant; their rights are to be respected, and life is to be made tolerable for them. Job lays great stress on this when speaking of his former righteous conduct: If I saw some one perishing for lack of clothing, and that he had no covering — if his loins have not blessed me, and if he were not warmed with the fleece of my sheep! (Job 31,19-20). It is an honorable obligation on the part of the great always to uphold the lesser, but it is more or less the duty of every Israelite.

An Israelite who is the slave of another is to be released after six years, unless he himself wishes to remain (Exod. 21,1-6; Deut. 15,12-18). An Israelitic slave-woman cannot be sold to strangers when she no more pleases her master, but in that case she shall be redeemed. If he takes others beside her, then he is not permitted to give her less than her due; if he does so, she is to be released. If he gives her to his son, she is to be treated as a daughter (Exod. 21,7-11); and something similar holds good of strangers (Deut. 21,14).

The "Law of Holiness" requires that an Israelite under no conditions is permitted to serve as a bondservant, but only as a hired servant, and as such he must be treated leniently, and in the year of *yōbhēl* he is to be set free. Slaves must be taken among strangers (Lev. 25,39-46). A slave who has escaped from his master must not be returned to him, but is to be treated kindly (Deut. 23, 16-17).

When an Israelite becomes poor and is obliged to borrow, interest must not be taken, and if his mantle is taken as a pledge, it shall be delivered to him in the evening, that he may cover himself with it for the night (Exod. 22,24-26). The "Law of Holiness" also enforces that one must not defraud nor rob one's neighbour, nor keep back the wages of the hired man (Lev. 19,13, cf. Deut. 24,14-15). And when a man is impoverished, one must not let him go down nor take interest on loans (Lev. 19,35-37). On this point all the codes are agreed. The Deuteronomy says that it is not permitted to lend upon interest to an Israelite; that one may do towards strangers (Deut. 23,20-21, cf. 15,1-8). One must not take the nether or the upper millstone to pledge, one must not penetrate into his house in order to get a pledge, nor keep his raiment in the night (Deut. 24,6.10-13).

The chief thing is everywhere to show mercy to those of the same covenant: One must not curse a deaf man, nor put a stumbling-block before the blind (Lev. 19,14), and in particular there are three kinds of weak people who should be protected: widows, fatherless and *gērīm,* clients; in short, all of the Israelitic community who are without a family to uphold them.

It is said in the Book of Covenant: Thou shalt neither vex a *gēr* nor oppress him; for ye were *gērīm* in the land of Egypt. Ye shall not afflict any widow or fatherless child. If thou afflict them in any wise, and they cry at all unto me, I will surely hear their cry; and my wrath shall wax hot, and I will kill you with the sword, and your wives shall be widows and your children fatherless (Exod. 22,20-23).

Another law ordains: And when ye reap the harvest of your land, thou shalt not wholly reap the corners of thy field, neither shalt thou gather the gleanings of thy harvest. And thou shalt not glean thy vineyard, neither shalt thou gather every grape of thy vineyard, thou shalt leave them for the poor and the *gēr:* I am Yahweh, your God (Lev. 19,9-10).

We find both of these laws combined in the Deuteronomy (24, 19-22), the same law which bids one not to shut one's hand against one's poor brother, but to help him willingly and give him all that he needs (Deut. 15,7-8). The *gēr* is to be acknowledged as belonging to the community. The Book of Covenant mentions twice that he must not be oppressed (Exod. 22,20; 23,9). In the "Law of Holiness" it is even said: Thou shalt love him as thyself (Lev. 19,33 f.). The *gēr* is entitled to this, because he is nearly an Israelite.

But *gēr,* client, is likewise every one who comes travelling and settles in a strange town for a shorter or longer period. He has claims to protection and full sustenance. The host must provide food both for him and his beasts (Gen. 18; 24; Judg. 13; 19,19; 2 Sam. 12,4); preferably, the fatted calf shall be killed, and new-baked bread and wine or curdled cream must be put before the guest. If the traveller arrives in a strange town, he goes to the gate or the open space within it, and here one of the inhabitants is sure to come to him and urge him to take up his abode in his house, as Abraham did when the three men came walking. Only depraved people, like the citizens of Sodom or Gibeah, violate the right of hospitality (Gen. 19; Judg. 19), but in both towns there was a client who knew the duties of a host, and in both cases he valued the right of hospitality so much that he was willing to sacrifice his daughter in order to protect the guest against the brutal townspeople. The observance of the right of hospitality is also mentioned by Job among his righteous deeds: The guest did not lodge in the street, but I opened my doors to the wayfarer! (Job 31,32). Even the slave who has escaped from his master in a foreign nation and dwells with the Israelites is not to be delivered, and shall not be oppressed (Deut. 23,16-17).

That which the law demands is in all cases the keeping of the covenant. The neighbour is to be maintained in his honour, the free development of his soul is respected, provided he does not disturb the growth of others. It must be extended to everyone who is included in the covenant of the people; he must have his share in the love of every Israelite: Thou shalt not hate thy brother in thine heart, thou shalt do justice to thy kinsman and not bear sin for his sake. Thou shalt not avenge nor bear any grudge against the children of thy people, but thou shalt love thy neighbour as thyself. I am Yahweh (Lev. 19,17-18). The covenant must be inspired by some of the instinctive feeling which connects the family.

Even from one's enemy one must not quite withdraw one's hand. Job looks upon it as an example of his righteousness that he never rejoiced at the destruction of him that hated him, nor wished a curse on his soul (31,29-30). In the Book of Covenant it is said: If thou meet thine enemy's ox or his ass going astray, thou shalt surely bring it back to him again. If thou see the ass of him that hateth thee lying under his burden, thou shouldst forbear leaving it to him; thou must release [1] it together with him (Exod. 23,4-5).

That it is here a question of a covenant-man or rather a fellow-townsman is a matter of course. The laws strongly maintain the validity of the covenant for the whole people; no one is permitted to go down when he has a share in the covenant, if only as a client. So strong is the tie of the covenant, and so closely united are the covenant-men. We have seen how in the old community it was a point of honour with the great to uphold the lesser. The claim for mercy towards the lowly is based upon the following argument: You have yourselves been clients and slaves in the land of Egypt, and therefore you must befriend clients and slaves. This remark is addressed to the mighty who consider themselves uplifted above and detached from the lesser elements of the community. It says that none is so great as to be superior to the covenant; the mark of the lowly is upon all of them from their history. No one is too great and no one too small to bear the rights and the duties which justice confers on him who has a share in the covenant.

All of the fundamental values can be traced back to their root in the soul. The happy development of the soul and its full harmony with the souls with which it is connected are not two different things, but both are peace, the totality of the soul. The power to maintain peace is the blessing, but the kernel of blessing and peace is righteousness, the health of the soul. Just as the righteous must maintain peace by acting towards members of the same covenant according to the laws of life, so he must necessarily also expand in the happiness of peace. Goodness and happiness are parallel expressions of the working of the healthy soul.

For righteousness is firmness and strength or, in other words, that which creates blessing, and this again is the integrity of the soul as an inner character, but one cannot normally have the entirety as an inner quality without having it in its full expansion in happiness. The manner of speech is stamped by it. The ordinary appellation of harmony and happiness, integrity in its full extent, is *shālōm,* but we have seen that *shālōm* denotes the soul as righteous or whole in the sense of inner health. Integrity as a quality of the soul, righteousness, is generally expressed by *tōm* and the corresponding adjective *tāmīm*, but both of these words also denote happiness. Job says that a man may die in the midst of his happiness *(tummō)*, in his full vitality (Job 21,23), just as the psalmist praises God because he makes his way whole (*tāmīm,* Ps. 18,33). "Let us swallow them up alive as Sheol, and those who stand in their full happiness *(ūthᵉmīmīm)* as those that go down into the pit", say the wicked (Prov. 1,12). When Ezekiel says to Tyrus: Thou wast *tāmīm* in thy ways from the day that thou wast created, till iniquity was found in thee (Ezek. 28,15), then it is not tautology, for in this place *tāmīm* not only denotes inner righteousness, but also the happiness which developed from it.[1]

Righteousness is the inner kernel of blessing and must always be penetrated by it; the righteous must develop, just as the healthy tree must grow unless hindered from without. "Surely it is well with the righteous; they eat the fruits of their doing", says the prophet (Is. 3,10). "The horn of the righteous is exalted" (Ps. 75,11). The pure "receives blessing from Yahweh, righteousness from the god of his salvation" (Ps. 24,5). "God is with the generation of the righteous" (Ps. 14,5), "a man of truth abounds with blessing" (Prov. 28,20). In psalms and proverbs it is described over and over again how blessings pour down over the righteous.

Righteousness manifests itself in all forms of blessing. It is the same as *victory*. When Yahweh intervenes and drives out the conquerors from Jerusalem, then "he fills Zion with righteousness and right" (Is. 33,5), for Yahweh's deeds of justice are his victories over the enemies of Israel (Judg. 5,11). In his immense righteousness he strikes down all enemies; he puts on righteousness as a breastplate (Is. 59,17); by his righteousness and strength Israel becomes just, exults while conquering its enemies (Is. 45, 24 f.; 59,18). "Can the prey be taken from the hero; can the spoil be wrested from the righteous?" asks the prophet (Is. 49,24).

Surely not! Righteousness is the power of victory, the blessing of the warrior in his fight against the enemy, a royal virtue. The mighty king who is to come and create the happiness of Jerusalem makes his entrance "just and having salvation" (Zech. 9,9), i. e. filled with the power of the conqueror and ruler.

Righteousness is *peace and salvation.* "Those who desire my righteousness shall exult and rejoice and say continually: Great is Yahweh who desireth the peace of his servant", it is said in one of the Psalms (35,27). All kinds of prosperity, wealth and well-being follow the righteous; he is delivered from all sufferings (Ps. 34,20; Prov. 10). Also in this respect is truth identical with righteousness (2 Kings 20,19; Is. 39,8). Righteousness is fertility. When "mercy and truth are met together, righteousness and peace have kissed each other", how then is the state of the country? The description reads as follows: "Truth springs out of the earth, and righteousness looks down from heaven. Yea, Yahweh giveth that which is good, and our land yieldeth her increase. Righteousness goes before him; peace [1] there is for the way of his steps" (Ps. 85, 12-14). Fertility, the rich growth, wells forth from the ground.

The king "judges" his people with righteousness, in that the mountains bring peace to the people, and the little hills righteousness (Ps. 72,3). The "peace" and "righteousness" with which the mountain sides are filled, are flourishing pastures and fertile fields. Righteousness drops down from above in the rain and springs up from the soil in the growth (Is. 45,8). For righteousness, i. e. for fertility, God lets the early rains come down over the fields (Joel 2,23).

All fundamental values are given with righteousness; it must create life. "In the way of righteousness is life" (Prov. 12,28), "righteousness tendeth to life" (11,19), "he that followeth after righteousness and love, findeth life [2] and honour" (21,21). Justice is what the Israelites are striving after; then they may live and inherit their land, says the law (Deut. 16,20). The righteous is to live, and just because of his very righteousness or, what comes to the same thing, his truth or faith (Hab. 2,4).

In old Israel righteousness is never an abstract demand which is put in the same way to all men, not something external, but the very constitution of the soul. The mighty has more righteousness than the weak, because he has greater strength; his goodness is greater, because he can put more into it; his claims, but also his duties are greater, because he has the power to give and take more. Therefore, not only right and duty are identical and expressed by the same word, but also the power and the will to maintain the covenant in its natural relations, the very same demands being made to the man, which must be put to him in the actual position obtained.

This is an inevitable consequence of the Israelitic conception of what belongs to the soul. The will is not a particular quality of the soul, but its very substance and working. And the action is not something sent away from the soul in order to make a result outside it. Result as well as action is the direct expression of the peculiar characteristics and power of the soul.

The close connection between the nature and conditions of the soul, reflected in the Israelitic manner of speaking of right and righteousness, also appears when he speaks of the *ways* of man. The ways of man are his actions, everything in which the nature, the strength, the ability and the will of his soul are manifested outwardly, his very manner of being or, in other words, nearly the same as *mishpāṭ*.[1] But at the same time the ways of a man are the conditions under which he lives — the happiness or lack of happiness incidental to his being.

It is expressed in a double manner: either that happiness is the destination towards which the way leads or that the very way is happiness. The way which "prospers" (Jer. 12,1; Ps. 37,7; Job 34,27) is the straight way (Ps. 37,14; Prov. 11,5), the one that leads to the goal. But the goal is given with the very character of the way. "The way of life and the way of death" (Jer. 21,8) are the manners of acting that result in life and death, but also those fraught with life or death. When it is said that Yahweh knows the way of the righteous (Ps. 1,6), then this implies, both that he rejoices over their manner of acting and that he maintains their happiness. The way of the wicked perishes. Their actions lead to nothing, their happiness is dissolved. "Their way is as the darkness", at any moment they are apt to stumble (Prov. 4,19);

to wander a way that is "dark and slippery" (Ps. 35,6) means to have a fickle and uncertain fate, which at any time may be changed into unhappiness.

To have a straight way is thus both to act rightly and to prosper. He who disturbs the happiness of a man, turns aside his way (Am. 2,7) and makes it crooked (Ps. 146,9). The way is thus the same as the "right", only with a slightly more external application. It is the nature of the soul, as it manifests itself outwardly in actions and conditions.

Just as the action is given with the nature of the soul, so the result of the action lies in the soul itself, as the fruit lies in the flower. This image is used by the Hebrew himself. He says that "there is fruit for the righteous" (Ps. 58,12); the fate which a man and a people get is the fruit of their doings (Is. 3,10; Jer. 17,10; 21,14; 32,19). When the people and country of Israel are destroyed, then it is the fruit of their doings (Mic. 7,13), the fruit of their thoughts (Jer. 6,19). Falsehood bears its bitter fruit. He who changes right into poison, reaps wormwood as his fruit (Am. 6,12, cf. Hos. 10,13). The very word denoting the action, *pōʿal* or *peʿullā*, also denotes the result obtained through the act. The man "gets his action" in that he obtains the result of it, just as he "gets his way". [1]

The whole of this conception of life presupposes the harmony supplied by the covenant, in that all its members support each other and uphold the community with their blessing. They must all be righteous and give what they are able to give, and this particularly applies to the great, the upholders of the covenant. But the harmony must go so deep that it includes the underlying forces of existence. Behind the community stands its god in whom the covenant rests. He is with the righteous and lays the blessing into him. On his justice the Israelite bases his confidence in the subsistence of the harmony, in the development of every man to the measure for which he is qualified. The strength of the members of the same covenant and of the god of the covenant is in the man's soul when he acts; if they fail his energy of action is gone. But they cannot fail as long as the man is righteous; that would be contrary to the very laws of life.

But if, nevertheless, God now fails the righteous, so that in the full strength of his righteousness he suddenly loses happiness, what then? As long as it is only a question of one of the lower members of the community, then the problem is not so painful. It may be the stronger members of the covenant, who are unrighteous and fail to do their duty to maintain the covenant. But if it is a chief, a man who upholds the community and whose righteousness penetrates all his actions, who supports the weak by his possessions and strengthens the strong by his advice; if suddenly, in the full strength of his righteousness, he fails and loses his happiness, is there then any other way but to declare that God has been unjust? Here is the painful problem to which the Israelites were constantly recurring; if God is unjust, in whom the whole of the covenant rests, then the very ground has been knocked from under existence. All harmony has been dissolved; the souls must perish, because the source of their own righteousness and vigour of life has been dried out.

It is this problem which is treated in the Book of Job. The author has used an old narrative of a happy man, Job, whom God permitted Satan to test in order to see whether he would remain faithful when happiness failed him. Against the background of this narrative he worked out a colloquy between Job and three of his friends, which is finally interrupted by God, who addresses them in a speech full of power. The book is no drama, for there is no progress in the action; it is not a philosophical discourse, for the thought does not progress. But each of the persons expresses his conception of the problem: How is one to judge, when a chief suddenly loses his happiness without apparent unrighteousness on his part?

Job is such a man. He lives in a small community, the upholder of which he is. In the covenant of the townsmen he is the leading will; to him the strong and the weak look for help, and no one goes away empty-handed. The small town forms an ideal Israelitic community; all is prosperity and harmony, upheld by a single man. Then in the full strength of his righteousness misfortune falls upon him, and he must sit naked in the dirt, more lowly than the lowliest of his own slaves.

Job himself cannot restore his happiness; his soul is despoiled and empty. Then he curses life, which did not grant him salvation. He praises the grave which at any rate will free him from suffering. He accuses God, who afflicts man endlessly and makes life one long suffering.

That which lends its peculiar character to the Book of Job is that it rests entirely in the old Israelitic conception of life. The speech in which Job describes his lost happiness (chap. 29) is a classical description of an old Israelitic community. In Job's soul there was peace, for the covenant was firm and the members of it thronged closely round him. There was honour, for he was the one to whom they all looked for help and support; his will was the will of the covenant. And there was blessing, for everything flourished round him in family and property; God was present in his soul. And there was justice, which penetrated him to such an extent that he "put on righteousness and it clothed him". His soul was healthy throughout, acting as it should according to its presuppositions. He was the great man, and therefore he upheld the others.

Happiness rested in the fact that all of these features were present in his soul. The blessing of the other covenanters must necessarily be there. God was there, and that which held the whole thing together was righteousness.

Then it happens that God deserts his soul, and it loses all. God withdraws his blessing from it, and thus takes its peace and its honour. In that way God infringes upon the righteousness of Job; he has taken it from him, for blessing is the natural development of righteousness. Righteousness without blessing is the same as health without strength, an inner contradiction.

Job maintains that this is unjust; his soul is righteous or, in other words, healthy, and when it is not permitted to develop it is a breach of the laws of life. "I am whole, but he made me crooked" (9,20). Job does not ask God for something which he has deserved; he does not demand happiness as a reward for something he has given. It is nowise the recapture of the outward happiness which comes to the front in his thoughts. In his speech the future does not play any prominent part; his attention is directed towards the injury done to him, i. e. that his righteousness has been unjustly taken away from him. That which he requires is restoration, the re-establishment of the law of the covenant, that the healthy should have his health and the right to develop.

No soul can be restored without being righteous, healthy in its root; but if it is so, the restoration must take place. Job does not deny that his righteousness may have certain flaws. Even the healthy may suddenly be afflicted with illness; thus also the righteous may become tainted with sin. How easily may man, this feeble being, be touched with evil and thus come to offend God! But Job positively denies having sinned so greatly that the sin should have affected his soul in its centre and dissolved his righteousness (7,17-21; 10,6.14 f.; 13,25-27; 14,16).

For if God should take away the blessing from human beings for the sake of such trifling transgressions, it would be unjust. Lesser transgressions are inevitable; they cannot destroy the blessing and ought not to offend God. Just as the chief forgives his subjects their minor transgressions, so God also must be able to forgive and wipe out the trifling transgressions of his faithful, transgressions which signify so little in the totality of the soul. In any case he must attract the attention of man to his sin, that he may take care to have it removed.

But God has not done so, and here we are at the crux of the matter. When Job stood in his strength, he upheld all within his covenant and maintained justice by providing for the prosperity of all the righteous. This Eloah has not done; he has failed his covenant. Instead of putting his blessing into the righteous he has withdrawn from him and deserted him, attacked him and made himself his enemy. Thus God is not different from perpetrators of violence. He is utterly unjust.

Job maintains that his case is not unique. God falls upon men whether righteous or unrighteous, nay, he is chiefly on the side of the unrighteous. He lets the wicked rule and unrighteous judges govern (9,24). The souls of the wicked thrive, as if they were healthy; they get flourishing and numerous progeny; they dwell in security, live their lives unto the grave in peace; they succeed in everything and never have any accidents with their flocks (21, 7-17). It is arbitrariness, lawlessness, of which Job accuses God; God has no love and therefore also lacks justice. He is not as the chief upholding his covenant, but as the despot who knows no other law than his own greatness and arbitrariness.

Job by no means puts himself on an equal footing with God. God is infinitely greater and mightier than man; it is therefore that he can do all he wants. But the claim of justice increases with greatness. The righteousness of Job manifests itself towards God in his fearing him and showing him all the honour that his greatness demands. This Job has fulfilled, but what can be demanded of God is that he should take care of the feeble creature who is delivered entirely into his hand, and this he has not fulfilled (chap. 10; 14,15-22). On the contrary, he considers him as an enemy and strikes him. It would be far better if Eloah left Job to himself, so that he might die in peace and pass into the oblivion of the grave (6,8-13; 7,15-16; 10,18-22; 14,1-6.13-14).

The humiliation under God Job will in no wise reject, but he will not deny his own truth. He knows that he is righteous, and it is that which he wants to maintain in the face of the whole world. What he demands is therefore proper judgment, a settlement between him and God, through which it is proved whether he himself has vitiated his righteousness, or whether God has taken it by violence, so that Job may claim it back (13,20-28; 23,1 ff.). He desires nothing more ardently than that God, his opponent, should write his indictment against him; then he would take it upon his shoulder in triumph and himself willingly set forth everything (31,35-37). But in this very particular God shows his injustice, making use of his power to strike Job, and then withdrawing so that Job cannot find him.

In his despair he calls upon his witness and defender in heaven to take care of him and to support his right towards Eloah, for soon he himself is going to die (16,18-22). His claim cannot perish; it is greater than himself. Therefore he wants his words to be written down, by preference to be graven in the rock for ever. Then, when he is dead, his case will be taken up by his *gō'ēl* who inherits his claims (19,23-25).

In these expressions the speeches of Job reach their climax. They are the cry of a great soul which is struck down and checked in its growth, and Job takes it as an injury, because he knows within himself that he is healthy and has all the qualifications of development. It is his right and duty to maintain his righteousness and thus to strive in order to keep himself. Job has lost blessing, honour and peace; his friends and kinsmen have deserted him, his own house considers him a stranger, his wife and children turn their backs to him, none of his servants do his bidding (19, 9-19). But righteousness he will not part with.

In a harmonious culture the values must have an inner kernel, round which they all centre. With the Arabians this centre is honour. Of course they cannot conceive of a normal life without harmony, unity with the tribe and progress in the world, but all this can be lost, as long as honour is maintained by courage and independence. When honour is preserved the man dies in peace, even if everything else fails, because he lives in it. It can never be taken away from him by another, because, after all, it is himself who is to maintain it. We have seen features of this kind in the oldest Israel, but with the average Israelite the kernel of life is righteousness. It is the innermost centre of the soul, and the only psychic value which always rests in the soul itself. Therefore Job can abandon everything else, but not that.

The psychology of the Book of Job is from first to last typically Israelitic. The Arabians would not be able to produce a writing of this kind, because a fate like that of Job would offer no problems to them. If, with them, a chief falls as decisively as Job did, then he may, if strong like Imra'alḳais, defy the god, and wander forth to seek his restoration; but if he does not possess this strength, then he is judged by his very fate. With the Israelites the sting of the problem arises out of the fact that the claim of justice is a claim on their god. The righteous soul must develop according to its health, but this it can only do because God puts his blessing into it. That this happens is the normal case, but it is God in whom it rests. Life has two poles, the righteousness of man and the justice of God, and they *must* be in harmony with each other. If God is unjust, then life is lawless, absurd.

It is this inference which Job draws, because he is by no means prepared to let go his righteousness. It is his maintenance of self, but more than his personal claim. It is an ideal claim, which *cannot* perish; it must live after him in his family and be maintained by his *gōʾēl;* it extends throughout the powers of life, and is bound to find a point of support in the divine beings surrounding Eloah in heaven, so that someone up there will maintain it against Eloah, until at last he himself gives way and acknowledges it. If only this is acknowledged, Job has obtained what he desires and is willing to pass into the grave, without happiness.

Job's pride does not go so far as that of the Arabian; he is unable to defy his god and look for happiness outside him. He cannot circumvent God, because everything depends on him, but his pride is to maintain himself — in his lowliness — against God and claim acknowledgment for himself. His pain is all the deeper, as the logical inference of his claim is that God is unjust, which cuts the ground from under existence.

Thus the Book of Job carries us to the limit of the Israelitic conception of life: where the righteousness of man and the justice of God clash, there is no way out, because life is based upon the complete harmony between the two.

The friends start from the same fundamental conception as Job. Also for them justice is what upholds life, and it is God who upholds justice. But they deny the possibility of any conflict. They constantly repeat that the righteous must maintain himself and prosper, whereas the unrighteous may now and then get happiness, but this is no rule, and their happiness has no deep foundation; they will quickly lose it again, and their fall then becomes all the greater. Therefore the wicked always travaileth with pain (15,20), his light shall be put out (18,5), and his triumph is short (20,5). This God accomplishes because he is righteous.

No man has the right to consider his fate as an exception from this law. If an otherwise righteous man is afflicted by evil, then he must consider that, however righteous, he nevertheless commits iniquity. Calamity is not something which comes from without; it always originates in the very soul of man. "Affliction cometh not forth of the dust, neither doth trouble spring out of the ground" (5,6); the soul of man being so imperfect as it is, it is born unto trouble (5,7).

Therefore man must hold himself responsible for the calamities befalling him; they are always due to his unrighteousness. And God is so great that he sees through man at once and deserts his soul when there is wickedness in it (11,11; 22). When Job has now fallen into trouble, he must have been unrighteous; he has not been faithful to his covenant. He is to abandon his claims, to recognize his unrighteousness, and humbly ask God to pardon him; then his happiness shall be restored to him.

Job and his friends are all the time at cross-purposes with each other. They want him to give up his claim to righteousness in order to obtain happiness. But for him the claim of righteousness is the very starting point; he does not, *eo ipso,* claim happiness, but only as a consequence of his righteousness. He starts from his righteousness and therefore declares God to be unjust; they start from the proposition that God's justice is supreme and irreversible and therefore declare him to be unrighteous.

The friends maintain that God cannot rob man of righteousness, because man has no righteousness with regard to God. Whatever God takes, it is something which belongs to him, because he gives everything. Man cannot claim anything from him, because he has nothing to give him; therefore God is always just. In particular this is emphasized several times by Eliphaz. He asks whether a man can profit God: "Is it any pleasure to Shaddai that thou art righteous? or is it gain to him that thou makest thy ways perfect?" (22,2-3). "Has mortal man a claim of justice on God? Is man more pure than his maker? Behold, he puts no trust in his servants; and he finds faults with his messengers. How much less in them that dwell in houses of clay, whose foundation is in the dust, which are crushed before the moth" (4,17-20, cf. 15,14-16). The angels have not sufficient strength to maintain anything against God, and how much less the still weaker human being! It is the same thought that is expressed by Bildad, when he says that the moon and the stars do not shine in God's sight (25,5). All strength shrinks before him and becomes weakness. Therefore no man can be so righteous as to make God unjust.

This reference to the strength of God Job dismisses scornfully. The very trouble is that God uses his power against man, so that he cannot maintain his justice, and yet if he possessed the love of the covenant, his very power should bind him to take care of mankind in its weakness. For God does not gain anything by striking down man, who is so much more lowly than he, and whom he even created himself (chap. 10). It is true that man in relation to him is only as a leaf driven to and fro, as the flower that quickly fades, as the shadow which disappears; but so much the greater is the arraignment against him, when he vexes this weak being instead of leaving it in peace (13,25-14,3).

In order to support their arguments the friends refer to the traditions of the fathers; but it would not be proper to characterize the relation between them and Job by saying that they represent the old conception, i. e. the unity of righteousness and happiness, while Job represents something new: righteousness without happiness. No less than the friends Job represents the old; also in his eyes righteousness and blessing normally belong together. He cannot show any new order of things where it is different; life for him is without law and meaning when the righteous cannot maintain himself.

What divides them is, when all is said and done, the relation between human and divine righteousness, the two poles of life. For Job the centre of gravity lies in the former, for the friends in the latter, but this implies a different conception of justice. Job stands firm in the old, fundamental psychological conception: righteousness is the firmness and integrity of the soul, its health. It manifests itself in the fact that man upholds the claims of the covenant, that he shows kindness to the other members of the covenant, and that he yields worship, fear and honour to the god of the covenant; but the justice of the god of the covenant must be in harmony with this by his respecting and supporting the righteous.

On the other hand God, in the eyes of the friends, is so powerful that he is raised above all claims; he is always just. Man may be righteous, as Job says he is, but he must in any case first and foremost humble himself before God and give him everything, even his righteousness; then God will raise him (8,5; 11,13 ff.; 22,3). There is thus the peculiarity about the position of the friends that they maintain, at the same time, that the righteousness of man avails nothing whatsoever, and that the righteous in any case will be upheld. The remainder of self-maintenance possessed by the normal Israelite they take away from him, leaving all to God; the inference is that God is not bound by human righteousness, and this they also maintain. But with that they have cut the ground from under their own assertion that God always lets the righteous prosper; God is above such lawfulness.

The standpoint of the friends lacks intrinsic logic, and Job is right when characterizing their words as empty phrases, assertions floating in mid air. They represent the flat optimism to which the Israelitic conception of life laid itself open when it aimed at making man merely receptive. God would give all to man, and he must be just.

In the speeches of Job there are no abstract arguments; his standpoint throughout rests upon a psychological basis and has its root in the totality-conception of old Israel. Justice is to him a reality, the health of the soul; his claim against God is not a doctrinary demand for happiness, but a claim for acknowledgment of a reality: the health of the soul and its right to a natural self-development, such as can only take place with the assistance of Eloah.

Therefore Job is in reality more deeply rooted in the old-Israelitic conception of life than his friends. They maintain the old in its extrinsic logic, i. e. the happiness of the just; but by denying its presupposition, i. e. the reality of human righteousness, they have hollowed out the kernel round which this shell has formed. It is characteristic that they refer to a tradition and doctrines about God; they are dogmatic, their point of view is determined by the very tradition, without being supported from within. On the contrary, in Job the kernel of the old conception of life is quite sound: happiness is the self-development of the healthy. But the logical result of justice does not follow, because God does not show the justice which is essential to the natural development of life.

The colloquy between Job and his friends is interrupted by God, who in his powerful speech describes his illimitable might (chap. 38). He has created heaven, earth and the unfathomable sea; the whole of the universe he holds in his hand; he has established its laws and maintains it all; great and small, he must uphold them all. And against him Job wants to make claims, against him he wants to maintain himself!

Job humbles himself before the speech of God, he puts his hand on his mouth and declares that he has spoken, without understanding, of things which he did not know. "I have heard of thee by the hearing of the ear; but now mine eye seeth thee. Wherefore I repudiate what I have said and repent in dust and ashes" (42, 5-6). One may wonder that God's speech should have this effect. Job has already rivalled with his friends in descriptions of the power of God. But the explanation must be that only now, when he sees God himself, does he get a real impression of his might, and in this instinctive transport he abandons all claims.

God's speech does not yield a comprehensive solution of the problems of the Book of Job, so as to make the final result appear directly from it; it is only an exhibit in which God guards himself against attacks. But in this exhibit thoughts are expressed which illustrate the poetical work in its totality.

To a certain extent it might seem as if the friends had carried the point. Did not they maintain that God is always just, and that man must submit to him? Did not they say that man cannot make God unjust, because the justice of God is above human righteousness? And yet this manner of judging the friends would be superficial. They are judged through the answers of Job to their speeches, and God gives them no satisfaction. The peculiar thing about their arguments is the very fact that they do not carry their point of the superiority of God to the righteousness of man; they say that wherever there is righteousness God will acknowledge it and let it develop in happiness. It is this superficiality which

Job lays bare in its emptiness, and it is entirely in the spirit of the poem when, in the epilogue, the friends are rebuked because they have not spoken rightly of God.

The argument of God is that man is never permitted to remonstrate with God and judge him. Man cannot claim to maintain his righteousness in all cases, because God, who is to maintain it, has a far wider sphere of activity than man, and his deeds are accomplished against a greater horizon. God's greatness makes his righteousness to pass beyond that of man.

It cannot be said that the Book of Job has shattered the old Israelitic conception of life. God does not say that man is to abandon his righteousness; it is the normal foundation of human life. And, unlike the friends, God does not demand that man shall confess to uncommitted transgressions when the blessing fails him. The Book of Job deals with the exceptions from the law of life, cases which must necessarily occur: that the righteousness of man was not in harmony with that of God. In such cases man, it is true, must not relinquish his own righteousness, nor must he relinquish God's. When man cannot maintain his own righteousness, then he must not think that it is lawlessness which prevails in the world. He must subject himself to the mighty will of God, trusting to the fact that man has *his* righteousness and God *his;* and when they do not harmonize, then it is not that God's justice goes against that of man and suspends it, but that it transcends it and goes deeper than man is able to penetrate. Even if the righteous fails, he must still believe in righteousness as the supreme law of the world, firmly resting in God. Thus the Book of Job ends in the apotheosis of righteousness.

That Job regains happiness, as occurs in the epilogue, is not an inevitable consequence of the poem, but it cannot, on the other hand, be said to be at variance with it.[1] God may yield the blessing to Job when it agrees with his justice, and the latter is impenetrable. But whether or not the righteous gets the blessing, he must humble himself before God, the great giver of everything, knowing that man who receives everything has no claim on his great giver. "Yahweh gave, Yahweh has taken away, blessed be the name of Yahweh", these words with which, according to the prologue, Job received the tidings of his calamity, ought to stand as a motto over the Book of Job.

The Israelites over and over again recur to the problem of justice, because to them it is the real problem of life, and their thoughts must, as in the Book of Job, constantly circle about the relation between human and divine justice. The thoughts we most frequently come across in later Israel are those represented by the friends of Job, which Job called empty: man is to be just, but first and foremost he must abandon himself entirely to God; then God, for his own sake, will support man. At the same time that Israel consolidates more and more closely, it holds more tightly to its God. Righteousness more and more becomes a definite manner of conduct, the kernel of which is loyalty and submission to the God of Israel, who must show his justice by blessing his faithful. When those placing themselves outside the circle prosper in life, then it can only be for some time. God must intervene and strike them down, and his faithful must be exalted. Otherwise he would not be righteous, and then life would perish.

Such is the predominant note of the Psalms: "Fret not thyself because of evil-doers, neither be thou curious against the workers of iniquity. For they shall soon be cut down like the grass, and wither like the green herb. Trust in Yahweh and do good, dwell in the land, and deal with truth. Delight thyself also in Yahweh; and he shall give thee the desires of thine heart. Commit thy way unto Yahweh; trust also in him, and he shall bring it to pass. And he shall bring forth thy righteousness as the light, and thy right as the noonday . . . Evil-doers shall be cut off; but those that wait upon Yahweh, they shall inherit the earth. For yet a little while, and the wicked shall not be; yea, thou shalt diligently consider his place, and it shall not be . . ." (Ps. 37,1-6.9-10). The poet is vexed at seeing the unrighteous thrive, but he once more finds peace in the certainty that God sets them "in slippery places, and casts them down into destruction" (73,18). If it does not happen now, it will happen soon.

The Psalms constantly proclaim that the arm of the wicked is broken, whereas Yahweh maintains the righteous; the latter live in wealth and satiety and have enough to lend to others, but the unrighteous cannot even redeem his loans, "for Yahweh loves justice and does not forsake his faithful" (Ps. 37,28). Therefore the pious, with full confidence, ask Yahweh to judge them according to their righteousness; they have given themselves to Yahweh, and so he must uphold them.

The change in the conception of justice has taken place gradually. It corresponds with the transformation undergone by the other fundamental ideas of the conception of life, and an important factor are conditions in the great cities, as we see them reflected in the speeches of the prophets, which are chiefly directed against the rulers of towns like Jerusalem, Bethel and Samaria.

Also Jerusalem was at one time the home of righteousness, says Isaiah, but the old harmony has been dissolved long ago. It is a strikingly uniform picture which the prophets draw of the life in the cities. The men of wealth pile up their treasures and live a life in luxury and voluptuousness, while letting the poor starve. They make light of the old claim of justice, that the mighty shall uphold the weak; they demand everything from the poor, but give nothing. The poor are righteous, because they have an unfulfilled claim; the rich are unrighteous, because they break the law of the covenant. The whole country suffers under their unrighteousness, the herbs of the fields wither, the beasts are consumed (Jer. 12,4). The whole thing is so absurd that every one suffers except the unrighteous, who because of their unrighteousness are responsible for the misery.

But the covenant is maintained by God. How can he uphold such a community which is not a community? Like the psalmists the prophets say that it is only for a little while. The unrighteous mighty will some day collapse in their unrighteousness. But why does it last so long? This is the painful question which every Israelite asks himself. Jeremiah says: Righteous art thou, O Yahweh, when I plead with thee; yet let me talk with thee of the right. Wherefore doth the way of the wicked prosper? Wherefore are all they happy that deal very treacherously? Thou hast planted them, yea, they have taken root; they grow, yea, they bring forth fruit; thou art near in their mouth and far from their reins... Pull them out like sheep for the slaughter, and prepare them for the day of slaughter. How long shall the land mourn, and the herbs of every field wither, for the wickedness of them that dwell therein? The beasts are consumed and the birds; because they said: He doth not see our last end (Jer. 12,1-4).

Righteousness is normally a common possession. The righteousness of the man acts through the community of which he is a member, and first and foremost through the family. Here and there thoughts crop up of a dissolution of the family-unity, and then the idea of righteousness triumphs over the idea of the family. The unrighteous should himself fall in his wickedness, says Job; what does he care for his house, when he is dead (Job 21,21), for he is not a normal man. In defiance of old-Israelitic sentiments we hear Hezekiah express his joy that the misery which he introduced into the family will only take effect in his successors. Most sharply such thoughts stand out in Jeremiah and Ezekiel, who prophesy a future when it can no more be said that "the fathers have eaten sour grapes, and the children's teeth are dulled". Every man is to have a fate, closely corresponding with his own righteousness (Jer. 31,29 ff.; Ezek. 3,20; 14,14.20; 18). But these attempts to set up man as an isolated individual are quite sporadic and nowhere carried out fully.

The natural idea in old Israel was that the righteous created happiness, because God and his blessing was with him. When the mighty lost the old standard of honour and became unrighteous, an intolerable state of affairs arose, which could not last. God had to act and to give to the righteous poor the blessing which the unrighteous had taken away. When the righteous become identical with the weak, it is God who must do everything and maintain justice. Thus the social development contributes increasingly towards shifting everything from man to God.

When righteousness becomes partly a certain conduct, partly devotion to God, it must necessarily split. The old identity between the mental presuppositions and their accomplishment is in danger of being superseded. Goodness and happiness are no more two parallel manifestations of righteousness. Righteousness is no more a faculty, but a condition, and happiness becomes *reward*. This development is to be found strongly accentuated in the Yahwist; but it finds complete fulfilment in Judaism, where it is one of the characteristic fundamental features.

MAINTENANCE OF JUSTICE.

THE normal state in old Israel is that the righteous are able to maintain themselves in life. If the integrity of a man is disturbed, then it is a question whether the disturbance comes from within or from without. The worst case is when it originates in the unrighteousness of the man. If it is only a slight tainting of the soul, then it can be cured, and everything will be well again; but if the soul is utterly vitiated, then no salvation is possible. If the disturbance comes from without, and the soul is sound and righteous, then it is to be healed through the restoration. This is a claim of justice, because it is a claim for a natural growth, and behind it stands the whole of the covenant, all the positive forces of life.

The greatest infringement that can be made upon men is that they are robbed of life. If a man is killed, then life is taken away, not only from him, but also from the family with which he has life in common. This breach must be healed by life being taken from him who robbed him, and this is done by means of blood-vengeance. In the history of blood-vengeance we see an illustration of the development of the idea of justice in Israel.

The most vivid narrative of blood-vengeance we find in the Book of Judges, chap. 8. It is told how Gideon victoriously drives the attacking hosts of Midianites back across Jordan and pursues them with his men. They succeed in catching the two Midianite chiefs, Zebah and Zalmunna. When they have been brought back, Gideon addresses the following question to them: "What manner of men were they that ye slew at Tabor?" And they answered: "As thou art, so were they; each one had the presence of the children of a king." And he said: "They were my brethren, even the sons of my mother; as Yahweh liveth, if ye had saved them alive I would not slay ye."

And we read further: And he said unto Jether his first-born: "Up and slay them!" But the youth drew not the sword; for he feared, because he was yet a youth. Then Zebah and Zalmunna said: "Rise thou and fall upon us; for as the man is, so is his strength." And Gideon arose, and slew Zebah and Zalmunna, and took away the crescents that were on their camels' necks (Judg. 8, 20-21).

The impressiveness of this scene is due to the calm and precision with which question, answer and action follow upon each other. There is neither sentimentality, fear nor malignant satisfaction; both parties are agreed that whatever happens *must* happen, and no one tries to shirk.

The two Bedouins do not want to run away from their deed, on the contrary! They say with pride that they were noble-looking chiefs whom they killed; that honour they are not prepared to forgo. They know the cost of it; they have taken their honour from Gideon. They have robbed him of life by taking the lives of his brothers; in that way they have made a breach upon him, lessened him, while at the same time they themselves have grown. Under other circumstances Gideon might have set them free, but now he cannot let them go, charged with life which they have taken from him. He must take it back, and thus himself become whole once more.

Gideon first tries to get double restoration for himself by letting his son, a boy who is not yet full-grown, take their lives. Thus the boy is to win man's honour, and they are to render up their man's honour by being struck down by a boy. But they are too mighty for him, and they themselves — the slayers of chiefs — demand to fall at the hand of a chief. "As a man is, so is his strength", this presumably means that a strong man is required in order to strike down strong men. Gideon not only takes their lives, he also robs them of their valuables. All that made their greatness he makes his own.

Every feature of the narrative shows that for Gideon the essential thing was not to remove the two men. His vengeance is something positive, to appropriate something, because they have taken something from him.

The object of blood-vengeance is to heal the breach of the violated. But how much is required in order to heal the breach? To the ancients life is not something uniform, a bare "existence", it is fashioned into a greater or a lesser honour. The great has more life than the small, therefore he must have more vengeance in order to become fully restored. Gideon might be content; a greater satisfaction than the lives of the two splendid chiefs he cannot demand for his brothers. In a community where honour is the upholding element, the claim may increase to indefiniteness, and a constant balance between the parties is never obtained, because both constantly demand more vengeance. We know from the Arabians what it means when, as they say, the grinding-mill of war is set going; it often continues till there is no more grain left.

This Bedouin spirit we have been confronted with in the oldest Israel, and we have a few examples of its expression in the demand for vengeance. Lamech speaks like a true Arabian when he recites the following song before his two wives: Adah and Zillah, hear my voice; ye wives of Lamech, hearken unto my speech! for I have slain a man to my wounding and a young man to my hurt. If Cain shall be avenged sevenfold, truly Lamech seventy and sevenfold! (Gen. 4,23-24).

So mighty is Lamech that seventy-seven are required to restore the loss he suffers in one, and even his slightest wound can only be healed by a human life. Lamech does not speak as the average Israelite, such as we known him; in him the narrator undoubtedly wanted to represent the type of the border peoples in the southern parts of Canaan; and the feelings of the Yahwist who preserved this little pearl in his narratives from olden times, are surely rather horror than admiration for his swaggering hero.

The words of Lamech show that the essential feature of vengeance is not to kill life, because life has been killed. He also avenges slight hurts. Every breach of honour requires restoration through vengeance. Of this we find confirmation when we look at Samson, one of the finest representatives of what may be called the Bedouin spirit in oldest Israel.

The life of Samson is taken up with valiant deeds, the connection of which is determined by the law of vengeance. When he has bespoken a bride from among the Philistines, but hears that her father has given her to another, he says: Now I am quits with the Philistines, when I do unto them mischief! (Judg. 15,3). They have infringed upon his right and honour, and so it is righteous that he should obtain satisfaction by causing them hurt. This he does by chasing three hundred jackals with firebrands at their tails into their fields.[1] When the Philistines hear of this, they burn his wife and the house of his father.

Now once more it is the turn of Samson; a new affront has been inflicted on him, and he declares that he will not rest before he has avenged himself. He smites them "leg upon thigh" with a great slaughter. The Philistines come to his family, and he is delivered into their hands that they may "do unto him as he has done unto them" (Judg. 15,10). But Samson makes himself free, and again vengeance is his. With the jawbone of an ass he smites them right and left.

And when at last by woman's wiles the Philistines succeed in stealing the strength of Samson, they humble him by putting out his eyes and set him to the ignominious slave-work of grinding in the prison house. They increase the ignominy by dragging him out for public derision at their feasts. But Samson once more asserts himself. When his strength has returned, he asks for strength to avenge himself on the Philistines for one of his eyes (16,28). And he carries out his vengeance by breaking the pillars upon which the house stands, so that it falls upon all who were present therein, killing them as well as himself.

Samson acts in the spirit which also animates Lamech. The whole of his history shows that vengeance is restoration, the maintenance of an honour which has been infringed upon. He is so great that he cannot be content with simple retaliation, to take quantitatively what the Philistines have taken from him. His honour is only healed by great exploits; therefore the relentless sequence of vengeance becomes interminable. But the great final ignominy inflicted upon him by the Philistines, for that he cannot receive full satisfaction: all the Philistines present only compensate for his one eye. Here we see the old idea of vengeance applied to the full, the man's filling in the breach which has been made in his soul. The grand deed which terminates the life of Samson reminds us of the story told by the Arabians of Muhalhil, who killed young Bujayr ibn ʿAmr to avenge the sandal-strap of his murdered brother.

When Samson requires vengeance, it is not for manslaughter. He who takes life, takes more than physical life, because the total contents of the soul belong together, shaped in honour. Therefore it is not the physical life which is the deciding factor. Everyone who infringes upon another takes life away from him, and the violated must demand satisfaction that he may once more become whole. We have an example of this in David's relation to Shimei.

When David had to flee before Absalom, there was a man of the house of Saul, Shimei, who came running and threw stones and dust after him, all the time uttering curses against him and calling out that David was a man of blood, who was now visited by misfortune, because he bore blood-guilt for the house of Saul (2 Sam. 16). When David returned with victory, Shimei asked for mercy, and in his joy the king swore that he would not kill him (2 Sam. 19,24).

But the affront rankled in the soul of David; the curse had been laid there, and the term "man of blood" stuck to him and preyed upon him. His soul had been lessened by it; Shimei by his curse had made a breach in his life, which was not essentially different from slaughter. Only by killing the author of the curse could he make the word void and of no effect, and thus restore his soul. But how could he get satisfaction without breaking his oath? The solution of this problem he left to his son Solomon, who naturally was as much bound by the oath as David himself.

Solomon did not fail the trust of his father. He forbids Shimei to leave the precintcs of Jerusalem, adding that if he breaks the interdiction he will be killed and his blood will be on his own head. This Solomon can ordain as a king, and Shimei confirms it solemnly, even with an oath (1 Kings 2,36-38.43). Of course Solomon knows that Shimei sooner or later will break the interdiction, and then he will have him in his power. For three years he waits patiently for his vengeance; then Shimei walks into the trap.

A couple of slaves have run away, and Shimei, who is beginning to feel safe, rides out to fetch them back. Now the hour of Solomon has struck. He calls Shimei before him and points out what must be the consequence of his action, by his own oath. "And the king said to Shimei: Thou knowest all the wickedness which thine heart is privy to, that thou didst to David my father; Yahweh now returneth thy wickedness upon thine own head; but King Solomon is blessed, and the throne of David is established before Yahweh for ever. So the king commanded Benaiah, the son of Jehoiada, which went out and fell upon him that he died" (1 Kings 2,44-46).

Solomon has obtained his end. The oath of David is unbroken, and yet he has avenged himself upon his enemy. Solomon was justly renowned for his wisdom. The story shows how necessary vengeance is in order to keep the soul whole and upright.

In the narratives of Gideon and Shimei the revenge is directed against the offenders themselves. Wherever this is possible it will always be the natural proceeding, but there are also other possibilities depending upon the unity of the family. When a man is guilty of manslaughter, his whole family shares his responsibility, its life being raised or lessened through the act. Therefore the avenger takes from the life of the slayer by taking the lives of his kinsmen.

It is told (2 Sam. 21) that once during the reign of David there was a famine for three successive years. By asking Yahweh David learnt that there was a blood-guilt on the house of Saul because he had killed some Gibeonites — of which event, however, we hear nothing — and the Gibeonites, who were Amorites, had entered into a covenant with Israel. It is then told: And David said to the Gibeonites: What shall I do for you, and wherewith shall I make the atonement, that ye may bless the inheritance of Yahweh? And the Gibeonites said unto him: We will have no silver nor gold of Saul, nor of his house; neither do we claim to kill any man in Israel. [1] And he said: What ye claim that will I do for you. And they answered the king: The man that consumed us, and that devised against us — we are so destroyed that we no more can remain within the territory of Israel [2] — let seven men of his sons be delivered unto us, and we will slay them [1] before Yahweh in Gibeah of Saul whom Yahweh did choose. And the king said: I will give them. But the king spared Meribbaal, [2] the son of Jonathan, the son of Saul, because of the Yahweh-oath that was between them, between David and Jonathan, the son of Saul. But the king took the two sons of Rizpah, the daughter of Aiah, whom she bare unto Saul, Armoni and Meribbaal; and the five sons of Merab [3] the daughter of Saul, whom she bare unto Adriel the son of Barzillai the Meholathite. And he delivered them into the hands of the Gibeonites, and they slew them in the hill before Yahweh. And they fell all seven together and were put to death together in the first days of harvest, in the beginning of barley harvest (2 Sam. 21,3-9). Further it is told, impressively and beautifully, how Rizpah guards her sons against beasts and birds of prey, until David lets them be buried together with the bones of Saul and Jonathan.

This narrative shows us the strength of the demand for vengeance. It is an ethical demand, on the maintenance of which fertility and blessing depend, because it is one with justice. Not until the person violated has been restored and blesses the offender does the normal state return once more.

The Gibeonites cautiously suggest what sort of satisfaction they will not be content with: a money fine is not sufficient, nor revenge upon *other* Israelites than the responsible house. It is true that Saul as the greatest chief held a very special position. The consequence of his deed extends far beyond his own house and calls down famine over the whole of the country. But the wrong particularly centres in the house of Saul, and from this the Gibeonites demand satisfaction.

The Greek translation has a peculiar rendering of the words of the Gibeonites unto David: The man (i. e. Saul) brought ruin upon us and pursued us, let us destroy him from remaining within the whole of the territory of Israel (2 Sam. 21,5). Whether this rendering, from a philological point of view, is the very earliest text is a question apart, but at any rate it must have some sort of old tradition behind it, for it is entirely in the spirit of old Israel. Thougn Saul long ago has fallen by his own sword on the mount of Gilboa, the Gibeonites still demand *his* destruction by killing his successors, for it is his life that lives in them.

They demand seven men, and they get them. Jonathan was the son who was nearest to the father, and therefore his son is mentioned first, as the one who, properly speaking, should have paid the penalty, but he has a covenant with David, and therefore he is spared. Then there are the two sons of Rizpah, a concubine (2 Sam. 3,7), and finally the five sons of Saul's daughter. The latter are included because all possibilities must be exhausted. They belong mainly to the house of their father, Adriel, but some of the life of Saul they have in them through their mother, and all the more as the family of Saul is stronger than that of the father. By the taking of their lives and, through them, of the life of Saul they obtain satisfaction for the breach which Saul committed on them by the taking of their lives.

They are not content to rob the house of the offender of its physical life; they also humble it, strike it down, rob it of its value in life. It would be interesting to know the actual meaning of the word indicating what was done to them. So much is sure that it must have been a humiliating death, for the dead bodies are not buried, but are exposed to the mutilations of birds and wild beasts; only when David hears how the mother faithfully guards the bodies of her sons does he have them buried.

We have a single example of vengeance being taken on a tribe, in that Benjamin makes common cause with one of his towns, Gibeah, when the latter has violated an Ephraimite, who is supported by the other tribes (Judg. 19-21). But in the older narratives we hear nothing of cases of that kind. Vengeance is always claimed by the family, meaning the father's house, because there is an absolute community of life and responsibility in it.

Vengeance within the family is a contradiction in terms, and yet it may occur. We hear of it in the sinister narrative of Amnon, son of David and Ahinoam; he fell in love with Tamar, who was also the daughter of David, but had another mother, Maacah from Geshur, who was also the mother of Absalom. Feigning illness Amnon lures Tamar to his bedside, and in spite of her prayers he violates her. But presently his love turns to loathing, and he brutally chases her out of his chamber.

Tamar is left with her shame, strews ashes on her head and cries out in her pain. Her brother Absalom takes care of her and comforts her, but for the time being he does not do anything in the matter. When a couple of years have gone by, and the event is presumably consigned to oblivion, Absalom invites his brothers to a feast, and on this occasion he lets his servants kill Amnon. He flies at once to his mother's family, but is subsequently recalled (2 Sam. 13).

The deed of Absalom presupposes a certain dissolution of the peace within the family. The usual state of affairs is that the whole house is a solid unity, but with the increasing scale of life in the king's palace the feeling of unity is weakened. A tendency is developing in the direction that community only exists to the full between those who have both the same father and mother. Thus half-families are brought into the same relation with one another as otherwise whole families. This tendency appears in the possibility of a marriage between half-brothers and half-sisters, which possibility forms the very presupposition of our narrative (v. 13), and it may thus also lead to the possibility of blood-vengeance.

And yet it cannot go further than a tendency. The division of the father's house is absurd, because all the sons have the life of the father in them, and it never became a rule in Israel that half-brothers avenged themselves upon each other. The very idea is unnatural. A man cannot take life away from his half-brother without taking it from himself. It also proves in this case that the vengeance cannot be acknowledged, and Absalom is bound to fly.

Fratricide can never become vengeance in the usual sense of the word; it is the principle of vengeance degenerated. But of course a conflict can spring up within a family, and then it is the duty of the father of the house to re-establish peace. Amnon's violation of Tamar is of such a serious nature that David, properly speaking, should have thrown him out of the family; this is also hinted at in the old translations of the Hebrew texts, which read as follows: When King David heard of this, he was very wrath; but he did not vex the spirit of his son Amnon; for he loved him, because he was his first-born (2 Sam. 13,21). David thus showed undue weakness towards his son.

The matter is more fully elucidated by the story of the manner in which Joab managed to get Absalom recalled. Towards him David first showed due firmness; he did not permit the return of Absalom to the family, the peace of which he had violated by slaying his brother. Then Joab sent a woman to David and made her tell him a story (2 Sam. 14). She was a widow, she said, and had two sons, who quarrelled with each other, with the result that the one lost his life. Now the family came to the fore and demanded the deliverance of the slayer in order that they might avenge the brother by slaying him, but in reality in order to remove the heir and possess themselves of the property of her husband, their deceased kinsman. In this manner the name of her husband would be exterminated, and the widow implores the king to help her, which he also promises to do.

After the king has given his promise, the woman exclaims: My lord, O king, the iniquity be on me, and on my father's house, and the king and his throne be guiltless (v. 9). The king then understands that she refers to Absalom.

The words of the woman imply an acknowledgment of the danger incurred by receiving the slayer of a brother into the family, but on the other hand his expulsion is not a pure demand for vengeance. The claim of the relatives is only a pretence in order to get the young man out of the way. There is thus some uncertainty; the slaying of the fratricide is not necessary from the point of view of vengeance, and cannot be so from the Israelitic conception of the family, as long as vengeance is restoration. But when it is at all possible that, in such a case as this, there can be a question of vengeance, we already here find a suggestion of the existence of other elements in the idea of vengeance than those implied by the old principle of restoration. Wherein they consist we shall see later on.

The history of David presents us with another example of a different kind, where the claim for blood-vengeance clashes with the covenant. When Abner had killed Asahel in order to free himself of the ignominy of being vanquished by the younger man, Joab, the brother of Asahel, got a claim of vengeance on him. However, he did not redeem it at once, but went away, apparently in peace. Some time afterwards Abner came to Hebron with twenty men, offering David his service and with it the kingdom of Saùl. They concluded a covenant, and had a meal together, whereupon Abner departed. Shortly afterwards Joab came, and when he heard what had taken place, he caused Abner to be brought back. Pretending that he wanted to speak to him quietly, he took him aside in the gate, and smote him there under the fifth rib "for the blood of Asahel, his brother" (2 Sam. 3,27).

The strange thing about this narrative is that Joab should reserve his vengeance for such a long time. We have already seen how there was sufficient ground for the deed of Abner; but its inevitable consequence must be the vengeance of Joab. Only when new factors make themselves felt, i. e. the fear of being superseded by Abner, Joab enforces his claim and even carries it out in a cunning and wily manner. But at that time the claim of Joab was not legitimate. Abner was at peace with David, and so also with Joab; in view of this peace all the men of David must suspend their claims of vengeance. Joab "laid blood in peace", and in its character his deed came near to fratricide. That it was really looked upon in that light, appears from the anxiety shown by David on his deathbed, that the guilt of Joab should take effect. Thus the claim of vengeance is not absolute; it is circumscribed by peace and cannot be carried out at the cost of the covenant established by one's lord. The consequence must then be that David should remove Joab as he later on removed Absalom; but also in this case David shirked the consequence.

Vengeance is first and foremost the claim of justice on the part of the person offended. If he is killed, then his blood cries for restoration from the ground, as it is said of Abel (Gen. 4,10). As long as it is uncovered by the earth, so long its claim sounds, it is "remembered". Therefore Job, who feels that he has unjustly been sent to death, asks that the earth may not cover his blood (16,18). Ezekiel threatens the inhabitants of Jerusalem that their blood shall come down into the earth, and be no more remembered (Ezek. 21,37), whereas, conversely, the blood they have shed shall lie upon the top of a rock without being covered, that it may be avenged (Ezek. 24,7, cf. Is. 26,21). Even as late as the time of the Maccabees we hear Jude and his fellows calling upon God to listen to the blood crying unto him (2 Mac. 8,3). The dead moans under injustice. His blood, his soul cries for restoration. Only vengeance is able to restore him, because it makes him righteous once more, and thus he gets peace.

Vengeance, *nāḳām,* is restoration *taken*[1] by the offended; he gets vengeance *from*[2] or *with*[3] the offender, just as it is said that the blood of the slain is *demanded* from the slayer.[4] One avenges, i. e. restores the blood which is shed[5] or the violated limb,[6] in that the injured person, by getting some of the life of the other, restores the loss he has suffered in his own honour.

Vengeance always has this connotation of self-maintenance, viz. the maintenance of honour, *ḳin'ā* (Prov. 6,34). The warrior obtains "vengeance" of his enemies when he conquers.[7] The victorious king performs acts of vengeance in reducing nations to his sway. David says that Yahweh will give him vengeance of Saul, thus implying that he is to be re-established, to prove victorious in the conflict between them, just as Jeremiah hopes that Yahweh will let him get the vengeance of his enemies which they hope to get of him.

He who gets vengeance breathes again, gets satisfaction, *niḥḥam.*[8] Even the old word for vengeance may sometimes be changed so that it only means this passion, hostility and hatred, and then the "avenger" actually becomes the passionate, spiteful enemy.[9] The sweetness of revenge is well known in Israel. "The righteous rejoiceth, he seeth the vengeance; he washeth his feet in the blood of the wicked" (Ps. 58,11), and when some day Yahweh is going to take full vengeance, then it will be to him an "acceptable year" (Is. 61,2).

Vengeance is the real restoration of the violated. His name has been lessened, his righteousness has been infringed upon, but the name revives when vengeance is done. If he can, then he must undertake the vengeance himself, like Lamech or Samson. But more frequently he is killed and cannot avenge himself, and then his kin intervenes. Just as the act of the offender rests upon the whole of his house, in the same manner the offence also falls upon the whole house and kin of the stricken person. [1] It is an exception when the family of Samson agree to deliver him into the hands of his enemies. The normal practice is that the whole of the kin share in the claim for vengeance, because it shares in the breach brought about by the act. The claim of the Gibeonites on the kin of Saul shows that also a town might claim vengeance.

In the olden time two families stand against each other in the vengeance; the one has taken something from the other, and the injured party is healed by taking something back. The man through whom the offended family acts is called the *gō'ēl,* and with him we are already acquainted; it is he who is to take over the property after his nearest of kin, when it is in danger of passing out of the family, or has already been lost, and to all intents and purposes it is also he who, through the Levirate marriage, is to secure the name of the man who has died without male issue. Thus he is the upholder of the family, its restorer. His task as an avenger is of exactly the same kind: he restores the name of the offended, and thus maintains the family of which he himself is a member.

The avenger is usually the son (e. g. Solomon, Amaziah) or the brother (Gideon, Joab); but he is always the nearest of kin. We know the order of succession: son, brother, father's brother, son of father's brother, etc. (Lev. 25,48 f.; Num. 27,10 f.). They step in, each in his turn; if the nearest fails, then the next takes his place. Where kinship ends, there is no longer an avenger. The lonely and kinless is like the accursed: anyone who comes across him may slay him. During his sedition Zimri deliberately exterminates the *whole* of the house of Baasha: he left him no kinsman *(rē'a)* and no avenger *(gō'ēl),* it is expressly stated (1 Kings 16,11). From that family he has no more to fear; only he did not take into account that there might be others who had the same ambition as himself, and this was what proved his bane.

The restorer is to intervene whenever the family is degraded and loses life. It may happen in the case of a brother becoming so poor that not only is he unable to maintain his property, but he must even go into slavery. Thus he drops out of the family; he has lost his freeman's honour, and also degraded the others, and he has passed into another family, the life and honour of which he must serve.

If he must deliver himself into the hands of one of his own people it is not so bad. In that case the "Law of Holiness" does not mention any obligations on the part of the restorer, while enforcing upon the master of the degraded that he must not treat him as a slave, but as a hired servant and client *(gēr),* and in the year of *yōbhēl* he shall be free (Lev. 25,35-43). If, on the other hand, the fall is so great that he must go into slavery, then the restorer must come to his rescue. Of this we read:

And if a *gēr* and client wax prosperous by thee, and thy brother that dwelleth with him wax poor, and sell himself unto such a *gēr* and client by thee, or to the dependents of a *gēr*'s family, then after that he has sold himself restoration *(ge'ullā)* must be made unto him; one of his brethren shall restore him, or his father's brother or the son of his father's brother shall restore him, or any other of his flesh, of his family shall restore him; or if he wax prosperous, then he may restore himself. Then he shall reckon the days with him that bought him, from the year that he was sold to him unto the year of *yōbhēl,* and the price of his purchase shall be reckoned, less the number of years he has served; his stay with him is to be reckoned in the same manner as the working days of a hired labourer. If there be yet many years left, according unto them he shall pay, as the price of his restoration, part of the sum that he was bought for. And if there remain but few years unto the year of *yōbhēl,* then that shall be reckoned to him; and according to the number of years he has served, he shall pay the price of his restoration, and as a yearly hired servant shall he be with him, the latter not ruling with vigour over him in thy sight. And if he be not restored in any of these ways, then he shall go out in the year of *yōbhēl,* both he and his children with him (Lev. 25,47-54).

The fundamental ideas of this law express the conception of life in Old Israel. The man is not to be upheld mechanically in the position he occupies, unless he is able to maintain it. But he must not go down entirely; it is the duty of the family to re-establish him, and this obligation rests with the nearest of kin. [1] The point of gravity is in the family; the object is its prosperity, but the responsibility for the latter lies with itself. The various families stand over against each other, giving and taking *inter se* and balancing each other; thus they manifest their righteousness. If a family takes too much from another, then the latter maintains its righteousness by getting satisfaction and re-establishing the equilibrium. It is at the same time the right and duty of the restorer to intercede, because he maintains himself while maintaining the family. If the family does not put forth claims, because it has not the strength to do so, then the claim drops, and the family is doomed. The basis of the law of restoration is throughout realistic, because it is the very instinct of preservation of the family that is its driving power.

The law of restoration belongs in a community which is not held together by external powers above it, but by inner forces creating the harmony. We find it in its typical form with the Arabians. The restoration is not regulated by mechanical laws; every tribe must take as much as is required, in order that its breach may be healed. Through the law of equilibrium the balance is maintained, and vengeance is the maintenance of the law.

Together with the law of restoration we find with the Israelites quite a different principle in the *law of retaliation,* which is clearly expressed in the well-known claim: Life for life, eye for eye, tooth for tooth, hand for hand, foot for foot, burning for burning, wound for wound, stripe for stripe, scar for scar, scratch for scratch (Exod. 21,23-25, cf. Deut. 19,21; Lev. 24,20). The law of retaliation does not place the point of gravity in the offended and his claim to have a breach healed. The point of gravity lies outside or, rather, above both parties, in a power maintaining justice for its own sake. Every action which deviates from the right must be balanced; it is just as necessary for the sake of justice that he who commits injustice should suffer a loss, as that he who suffers an unjust loss should receive satisfaction. Because the actions cannot be judged from within, they are measured and judged from a purely quantitative point of view, not according to what they signify in the totality of the two parties, but with their starting point in a third power, before which the parties must bend. The law of retaliation presupposes the legal state, which regulates all the acts of its citizens, and through this regulation maintains the idea of justice and so also itself. The free display of the forces, the unlimited right to take in accordance with one's power which characterizes a community like that of the Arabians, must, in the legal state, necessarily be replaced by artificial limitation and mechanical uniformity in the rights of the citizens.

It is the Babylonian legal state which most clearly carried out the principle of retaliation, and this principle forms the basis of Hammurabi's law. There is every probability that the principles of this law which we also find in the Assyrian Code, have been at work in Western Asia, and that, through the kindred Amorites, they have imbued West-Asiatic town-life. In any case Israel has adopted them, and one of its codes, the Book of Covenant (particularly Exod. 21) is entirely determined by the principle of retaliation. How much this code depends on Babylonian legal conception as represented in Hammurabi's law becomes clear from a comparison. The very formulation of the basic law: life for life, eye for eye, etc., agrees partly *verbatim* with the words of Hammurabi. The Hittites follow another principle, claiming restoration, not by blood, but by deliverance of four persons for freemen, two for slaves. [1]

It is the principle of restoration which has its root in old Israel; it corresponds with the construction of the whole organism, but the law of retaliation is taken up, runs parallel with the old law and is assimilated by it. Its foreign origin appears from the absence of its presupposition, i. e. the legal state; therefore it has never been possible to carry it out entirely in Israel.

The transformation of Israel, accomplished through its history, touched the very root of the old idea of restoration, and thus the assimilation of the principle of retaliation was furthered. This appears in the limitation of the claim for vengeance. How much vengeance may a man claim? The greater the honour, the more, according to the old conception, he must have in order to be healed. But with Israel in general, honour is prosperity and wealth, not the violent exertion in the deed of fighting man; the unsteady balance, the eternal rivalry which vengeance creates among the Arabians is intolerable to the Israelite. Vengeance is not so much a claim of honour as a claim of justice, resting in God before whom all are small; no one can arrogantly make himself great and take the law into his own hands. In later Israel this may lead to the thought that man is not to take vengeance, but to leave it to God, who will do it all the more thoroughly.[1] This fear of passing beyond the goal is in harmony with the meting out of the law of retaliation: life for life, eye for eye, etc.

The same fundamental thought leads to another consideration of the offender than the one implied in the law of restoration. The Arabian, it is true, can blame the perpetrator of violence, but it is a question between him and the violated only. If no claim is made on the offender, then there is an end to the whole affair, because the claim for restoration rests entirely with the tribe violated. With the Israelite justice rests in God; it is a claim above both parties, and for the sake of righteousness it is as essential that he who has committed an unjust action loses what he has taken in excess, as it is needful that he who has lost too much gets it back. Thus vengeance becomes two-edged, not only a restoration, as with the Arabians, but the reaction of the unrighteous act as in the law of retaliation. The offended "leads vengeance back" *(yāshībh)* to the offender (Gen. 50,15; Deut. 32,43, cf. 41). But this reaction is not purely mechanical; it is a consequence which injustice — in accordance with its essence — demands, or, rather, a complement that it may become whole.

Retaliation is frequently expressed by the verbal roots *shlm* and *gml,* both meaning totality. The former is already well known to us;[2] the latter means to get ready, ripe, whole (Is. 18,5), possibly "make ripe" (Num. 17,23), but generally to perform an action which either in itself is a complement or by its nature requires a complement. It thus partly denotes an action which is retribution, and partly an action which requires retribution, whether it be an act of charity or an act of violence; it is often difficult to distinguish if it is the one or the other.[1] When the word *g^emūl* is applied to vengeance (Is. 35,4), then it is evidence that vengeance is not only a claim with the avenger, but a necessary consequence of the unjust action itself.

Thus the inner development of the Israelites tends towards the assimilation of the extraneous principle of retaliation. But the Babylonian theory of retaliation they never carried out entirely, because they have no authority above them to take the full accomplishment of justice into its hands. Retaliation becomes a claim on the part of the violated, a definitely apportioned restoration. The old principle of restoration also has a negative side, viz. to strike him down in whom the wrong originates, to free oneself of him in whom one's misfortune is seated; Shimei is to be put to death, because the curse and the violation which he has laid into David has its root in him. In the law of retaliation this is regulated in the direction of the offender losing what he has taken. It is a kind of negative restoration for the injured. The offender has lessened the other, and now himself is to be made just as small. Instead of the positive object of the old law, i. e. that the righteous is to be made whole, stress is laid on the opposite, i. e. that the unrighteous is to be broken. In later Israel we feel a good deal of the exultation of the weak, when seeing that he who has raised himself above him is made weak like himself, nay, even weaker.

The peculiar mixture of Arabian and Babylonian types which Israel represents, expresses itself in the *law of manslaughter* and other injury. In the Book of Covenant it is ordained: He that smiteth a man, so that he die, shall be surely put to death. And if a man hath not done it purposely, God having led his hand, then I will appoint thee a place, whither he shall flee. But if a man act presumptuously against his neighbour, to slay him deliberately, thou may take him from mine altar, that he may die (Exod. 21, 12-14).

Here a distinction is made between deliberate murder and manslaughter, just as in the Hittite Code, where it is expressed in exactly the same terms. In the former case the law of retaliation inexorably demands that the perpetrator of the deed is to be killed; even from the altar he is to be dragged away. In the second case no penalty has been settled, as in the Hittite Code, which claims the delivery of the corpse and of two persons (half the penalty for deliberate murder), but he can flee to the sanctuary. [1] Now the question is: Who shall slay the slayer and possibly drag him away from the altar? There can be no doubt that it is *gō'ēl,* the avenger. He kills the slayer, and if the latter has reached the holy place, they are able to negotiate, and the guilty then does not need to leave the sheltering altar before the account is settled, as was the case with Adonijah (1 Kings 1,51).

This is confirmed by the other groups of laws. In the Deuteronomy it is ordained that three cities are to be selected in the land of Israel, that slayers may flee there (chap. 19; cf. 4,41-43). It may happen when people hew wood in the forest, and the head flies off from one man's axe and kills his comrade, then "he shall flee unto one of those cities and live, lest the avenger of blood pursue the slayer, while his heart is hot, and overtake him, because the way is long (to the sanctuary) and slay him; whereas he was not worthy of death, inasmuch as he hated him not in time past" (Deut. 19,5-6). "But if any man hate his neighbour, and lie in wait for him, and rise up against him, and smite him mortally that he die, and fleeth into one of these cities, then the elders of his city shall send and fetch him thence, and deliver him into the hand of the avenger of blood, that he may die. Thine eye shall not pity him, but thou shalt put away the guilt of innocent blood from Israel, that it may go well with thee" (Deut. 19,11-13).

The new feature of this law is the establishment of special cities of refuge, which regulation was made necessary by the simultaneous removal — ordained by the same law — of the many sanctuaries scattered about the country. The Priestly Code follows the same line (Num. 35,9-29; Josh. 20), though yielding a few more details. Six cities of refuge are established, three on each side of Jordan. The case of the fugitive must be examined and decided through witnesses, no fewer than two. [2] If he is found not guilty, then he may live in the city of refuge. It is a matter of course that only there does he enjoy protection; if he leaves the refuge, the avenger may kill him. On the other hand, he may return unhindered when the high priest of that period dies (Num. 35,28; Josh. 20,6), which regulation seems to signify that guilt is annulled on this occasion.

Nearly on a level with manslaughter is the stealing of human beings (for slavery); in that case the law ordains death for the evil-doer (Exod. 21,16; Deut. 24,7). The Hittite Code treats the same case, but, according to the principle of this code, the evil-doer is not killed, but is to give ample restitution, curiously enough ampler than in a case of murder (I 19 a. b.).

Thus the laws on one hand circumscribe vengeance, on the other hand they confirm it as a necessary retaliation. Between the offender and the offended a higher power intervenes, viz. the authorities of the city, though not like the authorities of the state of Hammurabi. It is not they who carry out justice, they only are to regulate it by establishing and upholding it. Retaliation is the just claim of the restorer and is accomplished by him, the slayer being delivered unto him.

It is not as in the olden time, when it rested with the family itself how much it would demand for a violation. In case a man is slain, nothing less than the life of the slayer can satisfy. This is demanded by the law of retaliation. The law which is called "life for life" holds such an important place in the Priestly Code that it is put before all others; it dates from the new order of things after the deluge. Man may kill beasts, but "surely the blood of your own souls will I require; from all living things will I require it, and from the men mutually [1] will I demand the soul of man. Whoso sheddeth man's blood, for [2] the man (i. e. the slain) shall his blood be shed; for in the image of Elohim made he man" (Gen. 9,4-6).

Blood-vengeance *shall* be accomplished. What, for instance, the Gibeonites considered a divine right against Saul, becomes by the law of retribution first and foremost a duty, not only towards the avenger himself, but, before all, towards a just order of things resting in God. It is expressly forbidden (Num. 35,31 f.) to settle a matter of that kind with a fine. Life is to be atoned for with life. From a still later period we have the claims of the Book of Jubilees (21,19 f., cf. 7,33): "Take no gift for the blood of man, that it is not to be shed unexpiated, without punishment; for the blood which is shed maketh the earth sin, and the earth cannot be cleansed of the blood of man except by his blood who shed it. And take no gift and no satisfaction for the blood of man. Blood for blood, that thou mayest be acceptable to the Lord, the supreme God." Here the last stage is reached, and every thought of the avenger vanishes. The retaliation is in itself demanded because of the very action; unrighteous manslaughter is *sin,* and this point of view is emphasized at the cost of all others.

Thus one of the pillars of the old blood-vengeance collapsed, i. e. the restoration of the violated; and, furthermore, attempts were made to overturn the other: the common co-responsibility of the family. It is ordained in the Deuteronomy: The fathers shall not be put to death for the children, neither shall the children be put to death for the fathers. Every man shall be put to death for his own sin (24,16).

This law, which is to annul the unity of the family and make the family crumble away into individuals, has been respected in spite of its radical tendency (2 Kings 14,6). It follows currents which made themselves felt through the metropolitan life developing in Jerusalem; but it is presumably also a consequence of the idea of retaliation. However, neither the Deuteronomy nor the contemporary Jeremiah nor the somewhat later Ezekiel have been able to carry out the revolutionary idea. The Deuteronomy only abandons solidarity where it is a question of guilt, not as far as the claim is concerned. The blood-avenger, the nearest of kin, still acts as in former times, though no evil has befallen him.

The Priestly Code and the Book of Jubilees dismiss the idea of penalty in the case of manslaughter, but the sharp wording of the very prohibition shows that the thought did not lie beyond their horizon. The Gibeonites refused to take silver or gold in satisfaction (2 Sam. 21,4), but also this is evidence that a fine has been taken for a life, even if it were held in lower estimate. It would also be striking if Israel should not have acknowledged a satisfaction of this kind, before it was prevented by the demands of the law of retribution and the fear of sin; it plays a great part among the Arabians and other peoples, where the claims of honour are much greater than in Israel. When the slayer fled to the refuge and began to negotiate with the violated, then it was surely the rule that the point of issue between them was settled with a fine. Where it is not a question of manslaughter, mention is, on several occasions, made of fines.

When Abimelech had violated Abraham by taking Sarah away from him, he tried to expiate his offence by sending to Abraham a great gift, consisting of cattle, slaves and slave-women. On sending away Sarah he says: "I have given thy brother a thousand shekels of silver; behold, it is to thee a covering of the eyes, regarding any claim set forth by thee and everybody, and thus thy case is settled" (Gen. 20,16). [1]

The substitution of a penal sum for blood-vengeance fits into the old conception of vengeance as an act of restoration, the loss of the offended being made good by a gift. It is true that the gift is not so much as a human life, but that it contains life and is more than a material satisfaction, of that we have sufficient evidence. By the fine the offended is satisfied; he abandons his claim. It is this which Abimelech expresses by saying that it is a covering for the eyes of Sarah, and of course also of Abraham. The wronged no more sees the offence; it does not exist for him. The usual denomination of such a penalty is *kōpher,* and this always denotes a gift which makes the receiver abandon a reasonable claim. [2] The fine makes the wronged give up his claim.

The penalty often implies that it makes the violated renounce a higher claim. It is said of the owner of a goring bull which has killed a man, that "if there be laid upon him a sum of money, then he shall give for the ransom of his soul whatsoever is laid upon him" (Exod. 21,30). "Ransom", *pidyōn,* is a term applied to the redemption of a slave. [3] The violated has acquired a claim on the life of the owner, in that his bull has caused manslaughter; but he may generously content himself with a gift of a reasonable size.[1] Thus the consideration of the psychical restoration of the violated plays a part also in the Book of Covenant, which is permeated with the law of retribution.

The laws of the Book of Covenant dealing with bodily injuries are stamped in the main by the spirit of Hammurabi, but modified according to Israelitic presuppositions (Exod. 21). The basic law is retaliation, and it must be understood that if a man inflicts bodily harm on another, the law entitles the person offended to destroy the corresponding limb of the offender. The law of retaliation even refers to animals. An ox which gores a man so that he die is to be stoned (Exod. 21,28). There is a distinct difference between these laws and the Hittite Code, where all kinds of bodily injury are atoned for by fixed fines; but in some special cases the three codes agree, and then it is not possible to decide if the Israelitic law is most influenced by the Babylonian (Amorite) or by the Hittite view.

Of men fighting each other it is said: If men strive together and one smite another with a stone, or with his fist,[2] and he die not, but keepeth his bed — if he rise again, and walk abroad upon his staff, then shall he that smote him be quit; only he shall pay for the loss of his time, and shall cause him to be thoroughly healed (Exod. 21,18-19). This law is Babylonian and Hittite. Hammurabi ordains that if two men fight, and the one strikes the other and takes an oath that it was done unintentionally, then he is to pay the physician (§ 206). In the Hittite Code the perpetrator of violence must in the same case pay the physician and a fine of 6 shekels, and find a substitute for him as long as he is unable to work (I 10). There is no question of psychic restoration in the old-Israelitic sense of the word, nor of a psychical balance between the two parties, but only of a certain compensation; how far removed are we here from Lamech, who claims a man for a wound and a boy for a hurt!

If men strive and hurt a woman with child, so that the fruit depart from her, and yet no other mischief follow, he shall pay a fine. The amount of the fine is fixed by the woman's husband

(Exod. 21,22); but it must of course be in accordance with reasonable requirements, i. e. custom, and this is presumably expressed in the following obscure words. [1] The priests were the natural guides in such cases (Deut. 21,5). Also this law is Babylonian and Hittite. The law of Hammurabi ordains, like the Sumerian law, that if a man strike another man's daughter who is with child, so that the child is killed, then he must pay ten shekels for it if she is a Patrician (§ 209), five if she is a Plebeian and two shekels if she is a slave (§§ 211.213). Also with the Hittites the evil-doer is fined ten shekels if the woman is free, and delivery is imminent; if in the sixth month, the fine is five shekels only. For slave-women half the fine is paid (I 17.18). With the Assyrians the evil-doer may be killed for manslaughter when the husband of the woman has no son; if the foetus is of female sex, he shall make full restitution for human life. [2] The particularly Israelitic feature of the law of Exodus is that the man himself determines the fine; it is not fixed by law. So his satisfaction and restoration are not thrown wholly into the background.

The law does not say what will happen if the woman dies; in Hammurabi's law retaliation in such a case takes the following course: the daughter of the slayer is to be killed if the slain is the wife of a Patrician (§ 210, cf. 230 f.; if her husband is a Plebeian, the evil-doer is fined with half a mine), and it is commonly expressed that the same must have held good in Israel. But this is not likely. According to the Deuteronomy it cannot be the case, as it is opposed to individual retaliation (Deut. 24,16). But the Book of Covenant also considers the law of retaliation in a different manner, which appears from the above-mentioned law of a bull in the habit of goring. If it kills a man or a woman, not only it, but also its owner is to be killed, and the same holds good if it kills their son or their daughter (Exod. 21,28-31). This shows that the law of retaliation is not carried out so mechanically and abstractly in Israel as in Babylonia. The Israelites put stress on the guilt, the injustice, directing themselves against its source, the responsible man, and, on the other hand, the point of view of restoration holds good to a certain extent. In the above-mentioned case the law of retaliation therefore comes into effect against the evil-doer himself, as in Assyria, where he is killed (§ 48). But in Israel the matter may have been decided by a fine, and this is always the case when the person slain is a slave (Exod. 21,32). The fine is thirty shekels.

If it is a question of slaying or damage done to a slave, Hammurabi demands satisfaction of his value for the master (§ 116), just as in the law of Israel (Exod.21,32). Hammurabi does not reckon with the slaying of one's own slave. The Hittites in this case claim half the fine of that fixed for freemen. In Israel "it is invariably to be avenged" if a man slays his slave or his slave-woman on the spot (Exod. 21,20). But who is to avenge it? It must be a question of an Israelitic slave, whose kin may claim a penalty. If the slave or the slave-woman dies only after some days, it is not manslaughter, and the vengeance drops. This shows that the Israelites have applied the law of retaliation with particular strength in the case of actual slaying. The shedding of blood is so terrible that it must be avenged; it creates guilt. Otherwise a slave has certain claims on his master. If the master strikes the eye of his slave or smites out a tooth, then he shall go free "for" the damaged limb (Exod. 21,26-27). This is his restoration.

We have already seen how the restorer must maintain the property of the family, just as he maintains their lives. This old Israelitic conception of property and its close relation to man is reflected in the law, where to move boundaries of the landed property of one's neighbour is strictly forbidden, and is mentioned among the great sins which call down the curse upon him who commits it (Deut. 19,14; 27,17). But in the chief part of the laws concerning property we find a different spirit. This spirit is in the main not that of Hammurabi. In Hammurabi's laws the right of property is maintained with such strength that death almost becomes the normal manner of dealing with the thief. [1] Of the Assyrians we know how they treated the man who annexed a large piece of his neighbour's field: he should give three times the field that he had appropriated, one of his fingers should be cut off, he should receive 100 lashes and for one month do "royal service". [2] Even here the reaction against the thief is very strong. As said above, the Israelites also condemned this kind of theft very severely. But the main principle of their laws about theft and other encroachment upon the property of the neighbour is that of *ample restitution.* This is found in some few cases with Hammurabi, while it is the main principle of the Hittite Code.

Strange to say, the dealing with theft of animals and chattels is milder in Canaan than in Asia Minor. When breaking into a house or barn a free man, among the Hittites, must replace that which he has stolen, and further pay 12 shekels silver (older law: one mine); a slave must pay 6 shekels (1, 95-98). The Book of Covenant in the same case demands restitution without stating how much; if the thief cannot pay, he shall be sold for his theft. If the theft takes place in the day, the slaying of the thief comes under the heading of blood-guilt. Only at night is it permitted to kill the thief (Exod. 22,1-2). In certain cases double restitution is required (Exod. 22,6).

If an ox, an ass or a sheep has been stolen and is found with the thief, it is, according to the Book of Covenant, to be restored together with an animal of the same kind. If the stolen animal is not found, the thief is to make good the ox fivefold, the sheep fourfold (Exod. 21,37; 22,3, cf. 1 Sam. 12,3). Curiously enough Hammurabi, in the case of domestic animals, adopted the rule of ample restitution, in that he demands thirty- or tenfold satisfaction (§ 8) and the thief is only to be slain in case he does not pay — but this exception would rather have been the rule. Also in the case of thefts of watering implements in the field Hammurabi is content with restitution (§§ 259-260). The severe Assyrians claim the deliverance of the stolen animals, fine the thief, give him 50 lashes and let him do royal service for some time. [1] The Hittite Code makes the same distinction as the law of Israel: A stolen ox, horse, mule or ass which is found in the possession of the thief is to be restored together with three others. Stolen animals which are not found the thief must replace, giving: for one ox, fifteen oxen; for one plough-ox, ten; for one horse, fifteen; for one sow, six; for one ram, fifteen head of small cattle; for a sheep or a buck, six. At an older period the number of animals to be given was on an average twice as great (I, 58-70). The Hittite Code contains a detailed list of fines for all kinds of theft (I 92 f. II 1-3.8.10 ff.).

The Israelitic law applies the principle of restitution in the following cases: If an animal falls into an uncovered cistern the owner must substitute another animal for the one perished, the carcass of which he is then allowed to keep (Exod. 21,33-34). A similar law also seems to be found with the Hittites (II, 35-37). If a man's ox gore another man's ox, and it dies, the owner of the former, if it was apt to gore, must make full restitution. Otherwise they are to divide the value of the two oxen (Exod. 21,35-36). A somewhat similar rule is to be found in Hammurabi's law (§§ 251-252).

Double satisfaction is demanded for property delivered on trust if it be lost, unless it can be proved by oath that it has been stolen; in that case the thief is to give double satisfaction (Exod. 22,6-8). So also Hammurabi (§§ 124-126, cf. Law of the Assyrians § 96), with whom the keeper always bears the responsibility and, possibly, must indemnify himself with the thief. This rule also holds good in Israel in the case of cattle. He who has received cattle on trust must make restitution for what is missing, even if it has been stolen. If, on the other hand, it is carried off by beasts of prey, or is lost in a similar way, the keeper of it is free, if he can prove his case (Exod. 22,9-12, cf. Am. 3,12). So also Hammurabi (§§ 266-267). Similar rules of responsibility prevail among the Hittites (I 46.61-63.76-79).

Rules of the same kind apply to him who borrows or hires an animal (Exod. 22,13-14), and here the law of the Israelites agrees with that of the Babylonians (Cod. Ham. §§ 244-249) and the Hittites (I 76).

In a special case we clearly see the Hittite law behind that of the Israelites. It is ordained (Exod. 22,4-5): If a man shall cause a field or a vineyard to be eaten off, and then shall leave hold of his cattle, and it shall graze in another man's field, the best of his own field and the best of his own vineyard, shall he give as a restitution. — If fire break out, and catch in thorns, so that the stacks of corn, or the standing corn, or the field, be consumed, he that kindled the fire shall make restitution for it. — Cod. Ham. does not take these special cases into account, but, it is true, others suggesting them, i. e. damage caused by water on the field of the neighbour by one who has not been careful with the bank of his canal, or by a shepherd making his sheep feed off the field of a neighbour. In both cases restitution is demanded in corn (§§ 53-58). The Hittites, on the other hand, have in their law exact parallels to the ordinances of the Hebrew Code, the content of which is the following: If a man makes fire on his field, and it catches the field of another man, the man who kindled the fire shall take over the burned field and instead of it yield up a good field, which he is bound to sow (II 6). Further: If a man leaves his sheep to run into the vineyard of another man, and they damage it, he shall pay 10 shekels per Kan, but in certain cases 5 (or even 3) shekels.[1]

The laws regulating the reparation of encroachments upon property and life and body clearly show the influence exercised on Israel by the foreign culture which they met with in Canaan. The genuine Israelitic conception is that every injury of this kind is an encroachment upon the honour of the family and must be restored by the latter. As for property, this principle has been maintained to the largest extent by the Arabians, with whom the infringement of property is always a breach of honour demanding satisfaction; and this close connection between man and property is still recognized by the eastern Semites, who react violently against every encroachment on property. In some special cases we are able to trace the influence of the eastern culture in the Israelitic laws about property; but upon the whole the Hittite influence has been more important in this respect. There can be no doubt that their view has contributed towards disintegrating the old Israelitic intimate conception of property.

As to injury of life and body, the Hittite influence is also to be traced in special cases. But on this point the Babylonian spirit exercised the greatest influence in Canaan. When comparing the laws on this point with the Israelitic documents, the conflict between two principles becomes evident, i. e. between restoration and retaliation. This conflict, however, is not an open one; the two principles act together and upon each other, with the result that many new nuances are created. And yet two entirely different types of society are to be traced behind them, which types we find clearly expressed, partly in the Arabian tribal organization, partly in the Babylonian state, and which compete with each other within Israel. The former could not maintain itself under the settled conditions and against the foreign influences at work; nor could Israel mould itself entirely on the other type, because a State-organization was never carried through in Israel as in Babylonia; but the imperial idea came to play a very great part in the development of the Israelitic conception.

The abstract Babylonian conception of right presupposes a solidly organized civil service, which represents the legal state and maintains it by passing sentences and carrying them out. An organization of this kind is not to be found in Israel; therefore the Israelitic *judicial proceedings* never had an established character. Litigations only concern the two parties, but the matter is frequently too complicated for them to decide alone; it should be decided justly, viz. according to the Israelitic tradition. On one hand the offence might be undefined, on the other the offended might be unable to obtain restoration unaided.

Unfortunately we cannot form any clear picture of the judicial procedure. It has generally been connected with the sanctuary. If a crime, e. g. a theft, had been committed without the criminal being known, then a curse was pronounced on him before the altar (1 Kings 8,31), but it might also be freely pronounced anywhere else (Judg. 17,2; Prov. 29,24). As a rule, however, there are two parties, viz. the accuser and the person accused, and they plead their cause before the priest, that he may determine justice for both of them. In one place mention is made of written bills of indictment (Job 31,35), but this has hardly been the rule, and it does not preclude that the manner of proceeding in all cases has been by word of mouth.

The procedure thus does not rest on external compulsion, but on the acknowl^dgment of all parties that it is the right which is to be pursued. And right is not something outside man; the question is who has the right within himself, so that he has the presupposition to maintain it. Therefore the external evidence does not play the principal part. The old means of proof is the *oath*. He who swears puts the whole of the substance and strength of his soul into the words he speaks; he concentrates himself entirely on his cause and strains himself to the utmost. If he be just, then his soul may also bear this tension and carry through its cause. If he has spoken untrue, then his soul which has centred entirely in falsehood, is wasted from within and dissolves; he must be struck down by misfortune.

In the olden time we must imagine the whole family as standing behind each of the parties; the individual must necessarily carry his family along and thus make every legal case a conflict between families. And the family faithfully supported its brother with the oath; in that manner it imbued his words with increasing strength, and together with him it staked its life to maintain itself in the fight against the opponent. This is a rule among the old Arabians, and in the Deuteronomy we have evidence of something similar, where the town, it is true, has taken the place of the family.

It is said in this place (Deut. 21) that if one is found slain in a field, the distance to the neighbouring cities is to be measured, and the one which is nearest to the man shall cleanse itself of the blood guilt. This takes place in the following manner: the elders and the priests of the city lead a heifer which has not drawn in the yoke down to an ever-running brook in an untilled valley. The elders and the priests then wash their hands over the heifer and affirm their innocence before Yahweh.[1] The guilt is common to the whole town; conversely, the elders and the priests, by their sayings, maintain the innocence of the whole town. This responsibility of the town is also acknowledged by the other old communities.[2]

The significance of the *oath* in the old rules of court shows that the legal conflict, as all other strife, first and foremost refers to the maintenance of the soul; the two parties carry on a mental combat, and he who is able to maintain himself in it has gained the day. The *witnesses* whose statements gradually became the decisive proof, subject themselves to these points of view. They are not "objective" informants, but they put their authority into the one or the other of the parties and place themselves by his side, as does the family in the old order of society. The law requires at least two witnesses (Num. 35,30; Deut. 17,6; 19,15).

Akin to the oath is the hypothetical curse pronounced by the priests on the woman accused of adultery (Num. 5). She drinks water which is charged with a curse, and if she is guilty her belly shall swell and her hip rot. But if she performs this ceremony unscathed, then she is innocent. [1]

With the oath the matter is settled. The task of the judge is to arrange about the taking of the oath, to decide which party is to swear, and to see that everything is done in the right manner.

In the case of an established guilt the task of the judge was only to determine its extent and the claims of restoration put forth by the offended. Then the priests passed sentence as those thoroughly versed in tradition, and in difficult cases they consulted the oracle. In all cases their decision was the decision of God (Exod. 18,16; 1 Sam. 2,25).

It was not external force, but tradition and the stronger power and insight which conferred authority upon the judge. Therefore the whole judicial system had a peculiarly free character. Instead of the priest one may also seek a man with prophetic gifts, who looks more deeply into things. Thus the Arabians went to their *kāhin*'s. It is told of Deborah that she was a prophetess and judged Israel, Israel laying their litigations before her. She was then wont to sit under a special tree, the palm of Deborah, which undoubtedly was holy (Judg. 4,4-5). And Samuel, a man with prophetic gifts, went about to certain towns deciding litigations, to Bethel, Gilgal and Mizpeh (1 Sam. 7,15 f.), and in his home at Ramah he received people and pronounced sentence. His authority was based on his power to "see". He could see where asses ran, and thus he was also able to see who had committed theft, etc.

When passing judgment the priest or the prophet puts his authority into him whom he declares to be right. Thus he increases his righteousness in relation to the other party so strongly that the latter must give way. The efficacy of the judgment rests in its mental authority, both as regards the winner and the loser. The rule must have been that the loser, without further ado, gave to the conqueror the satisfaction adjudged to him. For behind the claim of the latter was now the whole of the covenant. The words of the judge were an expression of the will of the covenant. We see that it is still so in the Deuteronomy, which ordains that difficult cases are to be laid before the priests of Jerusalem. And he who does not submit to their sentence shall die (17,8-13). Thus one must either voluntarily act according to the sentence or die; to revolt against the judgment is a breach of the covenant.

But in spite of this it might happen that the loser refused to give satisfaction. If the winner were too weak to follow up his victory, then his only resource was to turn to one stronger than himself and ask him for help. And, as already shown, the greatest obligation which honour laid upon the strong was to help the weak to obtain his right.

He whom one seeks is, as a matter of course, the most powerful man. He who upholds the community is responsible for the upholding of the covenant, and, as the mightiest, he has the power to "justify". Therefore one applies to the chief or the king when unable to vindicate one's right.

A characteristic story is the one in 2 Sam. 14, dealing with the woman from Tekoah who came to ask David for help, when she had lost her one son and was on the point of losing the other. It is, strictly speaking, just that the son who slew his brother is to be slain. But in the eyes of the king the helplessness of the woman is the greater consideration, and the saving of the son therefore a higher justice: The king must have the wisdom to distinguish between good and evil, in order to be able to decide where justice claims his help, and where it does not claim it (1 Kings 3,9). He himself must judge. It forms part of the activity of the king as well as of that of the priest and the seer. He must strengthen the people outwardly and maintain the covenant inwardly, the very thing which the Israelites understand by "judging".

There is no formal relation between the various judicial powers applied to, because they are natural authorities. One may first of all go to the priest, and then seek the king, if the loser refuses to give satisfaction. But one may also appeal directly to the king, or some other powerful man, and ask for his judgment, i. e. his help. Towards the judge both parties stand in the relation of applicants for help, as the two women stand towards Solomon (1 Kings 3,16-28). They both deliver themselves into his power, he "lays his hand upon them both" (Job 9,33). When he has spoken, it means that he unites his will with the person to whom he adjudges the right. The opponent offends him by not respecting his judgment. It is a good thing to have the judgment of a powerful man on one's side.

The Israelitic judicial system has, in a natural manner, grown out of a common respect of justice and the efforts of the violated to have their rights acknowledged; therefore it bears the impress of the irregularity of life. But there is a tendency towards creating organized authorities and courts of law; this makes itself most strongly felt in the Deuteronomy, which ordains the establishment of fixed courts of law in the towns (Deut. 16,18-20) and gives rules for the evidence of witnesses (17,6; 19,15). In certain cases the judge may sentence the criminal to being beaten in punishment, up to forty stripes, and then he himself may carry out the sentence (Deut. 25,1-3).[1] Here there is a suggestion of a formal judicial system, the judge having to maintain justice for its own sake and punishing the evil-doer in the manner so well known from the Assyrians; but, generally speaking, the Deuteronomy is also governed by the thought that the authority of the court of law is of a purely ideal kind, and that the offended himself must carry out his restoration (19,12).

But in certain cases a crime may be of such a nature that it does not only concern two parties, but threatens the justice and blessing of the whole community. In that case the upholders of the community pass sentence on the offender and destroy him among them when his crime has become established. For its own sake the community must purify itself of sins which are so great that they may consume its blessing. This point of view leads us to a consideration of sin and evil.

SIN AND CURSE.

THE old Israelitic conception of life bears the impress of the deep optimism of peoples not disintegrated by an artificial culture. The good action is the normal action, and if the act be normal and good, then according to its character it must succeed and produce good results. It means that the good and the healthy are the strongest factors of life, but not that they are the only ones. Not all actions are normal and good, and several are only partly so. Such actions the Israelite calls by the name of *sin.*

Sin is the opposite of righteousness, but these two conceptions cannot be set up as equal quantities. Only the righteous act can be termed an action in the proper sense of the word, because it has the characteristics of the normal. A sinful act is, properly speaking, no action, but a caricature.

Sin is the negative, that which preys upon the positive forces of life. One cannot sin with a whole heart, for sin is the very dissolution of the totality. If a soul is throughout sinful, then it means that it is entirely dissolved, decayed, and then it is no more to be reckoned a human soul.

The sinner lacks the firm centre of action; his soul is not a pure and firm organism, but full of inner strife, a dissolved mass. Therefore it staggers about aimlessly, like one intoxicated *(tāʿā, hithʿā)*. The soul of the sinner lacks firmness and strength, therefore falsehood is its characteristic feature.

For falsehood is the same as the splitting of the soul, to act without a whole and, thus, a clean heart. "With heart and heart they speak", says the Israelite (Ps. 12,3), thus denoting the duplicity of the soul of the liar. Just as he who speaks truth shows faithfulness towards his own being, and preserves the integrity of his soul, so the liar is he who fails himself, denies the substance of his own soul. "And also the God of Israel lieth not and repenteth not; for he is not a man that he should repent" (1 Sam. 15,29, cf. Num. 23,19). To "lie" is here the same as to betray one's word, to retract from one's resolve, and the same is meant when mention is made of "lying" against one's faithfulness (Ps. 89,34) or "lying" against one's covenant (Ps. 44,18).

He who lies against the covenant fails his soul, which is penetrated by its union with the neighbour. Therefore Abimelech asks Abraham not to "lie against me, nor against my progeny, nor against my posterity" (Gen. 21,23), that is to fail their common relation. A "witness of falsehood" (Exod. 20,16; Lev. 5,22; Deut. 19,18 *et al.)* is a witness who speaks otherwise than according to the actual substance of his soul.

As falsehood is that which is without basis in the totality of the soul, it is hollow and rootless. Just as truth is that which contains the strength of self-maintenance, so falsehood is that which cannot be maintained, that which must collapse, because it has not the vitality to give it strength and firmness.

The false is the same as the powerless, because it is not filled with the substance of a soul. It is said, characteristically, of the idols that they are falsehood; there is no soul *(rūaḥ)* in them (Jer. 10,14; 51,17; cf. Is. 44,20). "Horses are falsehood for salvation" (Ps. 33,17), i. e. inefficient, powerless, just as the false prophets see "falsehood" when their visions lack the strength of life. "Wind" and "falsehood" are brothers (Mic. 2,11). Falsehood therefore must be that which is futile. "For falsehood have I kept all that this fellow had in the desert", says David, when Nabal has refused his request for support (1 Sam. 25,21). To "work falsehood against one's soul" (2 Sam. 18,13) means to counteract it or to betray it, the opposite of maintaining it.

In all of the examples quoted the word used is *sheḳer,* the most ordinary Hebrew appellation of "falsehood", but what has been said above holds good of all the denominations; *kāzābh* follows it in all its shades. This word also means to betray one's word. "One thing have I sworn by my holiness, I will not lie unto David", says Yahweh, when speaking of his covenant with David

(Ps. 89,36). "For the vision hasteth towards the end and lieth not", says Habakkuk (2,3). Springs whose waters "lie" not (Is. 58,11) are springs which do not fail but always have the strength to run. "Falsehood and violence" are mentioned together (Hos. 12,2) because they both are a betrayal of the maintenance of the covenant. The hollow and empty is *kāzābh* as well as *sheḳer*. "Ye love the empty, seek after falsehood", says a psalmist (4,3), and another says: "The children of men are a breath, man is falsehood" (62,10). He who stakes his soul on some thing, but does not achieve it, his expectation becomes a falsehood (2 Kings 4,16; Prov. 30,6; Job 41,1). [1]

The powerless, empty juggling of falsehood the Hebrews often denote by *shāw'*. It is difficult to establish wherein the shade of difference between this and the other words consists, but perhaps it may be said that, whereas the other Hebrew stems equally denote the conflict within the soul and the powerlessness, this more one-sidedly denotes the latter, i. e. emptiness, delusion. The prophet uses this appellation for the sacrifices of the Israelites (Is. 1,13), because they are mere forms without any power of reality, and the same is said about the salvation of man (Ps. 60,13; 108,13). To make some thing *lashshāw'*, unto emptiness, is to do it aimlessly, without meaning and without result. To *shāw'* the Israelites offer sacrifices (Jer. 18,15), and the same the prophet says of their other efforts (Jer. 4,30) and of the attempts of their God to chastise them (2,30).

shāw' is chaos, *tōhū* (Is. 59,4), the confused mass to which life has not given the shape which makes it reality. [2] For chaos is not reality, for the very reason that it cannot realize; it lacks the construction of the living organism. He who acts for *shāw'* consequently throws his activity into empty space. It cannot work anything, but only dissolve. "The men of emptiness", about whom the pious says that he will not converse with them (Ps. 26,4, cf. Job 11,11), are men whose actions are of that kind, men like him "who lifts up his soul unto emptiness" (Ps. 24,4). Those who speak emptiness, every one with his neighbour (Ps. 12,3; 144,8.11, cf. Exod. 23,1), speak juggling words, inane verbage, without mental strength and the value of truth, like the visions of the false prophets (Ezek. 12,24; 13,6.7-9.23; 21,34 *et al.)*. He who swears by the name of Yahweh when he speaks such words, makes a caricature of an act. He fills himself with the supreme strength of life in order to produce that which is void of life! Such a use of the great name no true Israelite can undertake (Exod. 20,7; Deut. 5,1).

The soul that is full and rich does not know *shāw'*, but for others the time may become so void that the soul feels no joy of life. This kind of "months of emptiness" Job had apportioned to him (7,3). It is happiness which yields fullness, and unhappiness which yields emptiness; *shāw'*, the chaotic and empty, is identical with unhappiness. The pious psalmist prays that he may not see *shāw'* (Ps. 119,37). When Yahweh comes to judge, he shakes the peoples in the sieve of "emptiness", unhappiness spreads over the earth, and the world of peoples is drowned in chaos.

Falsehood has its root in the soul; from there it springs, and there it performs its work of dissolution. And all that has been said of falsehood applies to sin generally, for falsehood is typical of sin. Sin is the dissolution of the soul, an infringement upon its integrity and its firmness. It is also described as hardness and stiffness, for the normal soul is pliable and yielding, fit to subject itself to a totality with others. He who makes the heart hard *(ḥizzēḳ, 'immēṣ, hiḳshā)* or heavy *(hikhbīdh)* [1] kills love; he prevents the soul from linking itself with and submitting itself to other souls. And just as the righteous soul is upright, straight, so the sinful soul is "crooked", [2] deviating from the straight road and tottering backwards and forwards.

The three most commonly used denominations for sin are *ḥṭ'*, *'āwōn* and *pesha'*, partly characterizing sin as a failure, partly as an irregular, "crooked" action, partly as an infringement upon a psychic totality. The infringement applies to the psychic totality as a presupposition or inner quality *(tōm,* righteousness), just as *shebher* is an infringement upon the totality with regard to the expansion of the soul *(shālōm)*. In the use of the above-mentioned three words there is no difference of any importance.

That which upholds all life is the covenant; through that the totalities and organisms are formed in which life acts, and righteousness is the maintenance of the covenant. Sin, the essence of which is unrighteousness, consists in transgressing it, in acting outside its laws. It is sin to hate one's brother (Lev. 19,17). He who deals wrongly with his brother, sins against him (Gen. 42, 22; 50,17). If we look at the actions which are characterized by the name of sin, we will find that the breach of the covenant is the kernel of sin.

It is a "breach" to forget the brother-covenant, to violate the claim of kindred, and to sacrifice those with whom one has peace (Am. 1,6.9.11). Sin is every kind of violation of marriage, the taking of another man's wife (Gen. 39,9; Deut. 22,24) as well as the committing of incest (Lev. 20), because in the former case one violates the covenant of another, in the latter one's own. The Sodomites were great sinners; this was proved when they violated the right of hospitality, the covenant which strangers had with the town (Gen. 13,13; 19,6.15). Whenever one does not give to one's neighbour what he is entitled to according to the law of the covenant, one commits a sin; if, e. g., one does not at once give the hired labourer his wages (Deut. 24,15), or if one proves stingy towards one's neighbour, because the seventh year, in which debts are abolished, is at hand (Deut. 15,9).

Sin is thus determined by the relation between men. In any case it is a sin not to act according to the rule implied in the nature of the relation in question (Deut. 19,15). He who fulfils the claims of a relation, a covenant, is righteous; he who does not do it, sins with regard to his opponent. "What is my trespass, what is my sin that thou hast so hotly pursued after me?" Jacob asks Laban (Gen. 31,36), and a similar question David puts to Jonathan concerning his relation to Saul.[1]

The relation between Saul and David was of such a nature that it required of David that he put all his strength at the disposal of Saul, and of Saul that he rendered to David the honour and protection which he owed his subjects. The obligation was mutual as long as it was kept on both sides. When the conflict had broken out, David, whose position was that of the inferior, still attempted to keep the relation, and his friend Jonathan pleaded his cause before his father. Jonathan maintains that David has not sinned against Saul; on the contrary, his deeds have been very profitable to Saul, seeing that he has defeated the Philistines at the risk of his own life. He had also accomplished to the full what his relation to Saul demanded; this is what he means when he says that he has not sinned against him. The inference is that Saul would commit a sin against David by pursuing him and possibly killing him (1 Sam. 19,4). It is the same which David, at a later stage of the persecution, has the opportunity of bringing home to Saul when they have been in the same cave, and David is content to cut off the skirt of Saul's robe. He calls out to Saul that it is now clear that there is neither evil nor guilt in his hand, he has not sinned against him (1 Sam. 24,12). Then Saul acknowledges that David is righteous and that he himself has sinned (cf. 1 Sam. 26,21).

What is just towards the one may be a sin towards the other. It is not the external nature of the act which makes it sinful; the relation which creates the right also creates the sin. There is nothing wrong in cursing the evil and killing him who has forfeited his life against one. But it is wicked to curse or kill people with whom one stands in an unbroken covenant.

When David fled before Absalom up Mount Olivet, Shimei cursed him and called him a man of blood. There was nothing wrong in this. Shimei was of the family of Saul and had reason to rejoice, because the conqueror of his family had fallen. But when David returned victorious, Shimei was lost. The thing for him was to throw himself on the protection of David. From that point of view his curse was a sin, for it was directed against his own protector and master. He then appeared before David saying: Let not my lord impute iniquity unto me, neither do thou remember that which thy servant did perversely the day that my lord the king went out of Jerusalem that the king should take it to his heart. For thy servant doth know that I have sinned; therefore, behold, I am come the first this day of all the house of Joseph to go down to meet my lord the king (2 Sam. 19,20-21).

All lack of obedience towards superiors is sin, because the relation to them demands obedience. The Egyptian baker and cup-bearer who were in the same prison as Joseph, had been sent there because they had sinned against the king of the Egyptians (Gen. 40,1; 41,9).

The same applies to every deed which is in conflict with and dissolves a community. When the king of the Moabites (or Ammonites) attacked Israel, Jephthah sent word to him and explained that there had always been a relation of peace between the two peoples, and that the conquest of Israel in the border-regions had not infringed upon this relation. "I have not sinned against thee, but thou doest me wrong to war against me" (Judg. 11,27). The sin is a breach of the peace, of the covenant-relation between the peoples. When, on his expedition against the minor states of Western Asia, Sennacherib threatened Judah, Hezekiah sent a messenger to him, saying: I have sinned; return from me; that which thou puttest on me will I bear (2 Kings 18,14). The sin of Hezekiah consists in a violation of his vassal-duties. Such breaches of the covenant of peoples are generally called *pesha'* (1 Kings 12,19; 2 Kings 1,1; 3,5.7; 8,20.22).

A sinful act is thus an act through which a community is dissolved. In so far sin becomes a matter between two parties; one is a sinner in relation to another. In reality this way of looking at things is a feature of great moment. When the brothers of Joseph were starting for Egypt and absolutely wanted Benjamin to go with them, Judah took upon himself the responsibility for him over against his father, saying: "If I bring him not unto thee, and set him before thee, then I have sinned to you for ever" (Gen. 43,9, cf. 44,32). When Jeremiah was taken from the prison and placed before king Zedekiah, he asked: "What have I sinned against thee, or against thy servants, or against this people, that ye have put me in prison?" (Jer. 37,18).

The presupposition of such a speech is that he who does not fulfil his obligations in relation to another, gives his opponent a claim upon him. Thus "sinner", like "righteous", to a certain extent becomes a relative idea. The sinner is he who is wrong in his relation to another, in so far as he has not given what the latter was entitled to. And the demands are determined in a realistic manner by the actual conditions. When during the last days of David it looks as if Bath-sheba would not succeed in having her son Solomon appointed his successor, she declared before the king that the inference would be "when my lord the king shall sleep with his fathers, that I and my son Solomon shall be counted sinners" (1 Kings 1,21). For if another of David's sons were appointed king, they would be sinners against him, because they had counteracted him and, in actual fact, had been proved wrong.

One of the strong appellations of a sinner, *rāshā'*, is often used in this manner about him who is wrong in a special case, quite corresponding to *ṣaddīḳ,* which denotes him who is right.

When Moses saw two men fighting, he addressed the "sinner" (Exod. 2,13), i. e. he who was wrong. In the conflict between Yahweh and Pharaoh the latter declared that he had sinned: "Yahweh is righteous, and I and my people are the sinners *(hārᵉshā'īm)*" (Exod. 9,27). The law pronounces severely against yielding assistance to "the sinner" in a lawsuit (Exod. 23,1), which is equivalent to admitting that he is right, "justifying" him (23,7; Prov. 17,15).[1] To "make unrighteous", *hirshiᵃ,* is the opposite of "justifying", meaning to deem a person wrong in a certain case, and at the same time to carry out this judgment (Exod. 22, 8; Is. 50,9; Ps. 94,21; Job 9,20; 15,6; 34,29 *et al.).*

The idea is that in a mutual relation he is the righteous who maintains the duties which the fellowship implies for him; he does what he is bound to do, but when the other one does not do his duty, he will not get what is due to him according to the community. The violator of the covenant to a certain extent becomes the debtor of the righteous, and the latter is entitled to take what is due to him. This happens, as we have seen, through restoration, vengeance. This conception of sin is the principal one among the Arabians and, as appears from the preceding chapters, it is also true of Israel. But among the Israelites it is only one side of the matter.

The sinful deed is, by its very essence, a breach of peace. But it does not only mean that one neglects giving another what is due to him; it means that one's own soul is diseased. The soul only exists as a link in an organism with which it is intimately interwoven; the breach of peace is a result of the soul misjudging this reality and acting as if it were isolated, something apart. Such an act is called violence, *ḥāmās, shōdh* or encroachment, *'ōshek;* it is only a delusion, not a real action, because it does not proceed from a healthy soul, acting as a link in its totality, but from a soul living in an imaginary, exceptional position, as an isolated individual, one that does not act according to the law of totality.

'ōshek is often mentioned by the prophets. They constantly use it of the mighty who do not fulfil the claims of the poor members of the covenant to a tolerable existence, those who gain lucre by crooked ways, and counteract those who are in the right before the courts of law. It is one of the various words denoting the opposite of righteousness. Like the two other words, it is used to express the arbitrary deeds of violence, circumventing the rules of the community. They pertain to a community in a state of dissolution; in a healthy community they can only be an exception. Therefore violence *(ḥāmās)* and strife pertain to the same city (Ps. 55,10). Violence thrives in discord. "A violent man enticeth his neighbour" (Prov. 16,29). And violence is the same as falsehood (Exod. 23,1; Deut. 19,16; Ps. 27,12; 35,11), because both denote that which deviates from the straight and just, i. e. the abnormal, which does not spring from a healthy soul, and therefore has no root in reality. Violence is apparently an expression of strength, but the Israelite considers this strength a delusion, which can only exist for a time, because it does not draw directly from the source of strength, peace and its blessing, which rests in the divine forces. Sin originates in a dissolved soul, and must spread dissolution round it. But all sins are not equally great.

It follows from the psychological conception of the Israelites that a man is responsible for all his actions. Every action must exercise its effect, also in the soul of the person who acts. One may sin without knowing it. Abimelech sinned unwittingly by taking the wife of Abraham (Gen. 20,9). If a man falls down from a roof without a rail and is killed, then the owner of the house bears blood-guilt (Deut. 22,8). Balaam sinned when he wanted to urge his ass forward, *because* he did not know that Yahweh's *mal'ākh* stood before him (Num. 22,34). Thus the man always bears the responsibility, but more frequently that kind of sin will sink less deeply into the soul.

An offence included under this category the Israelite calls *sh^{e}ghāghā*. It is not its outward character which determines its essence. Even manslaughter may be of this kind (Num. 35,11.15; Josh. 20,3.9). The decisive thing is what is the relation of the action to the acting soul: does it arise in the central will of the soul, or does it merely lie in the periphery of the soul? If the latter is the case, then it can be wiped out and be removed before it gains ground. This is done in two ways; the infringement which is made upon the right of the others must be healed through their restoration; and the mental hurt which threatens the perpetrator of the deed is removed through the sacrifice (Lev. 4; 5; 1 Sam. 26,19). No human being is so perfect that he can avoid such breaches; even an essentially firm and whole soul may create irregular actions.

But if an infringement upon the law of righteousness is more deeply seated in the soul, then it is not to be removed. Sin implies guilt (*'āshām*). How the latter acts, we see most clearly when we consider the strongest form of the breach of peace, viz. unrighteous manslaughter.

He who commits an offence of this kind bears blood-guilt, or as the Hebrews merely say: blood. "He goes into blood",[1] he gets the "blood of the slain on his head".[2] Only if the slaying is righteous, the blood of the slain "comes over his own head".[3] He who sheds "pure blood" is a "man of blood". A man who shed a good deal of very pure blood was Manasseh.[4] But the prophets are still accusing those in power that "their hands are full of blood", the whole country is filled with it.[5]

If a deed of blood has been brought into the world, then the deed persists as a wicked poison, consuming the soul of the man who has committed the deed of blood. And, according to the fundamental law of the soul, the guilt must spread from him and be carried by the whole of his family. The poison follows the blood. If the perpetrator of the deed dies, then it is still in his brothers, passes to the sons and from them into the sons of the sons, until some day it comes out and destroys its victim. The violated family may be patient and wait until their hour strikes; it is not easy for its spoil to escape.

The deed has created a breach in the soul of the violated as well as in that of the perpetrator of the deed, but the breach of the violated can be healed, because it has struck him from without. Through the vengeance he takes life, just as he has lost life. But the position of the offender is different. His deed is not merely something which concerns him and his antagonist. Ruin awaits him, because its germs are in him. Even if there is no opponent to claim his death, misfortune must yet strike him. Thus it is not only the claim of retaliation which, in any case, demands the death of the slayer. On this point the artificial thought of retaliation meets with an idea which has much deeper roots in the whole of the Israelitic conception of psychic life: the absolutely wicked deed can only spring from a degenerate soul and must itself complete the ruin of the soul in question.

An illustration of this we find in the history of Abimelech. He was the son of one of the concubines of Gideon and so not a full member of his father's house. Therefore he had no share in the rule exercised by the seventy sons of Gideon in Ophrah. His mother came from Shechem, which was also under their rule, and he succeeded in winning the Shechemites, whose flesh and blood he had in him through his mother. By means of a hired gang he slew his half-brothers, and then himself became the ruler of Shechem. Only one of the brothers, Jotham, the youngest of them all, escaped death by hiding himself. One day he went and stood on the top of a rock near the town and told an instructive parable about the trees, the purpose of which was that the only tree which would be supreme ruler of the others, was the unfruitful and prickly bramble. And he concluded his narrative with the following words: "If ye then have dealt in truth and sincerity (integrity) with Jerubbaal (Gideon) and his house this day, then rejoice ye in Abimelech and he too will rejoice in you; but if not, fire shall come out from Abimelech, and devour the men of Shechem and the house of Millo, and a fire shall come out from the men of Shechem and from the house of Millo and devour Abimelech" (Judg. 9,19-20). After that he fled.

Jotham is not an avenger in the ordinary sense of the word. The slayer of his brothers is himself his brother, though as the son of a slave he does not quite belong to the house of his father. In so far vengeance might barely be taken of him, but what satisfaction can seventy noble men get from the son of a slave-woman? An Arabian would have made that kind of reflection, but such an idea is not suggested in our narrative. Its main point of view is not the restoration of the violated, but the guilt of Abimelech. If the deed be righteous, then all is well; but if it is an infringement upon the law of the covenant, then the new covenant which rests upon such a breach cannot persist, but must be dissolved from within and consume those taking part in it.

And this was just what happened. It is told: When Abimelech had reigned three years over Israel, then God sent an evil spirit between Abimelech and the men of Shechem; and the men of Shechem dealt treacherously with Abimelech, that the deed of violence towards the seventy sons of Jerubbaal came over and their blood was laid [1] upon Abimelech their brother, which slew them, and upon the men of Shechem which strengthened his hands towards the killing of his brethren (Judg. 9,22-24). The Shechemites lay ambushes for the caravans of Abimelech. At a festival they sit cursing him, and a swaggering youth, Gaal, undertakes to make away with him. But is was Abimelech who destroyed Gaal and the whole of Shechem; he beat it down and sowed it with salt.

Shortly afterwards Abimelech himself went to his destruction. While he was laying siege to another town, Thebez, a woman cast an upper millstone upon his head. However, he avoided the ignominious death by the hand of a woman by letting his armourbearer thrust his sword through him. "Thus God rendered (upon his head) the wickedness of Abimelech, which he did unto his father, in slaying his seventy brethren, and upon them came the curse of Jotham, the son of Jerubbaal" (Judg. 9,56-57).

It is God who visits Abimelech, and the curse of Jotham comes upon him and Shechem, but it does not mean that the misfortune is a punishment striking them from without. On the contrary. The curse of Jotham merely consists in his stating a fact, and his words are confirmed by God. Their community becomes inflamed, a wicked soul ("spirit") acts in it, it causes hatred and strife, and shortly afterwards they have destroyed each other. For the Israelitic conception it was a matter of course. A psychic whole founded on violence is a delusion and must be consumed from within. [1]

Another example of violence destroying its author we find in the history of Ahab. When, through the wiles of Jezebel, Naboth had been put to death, and Ahab had taken possession of his property, a double crime had been committed: a righteous man had been killed, and Ahab had unjustly appropriated the property of his family. Ahab knew what he had done. When Elijah proclaimed to him his own ruin and that of his family, he acknowledged that it was justice which had spoken (1 Kings 21,17 ff.). Three years afterwards came the war with Aram. The king went out to fight with evil omens. Micaiah ben Imlah saw his defeat. In vain he disguised himself as a common warrior; he could not avoid his fate. An arrow from a bow drawn at venture reached him and brought him death. But this was not the end. The whole of his family was tainted. It ruled for a few years more, until it collapsed and was wiped off from the earth by the hand of Jehu. But Jehu himself overshot the mark; a full century later Hosea says that the blood-guilt of Jezreel cleaves to his house and will ruin it (Hos. 1,4).

The man who is anxious to promote his own welfare takes care that the dangerous disease called "blood" does not enter into his family so as to undermine its vitality. David had good reason to praise Abigail, when by her wise behaviour she withheld him from killing Nabal and thus being brought "to slipping and the stumbling of the heart" and "to go into blood" (1 Sam. 25,26.31.33). When David lay on his deathbed he was troubled by the fear of such "blood" threatening his soul on the part of Joab. Just as he left to Solomon to liberate the family from the affront inflicted upon it by Shimei, Solomon also was to liberate it from the blood-guilt of Joab.

As to his David said to Solomon: Thou knowest also what Joab, the son of Zeruiah did to me, and what he did for the two captains of the hosts of Israel, unto Abner the son of Ner, and unto Amasa the son of Jether whom he slew and shed the blood of war in peace, and put the blood of war upon his girdle that was about his loins and his shoes that were on his feet (1 Kings 2,5). Here a reference is made to the vengeance which, in spite of their reconciliation, Joab took over Abner (2 Sam. 3) and to his slaying of Amasa (2 Sam. 20,10), whom David during the sedition had won for himself by promising him the post as captain of hosts in the place of Joab (2 Sam. 19,14).

To be sure David was not very sorry to keep the powerful Joab in lieu of the deserter Amasa, and, as long as he lived, he gladly made use of Joab. But the fear of "blood" was constantly in him. Soon after the death of Abner David exclaimed: "I and my kingdom are guiltless before Yahweh for ever from the blood of Abner the son of Ner. Let it rest on the head of Joab, and on all his father's house. Neither shall there fail from the house of Joab one that has an issue, or is a leper or that plieth the distaff, that falleth on the sword or that lacketh bread" (2 Sam. 3,28 f.). In these words one feels the eagerness to confine the blood-guilt to Joab himself. The guilt is there, and must work misfortune, but it must not touch the house of David. And yet the danger remained. Joab was the servant of David, one of his familiars. At any time the guilt might come out in the family of David; [1] this is the reason why Joab must be removed.

Solomon carried out the ordainment of his father, causing Benaiah to cut Joab down, even at the very horns of the altar, to which he clung. Of this it is told: And Benaiah came to the tent of Yahweh, and said unto him (i. e. Joab): Thus saith the king: Come forth! And he said: Nay, but I will die here. And Benaiah brought the king word again, saying: Thus said Joab, and thus he answered me. And the king said unto him: Do as he hath said, and fall upon him and bury him, that thou mayest take away the innocent blood which Joab shed from me and from the house of my father. And Yahweh shall return his blood upon his own head, because he fell upon two men more righteous and better than he, and slew them with the sword, my father David not knowing thereof, to wit, Abner the son of Ner, captain of the host of Israel and Amasa the son of Jether, captain of the host of Judah. Their blood shall therefore return upon the head of Joab, and upon the head of his seed for ever, but upon David, and upon his seed, and upon his house, and upon his throne, shall there be peace for ever from Yahweh. — So Benaiah the son of Jehoiada went up and fell upon him, and slew him. And he was buried in his own house in the "wilderness" (1 Kings 2,30-34).

There is a great difference between David's relation to Shimei and his relation to Joab. David desires to kill Shimei in order to obtain restoration for an offence done to him, and the wisdom of Solomon shows itself in finding an expedient by which he is able to kill the man and still keep the blessing, the slaying being righteous (1 Kings 2,45), whereas Joab must be done to death in order to keep the blessing, seeing that the latter is threatened from within by the guilt of Joab.

The fear of blood-guilt through unrighteous slaying becomes stronger and stronger in Israel. It contributes to the development undergone by the blood-vengeance; the community dare not make common cause with the slayer — as the Arabians always did — for fear of the guilt which it brought down upon itself. If a slayer flees to a city of refuge, the elders of his town must cause him to be brought back and then delivered to the avenger that he may be slain, and this they must do to purify themselves of innocent blood (Deut. 19,11-13). The result is that the slayer, providing he be guilty, must always be done to death, in order not to taint his own community. And the cities of refuge, which the Deuteronomy ordains, are founded to prevent the violated from incurring blood-guilt by taking too great a vengeance, i. e. by killing a man who only by chance has become the slayer of his relative. Also this law is given "in order that innocent blood be not shed in thy land, which Yahweh thy God giveth thee for an inheritance, and so blood be upon thee" (Deut. 19,10) — a point of view which is far from that of the Arabians, nor was it applied in the very oldest Israel.

There are other offences than "blood" creating such a guilt in the souls of their authors that it threatens to poison the community, and therefore must be done away with. This refers to those who commit a trespass upon the holy thing. The Book of Joshua (chap. 7) tells us how Achan had stolen of the spoil consecrated to

Yahweh, and was put to death, the offence being so violent that it tainted the whole people. It soon made itself felt in an inexplicable defeat. The strength of the people was undermined. When, through the throwing of lots, Achan had been found, he was stoned and burnt with the whole of his house, everything that in any way belonged to him. The taint had to be utterly removed.

Gross breaches of a cultic law smite with a violent guilt. This first and foremost refers to the adoption of foreign cults and the worshipping of strange gods. The whole of the history of Israel deals with this. According to the representations of the biblical authors, nearly all of the kings committed transgressions of this kind, and the sin must act through the whole of the people. They "made Israel sinful", as occurs over and over again in the Book of Kings, and they were the origin of all the misfortunes which came over the people.

The laws enumerate a number of transgressions which must entail extermination. This refers to him who sacrifices outside the sacred place (Lev. 17,4), who "eateth blood" (Lev. 17,10-14), who does not deal rightly with the flesh of the sacrifice (Lev. 7,20-27; 19,8), who sacrifices children (Lev. 20,2), who eats leavened bread during the feast of *maṣṣōth* (Exod. 12,15.19), who does not celebrate the passover (Num. 9,13), the priest who goes to the holy thing having his uncleanness upon him (Lev. 22,3), who profanes the holy oil and perfume incense (Exod. 30,33.38), who touches dead bodies without purifying himself (Num. 19,13.20), who acts as a soothsayer (Lev. 20,6), who works on the day of atonement (Lev. 23,30), who violates the law of the sabbath (Exod. 31,14; Num. 15,32-36) or of the circumcision (Gen. 17,14). The law of the cult must be kept most scrupulously, for upon that depends the growth and maintenance of life. The violation of that infects the transgressor with a pollution so dangerous that it threatens the whole of the community, and therefore he must be removed.

But this generally applies to all transgressions against the laws which more especially contribute towards upholding the community. He who strikes or curses his parents has broken the fundamental law of life and violated peace and blessing; he must surely die (Exod. 21,15.17; Lev. 20,9, cf. Deut. 21,18 ff.), and the same holds good of him who blasphemes the god of his people (Lev. 24,10 ff.), as, upon the whole, of any one who purposely sets himself against him (Num. 15,30).

Gross breaches of the honour and rights of others entail death, as in the case of him who violates another covenant in its most intimate relation, e. g. by abducting a man (Exod. 21,16) or by violating a "betrothed damsel" (Deut. 22,25). The relation between the sexes, the presupposition of the very formation and maintenance of the family, is so essential and fundamental that violation of its laws causes guilt which makes death necessary (Lev. 18; 20,10-24, cf. Deut. 22,20-22).[1]

Of the soul committing such a sin it is said that it is "exterminated from its kinsmen" because it has broken the covenant. It is a diseased member, which no more cooperates in the organism of the totality; it must be removed completely in order that the community of kinsmen may keep its health and blessing.

This amputation is sometimes called *heḥᵉrīm,* to "remove from the normal community", in one place *shērēsh,* "pull up by the root" (Ps. 52,7, cf. Ezr. 7,26). The chief thing is that the offender is wiped out entirely, and it is a matter of course that the sin is not merely seated in the individual from whom it has originated. All that belongs to him is affected. Sin can not merely be seated in the whole of the family, but also in the possessions belonging to them. It is seated in buildings (Lev. 14,52), nay, the very sacred place may become tainted by it (Lev. 8,15; Num. 18,1). Still it is not the rule — as in the case of Achan — that the whole family should be destroyed, with everything that belongs to them. It generally suffices to remove the very perpetrator of the deed in whom the sin centres.

The sinner is sometimes exterminated by *burning,* in particular in the case of sexual crimes (Gen. 38,24; Lev. 20,14; 21,9), just as it may happen that the sinner is first killed and then burned with fire, as was the case with Achan. The usual proceeding was to *stone* the sinner. He was led outside the town or the camp (Lev. 24,14; Num. 15,36; 1 Kings 21,10.13); the witnesses threw the first stones, and the other members of the community continued, until death occurred (Num. 15,35; Deut. 17,7; 22,21). Over the slain a heap of stones was raised (Josh. 7,26; 8,29). To be stoned was the ignominious death. Through that the sinner was placed entirely outside his community;[1] the ordinary burial, surrounded by one's kin, was out of the question; the heap of stones warned people against the tainted place. The dead body was sometimes hanged on a pole (Deut. 21,23), which fate a vanquished enemy was likewise sometimes made to suffer (Josh. 8,29; cf. 1 Sam. 31,10). In that way the dead body was exposed to be mutilated by birds and to other kinds of destruction, and it was denied the peace of the grave.

This extermination of the great sinners is not punishment in the sense that the perpetrator of the deed has "deserved" it according to the law of retaliation. It is not retaliation, though the principle of retaliation may have acted as a secondary cause. It is the manner in which the community liberates itself from elements threatening its growth. And this threat does not proceed so much from the direct harm done by the deed performed; it proceeds from the fact that such a deed can only be performed by a degenerate and unnatural soul, which will be a constant danger in a sound organism.

The various examples of guilt breaking out in misfortune are in no wise isolated. Righteousness must carry happiness, because happiness is created in the soul, and the righteous is the soul possessed of the power to create. Violence is falsehood and delusion, and all sin is in reality weakness.

Whereas "justify" means to give vitality, to make strong, so also "unjustify" means to weaken, to rob of the power to self-maintenance. When God in a law suit "unjustifies" *(hirshīᶜᵃ)* one of the parties (Exod. 22,8), then it means that he robs him of the power to maintain himself against the other (cf. Job 9,20; 10,2; 15,6; 34,29). The pious declares confidently that when Yahweh wants to help him, no one can "unjustify" him; all are worn out as a garment consumed by moths (Is. 50,9; cf. Ps. 102, 27). Those who "unjustify the covenant" (Dan. 11,32) are those who suspend it, make it invalid. Just as the justification is victory, so the unjustification is defeat. It is said of Saul in his days of prosperity that he was at war with the neighbouring peoples, and wherever he turned "he unjustified" (1 Sam. 14,47) the enemies, i. e. defeated them.[1]

How then was a sinner to maintain himself? He lacks all the presuppositions. It is righteousness which forms the frame-work of blessing and peace, but it is this very righteousness which the sinner lacks, righteousness and wisdom. The sinner is a *fool,* because he cannot devise plans which are worth anything. The fool belongs together with the perpetrator of violence (Ps. 94,8), with him whose soul lacks health. He goes about calumniating (Prov. 10,18), his substance is deceit (Prov. 14,8). His counsel lacks firmness and must collapse — an example is he who himself bore the name of "fool", *nābhāl*. Folly and disgrace, collapse, are synonymous.[2]

A very vivid description of the essence of the sinner we find in Is. 57,20. "The sinners are like the troubled sea", it is said in this place; "it cannot rest, and its waters cast up mire and dirt. There is no peace, saith my God, to the sinners" (cf. Is. 48,22). The soul of the sinner is like the water, without firmness and stability; therefore nothing but mire proceeds from the sin, peace and happiness it cannot create.

The Old Testament is filled with descriptions of the misery of the sinner, the most vivid of which is to be found in the Book of Job, more particularly in the speeches of the friends.

Bildad says:

"Yea, the light of the sinner[3] is put out, and the spark of his fire doth not shine. The light is dark in his tent, and his candle is put out with him. The steps of his strength are straitened, and his own counsel casteth him down.[4] For he is cast into a net by his own feet, and he walketh upon the toils. A trap taketh hold of his heel, and a snare layeth hold of him. The noose is hid for him in the ground, and the gin for him on the way. Terrors affright him on every side, and chase him at every step. His misery becomes greedy, and destruction is ready for his fall. For it devoureth the ... of his skin, even the firstborn of death devours his ...[5] His confidence is plucked out of his tent, ... he is marched to the king of terrors. In his tent dwelleth corruption,[6] brimstone is scattered upon his habitation. His roots are dried up beneath, and above his branch is withering. His remembrance perishes from the earth, and he has no name on the open plain. He is driven from light into darkness, and chased out of the world. He neither has posterity nor offspring among his people, nor any survivor in the place where he sojourned. They of the West are appalled at his day, they of the East take to shuddering. Surely such are the dwellings of the wicked, and this is the place of him that knoweth not God" (Job 18,5-21).

This speech is an illustration of the saying of Eliphaz, viz. that pollution does not arise out of the dust, and misery does not rise out of the earth, but has its origin in man himself (Job 5,6 f.). His root is withered, his soul confused, his counsel vain. Therefore he is barren, must stumble, lose his confidence, fear and fail. His wealth crumbles, he disappears without leaving a trace or a name. No progeny can keep his soul alive; the righteous rejoice that have no intercourse with him (cf. Job. 15,34; 20,4-29; 27,13-32).

The Israelites are agreed that such is the fate of the sinner, because it is given with the whole fundamental conception of the soul. "The sinners are destroyed in darkness" (1 Sam. 2,9), "the way of the sinners perisheth" (Ps. 1,6), "the desire of the sinners perisheth" (Ps. 112,10), their way is made crooked (Ps. 146,9), their years are shortened, their hope perishes (Prov. 10,27.28), they are put to shame and disappear in Sheol (Ps. 9,18; 31,18), evil slays them (Ps. 34,22), their names rot (Prov. 10,7). If all sayings of this kind were to be quoted, a very considerable part of the Old Testament would have to be copied out.

No Israelite denies that the sinner may flourish and display vigour for a time, for if not, acts of violence would be impossible. But that which he maintains is that it only will last for a time. The disease will come out, if not before, then in posterity. The sinner has no real strength because he is not rooted in the forces of the blessing.

There is something unnatural in the apparent strength of the sinner. It does not spring from normal sources, but is acquired by crooked means. Characteristic of the sinner's manner of acting is *witchcraft*. They are the very actions which seek their strength outside the normal paths. Witchcraft and whoredom are mentioned together (2 Kings 9,22; Nah. 3,4), because they both denote actions originating in a dissolution of psychic fundamentals. And, just as naturally, the two are mentioned together with unnatural cults (*ibid.* and Deut. 18,10; 2 Kings 17,17; Mic. 5,11), because it is the cult which creates the blessing and the power to act. Witchcraft is a capital sin, and all groups of laws demand the extermination of those who deal in it (Exod. 22,17; Lev. 20,27; Deut. 18,10). Balaam says that witchcraft and magic arts are not to be found in Israel, which gets everything from its God (Num. 23,23). An act due to witchcraft may look very well for a time, but it is like a tree, put into the ground without a root. Where there should be a root, there is wickedness and emptiness.

A deed of this kind the Israelite may call *'āmāl,* but the characteristic word is *'āwen.*[1] Properly speaking it denotes strength, but gradually it has chiefly come to be used of the false strength, the magic power, and therefore it has all the characteristics of sin. It is the evil, hollow act (Is. 1,13; 10,1), full of wickedness and hostility (Is. 32,6; 58,9; Ps. 6,9; 14,4; 28,3; 36,5 *et al.*), that which pursues its spoil by crooked ways, with deceit and secret arts or, briefly, that which is in reality vain and carries unhappiness in it (Num. 23,21; Jer. 4,15; Am. 5,5). The false gods are *'āwen* (Is. 66,3; Hos. 10,5.8).

The man who does that kind of thing is a man of *b^elīya'al.* The root *y'l* is one of the denominations of positive action: to carry through a good, normal action. With the negation *b^elī* it therefore denotes the negative action.[2] Men of *b^elīya'al* are the same as "empty men" (2 Chron. 13,7), beings without a soul, whose actions are rootless, wicked (Nah. 1,11); people who worship false gods (Deut. 13,14), who show wickedness against their brothers (Deut. 15,9), who violate the law of hospitality (Judg. 19, 22; 20,13); men of blood who violate the right (2 Sam. 16,7), who make false depositions (1 Kings 21,10.13; Prov. 19,28), who oppose themselves to the normal order of things (1 Sam. 10,27; 30,22). Such men were the sons of Eli (1 Sam. 2,12), such a man was Nabal (1 Sam. 25,17.25) and Sheba who opposed himself to David (2 Sam. 20,1). They are people who only think of doing harm. The good are afraid of having anything to do with them (Ps. 101,3), for corruption always springs up around them. The prophet proclaims the glad tidings to Judah of a future when there shall no more be *bᵉlīyaʿal* in it (Nah. 2,1). What *bᵉlīyaʿal* is appears most clearly from a psalm, where a man who is ill implores for healing and help. He says among other things:

"I say: Yahweh be merciful unto me; heal my soul, for I have sinned against thee. Mine enemy speaks evil of me: When shall he die and his name perish? And if he come to see me, he speaketh vanity *(shāwʾ)*, his heart he filleth with juggling *(ʾāwen)*, when he goeth abroad, he telleth it. All that hate me whisper incantations [1] together against me, against me do they devise hurt: A poison [2] of *bᵉlīyaʿal* is shed in him, and now that he lieth he shall rise up no more. Yea, mine own man of peace, in whom I trusted, which did eat of my bread, practiseth gross deception [3] against me" (Ps. 41, 5-10).

These violent arraignments are not unique. A man is prostrated on a bed of sickness; by their evil words and thoughts his enemies put misery into him; it is *bᵉlīyaʿal,* corruption itself which acts in him.

The sinner does not belong to the righteous community. He counteracts the positive forces which uphold community and have their roots in God. It is God who stands behind the law, the rule of the behaviour of healthy people. Therefore all sin is a violation of God. This is the dominant note with the prophets. "They have transgressed my covenant and trespassed upon my *tōrā*" says Hosea (8,1). It does not only take place by cultic transgression and direct sacrilege or apostasy to strange gods. All transgression offends Yahweh, because he is the soul of every Israelitic covenant, and it is he who is the author of the law. When David had violated the marriage-covenant of Uriah, he confessed that he had sinned against Yahweh (2 Sam. 12,13), just as it was a sin against God into which Potiphar's wife wanted to inveigle Joseph (Gen. 39,9). Therefore all sin is revolt and disobedience against Yahweh. [4]

This does not alter the fact that the whole Israelitic conception of sin is based on a psychological law; it confirms it, for Yahweh is inseparably bound up with this law. It is from him that the blessing radiates which upholds the healthy and strong; he acts in the soul of the righteous with his strength, and immediately withdraws from the unrighteous; he hates the sinful, which is at war with his essence. The psychological law agrees with his essence, because it rests in him. The sinner must fail, because his soul is weak, and it is God who, because of the offence against him, puts weakness into it.

In so far the misfortunes which strike the sinner are a punishment. God "remembers" or "visits" the sinful act. [1] Perhaps some time may pass, but one day God lets sin perform its work and breed unhappiness for its author. Job complains that God will not let his small sins disappear without leaving any trace. "For thou inquirest after mine iniquity and searchest after my sin" (Job 10,6, cf. 14,16). When Elijah was in Zarephath, the widow in whose house he sojourned lost her son; she complained that Elijah had come to call to mind her sin and thus cause the death of her son (1 Kings 17,18).

The punishment of Yahweh is thus not arbitrary. The person visited "bears his sin", sin and unhappiness being two manifestations of the same idea. "Our transgressions and sins be upon us, and we pine away in them", say the Israelites (Ezek. 33,10). He who bears a sin bears a poison within himself, which consumes his vitality. Thus it is said that he who commits incest, bears sin and shall die childless (Lev. 20,20). When it is said: There is sin in thee (Deut. 15,9; 23,22; 24,15), then it means that a dangerous disease has taken its abode in the soul and gnaws the blessing. Sin is identical with misfortune. Isaiah says woe unto them who "draw iniquity with cords of falsehood, and sin as it were with a cart rope" (5,18), and in the Book of Zechariah mention is made of the glorious future, when Jerusalem shall be the centre sought from all countries. He who does not go there shall be plagued with lack of rain; it shall be the sin of Egypt and the sin of all the people who do not go up to celebrate the feasts of tabernacles (Zech. 14,19). To bear sin thus means to bear misfortune. "For forty years shall ye bear your iniquities, and know my wrath", says Yahweh to the Israelites (Num. 14,34). The sinful bears his mischief on his head (Ps. 7,17), he obtains "his way upon his head" (1 Kings 8,32).

The old law of Israel, viz. that goodness bears blessing within itself, and that wickedness entails curse and misery, did not die. It was the law of justice, identical with the faith in Yahweh, and so in life. Wickedness might persist for a time, but it would not last for ever. According as the Israelites saw wickedness spreading more and more over the land, the whole of the basis of their culture and existence must collapse or possibly be renewed, or they must constantly maintain that this would only last for a time. It was the latter which happened. The prophets proclaimed that Yahweh would soon intervene and pass judgment, and misfortune would come over all sinners. When the powerful neighbouring states led their armies against the small people near the Mediterranean, then it was Yahweh who called down punishment over the sinners of his people. But Yahweh grew, and the law of justice came to apply to the whole of the world. Every people which opposed itself to the powerful guardian of justice, should be crushed in the violent judgment of peoples.

These thoughts are incessantly varied in all the prophetic speeches. The doom of the people at the destruction of Jerusalem was considered the confirmation of the idea of righteousness: the people had sinned and therefore were doomed. As long as the Israelite knew righteousness, the expectation of imminent judgment was the end of his spiritual strife to keep his belief in righteousness. It was still a riddle that sinners were at all able to exist, and many would ask with Jeremiah: "Wherefore doth the way of the wicked prosper?" (Jer. 12,1). The answer was in the main always the same. When the impatient called out: "How long, oh Lord?" as often happens in the Psalms, then the answer is: Wait only for another short hour, then it will be past. Then Yahweh will intervene, the sinners will be shamed and be sent down into Sheol, where they belong (Ps. 9,18; 31,18); they are to be wiped off from the surface of the earth (Ps. 104,35), to disappear in an instant with all their stolen happiness (Ps. 37.49.73); Yahweh wades in their blood (Ps. 58,11), and the righteous rejoices because he shall then be permitted to enjoy the splendours which the sinners so unrighteously have usurped (Prov. 13,22; Job 27,17). With terror the pious thinks of the possibility that he should be carried away together with the sinners (Ps. 26,9) and perish in the very catastrophe which should give him life.

Sin centred more and more in this one conception: *Disobedience against Yahweh.* All the germs of it we find in the old conceptions, but it makes a difference to have it made into practically the only argumentation and the only motive. It contains the possibility of obscuring the natural, mentally deep-going consideration of sin by a more outward, arbitrary one. The preaching of the prophets centre in the claim of obedience, and the same holds good of the admonitions forming the frame of the laws. The narratives of the Yahwist in the Genesis, illustrating how obedience leads to blessing and disobedience to curse, bear the same stamp. Man was disobedient when he ate of the tree which God had forbidden him to touch; therefore he was driven out of Eden, and his whole existence became cursed. Abraham was obedient even though what was demanded was contrary to the first demand of Israelitic ethics — therefore the blessing was given to him.

This manner of thinking falls in with the later conception of righteousness. The immediate consideration of sin does not know of any measuring of the misfortune entailed by sin. If poison has been instilled, then it acts as far as its operative power may penetrate into the life of the family. But is this righteous? According to the old view decidedly so, but later on there are those who say: There must be a fair proportion between offence and punishment, for it is Yahweh who decides it, and he is merciful. Yahweh will only visit the iniquity of the father unto the third and fourth generation while showing mercy to thousands (Exod 20,5-6; 34,7; Num. 14,18; Deut. 5,9).

The law of retaliation demands that the offender himself should be punished according to his sin. How strongly the sense of righteousness was influenced by this law appears from the fact that

Ezekiel arbitrarily establishes that so shall it be in real life. The law of the cohesion of the family, like all the old psychical laws, must give way before this postulate. "What mean ye that ye use this proverb in this land of Israel, saying: The fathers have eaten sour grapes, and the sons' teeth are dulled. As I live, saith the Lord Yahweh, ye shall not have occasion any more to use this proverb in Israel. Behold, all souls are mine, as the soul of the father so also the soul of the son is mine; the soul that sinneth, it shall die" (Ezek. 18,2-4, cf. 20; 33,18 and Jer. 31,29-30). The expression is clear enough: Yahweh is able to deal with man as he wants to, and he will follow the law of retaliation.

So far an abstract theory might deviate from the ground of the psychological presuppositions and reality. But it is only an isolated consequence. Ezekiel himself is sure that he bears the iniquity of the Israelites (4,4 ff.), and that the Israelites bear the iniquity of their fathers (16; 21,30.34; 35,5), and the same applies to Jeremiah (e. g. 14,20), in whose speeches, for that matter, the above-mentioned saying presumably does not at all belong.

Starting from the arbitrary and abstract law of justice, other problems can be raised. When a community consisting of sinners is visited and suffers destruction, it will inevitably involve in its ruin the few righteous who may be in it. Is this just? Also this question will be answered in the affirmative according to the old conception: the community is solidary. But the theorizing manner of thinking, so fully developed in the Yahwist, is shocked by this. It does not ask for reality, but deduces from its doctrines, and it says that Yahweh cannot sacrifice a few righteous people for the sake of the many unrighteous. He was willing to withhold his punishment from such a town as long as there were ten righteous men in it (Gen. 18). The problem, no less than its solution, is characteristic of the manner of thinking which dominated later Judaism.

But most important is the influence which the idea of retaliation came to exercise upon the relation of iniquity and misfortune. Sin demands misfortune as its punishment; misfortune is the righteous reaction against sin. To every sin must correspond a suitable amount of punishment: the two balance each other. Thus the way is paved for the idea that punishment is payment for the offence; when the sin has been paid for, it disappears, the sinner is a sinner no more. This quantitative measuring out of misfortune as punishment for iniquity leaves its traces in one of Yahweh's denunciations against the Israelites (Lev. 26), which speeches in other respects bear the old stamp. It is this consideration which causes the prophet of the exile to proclaim that the exile must be approaching its end, because the debt is paid, Israel having received a double measure of punishment in proportion to its sins (Is. 40,2).

That which characterizes all of these doctrines is their theoretical nature. The realities of life are treated as a sum in arithmetic, irrespective of the laws of reality. One thinks in abstractions and demands that reality should conform itself to them. But alongside of this the old real conception of Israel is maintained until a late period of its history.

Close to sin lies the *curse,* their mutual relation being as righteousness to blessing. The sinner is charged with the curse, for the curse is the dissolution which takes place in the soul of the sinner. It is as a poisonous, consuming substance that destroys and undermines, so that the soul falls to pieces and its strength is exhausted. This poisonous substance which spreads about is in Hebrew called *'ālā.* It consumes the earth, which loses its power of germination; the plants fade, towns collapse, the inhabitants wail and disappear from the surface of the earth (Is. 24,6-12), the whole of the country decays, all pastures are dried up (Jer. 23,10). A woman is penetrated with *'ālā,* and her belly is made to swell and her thigh to rot (Num. 5,21.27); children she cannot bear, and she becomes a curse among her people. When the Israelites came into Canaan, the blessing and the curse were to be put before them. The curse should come over sinners, and there is a very elaborate description of its substance. It reads as follows:

"Cursed be thou in the city, and cursed be thou in the field. Cursed be thy vessel and thy kneading trough. Cursed be the fruit of thy body, and the fruit of thy land, the increase of thine kine, and the flocks of thy sheep.[1] Cursed be thou, when thou comest in, and cursed be thou, when thou goest out. Yahweh shall send upon thee cursing, paralyzation, and rebuke, in all that thou settest thine hand unto for to do, until thou be destroyed, and until thou perish quickly, because of the wickedness of thy doings, that thou hast forsaken me. Yahweh shall make the pestilence cleave unto thee, until he have consumed thee from off the land, whither thou goest to possess it. Yahweh shall smite thee with a consumption, and with a fever, and with an inflammation, and with a burning of fever, and with the drought,[2] and with blasting, and with withering, and they shall pursue thee until thou perish. And thy heaven that is over thy head shall be brass, and the earth that is under thee iron. Yahweh shall make the rain of thy land powder and dust, from heaven it comes down upon thee, until thou be destroyed. Yahweh shall cause thee to be smitten before thine enemies; thou goest out one way against him and fleest seven ways before him, and becomest the horror[3] unto all the kingdoms of the earth. And thy carcass shall be meat unto all fowls of the air, and unto the beasts of the earth, and no man shall fray them away. Yahweh shall smite thee with the botch of Egypt, and with the emerods, and with the scab, and with the itch whereof thou canst not be healed. Yahweh will smite thee with madness, and blindness, and astonishment of heart. And thou shalt grope at noonday, as the blind gropeth in darkness, and thou shalt not prosper in thy ways; and thou shalt be only oppressed and spoiled evermore, and no man shall save thee. Thou shalt betroth a wife, and another man shall lie with her; thou shalt build a house, and thou shalt not dwell therein; thou shalt plant a vineyard, and thou shalt not gather the grapes thereof. Thine ox shall be slain before thine eyes, and thou shalt not eat thereof; thine ass shall be violently taken away from before thy face, and shall not be restored to thee; thy sheep shall be given unto thine enemies, and thou shalt have none to rescue thee. Thy sons and daughters shall be given unto another people, and thine eyes shall look and fail with longing for them all the day long, there being no might in thine hand. The fruit of thy land and all thy labours shall a nation which thou knowest not eat up; and thou shalt be only oppressed and crushed alway, so that thou shalt be mad for the sight of thine eyes, which thou shalt see. Yahweh shall smite thee in the knees, and in the legs with a sore botch that cannot be healed, from the sole of thy foot unto the top of thy head. Yahweh shall bring thee, and the king which thou shalt set over thee, unto a nation which neither thou nor thy fathers have known; and there shalt thou serve other gods, wood and stone. And thou shalt become an astonishment, a proverb, and a byword among all nations, whither Yahweh shall lead thee. Thou shalt carry much seed out into the field, and shalt gather but little in; for the locust shall consume it. Thou shalt plant vineyards and dress them, but neither drink nor store the wine, for the worms shall eat it. Thou shalt have olive trees throughout all thy estate, but thou shalt not anoint thyself with the oil; for thine olive shall cast his fruit. Thou shalt beget sons and daughters, but thou shalt not enjoy them, for they shall go into captivity. All thy trees and fruit of thy land shall the locust consume. The client that is within thee shall raise himself higher and higher above thee, and thou shalt sink lower and lower. He shall lend to thee, and thou shalt not lend to him; he shall be the head, and thou shalt be the tail...

And thou shalt eat the fruit of thine own body, the flesh of thy sons and of thy daughters, which Yahweh thy God hath given thee, in the straitness and the agony wherewith thine enemies shall distress thee. The man that is tender among you, and very delicate, he shall grudge giving his brother, and the wife of his bosom, and the remnant of his children any of the flesh of the children whom he shall eat; because he hath nothing left him in the straitness and sharp pain which thine enemies shall inflict upon thee in all thy gates...

And ye shall be left few in number, whereas ye were as the stars of heaven for multitude; because thou wouldst not obey the voice of Yahweh thy God. And it shall come to pass, that as Yahweh rejoiced over you to do you good and to multiply you, so Yahweh will rejoice over you to destroy you, and to bring you to nought; and ye shall be plucked from off the land whither thou goest to possess it. And Yahweh shall scatter thee among all people, from the one end of the earth even unto the other; and there thou shalt serve other gods, which neither thou nor thy fathers have known, even wood and stone. And among these nations shalt thou find no ease, neither shall the sole of thy foot have rest; but Yahweh shall give thee there a trembling heart, wearing out of eyes and dissolution of soul. And thy life shall seem to thee rootless; [1] and thou shalt fear day and night and shalt have none assurance of thy life. In the morning thou shalt say: Would God it were even! And at even thou shalt say: Would God it were morning! for the fear of thine heart, wherewith thou shalt fear, and for the sight of thine eyes which thou shalt see. And Yahweh shall bring thee into Egypt again with ships, by the way whereof I spoke unto thee: Thou shalt see it no more again; and there ye shall be sold unto your enemies for bondmen and bondwomen, and no man shall buy you" (Deut. 28,16-44.53-55.62-68).

In this classical description of the curse, which has its parallel in another code (Lev. 26), all the principal features are drawn with a sure and merciless hand. The cursed is the man for whom everything fails. The paralysis is in him, whatever he puts his hand to. Illness, drought, crop failure, defeat is the result. He is so dissolved and confused in his soul that he staggers on blindly. Whatever he touches is doomed to failure. If he takes a wife, then she is taken away by another; if he builds a house or plants a vineyard, others are to reap the fruits of his efforts, provided that there be any fruits. The power to create posterity fails, his people shrink into insignificance. It is shattered about the world, but nowhere it finds peace. All love disappears. When besieged by the enemy the cursed eats his own children. A greater perversity can hardly be imagined; the picture cannot become much blacker by the addition of his grudging his brother or wife to partake of the dreadful meal.

The dissolution is seated in the soul, which lacks the firm basis of all action. Therefore the cursed is rootless, full of fear in his empty life. So humbled he becomes that he who was under his protection shall rise far above him; he sinks deeper and deeper into actual slavery. Nay, the author of this gruesome description is so refined in his cruelty as to add that the cursed is not even to be considered worthy of this condition of life.

The curse acts within the soul, and it acts thoroughly. The whole of the soul is made empty by it, and all its fundamental values are undermined, honour as well as blessing and peace.

The curse and sin are so closely intertwined that they cannot be separated. Sin breeds the curse, and the curse breeds sin, but the horrible thing about the curse is that it can be put into the soul from without. Just as a man may utter the blessing into the soul of another, thus he can also utter the curse into it. Between souls which are together there must be a covenant, and this means that a common current of blessing passes through them; this is peace, and through this men uphold eachother. If evil thoughts or evil words come between them, then it is a curse; it counteracts the psychic community. The power of the curse is not *per se* implied in the wish or the word. It lies in the mysterious power of the souls to react upon each other. He whose soul creates something evil for another — be it in thought, in word or in deed — he puts the evil into the soul of his neighbour, where it exercises its influence.

If a man calls another a man of blood and a *b^elīya'al*'s man, as Shimei did (2 Sam. 16,7), then it is just as much a curse as when David says: Neither shall there fail from the house of Joab one that has an issue, or that is a leper, or that plieth a distaff [1] or that falleth on the sword, or that lacketh bread (2 Sam. 3,29), or when Yahweh says: Woe unto them! and: Confusion unto them! (Hos. 7,13). It is a curse to spit in the face of another (Num. 12,14; Deut. 25,9), to mock and debase, to make mouths (Is. 57,4), and to point the finger (Is. 58,9), all because it creates evil in the soul, counteracts the blessing and debases the honour. Sin and misfortune work together in the curse.

Therefore the striking power of the curse is particularly strong when it coincides with sin and injustice. With great effect one pronounces a curse against the unknown offender (Judg. 17,2; 1

Kings 8,31) And if violence has been done to someone, then his curse is dangerous for the perpetrator of violence; it acts together with the sin in the soul of the latter towards undermining it. A people which has been struck in this way must seek to remove the guilt as quickly as possible, that the good strength of the blessing may once more flow through it (2 Sam. 21,3). When Pharaoh was smitten with the death of all first-born because of his deeds of violence against the Israelites, then he let them go away and did not forget to ask them for their blessing (Exod. 12,32). He who has pronounced a curse makes up for his curse with a blessing (Judg. 17,2). If a curse has come upon one unjustly, then one is often able to maintain oneself in spite of that, but there is a danger. It is seated as an offence in the soul and is only removed through restoration by the humbling or death of its author, as appears from the example of Shimei.

Men of strong souls, like the prophets, speak stronger curses than ordinary people (2 Kings 2,24, cf. 6,16), and there are those who have special gifts for that kind of utterance, such as Balaam. There even seem to have been guilds of more or less professional cursers (Job 3,8). The strength of the word was increased by its being spoken from the holy place in front of the altar (1 Kings 8,31). And it seems a matter of course that the curse is particularly dangerous and horrid when proceeding from the most intimate circle, the blessing of which makes the very basis of existence for the man.

The best way to protect oneself against sin and curses is by acquiring blessing. The man rich in blessing is so full of good forces that evil cannot penetrate into him; he has the strength to dissolve the poison, and he has enough to spare for his friends. But the curse is always there, lying in wait as a danger. And it has its centres from which it spreads as well as the blessing. He who is charged with the curse, spreads it; first and foremost, of course, it spreads in the family, but it also infects all with whom he gets into touch, for souls must seek each other, and act upon each other. A cursed man becomes a curse for his surroundings (Num. 5,21.27; Deut. 28,37; 29,18; Jer. 42,18; 44,12), and therefore it is to be preferred that the cursed should be entirely removed. And when the wicked person is killed, his corpse must not be left to hang too long, for the curse is still in it, and may defile the land (Deut. 21,23). As everywhere else it holds good that the whole of the man has a share in and is responsible for what is in the soul, and that he may have to make amends for it. The man of misfortune who brings tidings of evil happenings and puts the evil into the soul of the king, runs the risk of being put to death. [1]

Thus there are sufficient circumstances which threaten to counteract the blessing and put the curse, with all its wickedness and misfortune, into the soul. It may rise in one's own soul, it may proceed from kinsmen and friends, from the evil thoughts, words and deeds of enemies, it may come from places where the curse lives. Without warning it is there with all its symptoms: discord and slackness in the soul, unhappiness, illness and misery.

When the Israelite is visited by disease or other misfortunes, he always sees it as a manifestation of this evil in the soul. The evil is only removed by removing its root. Then the question arises: Does it originate in my own sin or in the curse of others? And even though the latter be the case, then this will also put itself into the soul as a sin and make it responsible for it. When thus a man feels that he is "stricken in the soul" (1 Kings 8,38), then he goes to the temple in order to have his sin removed, and if he succeeds the blessing must return, whether the evil has come out in defeat, drought, famine, illness or in some other misfortune (1 Kings 8,33-40). We know that the Babylonians acted in the same way.

What a person "stricken" in that way has spoken, is also known to us, as part of the Psalms are prayers from such people asking to be liberated from evil. This in particular applies to the so-called psalms of "penitence" and "suffering". Characteristic is Psalm 6:

"Yahweh, rebuke me not in thine anger, neither chasten me in thy hot displeasure. Have mercy upon me, Yahweh, for I am weak; Yahweh, heal me, for my bones are paralyzed. My soul is also sorely paralyzed, but thou, Yahweh, how long? Return, Yahweh, deliver my soul; oh save me, for thy mercies' sake. For in death thy memory is not, in Sheol who praiseth thee? I am weary with my groaning; all the night make I my bed to swim; I water my couch with my tears. Mine eye is consumed because of my grief; it waxeth old because of all mine enemies. — Depart from me all of you who perform witchcraft; for Yahweh hath heard the voice of my weeping. Yahweh hath heard my supplication; Yahweh will receive my prayer. All mine enemies shall be ashamed and paralyzed; suddenly they shall be confused once more."

Closely related to this is Psalm 38:

"Yahweh, rebuke me not in thy wrath, neither chasten me in thy hot displeasure. For thine arrows stick fast in me, and thy hand presseth me sore. There is no soundness in my flesh, because of thine anger; neither is there any peace in my bones, because of my sin. For mine iniquities are gone over mine head; as an heavy burden they are too heavy for me. My wounds stink and fester, because of my foolishness. I am troubled, I am bowed down greatly; I go mourning all the day long. For my loins are filled with inflammation, [1] and there is no soundness in my flesh. I am feeble and sore broken; I have roared by reason of the disquietness of my heart. Yahweh, all my desire is before thee; and my groaning is not hid from thee. My heart panteth, my strength faileth me; as for the light of mine eyes, it also is gone from me. My lovers and my friends stand aloof from my sore; [2] and my kinsmen stand afar off. They pursue my life, lay snares for me, and they that plan my destruction speak mischievous things, and imagine deceits all the day long. But I am as a deaf man, in that I hear not, and I am as a dumb man that openeth not his mouth. I am as a man that heareth not, and in whose mouth are no reproofs.

For in thee, Yahweh, do I hope; thou wilt take charge of me, Yahweh, my Lord. For I said: Hear me lest otherwise they should rejoice over me; when my foot slippeth, they magnify themselves against me. For I am ready to halt, and my sorrow is continually before me. But I declare mine iniquity; I am depressed by my sin.

But my mortal enemies[1] are numerous; many are those that hate me wrongfully, that render evil for good, that are my adversaries, though I have followed the thing that is good. Forsake me not, Yahweh! O my God, be not far from me! Make haste and help me, Lord, my salvation!"

We might continue with other quotations, but these two are typical and contain all essential features. In conclusion we shall only add the beginning of Psalm 32, uttered by one who has been released from misery:

"Blessed is he whose guilt is taken away, whose sin is covered. Blessed is the man unto whom Yahweh imputeth not iniquity, and in whose spirit there is no slackness. When I kept silence, my bones were consumed through my roaring all the day long. For day and night thy hand was heavy upon me; my marrow was dried out by the heat of the summer. I acknowledged my sin unto thee, and mine iniquity I did not hide. I said: I will confess my transgressions unto Yahweh; and thou tookest away my guilt" (32,1-5).

Common to these and all the other psalms of suffering is the powerful description of psychical sensations. In all three psalms it is clearly a question of illness. He who is miserable implores Yahweh to heal him. His body is tormented with pain, he moans and calls aloud, his bed flows in tears. His whole body is sore, the poison, the arrows of Yahweh have penetrated into it, there is not one place where he feels "wholeness", "peace", i. e. health. He is filled with wounds, wasted, full of fear and throbbing of the heart. The glow of fever has consumed the essence of his strength, his marrow. Bodily suffering cannot be something isolated. It is the soul that suffers, being dissolved, powerless, devoid of vitality and the power to keep upright. He is "crooked" and cannot put his hand to anything. It is a matter of course that such a soul is full of sin. The sick man acknowledges it, and he prays that Yahweh will take away his sin and thus remove the root of his misery. In Psalm 32 a man who has recovered describes his joy at being liberated from the evil.

The state of the diseased is doubly miserable, because his illness removes his friends from him. This is a complaint which we know from Jeremiah and Job (Jer. 15,17; 30,14; Job 19,13-19); it recurs over and over again in the Psalms. His suffering strikes his friends with terror, so that they fly far off from the diseased and avoid his presence (Ps. 31,12; 88,9.19; 142,5). For the Israelite the most distressing feature about the disease is perhaps that he who only exists in the community of his kinsmen, is, by his misery, placed outside the community because, being affected by the poison of the curse, he conveys a danger to it. All who are able to do so avoid him; perhaps they even hurl a curse at him in order to guard themselves against his disease.

Isolation from kinsmen and friends, curses, derision and malignant exultation on the part of enemies, this is the experience of the miserable one. But the enemies are not merely accused of exulting at his pain and dishonour; they even help to create it.

The Psalms are constantly referring to *enemies.* Often they are called sinners, *r*ᵉ*shāʿīm.* According to the different kinds of Psalms the enemies also are different. In the royal psalms mention is chiefly made of strange peoples, external enemies, and the same is the case in other psalms which render the prayers of the people against its foes (Ps. 44; 46; 48; 60; 68; 74; 79; 83; 118). But as a rule it is clearly a question of domestic enemies. Now and again one gets the impression that these wicked, hostile sinners are the rich and mighty rulers (58; 94). When it is said that they murder widows, *gērīm* and fatherless and "unjustify innocent blood" (94,6.21) or that they take bribes (26,10), then it reminds us of the conditions described by the prophets, and in some psalms mention is also made of the happiness of the sinners in such a manner that they seem to belong to the mighty. But it would be wrong to see a homogeneous party or a certain order of society in them.

The sinners are those in whose souls wickedness abides, and this wickedness they show towards the man who complains. As a rule it is a case of purely personal matters; in a couple of psalms it is said that the enemies, the sinners, are former friends who have proved faithless (35; 55; 109). But in the eyes of him who complains, his own cause assumes enormous dimensions. In his isolated state he feels that he has the whole world against him; his release or recovery is not an individual matter, but the very victory of justice over sin and wickedness. By that the people are released from the unrighteousness and wickedness which his misery puts into it, nay, he proclaims his salvation loudly to the whole world, for the glorification of Yahweh, the god of justice.

Sometimes the miserable makes assurance that he is innocent of any iniquity (17,3-5; 18,21-25), and that all his misery is due to his enemies, but even though he be guilty, they still contribute to his misery. They may appear as false witnesses in a case, and thus cause him unhappiness (27,12; 35,11), but everything evil comes from them, lack of peace and, above all, disease.

His misfortunes are due to their curses. "The scourge of the tongues" which Eliphaz mentions (Job 5,21) is a dangerous weapon to be attacked with in Israel, and the inhuman beings of whom the Psalms speak know how to use it. They mock and curse the man who complains and whom they hate without reason. Their mouth is full of treacherous words; their tongue is a sharpened knife, a whetted sword (7,13; 52,4; 57,5; 64,4; 140,4), they vent their venom (140,4), send forth their wicked words as arrows (11, 2; 64,4; 120,4). Their throat is an open sepulchre from which curses and corruption are sent forth, an abyss of wickedness and destruction (5,10). With treacherous words they slander him, persecute his soul, whom they attempt to get into their power and to harm.

He is often thinking of individual persons. Sometimes he says that they come to him as friends with blessings, but when they are out of sight they speak their horrible curses, which cause him agonies (28,3; 41,7; 62,5). This duplicity is the most unpleasant feature of the picture given in these lamentations; the sick and "stricken" man becomes full of suspicion. When he sees people, to whom he has formerly shown friendship, keep away from him and avoid him in the street, nay, perhaps even gnash their teeth, roll their eyes and make mouths at him to keep him away (35,16.19.21), then he knows whom to thank for this suffering. They do not speak peace (35,20), and therefore they are the authors of his misfortune. His suspicion even extends to those who come to see him in his illness (41,7).

The enemies are constantly called the practicers of *'āwen,* which word, as we have seen, denotes the false strength, deeds involving disaster, witchcraft and magic arts. All that they do is *shāw'*, falsehood, corruption, acts which proceed from a sinful, inhuman soul and do harm. In secret they utter their fatal words, so that they themselves do not need to fear anything (10,8 f.; 64,5); mostly they send them forth during the night, the time when evil of all kinds has the strongest effect (11,2, cf. 36,5; 91,5). As wild beasts they are lying in wait for their prey (17, 12). By their wicked words they make snares as a fowler (91,3), dig pits and lay out nets (9,16; 10,9; 57,7; 140,6; 141,9; 142,4 *et al.).* We know these expressions from the Babylonians, where nets and snares are the current terms for the curse and the magic arts producing it, and the actual thing we not only know from the Babylonians, but from the different peoples outside modern culture. For them as for the Israelites illness and what pertains thereto either originates in one's own sin or in the curses and magic arts of evil-minded people. And so it must be from their conception of life.

The Israelite who is stricken with evil must do as the Babylonian in order to have it removed, i. e. turn to his God in his temple. He implores that his sin may be removed from his soul, and perhaps makes a sacrifice for it. And the magic arts must be removed, in that their authors, the wicked enemies, are struck down. Yahweh must help; it is the cause of Yahweh himself, justice, which is at stake. The sinners are *his* enemies. These assailants of life and righteousness merely make mock of Yahweh, they pretend ignorance of his existence. It is that which forms the background of our psalms.

In one of the Psalms the man who complains has a certain individual in view:

"Surely, he again whets his sword; he bends his bow and makes it ready. But for himself he hath prepared the weapons of death. He shapeth his arrows against... Behold he travaileth with witchcraft, and has conceived jugglery, and brought forth falsehood. He hath made a pit and digged it, but he falleth himself into the hole which he made. His jugglery comes over his own head, and his violence comes down upon his own pate" (7,13-17).

In another the wicked man is described in the following words: "The wicked in his overwhelming pride despiseth Yahweh. 'He interveneth not, there is no God', are all his thoughts. [1] His ways . . . at any time, thy requirements are far above him, as for all his enemies he puffeth at them. [2] He saith in his heart: I totter not; from generation to generation . . . not with evil. His mouth is full of cursing and deceit and fraud; under his tongue is jugglery and witchery. He sitteth in the lurking places of the villages; in the secret places doth he murder the innocent; his eyes spy after . . . He lieth in ambush secretly as a lion in its jungle; he lieth in wait to catch the afflicted; he doth catch the afflicted when he draweth him into his net" (10,4-9).

But most frequently they are mentioned as a gang of conspirators: "For I hear the slander of many, horror on every side; when they take counsel together against me, devise to catch my soul" (31,14). "Deliver me, Yahweh, from evil men; preserve me from violent men, which imagine evil things in their hearts, all the day they stir up wars. They sharpen their tongues like a serpent; adder's poison is under their lips. Keep me, Yahweh, from the hands of the wicked; preserve me from men of violent deeds who devise to trip up my feet. The reckless conceal traps for me and spread cords as a net; by the wayside they set snares for me. I say unto Yahweh: Thou art my God! hear the voice of my supplications, Yahweh. Yahweh, Lord, the stronghold of my salvation, thou coverest my head on the day of weapons. Grant not, Yahweh, the desires of the wicked, further not their wicked device . . . burning coals upon them, let them be cast into the pit, that they rise not up again. The men of tongues shall not persist in the country; evil shall hunt the men of violence — stroke by stroke. I know that Yahweh will maintain the cause of the afflicted, and the right of the poor. Surely the righteous shall praise thy name; the upright shall dwell in thy presence" (140).

This psalm is evidence of how the fight of the miserable becomes a fight for the right, which extends so far as to become a fight for all righteous. The following verses of a psalm are perhaps particularly characteristic:

"Hear my voice, O God, when I complain; preserve my life from dread of the enemy. Hide me from the secret counsel of the wicked, from the undertakings of the workers of witchcraft, who whet their tongue like a sword, aim with poisonous words for an arrow, that they may shoot in secret at the perfect; suddenly do they shoot at him without fear for themselves. Wicked words they make strong, recite them in order to lay hidden snares, they say: Who can see it? . . .[1] But God shall shoot against them with an arrow; suddenly[2] shall they be wounded. He makes them fall,[3] their tongue smites themselves. All that see them shall flee away.[4] And all men shall fear and shall declare the work of God and glorify[5] his deed. The righteous shall be glad in Yahweh, and shall trust in him, and all the upright in heart shall glory" (64, 2-11).

Through the Psalms we are acquainted with a community of strong discords, as it developed in towns like Jerusalem. People fight among themselves. Violence and transgression are the order of the day. But first and foremost it is a fight to preserve the blessing from being weakened. It is a fight of souls, carried on with thoughts and words. On one hand the fight is carried on by witchcraft and curses in order to paralyze the soul of the opponent, and the person attacked, on the other hand, guards himself by uttering curses on the cursers. If he is able to paralyze them, then also the source of his misery is stopped. Therefore he begs Yahweh to strike them with their own curse, so that they fall into the grave they dug for him; live coals are to rain on them; they are to sink down into Sheol. A couple of the most powerful of these curses of cursers read as follows:

"Their table shall become a trap before them, a snare unto men in the midst of peace. Their eyes shall be darkened that they see not; and their loins shall be continually shaking. Pour out thine indignation upon them, thy wrathful anger shall overtake them. Their habitation shall be desolate, and none shall dwell in their tents. For they persecute him whom thou hast smitten; and they talk to the grief of thy wounded. Add iniquity unto their iniquity, and let them not come into thy righteousness. Let them be blotted out of the Book of Life, and not be written with the righteous" (69,23-29).

"Set thou a wicked man against him, and let an adversary stand at his right hand. When he is judged, he shall come forth condemned, and his prayer shall become sin. His days shall be few, and another man shall take his office. His children shall be fatherless and his wife a widow. His children shall be continually vagabonds and beg, . . . from their desolate places. The extortioner shall lay snares for all that he hath, and the strangers shall spoil his labour. There shall be none to extend mercy unto him; neither shall there be any to favour his fatherless children. His posterity shall be cut off, and in the generation following his [1] name shall be blotted out. The iniquity of his fathers shall be remembered with Yahweh; and the sin of his mother shall not be blotted out. They shall be in sight of Yahweh continually, that he may cut off the memory of them from the earth. Because that he remembered not to show mercy, but persecuted the afflicted and poor and attempted to kill one whose heart was broken. As he loved cursing, so let it come unto him; as he delighted not in blessing, so let it be far from him. As he clothed himself with cursing like as with his garment, so let it come into his bowels like water and like oil into his bones. Let it be unto him as the garment which covereth him, and for a girdle wherewith he is girded continually. Let this be the reward of my pursuers from Yahweh, and of them that speak evil against my soul" (109,6-20).

The same features pervade all of these violent curses; the vitality of the soul is undermined, the ties which connect it with the organism from which it sucks strength and nourishment are gnawn asunder: peace, honour and blessing are lost.

Naturally there are degrees in the curse. The powerful absolute curse is the one which detaches the soul from its community, from the family, the town or the people. To put one under such a curse is called in Hebrew *'ārar*. If it acts throughout it must entail death and expulsion. That Cain was cursed *('ārūr)* from the tilled land meant that every connection with it was severed (Gen. 4,11), and that the serpent was cursed from the animals (Gen. 3,14) means that it was put outside their community. When a man has sinned so greatly that he must be removed from the community, then it is the curse which is carried out and, as we have seen, it is accomplished in a more or less radical manner, through expulsion, burning or stoning. The external acts are only the natural result effected by the substance of the souls of the sinner and the cursed. Its dissolution and corruption has solved it from the normal community. To be cursed is the same as to perish (Job 3,3).

In any case the curse gnaws the substance of the soul. It threatens to make light the "heavy" soul of him who is full of honour; to "make light" (*ḳillēl, hēḳal*) is the most frequent Hebrew term for it.[1] Its infringement upon honour and blessing may be stronger or weaker; but, when seated in the soul, even a weak curse has always the possibility of gaining strength, and eating its way so far in that it consumes righteousness. And he who is made quite "light", so that his soul is emptied of its whole substance, is no better off than the great sinner; the law of life does not act in him, and some day he must perish. Therefore the Israelite must make use of all his energy to keep every curse far from him.

THE WORLD OF LIFE AND DEATH.

THE Israelite calls the world "heaven and earth", meaning thereby the world that is imbued with life. But if everything is to be included, then the world falls into three parts: the heaven above, the earth in the centre, and the waters of the nether world. [1] The earth is a round plane (Is. 40,22); together with the heavens it forms a grand building, which to the Hebrew suggests a tent or a house, resting on pillars.

The heaven is stretched as the curtain of a tent (Is. 40,22; Ps. 104,2). This does not mean that it consists of a loose or fragile fabric; it is a firm vault, resting solidly on the circle of the earth (Am. 9,6), made fast to pillars (Job 26,11). On that sun, moon and stars are placed, each with its nature and wanderings, all connected with the light; for heaven is the home of light.

Above heaven are the mighty waters, the deep from which the rain pours down through the railings of heaven (Gen. 7,11; 8,2; 2 Kings 7,2) or its doors (Ps. 78,23). Up there rain, snow and hail have their chambers from which they are poured out upon the earth. [2] The poet can speak of the heavenly water-conduits (Job 38,25), and, like the Arabians, the Israelites speak of the clouds as water-bags sending forth their contents (Ps. 104,13; Job 26,8; 38,37).

Also below the earth the mighty ocean extends. [3] Into that are sunk the pillars upon which the earth rests; they are well fastened and do not totter; the pillars are the great mountains, the deep roots of which extend downwards into the ocean and form the foundations of the earth. Under the earth lies not only the ocean, but also Sheol, the habitation of the departed souls.

This conception of the universe is mainly the same as that of the Babylonians; it has surely been the prevailing one in the whole of Western Asia.[1] But it only shows us certain external sides of the Israelitic view of the world; their conception of the universe derives character and substance from their idea of the very world in which they live. The earth, *'ereṣ,* is the centre of the world, placed between the upper and nether waters, but it is not a homogeneous mass. The earth forms the basis of life; as such it is sometimes called *tēbhēl,*[2] but the characteristic word is *'adhāmā.*

This word, the relationship of which with *'ādhām,* man, is so obvious, applies to the land inhabited and cultivated by man (Gen. 2,5; 47,23; 2 Sam. 9,10).[3] The Israelitic conception of the nature of habitable land is determined by the natural conditions of Palestine, the country of agriculture and cattle-breeding. We often hear eulogies of the Israelitic land. It is called "a land that floweth with milk and honey",[4] land with "corn and young wine and oils" and pastures for the cattle (Deut. 11,10 ff.; Joel 1,10 *et al.),* "a good land of brooks and fountains and wells springing out in valley and on hill, a land of wheat, and barley, and vines, and fig-trees, and pomegranates, a land of olive-tree and honey" (Deut. 8,7-8). It partly consists of cultivated fields, partly of pastures.[5] It is the water which makes it what it is. The rain pours down from above, springs well from the ground, and together with brooks and rivers they are the creators of fertility. For the Israelite "the land" is the country where blessing abides.

This does not only mean that it is fertile land. The blessing is not identical with material fertility, but is the source of it. The blessing is the vital nerve, the positive value of life and the strength in all forms of life. The country is the place where the values abide, where the forces belong, where the law and order of the people of blessing prevails. With horror the Israelite thinks of the man who has been driven out of the country of blessing and now roams about in other places, where anyone can slay him, because there is nothing of what he understands by the law of man (Gen. 4,14).

The opposite of the land of man is the *desert-land.* It is the *evil* place "where there is no seed, nor figs, nor vines, nor pomegranates, neither is there any water to drink" (Num. 20,5). In the desert the good plants do not grow; its soil is full of stones and salt, covered with nettles, with thorns and thistle (Is. 5,6; 7,24; Zeph. 2,9). "Terrible" the Israelites call the desert; it consists of waterless wastes, inhabited by horrible beasts, such as serpents and scorpions (Deut. 8,15). From that comes the fiery, all-consuming storm (Jer. 4,11), not the mild winds which bring rain and fertility.

When the Bedouin speaks of the desert, he expresses his love of the free, unbounded expanses, a worthy scene for the valiant warrior who goes out to perform valiant deeds, and who cannot put up with the narrow fetters with which hard work constrains the life of the peasant. The Israelite who himself came from the desert must, at one time, have looked upon it in a similar way; traces of this view are to be found even at a very late period. For the sect of the Rechabites the life of the desert was the ideal one. But for the average Israelite the desert only appears as the direct opposite; he merely knows its terror.

For the Israelite the wilderness is the home of the curse. Wicked demons are at work here (Lev. 16,10.21 f.), but for human beings it is uninhabitable. Not only normal humans, but also the animals belonging to the world of man, keep far from it. There is no thoroughfare, no wayfarers, only the bellowing of animals which live far from the dwellings of man — wild asses, jackals, ostriches, owls and ravens. [1] When Jeremiah says that if he could find a lodging place in the wilderness, he would leave his people (9,1), then it means that he prefers the worst to his present surroundings.

A prophetic curse on Edom describes the appearance of such a desert land:

"And the streams thereof shall be turned into pitch, and the dust thereof into brimstone, and the land thereof shall become burning pitch. It shall not be quenched, night nor day; the smoke thereof shall go up for ever; from generation to generation it shall lie waste; none shall pass through for ever and ever. But the *kā'āth* bird and the hedgehog shall possess it; the owl [2] also, and the raven shall dwell in it; and he shall stretch out upon it the line of chaos and the stone-weight of confusion. [It is the haunt of satyrs] but its nobles [are not there]. [1] There is no kingdom, which they proclaim, and all its chiefs have disappeared. And its palaces shall be overgrown with thorns, its fortresses shall be filled with nettles and brambles. And it shall be an habitation of jackals and camping place [2] of ostriches. Wild cats meet with jackals, and the satyr shall cry to his fellow. Lilith [3] also shall rest there and find for herself a place of rest. There the poisonous adder makes her nest, [4] and lays and hatches and gathers under her shadow; there the vultures also gather; the one shall not miss [5] the other" (Is. 34,9-15).

This is a description, point by point, of a cursed country, where the blessing is lacking. The wilderness is the land of chaos, because the law of life does not operate there; we hear several times that the desert is *tōhū* or *tōhū wābhōhū*, the characteristic expressions of chaos, the lawless, the empty. He who wanders there may suddenly be led astray, for there is no road; how should a road leading to a goal be found in a "land" the essence of which is disorder and confusion? [6]

Through the powerful descriptions which the prophets give of the non-land, we get perhaps the strongest impression of what the good land, the land of man is. But the frontier line between the land of man and the desert-land cannot be drawn geographically. Every Israelite knows, it is true, that the desert land proper lies towards east and south, outside the frontiers of Canaan, but it sends its offshoots far into the land of man; for the land of the desert is to be found wherever the curse abides.

Within the habitated land there are patches of cursed land. The Israelite speaks with a shudder of Sodom and Gomorrah, where nothing living can dwell, because the sins of the people called down fire and brimstone over it. [7] There are towns which are laid waste in war, burnt and possibly strewn with salt. Thus Joshua made Ai a desert for ever, and he laid a curse upon the fallen Jericho; Abimelech broke down Shechem and strewed salt on the ruins. [8] These patches of cursed land, ruins and deserts, are to be found everywhere in the country. Human beings avoid them, but the sinful, those who are stricken with a curse, belong in such places, in "degenerate (strictly 'made a lie') cities and in houses which no man inhabiteth, which are ready to become heaps" (Job 15,28).

But even where the blessing grows, the curse is ever lying in wait; in the good fields it shoots up with thickets and thorn and thistle (Gen. 3,18), all of those things which have their home in the desert-land. Anywhere in the world of man the wilderness may crop up, but then the humans must flee, for the wilderness is not for man. As the good land is closely connected with the world of man, thus the "monsters" belong in the desert-land. In the Book of Job there is a picturesque description of this inhuman life: "For want and famine they are barren, they gnaw the desert, . . .[1] waste and wilderness. In the shrubs of the wilderness they gather mallow, and broom roots for their meat. They are driven forth from among men; they cried after them as after a thief. They must dwell in the valleys of horror, in caves of the earth and the rocks. Among the bushes they bray; under the nettles they gather together. They are the children of fools, yea, of nameless men, which are whipped out of the country" (Job 30,3-8).

Outside the world of man is the wilderness, and yet so close to it that man must constantly strive to keep it away. This means that the desert-land still lies as a threatening possibility in the very land of man. If sin and curse got such a hold of man that the blessing was reduced to nothing, then the wilderness would be there at once. And it is this possibility of which the prophets speak continually.

How far the conception of the universe is determined by the conception of the psychic whole appears from one of the denominations of the wilderness, *sh^e^māmā*. This word, in its verbal form, denotes the paralyzation prevailing in a soul touched by evil, whether it be a weaker touch, as by a passing vision of unhappiness, or whether it be a vital blow. It is used of a violated woman like Tamar, left alone in her misery (2 Sam. 13,20); also of the violated woman Israel, sitting in foreign parts in her exile, in childlessness and widowhood (Is. 54,1); of him whose soul is so perturbed that his self-control vanishes, and he must cry out in pain like a travailing woman (Is. 42,14); of the leaders of the people, standing there with nerveless hands, because their hearts shall perish in their misery (Jer. 4,9); of the heart of the miserable, when his will and strength is changed into nervelessness (Ps. 143,4), and of the enemy, whose strength is paralyzed (Ps. 40,16); but it is also used of him who stands dumb and stiff in horror at what he sees (1 Kings 9,8; Is. 52,14; Jer. 18,16; 19,8; 49,17; Ezek. 27,35; 28,19; Job 21,5 and many other places); possibly only of him who for a moment stands still in astonishment (Is. 63,5). In the same manner it is used of a town or a people which has lost its strength and its power to live (Lam. 1,13.16; 3,11), of fields that are no longer cultivated (Gen. 47,19), of the inhabited land which no more shelters human beings (Ezek. 33,28), of pastures in which there is no more life (Jer. 10,25; 49,20; 50, 45; Ps. 79,7).

These examples, which are taken at random from the different verbal forms, show us clearly enough the substance of the word. It denotes the effects of the curse in all its forms, and with this corresponds the various derived nouns. It is the paralysis, the terror, the destruction, the curse which is implied in them, and at the same time they denote the paralyzed, the destroyed, the accursed, the place on which the curse rests. *sh^{e}māmā* is the country lacking the blessing of the country of man, where no human beings but only jackals dwell (Jer. 32,43; 49,33), the dry land (Joel 2,20), the land of ruins, *ḥorbā.*[1]

There is an intimate connection between the nature of the land and the men who dwell in it. If man maintains the blessing, then it penetrates the land and makes it a land of man; the blessing is in the field and in the pastures. Mountains and hills are covered with peace and righteousness (Ps. 72,3) which fill barns and yield fodder for the cattle. The brooks carry water in abundance, the rain pours down, the valleys wave with the blessed grain, the hills are clothed with flocks of sheep (Ps. 65,10-14); the Israelite rejoices in the land where the mountains flow with new wine, and the hills flow with milk, and all the rivers flow with water (Joel 4,18; Am. 9,13).

All this is implied in the essence of the blessing, but it rests on an intimate companionship between people and land. The land is a "land of possession" (Lev. 14,34 *et al.)* that is, it is penetrated by the soul of the Israelites, they *know* it, as contrasted with other countries with which they have no psychic community (Jer. 16,13). If they maintain righteousness and thus preserve the blessing, then peace must likewise permeate them in their relation to the country; they act in harmony with it. It is this which the law expresses by saying that if they live according to its demands their days shall be long in the land (Exod. 20,12; Deut. 5,16; 32,47). Israel came into existence, in that it was received into the human land from the desert (Deut. 32,10; Hos. 9,10). It is just as wonderful as if one would go gathering grapes in the desert.

If sin gains the upper hand, the curse will be present immediately, and it must invariably react upon the country. It is defiled, profaned, filled with sin (Lev. 19,29; Num. 35,33; Jer. 2,7; 3,2.9). The curse entails the nature of the desert. If blood-guilt rests upon a land, then its fertility is gone, as appeared in the days of David (2 Sam. 21,1). All vegetation fades, animals and birds disappear (Jer. 12,4), the country is no more a habitation of human beings, but ends by pouring forth its inhabitants (Lev. 18,25; 20,22).

The connection between the nature of the country and the blessing which is to be maintained by man is so powerful that the country *is* a wilderness as soon as sin prevails. Even though desolation has perhaps not yet developed, it still lies under the surface, ready to burst forth. The prophet says: The earth is defiled under the inhabitants thereof; because they have transgressed the laws, violated the ordinance, broken an eternal covenant. Therefore the curse devoureth the earth, and they that dwell therein are desolate; therefore the inhabitants of the earth are scorched and few men left. The new wine drieth out, the vine withereth, all the merry-hearted do sigh ... The city of chaos is broken down; every house is shut up that no man may come in (Is. 24, 5-7.10). And in Jeremiah we read: I behold the earth and, lo, it is chaos; I look towards the heavens, and they have no light. I see the mountains and, lo, they tremble, and all the hills totter. I behold, and, lo, there is no man, and all the birds of the heavens are fled. I behold, and, lo, the fruitful place is a wilderness, and all the cities thereof are broken down. This comes from Yahweh and the blaze of his wroth (Jer. 4,23-26).

This conception of the country forms a natural link in the total Israelitic conception. Blessing and curse cannot exist peacefully beside each other; if, through their sin, the people have become penetrated with the curse, then this must act throughout and consume the blessing of the country. The Israelite thus cannot give himself up to the conviction that he lives in the blessed land, and that the wilderness is far away. The wilderness is wherever the curse lives; therefore there is no distinct borderline between that and the land of man. The land of man must be maintained, and the desert land must be kept out, in that the blessing is preserved.

It is the contrast between life and death which determines the Israelitic conception of the universe. Therefore the enemy of the good country is not only the desert-land, but also the land of the grave. The world which lies in the sun, where men are moving and working, is the land of life (Is. 38,11; 53,8; Ezek. 32,32). Below it extends the land of death, Sheol.

The dead dwell in the grave. There the corpse is laid; to die means the same as to go down into the grave (Ps. 16,10; 30,10; 55,24; Job 17,14 *et al.).* In the grave the dead remain, and there the survivors may look for them (see, e. g., Jer. 31,15).

But the individual grave is not an isolated world; it forms a whole with the graves of the kinsmen who make a common world and are closely united. Nor does the thought stop at this totality. Viewed from the world of light, all the deceased form a common realm, because they are essentially subjected to the same conditions.

This common realm the Israelites call *shᵉʾōl* or the nether world. Here the dead gather, lying on their beds of worms and corruption. Sheol is the deepest place in the universe, just as heaven is the highest (Is. 7,11; 57,9; Prov. 9,18 *et al.*). There is room for many, and he who has got down there, never returns (2 Sam. 12,

23; Job 7,9; 10,21; 16,22). Like the Greeks, the Israelites may speak of the nether world as a cruel animal; insatiable it opens its jaws wide in order to swallow man (Is. 5,14; Hab. 2,5; Prov. 27,20; 30,16). We find suggestions of the Babylonian descriptions of the world of the dead as a town or a great palace when mention is now and again made of the chambers of death (Prov. 7,27) and of the gates and bolts of Sheol (Is. 38,10; Ps. 9,14; 107,18; Job 17,16; 38,17).

What then is the mutual relation between the conception of the grave and that of Sheol? The attempt to unite them usually offers such difficult problems to the minds of scholars that they make a sharp division between them as two fundamentally different conceptions; the more general conception of Sheol being said to be of later, possibly foreign origin.[1] But he who is satisfied with this view will be disappointed if he proceeds to other peoples, for there he will constantly be confronted with the same problem.

The ideas of the grave and of Sheol cannot be separated. Every one who dies goes to Sheol, just as he, if everything happens in the normal way, is put into the grave. When the earth swallowed up Dathan and Abiram with all that belonged to them, they went straight down into Sheol (Num. 16,29 ff.), and Jacob now speaks of going into the grave (Gen. 47,30), now of going to Sheol (Gen. 37,35). The dead are at the same time in the grave and in Sheol, not in two different places.

In Ezekiel there is a description of how the king of Egypt suffers defeat and goes down to Sheol. It is proclaimed unto him that he must *lie* down in Sheol together with the uncircumcised, as the body is laid into the grave. All of the fallen form one kingdom. Ashur is there with all her company; "his (i. e. the Egyptian king's) graves are about him"; in them lie all his fallen giants, "her (Ashur's) graves are set in the sides of the pit, and her company is round about her grave".[2] There is Elam with all her graves, bearing shame with them that go down to the pit; and Meshech, Tubal, Edom and the princes of the north join them, all who formerly spread terror in the land of the living lie in Sheol, in the pit between graves and people who went down to the grave (Ezek. 32,19-32).

The relation between the grave and Sheol cannot be unravelled according to our conceptions of space. From the saying of Ezekiel one might get the impression that Sheol was a common world in which the graves formed compartments. But sometimes we hear that Sheol is deep down under the earth, though the grave is just below the surface; and all the chiefs of the above-mentioned countries — meeting in the realm of the dead — their graves are to be found far from each other in the various regions of the earth. Thus the fallen king of Babylonia also sits on his throne in the nether world, surrounded by shadows, at the same time abiding somewhere, decaying, devoured by worms, far away from the family-grave (Is. 14,19).

Sheol is the entirety into which all graves are merged; but no more than the other entireties which fill the Israelitic world of ideas, it is the result of a summing up of all the single parts, so that Sheol should be the sum of the graves. All graves have certain common characteristics constituting the nature of the grave, and that is Sheol. The "Ur"-grave we might call Sheol; it belongs deep down under the earth, but it manifests itself in every single grave, as *mō'ābh* manifests itself in every single Moabite. Where there is grave, there is Sheol, and where there is Sheol, there is grave.

The grave is both good and bad. In it dwell the fathers, and the family keeps its graves close by it; but, nevertheless, it is the home of death and in so far the enemy of life. In the grave is corruption (Job 17,14); it is the habitation of nothingness (Is. 38,17). Therefore the nether world is also called *'ᵃbhaddōn,* the place of corruption (Ps. 88,12; Prov. 15,11; Job 26,6; 28,22). Those who dwell there are weak and tottering (Is. 14,10; 59,10; Ezek. 26,20); they are called *rᵉphā'īm,* the slack (Is. 14,9; 26, 14.19; Ps. 88,11 *et al.*). "There is no action nor thought nor knowledge, nor wisdom in Sheol" (Eccles. 9,10); there one does not remember; it is the land of forgetfulness (Ps. 88,13).

The realm of the dead is the home of evil. There death and curse are concentrated. There illness and plagues belong. "Death, hither with plague! O Sheol, hither with disease!" says the prophet (Hos. 13,14); it is filled with misfortune, pain and trouble (Ps. 116,3). The desolation of the realm of death increased more and more in Israel, in the same degree as temporal prosperity became the ideal. And when the connection of the family was slackened, merely the desolation remained. The Psalms only know terror of the grave.

The realm of death is thus closely related with the desert-land. The two belong together as the opposite of the land of man, the land of light. At the same moment that Yahweh calls the plague up from Sheol, he calls the east wind in from the desert, that it may dry out the springs of the country and consume its riches (Hos. 13,15). That which characterizes both countries is chaos, the lack of strength, of firmness and law.

These two realms of death are gradually joined by a third, the immense deep, the ocean, which lies curbed under the earth. Also this is chaos, *tōhū* (Job 26,7), which lies lurking under the world of man. It has that in common with the realm of death that it is subterraneous, and the natures of the two worlds are so related that they merge entirely into one another. We cannot sharply define their spacial relation to one another. The conception of the ocean the Israelites have borrowed from the Babylonians, but they have assimilated it with their own total conception.

The ocean, *tehōm,* lies below (Gen. 49,25; Deut. 33,13), as also does Sheol. The mountains are sunk into the ocean, but it may be said of the realm of the dead that it is at the roots of the mountains (Jon. 2,7), just as it is said of the shades of the dead that they are under the waters (Job 26,5). And yet Sheol is identical with the grave, and when the earth opens, one plunges right into it.

He who is in Sheol is also in the ocean, because they both denote the subterraneous, negative power, the world of death and chaos. He is surrounded by its waters, which close over him; he wades in slime and seaweed (Ps. 40,3; Jon. 2,6); he is swallowed up by the ocean, the great deep, *meṣōlā*, attracts him to it (Ps. 69,3.16; 88,7). He is overwhelmed by the surges of death (2 Sam. 22,5) and desires to be pulled up from the *tehōmōth* of the earth, its ocean-deep (Ps. 71,20). Sheol and the ocean are fused in a unity, as the source of all that is evil. In Sheol flow the streams of *b^e^līya'al,* i. e. the waters of nothingness, those that do not produce anything good or positive (2 Sam. 22,5; Ps. 18,5).

The three non-worlds we find united in a prophetical description of the destruction of Tyre: When I shall make thee a desolate city, like the cities that are not inhabited, by leading *the deep* over thee, and when great waters shall cover thee, then I shall bring thee down with them that descend into the *pit,* with the people of eternity, and shall set thee in the land of *the nether world* like *ruins* from eternity, with them that went down to the pit: that thou be not inhabited and have a place [1] in the land of the living; I will make thee a terror, and thou shalt be no more; though thou be sought for, yet shalt thou never be found again (Ezek. 26, 19-21).

The living town is transformed into a dead one. It becomes a desert land, ruins, uninhabitable for human beings; it sinks into the nether world, overflown by the ocean. The "pit" into which it disappears, *bōr,* is the appellation both of a hole in the ground, filled with stones (Is. 14,19), and of the depths of bottomless corruption, filled by the slime of the ocean (Ps. 40,3).

Common to the three non-worlds is *darkness.* Its proper home is in Sheol. Job speaks of "the land of darkness and gloom, a land of darkness like blackness, gloom and confusion; its shining is a darkness" (Job 10,21 f.). The darkness actually becomes the characteristic term for the realm of the dead; in the speech of God to Job it sounds: Have the gates of death been opened unto thee? or hast thou seen the doors of the gloom? (Job 38,17). And the psalmist asks: Are thy wonders known in the dark? and thy righteousness in the land of forgetfulness? (Ps. 88,13). The dead are those who do not see light (Ps. 49,20); on the other hand, *ṣalmāweth,* "the shadow of death", is the strongest denomination of darkness. [2] But also in the depth of the ocean darkness prevails. "Thou hast laid me in the pit of the nether world, in darkness, in the deeps", it is said in a psalm (88,7). And so closely connected is it with the land that is hostile to life that it is also connected with the desert-land. Jeremiah speaks of the desert, the land of the steppe and the ravines, the land of desolation and darkness, where no one travels nor abides (Jer. 2,6, cf. 31). Outside *tēbhēl* darkness prevails (Job 18,18). He who is turned away from the land of man, into the trackless chaos *(tōhū)*, gropes about in the darkness as one intoxicated (Job 12,25).

In the world of man *light* belongs; it is inseparably united with life. Light is life, but life is, as we know, to possess the values of life. Therefore light is identical with blessing and peace, with righteousness and truth. Light radiates from the eye of the strong, spreading blessing about it. "In the light of the king's countenance there is life" (Prov. 16,15). The blessed wander in the light of life (Ps. 56,14; Job 33,30); the healthy see the light (Job 33,28). It is true that, to a certain extent, all men see light as long as they live (Job 3,20), but life may be so weak in one that it deserves only to be called darkness. Light one only has in happiness and prosperity. "Light is sown for the righteous" (Ps. 97,11), "unto the upright there ariseth light in the darkness" (Ps. 112,4), "the people that walked in darkness, see a great light" (Is. 9,1), "he will bring me forth to the light, and I shall behold his righteousness" (Mic. 7,9). We might continue with quotations of this kind, analogies of which are also offered by the Babylonians. When Israel enters into a "covenant with peoples", then it also becomes a light for the peoples, because it yields to them the happiness of peace (Is. 42,6; 49,6). And light is identical with righteousness and truth: "He brings forth thy righteousness as the light" (Ps. 37,6); the right *(mishpāṭ)* of Yahweh is to go out as the light of the peoples (Is. 51,4); "send out thy light and thy truth", the humble ask (Ps. 43,3).

Earth is penetrated by light, i. e. by vitality. It is upheld by the great reserve of power abiding in God; by his light it is that man "sees light" (Ps. 36,10). But not all that is in the world is light. The non-world sends its darkness into the world of man, where it eclipses the light and disappears in troubles, misery, death. The day of misery is the day of darkness. "It is darkness, not light" (Am. 5,18.20, cf. 8,9), "a day of trouble and distress, a day of destruction and corruption, a day of darkness and gloom" (Zeph. 1,15). Darkness is the evil in all its forms, both as sin in the soul, and as unhappiness. The sinners who call the evil good and the good evil "make darkness into light and light into darkness" (Is. 5,20). Therefore also "darkness of distress" will come upon the land, and the light will be darkened (Is. 5,30). Job in his misery is overwhelmed by darkness, covered with gloom (Job 23,17). Instead of the happiness he expected, he has gained unhappiness, for light darkness (30,26). Darkness is the element of sinners. They are the enemies of light, sneak about in the night, murder and steal in darkness (Job 24,13-16). Therefore they also belong to darkness. They perish in darkness (1 Sam. 2,9). The darkness which they themselves have chosen will not leave hold of them, but fall upon them with fear and sword and misery (Job 15,22 ff.).

The darkness wells forth from the non-world into the world of light. It abides with sinners and men of evil, for they themselves belong to the world of Sheol. "The sinners shall return into Sheol", it is said (Ps. 9,18), for there they belong. According as Sheol more and more becomes the concentration of evil, all sin must tend towards Sheol, because it belongs to its world. In the Proverbs there are some characteristic sayings of the loose-living woman: "Her feet go down to death, her steps are directed towards Sheol. She does not wander along the path of life, her tracks are uncertain, she has no knowledge" (Prov. 5,5-6); "her house is the way to Sheol going down to the chambers of death" (7,27). Her ways wind backwards and forwards, without firmness, and must therefore necessarily end in the non-world.

The sinner goes to Sheol, but in reality he is there already. Just as the wilderness crops up in the land of man and is to be found wherever evil abides, so also the nether world, after it has come to stand for the home of the wicked. Where there is darkness, there is also the nether world; for the nether world is wherever there is a nether world nature. He who is struck by evil, by unhappiness, disease or other trouble *is* in Sheol, and when he escapes from the misery and "beholds the light", then he has escaped from Sheol. The thought is so obvious to the Israelite, because he is always governed by the totality. If he has any of the nature of Sheol within him, then he feels it entirely. He feels the desolation of the grave, the oppressing darkness; nay, even the waves of the chaotic ocean he feels beating about him with their slime and mud.

This enables us to understand the fundamental cord struck in the many psalms of lamentation and thanksgiving. We may begin with a small psalm of thanksgiving in the Book of Job. A man has been ill and his flesh consumed away, "his soul drew near unto the grave, and his life to the destroyers" (33,22). But then he recovered, and he now goes to God in the temple and recites a song of thanksgiving, which reads: "He hath delivered my soul from going into the pit, and my life seeth the light. Lo, all these things worketh God oftentimes with man, to bring back his soul from the pit, to be enlightened with the light of the living" (Job 33,28-30). In other words: the man was so ill that he came near the grave; but the very disease was a sojourn in the grave, from which recovery brings him back.

A psalm of the same kind is to be found in chapter 2 of the Book of Jonah: "I cried by reason of mine affliction unto Yahweh, and he heard me. Out of the belly of Sheol cried I, and thou heardest my voice. For thou hadst cast me into the deep, in the midst of the seas, and the floods compassed me about; all thy billows and thy waves passed over me. Then I said: I am shut out from appearing before thine countenance; surely I will look continually toward thy holy temple. The waters compassed me about, even to the soul; the ocean closed me round about, the weeds were wrapped about my head. I went down to the roots of the mountains; the bars of earth were about me for ever; but thou hast brought up my life from the grave, Yahweh my God! When my soul fainted within me, I remembered Yahweh; and my prayer came in unto thee, into thine holy temple. They that have regard to idols of vanity forsake their own love. But I will sacrifice unto thee with the voice of thanksgiving; I will fulfill my vow. My salvation I owe to Yahweh."

What the trouble is which has given rise to his poem, is not said expressly, but it is probably illness, which consumes the strength of the miserable and makes him faint. He is in Sheol; in his dizziness he feels the waters of chaos pass over him. He is far down in the deep, far from life. Then he remembers

Yahweh. He cannot present himself before Yahweh, i. e. go up to the temple.[1] But, in order to get his share in the strength of the holy place, he turns towards it and directs his look towards the sanctuary. He sends his prayer towards the temple and promises a sacrifice unto Yahweh if he gets well. As this really happens, he goes to the temple to offer his promised sacrifice, but before the sacrificial act he recites this psalm and praises Yahweh as his saviour, the only one of the gods to whom it is worth while to cleave.

There are other psalms showing how misery and illness make the prayer go down into Sheol, e. g.: "I will extol thee, Yahweh, for thou hast pulled me up[2] and hast not made my foes to rejoice over me. Yahweh, my God, I cried unto thee, and thou hast healed me. Yahweh, thou hast brought up my soul from Sheol, thou madest me alive, when I had gone down in the pit" (30,2-4).

A vivid picture of such a sick and miserable man is given in Psalm 88: "Yahweh, God of my salvation! In the day[3] I cry, in the night I am before thee. Let my prayer come before thee, incline thine ear unto my cry; for my soul is full of troubles; and my living draweth nigh unto Sheol. I am counted with them that go down into the pit; I am as a man that hath no strength. Among dead . . .,[4] like those slain by the sword that lie in the grave, which thou rememberest no more; and which are cut off from thy hand. Thou hast laid me in the pit of the nether world, in darkness, in the deep. Thy wrath lieth hard upon me, and thou hast afflicted me with all thy waves.[5] Thou hast put away mine acquaintance far from me, thou hast made me an abomination unto them, I am shut up and cannot come forth, mine eye mourneth by reason of affliction.

Yahweh, I call daily upon thee, I stretch out my hands unto thee. Dost thou do great deeds to the dead? Do shades arise and praise thee? Is thy loving kindness declared in the grave? or thy faithfulness in Abaddon? Are thy great deeds known in the dark and thy righteousness in the land of forgetfulness? But unto thee I cry, Yahweh, and in the morning my prayer cometh towards thee.

Why castest thou off my soul? Why hidest thou thy face from me? I am afflicted and ready to die in the midst of my youth, while I bear thy terrors and am redeless.[1] Thy fierce wrath goeth over me; thy terrors cut me off. They come round about me all day like water, they compass me about together. Lover and friend hast thou put far from me, and mine acquaintance thou keepest away."[2]

The situation is similar to the one presupposed in Jonah, chapter 2, only that the diseased here has not as yet found recovery. In the midst of his youth he is stricken. His friends dare not approach him, because he is filled with the curse. We have the same duplicity in the sayings here as in the other psalms. His soul is near Sheol. He is still partly in the land of the living, but, nevertheless, so strong is the hold which misery has on him that he is in Sheol. He feels the darkness of the grave, the desolate lack of strength and blessing of the nether world, the gloom of the ocean.

In another psalm it is said: "The eye of Yahweh is upon them that fear him, upon them that hope in his mercy; to deliver their souls from death and to keep them alive in famine" (33,18 f.). Here it is hunger which holds the miserable in death.

An old man declares as his experience in life: "Thou showedst me[3] great and sore troubles, but thou madest me alive again, and broughtest me up again from the depths of the earth" (Ps. 71,20). All kinds of trouble lead unto Sheol and may give rise to prayers for deliverance. "He inclineth his ear unto me, therefore will I call upon him, as long as I live. The snares of death compass me. The troubles of Sheol get hold upon me; I find trouble and sorrow. But I call upon the name of Yahweh. O Yahweh, I beseech thee, deliver my soul! . . . Yea, thou hast delivered my soul from death, mine eyes from tears, and my feet from falling. I walk before Yahweh in the land of life" (Ps. 116,2-4.8-9).

He who in Psalm 69 utters the strong curses, is, like so many others, paralyzed by enemies. Here it seems as if he is the victim of legal prosecution ("that which I have not taken away, I shall restore" v. 5), but also he is sunk in the deep of the ocean. "Save me, God, for the waters are come in unto my soul. I am sunk in the mire of the deep where there is no standing; I am come into deep waters where the floods overflow me. I am weary of my crying; my throat is dried; mine eyes fail while I wait for my God . . . Deliver me out of the mire, and let me not sink; let me be delivered from them that hate me, and out of the deep waters. Let not the water-flow overflow me, neither let the deep swallow me up, and let not the pit shut her mouth upon me" (69,2-4.15-16).

In the same manner the king expresses himself when threatened by his enemies (2 Sam. 22 and Ps. 18, v. 5-6). The miserable man immediately thinks of the deep, because it fits into the tôtality of his feelings. Firmness and certainty are health; when the soul is diseased, then he feels how it wavers, unstable as the murmuring sea, pulled downwards in the slipping mire. Therefore the miserable man craves to put his foot on the rock, where he feels firm ground under him. "He pulled me up from the pit of corruption, out of the miry clay, and set my feet upon a rock, and established my goings" (Ps. 40,3).

Thus the sensations of the soul increase, because they all lead towards creating a totality, and this totality finds spacial expression, because there is complete accord between the Israelitic conception of the soul and the Israelitic view of the universe. Firmness, joy, strength, blessing belong to the world of light; slackness, sorrow, exhaustion, curses belong to the realm of the dead.

The Israelitic conception of the universe is an expression of the conflict between life and death, or, rather, the fight for life against death. The land of life lies in the centre, on all hands surrounded by the land of death. The wilderness lies outside, the realm of death and the ocean below, but they send in their tentacles from all sides, and make the world a mixture of life and death, of light and darkness. But life *must* be the stronger. The great terror of the Israelite is that some day evil shall get the upper hand, and chaos come to prevail in the world of man. The important thing is to have sufficient blessing to be able to keep evil down.

Thus the world must be upheld continually through the renewal of the blessing; in that manner the land of man, with its state of order, gains the upper hand over chaos. This the Israelites, like other peoples, express through myths, telling how their god forced back chaos and superseded it with law and order.

The old myths which the Israelites must have had, have not been preserved to us. If we look at the exposition of the Yahwist (Gen. 2-3), then it is partly fragmentary, in that it does not give us the whole of the creation of the world, partly combined with foreign matter, and partly stamped by the conception of later Israel, that the task of man is merely to show obedience.

But, behind it all, we see glimpses of the old Israelitic view of creation: First the world lay waste and desert, non-land, and there was no life. No human beings were there to till the land of man. Then the wells sprang forth from the earth and watered it; trees and bushes appeared, and then also man and the animals. The creation of the world is the creation of the peasant's world.

In the other descriptions of the creation water, as the element of chaos, plays a principal part. In Gen. chap. 1 it is told how first of all Chaos, *tōhū wābhōhū,* and the ocean, *t^ehōm,* prevailed, and that darkness was over all. The spirit of God hovered like a bird over the waters of chaos. Then God created light and divided it from darkness. And he divided the waters of chaos into the upper and nether waters, and from the latter he divided the firm land. Then plants were created, and heavenly bodies, beasts and man.

That this conception was adopted by the Israelites from without, has been proved long ago. [1] Its extraneous character appears from several features; e. g. the spirit of God is "hovering", but there is no indication that this hovering produces anything. The part played by the waters of chaos corresponds closely with the story of the deluge. Water is a dangerous element, which threatens to gain the upper hand and destroy life; therefore it is chaos. This conception of the water is not native to Israel, where water is only known as something good, and something which one may easily come to miss. The conception that the whole world is compassed with water, and that this implies a threat for it, originates in river-countries like Egypt and Mesopotamia, and from Mesopotamia

Israel has taken over these ideas. But we have seen that this view, setting up water and darkness as the elements of chaos, has entered into the Israelitic total conception.

The fundamental contrast — i. e. between life and death — is identical with the contrast between law and chaos. That which is not according to the law is "falsehood", something which does not live; therefore chaos is nothingness. Creation consists in establishing lawfulness out of confusion, and for the Israelites this becomes: to create habitable land out of desert land, light out of darkness, a continent out of the ocean. Thus a land fit for habitation takes the place of chaos (Is. 45,18).

A hymn describes to us how Yahweh overcomes the waters of chaos covering the whole world. With his voice of thunder he forced the water behind its established bounds (Ps. 104,6-9). It is closed behind firm gates, so that it cannot break the law appointed for it (Jer. 5,20-22; Job 38,8-11; Prov. 8,29).

The fight of Yahweh against the ocean of chaos, *t^e^hōm,* is sometimes described as a fight with a dragon, *tannīn,* called by the names of Rahab and Leviathan and surrounded by helpers (Job 9,13). The dragon is identical with the ocean as the waters of chaos. Yahweh fought against it and conquered; he pierced the dragon and split it, and this is identical with his setting up barriers against the lawless swelling of the ocean, thus saving the firm land: "Thou splittedst Rahab and piercedst the dragon and madest the sea dry" (Is. 51,9). "Thou rulest the raging of the sea; when the waves thereof arise, thou stillest them. Thou brokest Rahab in pieces like one smiteth by the sword; thou scatteredst thine enemies with thy strong arm. The heavens are thine, the earth also is thine, as for the world and the fulness thereof thou hast founded them" (Ps. 89,10-12).

The fight which took place at the creation is, in a condensed form, that which is constantly occurring. In the quotation above it is impossible to distinguish what belongs to the past and what belongs to the present. Leviathan still plays in the deep (Ps. 104, 26, cf. Is. 27,1; Ezek. 29,3; 32,2); chaos still threatens from the waters; watch must be set over the dragon (Job 7,12), the law of the bounds of the ocean must be constantly renewed.

The fight is everlasting, as truly as light fights darkness. We have sufficient examples that the darkness and the waters of chaos belong together; therefore the victory over the dragon is identical with the appearance of light: "He stilleth the sea with his power, and by his cunning he smiteth through Rahab. By his spirit the heaven becometh light; his hand pierceth the fleeing serpent" (Job 26,12-13). The fleeing serpent is here evidently the fleeing darkness of night. To curse the day with its light is the same as to raise up Leviathan (Job 3,8).

But the myth of God's victory over the dragon is an expression of the predominance of life and blessing. The ocean which, as chaos, is a curse, is changed into a blessing by being subjected to the law; for from the ocean comes the life-giving water.

All water belongs together. It is a matter of course, because that which is of the same nature always forms a whole. The heavenly ocean sends down the rain, from the subterranean deep springs and rivers well up, and the two oceans, which came into existence through the dividing of Rahab, form a unity. It does not mean that there is a spacial connection between them, any more than there is a spacial connection between the grave and Sheol in the deep.

The victory over chaos is therefore identical with the production of rain and springs. In immediate connection with the account of the subjugation of the ocean it is said in the hymn: Thou sendst springs into the brooks; they run between hills. They give drink to every beast of the field; the wild asses quench their thirst. Over them the fowls of the heaven have their habitation, and they sing among the branches. Thou waterest the hills from thy high place; the earth is satisfied with the fruit of thy works. Thou causest the grass to grow for the cattle, and herbs for the service of man, etc. (Ps. 104,10-14).

Still more clearly the context appears from another hymn: Thou didst divide the sea by thy strength, thou brakest the heads of the dragons in the waters. Thou brakest the heads of Leviathan in pieces, and gavest him to be meat to people and the beasts of the desert. [1] Thou openedst up fountain and brook, and thou driedst up everlasting rivers (Ps. 74,13-15). The confused mass of the ocean was, when split and broken, made into food for human beings, in that it sent forth its springs and brooks at the same time that dry land was produced from it.

Thus the feared and threatening *t^ehōm* must still help to uphold the world of man, which it would like to rule and destroy. "Blessings of heaven above, blessings of the *t^ehōm* that lieth under" (Gen. 40,25, cf. Deut. 33,13), that is the rain and the springs yielding to the Israelite the fruitfulness, which to him is peace and blessing, that which gives substance to life.

Land of man is to be found wherever there are human beings, but it has its centre where the Israelites live. The narrative that man originally lived in Eden far towards the east, is hardly of Israelitic origin. It is possibly connected with the stories of the common ancestor, Abraham, who brings about a connection between Israel and the eastern cultures. It is the man's living together with the land that gives to it its character of land of man. Therefore the land is not for him a homogeneous plane; there are parts which are closer to him than others. The starting point of the relation to the country is the family. The landed property of the family belongs to the psychic totality of the family and cannot be divided from it. Just as it determines the life of the family, so it is imbued with its blessing. It is not the individual alone who is to create the blessing upholding the property. He is a link in the family as extending through the generations.

But he also belongs to a national whole, and as the life of the family is connected with the inherited property, thus the life of the people is connected with the "land of inheritance". The two facts are perfectly analogous. It is history which makes Israel entitled to the land.

In the Book of Judges there is an account of negotiations between Jephthah and the king of Moab (or Ammon) concerning the ownership of the land between Arnon and Jabbok. Jephthah reasons as follows: Our fathers have not taken the land from

Moab, but from the Amorites, our God yielding it into our hands, and so you have no claim to it. This is not a formalistic discussion as to who was the first comer. The question is: To whom does it *de facto* belong? Whose is the life which left its impress upon it?

That the country is stamped by the life of Israel is the same as that it bears its blessing. But the blessing does not, to the same extent, abide everywhere. There are spots where the curse acts, and there are others where the blessing is concentrated. Such centres of power are the holy places, where the divine forces act; from these centres the blessing radiates and penetrates the country.[1]

By the Israelites Canaan is incessantly called the land of the fathers (Gen. 48,21; 50,24; Deut. 1,8; 6,23; 31,20-21 etc.). The expression meant still more to them than to us, and this is implied by their conception of history. To them a people is not a collection of human beings, more or less like each other. It is a psychical whole, and in so far an ideal quantity. "The people" is not visible. All common experiences are merged into the common soul and lend to it shape and fulness. Thus a psychic stock is created which is taken over from generation to generation, being constantly renewed and influenced by new experiences. It is lived wholly in every generation, and yet it is raised above it, is something which is given to it and makes claims to it. The connection between the generations of a people is just as intimate as that between the generations of a family. The soul of the people and the soul of the family belong equally to the individual; only their subject-matter differs.

The relation to the fathers becomes common life. They share their experiences with each other. What the fathers have handed down is inherited by the generations, and the experiences of the latter act in the fathers; therefore the responsibility is a common one. It is a thought with which we are constantly confronted in the prophets: the people bear the blessing of the fathers, but also their guilt. All events are connected, because they contribute towards forming a psychic whole, into which they are merged. Thus there rises out of the history of the people an invisible figure of grand proportions, bearing the impress of definite features, the features left by experiences. And this figure is identical with the ancestor.

When the Israelites speak of their ancestor, then it is not as a remote figure which has disappeared long ago. He constantly shares in what happens, the history of the people is his. The Israelitic narratives of the fathers is the condensed history of many generations. The experiences of the various generations have left their impress in their characteristics, because they are the centres in which the changing generations recognize the soul of the people.

That the land has been given to the fathers therefore means that it is indissolubly bound up with the soul of the Israelites and fused with it. The blessing of the Israelites and the blessing of the country are identical. When the successors maintain their right to the country, then it is a maintenance of their own soul, of which the country forms part.

The country of man and the people are so closely linked that their creation coincides. The creation of the people took place at the liberation from Egypt and is thus identical with the vanquishing of the dragon. "Awake, awake, put on strength, O arm of Yahweh; awake as in primeval days, in the generations of eternity. Didst not thou split Rahab, didst not thou pierce the dragon? Didst not thou make the sea dry, the waters of the great *tᵉhōm?* Thou that madest the depths of the sea a way for ransomed to pass over?" (Is. 51,9-10). The crossing of the Sea of Rushes is identical with the splitting of the dragon of primeval times. Therefore Egypt is identical with the dragon, Rahab (Is. 30,7; Ps. 87,4). Under the arms of the Nile it lies in wait (Ezek. 29,3; 32,2 f.); it manifests itself in the terrible monster from the Nile, called the crocodile (Job 40,25).

The deluge was chaos which broke loose once more because of the iniquity of man. And chaos is the great catastrophe which destroyed the people and carried it away from the land, out into exile. It is a return to the state of the wilderness. The country has become a desert, and the exiled people are in the wilderness (Is. 40,3-4; 41,18-19; 43,19-20; Jer. 31,2), in the darkness (Is. 42,16). Restoration is the transformation from the land of the desert to the land of blessing: "I open rivers in high places and fountains in the midst of the valleys; I make the wilderness a watering meadow, and the dry land springs of water. I plant in the wilderness the cedar, the accacia tree and the myrtle and the oil tree; I set in the desert the cypress, and the elm and the pine together" (Is. 41,18-19). And this act of creation is analogous with the creation of the people, when at one time they were taken up from the wilderness: "Remember ye not the former things, neither consider the things of old. Behold, I do a new thing; now it springs forth. Do ye not feel it? I even make a way in the wilderness, and rivers in the desert" . . . (43,18-19).

With "the former things" is meant the liberation from Egypt: ". . . He which made a way in the sea, and a path in the mighty water; which brought forth the chariots and horse, the army and the power; they lay down together, and rose not, they were extinct, they were quenched as a wick" (43,16-17). And this liberation from Egypt is, as we have seen, identical with the vanquishing of the monster of Chaos, Rahab. The piercing of the dragon of chaos is identical with the drying out of the Sea of Rushes, and with that is immediately bound up the liberation from Babel. "Thou piercedst the dragon, thou laidst dry the ocean", "thou madest the depths of the sea a way to pass over", "and the redeemed of Yahweh return and come with singing unto Zion" (Is. 51,9-11), these three events belong closely together. They mean the establishment of the people and its world.

The people form a firm and coherent whole. Outside it stand all the other peoples, each with their world. In the ancient time the Israelites recognized these worlds with their peculiarities and their gods for what they were, but being strangers they were unclean in the eyes of the Israelites. Instinctively they stand as enemies against each other, making firm psychic communities which all claim to be wholes. The clean is that which belongs in the totality of the soul, the unclean that which stands outside it. Where the worlds of the peoples meet, a tension arises which leads to constant explosions, wars in which the people fight to maintain their psychic whole. But the tension can be relieved in a milder form. The strange souls enter into an intimate relation with each other, and conclude covenants; they must assimilate so much of each other's mental entity that the souls can be united.

The intensity and depth of this covenant may, as we have seen, be of many different degrees, but the object of it must always be to balance differences and to create a certain community. Gifts are generally necessary, but also mutual good words have the same effect. Even the least connection creates a relation between both *totalities* and the forces contained in them. He who lives in a foreign country must enter into connection with the strange gods. Where the souls of peoples meet, the gods must necessarily be in it (1 Sam. 26,19). Thus the Israelites may live in foreign parts, with strangers among them, without the totalities being broken. But it is always a misfortune to be in a strange country with which one cannot altogether assimilate, and where one cannot be entirely absorbed in the people among whom one lives. Thus we hear that the Israelites of Egypt, in spite of all hospitality, could not eat with the Egyptians, to whom this was an abomination (Gen. 43,32). The longing for home, expressed in a few of the psalms, is very intense.

For the Israelites the question of the relation to other peoples became particularly acute, because in Canaan they lived side by side with others. We know that they followed the natural course, concluded covenants with them and drew upon the substance of their souls. But at a certain point, when Israel had become great through the covenants, it withdrew entirely from the strangers. It was not permitted to conclude covenants with the peoples and their gods, but they were to exterminate them utterly (Exod. 23,28 ff.; Deut. 7 *et al.*; Josh. 23). Now the country had become the country of Israel, and the honour of Yahweh did not permit of a union with other gods.

The readiness to acknowledge strangers and the ability to amalgamate with them became less and less with the Israelites. The Deuteronomy, the law which with such strength demanded the extermination of Canaanite life, excludes — apart from those who are to be exterminated altogether, as the Amalekites (Deut. 25,17-19) — certain peoples from being received into the community of Israel (Deut. 23,2 ff.). Gradually the "heathens" became so unclean that they should rather be avoided, nay, properly speaking, ought not to exist at all. Only by submitting themselves entirely to the Israelitic soul and bending before the Jewish god could they acquire the true right to live.

The close relation between the country and the life of the people is only possible because earth itself is alive. We know that the Israelites do not acknowledge the distinction between the psychic and the corporeal. Earth and stones are alive, imbued with a soul, and therefore able to receive mental subject-matter and bear the impress of it. The relation between the earth and its owner is not that the earth, like a dead mass, makes part of his psychic whole — an impossible thought. It is a covenant-relation, a psychic community, and the owner does not solely prevail in the relation. The earth has its nature, which makes itself felt, and demands respect. The important thing is to deal with it accordingly and not to ill-treat it.

Job says: If my fields (*ʾadhāmā*) have cried against me, or the furrows thereof likewise complain, if I have eaten the fruit thereof without silver or have extinguished the souls of their *baʿals,* then thistles grow instead of wheat, and cockle instead of barley (Job 31,38-40).[1] The task of the peasant is to deal kindly with the earth, to uphold its blessing and then take what it yields on its own accord. If he exhausts it, then he attacks its soul and kills it; after that it will only bring forth thorns, thistles and whatever else pertains to the wilderness.

This forbearance was consequently observed. Every seventh year the owner must refrain from all encroachments upon the life of the earth and leave it entirely to its own nature. "Yahweh spoke unto Moses in Mount Sinai saying: Speak unto the children of Israel, and say unto them: When ye come into the land which I give you, then the land shall keep a sabbath unto Yahweh. Six years thou shalt sow thy field, and six years thou shalt prune thy vineyard, and gather in the fruit thereof; but in the seventh year shall be a sabbath of rest unto the land, a sabbath for Yahweh;

thou shalt neither sow thy field, nor prune thy vineyard. That which groweth of its own accord of thy harvest thou shalt not reap, neither gather the grapes of thy vine undressed; for it is a year of sabbath unto the land. And the growth of the year of sabbath shall be meat for you; for thee, and for thy slave and for thy slave girl, and for thy bondman, and for thy *metik* that sojourneth with thee; and for thy cattle and for the beasts that are in thy land shall all the increase thereof be meat" (Lev. 25,1-7).

In a more condensed form the same law appears in the Book of Covenant: And six years thou shalt sow thy land, and shalt gather in the fruits thereof; but the seventh year thou shalt let it lie fallow and untilled, that the poor of thy people may eat; and what they leave the beasts of the field shall eat. In like manner thou shalt deal with thy vineyard, and with thine olive-tree (Exod. 23,10-11).

The subject matter of both of these laws is the same. The main object is to secure for the earth the rest which is necessary, if it is to maintain its life. But here it is not a question of rest in the sense that nothing is permitted to grow on it, as when our peasants let their fields lie fallow. The idea is that the earth is for a time to be free, so as not to be subjected to the will of man, but left to its own nature, to be like no-man's land. Therefore poor people and wild beasts are to be permitted to enter freely, and take what grows in it. [1]

Thus there are a number of rules to be observed in relation to the earth. Its blessing must be tended, its nature not violated, and yet it is to be kept close to the soul of man and received into it. If it is violated, it revolts and becomes a wilderness; and if the people lose the blessing, then it taints the earth and is spewed out of it (Lev. 20,22).

The earth is not only peopled by human beings. When, in the Old Testament, mention is made of the *animals,* they are sometimes classified as beasts of the water, of the air and of the earth, which classification is the one followed in the story of the creation (Gen. 1). This division is based upon the manner of living of the beasts. Fish and other dwellers of the sea, up to the great sea-monsters — to which, e. g., the crocodile belongs (Job

40,25) — have the community which is determined by life in the water. Beasts and insects are classed with birds, because they have the nature of the air and move on wings; they are all called *'ōph.* The beasts of the earth are divided into cattle, wild beasts and crawling things; it is mainly those which belong in the land of man, in the wilderness and the dust.

Most closely allied to man is the *cattle.* The Israelite can speak of the cattle as a whole: *behēmā, be'īr, miḳne.* The first of these terms denotes cattle as the dumb, and may also be used of other animals, whereas *miḳne* designates them as the property of man. As a rule the cattle is mentioned after its kind: ox, small cattle, i. e. sheep and goats and also ass, camel, horse. As property the cattle make part of the psychic entirety of the man. The relation between the man and his cattle can by Isaiah be compared with the relation between father and son. They *know* each other. "The ox knoweth his owner, and the ass his master's crib" (Is. 1,3), and so also: "righteous man regardeth the life of his beast, but the heart of the sinner is stubborn" (Prov. 12,10). The man has a covenant with his cattle, just as he has a covenant with his earth. In this covenant he makes the cattle his slave, keeps it under his will (Job 40,28). Just as he is not permitted to exhaust the earth, so he must not weaken the lives of the cattle. Cattle and servants shall be permitted to rest every seventh day (Exod. 23,12, cf. 20,10; Deut. 5,14); of the slave it is said that it is in order that he may be "ensouled". The same might be said about the cattle.

The *wild beasts* are called the "living of the earth", i. e. the souls which swarm abroad in the world. This implies something remote; the souls of the earth are those which have no covenant with man, such as the cattle. In the Book of Job God puts the following question to Job regarding the crocodile: "Doth he make a covenant with thee? dost thou take him for a slave for ever?" (40, 28). In a similar manner he asks about the wild ox: "Is it its will to serve thee, or abide by thy crib?" (39,9). It is a thought which pervades the whole of the speech: the world is full of life, which Job does not *know,* i. e. with which he does not have any covenant and upon which he does not exercise any influence and much less control. In contradistinction to the cattle the wild beasts have their own will, and maintain it against man (39,7-12; 40,32).

And they are entitled to it, because it is implied by their very being. They may justly claim their food, which maintains their souls. The lion and the eagle get their gory prey from God, just as all other beasts (Job 38,39; 39,30; Ps. 104,21). They all belong in the world created by God and were preserved from the flood, and their lives, each in their kind, is ensured in that they are in the covenant of God, upon which all life rests (Gen. 9).

The line which divides tame and wild animals is not the only line dividing the animal world in its relation to man. There are *clean* and *unclean* animals; the former are to be eaten, the latter not, their carcases rendering the partaker unclean. These regulations imply a history, which we are unable to grasp in its entirety. Clean is what belongs to the psychic totality, unclean that which counteracts it. He who eats an animal absorbs part of a strange soul, as truly as soul and body belong closely together. Therefore he can only eat what is assimilated into the soul, for if he does, he runs the risk of bursting it. The animals the Israelite can absorb are those which belong to his most intimate world. Through the regulations of cleanness we learn with which animals the Israelite is most familiar.

The clean animals are ox, sheep and goat, to which must be added deer, gazelle, several kinds of antilopes, ibex and wild goat; fishes with fins and scales, as well as locusts. Unclean are all other animals; in particular mention is made of the camel, hare, rock-rabbit, swine and all crawling things (Lev. 11; Deut. 14).

It is not possible to distinguish what lies behind all of these regulations. That sheep and goats are clean is a matter of course, seeing that they have at all times formed the most important part of the flocks of the Israelites. Camels are mentioned among the possessions of the patriarchs (Gen. 12,16; 24; 30,43, etc.), but have played no principal part. When they are unclean, then it is beyond a doubt because pre-Canaanite Israel did not possess camels, but only small cattle, like the poor tribes of Arabia until the present day.[1] For similar reasons the horse and ass are not clean. The ass was appropriated shortly after the immigration

(Judg. 5,10); horses, which already then were used by the Canaanites (Judg. 5,22), were only employed on a grand scale by Solomon, who introduced them from abroad (1 Kings 5,6-8; 10, 26-28). The ox and the pig are Canaanite animals; from the finds at Gezer we know that the pig was eaten and used as a sacrificial animal.[1] This was also the case with the ox, of which sufficient is told in the Old Testament; these stories are confirmed by the discoveries made.[2] The fact that the Israelites treated the two animals in a different manner may probably be explained by the pig being too indissolubly connected with cults which the Israelites could not adopt.

The clean wild beasts are few in number. It sounds like priestly systematization when it is said in the laws that the reason of their cleanness is that they are cloven-footed and chew the cud; but perhaps the explanation is that it is their relationship with the ox which makes them clean.[3] Locusts are to this day used for food, but as they are not to be found regularly in Palestine, this is probably another habit preserved from the desert.[4]

Though the Israelite thus only eats animals with which he is quite familiar, he must, however, forbear eating all parts of them. First and foremost he must forbear eating the blood. "But flesh with its soul, its blood, ye must not eat" (Gen 9,4). This prohibition is among the most important of the Old Testament, and the reason given is everywhere the same: "Ye shall eat the blood of no manner of flesh, for the soul of all flesh is its blood" (Lev. 17,14, cf. 19,26; Deut. 12,23; Ezek. 33,25 f.). The blood particularly contains the soul of the beast, and if they received it within themselves, they would get too much of the nature of the animal into their soul. For the same reason they are not permitted to eat other of the vital parts of the animal, more especially the fat covering the inwards, and the kidneys and the caul above the liver (Lev. 3,3-4.16-17; 7,23) in which life is particularly seated. We hear by chance that the Israelites likewise do not eat the sinew above the hip point socket (Gen. 32,33).[5]

However, this is only one phase of the matter; consideration is also to be given to the animals themselves. If the blood was taken, then man would take the soul from the animals and encroach upon their central life. By giving the blood to the holy place they return it to life, and are then satisfied with taking the parts of least importance to the latter. In the case of game it is sufficient to pour out the blood, and to cover it with dust (Lev. 17,13, cf. Deut. 12). On no condition is one permitted to appropriate it. It is the right of the beasts to maintain their lives that is expressed in these commandments. It is the same fundamental principle pervading a commandment, like the one that ordains not to take a bird together with its eggs or young, but that one of them must be left alone (Deut. 22,6-7). Life is to be respected; it may be curtailed, but not killed.

Everything the Old Testament tells us of the animal world — and for that matter it is not much — points towards the great difference which, in the eyes of the Israelite, prevails between animals close to him and animals far from him. The beasts are judged by their relation to man; for man is, in the eyes of the Hebrews, the goal of all created things. Towards the animals he feels like the ruler. Even if he acknowledges their nature and has a covenant with his domestic animals, he claims to be the absolute ruler in this covenant-relation. All animals must bend wholly before him. This is expressed by the Yahwist, who lets the animals be created entirely for the sake of man (Gen. 2,19), and in the Priestly Code it is said, in so many words, that animals are to be ruled by fear and terror in their relation to man (Gen. 9,2, cf. Ps. 8). There is here a tendency which may run counter to the old acknowledgment of the life of the animals, and we know that it has done so in Israel. The animals are only acknowledged, in so far as they directly serve the purposes of man. It is the same narrowing of the world with which we became acquainted when considering the mutual relation of men.

What right then have the wild beasts to live? As we have seen, this becomes a real question in Israel, perfectly analogous with the question of the right of existence of foreign peoples. And in both cases the answer points in the same direction. The tendency is that the wild beasts ought either not to live, or that they must subject themselves to the rule of man, enter into his covenant and will, like the tame animals, or in other words deny their own nature. The prophets are full of this ideal. We find it in Isaiah, in Ezekiel, in Hosea and Zechariah; it is part of their conception of peace. Eliphaz speaks of having peace with the wild beasts of the fields, which enter into a covenant with man, and serve him as domestic animals (Job 5,22-23), and if they do not, they are to be struck down: "Roaring of the lion and the voice of the fierce lion, and the teeth of the young lions are broken. The old lion perisheth for lack of prey, and the lion's whelps are scattered abroad" (Job 4,10-11).

It is the claim of the ruler which determines the relation of man to the animals. Even when the right of the wild animals is acknowledged, it is only a compulsory acknowledgment, a testimony to the impotence of man. This appears strongly in God's speech in the Book of Job. God maintains the right of the wild animals as links in the order of the universe, but it is an evidence against man. If he should receive them into his world, then it could only be imagined as a subjection of them; man should be able to tie the wild ox to his crib and make the crocodile the playfellow of his little girls.

The animals which are in the world each belongs to its kind, *min*. As a rule the kind, like all other wholes, forms a firm unity, a type which underlies and manifests itself in the individual specimens. The individual differences disappear before the type; when a serpent bites, then it is *the* serpent (Am. 5,19; cf. Gen. 3,1), just as it is *the* lion and *the* bear, which attacks the herd (1 Sam. 17,34-37). This unity of kind is stronger than all time; it expresses itself in every kind being created in primeval time, "after its kind". It is the maintenance of the kind which is the decisive factor; that the individual specimen disappears does not mean anything.

The Israelite in every possible way avoids mixing the kinds. It is the claim of totality which all the time is making itself felt; every kind claims to preserve its totality and must be protected against the breach of the latter by an intimate union with others.

It is a particularly horrible thing if human beings copulate with animals; it is such an abomination that they must both be killed (Lev. 18,23; 20,15 f.). But neither is it permitted to copulate animals of two kinds (Lev. 19,19). Ox and ass must not go before a plough together (Deut. 22,10). This principle is carried out in the minutest details. One must not sow two kinds of seed in the same field (Lev. 19,19; Deut. 22,9), one must not make a garment of two sorts, as woollen and linen together (Lev. 19,19; Deut. 22,11), a woman is not permitted to wear man's clothing or *vice versa* (Deut. 22,5). So strong is the claim of totality and the law relating to the purity of the kind.

That which applies to animals, also applies to plants and trees. Each makes a definite kind with its peculiarity, which must not be mixed up with others. And the great division in the world of plants is the one distinguishing those which belong to the Israelitic world of man, from those which do not. Thorn and thistle belong in the wilderness, and only through the curse are they made to crop up in the world of man. But to the world of thistles belong all kinds of strange plantings, which the Israelite does not know and has not received into his intimacy. A "strange planting" (Is. 17,10) is an evil growth.

But the Israelite knows that even the plants and trees have a life which is to be absorbed and exploited, but not violated. The fruit of a tree must not be taken the first three years after it is planted; in the fourth year the fruit is consecrated to Yahweh; only in the fifth year is man permitted to take it (Lev. 19,23-25). Thus the tree is slowly being made intimate with the world of man. And when the harvest comes, the owner must not plunder the seed or the trees of their full crop. He is to leave a corner of the field unreaped *(pē'ā)*; the fruits of the vineyard shall not be gathered fully, and in both places the gleanings are not to be gathered (Lev. 19,9-10; 22,22). Plants and trees are to be permitted to contain some of their wild nature, and poor people are to be able to gather and glean a little, as they are permitted to do with unoccupied fields and vineyards.[1]

To the swarm filling the world also belong the *sun*, the *moon* and the *stars*. They belong to the totality of the world of man and exercise their influence on it, in that they rule day and night respectively (Gen. 1,16; Jer. 31,35; Ps. 136,7-9). They are living beings, each having its own nature and consequently following its own laws. The sun follows its determined course every day, in that it leaves its tent and, having completed its circuit, returns to its starting point (Ps. 19,5; Eccles. 1,5). The stars have names and form a well-arranged army, in which every star has its place (Is. 40,26; Jer. 33,22; Ps. 147,4 *et al.)*. The significance of the celestial bodies is that they rule the forces of light; therefore the blessing is bound up with them. It is true that they may strike in their might (Ps. 121,6), but they are among the great upholders of life: "Blessed by Yahweh is his land, by the gift of dew from heaven, and by the ocean lying beneath, and by the gift of the crops of the sun, and by the gifts of . . . the moons" (Deut. 33,13-14). Fertility is indissolubly connected with the sun and the moon. If the light of heaven is darkened, then all blessing is seriously threatened; it is a suspension of the law upon which life rests. Therefore eclipses are only mentioned in the threatening speeches of the prophets, who presage the coming chaos. [1]

Thus the celestial bodies have a covenant with the land of man and all the good forces upholding it. The stars of the morning rejoiced together when the world was created out of chaos (Job 38,7), and from heaven the stars took part in the fight which was to maintain the position of Israel against the hostile powers (Judg. 5,20).

The rule of sun and moon consists in their governing *time*. [2] It does not mean that they are used to measure distances in time. For the Israelite time is not merely a form or a frame. Time is charged with substance or, rather, it is identical with its substance; time is the development of the very events. When the Israelite speaks of evil or good days, then it is meant literally, because the character of the time is always determined by that which happens. He may say: Time *is* rain (Ezr. 10,13), when the principal substance of time is rain. The law about lepers was given "in order to instruct concerning the day of the unclean and the day of the clean" (Lev. 14,57), meaning all which the latter are to do and which is to be done to them.

The time or day of the man or the people is therefore identical with his or its actions and fate. When mention is made of the day of Jerusalem, Jezreel or Midian, then it applies to events of decisive importance in their lives, just as the day of Yahweh is the violent actions, in which Yahweh more particularly manifests himself.[1] In his passionate maintenance of justice Job says: "My righteousness I hold fast, and will not let it go; my heart does not despise any of my days" (Job 27,6). The two sentences imply the same thing, because his days are identical with the unfolding of his soul in action. "To everything there is a time" (Eccles. 3,1.17; 8,6.9), because everything has its special nature. The close context between character and fate makes "time" cover both conceptions. In the above-mentioned place Job is thinking of the former; the pious who says that Yahweh takes care of the days of the righteous (Ps. 37,18), chiefly thinks of the latter.

Times of the same substance are therefore identical. He who gets new courage and new youth and strength may say that he "returns to the days of his youth "(Job 33,25). He might also have said that the days of his youth once more become alive, for the events with their character and substance make time alive. "When this time again becomes alive" means: in a year, when we have the same season as now, with its peculiar heat, harvest or whatever characterizes the time in question (Gen. 18,10.14; 2 Kings 4,16). When Hannah had left the sanctuary with the promise of a son, she bore him "at the turns of the days" (1 Sam. 1,20), i. e. when the same season recurred, or, in other words, a year later. One may curse a day or a night to be *barren,* so that it falls out of the month, is deprived of its substance and its joy (Job 3,6-8).

All that happens originates in souls and is directed against souls. Therefore all events move round centres, and the events which in that way centre round a man are his time. Thus there are as many times as there are souls. Everything has its time. The stork, the turtledove and the other birds know their times — whereas Israel does not know that which it has to do (Jer. 8,7). The world is a closely woven net of centres of action. When the sun rules during the day, then it means that all the events of the day are knit together with the sun and bear the impress of its quality: the quality of being light. It is the nature of the sun to follow a certain course, so that it comes and goes regularly; this is its contribution to the totality of the universe, hence its covenant with God (Jer. 33,20). A "day" is all that happens in connection with the sun. There are things which can only be done in connection with the sun, and there are things which can only be done in the night; there are deeds of light, and there are deeds of darkness.

Nor, when the day is divided, is it according to an abstract measure dividing it into equal lengths; the decisive factors are the different peculiarities of the sun which leave their different impress upon everything. "Morning" is everything connected with the sun's driving away the darkness with its rays; "high light" is everything which happens in connection with the clear noonday sun, also called the "glow of the day" or the "glow of the sun"; the "breeze of the day" is the time of the day which is characterized by the cool evening breeze of Palestine. The colourless idea of "hour", measuring time in a purely quantitative way, is far from the old Israelitic conception.

Sun and moon rule not only day and night, but also year and month, according to their peculiar life. The moon increases and decreases and subsequently disappears. Events which belong together with an entire moon-life form a whole apart, a month, and the four weeks are the four unities of time connected with the different phases of the moon. When the month is dead, a new one *(ḥōdhesh)* is born. Each of the various moons has its life, because each has a different substance. There is a "flood month", a "fruit month", an "ear (harvest) month", a "flowering month". [1] Every month revives again during the following year, when the same life is reborn. Together the many different months form the life of a year, which is again connected with the peculiarities of the sun. That which animates the year is all its events, all its growth. When the last harvest is completed, and life dies away, then "the year runs out" (Exod. 23,16). But it only revives in spring time, when life once more begins its growth. That time is called "the return of the year" (2 Sam. 11,1; 1 Kings 20,22.26).

How the old Israelites looked upon the interval, we do not know. They presumably considered it a dead time, seeing that the old year slumbered before the new year was born. [1]

That which characterizes the Israelitic conception of time is, thus, not so much the distances as the substance and context of the events. The conceptions of time and space are uniform; in both cases it is a question of wholes which are not sharply outlined, but determined by their character and quality. Like space, time also forms in certain centres round which the totalities are grouped. Each continuity of time, e. g. a month, is a sum of expansion of life, merged into a unity, and this is concentrated in certain days, chiefly the first day. Out of these festal days *(mō'ēdh)* the events develop. History is not considered a long chain of events, divided into special periods. It is true that one reckons with periods, but in that one sees the experiences gathering round a special feature which pervades the whole, an important event or a prominent man.

The term used for such a period is *dōr,* denoting a time with the events distinguishing it, and first and foremost the people who create it and its substance, or, as it is usually rendered: generation. [2] Noah's *dōr* is the whole of the contemporary period, which in the eyes of posterity is characterized by his personality. Every *dōr* bears its common impress; one is good, another evil. The meaning of *dōr* approaches that of *mishpāḥā,* a kind, a category. Those who seek God, together form a *dōr* (Ps. 24,6); the *dōr* of the righteous is blessed so that the wicked gnash their teeth in high fury (Ps. 112,2.10).

The strong naturally impress their period with their character, because it is they who bear its substance. In the Priestly Code it is said that the man who has committed manslaughter may leave the city of refuge and return in peace to his home on the death of the high-priest (Num. 35,25-28; Josh. 20,6); it means that a high-priest creates a period determined by him. Actions which are performed in his time are connected with him, and die with him. The importance of this fundamental idea in old Israel we are unable to distinguish, but we have a single suggestion of such ideas being connected with the life of the king (Is. 23,15).

History consists of *dōrōth,* each with their special stamp, but all the generations are fused into a great whole, wherein experiences are condensed. This concentrated time, into which all generations are fused, and from which they spring, is called eternity, *'ōlām*. Eternity is not the sum of all the individual periods, nor even this sum with something added to it; it is "time" without subdivision, that which lies behind it, and which displays itself through all times. That the throne of David is to remain eternally, means that it must be raised above or, rather, pervade the changing periods, in that it has its foot in primeval time itself, the stock from which all time flows.

Primeval time absorbs in it the substance of all time, and is therefore the beginning of all time; *'ōlām* is history and thus the world as a compact whole. History is upheld by the generations, and it springs from primeval time, concentrated in the fathers in whom the life of the family lives. Adam is primeval man, at the same time the first man, and the genus man into which all human beings are absorbed.

There is a peculiar solidity in the Israelitic conception of the universe. The world consists of a number of various lives which are intermixed, but can never become merged, because each has its special characteristic determining it. They can never become some incidental new thing, because everything individual is a direct expression of its type, and this type has its root in primeval time.

That which upholds all of these lives in the world, is the blessing resting in the divine powers. It is to be maintained by the Israelites, because it is their world, and they keep the blessing while preserving the covenant with their god. Therefore heaven and earth tremble at their sins, and if the curse were to prevail entirely in them, their world would collapse.

Therefore the object of the Israelite is to live so as to keep his world clean, and it is obtained through his living a normal life from birth to death. He cannot lead an untrammelled "natural life", but he must be shaped according to Israelitic custom and habit.

Foreign customs make him unclean (Deut. 14,1 f.; Lev. 19,27 f.). Immediately after birth he is named, and thus he is received into the community of the family. His growth is a growing into the community. A stage on the way is the weaning from his mother's breast. The importance of the event is marked by a festival and a meal (Gen. 21,6; 1 Sam. 1,24). The most important event in the life of the boy is circumcision.

According to the law, circumcision takes place as early as eight days after birth (Gen. 17; Lev. 12,3), and at a later period it coincided with the naming of the child. We have no certain evidence that it should formerly have been the rule to practise it at a later age, but it is possible to trace a context between circumcision and marriage in the term for bridegroom, *ḥāthān,* the corresponding verb of which in Arabic means to circumcise. There is also a short narrative which seems to suggest that marriage is sanctified by circumcision (Exod. 4,25). If we look at the use of this habit among other peoples, we find that it is practised in all ages from birth till the seventeenth year, and its universal feature is that it is an initiation into the community of men. With some peoples it is therefore connected with a long series of initiatory practices, changing the boy into a man, in that he passes through rigorous trials greatly taxing his moral strength, while at the same time he learns the secrets which uphold the life of the tribe.[1]

There can be no doubt that circumcision is an initiation into manhood. The boy becomes "purified", as the Arabians also call it (cf. Is. 52,1). This happens through an encroachment upon the typically male parts. It is undertaken by the man who is to receive him into the community, i. e. his father. And just as part of the fruit — its "foreskin" — must be withdrawn from ordinary use, thus also a part of his body is taken, the part where his male strength is seated. Therefore circumcision is the presupposition of taking one's place as a man and entering into marriage, just as it is upon the whole necessary in order to have a man's honour. From the Israelites we learn nothing of similar habits as far as the women are concerned.

No one can escape being touched with *uncleanness* throughout life. There are uncleannesses which in the main can be avoided, as everything connected with breaches of covenants; the laws of cleanness particularly mention the violation of the marriage covenant (Lev. 18,20; Num. 5,13, cf. Gen. 34,5.13.27). But some kinds of uncleanness human beings must always be affected by, for instance, the various kinds of issue from the body (Lev. 15). During such periods the man must not approach his wife (Lev. 18, 19; 20,18). When two foreign unities meet, there is always danger of uncleanness, as in the case of marriage. And the same is the case where new life is born (Lev. 12).

Uncleanness is closely allied with sin, for both terms apply to things which cannot be reconciled with the totality and contract guilt (Lev. 5,2; Num. 19,19). Only, uncleanness rather comes from without. Between uncleanness and the curse there is no essential difference. They both have the dangerous quality of being likely to spread, and therefore they must be stopped and exterminated as quickly as possible. He who touches unclean things is defiled (Lev. 5,2); this not only holds good of human beings, but of clothes, beds, vessels, ovens (Lev. 11,31-38; 15). If the uncleanness is incurable, then the individual in question must be irrevocably removed from the community, for the life of the latter must not be threatened by one person. So in the case of leprosy (Lev. 13). As long as the existence of the latter disease has not been proved for certain, then the afflicted is to be kept carefully isolated; but if it be proved that he has the plague within him, then "his clothes shall be rent, the hair of his head shaved off, and he shall put a covering on his upper lip, and shall cry: Unclean, unclean! All the days wherein the plague shall be in him, he shall be defiled; he is unclean; he shall dwell alone, outside the camp shall his habitation be" (Lev. 13,45-46). In other words: he is to be expelled from the community of man. The fear of leprosy is so great that the law also applies it to similar symptoms on apparel, leather and buildings (Lev. 13,47-59; 14,33-57).

All contact with death defiles. This applies to him who touches a corpse, the bones of a human body or a grave, and so also to him who comes into a house where there is a dead body (Num. 19, 13-16); unclean is also he who touches the bodies of fallen enemies (Num. 31,19), and he who touches the carcases of unclean animals (Lev. 5,2). Everybody gets into touch with death; he whose family is visited by death is stamped by its uncleanness.

The habits which in Israel are observed at deaths in the family express sorrow. Wailing and weeping are here as everywhere the natural attendants of sorrow. One cries: Ah, my brother! Ah, my sister! (Jer. 22,18; 34,5). The wailings are not spontaneous expressions of sorrow, but they have their conventional forms, based upon tradition. A good man may claim to be bewailed; the wailing means that he has filled his place and leaves a gap. There were certain men and women particularly practised in reciting the song of lamentation (*ḳinā,* Jer. 9,16 f.; Am. 5,16). Like other peoples the Israelites relieve their feelings in a regular and traditional form.

The mourning-rites express the humiliation and pain at having got into close touch with death. One tears one's clothes, [1] puts a piece of coarse sackcloth round one's loins, [2] flings oneself on the bare ground, [3] throws dust over one's head, [4] does not anoint oneself, [5] takes off one's sandals, [6] cuts off one's hair and beard or covers it, [7] slashes one's skin. [8]

It has been thought that these habits had nothing to do with sorrow, but this is only because we claim individual, spontaneous manifestations of feeling and have some difficulty in acknowledging it behind the established, traditional forms. Behind the mourning-rites lie sorrow, fear of death and much besides, but in their fundamental character they are an expression of the Israelitic sense of totality. Through contact with death he has been stricken by the evil, tainted with the world of curse, and of this he takes the consequence. If the misfortune, the curse is seated in his soul, then he cannot at the same time act normally, because the whole of his outward appearance must necessarily form a link in his psychic whole. Discords of any kind would only create new misfortunes and violate the normal life which he lightly connected with the curse. The instinctive feeling of what the mourning-state demands and the fear of hurting the blessing in life makes the family of the deceased place itself outside normal life and lets the dishonour and curse leave its impress on its habits. All attempts to explain the origin of the above-mentioned mourning-rites by roundabout ways and through external means are vain, because they are not merely used as death-rites, but make themselves felt in all cases when people are brought face to face with unhappiness and sorrow. Sorrows and misfortunes have a humbling effect. They attack both the substance and the vitality of the soul and remove the assailed from his community. He is in the world of uncleanness and curse and must necessarily act accordingly. The humiliated person, stricken by misfortune, tears his clothes and puts a sack round his loins [1] — just as a man, conversely, is subjected to humiliation by having his clothes rent. [2] He sits down in the ashes like Job or strews dust, the unclean, over his head. [3] He hides his head and his face, in which his honour most pronouncedly reveals itself, [4] shaves off the hair of his head and his beard, [5] slashes his skin, [6] in short, disfigures himself, makes a breach of all that is the manifestation of a normal soul. So also the leper, who has been placed outside the community, must go about with rent clothes, a covered beard and unkempt hair.

The mourning rites express that death is something evil. No Israelite will ever rejoice at the thought of having to die. Still, death is something normal and must be included in the conception of life. So it also is with the Israelites, to whom death is not always one thing. The death they fear is that which denotes an infringement on the normal development of life, to die in the midst of life before the possibilities are exhausted. It is this sudden and violent death which strikes the sinners, because it is an expression of the curse. And this is the decisive factor. He who preserves the blessing lives until he is full of years, then he falls like the ripe corn before the scythe. Such a death is "the death of the righteous" (Num. 23,10). It does not mean the cessation of blessing; the old man has got everything that the blessing can effect for him. If he sees it acting undiminished in the family, then he lies down calmly, for in the family his life is lived and his blessing acts. Against the life of the family that of the individual does not mean more than the burnt-out twigs falling from the fire.

He who dies in this manner dies in peace. For he dies in full harmony with life as well as with the family. His body is put into the grave together with those of the family who have gone before him.[1] To this the greatest weight is attached; the graves were in the closest connection with the house. It is told of Samuel that he was buried in his own house in Ramah (1 Sam. 25,1), and there is a similar account of Joab (1 Kings 2,34). Thus the deceased joins his kinsmen.[2] The survivors do not lose touch with him. There is a firm unity between the departed and the surviving kinsmen, which is maintained by their living together. The living have their lives in the living family, but in no point can this be distinguished from the common life with those who have gone before them, who have created the substance of life of the family and are still acting in it. That which happens through normal death is therefore only that a kinsman passes from one department of the family to another. His soul lives a life among the shades of Sheol, but its substance is still acting in the blessing of the family. As long as his memory lives, his personality is not wiped out. But it generally dwindles more and more, and at last he is merged entirely in the great stock of life, which upholds the family, that which is called the fathers. From them he has sprung, and to them he returns.

NOTES.

Page 5 [1]. Concerning the older history of Palestine and the position of Israel in the latter, *vide* H. R. Hall, *The Ancient History of the Near East,* 5. edition, 1920; *The Cambridge Ancient History* vol. 1-2, 1923, 1924; R. Kittel, *Geschichte des Volkes Israel* I, 5.-6. ed., 1923; F. Böhl, *Kanaanäer und Hebräer,* 1911; O. Procksch, *Die Völker Altpalästinas,* 1914; F. Albright in *The Journal of the Palestine Oriental Society* vol. 1-2.4, 1921, 1922, 1924; A. Ungnad, *Die ältesten Völkerwanderungen Vorderasiens (Kulturfragen* Heft 1), 1923; Ed. Meyer, *Die Israeliten und ihre Nachbarstämme,* 1906. As for archaeology, *vide* S. R. Driver, *Modern Research as Illustrating the Bible (The Schweich Lectures* 1908), 1909; H. Vincent, *Canaan,* 1907; H. Thiersch in *Archäologischer Anzeiger* 1907, 1908, 1909; P. Thomsen, *Kompendium der palästinischen Altertumskunde,* 1913; S. P. Handcock, *The Archæology of the Holy Land,* 1916; P. Karge, *Rephaim, die vorgeschichtliche Kultur Palästinas und Phöniziens,* 1917; Kittel's *Geschichte;* A. Bertholet, *Kulturgeschichte Israels,* 1920; in these works references will be found to special works and descriptions of the excavations at Tell el-Hesy, Gezer, Ta'annek, Jericho, Tell el-Mutesellim, Samaria, Jerusalem, etc. Concerning the other old cultures, some of the principal handbooks are: Ed. Meyer, *Geschichte des Altertums* I, 1909; *The Cambridge Ancient History;* L. W. King, *A History of Sumer and Akkad,* 1916, and: *A History of Babylon,* 1915; A. T. Olmstead, *History of Assyria,* 1923; J. K. Breasted, *A History of the Ancient Egyptians,* 1920; Erman, *Aegypten und ägyptisches Leben im Altertum,* 1885, new ed. by H. Ranke, 1923; B. Meissner, *Babylonien und Assyrien* vol. 1-2, 1920, 1924; J. Garstang, *The Land of the Hittites,* 1911; Ed. Meyer, *Reich und Kultur der Chetiter,* 1914; J. Friedrich and E. Forrer in *Zeitschr. d. deut. Morgenl. Ges.* vol. 76, 1922; R. A. S. Macalister, *The Philistines, their History and Civilization,* 1914.

As for the ancient law-codes, the *Codex Hammurabi* is edited (with a transcription) by Scheil, 1902, by Harper, 1904, with a French and an English translation respectively. It has further been translated into English by C. H. W. Johns, *The Oldest Code of Laws in the World,* 1903; into German by H. Winckler, 1904 and 1906, by

J. Kohler and F. E. Peiser, *Hammurabi's Gesetz,* 1904, by A. Ungnad in H. Gressmann, *Altorientalische Texte und Bilder,* 1909. The paragraphs quoted in this book are those of Kohler and Peiser. The relation between Cod. Ham. and the Old Testament has frequently been discussed, cf. D. H. Müller, *Die Gesetze Hammurabi's und die mosaische Gesetzgebung,* 1903; S. A. Cook, *The Laws of Moses and the Code of Hammurabi,* 1903; C. H. W. Johns, *The Relation between the Laws of Babylonia and the Laws of the Hebrew Peoples (Schweich Lectures* 1912), 2. ed. 1917. For the Assyrian Laws, *vide* V. Scheil, *Recueil de Lois Assyriennes,* 1921 (transcription with French translation); H. Ehelolf in *Mitteilungen aus der Vorderasiatischen Abteilung der Staatlichen Museen zu Berlin* I 1922; engl. translation by K. Tallquist in *Finska Vetenskaps-Societetens Förhandlingar,* Bd. LXIII, 1920—1921, Avd. B no. 3, Helsingfors, 1921. Transcription, Norwegian translation and notes by A. G. Lie in *Vitenskapsselskapets Skrifter* II, Hist.-Filos. Kl. 1923, Kristiania, 1924. Discussions by Koschaker in *Mitteilungen aus der Vorderasiat.-Aegypt. Gesellsch.* 1921, 3, and E. Cuq in *Revue d Assyriologie* vol. 19, 1922. The quotations of the Hittite Laws are from the translation by H. Zimmern, unter Mitwirkung von J. Friedrich *(Der Alte Orient,* 23. Jahrg. 2. Heft), 1922, compared with F. Hrozný, *Code Hittite provenant de l'Asie Mineure,* 1re partie *(Hethitica* tome 1), 1922. Discussion by E. Cuq in *Revue Historique de Droit Français et Étranger,* 1924. For the relation to the Old Testament, *vide* A. F. Puukko, *Die altassyrischen und hethitischen Gesetze und das Alte Testament (Studia Orientalia* I, Societas Fennica), Helsingforsiae 1925, and the article by the present author in "*Studier tilegnede Frants Buhl*", Copenhagen, 1925 (Danish). — The Amarna letters are quoted from J. A. Knudtzon, *Die El-Amarna-Tafeln (Vorderasiatische Bibliothek* II) 1915.

P. 6 [1]. Am. 290, 15 f. *bīt-NIN. IB* is mentioned as "one of the towns of Jerusalem". According to Dhorme *(Revue Biblique* 1918, p. 517) *NIN. IB* is not the well-known god (Urta, Ninurta), but a goddess *'nt;* O. Schroeder has pointed out *(Orient. Litt. Zeit.* 18, 1915, 294 f.) that the name of the goddess is Lakhama, and the town *bīt-Lakhama* is identical with Beth-lehem. In the Old Testament cf. Num. 21,25.32; 32,42; Judg. 11,26 *et al.* The question of the city-states and the territories of administration is treated by A. Alt in *Beiträge zur Wiss. vom Alt Test.* 13, 1913 and in a programme of the University of Leipzic *(Die Landnahme der Israeliten in Palästina)* 1925.

P. 7 [1]. Canaanite kings are mentioned in Josh. 2; 10; 11; Judg. 1,5-7; 5,19. "The men of Gibeon" are mentioned as acting on behalf of the town without any king, Josh. 9,3. The authorities of Succoth are its men, its elders and its princes, Judg. 8,6 ff.; cf. the note p. 39 [1].

P. 7 [2]. The inhabitants themselves write from Tunip, Am. 59, from Irkata, Am. 100. Tunip possibly belongs to the empire of the

Amorite Aziru, cf. 161, 12. 34; 165, 39. 41; 166, 25; 167, 23. Irkaṭa normally has a king, cf. 139,15; 140,10. The king of Gubla, Ribaddi, mentions the "city lords" of his town 138, 49 probably meaning a kind of elder. A special social class is represented by the *khubshu,* who are generally supposed to be the peasants, cf. Index to Knudtzon's edition. It seems to be a class of great importance, not mercenaries, but making part of the population, and so in all likelihood aristocrats. As *khabshu* is used as a Canaanite gloss for *ZAG,* meaning *emūḳu* "power" (Albright in *Journ. Pal. Or. Soc.* IV, p. 169—170), it means the same as the Hebrew *ḥayil,* and so *khubshu* would correspond with the Hebrew *gibbōrē ḥayil,* and *ḥophshī* would be the individual representative of the *khubshu.* In the Old Test. we find *ḥophshī* as the designation of an aristocrat, raised above the common freemen, 1 Sam. 17,25; but ordinarily it only means a freeman in opposition to a slave, cf. Exod. 21,2.5.26.27; Deut. 15,12.13.18, etc., and so also a released slave. In Assyria, on the other hand, at the time of Salmanassar and Sargon, *khubshu* means soldiers who are not freemen. That they are soldiers appears from Salmanassar II, Balawat Inscription V 3 (Amiaud et Scheil, *Les inscriptions de Salmanassar* II, 1890, p. 48 f. 102) and Sargon, *Khorsabad-Inscr.* 1.33 and other inscriptions (Thureau-Dangin, *Huitième campagne de Sargon,* p. 7,1.26; p. 40,1.258). Their not being freemen appears from another inscription of Sargon, where he complains that *corvée* has been laid on the city of Ashur and that its inhabitants have been treated as *khubshu* (H. Winckler, *Altorientalische Forschungen* I, p. 404,1.31 ff.).

P. 7 [3]. Am. 138,40-42, cf. 136,8 ff. Ribaddi was finally expelled when his ambassador returned from Egypt without having obtained a result, Am. 137. Also Tyre revolted against its king, Am. 89.

P. 7 [4]. Am. 92,44; 106,20.

P. 7 [5]. Am. 100,9 f.; 220,16; 267; 268; 294,9 f.; 325,10 f.; the yoke of the king 296,38.

P. 7 [6]. Am. 64,7; 65,5; 211; 213; 215; 232; 233; 298; 320; other expressions 60,3.7; 61,3; 84,5; 106,6; 116,60; 141; 142 *et al.*

P. 7 [7]. Am. 4,8.

P. 8 [1]. Am. 52,4.

P. 8 [2]. *Vide,* e. g., 275-283; especially interesting is the plur. *ilānu, ilāni-ia* reminding of the Hebrew *'elōhīm.* The king is called "an eternal sun" 155,47; he is like Adad and Shamash 149,6-7; 159,7-8. A hymn in his honour as the sun, *vide* 147,5-15.

P. 8 [3]. Am. 162,49; 163,3; 292,10 ff.; 296,14 ff. The psychic power is called *shāru* or *shēkhu.*

P. 8 [4]. Am. 107,22-23, cf. Gen. 41,42. Obedience towards the *rabiṣu* is enforced 211,21 ff.; 216,12 ff.; 218; 294,8 ff. The *rabiṣu* is counsellor, 94,72, judge 113,17 f.; 116,30 ff.; 117,64 ff.; 118,13 ff. 50 ff.; he receives reports, 62, undertakes travels of inspection, 220,

16 ff.; 225,10; 234,33 ff.; 272,18 ff. *et al.* Abimilki of Tyrus calls himself the *rabiṣu* of the king, installed by the king; so he is the inspector of the king, and accordingly gives reports, 149,14.47 f. Māia, the *rabiṣu* of the king (216,12 ff.; 218) is accused of having installed his *rabiṣu* in the city of Addudāni, 292,35, presumably meaning one of his subordinate inspectors. Addudāni himself belongs to another *rabiṣu,* Rianap; he entreats the king to bid this officer to regain the rulership for him.

P. 8 [5]. Am. 160,33 ff.; 288,19 f.; 301; 313 *et al.*

P. 8 [6]. Am. 287,53 ff.; 295 rev. 8 ff.

P. 8 [7]. Am. 88,45 ff.

P. 9 [1]. Am. 226; 255 *et al.*

P. 9 [2]. Am. 193; 201-206; 324-325.

P. 9 [3]. Am. 161. — Concerning the treaty concluded by Aziru with Shubbiluliuma, king of the Hittites, *vide* E. F. Weidner, *Politische Dokumente aus Kleinasien (Boghazköistudien* ed. O. Weber 8, 1923) p. 70-75.

P. 9 [4]. *SA-GAZ,* mentioned in the Amarna letters in a similar way as Khabiru, is philologically to be read *khabbatum,* "marauders". It is essentially identical with Khabiru, as shown by the analogous use of the two terms in the Boghazkeui-Documents, *vide* Weidner, *Politische Dokumente aus Kleinasien,* 1923, p. 31, n. 5; yet it is possible that *SA-GAZ* is a more comprehensive term than Khabiru. Both terms are regarded as meaning certain peoples, who are used as mercenaries in Canaan and Syria, and evidently also in Asia Minor. In the same manner they are employed by Warad-Sin and Rim-Sin of Larsa shortly before 2000 B. C., and so also by Hammurabi, *vide* S. H. Langdon in *The Expository Times* vol. 30, 1920, p. 324-329. This being so, it does not seem probable that the Khabiru represent the native nomad and peasant population of Canaan, revolting against the foreign influence, cf. Dhorme in *Revue Biblique* 1909, p. 67 ff.; 1924, p. 14 ff.; in *Journ. of the Palestine Orient. Soc.* vol 4, 1925, p 162 ff. Their position is analogous to that of the Sutū, from whom they are, on the other hand, distinguished, *vide* Am. 195,27-29; 318,11-13. The Sutū are known as Aramæan nomads of the Syrian desert; so it is not improbable that the *SA-GAZ*-Khabiru belong to those Aramæan tribes who at the end of the second millennium B. C. invaded the borderlands of Mesopotamia and Syria from the desert. They are employed by the cunning Amorite princes Abdi-Ashirta (Am. 71; 73; 79) and Aziru (Am. 132, 20 f.) but also by a man of Pharao like Namiawaza Am. 195). Many towns surrender to them (Am. 74; 76; 77; 79; 85,69 ff.; 144). Gezer, Ascalon and Lachish are said to support them (Am. 287,14 ff.), but the Prince of Gezer asks for assistance against them. From a philological point of view Khabiru can be identified with *ḥābhēr* "fellow" or with *ʿibhrī* "Hebrew", but these identifications are doubtful, cf. Landsberger in *Zeits. f. Ass.* vol. 36, N. F. 1, 1924, p. 213[1]. They may be identical with the invading Israelites, or they may be their forerunners, Hebrew being a more comprehensive term than Israelite, cf. 1 Sam 14,21 and the genealogy Gen. 10. For full evidence, *vide,* beside the above mentioned, Knudtzon, *Die El-Amarna-Tafeln,* p. 45-52, and Weber, *ibidem* p. 1146 ff.; 1336; F. Böhl, *Kanaanäer und Hebräer,* 1911, p. 83-96; C. F. Burney, *Israel's Settlement in Canaan (The Schweich Lectures),* 2. ed., 1919, p. 66-81 and *The Book of Judges,* 1918, p. LXXIII ff. and the literature there quoted; *The Cambridge Ancient History* 2 (Index).

P. 15 [1]. Gen. 35,21 f.; Josh. 15,6; 18,7 *et al., vide* C. Steuernagel, *Die Einwanderung der israelitischen Stämme in Kanaan,* 1901, p. 15-21.

P. 15 [2]. Jacob-el, *v.* W. M. Müller, *Asien und Europa,* p. 157 ff. and in *Mitteilungen der Vorderas. Ges.* 1907, 1. The equivalence of Y-š-p-ʾ-r and Joseph-el is more doubtful; cf. Kittel, Geschichte 5-6. ed., p. 261 note 1; Burney, *Israel's Settlement,* p. 61. According to Ed. Meyer, *Die Israeliten,* p. 282, Jacob-el may be sought in Transiordania. The name does not prove that the Israelitic tribe had settled in Canaan about 1500 B. C.; it is probably a Canaanite word adopted by the later invaders. The blessing, Gen. 27,29: "Be lord over thy brethren, that thy mother's sons bow down to thee", implies that Jacob was a tribe among others; but perhaps we ought not to attach too much weight to this expression. — As for *Israel* in the inscription of Merneptah v. F. Petri, *History of Egypt* vol. 3, p. 114; Spiegelberg in *Aegyptische Zeitschrift* vol. 34, p. 1 ff.; Breasted, *Ancient Records of Egypt* vol. 3, 602 ff., and *infra* note 17 [2].

P. 16 [1]. Cf. concerning the relation between Aramæans and Israelites Ed. Meyer, *Die Israeliten,* p. 235-249; Burney, *Israel's Settlement,* p. 76 f., 85.

P. 16 [2]. For the Israelitic tradition, *vide* above all Gen. 36,6-7. For the relation of Aram and Edom, *vide* H. R. Hall, *Ancient History,* 4. ed., p. 420 f.

P. 17 [1]. It is impossible to determine where Sinai was situated and what was its relation to Horeb. The Christian tradition places Mount Sinai in the South-West of the Peninsula named Sinai. From the beginning of the 4th century A. D. (Eusebius *et al.)* it was identified with Jebel Serbāl, from the 6th century with Jebel Mūsā. In these parts there was an old cultic centre, cf. B. Moritz, *Der Sinaikult in heidnischer Zeit (Abh. d. Ges. d. Wiss. Göttingen,* Phil.-Hist. Kl., Neue Folge Vol. XVI), 1916. But there is no link between the Christian and the old Israelitic tradition. Some scholars emphasize the connection of Sinai with Midian, the home of the father-in-law of Moses, and with Edom (Deut. 33,2; Judg. 5,4; Hab. 3,3) and place it in the *ḥarra* of North-West Arabia, *vide* v. Gall, *Altisraelitische Kultstätten,* 1898, p. 1-22. So also, emphasizing its volcanic character, Ed. Meyer, *Die*

Israeliten und ihre Nachbarstämme, p. 60-71; A. Musil, *Im nördlichen Heǧaz,* 1911; H. Gressmann, *Mose und seine Zeit,* 1913, p. 409-419, cf. P. Haupt in *Zeitschr. d. deut. Morgenl. Ges.,* 1913, p. 506 ff. The volcanic character of Sinai is, however, very doubtful, and the references quoted, above all Deut. 32,2, rather suggest that it is not far from Kadesh, i. e. in the Peninsula; for Kadesh is, according to the investigations of Trumbull *(Kadesh-Barnea,* New York, 1884), to be looked for in an oasis east of *wādī jerūr,* north of the Peninsula proper, cf. R. Weill, *La Presq'île du Sinai (Bibl. de l'École des Hautes Études),* 1908, p. 210-217; B. Moritz *op. cit.,* p. 34 note; R. Kittel, *Gesch. d. Volkes Israel* I 5.-6. ed., 1923, p. 343-349. — v. Gall, Ed. Meyer *et al.* seek Horeb far from Sinai, on the Peninsula, owing to the itinerarium of the Exodus *(vide* v. Gall *op. cit.,* p. 3-4). According to Exod. 17,6 this mountain must be near Kadesh, but according to Deut. 1,2 it is 11 days' journey from it. More expressly than with Sinai it is connected with Midian, Exod. 3,1; 18,1. As it is the mountain of the law-giving in Deut., it is probably not different from Sinai. — Since Naville, *The Store City of Pithom and the Route of the Exodus,* 1885, the place where the Israelites passed over the Red Sea is generally sought at Lake Timsāḥ, *vide* the discussion in Kittel, *op. cit.* p. 349-353; 369-370.

P. 17 [2]. Cf. Ed. Naville, *The Store City of Pithom and the Route of the Exodus,* 4. ed., 1903. If Raamses II was the builder of the city excavated in Tell el-Maskhūta by Naville, and this city was Pithom, the successor of Raamses, Merneptah, would naturally be the "new Pharaoh" of Exod. A difficulty in the way of this theory is the Israel-stele mentioned *supra* note 15 [2]. Here Merneptah boasts of having exterminated the seed, i. e. the posterity, of *Isirail* in Canaan. As Israel is here a settled Canaanite people, the possibility of Merneptah being the Pharaoh of the Exodus seems excluded. This has given rise to the hypothesis that only the Rachel-tribes represented Israel which had been oppressed in Egypt, whereas the Leah-tribes had settled at an earlier period in Palestine, the latter being the Israel mentioned by Merneptah. The mixed character of Israel makes it a matter of course that not the fathers of the whole of later Israel, but, as emphasized above, a prehistoric Israel was in Egypt. But it is not probable that the division into Leah-tribes and Rachel-tribes has anything to do with this. The name of Israel is in the older period not connected with the leading Leah-tribes, but with the Rachel-tribes. It must be admitted that the hypothesis of Naville is not so solid as supposed by most scholars, and the names of Pithom and Raamses Exod. 1,11 may be of rather late origin. The starting point must be the Israel-stele, showing that Israel (or rather its nucleus) had settled in Canaan at the time of Merneptah, about 1200 B. C. If the immigration of the Israelites was identical with or connected with that of the Khabiru, it took place about 1400 B. C. or a little later. The period between 1400 and 1200 is the time of the decline of the Egyptian power in Canaan. Sety I (about 1300) undertakes two campaigns to Palestine, where "the vanquished Shasu" had revolted. It is likely that these Shasu (the Egyptian term for Asiatic nomads) were the same as the *SA-GAZ*-Khabiru, cf. Burney *op. cit.* p. 81. Sety and Raamses both mention a district 'Asaru in the North, but we do not know whether it is Israelitic or still Canaanite. The story of Wenamon shows the total decline of Egyptian authority in Canaan, under Raamses XII (about 1100 B. C.), *v.* Erman in *Aegyptische Zeitschrift* vol. 38, p. 1 ff.; Breasted, *Records* vol. 4,557 ff. The *'Apuriu* are mentioned under Tutmosis III (c. 1501-1447) and Raamses II-IV (c. 1292-c. 1161) as foreigners, and they are represented as labourers occupied with building. They have often been identified with the Hebrews, though the representation of a Hebrew *b* by an Egyptian *p* is anormal, *v.* Chabas, *Mélanges Égyptologiques* I, 1862, p. 42 ff.; II, 1864, p. 108 ff.; Heyes, *Bibel und Aegypten,* 1904, p. 146, p. 108 ff.; Heyes, *Bibel und Aegypten,* 1904, p. 146 ff. The 'Apuriu being mentioned so late they must in any case represent a wider aspect than Israel. — For the whole question, *v.* W. Spiegelberg, *Der Aufenthalt Israels in Aegypten,* 1904; B. Eerdmans, *Alttestamentliche Studien* II, 1908; Burney, *Israel's Settlement;* Kittel, *Geschichte* I; Hall, *Ancient History,* 5. ed., 1920, p. 403 ff.; Albright in *Journ. Pal. Orient. Soc.* I, 1921, p. 49 ff.; *The Cambridge Ancient History* vol. 2, p. 358-369. A new and comprehensive treatment is to be found in A. Mallon, *Les Hébreux en Égypte,* 1921.

P. 19 [1]. The Korahites were keepers of the gates, 1 Chron. 9,19; 26,1.19; singers, 2 Chron. 20,19; incense-makers, 1 Chron. 9,31.

P. 20 [1]. *Vide* note p. 9 [4].

P. 20 [2]. Caves as dwellings are mentioned in Judg. 6,2; 1 Sam. 13,6; 14,11.

P. 21 [1]. *Vide* Jer. 35,7. For the tent as appellation for dwelling, cf. the phrase "to go to one's tents", Judg. 20,8; 1 Sam. 13,2; 2 Sam. 18,17; 19,9; 20,1.22; 2 Kings 14,12.

P. 24 [1] Concerning the year of Samaria's fall, *v.* Olmstead, *History of Assyria,* 1923, p. 205; *Am. Journ. of Sem. Lang.,* 1905, p. 179 ff.

P. 31 [1]. Cf. about Jair Ed. Meyer, *Die Israeliten* p. 517.

P. 31 [2]. This view has been generally adopted since it was set forth by B. Stade in *Zeitschr. f. d. Alttestamentl. Wissensch.,* 1881, p. 112-116 and *Geschichte des Volkes Israel* I, 1887, p. 145-148. It is most consistently carried through by Guthe, *Gesch. d. Volkes Israel,* 3. ed. § 1 and C. Steuernagel, *Die Einwanderung der isr. Stämme in Kanaan,* 1901.

P. 32 [1]. Cf. Ed. Meyer, *Die Israeliten* p. 428 ff.; B. Luther, *Die israelitischen Stämme,* in *Zeitschr. f. d. Alttestament. Wiss.* 1901, p.

22-23. Israel and Judah are constantly mentioned beside each other as two different parts, cf. especially 2 Sam. 19,44.

P. 32 [2]. M. Müller, *Asien und Europa,* p. 236 f., cf. note 17 [2]. The term "*in* all the tribes" is of frequent occurrence, e. g. 2 Sam. 15,10, cf. Is. 8,23. To this question, cf. B. Luther, *op. cit.* p. 11.21.

P. 32 [3]. The blessing of Jacob must mainly refer to the post-Davidic situation, as shown by the statement about Judah.

P. 33 [1]. It is obvious that, as suggested by Kuenen, an old narrative underlies the story. The commentators generally try to separate the original elements through an analysis of the story and so arrive at two sources. But this attempt, inaugurated by K. Budde, *Die Bücher Richter und Samuel,* 1890, has not led to anything definite, cf. the commentaries of Moore, Budde, Nowack and of Burney (whose analysis is quite different from that of the others). The story is badly related, full of repetitions and obscurities, which no analysis has been able to remove. Sentimentality mixed with cruelty is the characteristic feature of this secondary product.

P. 35 [1]. As to this rite and its analogy with the *ḳasāma* of the Arabians, see the author's *Der Eid bei den Semiten (Studien zur Geschichte und Kultur des Islamischen Orients* ed. C. H. Becker, 3), 1914, p. 186. The people go to war city by city, Am. 5,3.

P. 35 [2]. The elders acting as judges on all these occasions, it is not probable that "the judges" mentioned in the Deut., e. g. 16,18, should be different from the elders. This appears also from Deut. 21,1-9 where it is said, v. 2, that elders and judges shall go out together to the place of murder, whereas the following narrative only mentions the elders as participating.

P. 37 [1]. So the elders of the priests are mentioned in 2 Kings 19,2; Is. 37,2; Jer. 19,1.

P. 39 [1]. *śar* is related to Akkadian *sharru,* but it is doubtful if it is a loan-word, cf. Zimmern, *Akkadische Fremdwörter,* 1915, p. 7. The *śar* of the army is mentioned in 1 Sam. 14,50; 2 Sam. 2,8; 1 Kings 1,19; 2,32, etc.: *śar* of thousand 1 Sam. 8,12; 17,18; 18,13; 2 Sam. 18,1: of hundred 1 Sam. 22,7; 2 Sam. 18,1; 2 Kings 11,19: of fifty 1 Sam. 8,12; 2 Kings 1,9-11.14; Is. 3,3: of the cars 1 Sam. 22,31; 2 Kings 8,21: of the guard 1 Kings 14,27. This seems to suggest that they are military leaders (cf. the commentaries of Moore and Burney to Judg. 8); but they are not exclusively so, as shown by Job 29,9. In Judg. 8,6 ff. the *śārīm* and the elders of Succoth are mentioned indiscriminately, and upon the whole the relation between *śārīm* and elders in the old time is not clear. The king and the *śārīm* are mentioned together, Jer. 4,9; 49,38; Hos. 3,4; 13,10; Am. 1,15; as a class distinct from the people they are mentioned in Jer. 26,11.12.16; 34,10, the two classes having separate cemeteries, 2 Kings 23,6; Jer. 26,23. Another appellation of the aristocracy is *ḥōrīm,* which is only known from the time of the Monarchy. As for *ḥophshī, vide* note 7 [2].

P. 44 [1]. It may be suggested that the term *tōshābh* originally designates the released slave; there is no clear difference between this term and *gēr,* Gen. 23,4; Exod. 12,45; Lev. 22,10; 25,6.23.35. 40.45.47; Num. 35,15; Ps. 39,13; 1 Chron. 29,15; cf. the various opinions in A. Bertholet, *Die Stellung der Israeliten und der Juden zu den Fremden,* 1896, p. 156-163.

P. 47 [1]. So B. Luther in *Zeitschr. f. d. Alttest. Wiss.* 1901, p. 2.

P. 47 [2]. If the plur. "tribes of Benjamin" 1 Sam. 9,21 be correct, it would be a further testimony to the indefinite character of the tribe; but it probably should be read *shēbheṭ,* "tribe".

P. 48 [1]. For instances of uncertainty in the distribution of families, *v.* Steuernagel, *Einwanderung* p. 18 f.

P. 49 [1]. So Jer. 1,15; 25,9; Ezek. 20,32; Nah. 3,4; Psalm. 22,28; 96,7; 107,41; 1 Chron. 16,28.

P. 50 [1]. *ḥayyā,* 2 Sam. 23,13, in connexion with the Philistines; *ḥawwā,* Num. 32,41; Deut. 3,14; Josh. 13,30; Judg. 10,4; 1 Kings 4,13 about the city-community of Jair in Northern Gilead. The two words mean the same and are related to the Arabic *ḥayy.* 1 Sam. 18,18 reads *ū-mī ḥayyay mishpaḥath ʾābhī beyiśrāʾēl;* some scholars eliminate *mishpaḥath* and read *ḥay* "what is my father's family in Israel?" *v.* the commentaries of Nowack and H. Preserved Smith; but most commentators omit *mishpaḥath ʾābhī* and read *ḥayyī* "what is my family in Israel?" *v.* Wellhausen, *Text der Bücher Sam.,* p. 111; Budde in his commentary; Robertson Smith, *Kinship,* 2. ed., p. 46. Still, the Massoretic text is good: "what is the life of my father's family in Israel?" i. e. what is its inner value? Like *mī* so *ḥayyay* may be an archaic form, but we may also read it *ḥayyē.*

P. 51 [1]. Also used Exod. 18 (JE). The root means in the different dialects "to be bound together, to be familiar with, appropriate, know". The relation to *ʾeleph,* "ox", is obscure, but the community may have derived its denomination from this animal. At any rate, the use of the word as a number "thousand" must be derived. It is characteristic that in Ethiopic it does not denote 1000, but 10,000. So the military organization does not give us the key to the understanding of the original meaning of the word, cf. the view of Ed. Meyer in *Israeliten,* p. 498 ff. The term *ʾummā,* well known in Arabic, is only used in Gen. 25,16; Num. 25,15; Ps. 117,1; perhaps it is an Akkadian loan-word, cf. Zimmern, *Akkadische Fremdwörter,* p. 46.

P. 51 [2]. For the Assyrian, cf. Zimmern in *Zeitschr. f. Assyr.* 6, p. 247. In the Amarna letters (e. g. 9,5; 136,8) *bīt* denotes the members of the house. The term *bīt abi* also occurs, so 33,11; 49,18; 74,11; 116,66; 179,29; 189,10; 288,15. But in 189,10 it denotes the inherited domain; in some of the other passages it may have the same meaning as in Hebrew, but it may also mean the palace. In Arabic *bayt* is often used as denoting family.

P. 54 [1]. 1 Kings 20,35; 2 Kings 2,3.5.7.15; 4,1.38; 5,22; 6,1; 9,1; Am. 7,14.

P. 55 [1]. The same is the case in Arabic. A word like *baʿd* denotes part of a whole, but it is immaterial whether it is one or more; *ḳaum* is like *ʿam,* a people, a tribe, but is also used of a single person, e. g. *Bukhārī* ed. Krehl 1,103,1; *ʾahl* denotes a related whole, tribe (*Mutalammis* ed. Vollers 7,1) as well as family (*Bukhārī* 1,159,6; 2,38, 2; 126,3; 188,17, etc.); further, a single individual, especially the wife (*Bukhārī* 2,138,2 ff.; 146,2 infra; 155,6), but also others (*Ibn Ḳais ar-Ruḳayyāt,* ed. Rhodokanakis 2,16, *Labīd* 14,15, etc.; *ʾahl* may, like *ʿam,* be used in plur. Correspondingly, *ʿamm* in Arabic both denotes the community of kindred and the individual member; the individual can also be called *ibn ʿamm.* A discussion as to whether it first denoted the community or the individual leads to no result; cf. Juynboll in *Orientalische Studien Th. Nöldeke gewidmet,* ed. Bezold, 1906, I p. 353-356, where references are made to the views of Wellhausen, Robertson Smith and Nöldeke.

P. 55 [2]. City Gen. 19,4; Judg. 9,29 ff.; 1 Sam. 5,10 f.; Jer. 37, 12; Ruth 3,11; tribe: Joseph Josh. 17,14.17; Dan: Gen. 49,16; Gilead: Judg. 11,11; Zebulun: Judg. 5,18; Judah: 2 Sam. 18,6; 2 Kings 14,21; Jer. 25,1.2; 26,18, etc. Used of the Northern kingdom 1 Kings 12,27, of Israel through the whole of the Old Testament.

P. 56 [1]. Gen. 14,16; Josh. 8,1.3; 10,7; 11,7; Judg. 4,13; 7,1.8; 1 Sam. 13,5, etc.; the cultic community 1 Sam. 9,12; 1 Kings 21,9.12.

P. 57 [1]. *ʿam* is nearly always used about Israel as the people of its god, similarly about Moab as the people of Chemosh, cf. Num. 21,29; Jer. 48,46; *gōy* and *leʾōm* are not so deeply rooted in the family-feeling as *ʿam.* The words *ḳāhāl* and *ʿēdhā* are mostly used about momentary meetings, e. g. for worship; but both are also used about the permanent community to which one belongs, e. g. the nation; Job 16,7 *ʿēdhā* seems to be used about "the house".

P. 57 [2]. *ʿāmīth* is used beside *ʾāḥ,* Lev. 25,14 f., with *rēʿa,* probably Zech. 13,7; *ʾāḥ* and *rēʿa* are used indiscriminately, Exod. 2,11-13; 32,27; Deut. 15,2; Is. 19,2; Jer. 31,34; 34,17; Ps. 35,14; Job 30,29 *et al.*

P. 58 [1]. The Massoretic *ʾaḥē* "brethren", Gen. 24,27, is as good as the emendated *ʾaḥī* "brother". Similarly Judg. 14,3 "among the daughters of thy brethren" *bibhenōth ʾaḥēkhā,* ought not to be changed in *bebhēth ʾābhīkhā* "in the house of thy father" (so Budde and Nowack in their commentaries after Peshitta). The word has kept its old application. Ruth rabba 3,21 it is said: No man refuses to call his uncle his brother.

P. 59[1]. It is found in Lev. 5,21; 18,20; 19,11.15.17; 24,19; 25, 14 f. 17; Zech. 13,7; with *ben-ʿammī,* Gen. 19,38; 23,11.

P. 60[1]. Thus *rēʿa* is used about the man with whom one has to deal in a certain situation, like the Arabic *ṣāḥib,* Gen. 11,3.7; Exod. 11,2; Judg. 6,29; 10,18; 1 Sam. 10,11, etc.; even about things, Gen. 15,10. The "fellowship" may be of a peculiar kind, as a fight; therefore *rēʿa* may denote the opponent with whom one fights, 1 Sam. 28,17; 2 Sam. 2,16; 12,11. In a similar, weakened sense also *ʾāḥ* is used, Gen. 26,31; Exod. 10,23; 16,15; 25,20; 37,9; Jer. 23,35, etc. *ʾallūph* "a fellow" has not the significance we might expect, it being derived from one of the terms for family, *ʾeleph.* It is not used of a real fellow-kinsman.

P. 63[1]. *baʿal hab-bayith,* Exod. 22,7; Judg. 19,22.23; the *baʿal* of the wife, Exod. 21,3.22; Deut. 24,4; 2 Sam. 11,26; Prov. 12,4 *et al.* The verb *bāʿal* "to take as a wife", Deut. 21,13; 24,1; the wife is *beʿūlā* "taken by a *baʿal*", Gen. 20,3; Deut. 22,22; Is. 54,1; 62,4; *baʿal* of domestic animals, Exod. 21,28.29.36; 22,10; 2 Sam. 1,6; Is. 1,3; of property, Exod. 21,34; Eccles. 5,12; *ʾādhōn* of a slave, Exod. 21,4 ff. There is no object in raising the question whether it first meant one thing or the other.

P. 66[1]. *v.* Zimmern u. Friedrich, *Hethitische Gesetze* I 37; II 73.75 f. 80.85; Hrozný §§ 36.187.189 f. 194.199; cf. the additional note, *infra.* Among the Jews it has been a matter of discussion if a man is allowed to marry his niece, cf. Sam. Krauss in *Studies in Jewish Literature issued in Honor of Professor K. Kohler,* 1913, p. 165-175.

P. 66[2]. For Egypt, *vide* Erman, *Aegypten und ägyptisches Leben* 2. ed., 1923 (by Ranke), p. 180, for the Phænicians R. Pietschmann, *Geschichte der Phönizier,* 1889, p. 237, cf. Robertson Smith, *Kinship and Marriage,* new ed., 1907, p. 192. Of course not only Hittite, but also Egyptian influence on the Phænicians in this respect is possible. For the Israelites, *vide,* beside Lev. 18,9.11; 20,17, also Deut. 27,22; Ezek. 22,11. According to Lev. 18,18 it is forbidden to marry a woman and her sister together, but this is not acknowledged in the story of Jacob marrying Leah and Rachel. According to the genealogy, Num. 26, 58-59, the mother of Moses, Jochebed, is the sister of her husband's father, which is against Lev. 18,12. It is against Lev. 18,8 that the heir of the throne should take his father's wives, 2 Sam. 16,22; 1 Kings 2,13 ff., cf. Robertson Smith, *Kinship,* new ed., p. 109-111. It is possible that he only took the childless wives, as with certain African peoples.

P. 69[1]. *shillūḥīm,* Exod. 18,2; 1 Kings 9,16; Mic. 1,14, cf. Judg. 1,13 ff. As for *mōhar,* cf. Gen. 34,12; Exod. 22,16; 1 Sam. 18,25. From Deut. 22,29 compared with Exod. 22,15 f. we may conclude that its normal price was 50 shekels. Instead of money work may be yielded, as in the case of Jacob; a chief may claim valiant deeds as *mōhar* for his daughter, cf. Josh. 15,16; Judg. 1,12; 1 Sam. 17,25; 18,20 ff.

P. 70 [1]. A woman is even called *raḥam,* "womb", Judg. 5,30, as in the Mesha-stele 1.17, cf. the Arabic *farj.*

P. 72 [1]. *v.* Roscoe, *The Northern Bantu,* p. 174.

P. 75 [1]. Gen. 19,12 the sons-in-law of Lot seem to live with him, but this means: in the same town; according to v. 14 Lot "goes out" to them. It was not uncommon in the ancient Orient that a slave married a free woman, cf. for the Babylonians Cod. Ham. §§ 175-176, for the Hittites the law I 33.35. This agrees with the development of the social order, cf. above p. 44.

P. 76 [1]. Judg. 8,31; 14-15 are generally taken as evidence of the existence of the matriarchate in Israel, cf. the commentaries of Moore, Budde, Nowack, Burney and Benzinger, *Hebräische Archäologie,* 2. ed., p. 104. After Robertson Smith, *Ḳinship* (new ed. p. 93 f.) such a marriage is called *ṣadīḳa*-marriage, its principal feature being that the wife lives with her own kin and is independent of her husband. The Assyrian law, which shows that a wife living with her own family is very dependent on her husband, occurs in their code IV 50-55, cf. note 78 [1] and the additional note.

P. 77 [1]. As the whole matter is apparently an affair of the city, this term must mean "in the same town". Dillmann in his commentary understands it "in gemeinschaftlichem Hauswesen", but this sense seems to be too narrow. Ehrlich, *Randglossen zur Hebräischen Bibel* vol. 2, 1909, p. 322 f. translates "live contemporaneously". His translation, inspired by *Sifrē,* is based upon the rabbinical conception that the word excludes the case of a brother not yet born when the sister-in-law became widowed, cf. the paper of Mattuck quoted in the note 77 [5].

P. 77 [2]. So it must be translated. LXX *σπέρμα,* Matth. 22,24 *τέκνα* gives it a wider application, cf. Josephos, *Antiquitates* IV 8,23, who speaks of a childless wife (*τὴν ἄτεκνον*); this also occurs in *Mishna Yebhāmōth* II 5, in accordance with the later conception of the law, *v.* note 5.

P. 77 [3]. "Without", i. e. away from the kin.

P. 77 [4]. "Stand upon the name of his deceased brother", i. e. exist on the strength of it, maintain it and continue it. The Rabbis take the brother as the subject of this sentence; he is supposed to be designated by the word "the first-born". For other conceptions of the sentence, *v.* the commentaries.

P. 77 [5]. In the Jewish conception set forth in *Yebhāmōth* the law means that if a man dies without heirs, viz. sons or daughters (on behalf of Num. 27) the eldest brother shall take over the inheritance and with this also the widow (that belonged to the property); she is his wife by virtue of her former marriage. This is to be understood in the sense that the law of incest, Lev. 18, is suspended in the interest of the widow, when she is childless. But when the marriage is excluded by other laws, the *ḥalīṣā,* being equal to a divorce, is necessary. Some

Rabbis pretend that it is always necessary; cf. Joh. Selden, *Uxor Ebraica,* 1712, p. 67 ff. (cap. XIV); Israel I. Mattuck, *The Levirate Marriage in Jewish Law* in *Studies in Jewish Literature issued in Honor of Professor Kaufmann Kohler,* 1913, p. 210-222; H. Strack u. P. Billerbeck, *Kommentar zum Neuen Testament aus Talmud und Midrasch* I 1922, p. 886 f. Josephos is nearer to the original sense, *v. loc. cit.,* note 2.

P. 78 [1]. The Levirate Law, like the passages of Judg. quoted note 76 [1], has been of importance in the discussion carried on about the character of the marriage with peoples outside modern Europe. J. F. McLennan, *Studies in Ancient History* 1876 (comprising a reprint of *Primitive Marriage* from 1865; new, posthumous, series 1896) advanced the theory that marriage was originally a polyandry, of which two types exist. In the Nair type the woman remains with her own kin, and receives husbands of various kins; the paternity being uncertain, her child must claim kin with its mother. In the Tibetan type a group of kinsmen keep a common wife. It is suggested that the child was first reckoned as of the kin of the husband, but later (so in Tibet) the eldest kinsman is regarded as the father, and then the idea of individual fatherhood arose. The Levirate marriage would belong to the Tibetan type of polyandry. This theory was applied to the Semites by W. Robertson Smith, *Kinship and Marriage in Early Arabia,* 1885 (new edition 1903 by Stanley A. Cook, reissued 1907), cf. G. A. Wilken, *Het Matriarchaat bij de oude Arabieren,* 1884. Also other scholars look upon the Levirate as a survival of an original group marriage, though with a modified view, cf. J. G. Frazer, *Totemism and Exogamy* vol. 1, pp. 501 ff. and *Folk-Lore in the Old Testament* 2, 1918, pp. 263-341. Where group marriages were abandoned, the Levirate, according to Frazer, assumed a new character, partly economic, the widow being a valuable part of the inheritance, partly religious, offspring being necessary for the deceased to perform the rites for him. These two points of view are generally found with scholars treating the Hebrew law of the Levirate. The purpose of securing the rites for the deceased is emphasized by B. Stade, *Geschichte des Volkes Israel* 1, 1887, p. 394; *Biblische Theologie* 1, 1905, p. 188; Schwally, *Das Leben nach dem Tode,* 1892, p. 28; Marti, *Gesch. der isr. Rel.,* 5. ed., 1907, p. 57 f.; Bertholet, Commentary on Deut. 25,5 ff. and Ruth 1,11-13; 4,5 *et al.* The economic point of view is maintained by Driver on Deut. 25 in *International Critical Commentary,* and by Benzinger in Herzog-Hauck, *Realencyclopädie,* 3. ed. vol. 5, p. 745 f. and *Hebräische Archäologie,* 2. ed. p. 113.288 f. with slight variations. The consideration of the widow is emphasized by Mattuck *op. cit.* in accordance with the later Jewish conception, and by Ed. König in his commentary on Deut. 25. None of these points of view is quite wrong nor is any of them sufficient; they all must be viewed under a wider angle. The duties of the members of the family, the conception of its property and the position of the wife — all this can only be understood as links of an organic culture that must be taken as a whole, without being split up by narrow explanations adopted from without. So also the Levirate has its natural place in Hebrew culture, and theories as to what it is or has been under quite different conditions are of little use to elucidate what it really means in Israel.

P. 81 [1]. The genealogy Ruth 4,18-21, giving the boy the name of Boaz, goes against this expressly formulated purpose, cf. also p. 93.

P. 85 [1]. So it seems most natural to understand *laḥ^a^lîḳ* Jer. 37,12; it does not otherwise appear in Hiphil, cf. Duhm and Giesebrecht in their commentaries; Volz, in his commentary "eine Erbsache zu besorgen". If we translate "partake in the distribution by lot", cf. Gesenius-Buhl, *Handwörterbuch* s. v., this passage can not be connected with Jer. 32,6-15. The translation of the English revised version "to separate himself thence" is very doubtful.

P. 85 [2]. Some scholars suggest that there was some common property which was regularly disposed of by lot. They refer, i. a., to Jer. 37,12; Mic. 2,5, expressions like Ps. 16,6 and the frequent mention of the lot, cf. Wellhausen, *Die kleinen Propheten* on Mic. 2,5; Buhl, *Die socialen Verhältnisse,* p. 56 ff. If this is right (but Jer. 37,12 is uncertain, *v.* above), these fields must belong to the city.

P. 86 [1]. Dillmann, Driver and König (*v.* their commentaries, where further references are given) are of opinion that the law does not abolish, but only suspends the debt, in that it is not claimed in the seventh year. But this is not implied by the text and is hardly consistent with 15,9. Also Philon, *De special. legibus* II, p. 277.284, Josephos, *Antiquitates* III, 12,3 and probably *Mishna* (*Sh^e^bî'îth* X, 1) take it as full remission, cf. the commentaries of Bertholet and Steuernagel; Nowack, *Archäologie* 1, p. 355; Benzinger, *Archäologie,* p. 293. The Jews of a later period evaded this ordinance by a declaration in advance, prosbol, προσβολή, that is ascribed to Hillel, *v. Mishna Sh^e^bî'îth* X, 4; *Giṭṭin* fol. 36. It is implied in v. 9 that the law reckons with a common year of release, not a special one for every case.

P. 86 [2]. *minnaḥ^a^lāthō.*

P. 86 [3]. *w^e^shābhā.*

P. 86 [4]. *naḥ^a^lath.*

P. 89 [1]. The historical value of the whole of Neh. 10 is disputed, cf. S. Mowinckel, *Ezra den Skriftlærde,* 1916, p. 159 ff. Neh. 5,1-13 treats of a special case, not something of regular recurrence.

P. 89 [2]. Against the general conception of the *yōbhēl*-year as a late institution, Dillmann in his commentary and Eerdmans, *Alttestamentliche Studien,* vol. 4, maintain that this law must be old. But it cannot be inferred from the conservative tendency of the law that it is old in itself. Henry Schaeffer, *Hebrew Tribal Economy and the Jubilee,* 1922, is of opinion that the law is a compromise between an original group-ownership and the institution of private landownership.

P. 90[1]. Gen. 15,3 is very extraordinary, being without analogy in the Israelitic law. Abraham is not devoid of kinsmen; at any rate he has Lot. In view of *yelīdhē bhēthō* Gen. 14,14; 17,27 it can hardly be doubted that *ben bēthī* means "slave". Bertholet, *Die Stellung der Israeliten und Juden zu den Fremden,* p. 55 f. suggests that *ben bēthī* should mean a son of the husband and a handmaid, but this is excluded by v. 4. A. Lods, *Le culte des ancêtres dans l'antiquité hébraique,* 1906, p. 69, suggests with reference to L. G. Lévy, *La famille dans l'antiquité israélite,* 1905, that the slave was adopted. Perhaps it is only to be taken as an outcry of despair.

P. 91[1]. We may read *mōkherā* or *mākhera;* both of them can be translated "sells now". The interpretation that she has already sold the field, but now formally gets the money, is too artificial; cf. Nowack and Bertholet in their commentaries.

P. 91[2]. Read *tighʾal* 4,4.

P. 91[3]. Read *gam ʾēth* instead of *ūmēʾeth* and *ḳānīthā* instead of *ḳānīthī* 4,5.

P. 95[1]. In the Babyl. Talmud this law is only taken as valid for the first period, or it is merely reckoned as advice, *Bābhā bāthrā* fol. 120 a. But in the Jerusalem. Talm. it is strongly enforced, cf. Grätz in *Monatsschr. f. Gesch. u. Wiss. d. Judenthums,* 1879, p. 509.

P. 100[1]. Gen. 1,20.21.24; 2,19; 9,10.12.15.16; Lev. 11,10.46; 24, 18; Ezek. 47,9.

P 100[2]. To hear Gen. 2,19; Exod. 20,18; feel warm Is. 44,16; see good Ps. 34,13; see evil Ps. 90,15; see hunger Jer. 5,12; see sleep Eccles. 8,16; see life Eccles. 9,9; see death Ps. 89,49, or the grave Ps. 16,10; 49,10, cf. Gesenius-Buhl, *Handwörterbuch.*

P. 101[1]. Gen. 34,30; Exod. 5,21; 1 Sam. 13,4; 2 Sam. 10,6; 16, 21; Eccles. 10,1; 1 Chron. 19,6; the root *bʾsh,* "stink", in related languages means to be abominable, wicked.

P. 102[1]. Read *ḳōr* for *ḳīr.*

P. 103[1]. Some MSS. read 2 Kings 9,15 "with your soul". Both readings are equally good.

P. 103[2]. Or read 1 Sam. 14,7 with a small alteration according to LXX: "Do what thy heart inclines towards; I shall go with thee. As thy heart so is my heart", cf. the commentaries. It should be emphasized that the Massoretic text is as good as that of the LXX. To *neṭē lākh* in M. T., cf. 2 Sam. 2,21.

P. 107[1]. LXX renders it correctly by διαβούλια, counsels, resolutions. It is superfluous, on account of LXX to alter *maʿalōth* into *mōʿaṣōth.*

P. 107[2]. Jer. 12,11 with *ʿal,* 2 Sam. 19,20 with *ʾel.*

P. 108 [1]. Exod. 7,23 *shīth lēbh le;* otherwise *šīm* with *le, 'al* or *'el, nāthan* with *le* in Eccles. 1,13.17; 7,21; 8,9.16; as to "speak upon the heart of someone", cf. also Is. 40,2; Hos. 2,16.

P. 109 [1]. The terms for "investigate" are *biḳḳēr, ḥāphaš, ḥāḳar, dārash, biḳḳēsh, tūr* (Grecism).

P. 112 [1]. Herder, *Sämmtl. Werke. Zur Religion und Theologie* I, Tübingen 1805, p. 30.

P. 114 [1]. A summary of the discussion of these problems as well as an independent contribution is given by J. A. Knudtzon, *Om det saakaldte Perfektum og Imperfektum i Hebræisk,* Kristiania 1889, cf. *Actes du 8e Congrès Internationale des Orientalistes, tenu en 1889 à Stockholm et à Christiania. Section Semitique* B (1891), p. 73 ff. The fact that the perfect and imperfect do not indicate the time of the action, but its character, is most strongly emphasized by Driver, *A Treatise of the Use of the Tenses in Hebrew,* 1874; he says of the two forms: "They do not in themselves determine the *date* at which an action takes place, they only indicate its *character* or *kind*" (p. 3). This basic thought has been acknowledged in principle by most scholars. However, both in the book of Driver and in later treatments, it has proved very difficult to break away from the temporal view. This is quite natural; we cannot translate a Hebrew sentence without employing the present, the perfect, the pluperfect, the future or some other of our tenses, determined by the temporal view. Therefore, the tense to be used to indicate the Hebrew form must for us always remain a problem. If we break away entirely from our own temporal conception, we find that there is no difficulty in the so-called consecutive forms, cf., as far as the perfect is concerned, Burney, in *The Journal of Theological Studies,* vol. 20, 1919, p. 200-214. The "consecutive" forms represent a fixed connexion as contrasted with the loose connexion expressed by means of *wāw copulativum,* cf. the author's article, *Die Semiten* in Ebert, *Reallexikon der Vorgeschichte.* A fresh attempt to elucidate the relation between the perfect and the imperfect appears in H. Bauer, *Die Tempora im Semitischen (Beitr. zur. Assyr. u. sem. Sprachw.* VIII,1), 1910, further elaborated by H. Bauer and P. Leander in *Historische Grammatik der hebräischen Sprache,* 1922. His view is the following: The verbal form proper is the imperfect (Bauer: Aorist), therefore originally the only one, and comprising all tenses. Of later occurrence was the perfect (Bauer: Nominal), a verbal noun connected with a pronoun. As a verbal noun it must, wherever it is a question of "punctual" actions, indicate the perfect ("he is a murderer" = "he has murdered"), in other cases it must mean the same as the ptcp. present ("he is a wanderer"), thus indicating the present as well as the past tense. So far in Proto-Semitic. In Western-Semitic, however, the perfect (Nominal) essentially came to be used for the past tense. Thus the imperfect (Aorist) was supplanted from this domain and chiefly came to be used for the present and the future, though both retained certain enclaves within the domains of the other, particularly in the consecutive forms. — The peculiarity about this construction is that it takes the temporal conception of the Latin and modern European languages for granted, and therefore presupposes it with the Semites. When the Semites are originally supposed merely to have had one verbal form Bauer is consequently only able to look upon it in the way that this one form expresses all our tenses (cf. "zeitlos, d. h. allzeitig", *Die Tempora* p. 10), which are then distributed on two forms. In reading a text it will, however, appear that, whatever the rules made, its verbs never subordinate themselves to the temporal conceptions which we are used to. The Semitic languages are as perfect expressions of Semitic thinking as the European languages of European thinking. If European ideas are imposed upon the Semitic languages, a crippled product results, with a manner of expression which is awkward as well as uncertain and is neither European nor Semitic.

P. 116 [1]. That *lā* in *lākhēn* is the preposition *la* and not another Proto-Semitic *lā* (so Barth, *Pronominalbildung, p. 75),* appears from the very form, seeing that it would otherwise have to be *lōkhēn* (cf. Brockelmann, *Vergl. Gramm.* II 480). Haupt distinguishes between four different kinds of *lākhēn,* of which one is an emphatic *l* + dem. *kēn,* "thus" *(Zeitschr. d. Deut. Morgenl. Ges.* vol. 64, p. 714; vol. 65, p. 565; *Journal of Biblical Literature* vol. 29, p. 104). In exactly the same manner as *lākhēn* also *lezō'th* is used, Gen. 2,23; in the same manner the Aramæans say *bekhēn,* which also occurs in Eccles. 8,10; Esth. 4,16. *kēn* is hardly different from the *kēn* signifying standing place (Gen. 40,13; 41,13; Dan. 11,7.20.21.38); thus P. Jensen in *Zeitschr. f. Assyriologie* vol. 7, p. 175. Others take it as an extension of the demonstrative *k,* cf. Gesenius-Buhl, *Handwörterbuch s. v.*

P. 116 [2]. A similar passage occurs in Jer. 23,30.

P. 117 [1]. LXX adequately renders *lākhēn* by οὕτως Ezek. 21,9.

P. 117 [2]. On the other hand, there is no reason to alter the text to *lō' khēn* in Gen. 4,15.

P. 118 [1]. Gen. 11,9; 19,22; 25,30; 29,34; 31,48; Judg. 15,19; 1 Sam. 23,28; 2 Sam. 5,20 *et al.* We must abandon "therefore" as an absolute rendering of the word, and ought not to use it in the expression *kī 'al-kēn* Gen. 18,5; 19,8; 33,10; 38,26; Num. 10,31; 14,43; Judg. 6,22; 2 Sam. 18,20 *(Ḳerē);* Jer. 29,28; 38,4. Here "because" would be more adequate than "therefore", but it is best rendered by "seeing that" or the like. The word only indicates a context. Jer. 38,4 reads: "Let this man be killed *kī 'al-kēn* he weakens the hands of the warriors." The point of gravity is in the first sentence, the second being attached to it. Jeremiah is to be killed, for he weakens the soldiers.

P. 118 [2]. *'asher* is thus closely related to *kēn,* and so the remonstrance of Brockelmann *(Vergl. Gramm.* II, p. 566, note) that it is without any analogy in the Semitic languages falls away. It is difficult to explain the word as an extension of *sha,* cf. the literature referred to in Gesenius-Buhl, *Handwörterbuch s. v.*

P. 119 [1]. Other demonstrative words which can be used in a similar manner are *hinnē* or *hēn* and *'attā*. Judg. 13,12 the latter can be translated by "when"; Judg. 11,23 by "thus", Gen. 21,23; 26,29; 2 Sam. 7,29 by "then". *hēn* approaches *kī* and *ya'an.*

P. 124 [1]. *Vide* the commentary of Driver *(Cambridge Bible) et al.* V. 4 does not mean that the lion only roars when it gets prey, but, on the contrary, that it always gets prey when it roars in the hunt. The young lion growls with satisfaction when it has got prey. V. 8 is closely connected with 3-6, whereas v. 7 does not agree with the context. It may be a gloss to v. 8.

P. 126 [1]. Cf. further Is. 59,3; Ps. 37,30; 71,24; Prov. 8,7; Job 27,4.

P. 126 [2]. Judg. 5,10 can be translated: Attention! or: Listen!

P. 127 [1]. Perhaps in Ps. 139,14 we should vocalize *yādha'tā* "you know my soul". Prov. 19,2 is in all probability to be rendered by: "In non-knowledge a soul is not good", i. e. without wisdom the soul fares ill. The continuation shows that knowledge here is the same as caution.

P. 132 [1]. Lévy-Bruhl, *Les fonctions mentales dans les sociétés inférieures,* p. 426.

P. 135 [1]. H. Zimmern, *Babylonische Busspsalmen,* Leipzig 1885, p. 101. Gen. 28,12 should be translated: He saw in dreams a ladder. Not: He dreamt that he saw a ladder. The ladder of his dreams is as real as any other.

P. 140 [1]. Josephos, *Antiquit.* XVII, 6,4. The Hellenistic Sirach, chap. 31, warns against attaching importance to dreams.

P. 145 [1]. *hēkhīn lēbh* therefore means to have the power to create action, i. e. nearly the same as *hō'īl.* Judg. 12,6: He did not have the power to say thus. The alteration of *yākhīn* to *yābhīn* is as superfluous here as 1 Sam. 23.22, where it means: take upon yourselves to... With implied *lēbh, hēkhīn,* like *śīm,* is used of the pulling together of the soul to action, Judg. 19,30; Is. 41,20; Job 4,20; 23,6; 24,12; 34,23.

P. 150 [1]. *'āṭaph* in this sense agrees well with the Arabic *'aṭafa,* "bend".

P. 151 [1]. The crushing is expressed by forms of *shbr* or *dk'* or *nk';* (for this, cf. Prov. 15,13; 17,22; 18,14).

P. 152 [1]. Köberle, *Natur und Geist nach der Auffassung des alten Testaments,* p. 180.

P. 153 [1]. See in details the last chapter of this book, p. 457 ff.

P. 153 [2]. Ezek. 47,9 "to live" is parallel with *yērāphē',* "be healed"; cf., further, 2 Kings 20,7; Is. 38,21; Ps. 30,4.

P. 155[1]. Gen. 26,19; Lev. 14,5.6.50.51 f.; 15,13; Num. 19,17; Jer. 2,13; 17,13.

P. 157[1]. The words "all that was in his heart" 1 Sam. 9,19 do not suggest what momentarily occupied the mind of Saul, viz. the asses, for this is settled at once, v. 20.

P. 157[2]. As to the psychology of the prophets, cf. G. Hölscher, *Die Propheten. Untersuchungen zur Religionsgeschichte Israels,* Leipzig 1914; H. Gunkel, *Israels Profeter* translated by S. Mowinckel, Kristiania, 1916. Also J. H. Kaplan, *Psychology of Prophecy,* Philadelphia, 1908.

P. 160[1]. The preposition *'al* is also elsewhere used of psychic conditions, 1 Kings 17,21; Ps. 7,9; 42,5.6.7.12; 43,5.

P. 162[1]. *shāḳēdh,* almond tree, *shāḳadh,* guard, Jer. 1,12; *ḳēṣ,* end, *ḳayiṣ,* summer (fruit) Am. 8,1 f.

P. 163[1]. Or read: "the seer calls", etc. In any case the Mass. text: "a lion" can hardly be correct.

P. 163[2]. So Duhm in his commentary to Isaiah; see also Hölscher: *Die Propheten,* p. 70. Buhl attempts to remove this division between the prophet and the spy by an alteration in the text *'omdhā meṣappe,* "act as a spy", cf. *Zeitschr. f. d. Alttestl. Wiss.* vol. 8, p. 157-164.

P. 164[1]. Robertson Smith and Frazer compare this passage with the many analogies from other peoples, *v. Journal of Philology* XIII, p. 286 and Frazer, *The Golden Bough* I, p. 285 note, as well as: *Folklore in the Old Testament* II, 1918, p. 510-13; cf. A. Lods, *La croyance à la vie future,* 1906, p. 46 f.

P. 164[2]. The meaning of *lephōreḥōth* in this passage and somewhat further down is unknown.

P. 168[1]. *Vide,* further, Gesenius-Buhl, *Handwörterbuch* and Buhl in the "Festschrift" of Vilh. Thomsen, p. 32 ff. Also the Aramæan *millā,* which occurs as a loan-word in Hebrew, is used in the same manner, Dan. 2,11.15.17; 6,15. The other terms for case and thing refer to the same unity between the external and the psychical element; *ḥēpheṣ* signifies the soul's pleasure in or desire of something, but also a matter, a case, Is. 58,3.13, or an object, Eccles. 3,1.17; 5,7; 8,6; *'inyān,* which also means to direct the soul towards something, at the same time indicates the external manifestation, the result, either an event, Eccles. 5,13, or an object, Eccles. 3,10; 4,8; 8,16.

P. 170[1]. This is probably what is meant by *bātē han-nephesh,* which is mentioned in Is. 3,20 together with *leḥāshīm,* another kind of amulet. As to this, *vide* Frazer, *Folklore in the Old Testament* II, S. 513. Others take it to mean scent-boxes, cf. Genius-Buhl, *Handwörterbuch s. v.*

P. 173[1]. A vivid description of how the sensations are felt in the various parts of the body is to be found in "The Testament of the

Patriarchs" (test. Sebulon 2) "... I felt pity and began to complain; my liver opened towards me and the foundation of my bowels swelled upwards towards my soul. And Joseph complained and I with him, and my heart resounded, and the joints of my body refused to do service, and I had no strength to stand upright".

P. 173[2]. In anger they quiver, 1 Mac. 2,24. It is not known what parts of the bowels are indicated by *ṭuḥōth* (Ps. 51,8; Job. 38,36).

P. 174[1]. Also Prov. 7,23 may perhaps be mentioned; here, however, it may be a question of a bird pierced by an arrow. As to the alteration of *kābhōdh* into *kābhēdh,* see note 239[1].

P. 177[1]. This must be the meaning of *ḥayyē bhᵉśārīm,* Prov. 14,30. The ordinary translation: "life for the body" seems too narrow, as the word occurs in the plural. Wildeboer (in Marti's *Hand-Kommentar)* takes the plural as "ein Abstraktum = Leiblichkeit".

P. 180[1]. During the last generation the problem of the dead soul, curiously enough, has claimed the attention of scholars to a larger extent than that of the living. This is, however, to be explained by the influence exercised on the view of cultural history within those years by the work of E. Tylor, *Primitive Culture,* 1871. Following the lines laid down by Tylor and Spencer *(Principles of Sociology,* 1876) a starting point was found for the understanding of what was called "primitive man" in his conception of the dead. Thus individual phases of his psychic view were isolated and subordinated to a theory, that of "animism", which was supposed to represent an original stage of manhood, a stage from which all culture had developed. According to this theory the soul is conceived as an image of man without a solid substance, a kind of film or shadow placed in the body and producing life and thought, but moving independently of the body and also existing after the death of the latter. This is not the place to trace the importance of the said theory for the investigations of the cultures and religions, nor its subsequent combination with other conceptions, like that of "preanimism" or "animatism". As for Israel, the animistic theory was employed by Joseph Halévy in *Mélanges d'épigraphie et d'archéologie sémitiques,* 1874. While holding different opinions of its importance as basis of the cult the following writers represent the same view: J. Lippert, *Der Seelenkult in seinen Beziehungen zur althebräischen Religion,* 1881; Oort in *Theologisch Tijdschrift,* 1881; B. Stade, *Geschichte des Volkes Israel,* 1887, and *Biblische Theologie des Alten Testaments* I, 1905; Schwally, *Das Leben nach dem Tode nach den Vorstellungen des Alten Israel und des Judentums,* 1892; J. Frey, *Tod, Seelenglaube und Seelenkult im Alten Israel,* 1898; R. H. Charles, *A Critical History of the Doctrine of a Future Life in Israel, in Judaism and in Christianity,* 1898-1899; A. Bertholet, *Die israelitischen Vorstellungen vom Zustande nach dem Tode,* 1899; C. Grüneisen, *Der Ahnenkult und die Urreligion Israels,* 1900; A. Lods, *Le culte des ancêtres dans l'antiquité israélite,* 1906. It is obvious that the conception of the living and the dead soul is to be taken as a whole; if the phenomena bearing upon the dead soul are separated, and thereafter made the starting point for the understanding of the soul as a whole, neither the conception of the dead nor that of the living soul can be rightly grasped. The peculiar thing is that in spite of the stress laid on the strange phenomena presented by "animism", the scholars, nevertheless, usually take it for granted that the manner of thinking and feeling of the Israelites is in the main like that of modern Europeans.

P. 187[1]. This forceful and striking term ought not to be altered into the colourless "enemy" *('ōyēbh* for *'ōrēbh),* which for that matter hardly gives sense.

P. 192[1]. Whereas Dillmann and Holzinger in the main look upon Gen. 30,25-43 as a unity (apart from v. 26.28), Wellhausen *(Composition des Hexateuchs,* 3. ed., p. 38—40) and Gunkel (in his commentary) have undertaken an exhaustive division of the narrative into two sources. The view of Gunkel is the following: According to the one source, Jacob was at once to take everything that was ring-streaked and spotted as his wages. "To-morrow" (v. 33) he is to prove that he only takes that. According to the other he is *in future* to have all that is ring-streaked and spotted, after setting apart all that at present is ring-streaked and spotted. Then "the black among the lambs", v. 32. 33.35.40, would not belong to any of the narratives, but would be inserted later — but for what reason? The sharp distinction between what is to be done now and in the future is artificial. *māḥār,* v. 33, does not imply new regulations "to-morrow", the sentence only means that Laban may control the accomplishment of the agreement to-morrow (and further on). The only obscure point is that v. 32 should read: take away from them all spotted and ring-streaked animals [among the goats, and all the black animals among the lambs]. The words in brackets are necessary for the sake of the context, but apparently have fallen out, because they are repeated immediately afterwards. It appears from v. 37 ff. that the herd, as it is probable, chiefly consists of goats, and in v. 39 the word *ṣō'n,* "small cattle", is used *a potiori* about these. Then v. 40 mentions the copulation of the lambs *(kebheś* not only signifies new-born lambs but also fully grown lambs).

P. 198[1]. The word *śkl* only in 1 Sam. 18,30 occurs in Ḳal, otherwise in Hiphil.

P. 199[1]. A term for "the life-power", which particularly occurs in the Book of Job, is *tūshīyā,* the origin of which is obscure. It essentially means the same as blessing, in particular as the latter manifests itself in the counsel or, mainly, the same as "the wisdom". The proverb advises to keep *tūshīyā* and wisdom, Prov. 3,21. Yahweh paralyzes the devices of the crafty, so that their hands cannot perform *t.,* Job 5,12. From these examples it appears that *t.,* like *berākhā*, at the same time indicates the productive power of the action and the action itself. Yahweh himself has "strength and *t.*", Job 12,16; his *t.* is wonderful, higher than heaven and deeper than Sheol, Job 11,6. Strength, counsel, understanding *(bīnā)* and *t.* are all manifestations of the strong soul, Prov. 8,14; 18,1. The strong has counsel and *t.,* Is. 28,29, and out of that he gives to others, Prov. 2,7; Job 26,3. The miserable who has lost the blessing complains that he has been deprived of his *t.,* Job 6,13. — Another related term, which only occurs in later writings, is *kōshārā,* Ps. 68,7. The corresponding *kishrōn* is at the same time the energy, Eccles. 2,21; 4,4 and the happiness, Eccles. 5,10. The verb means to succeed, Eccles. 11,6; Esth. 8,5, in Hiphil Eccles. 10,10.

P. 199 [2]. The form *pā'ūl* is not infrequently used in this manner, in Hebrew as well as in Arabic, e. g. *'āṣūm,* strong, *bāṭūaḥ,* confident, *'ānūsh,* malicious, *zākhūr,* remembering, *'āmūn,* reliable, *yādhūa',* knowing, perhaps Deut. 1,13.15 and, beyond a doubt, Is. 53,3; *pā'ūl* thus signifies he who is possessed of something. Otherwise there is hardly any difference between this and the passive meaning, e. g. *ḳāṭūl* is to be understood as he who has murder in him. *Vide* other examples in Lagarde, *Uebersicht über die im Aramäischen, Arabischen und Hebräischen übliche Bildung der Nomina,* p. 59 f.

P. 204 [1]. *berākhā* should then be connected with *berekh,* knee, the latter having to be construed as a term for the abdominal region, the seat of the power of reproduction. So in Assyrian *(tarbit birki-ia* "the seed of my knee", i. e. a son, cf., further, Delitzsch' Assyrian dictionary s. v. *birku),* cf. Gen. 30,3; 50,23; Job 3,12.

P. 206 [1]. This phrase is generally considered an insertion, but it is not certain. The chief argument, i. e. that *hū'* in this place should mean Solomon, whereas it is otherwise a question of the entire progeny of David, does not hold good, as it depends upon a sharp distinction between a whole and its individual parts, which is foreign to Old Israel.

P. 213 [1]. In Job 29,10 we must read *ne'elām* or *nikhlā',* or the like, instead of *neḥbe'ū.*

P. 219 [1]. According to Wellhausen, *Composition des Hexateuchs,* 3. ed. p. 224 this narrative (Judg. 12,1-6) is quite irrelevant and "ein reiner Abklatsch" of the other one, 8,1-3 (Kittel holds the opposite view), an example of the abstract character of a purely literary criticism. On the contrary, it is surprising that we do not have more of this kind of narrative.

P. 219 [2]. Instead of *wayyōdha'* it is common to read *wayyādhōsh* after v. 7. By means of LXX A and L and Syr. hexapl. Burney in his commentary makes the following emendation of the text, viz. "And he took the elders of the city and threshed them together with thorns of the desert and thistles", a text similar to that in v. 7. It would then mean that they were laid on thorns and then trampled down by oxen, or that a threshing-sleigh was rolled over them, cf. Am. 1,3.

P. 222 [1]. As for further details relating to the whole chapter see the note p. 423 [1].

P. 223 [1]. The best vocalization of Judg. 15,16 is that of Burney: *ḥămōr ḥimmartīm;* he considers it a word-play: "I have made them red" and "I have treated them as asses".

P. 227 [1]. Cf. Gen. 4,6; Ezr. 9,7.

P. 227 [2]. Diadem *(nēzer, ʿaṭārā)* and sceptre *(maṭṭe, shēbheṭ)* are among the old oriental regalia. The scepter in all probability is the shepherd's crook. In 2 Sam. 12,30 it is said that David took the crown of the Ammonite king or perhaps, rather, that of Milkom (for *malkām)* and placed it on his own head — probably fastened above his throne. Thus he appropriated the honour of Moab.

P. 228 [1]. *miḳne,* like the Arabic *māl,* frequently denotes cattle.

P. 231 [1]. 1 Sam. 1,6: "And her misery also provoked her sore, causing her to be in great agitation, because the Lord had shut up her womb". *harʿīmāh,* by the commentators unjustly considered without sense, means "make roar", move violently, a typical expression of the dissolution of the soul in grief and pain.

P. 237 [1]. Of Israel Hos. 5,5; 7,10; Am. 6,8; the Philistines Zech. 9,6; Ashur 10,11; Moab Is. 16,6 = Jer. 48,29.

P. 237 [2]. Also other words with the meaning of ornament are used to denote honour, as *yeḳār, ṣebhī* and *ʿadhī*; the latter seems to be used about the immense display, Ezek. 7,20; 16,7; and when Ps. 103,5 it reads: he "satisfieth thy glory with good things", then we evidently, in this place, have a term for the soul of the same kind as *kābhōdh.*

P. 238 [1]. *mashḥīth* "misery", as Ezek. 25,15.

P. 238 [2]. With this agrees the translation of LXX, viz. πνεῦμα. From a linguistic point of view it is also possible to translate it by: fresh complexion, cf. Gesenius-Buhl, *Handwörterbuch s. v.* The Aramæan *zīw,* Dan. 5,6.9.10; 7,28, which is rendered in a different manner in LXX, might mean the same as *hōdh,* Dan. 10,8.

P. 239 [1]. The alteration made in a number of the passages quoted, viz. from *kābhōdh* to *kābhēdh,* "liver", must therefore at the least be looked upon as superfluous. The use of the liver as denoting the soul would naturally in itself be possible, but it is of rare occurrence in the Old Testament and would, at any rate, hardly be used in Gen. 49,6. As it agrees with the essence of *kābhōdh* to be used in this manner, and as it is constantly used about Yahweh, there is no reason to make the problematic alteration.

P. 244 [1]. Shame is in the Hebrew denoted by various words, most frequently by *bōsheth.* This word, which also occurs in Akkadian *bushtu,* is undoubtedly somehow related with *b'sh,* meaning stinking, wicked, but the connexion cannot be traced in detail. Farthest out in the idea of the word lies the significance "delay" *(bōshēsh)* which, however, does not leave the domain of shame: not to carry through, to be checked. Sometimes the root *ḥfr* occurs, but more frequently *ḥrf*. The latter may perhaps have some connexion with the Arabian *khrf* "pluck, tear off", seeing that shame is looked upon as a plucking out; at any rate shame is, in Arabic, termed a pealing off (see *Der Eid bei den Semiten* by the present author, p. 85). *zimmā* is more particularly used of shame in connexion with sexual violations. Sexual shame is called *'erwā,* i. e. laying bare, in a single place *ma'ar* from the same root (Nah. 3,5). *k^elimmā* may be connected with the Arabic word "wound", as well as with the Assyrian *kalāmu,* "shorten", "make small", to which reference is made by Fr. Delitzsch. *ḳālōn* from the root "be light" is the opposite of *kābhōdh,* "heaviness". As for all of these words, cf. the dictionaries. An actual difference between them it is difficult to define; they all denote shame in all its forms, as something internal and external. Add to these words like *zōlēl* "despised", "valueless", *ni'ēr* "disdain", and the many words denoting scoffing. *rēḳ* is the man without honour, the dishonourable man, Judg. 9,4; 11,3; 2 Sam. 6,20, properly speaking the empty, he whose soul lacks the fulness of honour.

P. 249 [1]. It is more particularly Gunkel who, in his commentary, has attempted a division of the narrative into sources. For him the starting point is that Yahweh (v. 5) descends, and in v. 7 it is said that he is now going to descend. Further, that he cannot reconcile the two things that one builds in order to get a name and in order not to disperse. He therefore distinguishes between a "Stadtrezension" (to get a name) and a "Turmrezension" (not to spread, seeing that the tower is visible from everywhere). But the latter starting point is based upon a misconception of the idea contained in the name, and the former on an exaggeration of the difficulty of Yahweh's moving between heaven and earth.

P. 250 [1]. That a name is better than much wealth (Prov. 22,1) means that the name is more than wealth in itself. In Eccles. 7,1 it is said that a name is better than good oil, unless, with regard to the context, *shēm* should be taken as a misscript for *šāḳ*.

P. 250 [2]. *Vide* the author's *Der Eid bei den Semiten,* p. 105, note 4.

P. 251 [1]. A hand is frequently depicted on stelæ, *vide Corpus Inscriptionum Semiticarum* vol. 1,2 tab. 43.45.47.49.

P. 252 [1]. *Vide* G. Buchanan Gray, *Studies in Hebrew Proper Names, London,* 1896, p. 2 ff.

P. 255 [1]. Cf. in the Old Testament Neh. 2,3; Dan. 2,4; 3,9.

P. 256 [1]. Suggested *b^elēḥō* "with its marrow".

P. 258 [1]. As to adoption among the Sumerians, Babylonians and

Assyrians, *vide* B. Meissner, *Babylonien und Assyrien,* vol. 1, 1920, p. 150 f., 161, 181.

P. 265 [1]. There is nothing to prevent the use of *shālōm,* Jer. 13, 19; Ps. 55,21; 69,23, about persons who are possessed of *shālōm,* in the same manner as he who has blessing *is* blessing. Otherwise *shōlēm,* or *shālēm,* and *ʾīsh shālōm,* or *ʾenōsh shālōm,* are used to denote him with whom one has peace.

P. 267 [1]. Both *bāśār* and *sheʾēr* are used, possibly in the form *sheʾēr besārō,* Lev. 18,6; 25,49.

P. 276 [1]. The same problem is touched upon in Num. 16,22: Shall one man sin and wilt thou be wroth with all the congregation. Speculations on the problem occur in Gen. 18.

P. 276 [2]. Or: (unnumbered) families. It occurs in Exod. 20,5; 34,7; Deut. 5,9, cf. Num. 14,18.

P. 277 [1]. This is an essential point in Durkheim, *Les formes élémentaires de la vie religieuse,* 1912.

P. 285 [1]. On *berīth* and its etymology see the author's *Der Eid bei den Semiten,* p. 31 ff., p. 45 [1].

P. 285 [2]. So *massēkhā,* Is. 30,1, which in all probability means interweaving. Possible is also the meaning "pouring out", viz. of the covenant-making sacrifice. Or *ʾamānā,* the firm, the reliable, Neh. 10,1; *ḥōze,* Is. 28,15, is of obsure origin. In *nāḥā,* Is. 7,2, an attempt has been made to trace a contracted *naʾaḥā,* brotherhood, but this attempt is not fully justifiable. To make a covenant with one is called to "make peace", *hishlīm,* Deut. 20,12; Josh. 10,1.4; 11,19; 2 Sam. 10,19; 1 Kings 22,45; further, *kārath, hēḳīm, nāthan* or *śīm berīth,* possibly *bārā,* see *Der Eid bei den Semiten,* p. 44 ff. The same meaning seems to be attached to *ṣmd* in Niphal, Num. 25,3.5; Ps. 106,28; properly speaking it means to be tied to.

P. 290 [1]. The verbs *dābhaḳ* and *ḥāshaḳ* denote this intimate connexion.

P. 291 [1]. Gen. 34 is not among the chapters where literary criticism has been attended by success. Ed. Meyer says that it is the part of the Hexateuch which perhaps puts the greatest difficulties in the way of the critic. But in one respect all recent critics (with the exception of Eerdmans, *Alttestamentliche Studien* I, 1908, pp. 62-64) are agreed, viz. that the chapter is composed of two irreconcilable sources. The basis of this view was laid down in 1875 by Dillmann (in his commentary to Genesis, latest ed. 1892) and in 1876 by Wellhausen in his treatises in *Jahrbücher für deutsche Theologie,* subsequently collected in *Die Composition des Hexateuchs und der hist. Bücher des A. T.,* 3. ed., 1889. They look upon it as a contradiction that it is now Hamor, now Shechem who carries on negotiations, and that it is now a question of an extensive connubium, now an individual, Shechem, who desires a particular woman. Dillmann points out two accounts: 1) 1a.2a.4.6.8-10.15(14)-17. 20-24: Hamor offers connubium to which Israel agrees, but this is prevented in some way or other unknown to us. 2) 2b.3.5.7.11-13(14).19.25*.26.30 f.: Shechem carries away and violates Dinah and then proposes marriage. The brothers stipulate that he is to be circumcised, and when he is suffering from wound-fever, Simeon and Levi murder him, for which they are reproved by their father. The former of these accounts is referred to the Priestly Code (which Dillmann calls A) and the other to the Yahwist (Dillmann B), but the redactor has inserted a number of verses, in which the two accounts are intermixed, i. e. 13 f. 18.27-29, and perhaps 14 b, as well as a few minor things. Wellhausen takes his starting point in v. 26, where Simeon and Levi kill Hamor and Shechem, and then go. This is said to be irreconcilable with 27, seeing that it contains an account of how the sons of Jacob come and spoil. On the other hand, 26 agrees with 30, where Jacob reproves Simeon and Levi. But this is irreconcilable with 27-29, for Jacob is tantamount to all Israel, and so cannot condemn what all the Israelites do. In the one account (3.11.12.19.25 f. 30 f.) Shechem is a private individual who violates Dinah; she is given to him for wife, on conditions which are not communicated to us, but he is killed by Simeon and Levi. Over against this narrative by the Yahwist stands another, where it is not a question of family as against family, but of all the sons of Hamor, who want to enter into relation with all Israel; the Israelites craftily demand that they should let themselves be circumcised, and then kill them all. This account is said to be due to the Elohist. This division is adopted by Kuenen *(Theol. Tijdschrift,* 1880, reprinted in *Gesammelte Abhandlungen,* 1894) who, however, is of opinion that the second account belongs to the Priestly Code and is very late, the latter because of the part played by the circumcision. Cornill *(Zeitschr. f. alttestl. Wiss.* 1891) tries to show that Wellhausen is right, and his very detailed division recurs to all intents and purposes in Holzinger's commentary of 1898. Also Gunkel follows Wellhausen in a division into Yahwist and Elohist, and the view of Wellhausen seems upon the whole to have been most widely adopted, as in commentaries by Skinner, Driver and Procksch. However, Sievers in *Metrische Studien* II 332 ff. finds two Elohistic accounts, one of which is said to have a peaceable ending, some of the worst obstacles in the way of this supposition being removed as spurious, and, finally, Ed. Meyer, *Die Israeliten und ihre Nachbarstämme,* 1906, p. 412 ff. denies that we are dealing with the sources J. and E., at the same time considering it "deutlich erkennbar" that it is a composite narrative.

In opposition to this essential concord it should be maintained that it rests upon a false conception of the Old Israelitic relation between the individual and the community. The private individual Shechem does not exist. If he contracts marriage with an Israelitic girl, then there is connubium and, generally speaking, a common life between the entire communities to which the two belong. "Now it is Shechem speaking, now Hamor; then again it is now Jacob, now the sons". Yes, but it is strange that none of the commentators seem to remember that this is the very manner in which a man prefers his suit in the Orient as well as elsewhere on the globe. The whole of this scene stands out so vividly and clearly that one seems to be face to face with a narrative of the Bedouins or Fellahs of the present day, but it must be borne in mind that their ideas of the significance of the events taking place are different from ours! — A further objection made to the unity of the narrative is that Simeon and Levi cannot murder the entire male population of a town (lying half dead with wound-fever!) and that it cannot be said, after that, that the sons of Jacob spoil the city; it should have been the other sons of Jacob. Kuenen even says that only a poor narrator could have made such an account! These more or less pedantic remarks about the old narrator would hardly have been set forth unless it had been an established fact in the eyes of the critics that there were irreconcilable elements in the text. One incident might be mentioned with a show of justice: v. 26 presupposes that Shechem has Dinah with him, which has not been told in the preceding. But this is an example of the concise Hebrew manner of telling a story. It is implied in v. 19, according to which Shechem has fulfilled what was required of him in order to get her. — The most natural reading of 29 seems to be: "and they spoiled all (*'ēth* instead of *we'ēth*, cf. Kittels ed.) that was in the houses", *babbāyith* representing an undefined number, and corresponding with *bā'īr* ("in the town") and *baššādhe* ("in the field") in v. 28.

P. 297 [1]. This appears with great probability from Deut. 22,29 as compared with Exod. 22,15. He who violates a woman must, according to the former passage, give 50 shekels, according to the latter the bridal gift, *mōhar*. This corresponds with the Babylonian price in Codex Hammurabi §§ 138.139; *vide* Benzinger, *Archäologie,* 2. ed., p. 106.

P. 301 [1]. Whereas the separation of the Priestly Code and the Deuteronomy is as a rule evident, this is far from being the case when it is a question of the Yahwist and the Elohist; and this applies in a very high degree to the Jacob stories. It has been demonstrated above that Gen. 30,25-43 and Gen. 34 in reality form uncompounded wholes. The same holds good of the narrative of Jacob's meeting with Esau, Gen. 32,4-33,17. The first part of the narrative, 32,4-14, contains a description of Jacob's preparations for a possible fight, the following a description of his endeavours to avoid it. These two passages are, it is true, not necessary beside each other, but, on the other hand, they do not exclude each other. Jacob's prayer, 10-13, agrees entirely with the spirit of the narrative. Gunkel wants to eliminate it, because it shows a "deep religious feeling", whereas the remainder of the narrative is "quite profane". This distinction between profane and religious is not Israelitic. The Jacob addressing his god in his prayer is exactly the same as the Jacob who acquires wealth at the cost of Laban, because his god is with him. Closely connected with the account of the preparations is the description of the carrying out of the plan, 33,1-16. Between these two continuous passages is inserted the account of Jacob's fight, 32,23-33. Its position is conditioned by the fact that the fight must take place before Jacob enters Canaan. In itself it forms a whole. Holzinger, Gunkel and others consider it a double account. Gunkel's reasons are: 26a the hip of Jacob comes to be out of joint by means of a blow, 26b "by chance" during the wrestling. 2) The giving of a name in 28 f. is itself a blessing, and therefore it does not agree with v. 30 "and he blessed him there". 3) v. 29 Jacob departs, v. 31 Jacob barely escapes with his life. When applying an analysis so subtle as this it is surely possible to dissolve any narrative into sources. — It would carry us too far to enter into an analysis of the other Jacob stories.

P. 302 [1]. Cf. Judith 1,11.

P. 302 [2]. This is of course the case even if the word should happen to be a loan-word from Akkadian *shulmānu,* "gift".

P. 303 [1]. One ought not to raise the problem whether the kiss is an instinctive action or whether it tends to confirm the covenant. Nothing is more instinctive than the covenant and its manifestations; but for the Israelites and other peoples of similar cultural conditions there is a greater reality in such things than for modern man, and they fully accept the consequences of their instinctive actions. The vanquished kisses the victor, just as he confers gifts upon him, Ps. 2,12, the worshipper upon the gods, 1 Kings 19,18; Hos. 13,2. The prophet kisses the king whom he consecrates, 1 Sam. 10,1. One kisses people in order to attract them, 2 Sam. 15,5; before blessing Gen. 27, 26 f.; when meeting, Gen. 29,11; 33,4; Exod. 4,27; 18,7; 2 Sam. 14,33; possibly in dissimulation, 2 Sam. 20,9; when taking leave, Gen. 50,1; 2 Sam. 19,40; 1 Kings 19,20; Ruth 1,9.14.

P. 304 [1]. According to the general fundamental conception *shā'al lō l^eshālōm* cannot merely mean: to ask how one fares. There must be a positive "giving" in it, implied in the energy of will expressed by the verb. The same is the case in Akkadian, where exactly the same expression occurs, i. a. with the gods as its subject (e. g. Amarna letters 96,4 ff.; 97,3) and so it also is in southern Arabic, according to Weber (see the note in the above-mentioned work, p. 1190) who translates it by "sorgen für". The Akkadian *sha'ālu* means, according to Delitzsch, *Handwörterbuch* also to make counsel. The expression occurs in Gen. 43,27; Exod. 18,7; Judg. 18,15; 1 Sam. 10,4; 17,22; 25,5; 30,21; 2 Sam. 8,10; Jer. 15,5.

P. 306[1]. See *Der Eid bei den Semiten,* p. 25.48 f. As to the possibility of a connexion between *berīth* and *bārā,* "eat", see *ibid.* p. 45, note 1. A number of covenant rites are described by H. Clay Trumbull, *The Blood Covenant,* New York, 1885, and *The Threshold Covenant,* Edinburgh, 1896.

P. 307[1]. See *Der Eid,* p. 53 note 1. As to the handshake of surety see *ibid.* (Prov. 6,1; 17,18; 22,26; Job 17,3).

P. 307[2]. So Jer. 6,11; 15,17; Ps. 64,3; 111,1. On the community of the angels Ps. 89,8. The word is used of the counsel resulting in such a narrow covenant, Am. 3,7; prophets take part in *sōdh* with God, Jer. 23,18.22.

P. 309[1]. As regards the linguistic character of the term, which agrees entirely with its realities, cf. the exposition in *Der Eid bei den Semiten,* p. 31 ff.

P. 309[2]. The use of the word is possibly also connected with the fact that the central feelings are localized in the abdominal region, of course because they are felt there. It is sometimes difficult to decide whether it is a question of the feeling itself or of its seat in this part of the body, e. g. Gen. 43,30; 1 Kings 3,26; Prov. 12,10. This is not strange, as the Israelites do not distinguish between the psychic contents and its external manifestation. Brockelmann's remarks in *Grundriss der vergl. Grammatik* II, p. 60 therefore rest upon an artificial distinction of things which belong together. — *ḥēn* is related with the Arabic *ḥanna,* which is used of the mother camel's call to her young. In Israel it is mostly used of the kindness of the superior. *'āhabh* is possibly related with the root *whb,* "give", (as to the transition between Aleph and initial *w vide* Nöldeke, *Neue Beiträge zur semitischen Sprachwissenschaft,* 1910, p. 179 ff.). *ḥesedh* is etymologically obscure (*vide* Nöldeke, *op. cit.* p. 93).

P. 309[3]. Cf. Gen. 21,23; 1 Sam. 20,8; Is. 54,10; Jer. 16,5; Dan. 9,4; Neh. 1,5; 9,32; 2 Chron. 6,14. "Speak peace" or "to peace" Gen. 37,4; Jer. 9,7; Ps. 28,3; 35,20; 85,9; 120,6.

P 312[1]. *leshālōm* properly speaking "appertaining to peace"; the preposition is used as in *lebhadh* and *lābheṭaḥ.* In reality *le* here means the same as *be*.

P. 312[2]. Gen. 44,17; Exod. 4,18; 1 Sam. 1,17; 29,7; 2 Sam. 3,21 ff.; 15,9; 1 Kings 22,17 *et al.*

P. 313[1]. Cf. also Ezek. 32,28; Am. 6,6; Nah. 3,19; Prov. 15,4; 16,18; 17,19; 18,12. Another term for destruction and misery, *shōdh,* in all probability rests upon a similar fundamental thought: to stop, to check.

P. 314[1]. So 2 Sam. 17,3 according to LXX.

P. 315[1]. Is. 38 is full of obscure passages. In 13 and 14 the sentence occurs: From day to night *tashlīmēnī*. Duhm, Cheyne, Buhl and Marti in their commentaries propose the translation: "You desert me" which has been concluded from the Aramæan. It would agree well with the meaning of *shlm* to take it in the sense: "You make me sound". But then the line is in the wrong place, which must at any rate be the case in one of the two verses. It would go best after 17 a.

P. 315[2]. *ḥṭ'* here must be interpreted as "miss", "fall short of" and *ben* is to be elided, cf. Gesenius-Buhl, *Handwörterbuch s. v.*

P. 319[1]. It should be noticed that the narrative of the Gibeonites upon the whole has a secondary character, and it is extremely problematic whether in this case the difficulty is solved by a distribution on sources. The starting point of the division of the narrative is the following: 1) 6-7 *'īsh yiśrā'ēl* and *ḥiwwī* occur; with 8 a fresh start is made and here Joshua appears. 2) It is told twice that the Gibeonites are spared, 18 and 26; twice that they are made slaves of the temple, 21 and 27. As 17-21 make one context, it is an independent passage, and it belongs to P., as it is the *neśī'īm* of the community who act. With this then belongs the end of 15, where the same authority is mentioned. On the other hand, in 22 ff. it is Joshua who acts. In the remainder of the narrative two accounts are separated, but the division is very different with the various investigators, and so also the determination of sources. Wellhausen *(Composition des Hexateuchs,* 3. ed., 1899, p. 125) traces two Jehovistic sources and some Deuteronomic verses. By the Yahwist are 4-7. 12-14 where not Joshua, but "the Israelitic man" acts. Steuernagel (in his commentary) refers 6-7 to J. The remainder is referred to D[2] as based upon E. Like Budde, Holzinger (in his commentary) finds two Yahwistic sources besides D and P, Driver (in his *Introduction)* finds JE, D[2] and P; Procksch *(Das nordhebr. Sagenbuch,* p. 141 f.) finds J, E, D[2] and P. Nor are scholars agreed as to the distribution of the verses on the individual sources, which shows that the distinction is not immediately apparent. As a matter of fact, the separation of sources rests upon a very loose foundation. 17-21 is not repeated in the following; these verses mention the resolution taken within Israel, the following its carrying out by Joshua. As to the former point it must be borne in mind that the Israelitic community thoughout the narrative is made up of three elements: the Israelitic man, the chiefs of the community and Joshua; they are not sharply separated but act in harmony with each other, as appears from 14. It is the same social division which we know from the Priestly Code in the Pentateuch where the position of Moses is like that of Joshua in this place, and the narrative probably originates in the priestly circles of the temple of Jerusalem. That it is really throughout a late product appears from the fact that it is impossible to separate any part of it which is not determined by the view of later Israel, who looked upon immigrating Israel as the irresistible conquering people, and there is no reason to dissolve the unity of the narrative.

P. 320 [1]. Read: *shadh* for *shōdh.*

P. 321 [1]. The blessing of Moses, as we know it, is probably post-exilitic, see K. Budde, *Das Lied Mose's,* Tübingen, 1920.

P. 322 [1]. This probably means from one of the bounds of the earth to the other, the earth being surrounded by the ocean (*'ephes* = Ass. apsu) *vide* Wensinck, *The Ocean in the Literature of the Western Semites (Verh. d. kon. Akad. v. Wet. te Amsterdam, Afd. letterk. nieuwe reeks,* XIX, no. 2), p. 21 f.

P. 323 [1]. Hypothetical reading *hag-gīlā.*

P. 324 [1]. It must be expressly stated that the so-called Universalism of Deutero-Isaiah bears the same character. It is the God of Israel who has become the strongest, who leads foreign princes, and before whom even the Gods of Babylon sink. Other kings must prostrate themselves before him, and the "heathens" are only able to share in the light by adopting the ways of Israel.

P. 324 [2]. This was in all probability the original text. The Massoretes vocalize somewhat differently and interpret it "I want to excite". Thus peace would be won, in that all peoples outside Israel make away with each other. But this is hardly what is meant, as it jars with 21. The bygone time is referred to.

P. 326 [1]. The meaning of *me'ūrath* Is. 11,8 is uncertain; cf. the commentaries and Gesenius-Buhl, *Handwörterbuch s. v.*

P. 328 [1]. The same figure Jer. 11,19; Ezek. 17,8 ff.; 19,10 ff.; Ps. 1,3; 37,35; 52,10; Job 29,19 *et al.*

P. 330 [1]. Other terms for happiness are those connected with the roots *rḥb* and *rwḥ* which, like *ysh',* mean being wide, spacious. The former denotes the state of Israel when it has acquired all the treasures of the world, Is. 60,5; the pleasure in striking down enemies, Deut. 33, 20; in fertility, Gen. 26,22; in all progress, Prov. 18,16; in security, Ps. 18,37; cf., further, Ps. 4,2; 119,32. The latter is used about the easing of the diseased mind, 1 Sam. 16,23; of the victory and delivery of the Jews, Esth. 4,14. *'shr* lies between *shālōm* and *berākhā.* "In my happiness *('oshrī),* nay, young women call me happy *('ishsherūnī)*", says Leah, Gen. 30,13. *'ushshar* is used about him who thrives, Ps. 41,3. The happy person is extolled, just as he is blessed, Ps. 72,17; Prov. 31,28; Job 29,11; Cant. 6,9. But it implies more of a homage, an acknowledgment of the actual possession of the happy man than *bērēkh,* see, e. g., Mal. 3,15. *sha'anān* more particularly emphasizes the security, but at the same time approaches *gā'ōn,* happiness as honour, 2 Kings 19,28; Is. 37,29; Ps. 123,4. Quite close to *shālōm* is *shalwā,* and it seems likely to assume an original relationship between the two stems. It denotes vigorous, rank growth and occurs both as a substantive, an adjective and a verb. Jeremiah complains that the wicked *shālū,* thrive and bring forth fruit, 12,1 f. Job speaks of him who is vigorous *(shal'anān)* and rank *(shālēw),* 21,23 cf. 16,12. One of the friends says of the wicked: He knows nothing rank *(shālēw)* in his belly (i. e. soul), Job 20,20. *shalwā* is health, Ps. 30,7 cf. 3; it is victory, Lam. 1,5; but also rest and security, Ezek. 16,49; Job 3,26; 12,6; Prov. 17,1. And upon the whole it is, like *shālōm,* all kinds of happiness, Jer. 22,21; Ps. 122,6 f. Other terms for happiness are *nō'am,* the well-being of the soul; *rāṣōn,* its growth in accordance with its own desire. That also *yāmīn,* "right", as in Arabic has denoted happiness appears from Gen. 35,18. We cannot see what was the part played by *gadh* (Gen. 30,11). Is. 65,11, it is a god of fortune.

P. 331 [1]. *hōshī'ā,* later *hōshī'annā.*

P. 332 [1]. When Duhm wants to remove v. 10 from the context, it is probably due to a too narrow conception of salvation.

P. 333 [1]. On the suggestion of several interpreters *'ashrē* is inserted and in v. 2 *'ōmēr* is read.

P. 333 [2]. *sōḥērā* must be some weapon or other.

P. 333 [3]. Read *maḥsekhā.*

P. 334 [1]. The covering taken from the faces of the peoples is by Duhm considered a mourning cloth. It would, however, in this context be more likely to take it as a cover preventing them from seeing the greatness of little Israel. But the whole verse is so obscure that an exact understanding is excluded, cf. Schwally, *Das Leben nach dem Tode,* p. 118.

P. 335 [1]. As to the meaning of delivery from Sheol see the last chapter of this book.

P. 335 [2]. Read plural.

P. 337 [1]. With *tōm,* Ps. 26,1.11; Prov. 19,1; 28,6. It is also called *tummā,* Job 2,3.9; 27,5; 31,6.

P 337 [2]. *tām* Prov. 29,10; Job 1,1.8; 2,3; 9,22; *tāmīm* Gen. 6,9; Ps. 37,18; 119,80; Prov. 2,21; 11,5; 28,10. It is used of a whole object, Lev. 3,9, and a whole period, Lev. 23,15; 25,30; Josh. 10,13, and more particularly of sacrificial animals which are fully and normally developed and unhurt. As the corresponding adjectives of *'mn* and *ṣdḳ* are never used as substantives, there is reason to ask whether *tāmīm,* where used in this manner, e. g. Josh. 24,14; Judg. 9,16.19; Am. 5,10; Ps. 18,26; 84,12; 101,2.6, should not be plural of *tōm* on the analogy of *yāmīm* from *yōm,* seeing that it is used in plural in the same manner as *ne'īmīm, shelāmīm, 'emūnīm, 'emūnōth,* although the regular plural form is *tummīm.* The line between substantive and adjective is undefined. When, e. g., it is said "to wander *tāmīm*", Ps. 15,2; Prov. 28,18, then it may be an adjective, though, according to the Hebrew *usus loquendi,* it is more likely a substantive, which supposition is borne out by the analogous "wander in *tāmīm*", Ps. 84,12.

P. 337[3]. *kēn,* Gen. 42,11.19.31.33.34; of the normally exercised strength, Jer. 23,10; of the action, 2 Kings 7,9; of the fitting word, Exod. 10,29; Num. 27,7; 36,5; 2 Kings 17,9; Is. 16,6; Jer. 8,6; 48,30; Prov. 15,7. — *nākhōn* of the righteous heart, Ps. 51,12; 57,8; 108,2, of its ways Ps. 119,5; of the action, Exod. 8,22, of the word, Ps. 5,10; Job 42,7.8.

P. 337[4]. *yāshār* denotes all that is straight: a road, a leg, an even plain, a sheet. Of the heart, Ps. 7,11; 11,2; 32,11; 36,11; 64, 11; 94,15; 97,11. It is mentioned in parallelism with the integrity of the heart, 1 Kings 9,4; Job 1,1.8; 2,3, and with its purity, Job 8,6; of the actions, 1 Sam. 12,23; Mic. 3,9; Prov. 21,8; of the words, Ps. 33,4; Prov. 8,9. — *nākhōaḥ* is properly speaking the obvious, thus it is used with *le*. It is used of righteousness, Is. 26,10; 57,2; 59,14; Am. 3,10, of words, 2 Sam. 15,3; Prov. 24,26.

P. 338[1]. Read: *lekhol dōr yābhō'*.

P. 340[1]. The article to *gephen* must be left out; perhaps it belongs to the preceding word which, however, is not quite clear.

P. 340[2]. *'āmēn* occurs in Num. 5,22; Deut. 27,14 ff.; 1 Kings 1,36; Jer. 11,5; 28,6; Neh. 5,13; 8,6; 1 Chron. 16,36. We are in none of these passages dealing with a confirmation of an already accomplished fact, but truth naturally also denotes this, e. g., Gen. 42,16; Deut. 13,15; 17,4; 22,20; 1 Kings 10,6; Is. 43,9.

P. 341[1]. *shālēm 'im* 1 Kings 8,61; 11,4; 15,3.14; "before" 2 Kings 20,3 = Is. 38,3. To seek with a whole heart, Deut. 4,29; 6,5; Ps. 119,2.34.58.145. *tāmīm 'im,* Deut. 18,13; Ps. 18,24; *tāmīm le,* 2 Sam. 22,24; *kēn 'im,* Ps. 78,37; 89,22; Prov. 19,29; Job 12,5; 18,12; *kēn le,* 2 Chron. 20,33; *kēn 'el* 1 Sam. 7,3; *nākhōaḥ le,* Prov. 8,9.

P. 341[2]. The text should possibly read a little differently: Is thy heart righteous towards me? ...

P. 341[3]. Here the derivation *mīshōr* is used, being mostly applied to the straight, i. e. the level plain; the straight is opposed to the crooked, Is. 40,4; 42,16. Of righteousness, Is. 11,4; Ps. 45,7. In the same manner another derivation is used, i. e. *mēshārīm,* Dan. 11,6 and *yeshārīm,* Dan. 11,17; the latter is preferably to be taken as the plural of *yōsher,* cf. *zenūnīm, nedhūdhīm, kippūrīm,* etc. An alteration is thus superfluous.

P. 342[1]. Gen. 24,49; 47,29; Hos. 4,1. The truth and love of Yahweh towards his covenant people, Ps. 25,10; 33,4; 36,6; 85,11; 89,2 f. 15.25.34 f.

P. 346[1]. To justify in this sense is called *hiṣdīḳ,* whereas Piel is used, Jer. 3,11; Ezek. 16,51 f.; Job 32,2; 33,32, where it is only a question of the right to maintain a claim. Connected with *min* is *ṣdḳ,* where it is a question of being just in one's relation to another. The root, as probably *'mn,* is common to all Semitic languages. In Aramæan it occurs, e. g., *Corp. Inscript. Sem.* vol. 2, 145 A 5;

Elephantinepap. 2,27; *Nerab* 2,2; *Taima* 15. It is exhaustively treated in E. Kautzsch, *Ueber die Derivate des Stammes, ṣdḳ im alttestl. Sprachgebrauche,* 1881.

P. 348 [1]. *hiṣdīḳ 'ēth,* but *he'emīn be,* e. g. Num. 14,11; 20,12; Deut. 1,32; 1 Sam. 27,12; 2 Kings 17,14; Ps. 78,22.32; 106,12; 119,66; *he'emīn le,* Exod. 4,1.8; Deut. 9,23; 1 Kings 10,7; Is. 43,10; Ps. 106,24; Prov. 14,15; *he'emīn beḥayyāw,* Deut. 28,66; Job 24,22, properly speaking to put truth, security into one's life, i. e. to be sure to live.

P. 348 [2]. That this is the meaning of *ḥāshabh le* appears abundantly from Gen. 38,15; 1 Sam. 1,13.

P. 348 [3]. This word is related with *nōkhaḥ* "that which is lying right before one".

P. 349 [1]. In Hebrew it is a common practice that the prefixes *mi* and *ma* indicate the manifestation of the action expressed in the verb, viz. place as well as time and the action itself. This *ma* is perhaps originally identical with or related to the interrogative and the indefinite *mā,* cf. Brockelmann, *Grundriss* I § 195.

P. 349 [2]. Legal procedure, Deut. 1,17; 2 Sam. 15,2.6; Prov. 18,5; Job 9,32; 22,4; 34,23. Words of judgment, 1 Kings 3,28; Jer. 1,16; 4,12; Zech. 8,16; act of judgment, Ezek. 5,8; Hab. 1,12. Here it is only a question of various shades within the same meaning; in particular it is impossible to disentangle the two last mentioned shades.

P. 351 [1]. Gen. 40,13; Exod. 21,31; Josh. 6,15; 2 Kings 11,14; it is used in a similar manner in Lev. 5,10; 9,16; Num. 15,24; 29,18-37 passim; Neh. 8,18.

P. 358 [1]. The reading of Exod. 23,5 is uncertain. The difficulty is the twice occurring *'āzabh.* In the former place it is natural to imply "the matter" and to take *lō* about the owner. "You must desist from leaving the matter to him (the owner)" (and, on the contrary, help him); cf. Dillmann's commentary. But in that case *'zb* cannot be translated in the same manner in the following; here the burden must be the object of the verb meaning "to unload, make free". Most commentators adopt the old correction *'āzōr ta'azōr* "you shall help together with him". In both places it is possible to take the animal as the object: You must desist from leaving the animal to him, but you may, on the other hand, leave it together with him, i. e. if he can do nothing himself. A similar ordinance, though more clearly expressed, we find in Deut. 22,4.

P. 359 [1]. This appears from the general context of the statement. That the root *tmm* in itself contains "happiness" also appears from Ps. 73,4 *(lāmō thām),* and it is proved by the fact that it denotes the bodily health and normal development, e. g., as far as the sacrificial animals are concerned. We must also include this shade in the word Gen. 17,1, where Elohim says to Abraham that he must wander before him and be *tāmīm.* He who discharges an arrow at random does so *l^e^thummō* (1 Kings 22,34; 2 Chron. 18,33). This use is probably conditioned by the meaning of "happiness" rather than by that of "innocence"; the same must be the case in 2 Sam. 15,11: some people came walking at random, *l^e^thummām.* — Attention may also be directed to the fact that *nākhōaḥ,* one of the terms for the righteous, is related to the Arabic *najaḥa,* succeed, *v.* Nöldeke, *Neue Beiträge zur semitischen Sprachwissenschaft,* p. 190 f., cf. Gesenius-Buhl, *Handwörterbuch s. v.*

P. 360 [1]. Read *shālōm* for *w^e^yāsēm* v. 14.

P. 360 [2]. "justice" should in all probability be left out in the second hemistich, though it might for that matter in itself make good sense.

P. 361 [1]. *derekh* occurs in numerous places in this manner, i. a. Gen. 6,12; 1 Kings 2,4; 13,33; 16,26; 22,43; 2 Kings 22,2; Jer. 6,16; 10,2; 18,11; 25,5; 26,3; Ezek. 3,18; 13,22; 33,8.9.11; Jon. 3,8; Job 28,23. The way means the custom of a country, Gen. 19,31 (about the manner of acquiring a bride). "The way of women" is the peculiarity attached to the female sex, Gen. 31,35. In the same manner *'ōraḥ* occurs in Is. 26,7; Ps. 17,4; 119,9. 101.104.128; Prov. 2,13.15.20; 4, 14.18; 8,20; Job 13,27; 33,11; 34,11 *et al.* Women's *'ōraḥ* of the menses, Gen. 18,11. In the same manner this term is also used about destiny, fortune, "the *'ōraḥ* of life", Ps. 16,11; 25,10; 27,11; Prov. 2,19; 3,6; 5,6; 10,17; 15,24; Job 19,8. The alteration to *'aḥ^a^rīth,* Prov. 1,19; Job 8,13 is no improvement, being only an insertion of another word which bears the same meaning.

P. 362 [1]. *pō'al* of the income of the day-labourer, Jer. 22,13; Job 7,2; *p^e^'ullā* of the same, Lev. 19,13. Israel gets its *p^e^'ullā* on being liberated from Babylonia, Is. 40,10; 49,4; 61,8; 62,11; as *p^e^'ullā* Nebuchadnezzar on his western campaign acquires Egypt, Ezek. 29,20; the righteous obtain life as *p^e^'ullā,* the wicked misery, Is. 65,7; Ps. 109,20; Prov. 10,16; 11,18.

P. 373 [1]. There is no natural context between the poem and the prologue-epilogue, so it seems most probable that they are independent productions. That the Elihu speeches do not form part of the original poem is probable for purely formal reasons; but as to their contents they fit so well into the general scheme that they are probably a rough draught made by the poet himself. With great unction and circumstantiality they render the same thoughts which are set forth in the speeches of the friends. Elihu lays slightly more stress upon the idea that misery should lead to righteousness, but the same thought is set forth by Eliphaz, 5,8 ff. 17 ff. It is strange that the interpreters should have taken these speeches as the valid expression of the views of the author, though the big words are clearly charged with irony; if so, the speeches of the friends would also have to be taken as the serious opinion of the author.

P. 381 [1]. A similar proceeding is reported from the Mameluke period in al-ʿUmarī's state manual, *vide* R. Hartmann in *Zeitschr. f. alttestl. Wiss.,* 1911, p. 69-72.

P. 383 [1]. The sentence (2 Sam. 21,4) is generally translated: We must not kill any man... (Budde, Nowack, Kittel) which meaning it may have, but the homogeneous construction points in the direction of taking *lānū* in the same sense as at the beginning of the verse; so it is also understood in Targum, whereas LXX is ambiguous. According to this the meaning would then be: We do not claim any common man.

P. 383 [2]. This parenthetical exaggeration, 2 Sam. 21,4, agrees very well with the situation. The conjecture based upon the greatly deviating text of LXX is naturally also possible, i. e. *lᵉhashmidhēnī,* "who plotted in order to destroy us".

P. 384 [1]. Hiphil from *yḳʿ* which is used here, v. 6 and 9, as well as Num. 25,4, must denote a special way of killing.

P. 384 [2]. So for Mephibosheth, v. 7 and 8.

P. 384 [3]. As is done by most interpreters "Merab" should be read for "Michal", who, according to 2 Sam. 6,23, was childless; according to 1 Sam. 18,19 it was Merab who was given to Adriel.

P. 389 [1]. Is. 47,3, I "take" vengeance.

P. 389 [2]. With *min,* 1 Sam. 14,24; 24,13; Is. 1,24; Jer. 15,15; 46,10; Esth. 8,13; with *mēʾēth,* Num. 31,2; *mīyadh,* 2 Kings 9,7.

P. 389 [3]. With *bᵉ,* Num. 31,3; Judg. 15,7; 1 Sam. 18,25; Jer. 50,15; Ezek. 25,12.14.

P. 389 [4]. With *biḳḳēsh,* 1 Sam. 20,16; 2 Sam. 4,11; Ezek. 3,18.20; with *dārash,* Gen. 9,5; Ezek. 33,6; Ps. 9,13.

P. 389 [5]. Deut. 32,43; 2 Kings 9,7; Ps. 79,10.

P. 389 [6]. Judg. 16,28.

P. 389 [7]. Judg. 11,36; 1 Sam. 14,24; 18,25. When the verb, Josh. 10,13, is used with "enemies" as an object, it has actually acquired the meaning "to conquer". Of the King, Ps. 18,48 = 2 Sam. 22,48. David to Saul, 1 Sam. 24,13; Jer. 20,10.

P. 389 [8]. Ezek. 5,13; Lam. 2,13; in Hithpael, Gen. 27,42. Is. 1,24, it is actually used of inflicting vengeance.

P. 389 [9]. Lev. 19,18; Ps. 8,3; 44,17; cf. Lam. 3,60.

P. 392 [1]. It would in this context be interesting to know what is the age of the institution of the year of *yōbhēl.* The Book of Covenant and the Deuteronomy reckon with Hebrew slaves among the Israelites; they are to be liberated after six years, Exod. 21,2; Deut. 15,12. In Jer. 34,14 reference is made to this law.

P. 393 [1]. *Vide* the Code of Hammurabi, §§ 116.196.197.200.210. 230. Of particular interest is § 196: When a free man knocks out the eye of a free man, his eye must be knocked out. § 197: When a man breaks the bones of a free man, his bones must be broken. § 200: When a man knocks out the tooth of a man who is his equal, his tooth is to be knocked out. As for the Assyrians, *vide* their law-code I 88-96; VII 87-91; VIII 6-41; as to the Hittites, see the first paragraphs of their law-code.

P. 394 [1]. In particular Prov. 25,21-22: If your enemy hungers, then give him food to eat, and if he thirsts, then give him water to drink. Then you heap coals of fire upon his head, and Yahweh will requite you. — One must show kindness towards one's enemy in order to make his guilt the greater; then Yahweh will grant all the greater vengeance.

P. 394 [2]. *shillēm,* Deut. 32,35; *shillūm,* Hos. 9,7; *shillūmā,* Ps. 91,8; *shillūmīm,* Is. 34,8, here and Deut. 32 parallel with *nāḳām.* As a verb in Piel, Deut. 32,41; Is. 59,18; 66,6; Jer. 51,6.56; Joel 4,4; Ps. 137,8; Prov. 19,17.

P. 395 [1]. Ps. 18,21 = 2 Sam. 22,21: Yahweh *yighmᵉlēnī* after my justice. Here it is clear that the act of Yahweh is the complement. For instance, in Joel 4,4 it is used about an act demanding retribution: Are you willing to repay *(mᵉshallᵉmīm)* me an action demanding retribution *(gᵉmūl),* or do you yourselves want to perform an action demanding retribution *(gōmᵉlīm)* towards me. In a similar manner, Gen. 50,15.17 (a wicked act); Judg. 9,16 (a good act); Is. 3,11 (evil); 63,7 (good); 66,6 (evil); Jer. 51,6; Ps. 103,2 (good); 137,8 (evil); Prov. 3,30; 12,14. As to retribution, Deut. 32,6; Jer. 51,56; Ps. 94,2; 103,10; 116,7. On the other hand, 1 Sam. 24,18 it is not a question of either of the two shades in particular.

P. 396 [1]. Manslaughter at the very altar would be too great an infringement of its sacredness. Still it happened in the case of Joab, 1 Kings 2,30 ff. When in Exod. 21,13 it is said: "I will appoint thee a place whither he shall flee", then the word "place" here, as probably in many other passages, refers to the sacred place, then denoting any kind of sanctuary. Thus "the place" in v. 13 becomes identical with the "altar" in v. 14. As to the Hittite law with the expression "(if only) his hand sins", *vide* the translation of Zimmern and Friedrich I 3.

P. 396 [2]. According to Num. 35,12; Josh. 20,6 he shall stand before the "congregation" for judgment. Dillmann takes this in the sense of his native place, Baentsch in the sense of city of refuge, Holzinger in the sense of the whole of the people (*v.* their commentaries). As it is said, Num. 35,24 f., that the congregation is to take him back to his city of refuge, when it has proved him to be without guilt, then it possibly means that he is taken back to his own city for legal proceedings.

P. 397 [1]. This is the common interpretation of the passage, as Zech. 7,10. 8 MSS. and some old translations have *īsh wᵉʾāḥīō* "at the hands of a man and his brother", an excellent text referring to the solidarity of relatives as regards the demand for vengeance.

P. 397 [2]. *bāʾādhām* is certainly to be understood in this way, not "by man", which would be called *bᵉyadh ʾādhām.* For one thing, it is natural that *'ādhām* in this passage is the same as the immediately preceding, for another, *b^e* is used in this very sense in Deut. 19,21; 2 Sam. 3,27; 1 Kings 16,34; cf. Lam. 1,11; Neh. 5,15 *et al.*, cf. in Arabic *ḳatala bi.*

P. 399 [1]. The translation is uncertain. Dillmann: "Es ist für dich eine Augendecke allen, welche bei dir sind (so that they do not see the injury any more) und bei allen — so bist du dargethan im Recht". So also Kautzsch, whereas Gunkel makes the alteration to *'āthāk* and in the following to *we'att kullō:* "Das soll dir eine Vergütung sein für alles was dich betroffen hat; du aber bist in allem gerechtfertigt". A peculiar conception is that of Eerdmans *(Alttestamentliche Studien* I, p. 41); he makes the words "regarding all that is with thee" *(lekhol 'asher 'ittākh)* v. 16 refer to pregnancy caused by Abimelech, the object of the gift being to compensate that. In the above translation *'t* is taken in the same manner as the Arabic *'inda* of having a claim, and the statement must be taken as a legal formula, by which the offender declares his penalty to be decisive and the matter to be settled by it.

P. 399 [2]. *kōpher* is used of the bribe received by the judge, seeing that he is thus made to close his eye or, in other words, as *shōḥadh* (1 Sam. 12,3; Am. 5,12), with which it is parallel, Prov. 6,35. The rich man is able to give *k.* for himself, while the poor man is not, Prov. 13,8. By a *k.* Israel must redeem itself from Yahweh, to whom it belongs, Exod. 30,12. Ps. 49,8 says that no man by *k.* can redeem his brother at the hands of God. Yahweh gave Egypt as *k.* for Israel, Ethiopia and Seba in lieu of it, Is. 43,3. At the judgment the righteous are set free, because Yahweh takes the wicked as *k.* for them, Prov. 21,18 cf. 11,8. Man can by *k.* be redeemed from the grave, Job 33,24; obscure 36,18. The passionate avenger refuses *k.* (he wants the man himself), Prov. 6,35. With k. corresponds Arab. *fidā'.*

P. 399 [3]. Exod. 21,8; Lev. 19,20; also of the ransom of a person consecrated to Yahweh, Lev. 27,29.

P. 400 [1]. Lev. 27,2 ff. contains a list of rates for the ransom of persons consecrated to Yahweh. For fully-grown men (20-60 years) 50 shekels of silver; for women 30; for youths (5-20 years) 20 shekels; for young girls 10; for boys (1 month-5 years) 5 shekels; for girls 3; for old men (above 60 years) 15; for old women 10. These, no doubt with full justice, have been taken as evidence of the old rates of blood-money. Also with the Arabians a certain precedent has developed. For atonement *(diya)* of an average man 100 mares of camels can be demanded, which is a direct compensation for the life of the person killed.

P. 400 [2]. This is the translation of *'eghrōph* from LXX in accordance with later Hebrew. Other translations have been suggested, *vide* the dictionaries.

P. 401 [1]. *w^e^nāthan biph^e^līlīm.* The commentators generally adopt the ingenious correction of Budde, viz. *n^e^phīlīm* "miscarriage".

P. 401 [2]. *Vide* the Assyrian law, KAV 1, VII 63-82; according to II 98-104 a man who strikes a man's daughter and brings about a miscarriage shall pay 2 talents and 30 manas of lead, receive 50 lashes and do one month's royal service. The relation between the two paragraphs is not clear. How closely related the codes are, appears from special cases. In the Assyrian law the case is foreseen that if a woman in a brawl injure a man's testicle, then one of her fingers shall be cut off (I 78-87); in Israel a woman who in a brawl touches a man's testicle shall lose her hands, Deut. 25,11 f.

P. 402 [1]. Hammurabi not only demands death on those who steal from the temple and the king (§ 6) but also on him who surreptitiously appropriates the property of another through his son or slave (§ 7) or he who breaks into a house (§ 21) or steals during a fire (§ 25) or he who steals and then sells (§§ 9-11). And where the offence is not punished by death, the compensation becomes so great that it has hardly been possible for a common thief to provide it (§ 8). Thus with Hammurabi the laws of property do not come under the principle of compensation, the latter only holding good in the case of manslaughter and bodily injury. The law of trust property is nearly the same as in Israel (§§ 125-126).

P. 402 [2]. *Vide* KAV 2, IV 11-28.

P. 403 [1]. *Vide* KAV 6, rev. 3-9.

P. 405 [1]. Cf. Hrozný §§ 106-107. As the same verbal root *b'r* is used in the two verses, Exod. 22.4 and 5, they are generally taken in one sense, both verses dealing with fires. From this presupposition *b^e^'īrō* "his cattle" v. 4 must be altered (cf. G. Hoffmann, *Zeitschr. f. alttestl. Wiss.*, 1883, p. 122). The Hittite law shows that the Mass. text is good. Beside M. T. we find a tradition in LXX and text. samar. which is certainly good: if only part of the field is fed off, restitution shall be made according to its crops, i. e. that of the damaged field, but if the whole field is fed off this basis of estimation is lacking and then the restitution shall be according to the best standard. If this is an old tradition *mēṭābh* means "the best of the crops", but not the best of the ground; in that case there is an interesting difference between the Hittite and the Israelitic law, the latter less easily transferring landed property from one man to another.

P. 407 [1]. *Vide* the author's *Der Eid bei den Semiten,* p. 186.

P. 407 [2]. *Vide* Cod. Ham. §§ 23-24; Hitt. code I 6, red. 4.

P. 408 [1]. This rite has been analysed in *Der Eid,* etc., p. 104 f. With the Assyrians such a case is settled by ordeal, *vide* the law-code II 67-71; II 105-III 13 and Meissner, *Babylonien und Assyrien* I, p. 406.

P. 410 [1]. Flogging is used in Cod. Ham. in one case, viz. if an inferior strikes a superior, *vide* § 202. In the Assyrian law this punishment is very common, cf. also Meissner, *Babylonien und Assyrien* I, p. 176.

P. 413 [1]. Similar reflections can be made on the root *kḥsh,* which denotes leanness, wasting away, Ps. 109,24; Job 16,8; to fail, Hos. 9,2; Hab. 3,17; more particularly in a covenant relation, Josh. 24,27; Is. 59,13; Jer. 5,12; Job 8,18; 31,28; further, to declare to be unreal, Gen. 18,15; Lev. 5,22; Josh. 7,11; finally, to utter falsehoods, viz. to pronounce the real to be unreal or *vice versa,* Lev. 19,11; 1 Kings 13, 18; Hos. 4,2.

P. 413 [2]. Chaos is called *tōhū,* Is. 29,21; 40,23; 45,18; 49,4; 59,4; *tōhū wābhōhū,* Gen. 1,2; Is. 34,11; Jer. 4,23. In Is. 49,4 *tōhū* is parallel with *hebhel,* Is. 59,4 with *shāw'*. The two latter words mean nearly the same thing.

P. 414 [1]. *ḥzḳ,* Exod. 7,13.22; 8,15; 9,35; Ezek. 2,4; with Yahweh as agent, Exod. 9,12; 10,20.27; 11,10; 14,4.8.17; *'immēṣ,* Deut. 2,30; 15,7; *hiḳshā,* Exod. 7,3; Deut. 2,30; Ps. 95,8; *kbd,* Exod. 7,14; 9,7; in Piel, 1 Sam. 6,6; in Hiphil, Exod. 10,1; *sheriruth,* stiffness, Deut. 29,18; Jer. 3,17; 7,24; 9,13 *et al.*

P. 414 [2]. Crooked *'iḳḳēsh,* Piel Is. 59,8; Prov. 10,9, as adjective, e. g. Deut. 32,5; 2 Sam. 22,27; Ps. 18,27; 101,4; Prov. 8,8; 11,20; 17,20 i. a. *'āḳōbh,* uneven, is used, Jer. 17,9, of the sinful; *nālōz,* wrong, twisted, Is. 30,12; Prov. 2,15; 3,32; 14,2; *sūr,* deviate, is frequently used of sinning, in a few cases *nāṭā:* Ps. 44,19; 119,51.157; Prov. 4,5.27; Job 31,7; so also *śāṭā,* Num. 5,12.19.20.29 and the adjective *śēṭ,* Hos. 5,2. Also the root *'wl* means twisting or deviation, and *'iwwēth* as well as *'iwwā* mean "bend", the three latter words frequently denoting injustice; with the latter belongs *'āwōn,* one of the most frequent appellations for sin.

P. 415 [1]. In these two places occur the three main appellations for sin, *ḥaṭṭā'th* (both places), *pesha'* (Gen. 31,36) and *'āwōn* (1 Sam. 20,1).

P. 418 [1]. Other passages where *rāshā'* is used in this manner are Deut. 25,1; 1 Kings 8,32; Is. 5,23; Prov. 24,24; Job 34.18, cf. the dictionaries. As to appellations for falsehood, sin, nothingness, *vide* further S. Mowinckel, *Psalmenstudien I Awän und die individuellen Klagepsalmen [Videnskapsselskapets Skrifter Hist. phil. Kl. Kristiania]* 1921, p. 39 ff.

P. 420 [1]. *bō' bhedhāmīm,* 1 Sam. 25,26.33.

P. 420 [2]. *dāmō bherō'sho,* Josh. 2,19; 2 Sam. 1,16; 1 Kings 2,37; *'al rō'shō,* 1 Kings 2,32; with *'al,* 2 Sam. 16,8; Jer. 26,15. It has been maintained that the term "blood on his head" should originate in a Greek custom, the murderer wiping his bloody sword on the head of the murdered, saying: *σοὶ εἰς κεφαλήν, vide* E. Merz, *Die Blutrache bei den Israeliten,* Leipzig, 1916, p. 52. But the presupposition of the

Hebrew phrase as well as of the Greek habit is that the head denotes the person as he who bears the responsibility.

P. 420 [3]. Josh. 2,19; 2 Sam. 1,16; 1 Kings 2,37.

P. 420 [4]. "Pure blood", Deut. 19,10; 21,8; 27,25; 1 Sam. 19,5. "Man of blood", *'īsh dāmīm,* 2 Sam. 16,7.8; Ps. 5,7; in plur., Ps. 26,9; 55,24. "Manasseh", 2 Kings 21,16; 24,4. The "man of blood" is he who sheds "pure blood" "without reason", *ḥinnām,* 1 Sam. 19,5; 25,31.

P. 420 [5]. Is. 1,15; 59,7; Jer. 7,6; 22,3; 26,15; Joel 4,19; Jon. 1,14; Prov. 1,16 *et al.* "The country full of blood", Ezek. 7,23; 9,9.

P. 422 [1]. Strictly trans., very peculiar beside *lābhō'*. Perhaps it should be read *lāshūbh.*

P. 423 [1]. Judg. 9 forms a unity, and there is nothing which necessitates or justifies a division into sources. A division of this kind was first undertaken by Winckler *(Altor. Forsch.* I 1893, pp. 59-62) and after him attempted by the commentators, with the exception of Lagrange (Moore, Holzinger, Budde, Nowack, Burney), though without obtaining agreement as to details. The starting point of the division is the following: Discord arises in v. 23 owing to an evil spirit, v. 26-29 it is roused by Gaal (whose name Ga'al generally, without any reason, is altered to Go'al). Abimelech receives information and his intervention is expected, 25b, but, before it takes effect, the episode with Gaal 26-41 is narrated. So Moore and Burney reason, whereas the other scholars go into greater detail. Winckler emphasizes the peculiarity of Gaal standing at the gate talking quite cordially with Zebul, the trusted man of Abimelech, at the same time that the latter is marching against the town. Budde maintains that there cannot very well be two attacks on the town, as the former (34-40) proves victorious; at any rate, the inhabitants, after that, will not court disaster a second time (41-44), and an accomplishment of the victory, such as the destruction of the "tower of Shechem" (46-49), is consequently not to be expected. 34-40 there are four companies, 41-44 only three. We thus get one source with Gaal and the conquest of Shechem's tower (26-40.46-49) and another according to which the discord, in connection with Jotham's parable (7-20), originates in an evil spirit (23-25), with which is connected the account of the fight 42-45 and the end 56-57. — On the other hand, Nowack finds two threads running parallel throughout the whole narrative (1) 26.27b.28.29a.30.31.29b.33b.34b.35a-40.46-49. (2) 27a.32.33a.34a.43a.42a.35a.44.45.56-57. Redactor: 16b-19a.22.25b.41.43b. By dividing and in part transposing the verses and by leaving out some he succeeds in obtaining two fairly good accounts, but neither of these can compare with the narrative when taken as a unity. The starting point of the division is false. That an empty boaster like Gaal may win the souls of the Shechemites is the very manifestation of the evil spirit acting in them; led by the latter they must choose a chief leading them towards ruin. Abimelech's conduct of the fight and Gaal's relation to Zebul may seem absurd to us, but no one familiar with the warfare of the Bedouins should find it surprising. The history of Muhammad alone offers several analogies. 46-49 must, as realized by Moore and Burney, treat of a fight outside Shechem, "the tower of Shechem" being a small town in the neighbourhood. This appears from the fact that the "tower of Shechem" had a thousand inhabitants; the temple to which they resort cannot be situated in Shechem itself, which has been destroyed. And if it were a question of a stronghold in the latter town, it would offer the best means of protection. Add to this that the remark in v. 46: "and when all the men of the tower of Shechem heard that" definitely excludes the possibility that it may be a question of the stronghold of Shechem.

The progress of the narrative is as follows: An evil spirit comes between Abimelech and the inhabitants of Shechem. They curse him at a festival, and Gaal promises to strike him down if they agree to make him their leader. Zebul reports the matter to Abimelech. He arrives during the night with his men, ready to make a sudden attack on the town in the morning. By his own words Gaal is now forced to measure his strength against that of Abimelech. He leads out his men, but they are defeated by Abimelech, this settling the fate of Gaal. Zebul chases him out, and Abimelech withdraws. But the Shechemites in their turn did not submit to this decision. On the following day they went out into the field (in order to resume the combat), "the people", *hā'ām,* here, as frequently elsewhere (i. a. everywhere in this narrative), being the warriors. This appears from the continuation: "they told Abimelech" (v. 42), as there was no occasion to tell him that ordinary people went in and out of the town as usual. Abimelech now returned and with a company pressed towards the gate of the city, thus cutting off retreat, whereas two other companies fell upon the Shechemite warriors who had left the town. Then, enraged by this new insurrection, he destroyed the city and sowed it with salt. This accomplished, he went straight for the "tower of Shechem", the inhabitants of which had gathered in the hold of a temple. and annihilated them entirely — and then, in his turn, he went to his doom.

P. 424 [1]. The co-responsibility of David is clearly expressed in the Greek translation of 1 Kings 2,5, where David says that Joab "put the blood of war upon my girdle and my sandal". For that matter, David, Joab and Amasa are related, seeing that the mother of Amasa is Abigail, the sister of Joab's mother, Zeruiah (2 Sam. 17,25), both of them being the daughters of Jesse according to 1 Chron. 2,16 and 2 Sam. 17.25 LXX Ms. L.; but this does not seem to play any part in the narrative.

P. 427 [1]. Cf. *Additional Note.*

P. 428 [1]. This view of the stoning also holds good as far as the Greeks are concerned, *vide* Hirzel's treatise in *Abh. d. sächs. Ges. d. Wiss.* vol. 27, no. 7, p. 221-266.

P. 429 [1]. It is unnecessary to alter *yarshīaʿa* to *yiwwāshēaʿ*. The victory over enemies is, to the Hebrew mind, not different from victory in judicial proceedings. Besides the passages mentioned in the text, may be quoted Exod. 22,8; Deut. 25,1; 1 Kings 8,32; Ps. 37,33; Prov. 12,2; 17,15; Job 40,8. Quite analogous is, further, Is. 54,17: No weapon that is formed against thee shall prosper *(yislaḥ);* every tongue that shall rise against thee in judgment thou shalt vanquish *(tarshīʿī).* In the same manner Hiphil of *ḥṭʾ* is used in one place of vanquishing by judicial proceeding, Is. 29,21: those that "make men offenders" by words and lay a snare for him that proceeds in the gate and "bend" the just by "voidness" *(tōhū,* chaos, the opposite of righteousness). Also *ʿiwwā,* "bend" from which *ʿāwōn* is derived, means to call down misery over one (Lam. 3,9, cf. Is. 24,1). *ḥāmas* means to counteract, to annul, Ezek. 22,26; Zeph. 3,4; "he that misseth me counteracts his own soul", says wisdom (Prov. 8,36).

P. 429 [2]. The most frequent terms for the fool are *kesīl, ʾewīl, nābhāl* and *sākhāl*; *nābhal* as a verb means "to fade, to collapse" and so in Piel "to shame, to condemn". Closely connected with this is the meaning of "corpse". *sākhal* "to act foolishly", in Piel 2 Sam. 15,31 of frustrating a plan.

P. 429 [3]. Read sing., the following forms being in the singular. The expression used is well known, Prov. 13,9; 20,20; 24,20; Job 21,27.

P. 429 [4]. Possibly read *wethakhshīlēhū* "makes him stumble" v. 7.

P. 429 [5]. The meaning of *baddāw* in 13 cannot be determined. In the following verse something seems to have fallen out.

P. 429 [6]. Probably *belīyaʿal,* v. 15.

P. 431 [1]. A similar view as regards *ʾāwen* has been set forth by Mowinckel in his above-mentioned work (see the note, p. 418 [1]) cf. his remark in A. Fridrichsen, *Hagios-Qados,* Kristiania, 1916, p. 68. He is certainly right that the word is the same as *ʾōn,* meaning power, especially the procreative power (Gen. 49,3; Deut. 21,17; Ps. 105,36) and wealth (Hos. 12,4; Job 20,10).

P. 431 [2]. The verb *yʿl,* it is true, only occurs in Hiphil which, however, presupposes a Kal, and this etymology agrees so well with the general conception that there is no reason to look for other explanations, e. g., that it should be derived from *yaʿale* "comes up"; *vide* further Gesenius-Buhl, *Handwörterbuch s. v.* and the commentaries to Judg. 19,22 by Moore and Burney. That the expression "currents of *belīyaʿal*", meaning those of Sheol (2 Sam. 22,5), agrees very well with this, appears from the following chapter.

P. 432 [1]. It is probable that *yithlaḥashū,* v. 8, means "whisper incantations", even though it is also used in a more neutral sense, 2 Sam. 12,19.

P. 432 [2]. *d^e^bhar b^e^līya'al,* v. 9, strictly "a matter of *b.*". It has been suggested to read *debher,* "pestilence".

P. 432 [3]. *'āḳēbh,* v. 10, seems to be used in the same sense as otherwise *'āḳōbh,* but it is not certain.

P. 432 [4]. Verbs like *mārā, māradh, bāghadh, mā'al* are used.

P. 433 [1]. The words *zākhar* and *pāḳadh* are used interchangeably, e. g. Exod. 20,5; 34,7; Num. 14,18; Is. 13,11; 26,21; 64,8; Jer. 14,10; 25,12; Hos. 8,13; 9,9; Am. 3,2; Ps. 25,7.

P. 438 [1]. Both *sh^e^ghar* and *'asht^e^rōth,* v. 18, are obscure.

P. 438 [2]. Read *baḥōrebh* instead of *baḥerebh,* v. 22.

P. 438 [3]. *l^e^za'^a^wā,* v. 25 is uncertain.

P. 441 [1]. *pelekh,* "a distaff", also Prov. 31,19. The presupposition must be that spinning is the work of women or slaves, possibly of cripples. LXX's translation *κρατῶν σκυτάλης* "who catches (leans on) a staff" must denote cripples, but is hardly correct.

P. 443 [1]. This is implied in 2 Sam. 18,20.

P. 444 [1]. So *niḳle,* v. 8, from *ḳālā,* "burn", (Duhm, Buhl *et al.).* The old translations which, among others, Baethgen follows, have "shame". To all intents and purposes the meaning, in both cases, is the same, viz. illness.

P. 444 [2]. *nigh'ī,* v. 12; the corresponding verb means "to strike".

P. 445 [1]. The exact translation: "My enemies in respect of my life", v. 20. Perhaps it should be read *ḥinnām,* "without reason", instead of *ḥayyīm,* "life".

P.449 [1]. The words are here divided somewhat differently from the division followed in the M. T., cf. the edition of Kittel; *gōbhah 'appō,* "the highness of his nose", i. e. his haughty pride, cf. for the analogous Assyrian expression Holma, *Die Namen der Körperteile im Ass.-Bab. (Ann. Acad. Sc. Fennicæ ser. B, tom. 7,1)* Helsinki, 1911, p. 19.

P. 449 [2]. To "blow" is one of the most frequently occurring forms of witchraft. If the text is correct, it is probable that this refers to something in that line, cf. Arab. *nafatha. Vide* Doutté, *Magie et religion dans l'Afrique du Nord,* 1908, p. 89, cf. Mowinckel, *op. cit.,* pp. 26 f. 169 f.

P. 450 [1]. Is it possible that their charm should be contained in the unintelligible v. 7?

P. 450 [2]. This is how the verse should be divided. The last word of the sentence is not quite correctly transmitted.

P. 450 [3]. Read *wayyakshīlēmō,* v. 9; thereafter follows "their tongue is against them (selves)".

P. 150 [4]. Read *yithnōdhēdh,* v. 9.

P. 450 [5]. *hiśkīl,* v. 10, seems to have the same meaning as *hiṣdīḳ,* "to justify, to countenance".

P. 451 [1]. Ps. 109,13 read *sh^e^mō* instead of *sh^e^mām.*

P. 452 [1]. *Vide* the author's *Der Eid bei den Semiten*, p. 80. In the same work there is a more detailed description of the essence of the curse, and also of the linguistic peculiarities.

P. 453 [1]. The three "storeys" are mentioned in Exod. 20,4. Both "heaven and earth" and "earth and heaven" occur.

P. 453 [2]. Jer. 10,13; 51,16; Ps. 78,23 f.; 104,3; 135,7; 148,4; Job 9,9; 37,9; 38,12.22. "The waters of heaven", e. g., Ps. 29,3; 33,7; Job 36,27.

P. 453 [3]. Gen. 8,2; 49,25; Deut. 33,13; Ps. 18,16; 24,2; 136,6; Job 38,16. The mountain pillars in the ocean, 1 Sam. 2,8; Ps. 46,3; 75,4; 104,5; Job 9,6; 38,6; their firmness, Is. 40,12 ff.; Job 26,7 ff.; Prov. 8,25. The foundations of the earth, *mōsᵉdhē hā'āreṣ,* 2 Sam. 22, 16; Is. 24,18; 40,21; Jer. 31,37 *et al.;* the same word is used of the foundation of a building, Jer. 51,26.

P. 454 [1]. As to the Babylonian picture of the world, *vide* Jensen, *Kosmologie der Babylonier,* Strassburg, 1890. Meissner, *Babylonien und Assyrien* II, p. 102 ff.

P. 454 [2]. *tēbhēl* is probably taken over from the Babylonian *tābalu, vide* Zimmern, *Akkadische Fremdwörter,* Leipzig, 1915, p. 43.

P. 454 [3]. The actual relationship of the two words is very probable; also from a purely formal point of view it is likely that *'ᵃdhāmā* is the derivation. As a rule the two words are separated, *'ᵃdhāmā* being explained as crust, surface, from the Arabic *'adam* ("skin") (Nöldeke in *Zeitschr. d. deutsch. Morgenl. Ges.* 40, p. 737 and formerly Fleischer); for these and other explanations, *vide* Dillmann's and Stinner's commentaries to Gen. 2,7. Of course the matter in itself is independent of the explanation adopted concerning the linguistical relation of *'ādhām* and *'ᵃdhāmā.*

P. 454 [4]. Exod. 3,8; 13,5; 33,3; Lev. 20,24; Num. 13,27; 14,8; 16,13 f.; Deut. 6,3; 11,9; 26,9.15; Jer. 11,5; 32,22 *et al.* Behind the form of the expression lies perhaps an old oriental tradition, *vide* Gressmann, *Ursprung der isr.-jüd. Eschatologie,* p. 210 ff. and A. Jirku, *Materialien zur Volksreligion Israels,* 1914, p. 29-40.

P. 454 [5]. Both called *śādhe,* the open country.

P. 455 [1]. Jer. 4,23-28; 9,9-11; 10,22; 16,6; 22,6; 32,43; 33,10.12; Mic. 1,8; Zeph. 2,14; Job 30,29.

P. 455 [2]. The meaning of *yanshōph,* here rendered "owl", is as uncertain as that of *ḳā'āth, vide* the dictionaries.

P. 456 [1]. The bracketed word, v. 12, is included according to LXX. In M. T. the word "their nobles" stands isolated.

P. 456 [2]. Read *ḥāṣēr,* v. 13, with LXX.

P. 456 [3]. Lilith is a female demon, well known from Assyria.

P. 456 [4]. *ḳippōz* designates a certain species, serpens jaculus, *vide* Gesenius-Buhl, *Handwörterbuch s. v.*

P. 456 [5]. Read *lō' phāḳādhū* v. 15.

P. 456 [6]. "He leads them astray in *tōhū,* where there is no way", Ps. 107,40; Job 12,24. Caravans "go up to *tōhū* and perish", Job 6,18; *tọhū* is classed with the howling of the waste, Deut. 32,10.

P. 456 [7]. Gen. 19; Deut. 29,22; 32,32; Is. 1,9 f.; 13,19 *et al.*

P. 456 [8]. Salt, which also elsewhere is used in this manner, is the unfertile, that which is characteristic of the desert, Deut. 29,22; Zeph. 2,9; Ps. 107,34; cf. Burney, to Judg. 9,45. By putting salt on land one consequently puts desert nature on it.

P. 457 [1]. The meaning of *'emesh,* which otherwise means "yesterday", is obscure, Job 30,3.

P. 458 [1]. There is an intimate connexion between the two meanings "to be dry" and "to be waste" of the root *ḥrb.* — Besides *shᵉmāmā* there are various nominal derivations from *shmm,* viz. *shammā, mᵉshammā, shimmāmōn,* all governed by the essential meaning of the word. *yᵉshīmōn* and *yᵉshīmōth,* denoting the desert land and the destruction, are derived from the secondary form *yshm. shō'ā* and *mᵉshō'ā,* which also denote the destruction and the destroyed land, are connected with *shāw'.* These roots are in all probability related to *shā'ā,* which denotes inner perturbation, noise, destruction. Other terms for the desert land, *midhbār,* the steppe, and *ʿᵃrābhā* (presumably the land of the Arabians) imply the same meanings, but here the fundamental meaning is a different one. *tōhū* has been dealt with above.

P. 460 [1]. The nether world, *taḥtīyā* or *taḥtīyōth,* Deut. 32,22; Is. 44,23; Ezek. 26,20; 31,14; 32,18.24; Ps. 86,13; 88,7; 139,15; Lam. 3,55.

P. 461 [1]. *Vide,* e. g., B. Stade, *Geschichte des Volkes Israel* I, 1887, p. 418 and: *Biblische Theologie des alten Test.* I, 1905, p. 183; F. Schwally, *Das Leben nach dem Tode,* 1892, pp. 59-62; Marti, *Gesch. d. isr. Rel.,* 3. ed., 1897, p. 117; R. H. Charles, *A Critical History of the Doctrine of a Future Life in Israel,* etc., 1899, p. 33; E. Kautzsch, *Biblische Theologie des alt. Test.,* 1911, p. 178 f., *et al.* That grave and Sheol are not to be separated is emphasized by E. Aurelius, *Föreställningar i Israel om de döda och tillståndet efter döden,* Uppsala 1907, pp. 27-44, as well as A. Lods, *La croyance à la vie future et le culte des morts dans l'antiquité israélite,* Paris, 1906 pp. 207-212. A different matter is that foreign (Babylonian) ideas have influenced the Israelitic conception of the nether world.

P. 461 [2]. The interchange of suffixes of masc. ("his") and fem. ("its") Ezek. 32,20 ff. is probably due to the fact that it is now the king, now the land to which reference is made, and the two became merged.

P. 464 [1]. Hypothetical reading, Ezek. 26,20 *wᵉtithyaṣṣᵉbhī.*

P. 464 [2]. This conception of *ṣalmāweth,* which is the traditional one, is not uncontested. Many derive it from *ṣlm* "overwhelm", *vide* the dictionaries s. v.; *ṣalmāweth* in Sheol, Job 10,21; 38,17.

P. 468 [1]. When read in this manner, v. 5 gives sense without altering the text. As a rule *'akh* in v. 5 b is emendated to *'ēkh* (so already Theodotion): "how can I again look towards your holy temple". The orientation towards the sacred place is well known from the *ḳibla* of the Jews and the Muslims.

P. 468 [2]. The word *dillā* is properly speaking used of pulling a pail up from the well.

P. 468 [3]. Read *yōmām* v. 2

P. 468 [4]. The meaning of *ḥophshī*, v. 6, is uncertain. As to this word, cf. note 7 [2].

P. 468 [5]. The construction of v. 8 is not certain; perhaps we should read *b^ekhol* instead of *w^ekhol.*

P. 469 [1]. *'āphūnā*, Ps. 88,16, is uncertain, but LXX has *ἐξηπορήθην;* some scholars read *'āphūghā* "I am faint".

P. 469 [2]. "is darkness", v. 19, cannot be correct; hypothetical reading *ḥāśakhtā.*

P. 469 [3]. *K^ethībh* reads "us", which does not make any difference.

P. 471 [1]. This is one of the oldest results gained by the Old Testament research from the cuneiform-inscriptions. Important works on the subject are H. Gunkel, *Schöpfung und Chaos in Endzeit und Urzeit,* 1895, and his commentary to the Genesis (3. ed., 1910). Further: A. J. Wensinck, *The Ocean in the Literature of the Western Semites (Verh. d. kon. Akad. v. Wetensch. te Amsterdam, Afd. Letterkunde, nieuwe reeks, deel XIX, no. 2, 1918).* W. here points out the connexion between Ocean, Sheol and the desert and the double conception of the ocean as good and evil. This double conception is an expression of the actual double nature of water.

P. 473 [1]. *ṣī* denotes a kind of desert animal. The idea is in all probability that even the dwellers of the desert are to a certain extent animated by the water, or that human beings, without water, would be (like) animals of the desert.

P. 475 [1]. This subject, which here could only be touched, is treated in detail by A. J. Wensinck, *The Ideas of the Western Semites Concerning the Navel of the Earth (Verh. d. kon. Akad. v. Wetensch. te Amsterdam, Afd. Letterkunde, nieuwe reeks,* XVII no. 1, 1916) and J. L. Palache, *Het heiligdom in de voorstelling der semietische volken,* Leiden, 1920.

P. 479 [1]. The only difficulty in Job 31,38-40 is caused by *b^elī kheseph,* "without silver". It must mean that he has shown fairness in the cultivation and given their wages to the labourers. One would expect "beyond the measure" or something in that direction. In his commentary Duhm here, as in many other cases, avoids the difficulty by eliciting the whole verse. Budde is of opinion that it is a question of appropriating a field by murder. In most modern interpretations *b^e'ālēhā* is taken of the owners, cf. also the commentaries of Driver & Buchanan Gray *(Internat. Crit. Comm.)* and of C. I. Ball *The Book of Job,* 1922.

P. 480 [1]. Exod. 23,11 is somewhat abrupt. It cannot mean that only the poor and the wild beasts are permitted to eat, whereas the owner is not allowed to get anything. Leviticus here seems to yield a better and a more complete text, and renders more clearly the exact meaning of the fallow-year. In Exod. 23,11 the verbs, properly speaking, denote to "pull out", viz. to suspend the common routine, the normal working. The object is the earth. When some of the commentators want to make "the crop" the object, it depends on their looking upon the law as a "humane" law, according to which the soil is to be tilled as usual, while the crop is to be rendered up. See in particular Wellhausen, *Prolegomena zur Gesch. Israels,* 5. ed. 1899, p. 114 ff. Whether it really is so that the seventh year in Exod. 23 is different for the different owners, whereas in the Leviticus they are equal for all, cannot be proved; see Wellhausen, *op. cit.,* Baentsch and Bertholet in their commentaries, Nowack, *Archäologie* II, p. 162, *et al.* Otherwise in Dillmann's commentary. Later on the seventh year was made common to all, *vide* Schürer, *Geschichte des jüdischen Volkes im Zeitalter Jesu Christi* I, 3.-4. ed., 1901, p. 35 ff.

P. 482 [1]. Musil, *Arabia Petræa* III, 22 f.

P. 483 [1]. Macalister, *The Excavation of Gezer* II, 1912, p. 379 f. Vincent, *Canaan,* p. 188 note 1; 202. Among the Babylonians, the wild swine was eaten, cf. Jensen in *Zeitschr. f. Assyriologie* vol. 1,310; according to Lucian, *De dea Syria* 54 this animal was sacred among the Syrians, cf. Robertson Smith, *Religion of the Semites,* p. 291. Also among the Phænicians it seems to have been a sacrificial animal, *vide* Pietschmann, *Gesch. d. Phönizier,* p. 219.

P. 483 [2]. Vincent, *Canaan,* p. 188 note.

P. 483 [3]. Cf. John Roscoe, *The Northern Bantu,* Cambridge, 1915, p. 108: . . . there are a few kinds of wild animals they will eat, though these are limited to such as they consider related to cows, for example, buffalo and one or two kinds of antelope, water-buck and hart-beest. — The principal clean wild beast (hart, gazelles, antelopes and the like) are mentioned in Deut. 14,5.

P. 483 [4]. They are of frequent occurrence in Moab, Jaussen, *Coutumes des Arabes,* p. 249 f. A description of the great invasion of locusts in Palestine, 1915, with photographs, was given in *The Illustrated London News,* Feb., 1920, by John D. Whiting.

P. 483 [5]. *nervus ischiadicus.* A parallel is given by Frazer, *Folk-Lore in the Old Testament* vol. 2, 1918, p. 423 f. Rob. Smith, *Lectures on the Religion of the Semites,* new. ed., 1914, p. 380[1] is of opinion that the custom is based upon the conception of the lumbar power being the procreative power. The Israelites are not permitted to eat animals that are dead of themselves or torn by beasts of prey, Exod. 22,30; Lev.

7,24; 17,15 f.; Deut. 14,21; though the uncleanness is merely passing and can be purged away (Lev. 17,15). Such meat is generally to be given to dogs (Exod. 22,30) or to *gērīm* and strangers (Deut. 14,21). This shows that the law in this case is not determined by the fear of eating blood, which is the common view (as set forth by Stade, *Biblische Theologie,* p. 141; Benzinger, *Archäologie,* 2. ed. p. 408), for, like the Israelites themselves, strangers were not permitted to eat blood. The reason was probably the fear of the abnormal.

P. 486 [1]. The consideration of the latter achieves an independent significance and becomes the dominating factor in Deut. 24,19-22.

P. 487 [1]. Is. 13,10; Joel 3,3 f.; 4,15; Am. 8,9; Mic. 3,6; Job 3,5.

P. 487 [2]. About the time, cf. the note to 114 [1].

P. 488 [1]. The day of Jerusalem, Ob. 12; Ps. 137,7; of Jezreel, Hos. 2,2; of Midian, Is. 9,3; the day of Yahweh, Joel 1,15; Am. 5,18; Zeph. 1,7.14; Mal. 3,23. The day of a man, meaning a day of his misfortune, 1 Sam. 26,10; Job 18,20 *et al.*

P. 489. These renderings of *'ēthānīm, būl, 'ābhībh* and *ziw* are only partly reliable. In Gezer has been found a list of eight months: month of fruit-harvest, sowing, late sowing, flax-gathering, barley harvest, full harvest, clipping (?), summer fruit *vide Zeitschr. f. alttestl. Wiss.* vol. 29, 1909, p. 222-229 and Lidzbarski, *Ephemeris für semitische Epigraphik,* vol. 3, p. 36-43.

P. 490 [1]. Peoples with whom the seasons are the dominating factor may reckon the beginning of the year from harvest or from sowing, cf. Martin P. Nilsson, *Primitive Time-Reckoning (Acta Societatis Humaniorum Litterarum Lundensis* I), Lund, 1920, p. 92. The Gezer calendar begins with the harvest, which Nilsson takes as a proof of the year beginning with it, *op. cit.,* p. 234. It is not known how in the olden times the lunar year was equalized with the solar year. In later Judaism a leap-month was intercalated when the disagreements became too large, cf. the letter of Rabban Gamaliel in Dalman, *Aramäische Dialektproben,* 1896, p. 3; undoubtedly this was an old custom.

P. 490 [2]. The connexion of *dōr* with the Arabic *dahr* is probable; it implies the time with its contents, fate.

P. 492 [1]. An instructive description of the rites of circumcision with the Thonga-people is thus to be found in Junod, *The Life of a South African Tribe,* vol. 1, p. 71-92. As to another Bantu people, *vide* J. Roscoe, *The Northern Bantu,* p. 184-86. A summary for orientation is to be found in the article on "Circumcision" in Hastings, *Encyclopedia of Religion and Ethics.* Circumcision of older persons occurs in Gen. 34,14-25; Josh. 5,2-9, but these cases are exceptional.

P. 494 [1]. 1 Sam. 4,12; 2 Sam. 1,2.11; Jer. 41,5.

P. 494 [2]. Gen. 37,34; 2 Sam. 3,31; 21,10; Jer. 6,26 *et al.*

P. 494 [3]. 2 Sam. 13,31.

P. 494 [4]. Josh. 7,6; 1 Sam. 4,12; 2 Sam. 1,2; 15,32 *et al.*

P. 494 [5]. 2 Sam. 14,2; Is. 61,3.

P. 494 [6]. 2 Sam. 15,30; Ezek. 24,17.

P. 494 [7]. Lev. 21,5; Deut. 14,1; Is. 15,2; Jer. 7,29; 16,6; 41,5; 48,37; Job 1,20; cover: Ezek. 24,17.

P. 494 [8]. Lev. 19,27 f.; 21,5; Deut. 14,1; Jer. 16,6; 41,5; 47,5; 48,37.

P. 495 [1]. Gen. 37,29; 44,13; Josh. 7,6; 2 Sam. 13,19.31; 1 Kings 21,27; 2 Kings 5,8; 6,30.

P. 495 [2]. 2 Sam. 10,4.

P. 495 [3]. 2 Sam. 13,19 (Tamar); Is. 58,5; Jer. 6,26; Jon. 3,6; Job 2,8.12; Lam. 2,10; Esth. 4,1; Dan. 9,3.

P. 495 [4]. 2 Sam. 15,30; Jer. 14,4; Esth. 6,12.

P. 495 [5]. Is. 3,24; 22,12; Jer. 41,5; Mic. 1,16.

P. 495 [6]. Jer. 41,5; 47,5. — As to the whole of this problem, cf. the works quoted in the note 180 [1] and the author's *Der Eid bei den Semiten,* p. 101 f. The correctness of the fundamental view of the rites set forth in this work does not exclude the concurrence of other elements. An expression of "awe" for the deceased who have passed into the divine sphere, Wensinck traces in the Semitic ceremonies; he is certainly right in his supposition as to the existence of these moments; *vide* A. J. Wensinck, *Some Semitic Rites of Mourning and Religion (Verh. d. kon. Akad. v. Wetensch. te Amsterdam, Afd. Letterkunde, nieuwe reeks, deel XVIII* No 1, 1917).

P. 496 [1]. "In his father's grave", Judg. 16,31; "with the fathers", Gen. 49,29, cf. 2 Sam. 19,38; 21,13; 1 Kings 13,22.

P. 496 [2]. Gen. 25,8; 35,29; 49,33; Num. 27,13; Deut. 32,50; "to the fathers", Judg. 2,10.

ADDITIONAL NOTE.

Some Characteristics of Marriage in the West-Asiatic Cultures.

Among all the peoples surrounding Israel marriage was of the *patriarchal order.* Monogamy is the prevailing, but by no means the only form of marriage. The Babylonians maintain that one woman must be the chief wife. There are even examples of a man taking two sisters to wife at the same time, the one being subordinated to the other (Meissner, *Altbab. Privatrecht* p. 89; C. H. W. Johns, *Babylonian and Assyrian Laws, Contracts and Letters,* 1904, p. 138 ff.). The example of Jacob shows that an Israelite might also marry two sisters, but on equal terms. In other circles it is forbidden, Lev. 18,18. Intermarriage between the social classes is not forbidden; it even happens that a slave may marry a free woman, 1 Chr. 2,34 f., cf. Cod. Ham. §§ 175-176, Hittite Code I 34. Her children were free, according to Ham., and inherited her property and half of that of the slave-father. As still frequently happens in the Orient, the young people may have lived in the house of the bridegroom's father. Among the Assyrians the married wife not infrequently lived with her father (KAV 1, III 82-108; IV 50-70.82 f.), cf. Gen. 31,31; Judg. 14,10 f. According to Hrozný the same custom prevailed with the Hittites (§ 27 of his edition), but Zimmern and Friedrich understand the text (their translation I 28) in another sense. When the *bride-gift* has been paid, the parties are bound. If the suitor withdraws, the father of the bride, according to Cod. Ham., is entitled to retain the bride-gift, whereas the father of the bride, in case he changes his mind, must pay the suitor twice the amount received (Cod. Ham. §§ 159-160). The Hittites have similar provisions (I 30-31); but there is no compensation on the part of the bridegroom in case he is carried away by illness (I 38). Former agreements may also be broken, the new suitor indemnifying his predecessor (I 29 a).

In this context the Hittites and the Assyrians have a provision which is of particular interest. The Hittites provide: If a man marries a woman and then dies, then his brother may (or must) marry her; secondarily, his father. When the father dies, a brother may (or must) marry her, whatever his marital relations (Zimmern II 79, Hrozný §

193). The latter remark might point in the direction that the first-mentioned brother is at any rate not under obligation to take over the widow, if already married. The Assyrian provision is of a similar kind: If a man has solemnly designated a bride for his son, and this son dies or flees, then he may give her to anyone of his remaining sons who is ten years of age. If the father and his son, for whom a bride is designated, die, and there is a son of the latter, he shall marry the wife of his deceased father, if at least ten years of age. If not, the father of the bride may break the engagement and give back all he has received except food (KAV 1, VI, 19-39). A parallel between these provisions and the Israelitic law on the *Levirate marriage* (Deut. 25,5 ff.) suggests itself, but it is necessary to observe the points of difference. Among the Israelites it is a case of a *childless* widow, and the object of the Levirate marriage is to procure progeny for the *deceased.* But this is not so either among the Hittites or the Assyrians. With the latter the rule also applies, in case the first bridegroom flees. Other Assyrian provisions throw a clearer light upon the matter: A widow living in her father's house with a child may be married to her father-in-law; if her father-in-law, as well as her husband, is dead, and she has no son, she may go wherever she pleases (KAV 1, IV 56-70). If a man has paid the bride-gift to his father-in-law, and his bride dies, then he may marry one of the sisters of the deceased, or he may take the silver he has given, but not food (KAV 1, IV 40-49). Further: If a man has given the bride-gift on behalf of his son, and another son dies before the marriage, then he may marry the wife of his dead son to his first-named son. The first betrothal can then be broken, and the bride-gift — excepting food — must be repaid (KAV 1, IV 20-39). The point of view of the Assyrians is that an engagement established through marriage between two families should be maintained; an older engagement should not be rendered superfluous by a later one, which is not yet fulfilled. And if a widow has a child, she is so intimately connected with the family of the man that she is taken over by the father of the deceased husband. Similar points of view underlie the Hittite law. From the Hittite and Assyrian laws it appears that the Levirate marriage was a common feature in Western Asia, but the Israelites stamped this custom with quite a different character. This should be a warning to scholars who want to solve such problems all over the world with one single formula. According to the Rabbinical theory the Levirate marriage is closely connected with the question of inheritance; but because of Lev. 18,16.20.21, which forbids marriage with the sister-in-law, the law of the Levirate marriage is strickly limited; Abbā Shā'ūl is even of opinion that *ḥalīṣā,* renunciation, is always a duty, *vide* Talmud, *Yebhāmōth* and its treatment by Israel I. Mattuck, *The Levirate Marriage in Jewish Law* in *Studies in Jewish Literature issued in Honor of K. Kohler,* Berlin, 1919.

The principal *view concerning the wife* is the same with the Eastern Semites as with Israel. She belongs to her own family, but is given to that of her husband with the main purpose of bearing him children. If she dies childless, the bride-gift must be restored to her husband, Cod. Ham. § 163. The Assyrians ordain that if the wife, of her own accord, brings about a miscarriage, she shall be impaled on a stake and left unburied (KAV 1, VII 92-VIII 105). If she has a child, she is more closely connected with the family of the husband. With the Assyrians, this has, for instance, the above-mentioned consequence, viz. that a widow who has a child is to be taken into marriage by the head of the husband's family, i. e. his father, and it is important in respect of the order of inheritance that she has a child. Though the wife does not belong to the family of her husband in the proper sense of the word, she has a large share in the responsibility of his house. According to the Babylonians the wife is co-responsible for the debt contracted upon the house during the time of her marriage (Cod. Ham. § 152), and her husband may hand her over to the creditor to work off the debt (§ 117). With the Assyrians her state of dependency is still more pronounced: Even if she lives in her father's house, the wife is responsible for her husband's debts, penalty and sin (KAV 1, IV 50-55), whereas it is stated in several cases that the husband is not responsible for his wife (KAV 1, I 14-73); the husband is a despot who may cut off her ears, etc. (*ibid.* VIII 58-63). If a man ravishes a virgin, her father may take the wife of the evildoer and ravish her (KAV 1, VIII 15-29); the Babylonians, on the other hand, provide that if a man beats a pregnant woman and she dies, his *daughter* shall be killed (Cod. Ham. § 210). This is quite logical, because his daughter is nearer to him than his wife. If the wife bears no children, she may be divorced, but also without this presupposition the man is entitled to divorce his wife, not *vice-versa,* and this holds good of all the Semitic peoples.

Sexual crimes are judged according to this conception of marriage. If a man is seized in adultery with the wife of another, both of them shall be killed, in Babylonia (by drowning Cod. Ham. § 129), in Assyria (*K*AV 1, II 25-29), with the Hittites (Zimmern II 83-84; Hrozný §§ 197-198), as in Israel (Lev. 20,10; Deut. 22,22), although the offended husband may sometimes pardon the crime. If the wife has not sinned of her own accord, she goes free, and only the ravisher is killed. This principle is practised in some special laws. Thus, in Assyria a married woman who has been ravished in the open air is guiltless, and only the man is to be killed, whereas both of them are killed if they are seized in the man's dwelling (KAV 1, II 14-29). If they are seized in public places, the man is guiltless if he does not know that the woman is married (i. e. thinks that she is a hetæra); but if he knows it, the husband of the woman shall treat both of them in the same manner (II 30-40); in a special case, which is not quite clear, the adulterer goes free (II 58-66). The Hittites have a law similar to the Assyrian one mentioned above: If adultery takes place in the mountains, only the man is to be killed, but if it takes place in the house, both forfeit their lives. The husband is entitled to kill them on the spot, but he may also take them to the gate of the palace, and then allow them both to live. Also the king may pardon them (Zimmern II 83-84, Hrozný §§ 197-198). This law, prevailing with the Northern peoples, is adopted by Israel, stating that if a man is seized with a betrothed woman in the city, they shall both be stoned; but if it takes place in the open air, only the man shall die, because she may have cried for help without being heard (Deut. 22,23-27).

If a man has ravished a betrothed virgin, he shall be killed, but she shall go free according to Cod. Ham. § 130. In Assyria he shall give his wife to be ravished and is bound to marry the injured woman; if he has no wife, he shall pay three times the bride-gift for her (KAV 1, VIII 6-41). The Assyrian principle is recognized in Israel, which provides that if a man ravishes an unbetrothed virgin, he shall pay the bride-gift to her father, who may nevertheless refuse to give her to him (Exod. 22,15-16). According to the Deuteronomy the evildoer shall pay 50 shekels for her and marry her, without the right to divorce her (22,28-29). It is the honour of a wife to fulfil her engagement towards her husband and to know no other man. If a woman is charged with unchastity by her husband without evidence, she shall in Babylonia swear to her innocence and then return to her house (Cod. Ham. § 131). If the charge is brought against her by another man, the matter is settled by the river-ordeal (§ 132), and this is also the Assyrian law (KAV 1, II 67-91); similarly, if she has charged a man with adultery, he must go to the river (II 105-III 13). He who has brought a false charge of that kind against a woman shall receive 40 lashes, do royal service for one month, be mutilated and pay one talent of lead (II 72-81). The Israelitic laws take into consideration that the husband may charge his wife with not being a virgin at the time of the wedding; if her parents can prove her innocence with the tokens of her virginity, he shall pay 100 shekels to her father, and is never allowed to divorce her. If the cloth cannot be brought forth, she shall be stoned (Deut. 22,13-21). Any suspicion on the part of the husband is settled by a special ordeal (Num. 5). According to Koschaker, Cod. Ham. treats a similar case §§ 142-143 (*Zeitschr. f. Ass.* N. F. I, pp. 199-212). He takes *naṣrat* "preserved" to mean "a virgin" and traces a right for the young wife to leave her husband before the consummation of the marriage in case she is a virgin; if not, she shall be drowned. This interpretation presupposes an emendation of the text, which cannot be discussed here. The right of the wife, in certain cases, to leave the husband is acknowledged by the Sumerian law (*vide* op. cit., p. 210).

The position of the wife is clearly expressed in *her relation to the property,* as laid down in the laws of the Eastern Semites. The family of the husband pays to the family of the wife the bride-gift (in Cod. Ham. *tirkhātu),* and she brings with her a personal gift from her family *(shiriḳtu)*; these are always kept apart. So in Israel the bridegroom pays a *mōhar* to the family of the bride, and she gets a gift, *shillūḥīm,* from her relations, cf. above, p. 68.69. In a third category are the gifts which the husband may give her *(nudunnū),* cf. in Israel Gen. 24,53. As to the *tirkhātu,* it rests with her family; but according to Cod. Ham. § 163 it shall be restored if the wife does not fulfil her task, i. e. to bear children. It is the duty of the husband to keep her, and, as mentioned above, she is co-responsible for his debt. But her family property, the *shiriḳtu,* is always her property. She gets it when her husband dies (Cod. Ham. §§ 171.172); if she dies childless, it returns to her father (Cod. Ham. § 163), but otherwise it is inherited by her children (Cod. Ham. §§ 162.167.173.174). So also in Assyria; what the bride brings with her *(shirḳu)* and what her father-in-law gives her, belongs to her and her children, but her husband is entitled to take it (or perhaps only that given by her father-in-law?) and to give it to the children he prefers (KAV 1, IV 11-19); if she lives in her father's house, he is not entitled to take anything that belong to it (III 103-108). The *nudunnū,* the husband's gifts to his wife, belong to her, but are, according to Cod. Ham. §§ 171-172, to be given to her children after her death. In Assyria it is stated that the man is at any time entitled to take back the *nudunnū* he has given her (KAV 1, III 103-108; V 20-25). If he dies, and she is childless, she must deliver whatever ornaments he has given her to his family (KAV 1, III 82-102). Though no law to this effect has been preserved in Israel, everything indicates that the same principles have prevailed here as with the Eastern Semites.

It is a matter of course that the wife has no general right to *inherit* her husband. Nevertheless, the Babylonians give to a widow with children a share like that of one son (§ 172), if she stays in the house of the deceased. In the New-Babylonian period, a childless wife might get a share of the inheritance of her deceased husband (cf. Meissner, *Babylonien und Assyrien* I, 1923, p. 423). This treatment of the widow in Babylonian custom is undoubtedly due to Sumerian influence (cf. P. Koschaker in *Zeitschr. f. Ass. N. F.* I, 1923, p. 192-98). Even the divorced, but not guilty, wife is in Babylonia entitled to some assistance as in Sumerian law (Cod. Ham. §§ 137-140). In Assyria she is not entitled to anything in case of divorce (KAV 1, V 15-19), nor does she get any inheritance; she must rely upon her sons (VI 89-112, cf. Ham. § 172), or return to her family. Also other sons of her husband might take care of her, and even marry her (VI 89-112). The position of the widow in Israel is on the whole similar to that of the widow in Assyria.

There are certain suggestions in the Hittite law indicating a different conception of marriage and property. The wife has the right to inherit her husband (Zimmern II 78, Hrozny § 192). As Zimmern understands I 28, the family of the wife inherits, after her death, the chattels given to her by her husband, whereas the latter takes back what he has given her by way of landed property. From Zimmern I 32, Hrozný § 31 we way infer that in case of divorce the children were divided.

Even though the man can not break his own marriage, he can violate, not only other marriages, but also other relations by sexual intercourse. The Babylonian law punishes sexual intercourse with a daughter-in-law by drowning (§ 155), but only with the penalty of ½ mina, if the marriage has not yet been consummated (§ 156), whereas sexual intercourse with mother, daughter and stepmother is punished by burning, expulsion from the city and cutting off from the father's house respectively (§§ 157.154.158). From the Assyrian law it only appears that the pederast shall be castrated (KAV 1, II 93-97). In Egypt marriage with a sister was common, cf. Erman-Ranke, *Aegypten,* 1923, p. 180. The Hittites punish the ravishing of mother, daughter or son (Zimmern II 75, Hrozný § 189); but if the act is performed of their own accord it is not punished, nor is the ravishing of the stepmother (or mother-in-law) to be punished (Zimmern II 76, Hrozný § 190). Sexual intercourse of a freeman with slave-women or with his own relatives shall not be punished; and the same is the case when father and son have intercourse with the same slave or hetæra (Zimmern II 80, Hrozný § 194). Bestiality is punished with death, but the king may pardon the offender (Zimmern II 73.85, Hrozný §§ 187.199). From Zimmern II 76 as compared with II 75 (Hrozný §190 and 189) we may infer that pederasty is not punished. If Zimmern and Friedrich have rightly understood I 37 (Hrozný § 36), it has been possible to conclude a pederastic "marriage"; Hrozný takes it so that a man may give a young man the marriage gift to get him as a husband for his daughter, but this understanding is not probable in itself, and the main point "for his daughter" does not occur in the text. These Hittite laws are good illustrations of Lev. 18.20; Deut. 27,20-23.

INDICES

I. GENERAL INDEX

II. INDEX OF HEBREW WORDS.

(The order of the English alphabet is followed).